Introduction to Ada

Introduction to Ada

J. E. Cooling
Department of Electronic and Electrical Engineering
Loughborough University of Technology

N. Cooling
Scientific and Engineering Software UK Ltd

and

J. Cooling
Cadre Technologies Ltd

CHAPMAN & HALL
University and Professional Division
London · Glasgow · New York · Tokyo · Melbourne · Madras

Published by Chapman & Hall, 2–6 Boundary Row, London SE1 8HN

Chapman & Hall, 2–6 Boundary Row, London SE1 8HN, UK

Blackie Academic & Professional, Wester Cleddens Road, Bishopbriggs, Glasgow G64 2NZ, UK

Chapman & Hall Inc., 29 West 35th Street, New York NY10001, USA

Chapman & Hall Japan, Thomson Publishing Japan, Hirakawacho Nemoto Building, 6F, 1-7-11 Hirakawa-cho, Chiyoda-ku, Tokyo 102, Japan

Chapman & Hall Australia, Thomas Nelson Australia, 102 Dodds Street, South Melbourne, Victoria 3205, Australia

Chapman & Hall India, R. Seshadri, 32 Second Main Road, CIT East, Madras 600 035, India

First edition 1993   N.S. Ball 1995

© 1993 J.E. Cooling, N. Cooling and J. Cooling

Typeset in 10/12pt Sabon by Graphicraft Typesetters Ltd., Hong Kong

Printed in Great Britain by Page Bros, Norwich.

ISBN 0 412 44810 0

Apart from any fair dealing for the purposes of research or private study, or criticism or review, as permitted under the UK Copyright Designs and Patents Act, 1988, this publication may not be reproduced, stored, or transmitted, in any form or by any means, without the prior permission in writing of the publishers, or in the case of reprographic reproduction only in accordance with the terms of the licences issued by the Copyright Licensing Agency in the UK, or in accordance with the terms of licences issued by the appropriate Reproduction Rights Organization outside the UK. Enquiries concerning reproduction outside the terms stated here should be sent to the publishers at the London address printed on this page.

The publisher makes no representation, express or implied, with regard to the accuracy of the information contained in this book and cannot accept any legal responsibility or liability for any errors or omissions that may be made.

Library of Congress Cataloging-in-Publication data

Cooling, J.E.
   Introduction to Ada / J.E. Cooling, N. Cooling, J. Cooling.
     p. cm.
   Includes index.
   ISBN 0-412-44810-6
   1. Ada (Computer program language)   2. Real-time data processing.
I. Cooling, J. II. Cooling, N.S. III. Title.
QA76.73.A35C67   1993
005.13'3–dc20   92-39743
                                                                                  CIP

∞ Printed on permanent acid-free text paper, manufactured in accordance with the proposed ANSI/NISO Z 39.48-199X and ANSI Z 39.48-1984

Contents

Preface		x
Acknowledgements		xiii

1	**An introduction to Ada**	1
1.1	A very broad view of Ada's structure	1
1.2	Naming objects – identifiers	11
1.3	Comments	13
1.4	Console communications	13
1.5	Numeric constants	18
1.6	Basic data types	20
Review		24

2	**Elementary arithmetic and logic**	25
2.1	Statements and expressions	25
2.2	Arithmetic expressions	26
2.3	Boolean expressions	40
Review		43

3	**Program control structures**	44
3.1	The three basic control structures	44
3.2	Selection	45
3.3	Repetition or 'loop control'	57
3.4	The **goto**	68
Review		70

4	**Subprograms in Ada – procedures and functions**	71
4.1	How to handle large jobs	71
4.2	Introduction to the procedure	76
4.3	Using variables in procedures – scope and locality	78
4.4	Procedures with parameters	85
4.5	Functions	94
4.6	Nesting and recursion	99
4.7	A return to parameters – named and default types	100
4.8	Procedures and functions – body, specification and declaration	104

4.9	The block control structure of Ada	106
4.10	Overloading of subprograms	111
4.11	A last comment	115
Review		115

5 Types revisited — 116

5.1	Setting the scene	116
5.2	Data types – basic concepts reviewed	117
5.3	A brief review of Ada types	120
5.4	Predefined types	121
5.5	Inventing your own data types	136
5.6	Conversion of data types	157
Review		157

6 Number crunching in Ada — 159

6.1	Setting the scene	159
6.2	The limitations of finite number systems	165
6.3	Handling real number types in Ada	176
Review		185

7 Modular construction, information hiding and the package — 187

7.1	Fundamental ideas	187
7.2	Software construction methods	192
7.3	Building software the Ada way – the package concept	193
7.4	Building and using the package	199
7.5	Global items – a warning	219
Review		222

8 Composite data types – the array — 223

8.1	Introduction to structured variables	223
8.2	Arrays	226
Review		272

9 Composite data types – records — 273

9.1	Records – basic types	273
9.2	Introduction to discriminants	293
9.3	Record components – setting their size	295
9.4	More on discriminants	296
9.5	Records with variant parts – 'variant records'	306
Review		314

10	Dynamic data types	316
10.1	Introduction to dynamic data structures	316
10.2	Dynamic variables and pointers	318
10.3	Working with dynamic variables	319
10.4	Access types and objects – some features	327
10.5	Linking data items – declaration issues	330
10.6	Building and manipulating linked lists	332
10.7	Implications for real-time systems	336
Review		343

11	Information hiding, data abstraction and private types	344
11.1	Setting the scene	344
11.2	Introduction to the private type	348
11.3	The 'normal' private type	351
11.4	Constants as private types	352
11.5	A practical application example of private types	355
11.6	Limited private types	357
11.7	A practical application example of the limited private type	359
11.8	Miscellaneous points	363
Review		364

12	Exceptions	365
12.1	Exceptions – what and why?	365
12.2	Dealing with exceptions – the Ada way	367
12.3	Frame constructs – subprograms and packages	377
12.4	Scope and visibility aspects	384
12.5	Propagation of exceptions	386
12.6	Raising exceptions in the exception handler	394
12.7	Exception raising during declaration elaboration	396
12.8	Suppressing exceptions	398
12.9	Exception handling in embedded systems – a comment	401
Review		401

13	Generics	402
13.1	Concepts	402
13.2	Generics and Ada	404
13.3	Introduction using the generic procedure	407
13.4	Generic formal parameters – types	412
13.5	Generic formal parameters – objects	416
13.6	Generic formal parameters – subprograms	420
13.7	Generic functions	424

viii   Contents

13.8	Generic packages	425
13.9	Putting versatility into the generic unit	432
Review		438

14 Concurrency – the Ada task   441

14.1	Concurrency – an introduction	441
14.2	Interdependent and independent tasks – their co-ordination	444
14.3	Introducing the Ada task	447
14.4	Interdependent tasks, synchronization and the rendezvous	452
14.5	Executing code during the rendezvous	457
14.6	Synchronization and data transfer	459
14.7	The selective rendezvous	461
14.8	The calling task – conditional and timed entries	473
14.9	Task types	475
14.10	Task entry families	479
14.11	Termination and exceptions	481
14.12	Task priorities	487
14.13	Task and entry attributes	490
14.14	Tasks in packages	491
Review		495

15 Low-level issues   496

15.1	Introduction – the need to access machine facilities	496
15.2	Facilities needed to access machine resources	498
15.3	Low-level facilities in Ada – an overview	503
15.4	Mapping Ada on to the machine – representation clauses	503
15.5	Unchecked programming	520
15.6	Machine code insertions	524
15.7	Interfacing to other languages	525
Review		525

16 Data input–output   527

16.1	Inputting–outputting of data – an overview	527
16.2	File management	528
16.3	Readable text	535
16.4	Sequential input–output of machine-readable data	561
16.5	Direct input–output of machine-readable data	564
16.6	Low-level input–output	568
16.7	Exceptions in input–output	570
Review		570

17	**Program structure and compilation issues**	571
17.1	Introduction – compilation units	571
17.2	Library units	574
17.3	Secondary units	578
17.4	Compilation dependencies and order	583
17.5	Declaration and elaboration	588
17.6	Renaming Ada entities	593
Review		596

Appendix: Reserved words		597
Index		598

Preface

WHAT IS THIS BOOK ABOUT?

The purpose of this book is to give a comprehensive introduction to Ada. It covers all basic aspects of the language, with special emphasis on real-time systems design.

WHO SHOULD READ IT?

It is written with three groups of readers in mind:

- The novice programmer;
- Programmers meeting Ada for the first time who lack experience with modern high-level languages;
- Even for experienced programmers, certain topics – generics, tasking, exception handling and low-level features – may be unexplored territory. This text provides a comprehensive introduction to such aspects as they apply to Ada.

WHAT WILL IT DO FOR ME, THE READER?

It will introduce Ada in a painless way as a learning process. It carefully and clearly explains the structure and rules of the language, highlighting in particular its applicability to real-time systems.

WHY THE EMPHASIS ON REAL-TIME SYSTEMS?

The whole design concept of Ada is geared to the programming of real-time systems. Further, one of its main application areas has been that of real-time embedded systems. For such functions – where the computer is seen as merely one component within the total system – reliability, safety, deterministic behaviour and (usually) fast responses are paramount.

HOW DOES THIS AFFECT THE CONTENTS AND COVERAGE OF THE TEXT?

Appropriate emphasis is placed on the 'low-level' facilities which are needed to interact with computer hardware, and on concurrent ('tasking') processing. Dynamic and advanced data structures are treated only as an introductory topic.

WILL IT TEACH ME ANYTHING ABOUT SOFTWARE DESIGN AND PROGRAMMING STYLE?

Yes, but this is not its main objective. Its aim is to get you actually writing Ada programs as soon as possible. The relationship between design requirements and language support for such factors is always shown. Otherwise it's impossible to understand why the structures of Ada give us the means to produce first-class software.

ARE THERE ANY OTHER SPECIAL FEATURES ABOUT THIS BOOK?

Yes – it is designed as a learning guide. The text is built on the development of small but illustrative programs which you should work on. All the specimen programs have been tested.

SOME IMPORTANT POINTS

(a) The fundamental idea here is that students learn how to program in Ada via practical work. As such, they will first have to learn how to handle their computing equipment. In the writing of this text we assume they have that knowledge.
(b) They will also need to become familiar with their Ada compiler or program environment to carry out practical work. All compilers known to us include comprehensive documentation relating to predefined Ada features (such as the language attributes, pragmas and packages). We assume that students have access to this information, and we have therefore not included it in this text.
(c) Our experience is that novices do not really appreciate the broad, fundamental concepts of Ada on first meeting it. Therefore we have taken a very pragmatic approach. We start with the simple things, those which can be related to many other languages. The basic objective is to give the

students confidence with hands-on experience. Then we make a conceptual and implementation step-change by introducing the package. We coast through structured data types, following this with the more difficult topic of dynamic data types. The all-important concepts of information hiding and data abstraction are then studied in detail. After this we meet a set of topics which are relatively advanced for the novice programmer – exceptions, generics, tasking and low level. Data input–output follows, giving a detailed examination of that topic (this could be taught earlier if so desired). Finally, the text is rounded off by looking at program structure and compilation issues.

Note: Formatting of our program listings was carried out using Cadre's Ada Design Sensitive Editor.

Acknowledgements

Many thanks to Tim Court for taking the time and effort to read and comment on the draft manuscript.

Also, thanks to our heroine draftswoman, Janet Redman.

We especially wish to thank Dr Richard Beeby of Paisley College for his excellent and most helpful review of the draft manuscript. Its value cannot possibly be underestimated.

Jo and Niall are deeply indebted to Joan and Pauline for the copious amounts of cleaning and ironing they have done during the preparation of this text.

And finally, for some people who rarely get praise but have played an important part in seeing this into print: the staff of Chapman & Hall. In particular we should mention Dominic Recaldin for his unfailing courtesy and good humour (even as deadlines came and went and the book got bigger and bigger); Una-Jane Winfield for her very efficient and cheerful support; and Dave Hatter for his professional help and dogged perseverance in the latter part of this project.

Jim, Niall and Jo

To our Mums – thanks for everything.
Jo and Niall

Chapter One
An introduction to Ada

The purpose of this chapter is to introduce the reader to the simpler aspects of Ada together with specific points needed for future reading. After studying this you should be able to:

- Define the general layout of an Ada main program;
- Identify the use of program declarations and statements;
- Describe the use of identifiers, variables, constants, reserved words and comments;
- Understand the concepts of block structuring and data typing;
- Create a complete, compilable Ada program that you interact with from your computer console.

1.1 A VERY BROAD VIEW OF Ada's STRUCTURE

1.1.1 Structure – why?

It may seem strange to start off talking about structure when the main concern of this book is the Ada language, but the fundamental design of Ada forces us to use structure and organization in our software. So why should this be so important? Just look around and see the ordered form of the everyday things in our life; books, churches and motorway systems all have these properties. We tend to take these for granted; yet without proper organization and design they'd be almost useless. All right then, let's look more closely at a book example to see why structuring is so important. It's also quite meaningful because, in many ways, software design can be related to it.

The objective of a book is to communicate information. It doesn't matter whether the subject is 'Gardening for Beginners', a James Bond novel, or 'Electromagnetic Compatibility'; it's pointless printing it unless the reader can understand it. Those of you who've been unfortunate enough to read grindingly boring reports will appreciate this fact. So let's introduce some organization into our book design as shown in Fig.1.1.

2 An introduction to Ada

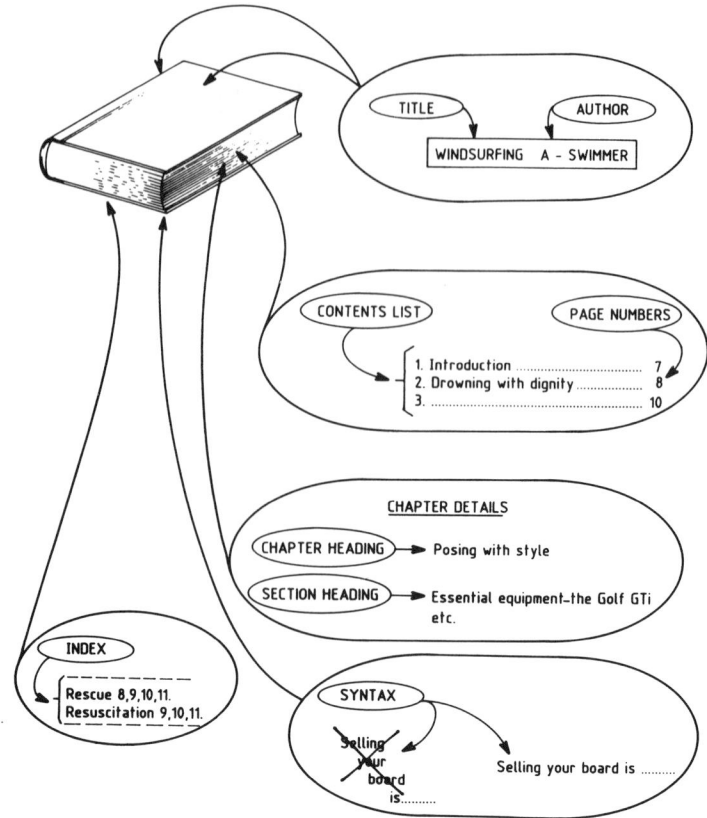

Fig.1.1 Structure – an essential ingredient.

Once the text has been produced we bind the book and put covers on it. On the cover we include the most important items of information: the title and author. Now it is easy to catalogue, store and reference the book. And everybody uses the same system. On opening the covers we find that the contents are arranged into chapters. For non-fiction work, logically related items are normally collected together in specific chapters. It then becomes a simple job to use the book as a reference source. But we still need to find our way around the book; that's where the contents list comes in. A quick glance at this will tell us immediately where the relevant information is held. It's also useful when we first come to decide whether or not to buy a book. When we get down to detailed referencing and cross-checking, the index comes into its own. Try using a technical working text which hasn't got an index; painful is the best description that can be applied to such a case. Finally, the text itself has to obey the rules of grammar and layout; that is, the syntax of the language.

We end up with an item which has a clearly understood function. If we go to the library we know how to track it down. Once in our hands we can quickly decide whether it's of interest to us from the contents list. Assuming that it is what we want, using it should be a straightforward task. Finally, we hope that it is written in a good, clear and correct style. If it does all these then it will truly convey information.

Software should be designed with the same aims in mind. Unfortunately, past experience shows the reverse case. Three interesting quotations, spanning roughly a 15 year period, illustrate this. The first castigates software developers for having an unprofessional and slap-happy approach. The second neatly highlights the absence of design as part of the software production process, while the last one shows just how little attention is given to the needs of the end user.

You software guys are too much like the weavers in the story about the Emperor and his new clothes. When I go out to check on a software development the answers I get sound like, 'We're fantastically busy weaving this magic cloth. Just wait a while and it'll look terrific.' But there's nothing I can see or touch, no numbers I can relate to, no way to pick up signals that things aren't really all that great. And there are too many people I know who have come out at the end wearing a bunch of expensive rags or nothing at all.

A USAF decision maker

If builders built buildings the same way that programmers wrote programs, the first woodpecker would destroy civilisation.

Gerry Weinberg

Most so called user-friendly systems are about as friendly as a cornered rat.

Eddie Shah

We've realized our mistakes of the past; now we're trying to get it right in the first place. At last software engineering has become a recognized discipline in its own right. But any profession needs the right tools if the jobs are going to be done properly. And one of the major tools is the programming language; enter Ada.

1.1.2 Ada – a gentle introduction to program structure

Ada is a large, powerful and complex language. These features make it a difficult language to learn – especially for those without experience of high-level languages (HLLs). So what we're going to do is to work our way through its structure and rules at a gentle pace. This means that, at each stage, only part of the complete Ada picture is revealed. But it will be

4   An introduction to Ada

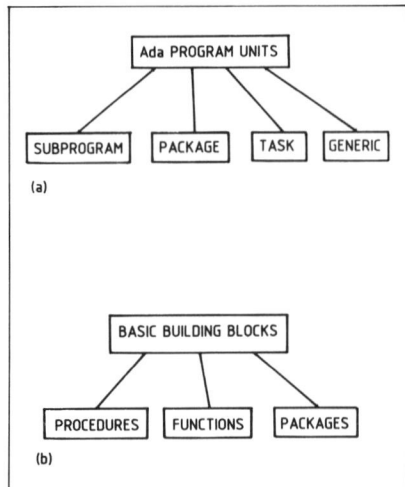

Fig.1.2 The major program units of Ada.

sufficient for you to begin writing programs straight away. Naturally these will be very simple in the early stages. But, as time goes by, the more complex and advanced features of Ada can be tackled from this solid initial base. Our starting point is to see how Ada programs are structured.

The form and meaning of Ada programs are specified in a document called 'The Reference Manual for the Ada Programming Language' (usually referred to as the LRM). This defines Ada programs to be a set of program units: subprograms, packages, tasks and generics, Fig.1.2a.

However, there is a second way of looking at Ada programs: the basic building blocks (compilation units) of the language. These come in three shapes: procedures, functions and packages, Fig.1.2b (procedures and functions are collectively known as subprograms). The relationship between the program units and the building blocks will become clear as the various topics are discussed. It will also become clear why we choose to describe Ada using these two approaches. For the moment, though, it is enough to know that they exist. If, at this stage, you know little about compiling source code and related aspects, see section 17.1. This contains a brief introduction to the topic.

For the next few chapters we're going to limit ourselves to the simplest executable program unit of Ada. This, defined to be the 'main program unit', is constructed using the procedure, Fig.1.3.

The other building blocks – which provide software services to the main program – are used extensively in the specimen programs in the text. What these services are will gradually become clear through regular use in the program examples. Details of their features, structures and implementations

A very broad view of Ada's structure 5

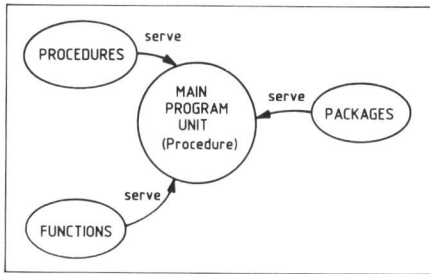

Fig.1.3 The elements of an Ada main program.

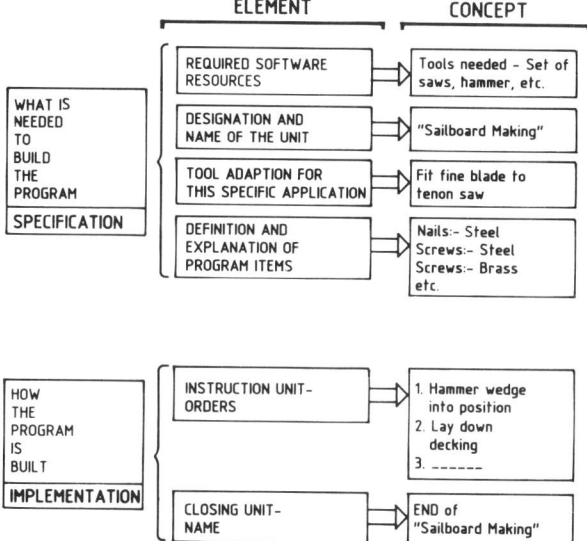

Fig.1.4 Ada main program – general structure.

can be left until later. Note also that the language provides, as standard, a wide range of software services.

Ada main programs have a defined structure (Fig.1.4).

This figure shows in very simple terms what tools are needed to build the program and how the program is formed. Read through this figure carefully and assimilate the concepts involved. These are basic to Ada programming.

In more concrete terms, an Ada main program usually has the form shown in Table 1.1.

First, a general point. All high-level languages (HLLs) use certain words to carry out specific actions; Ada is no exception. These words, called reserved words, may only be used for their defined purpose. They will be introduced

6   An introduction to Ada

Table 1.1 Ada main program – basic format

> **with** THINGS_THAT_ARE_NEEDED
>
> **procedure** PROCEDURE_NAME **is**
>
> ADAPTION REQUIREMENTS
>
> DEFINITION AND EXPLANATION
> OF PROGRAM OBJECTS
> **begin**
>   STATEMENTS FOR EXECUTION BY
>   THE PROGRAM ARE INSERTED HERE
> **end** PROCEDURE_NAME;

- **with** is used to define any external software resources needed by this particular program.
- **procedure** defines this software text (more correctly, a compilation unit) to be of class procedure (we will meet procedures in chapter 4).
- **PROCEDURE_NAME** is the name given by the author to the program.
- **ADAPTION REQUIREMENTS**: Often we need to tailor the facilities of external software resources to meet particular program needs. Such adaptations produce 'derived' units from parent types (this process is called 'instantiation').
- **DEFINITIONS AND EXPLANATIONS** ('Declarations'): What is their purpose? For the compiler to work correctly it must be given information about the objects used in the program. Such information is written in this section, the 'declarative part'. We normally call the contents of the declarative part the 'declarations'. Declarations are needed only for the compilation phase of program development; they take no part in the execution of the finished product.
- **EXECUTABLE STATEMENTS**: These are the set of instructions which are carried out (executed) by the program when it is run, defined as the program STATEMENTS.

---

as and when they are needed in these notes. The reserved words here are **with, procedure, begin, is,** and **end** (Fig.1.5).

Appendix A gives a full listing of such words. Note that Ada is not case sensitive; that is, 'END', 'End' and 'end' have the same meaning.

Ada is a typed language. That is, all program objects must belong to a defined type. The general concepts of types and their attributes are illustrated by Fig.1.6.

As a specific example, consider type INTEGER. All numbers defined to belong to this type must have whole values (i.e. no fractional part). Note that type information is given in the declarations section of the program.

A very broad view of Ada's structure   7

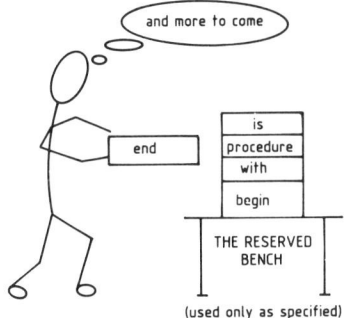

Fig.1.5 Reserved words.

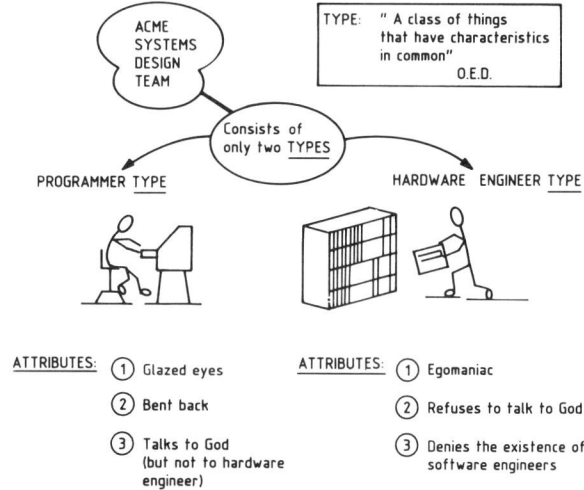

Fig.1.6 Types – concept and attributes.

1.1.3 Declarations and statements

Let's consider a very simple program to carry out the task:

"Compute   Y = X1 + X2"

Before the program can be compiled we must define:

- What external resources are needed.
- If any special adaption of these resources is required.
- The existence and the type of the three items Y, X1, X2. We 'declare' them, the relevant facts being written in the declarations section.

8 An introduction to Ada

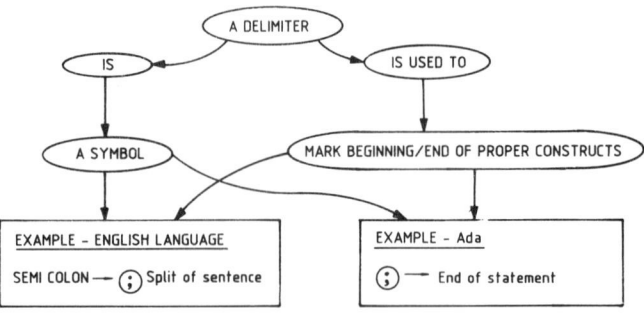

Fig.1.7 Delimiters.

We then write the program statement in the instructions section. Let us first take the simplest possible case where external resources aren't required (this is for demonstration only – the program won't actually do anything). For this case the program structure is

```
LINE 1    procedure EXAMPLE is
LINE 2       X1, X2, Y : INTEGER;
LINE 3    begin
LINE 4       Y := X1 + X2;
LINE 5    end EXAMPLE;
```

Line numbers have been put in for ease of reference only.

LINE 1: This starts with the reserved word **procedure**. The name of the program ('EXAMPLE') is inserted next, and the line finished with the reserved word **is**.

LINE 2: Here we list the items used in the program. In this case the items (X1, X2, Y) are defined (by their declaration method) to be variables; that is, their values can change as the program runs. The collection of variables is called the *variable list*. Observe that the list is terminated by a colon (':'), then followed by the word INTEGER, the whole lot being finished off with a semi-colon (';'). Both ':' and ';' belong to the set of Ada units called *delimiters* (Fig.1.7).

INTEGER defines X1, X2, Y to be of the 'type' INTEGER and has a specific meaning (as already shown) in Ada. Hence it can be seen that in the declarations section we must list all program items and define their type.

LINE 3: The use of **begin** indicates the start of the executable statements.

LINE 4: Here we meet the assignment symbol ':='. This can be read as 'is given the value of'. For this example Y is given the value of the

A very broad view of Ada's structure 9

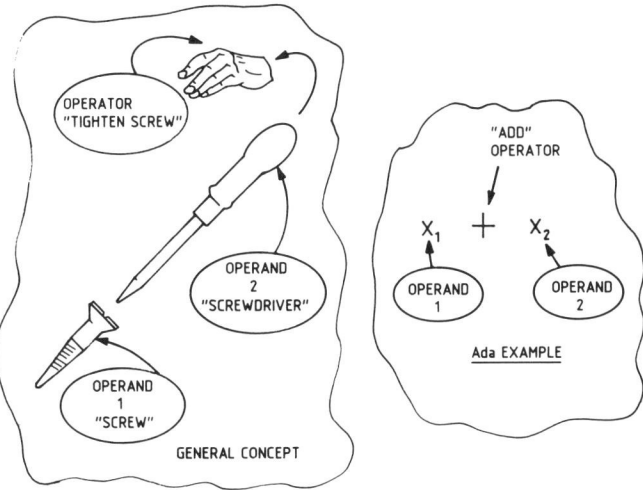

Fig.1.8 Operators and operands.

result of the addition of X1 and X2. Strictly speaking, we evaluate the expression on the right-hand side of the symbol and assign it to the variable on the left-hand side. In this statement X1 and X2 are defined to be operands; '+' is an operator (Fig.1.8). Once more note the use of the delimiter ';'.

LINE 5: The reserved word **end** followed by the name of the program and finished off with ';' defines the end of the executable statements.

In general (and more formal) terms the example consists of

```
procedure PROGRAM_NAME is
    IDENTIFIER_LIST : TYPE;
begin
    STATEMENTS
end PROGRAM_NAME;
```

Normally a program makes use of external resources, as described earlier. Often these external resources need to be tailored to suit our particular needs within the program. This is a rather more complicated aspect of Ada, covered in more detail in later chapters. For now it is enough to point out which part of a program is involved in tailoring external resources and to ask you to take this on trust.

For example, a common external resource is the package TEXT_IO. When we use it our program may start as follows:

10   An introduction to Ada

```
with TEXT_IO
procedure EXAMPLE1 is
   package INT_IO is new TEXT_IO. INTEGER_IO (INTEGER)
```

TEXT_IO is an external software resource (actually a package), being called up by the **with** operation. This is clear enough. By comparison the final line is pretty well incomprehensible. In simple terms (which is good enough for now) it says that we:

- First define a new package (INT_IO) within the procedure EXAMPLE1.
- Take a particular service package (INTEGER_IO) within the package TEXT_IO.
- Tailor it in a specific way (INTEGER).
- Allocate the tailored functions to the package INT_IO (instantiate).

This enables us now to use the package INT_IO to input and output data items of type INTEGER.

Similar statements will appear in the following examples. It is enough for now to recognize them (without a full explanation being given) to enable you to start programming in Ada. This won't in any way hinder you in developing the example programs; all will become clear in due course.

1.1.4   Block structure

Basically the block structure within Ada is provided by the matching **begin** and **end** words. Structuring of this nature supports program modularity and visibility, and also simplifies the use of variable names in large programs (see later, chapter 4, *local* and *global* variables).

1.1.5   Formally describing Ada features

Within the main body of this book Ada and its features are introduced in a gradual manner. Note that we use syntax diagrams to show the overall structure of Ada and to highlight specific language points. The interpretation and use of these diagrams is self-explanatory. As used here they give only part of the language syntax. A complete language definition is presented in the 'Ada Language Reference Manual'.

Consider how the general structure of an Ada program may be expressed using a syntax diagram (Fig.1.9).

We can now clearly see that we place the program declarations between **is** and **begin**; the program statements go between **begin** and **end**. It can also be seen that a subprogram may be written which has no declarations.

Naming objects – identifiers 11

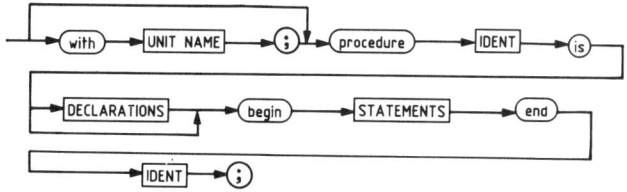

Fig.1.9 Ada main program – general structure (syntax diagram).

1.2 NAMING OBJECTS – IDENTIFIERS

IDENTIFIERS are symbolic names used to represent items (or objects) within the program (Fig.1.10).

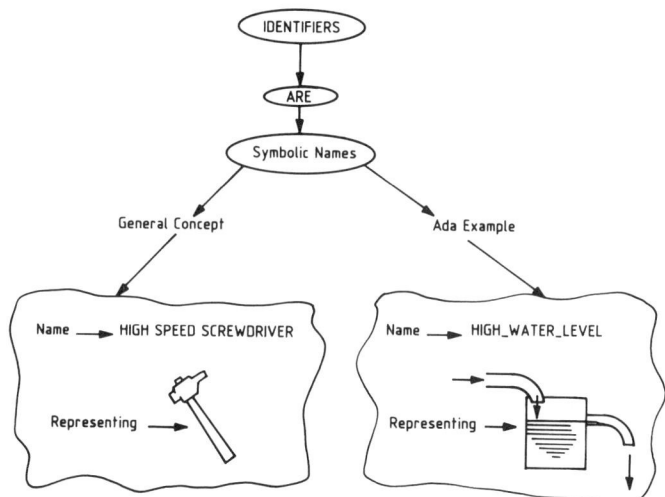

Fig.1.10 Identifiers.

For instance, in the earlier example, we used three identifiers – X1, X2, and Y – to represent program variables. The format for identifiers is given in the syntax diagram of Fig.1.11.

From this information it can be seen that an identifier MUST start with a letter. It may consist of only one letter, or may be followed by other letters and digits, including the underscore character. Examples of acceptable (legal) identifiers are

> A   a   A1   A11   AB   AB1   A_B   AbCD_11afG   etc.

12 An introduction to Ada

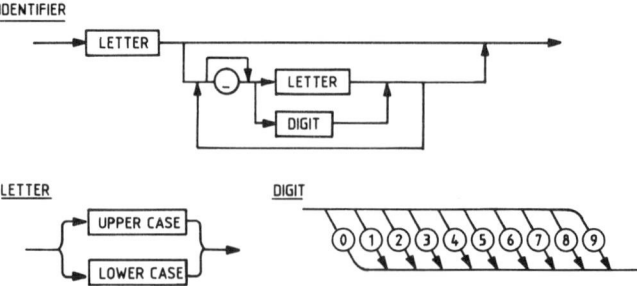

Fig.1.11 Syntax diagram – identifier.

Note that although the underscore character may be used, other special characters such as '/', '!', '[' etc. are not allowed (not legal). Reserved words MUST NOT be used as identifiers as this will cause errors at compile time.

Ada text, as stated earlier, is not case sensitive. The programmer is free to write in upper or lower case as he or she sees fit. Thus ALARM_GROUP, Alarm_group and Alarm_Group are identical identifiers (but AlarmGroup is different – why?). However, a *de facto* convention has grown up in the Ada world: lower case is used for reserved words, upper case being used elsewhere.

Later on you will come across items identified using dot notation, as in 'UNIT1.ALARM'. In Adaspeak this is defined to be a *selected component*. Here the identifier 'ALARM' is prefixed (or confined) by the name 'UNIT1'. This forms what we might loosely call a compound identifier. As such, identifiers 'UNIT1.ALARM' and 'UNIT2.ALARM' are regarded as two quite different items. Again, the use of this will be shown later; just be aware of it for now.

Ada doesn't put a limit on the number of characters which may be used as an identifier name – as long as it fits on a single line. In practice the maximum line length may be compiler dependent.

Names used for program identifiers should be clear and meaningful. For instance, 'PRIMARY_FUEL_FEED' and 'CURRENT_BANK_BALANCE' carry much more meaning than 'PF1' or 'CBB'. Typing in such names may, at first, seem to be a relatively boring and thankless task. Just remember, though, that programs generally have to be maintained for many years. During this time they will be read by many different people. How easy will it be for them to work out exactly what the software is trying to achieve? Even if this doesn't concern you very much, look at it from a selfish point of view. YOU might be the person given the task of revamping the software years after its initial production.

1.3 COMMENTS

Comments have one function only: to make the program easier for the reader to understand; they are ignored by the compiler. A well-designed program will always use comments liberally but selectively, that is use them for positive reasons. In Ada, comments are inserted into the program on a line-by-line basis. Each comment starts with two hyphens, then the text is added, as in

>   -- this is a comment

The comment extends only to the end of the line. If a long comment is needed then it must be spread over several lines, as, for instance,

>   -- This is the first line of the comment
>   -- and this is the second one.

Comments do not have to start on a new line; they may, for instance, be added to a program statement line, etc. (examples are given later). But it is not legal to insert a comment WITHIN the text of line statements.

Finally, note that there mustn't be any spaces between the two hyphens.

1.4 CONSOLE COMMUNICATIONS

1.4.1 Introduction

In general, programs are developed for two different applications. They may be developed for use on standard equipment, such as personal computers, workstations, etc. The other extreme is where they are intended for use within target (usually microprocessor-based) machines. For the moment we'll limit ourselves to standard platforms, dealing with targeted systems later.

With standard systems it is very easy to use interactive console operations to demonstrate program operations (you may know the console under a different name, e.g. terminal, or VDU and keyboard). Here program input data is usually obtained from a console operator, output information normally being sent to the console, printer, plotter or similar output device.

1.4.2 Outputs

Why start with output operations? Well, usually the computer must provide some information to the operator before any interactive processes take place.

Generally, outputs consist either of text messages for the operator or else numerical values, say the results of calculations.

For messages the output is a text string, that is a sequence or 'string' of printing characters. In Ada, to send a text string to the console we normally use a software operation called 'PUT'. For instance, the program statement

```
PUT ("Hello");
```

will lead to the word *Hello* being displayed on the console screen. Note that the character sequence is enclosed between (" and ").

A second write operation will be introduced here, that of 'NEW_LINE'. Its function is to send an end-of-line sequence to the terminal device, that is a carriage return/line feed action. The line statement NEW_LINE causes the screen cursor to move on to the next line. NEW_LINE (2) moves it two lines, NEW_LINE (4) moves it four lines, and so on.

A trivial example of a screen write operation is given below in Listing 1.1.

```
with TEXT_IO;
procedure ONE is
  use TEXT_IO;
begin
  PUT ("Hello");
  PUT (" to Ada programming");
  NEW_LINE;
  PUT ("Goodbye");
  NEW_LINE;
end ONE;
```

Listing 1.1 This is a trivial program to print out text on your screen.

You may well wonder where these magical quantities PUT and NEW_LINE come from and how the program recognizes them. They are, in fact, part of a software package TEXT_IO provided within the Ada library of standard functions. Library features are very common in high-level languages which run under standard operating systems. They are also found in microprocessor development systems (MDSs) for assembly language programming. Unlike some programming languages (e.g. Fortran), Ada library units must be explicitly brought into the program – the function of the **with** construct (the *context clause*). For the moment there is no need to know how they work in detail, only how to use them. Consult your Ada compiler handbook or the language reference manual (LRM) to see what library features are available.

We brought in the services provided by the package TEXT_IO using the **with** clause. Fine. But, when the program meets the statements PUT and NEW_LINE, how does it know where to find these? It can't, unless we tell it where to look. THAT is the function of the **use** clause.

Console communications 15

Read through this listing, decide what should be written on the screen of your computer, then compile, link and run the program. You should do this with all the examples given in the text as there is no substitute for practical experience.

A second version of the same program is given in Listing 1.2.

```
with TEXT_IO;
procedure FIRST is
begin
  TEXT_IO.PUT ("Hello");
  TEXT_IO.PUT (" to Ada programming");
  TEXT_IO.NEW_LINE;
  TEXT_IO.PUT ("Goodbye");
  TEXT_IO.NEW_LINE;
end FIRST;
```

Listing 1.2 This is almost the same as Listing 1.1.

You will see that now the operations PUT and NEW_LINE are prefixed or qualified by TEXT_IO. Using the qualified form allows us to dispense with the use directive; the locations of PUT and NEW_LINE are clearly specified. Generally, the use of the qualified or the unqualified form depends entirely on individual circumstances.

Let us now look at how numerical values are output from a program to a console. First, though, a short digression. Consider the requirement to print out the integer number 55. For this we write

```
PUT (55, X);
```

where X sets the minimum numbers of characters which are output to the screen, the so-called 'fieldwidth' (Fig.1.12).

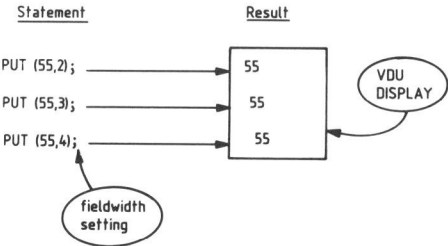

Fig.1.12 Use of the fieldwidth setting.

If we were to write PUT (55) the compiler would use a predefined (default) setting for the fieldwidth. We can now apply this to a practical example, Listing 1.3.

16   An introduction to Ada

```
with TEXT_IO;
procedure PRINT_NUM is
  package INT_IO is new TEXT_IO.INTEGER_IO (INTEGER);
begin
  TEXT_IO.PUT_LINE ("Hello");
  INT_IO.PUT (55, 2);
  -- note the fieldwidth setting
  TEXT_IO.NEW_LINE;
  INT_IO.PUT (55);
  -- default fieldwidth setting used
  TEXT_IO.NEW_LINE;
end PRINT_NUM;
```

Listing 1.3 This simple program prints out text and numbers on your screen.

Once more the service software which provides the PUT operation is located in package TEXT_IO. More precisely, it is housed in a package called INTEGER_IO which itself is contained within TEXT_IO. Some configuration of this package needs to be carried out before it can be used in the main program. We do this by using the declaration

package INT_IO **is new** TEXT_IO. INTEGER_IO (INTEGER);

Here we take the package INTEGER_IO and then tailor it to our application using INTEGER (to print out integer numbers). We then allocate all its features to the package INT_IO. In the program itself we use the facilities of INT_IO, as shown in Listing 1.3.

The name INT_IO is not predefined and we may use any suitable name; **new** is another Ada reserved word. This example has also introduced another standard procedure, PUT_LINE, which is merely a combination of PUT and NEW_LINE.

Observe also that qualified notation has been used here, as in TEXT_IO.PUT and INT_IO.PUT. Why this construct? The answer is that the PUT from package TEXT_IO is not the same as that in package INTEGER_IO. By qualifying each PUT we define which one should be used.

For the moment take this and similar constructs on trust. Use them when programming the examples in the text. Just treat them as tools which are needed to build the programs, because, at this stage, that is the main objective.

One final point: when writing Ada code, operation of the space bar produces the so-called 'white space'. Generally such spaces are ignored by the compiler UNLESS their use is prohibited in a particular construct (as between the two hyphens at the start of a comment).

1.4.3 Inputs

How do we get information into the program in the first place? Again we use standard library operations, here applying GET. From now on, these will be used without a full explanation being given in the text. The meaning of any such construct should be obvious from its use; but you SHOULD consult the LRM for full information.

In the following example (Listing 1.4) our very simple program is extended to take in the values of the variables X1 and X2 from the keyboard. Note that comments are also included in the program statement area.

```
with TEXT_IO;
procedure GET_AND_COMMENT is
  package INT_IO is new TEXT_IO.INTEGER_IO (INTEGER);
  X1, X2, Y        :     INTEGER;
begin
  TEXT_IO.PUT ("Enter first number  X1 => ");
  INT_IO.GET (X1);
  -- GET is a function which reads a value (X1)
  -- from the keyboard and verifies that it is
  -- an integer.
  TEXT_IO.SKIP_LINE;
  -- skip on to the next line
  TEXT_IO.PUT ("Enter second number X2 => ");
  INT_IO.GET (X2);
  -- now we read in X2 from the keyboard
  TEXT_IO.SKIP_LINE;
  Y := X1 + X2;
end GET_AND_COMMENT;
```

Listing 1.4 This is a simple example of inputting data and using comments.

Another new procedure, SKIP_LINE, has also been introduced.

Do not be surprised if error messages are generated when the program is run. These run-time errors (*exceptions*) have a number of possible causes:

- Entering a non-integer value;
- Entering too large a value as an integer;
- Computing a result which is too large for type integer.

Now let's further extend the program to provide interactive working with the console (Listing 1.5).

Note that the text between **begin** and **end** is indented; this makes the program structure clear.

Where text and numerical values are to be mixed we could, for instance, add the following to Listing 1.5:

18   An introduction to Ada

```
with TEXT_IO;
procedure CONSOLE_COMMS is
  package INT_IO is new TEXT_IO.INTEGER_IO (INTEGER);
  X1, X2, Y         :      INTEGER;
begin
  TEXT_IO.PUT ("Enter first number  X1 =>  ");
  INT_IO.GET (X1);
  TEXT_IO.SKIP_LINE;
  TEXT_IO.PUT ("Enter second number X2 =>  ");
  INT_IO.GET (X2);
  TEXT_IO.SKIP_LINE;
  Y := X1 + X2;
  TEXT_IO.PUT ("X1 + X2 = ");
  INT_IO.PUT (Y);
  -- the value of Y is written out
  -- it has the default fieldwidth setting
  TEXT_IO.NEW_LINE;
  TEXT_IO.PUT_LINE ("Calculation finished");
end CONSOLE_COMMS;
```

Listing 1.5 This program illustrates the use of comments and various read and write functions.

```
TEXT_IO.PUT ("The value of y is");
INT_IO.PUT (Y);
TEXT_IO.NEW_LINE;
```

Assume that the calculated value of Y is 36. When the program is run the following appears on the screen:

```
The value of y is  36
```

1.5 NUMERIC CONSTANTS

1.5.1 Literal constants

Often it is required to carry out a calculation using a fixed or constant value. One line of a digital filter computation might read

```
Y_NEW := 8.5 + Y_OLD;
```

The number 8.5 is said to be expressed as a literal constant (literal – a word or symbol that stands for itself rather than as a name for something else).

1.5.2 Named constants

While the literal form is perfectly all right, a much more flexible technique is to use names for constants. The names are defined (declared) in the declarations section; they are also assigned their actual or literal values at this point. In the program itself the identifier name (and not the value) is used, this being called a named constant. Thus instead of using the literal constant 8.5 in the computation we could use the named constant 'DEMAND', giving

```
Y_NEW := DEMAND + Y_OLD;
```

where DEMAND represents the value 8.5. This is done in the source program in the following way:

```
procedure P1 is
    DEMAND : constant := 8.5; -- note that we use
                              -- the assignment symbol
begin
    .
    PROGRAM_STATEMENTS
    .
end P1.
```

The word **constant** means just that – a constant value. It is another reserved word. The main point to remember is that constants are fixed; that is, they NEVER change during the execution of a program. Contrast this with variables.

The value to the right-hand side of the ':=' sign is, in this example, called a *universal static expression*. The following is a valid constant declaration construct:

```
SIX   : constant := 6;
THREE : constant := 3;
NINE  : constant := SIX + THREE;
```

The advantages gained by using a named constant are that, if the value of the constant has to be changed, then:

- Only one alteration has to be done;
- The workload is reduced;
- The likelihood of forgetting to carry the change through the program is eliminated.

1.6 BASIC DATA TYPES

1.6.1 Introduction

We organize variables and constants in Ada into various categories or TYPES, though so far we have only discussed type INTEGER. One reason for forming types is to let the compiler know how much memory space is needed for such data values. But once having done this we can then get the compiler to look for program errors caused by using types incorrectly. The use of data typing is a major aid for the elimination of syntax errors in Ada software.

Two important classes of data types are the scalar (or simple) and composite (structured) ones. At this stage only some of the scalar ones will be considered, a full discussion on types being kept until later (chapter 5).

1.6.2 INTEGER

Integers are defined as numbers without a decimal point, such as 55, 276, −49, etc. In Ada, type INTEGER is defined to be a contiguous set of such numbers – which can be precisely represented on computer hardware. The maximum integer value which a computer can handle depends on the particular machine or compiler implementation. For instance, in many machines integers are represented using 16 bits (2 bytes), giving a number range of −32 768 to +32 767. You must make sure that your programs (as in Listing 1.6) don't

```
with TEXT_IO;
procedure INT_MATH is
  package INT_IO is new TEXT_IO.INTEGER_IO (INTEGER);
  X1, X2, Y      :        INTEGER;
  DEMAND         :   constant       := 50;
begin
  TEXT_IO.PUT ("Enter first number  X1 => ");
  INT_IO.GET (X1);
  TEXT_IO.SKIP_LINE;
  TEXT_IO.PUT ("Enter second number X2 => ");
  INT_IO.GET (X2);
  TEXT_IO.SKIP_LINE;
  Y := X1 + X2 + DEMAND;
  TEXT_IO.PUT ("The value of Y is ");
  INT_IO.PUT (Y);
  TEXT_IO.NEW_LINE;
  TEXT_IO.PUT_LINE ("Calculation finished");
end INT_MATH;
```

Listing 1.6 This illustrates the use of data type INTEGER with both variable and constant values.

try to generate numbers greater than these values. Otherwise overflow errors will occur, causing the program to fail at run time.

To cater for the range of numbers met in practice, the LRM states:

An implementation may provide additional predefined integer types. It is recommended that the names of such additional types end with INTEGER as in SHORT_INTEGER or LONG_INTEGER.

1.6.3 Type real

Numbers which include decimal points are defined as *real* types. These can be expressed in two ways:

(a) Fixed point form: 5.1, 793.29, −6.508, etc.
(b) Floating point form: 2.0E+1   (meaning $2.0 * 10^1$),
                            5.2E−2   (meaning $5.2 * 10^{-2}$), etc.

A fuller discussion on real types is held over to Chapters 2 and 6, as this is not a straightforward item (not in Ada, that is). Strictly speaking there isn't a type defined as REAL in the language. There are, in fact, two types – FLOAT and FIXED. For the moment we will confine ourselves to type FLOAT, used for the handling of floating point numbers. Listing 1.7 gives a simple example of its application.

```
with TEXT_IO;
procedure REAL_MATH is
  package REAL_IO is new TEXT_IO.FLOAT_IO (FLOAT);
  X1, X2, Y       :      FLOAT;
begin
  TEXT_IO.PUT ("Enter the first number X1 (real number only) => ");
  REAL_IO.GET (X1);
  -- (X1) is read from the keyboard and verified
  -- that it is a real value
  TEXT_IO.SKIP_LINE;
  TEXT_IO.PUT ("Enter the other number X2 (real number only) => ");
  REAL_IO.GET (X2);
  -- now we read in X2 from the keyboard
  TEXT_IO.SKIP_LINE;
  Y := X1 + X2;
  TEXT_IO.PUT ("X1 + X2 = ");
  REAL_IO.PUT (Y, 10);
  -- note the larger fieldwidth setting
  TEXT_IO.NEW_LINE;
end REAL_MATH;
```

Listing 1.7 Here is a simple numeric example using floating point numbers.

The program variables X1, X2 and Y are all declared to be of type FLOAT. Moreover, a new package REAL_IO has been declared to exist in the subprogram REAL_MATH. This has been endowed with the properties of the package FLOAT_IO, tailored for type FLOAT.

WARNING: If your program generates error messages check that values are being entered correctly. For instance, decimal ten in real form is '10.0', not '10'.

1.6.4 Logical operations – type BOOLEAN

The Boolean type has only two values, TRUE or FALSE. The use of these will be discussed later; for the moment only the method of declaration is shown. It follows the usual form so that for a Boolean variable called 'TEST' the declaration is

> TEST : BOOLEAN;

1.6.5 Character operations – constants

We have already met the use of text characters for printing out messages to a console. The sequence of characters enclosed by the quotation symbols is defined to be a string. These messages are set at the time of writing the program; only by rewriting can they be changed. Thus they are known as *string literals*. As an example consider the declaration

> CAN29 : **constant** STRING := "SAE 20 oil";

The presence of the quotation marks (also called string brackets) defines that the enclosed items are printable characters. So when we write

> PUT (CAN29);

the text printed out on the screen is that shown between the string brackets, that is SAE 20 oil.

NOTE: A construct of the form "SAE 20 oil" is called a string literal.

1.6.6 Character operations – type CHARACTER

There are many cases where we want to interact with programs, as for instance to manipulate text and variables or to give simple YES/NO answers.

Likewise we may want to output information which depends on the results of a program run. It can be seen that using character constants presents the same difficulties as those found in the use of numeric constants.

Ada eases this burden and gives much greater flexibility by supplying another data type, the CHARACTER. Any variable defined as being of type CHARACTER can hold one – and only one – printable character (strictly there are also non-printing characters of this type; for the moment we'll ignore them). This now makes it possible to define and change printing characters under program control, something which can't be done with character constants.

Declarations of character variables are done in the usual way, e.g.

```
ALPHANUM : CHARACTER;
```

Then, within the program, we can assign any character value to the variable, as follows:

```
ALPHANUM := '7';
ALPHANUM := 'W';
```

As an example (Listing 1.8) let us consider the problem of reading in two characters from a keyboard and printing them back in reverse order.

```
with TEXT_IO;
procedure CHAR_IO is
   CHAR_1, CHAR_2 :    CHARACTER;
begin
   TEXT_IO.PUT ("Enter two characters => ");
   TEXT_IO.GET (CHAR_1);
   TEXT_IO.GET (CHAR_2);
   TEXT_IO.SKIP_LINE;
   TEXT_IO.PUT ("The reverse order is => ");
   TEXT_IO.PUT (CHAR_2);
   TEXT_IO.PUT (CHAR_1);
   TEXT_IO.NEW_LINE;
end CHAR_IO;
```

Listing 1.8 Here is an example of the use of the data type CHARACTER.

The more extensive use of this type is discussed later in chapter 5.

NOTE: the construct form 'X' is called a *character literal*.

REVIEW

Can you now:

- Define the general layout of an Ada main program?
- Identify the use of program declarations and statements?
- Describe the use of identifiers, variables, constants, reserved words, and comments?
- Understand the concepts of block structuring and data typing?
- Create a complete, compilable Ada program that you interact with from your computer console?

Chapter Two
Elementary arithmetic and logic

If you have fully understood Chapter 1 you are now in a position to learn how to manipulate data, both arithmetically and logically. On completing this chapter you will be able to:

- Define and use EXPRESSIONS;
- Carry out type changing between reals and INTEGERs;
- Perform addition, subtraction, multiplication, division and exponentiation;
- Understand and control the precedence of operations;
- Understand the structure and use of Boolean expressions.

2.1 STATEMENTS AND EXPRESSIONS

We have already met statements and expressions in quite a number of examples so far. These have been handled in a fairly informal way; now let's define them more precisely. A statement is 'the unit from which a high-level language program is constructed; a program is a sequence of statements'. Another view is that statements are instructions which cause something to happen when the program runs. One form of statement is typified by 'PUT_LINE', another by the assignment operation, as in 'X := 25'.

Consider the program statement

```
K := X1 + X2;
```

(Fig.2.1).

The total right-hand side of the statement is an example of an expression, where X1 and X2 are defined to be operands and + is an operator. More formally, an expression can be defined as 'a sequence of operators and operands which can be evaluated to produce a result'. This result may be either numeric or Boolean; the first case arises from arithmetic operations, the second from logical ones.

In this section we are going to look at the ways in which valid expressions may be formed (the syntax rules); then we'll consider the way these are evaluated by the processor (the semantics of the language).

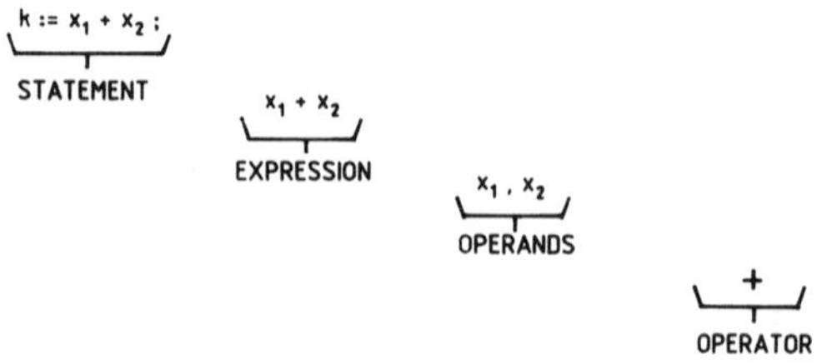

26 Elementary arithmetic and logic

```
k := x₁ + x₂ ;
_____/
STATEMENT       x₁ + x₂
                \_____/
                EXPRESSION      x₁ , x₂
                                \_____/
                                OPERANDS
                                                +
                                                \_/
                                                OPERATOR
```

Fig.2.1 Statements and expressions.

2.2 ARITHMETIC EXPRESSIONS

2.2.1 Introduction

The simplest form of expression only has one operand, as in

```
K := 55;   or
W := −36.2;
```

Clearly the value of the expression always stays the same. In most situations it is best to use a symbolic name (as described earlier), giving, for example

```
HIGHTEMP : constant := 55;
```

More complex expressions are formed by using a number of operands linked together by arithmetic operators. In Ada we can carry out the following (Fig.2.2):

```
(a) addition . . . . . . . . . . . '+'
(b) subtraction . . . . . . . . . '−'
(c) multiplication . . . . . . . . '*'
(d) division . . . . . . . . . . . '/', 'rem', and 'mod'
(e) exponentiation . . . . . . . '**'
(f) absolute . . . . . . . . . . . 'ABS'
```

Use of these is straightforward as long as the rules concerning type mixing are followed. For instance, the literal '2' is treated as an integer value; '2.0' is considered to be a real value. The statement

```
Y := 2 + 2.0;
```

Arithmetic expressions   27

FUNCTION	MATHS NOTATION	Ada NOTATION
ADDITION	x + y	x + y
SUBTRACTION	x − y	x − y
MULTIPLICATION	(x x y) or (x • y)	x * y
DIVISION	(x / y) or (x ÷ y)	x / y x rem y x mod y
EXPONENTIATION	x^y	x ** y
ABSOLUTE VALUE (MODULUS)	abs x or |x|	abs (x)

Fig.2.2 Arithmetic operations.

is illegal in Ada because it involves different types. In general, type mixing is not allowed. In this example type conversion must be performed until the statement contains one type only. And, in an effort to keep errors to a minimum, this must be done explicitly.

Much greater coverage is given to this aspect of program development in chapters 5 and 6.

2.2.2 Working with reals and INTEGERs − type conversion

Although it is best to work only with quantities of the same type, in practice it is often necessary to convert from real to INTEGER and vice versa.

Consider, for instance, carrying out digital filtering of analogue signals. The input is obtained from an analogue-to-digital converter (ADC) whilst the output is provided by a digital-to-analogue converter (DAC); in each case the digital version of the analogue value is in INTEGER form. Normally it is much simpler from the computation point of view to work with real numbers. Therefore, before mathematical operations are carried out on the input signal, an INTEGER to real type conversion must be performed. Likewise, a conversion back to INTEGER form is needed before the result is sent to the DAC.

An example of such type changing is shown below in procedure TYPE_CHANGE, Listing 2.1.

Here the INTEGER variable X1 is converted to real (floating point) form by writing

```
X1R := FLOAT (X1);
```

```
with TEXT_IO;              use TEXT_IO;
procedure TYPE_CHANGE is
  package INT_IO is new INTEGER_IO (INTEGER);
  package REAL_IO is new FLOAT_IO (FLOAT);
  use INT_IO;
  use REAL_IO;
  X1                :     INTEGER;
  X1R               :     FLOAT;
begin
  PUT ("Enter a number - integer value only => ");
  GET (X1);
  SKIP_LINE;
  X1R := FLOAT (X1);
  -- X1 is converted from INTEGER to FLOAT
  PUT ("The real value of the number is");
  PUT (X1R, 9);
  -- note the larger fieldwidth setting
  NEW_LINE;
  PUT ("Enter a number - real value only => ");
  GET (X1R);
  SKIP_LINE;
  X1 := INTEGER (X1R);
  -- X1R is converted from FLOAT to INTEGER
  PUT ("The integer value of the number is");
  PUT (X1, 7);
end TYPE_CHANGE;
```

Listing 2.1 Here is an example of type changing between INTEGER and FLOA types.

and the reverse process defined by the statement

```
X1 := INTEGER (X1R);
```

Note that variables X1 and X1R do not usually use the same amount of data storage space (normally specified in bytes). Note also that the number of bytes used for data representation may vary from compiler to compiler.

2.2.3 Elementary maths operations

(a) Addition

The addition operator '+' has been used on a number of occasions in the specimen programs and has the same meaning as the algebraic symbol. Strictly speaking it is defined to be a binary operator, that is it has two operands. Both operands must be the same type. The resulting value has the same type as the operands.

Arithmetic expressions   29

(b) **Subtraction**

The operator is '−'; again it has the same meaning as its algebraic counterpart. It also is a binary operator, having the same type rules as the addition function.

(c) **Multiplication**

The symbol for multiplication is '∗'; operations are similar to the algebraic 'x'. This also is used as a binary operator, where both operands must be the same type. The result of the calculation has the same type as the operands.

An example of simple addition and multiplication operations is given in Listing 2.2.

```
with TEXT_IO;             use TEXT_IO;
procedure ADD_MUL is
  package INT_IO is new INTEGER_IO (INTEGER);
  package REAL_IO is new FLOAT_IO (FLOAT);
  use INT_IO;
  use REAL_IO;
  X1, X2, Y1        :    INTEGER;
  Y1R               :    FLOAT;
  TG                :    constant    := 6.3;
begin
  PUT ("Enter first number - integer value only => ");
  GET (X1);
  SKIP_LINE;
  PUT ("Next number - integer value only => ");
  GET (X2);
  SKIP_LINE;
  NEW_LINE;
  Y1 := X1 + X2;
  -- addition of integers
  Y1R := FLOAT (Y1);
  Y1R := Y1R * TG;
  -- multiplication of REALS
  PUT ("The real value of Y is");
  PUT (Y1R, 2);
  NEW_LINE;
  Y1 := INTEGER (Y1R);
  PUT ("The integer value of Y is");
  PUT (Y1, 7);
  NEW_LINE;
end ADD_MUL;
```

Listing 2.2 Addition and multiplication of INTEGER and FLOAT types are performed in this example.

(d) **Division − reals**

For both INTEGER and real division we use the operator '/'. For real division, the '/' operation acts exactly the same as the divider in normal arithmetic. In this case

$$5/2 = 2.5 \quad \text{and} \quad 9/3 = 3$$

However, in Ada, real numbers must include a decimal point. This allows them to be distinguished from INTEGERs. Further, the result of the calculation must have the same type as the operands (as in the addition and multiplication operations). Therefore the equivalent Ada calculations would be

$$5.0/2.0 = 2.5 \quad \text{and} \quad 9.0/3.0 = 3.0$$

(e) Division – INTEGER

Consider the operation 'divide 10 by 4'. We define '4' to be the divisor and '10' to be the dividend. In formal mathematical terms we are trying to determine how many times the divisor is contained in the dividend. The result, of course, is 2.5. Fine. But how do we handle this result if we have already defined that all working should be done using whole numbers only – precisely the situation with INTEGER operations in Ada?

The solution adopted is a simple one. The result of integer division can always be represented in two parts: a whole number and anything remaining from the division. The whole number is equivalent to the truncated value found by using normal division. For instance,

$10/4 = 2 \quad$ the truncated part of 2.5 (rounding is not allowed)
$-10/4 = -2 \quad$ (truncation is towards zero)

Of course, INTEGER division frequently produces whole number results, as in $12/4 = 3$.

Now what about the remainder of any division operations? Are they of interest to us? The answer is, quite often, yes. But the form in which we want the remainder expressed depends on the mathematics being used. Specifically, are we concerned with 'normal' (Eulerian) arithmetic or with Modulo arithmetic?

For the first case we obtain the remainder by using the 'rem' operation. For the second, 'mod' is used. To find the remainders for the calculation (10 divided by 4) we'd have written

```
10 rem 4
10 mod 4
```

Both **rem** and **mod** are reserved words.

The rules for calculating the rem and mod values are given below. Assume that the required calculation is 'divide X (the dividend) by Y (the divisor)':

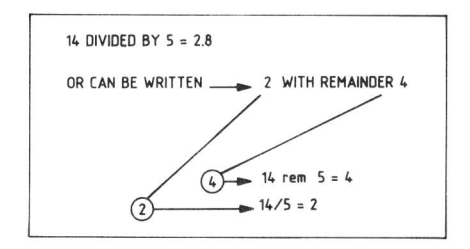

```
                    14 DIVIDED BY 5 = 2.8
              OR CAN BE WRITTEN ──→ 2 WITH REMAINDER 4

                              ④──→ 14 rem 5 = 4
                          ②──────→ 14/5 = 2
```

Fig.2.3 General concept for '/' and 'rem' operators.

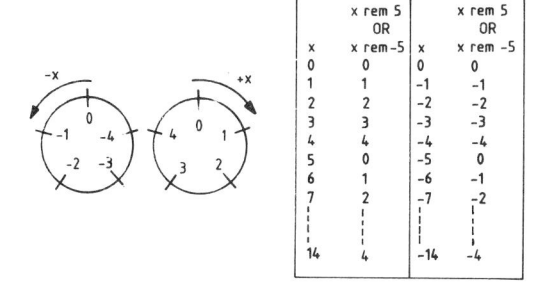

	x rem 5 OR x rem −5		x rem 5 OR x rem −5
x		x	
0	0	0	0
1	1	−1	−1
2	2	−2	−2
3	3	−3	−3
4	4	−4	−4
5	0	−5	0
6	1	−6	−1
7	2	−7	−2
⋮	⋮	⋮	⋮
14	4	−14	−4

Fig.2.4 Conceptual calculation for X rem Y.

```
( X / Y )    gives the INTEGER quotient value (Q_t)
( X rem Y )  gives an INTEGER remainder = X − (Q_t * Y)
( X mod Y )  gives an INTEGER remainder
```

These points are demonstrated in Figs 2.3, 2.4 and 2.5, and in Listing 2.3. Four cases have to be considered:

- X positive and Y positive
- X positive and Y negative
- X negative and Y positive
- X negative and Y negative

In all cases the integer quotient values differ only in their sign (plus or minus). To derive this use the rules of normal mathematics.

The sign of the remainder obtained using rem depends ONLY on the sign of the dividend. That is, a positive dividend gives a positive rem remainder. Likewise, a negative one produces a negative remainder value. This rule, and the resulting values of the rem remainder, are illustrated in the diagram of Fig.2.4.

32 Elementary arithmetic and logic

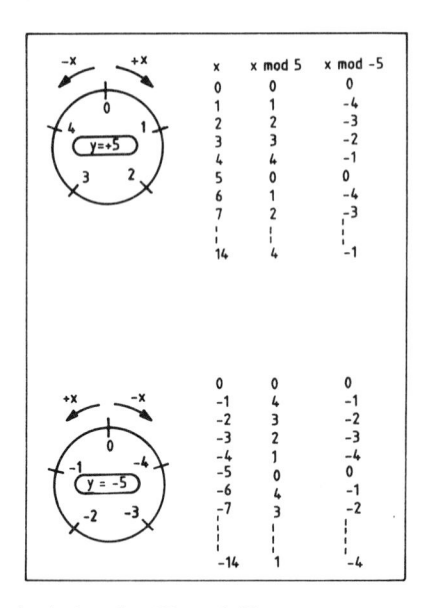

Fig.2.5 Conceptual calculation for X mod Y.

For instance, to calculate 6 rem 5, start at the zero location on the left-hand circle, and move six steps anti-clockwise. You will end up at the value '1'.

Modulo arithmetic is more complex, but its rules can be explained in the same way, Fig.2.5.

Here we have to take into account not only the sign of the dividend but also that of the divisor. Experiment with the program of Listing 2.3 to convince yourself of the correctness of this solution.

(f) Exponentiation

In mathematics we often have to evaluate expressions such as

$$10^2, \quad 2^{16}, \quad X^Y, \quad aX^2 + bX + c$$

and the like. The operation performed in calculating X^Y is defined to be 'exponentiation'. Here the first operand (X, the 'radix' or 'base') is raised to the power of the second (Y, the 'exponent').

Some limitations are placed on the mixing of the numeric types in this operation. Consider the following:

$4^2 = 16$ (the operands and result are whole numbers)
$4^{-2} = 0.0625$ (the operands are whole numbers, but the result is a decimal fraction)
$4^{1.2} = 5.278\ 031\ 643$ (a weighty calculation)

```
with TEXT_IO;              use TEXT_IO;
procedure INT_DIV is
  package INT_IO is new INTEGER_IO (INTEGER);
  use INT_IO;
  X1, X2, Y1, Y2, Y3 : INTEGER;
begin
  PUT ("Enter first number X1 - integer value only => ");
  GET (X1);
  SKIP_LINE;
  PUT ("Next number X2 - integer value only => ");
  GET (X2);
  SKIP_LINE;
  NEW_LINE;
  Y1 := X1 / X2;
  -- division of integers
  Y2 := X1 rem X2;
  -- calculating the euler remainder
  Y3 := X1 mod X2;
  -- calculating the modulus remainder
  PUT ("The truncated value of Y = X1 / X2 is");
  PUT (Y1, 7);
  NEW_LINE (2);
  PUT ("The Euler remainder REM of Y is");
  PUT (Y2, 7);
  NEW_LINE (2);
  PUT ("The modulus remainder MOD of Y is");
  PUT (Y3, 7);
  NEW_LINE (2);
end INT_DIV;
```

Listing 2.3 Division of INTEGER types is performed in this example.

As a result the rules in Ada state that if both operands are INTEGERs, then the power must be a positive INTEGER value (this includes zero). If the first operand is a real value, then the second one must be an INTEGER (reals are forbidden), but its sign doesn't matter. An example of the exponentiation operation is given in Listing 2.4.

NOTE: For the more general form aX^Y, 'a' is defined to be the 'mantissa'.

(g) **Absolute values**

It is fairly common in mathematics to work with the absolute value of a number. This, also called the modulus, is defined to be its positive value (sign is ignored). In Ada programming we use the ABS function (a standard predefined function) to calculate such absolute values. ABS has only one operand, as for instance

    ABS (35)   (gives the result '35')
    ABS (–35) (result is also '35')

34 Elementary arithmetic and logic

```
with TEXT_IO;              use TEXT_IO;
procedure EXPONENT is
  package REAL_IO is new FLOAT_IO (FLOAT);
  package INT_IO is new INTEGER_IO (INTEGER);
  use INT_IO;
  use REAL_IO;
  X1, X2, X3, X4, Y1, Y2 : INTEGER;
  X1R, Y1R               :       FLOAT;
begin
  PUT ("Enter base value X1 - integer value only => ");
  GET (X1);
  SKIP_LINE;
  PUT ("Enter exponent X2 - integer value only => ");
  GET (X2);
  SKIP_LINE;
  NEW_LINE;
  Y1 := X1 ** X2;
  PUT ("X1 ** X2 = ");
  PUT (Y1, 5);
  NEW_LINE (2);
  PUT ("Next base value X1R - real value only  => ");
  GET (X1R);
  SKIP_LINE;
  PUT ("Enter exponent X3 - integer value only => ");
  GET (X3);
  SKIP_LINE;
  NEW_LINE;
  Y1R := X1R ** X3;
  PUT ("X1R ** X3 = ");
  PUT (Y1R, 5);
  NEW_LINE (2);
  PUT ("Enter mantissa X4 - integer value only => ");
  GET (X4);
  SKIP_LINE;
  NEW_LINE;
  Y2 := X4 * X1 ** X2;
  PUT ("X4 * X1 ** X2 = ");
  PUT (Y2, 5);
  NEW_LINE (2);
end EXPONENT;
```

Listing 2.4 This example shows the use of the exponentiation function.

The operand may be either INTEGER or real. In each case the absolute value has the same type as the operand.

2.2.4 Operator precedence

Establishing precedence is something found all the time in everyday maths. Consider the problem stated in plain language in Fig.2.6.

It is then restated using a formal language or notation – algebra. But the formal statement can only be understood provided we know:

- The meaning of the operator symbols.
- The rules of operator precedence.

Arithmetic expressions 35

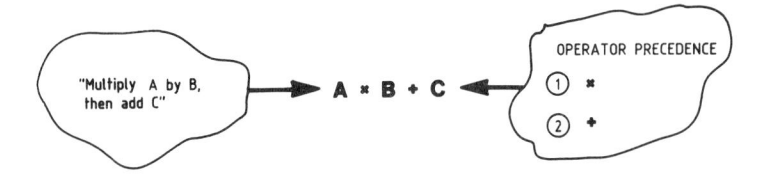

Fig.2.6 Operator precedence.

We meet a similar problem when carrying out mathematical operations in Ada. Consider the following expressions:

$$3 + 4 + 9$$
$$A - B - C$$
$$X * Y * Z$$

In each expression only one class of operator is used. How does Ada set about evaluating the result? Quite simply, it works from left to right in the expression. This may seem to be so self-evident and trivial that it doesn't deem a mention. True, in many situations the order won't matter; in others it is vital to get it right. Consider the statement

$$X1 = 300 - 400 + 150 \quad \text{and} \quad X2 = 300 + 150 - 400$$

In computer-based systems we can normally handle only two operands simultaneously. Thus, for each case the intermediate results are

$$X1 = -100 + 150 \quad \text{and} \quad X2 = 450 - 400$$

The final values are

$$X1 = 50 \quad \text{and} \quad X2 = 50$$

Both calculations give the same final result, but the intermediate values are different: that for X1 now includes a negative value (do not confuse subtraction with a negative sign). Consider now what will happen if the number type used to represent X1 and X2 does not include negative values. X2 will compute correctly, but X1 will fail at the intermediate stage.

Clearly, when mixed operators are used, we have to set rules for the precedence of operators. These should state precisely what is supposed to happen, similar to algebraic operations. Otherwise results are unpredictable.

We do this by splitting the operators into a number of precedence classes. As far as arithmetic is concerned the order is

```
Highest  **
         *  /  rem mod (equal precedence for these)
         +  -  when used as unary operators (equal precedence)
Lowest   +  -  when used as binary operators (equal precedence)
```

One small point should be mentioned here: the difference between the unary and the binary operators. The binary operator, as mentioned earlier, takes two operands. In contrast, the unary operator has a single operand, as in

```
+75, +201.3, -75, -201.3
```

Unary '+' appears to be redundant. Unary '−' changes the sign of the number.

Listing 2.5 demonstrates many of the points discussed above.

Just to reinforce the point that maths operations should always be carefully checked, consider the following calculations:

$$Y1 = 8000 \times 9 / 4 \quad \text{and} \quad Y2 = 8000 / 4 \times 9$$

Intermediate results:

$$Y1 = 72\,000/4 \qquad Y2 = 2000 \times 9$$

Final results:

$$Y1 = 18\,000 \qquad Y2 = 18\,000$$

The intermediate result for Y1 is too large for type INTEGER when implemented using a 16 bit number within the computer. Hence, if we wrote this in Ada using INTEGER arithmetic, Y2 would compute perfectly well but Y1 would give an overflow problem (a small point; if you try this out do not use literal values for the numbers – the compiler will eliminate the overflow condition).

Using reals will eliminate this particular problem. However, when very large and very small numbers have to be handled in the same expression, great care must be taken. A floating point system may have a very large

Arithmetic expressions 37

```
with TEXT_IO;              use TEXT_IO;
procedure PRECEDENCE is
  package INT_IO is new INTEGER_IO (INTEGER);
  use INT_IO;
  X1, X2, Y1, Y2, Y3, Y4, Y5 : INTEGER;
begin
  PUT ("Enter first number X1 - integer value only => ");
  GET (X1);
  SKIP_LINE;
  PUT ("Next number X2 - integer value only => ");
  GET (X2);
  SKIP_LINE;
  Y1 := X1 + X1 / X2;
  Y2 := X1 / X2 + X1;
  Y3 := X1 / X2 * X2;
  Y4 := X1 rem X2 + X1;
  Y5 := X1 + X1 rem X2;
  NEW_LINE (2);
  PUT ("X1 + X1 / X2   = ");
  PUT (Y1, 5);
  NEW_LINE (2);
  PUT ("X1 / X2 + X1   = ");
  PUT (Y2, 5);
  NEW_LINE (2);
  PUT ("X1 / X2 * X2   = ");
  PUT (Y3, 5);
  NEW_LINE (2);
  PUT ("X1 rem X2 + X1 = ");
  PUT (Y4, 5);
  NEW_LINE (2);
  PUT ("X1 + X1 rem X2 = ");
  PUT (Y5, 5);
  NEW_LINE (2);
end PRECEDENCE;
```

Listing 2.5 This demonstrates the precedence aspects of arithmetic operators.

dynamic range (i.e. smallest to largest number), but that doesn't mean that the smallest and the largest values can be handled simultaneously. These points are further discussed in chapter 6.

2.2.5 The use of parentheses

How do we implement the following: 'add A to B, then multiply the result by C'? If we write 'A + B * C' then the computation will result in B being multiplied by C and then having A added to that value. We could take the following line of attack:

```
Y := A + B;          Y := A + B;
K := Y * C;    or    Y := Y * C;
```

38 Elementary arithmetic and logic

```
with TEXT_IO;               use TEXT_IO;
procedure ARITH is
  package REAL_IO is new FLOAT_IO (FLOAT);
  use REAL_IO;
  X1, X2, Y1, Y2, Y3, Y4 : FLOAT;
  TG                     :    constant    := 6.0;
begin
  PUT ("Enter first number X1 (real number only) => ");
  GET (X1);
  SKIP_LINE;
  PUT ("Next number X2 (real number only => ");
  GET (X2);
  SKIP_LINE;
  Y1 := X1 + X2 * TG;
  Y2 := (X1 + X2 * TG);
  Y3 := X1 + (X2 * TG);
  Y4 := (X1 + X2) * TG;
  NEW_LINE (2);
  PUT ("X1 + X2 * TG   = ");
  PUT (Y1, 5);
  NEW_LINE (2);
  PUT ("(X1 + X2 * TG  = ");
  PUT (Y2, 5);
  NEW_LINE (2);
  PUT ("X1 + (X2 * TG) = ");
  PUT (Y3, 5);
  NEW_LINE (2);
  PUT ("(X1 + X2) * TG = ");
  PUT (Y4, 5);
  NEW_LINE(2);
end ARITH;
```

Listing 2.6 Just some more arithmetic, demonstrating the use of parentheses.

Generally it is better to use parentheses (brackets) to avoid confusion. So for the above example we have

$$Y := (A + B) * C;$$

Parentheses take precedence over the other operators; within the brackets normal rules apply (Listing 2.6).

One final point needs to be mentioned. Arithmetic operators cannot be placed next to each other; for instance

$Y := X * -10;$ is illegal. Rewrite as $Y := X * (-10);$

To summarize the evaluating of arithmetic expressions:

(a) If an expression contains nested parentheses (brackets within brackets) then work on the innermost pair first.

(b) Carry out all multiplications and divisions within these brackets, remembering that these operators have equal precedence. In such cases execute the operations working from left to right.
(c) Now perform all additions and subtractions.
(d) Repeat this sequence within each matching set of parentheses until the complete expression is finally evaluated.

A range of maths functions may be provided in the Ada library. These are not part of the language, and so are not portable between machines. Find out exactly what mathematical support is given by the library of your Ada compiler.

2.2.6 Some terminology

Expressions are defined as being made up of a number of component parts according to the following rules (Fig.2.7):

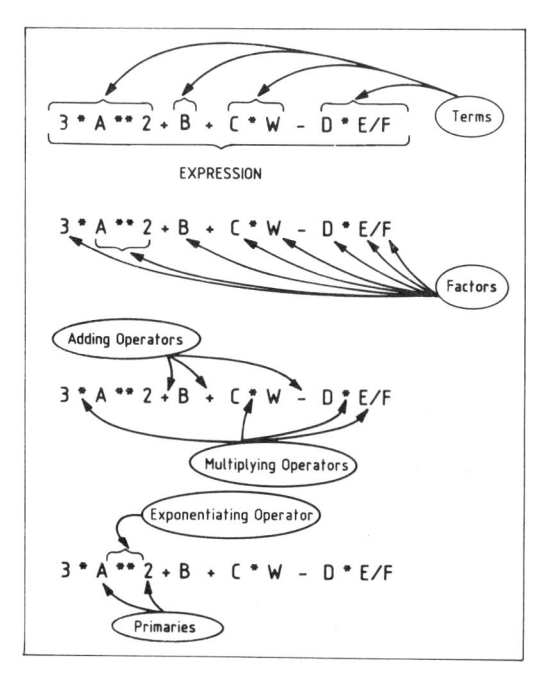

Fig.2.7 Make-up of a simple expression.

Example:

| Y := 3*A**2 + B + C*W − D*E/F | An Ada statement. |

| 3*A**2 + B + C*W − D*E/F | The whole right-hand side is defined as an EXPRESSION. |

| 3*A**2
B
C*W
D*E/F | These are defined as the TERMS of the expression. |

| 3
A**2
B,C,D,
E,F. | These are defined as the FACTORS of the terms. |

| *,/ | These are multiplying operators. |

| +,− | These are adding operators. |

| A, 2 | These are the primaries of the factors. |

In this particular example, strictly speaking B, C, D, E and F are also primaries.

2.3 BOOLEAN EXPRESSIONS

2.3.1 Introduction

Boolean expressions are defined as those which have only one of two values, true or false (Fig.2.8). A variable can be defined as type BOOLEAN and used in the program as required. It is important to realize that such variables are normally used in conjunction with other program statements to make logical decisions. For instance, a control system may have to shut down if a particular alarm occurs; the control processor would make a logical decision based on the state of the alarm signal to define a subsequent course of action.

As the use of Boolean functions is highly dependent on program requirements only the basic features will be discussed here. It is looked at in much greater depth in chapter 5.

Boolean expressions 41

Fig.2.8 Values of Boolean variables.

2.3.2 Logical operations

Two sets of operators are used in Boolean logic – the logical and the relational operators. The first one describes the logical operations which may be carried out in Ada. It comprises the 'and', 'or', 'xor' (exclusive or) and 'not' operators, as shown below.

Logical operations

Operator	Logical function
and	Conjunction
or	Inclusive or
xor	Exclusive or
not	Negation

The second set is used when relationships between operands need to be determined. These, the relational operators, consist of:

Relational operations

Symbol	Operation
=	equal to
<	less than
>	greater than
/=	not equal to
>=	equal to or greater than
<=	equal to or less than

The following simple problems illustrate two basic types of logical operations which are regularly carried out:

(a) Task A: Evaluate the logical value of

Y = A and B and C or D

42   Elementary arithmetic and logic

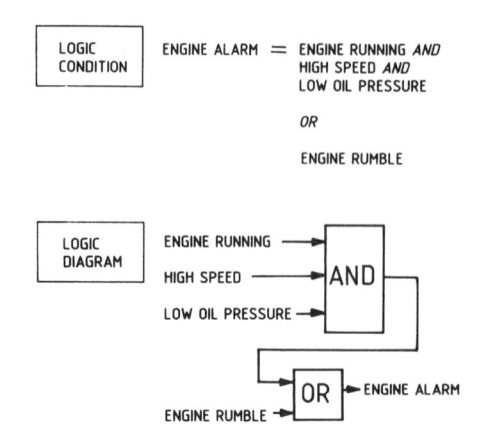

```
LOGIC       ENGINE ALARM = ENGINE RUNNING AND
CONDITION                  HIGH SPEED AND
                           LOW OIL PRESSURE

                           OR

                           ENGINE RUMBLE
```

```
LOGIC       ENGINE RUNNING ──┐
DIAGRAM     HIGH SPEED ──────┤AND├─┐
            LOW OIL PRESSURE─┘     │
                                   ├─►OR─► ENGINE ALARM
            ENGINE RUMBLE ─────────┘
```

Fig.2.9 Logical operations using Boolean variables.

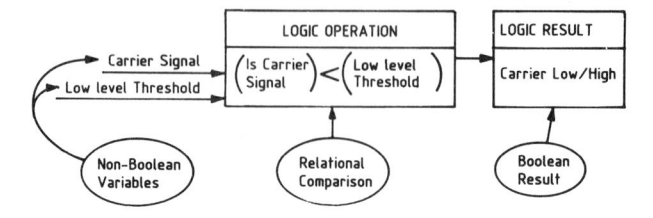

Fig.2.10 Decisions using the relational operator.

(b) Task B: If X is less than Y then carry out sequence Z.

Consider task A. First, What type of operand is involved? Second, what is the result type? Third, what is the order of precedence for the Boolean valuation? Clearly, all operands are of type BOOLEAN. So is the result. But the order of precedence is not what one would expect from the rules of Boolean algebra. In this particular example all operators have equal precedence (discussed later in chapter 5).

A practical use of BOOLEAN logical operations is shown in Fig.2.9.

Now look at task B. Here no Boolean evaluation is involved as we are only comparing the values of two variables. But note that the RESULT of the evaluation is a Boolean quantity. Hence the relational operators can be used with other variable types as well as with Boolean operands. In each case the result is always a Boolean one. Consider the following application as an example of this operation. Our purpose is to monitor a carrier signal in a data communications system where it is essential to flag up low-signal conditions (Fig.2.10). The method used is to compare the actual signal level (a program variable) with a predefined condition (another program variable) and produce a Boolean result from the comparison; this result defines the subsequent action by the program.

A variable used as a Boolean must be declared in the normal way, the format being

```
HIGH_LEVEL : BOOLEAN;
```

Demonstration programs which use BOOLEANs are left until Chapter 5.

REVIEW

Do you feel you can now:

- Define and use EXPRESSIONS?
- Carry out type changing between reals and INTEGERs?
- Perform addition, subtraction, multiplication, division and exponentiation?
- Understand and control the precedence of arithmetic operations?
- Understand the structure and use of Boolean expressions?

Chapter Three

Program control structures

Up to this point all program examples have followed the same pattern with statements executed one after the other. This is called the SEQUENCE control structure, and in the examples here has been implemented using mainly the straightforward assignment statement. Unfortunately this won't get us very far in practical situations, especially where calculations and decision making are concerned. Very broadly we can say that the sequential operations are disturbed as soon as we have to answer one or more of the following questions:

- Should this action be performed?
- Should action A or action B be carried out?
- How often should an action be carried out – 1? (FOR a fixed set of conditions carry out a task.)
- How often should an action be carried out – 2? (WHILE a condition is true do something.)
- How often should an action be carried out – 3? (REPEAT something until a terminating condition is reached.)
- How often should an action be carried out – 4? (EXIT from the task when a special terminating point is reached.)

On completing this chapter you should be able to:

- Define the basic control structures of sequence, selection and repetition used in Ada;
- Understand how and why they are used;
- Write simple programs using these structures.

3.1 THE THREE BASIC CONTROL STRUCTURES

It may sound like a gross simplification to say that all programs can be written using only the three basic control structures of sequence, selection and repetition (iteration), yet this really is the case in well-designed software, the only exception being the need on rare occasions to take unusual steps to get out of difficulties. And even that should be precisely controlled.

These three structures form the basic syntax for structured programming techniques; all programs can be constructed using just these. Most older programming languages allow the programmer to transfer program control

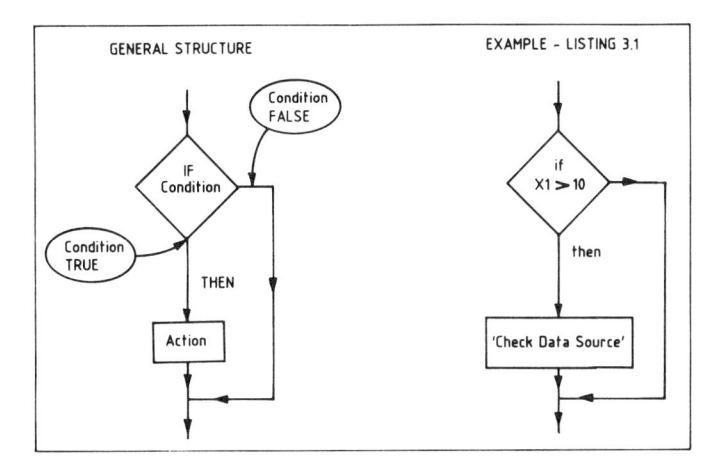

Fig.3.1 Flow chart of the 'if–then' operation.

unconditionally, usually by using the GOTO function. This is also available in Ada, which experienced programmers may find surprising.

3.2 SELECTION

3.2.1 The **if–then** statement

This is the simplest version of the selection statement, having the following informal form:

> **if** <condition A> **then** <action W> **end if**;

The program evaluates the condition A; if the Boolean result from this is TRUE then the action (statement) W is carried out and program flow continues to the next statement. If the result is FALSE the action is not carried out; instead the next sequential statement in the program is executed. Fig.3.1 shows the flow of operations for a simple **if–then** statement, the following program (Listing 3.1) being an example of this action.

Fig.3.2 gives the statement syntax.

3.2.2 The **if–then–else** statement

In the example above, if the test condition is evaluated as false, no action is taken. However, we often want to carry out alternative actions as a result of

46 Program control structures

```
with TEXT_IO;                    use TEXT_IO;
procedure IF_THEN is
  package REAL_IO is new FLOAT_IO (FLOAT);
  use REAL_IO;
  X1, X2, Y           :      FLOAT;
  HIGH_VALUE          :      constant      := 10.0;
begin
  NEW_LINE (2);
  PUT ("Enter first number X1 (real number only) => ");
  GET (X1);
  SKIP_LINE;
  PUT ("Next number X2 (real number only) => ");
  GET (X2);
  SKIP_LINE;
  NEW_LINE;
  if X1 > HIGH_VALUE then
    PUT_LINE ("Check data source");
  end if;
  Y := X1 + X2;
  NEW_LINE;
  PUT ("X1 + X2 = ");
  PUT (Y);
  NEW_LINE;
  end IF_THEN;
```

Listing 3.1 This shows the use of the 'if-then' statement.

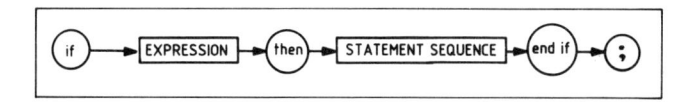

```
if ──▶ EXPRESSION ──▶ then ──▶ STATEMENT SEQUENCE ──▶ end if ──▶ ;
```

Fig.3.2 Syntax of the 'if–then' statement.

the evaluation, one set for true, the other for false. For instance, 'if autopilot shows heading error greater than 5° then move rudder left for starboard error else move rudder right'. To cater for this we have the **if–then–else** control structure.

```
if <condition A> then <action X> else <action Y> end if;
```

If the condition is found to be true the action X will be done, if false Y will be carried out. The flow chart explanation of the selection process is given in Fig.3.3, whilst the syntax is described in Fig.3.4.

Procedure 'IF_ELSE' (Listing 3.2) shows how this is used.

Here the evaluation '**if** X1 > HIGH_VALUE' gives a Boolean result; it's either true or false. If true, the statements following **then** are executed, otherwise those following **else** are carried out.

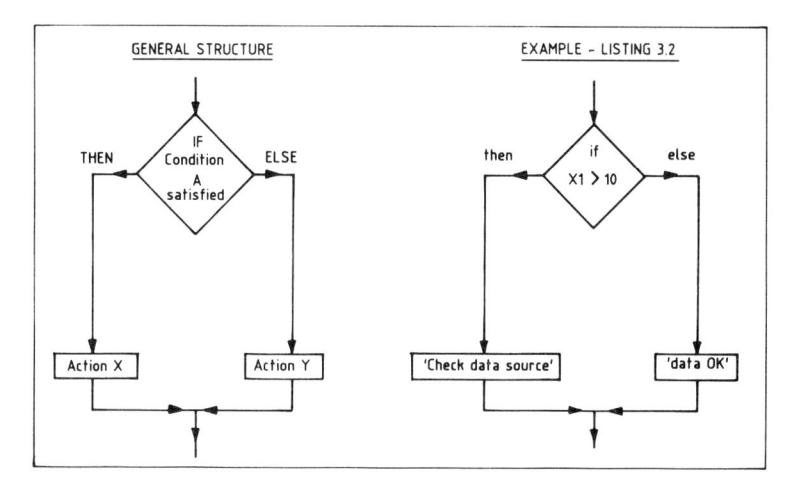

Fig.3.3 Flow chart of 'if–then–else' sequence.

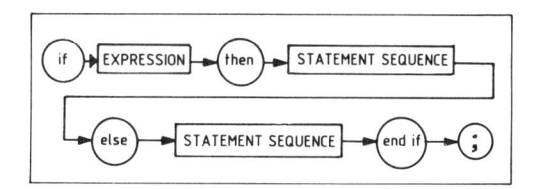

Fig.3.4 'if–then–else' syntax diagram.

```
with TEXT_IO;          use TEXT_IO;
procedure IF_ELSE is
  package REAL_IO is new FLOAT_IO (FLOAT);
  use REAL_IO;
  X1, X2, Y        :  FLOAT;
  HIGH_VALUE       :  constant        := 10.0;
begin
  NEW_LINE (2);
  PUT ("Enter first number X1 - real value only => ");
  GET (X1);
  SKIP_LINE;
  PUT ("Next number X2 => ");
  REAL_IO.GET (X2);
  SKIP_LINE;
  NEW_LINE (2);
  if X1 > HIGH_VALUE then
    PUT_LINE ("Check data source");
  else
    PUT_LINE ("data OK");
  end if;
  -- end of X1 > HIGH_VALUE
  NEW_LINE (2);
  Y := X1 + X2;
  PUT ("X1 + X2 = ");
  REAL_IO.PUT (Y);
  NEW_LINE;
end IF_ELSE;
```

Listing 3.2 Here is a simple example of the 'if-then-else' decision.

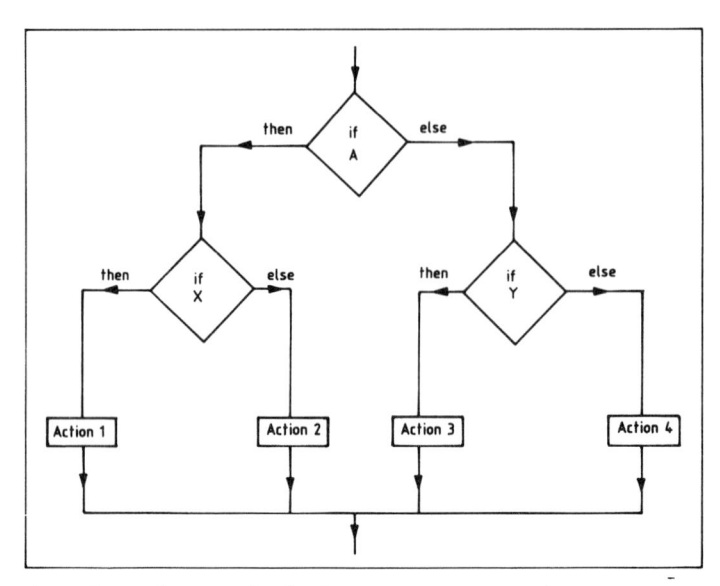

Fig.3.5 Flow chart of a nested selection sequence.

3.2.3 Nested **if** statements

There are situations where we have to perform not one, but a number of checks. Further, subsequent checking operations depend on the outcome of previous check results, Fig.3.5.

Using the **if** statement we can do it as follows:

```
if <condition A> then
    if <condition X> then <action 1> else <action 2> end if;
else
    if <condition Y> then <action 3> else <action 4> end if;
end if;
```

This is described as a *nested if* sequence (Fig.3.5). Note in passing that **if**, **then** and **else** are reserved words. The following listing (3.3) is an example of the nested **if** statement.

When nesting is used it can become quite difficult to decide which are the matching pairs of **if** and **end**. It is therefore good practice to use comments to help pick these out, as shown in Listing 3.3. Further, always align **if** and **end if** in the listings.

3.2.4 Multiple choices – **elsif** and **case** statements

Quite frequently we have to deal with multiple choices when making decisions. Typically this occurs in console interactions where the response from

```ada
with TEXT_IO;                  use TEXT_IO;
procedure NESTED_IF is
  package REAL_IO is new FLOAT_IO (FLOAT);
  use REAL_IO;
  X1, X2, Y         :      FLOAT;
  HIGH_VALUE_X1     :      constant      :=  10.0;
  LOW_VALUE_X2      :      constant      :=  20.0;
begin
  NEW_LINE (2);
  PUT ("Enter first number X1 (real number only) => ");
  GET (X1);
  SKIP_LINE;
  PUT ("Next number X2 (real number only) => ");
  GET (X2);
  SKIP_LINE;
  NEW_LINE (2);
  if X1 > HIGH_VALUE_X1 then
    if X2 < LOW_VALUE_X2 then
      PUT_LINE ("Bad data");
    else
      PUT_LINE ("Check data source, X1");
    end if;
  -- (end X2 < LOW_VALUE_X2)
  else
    if X2 >= LOW_VALUE_X2 then
      PUT_LINE ("Data OK");
    else
      PUT_LINE ("Check data source, X2");
    end if;
  -- (end X2 > LOW_VALUE_X2)
  end if;
  -- (end X1 > HIGH_VALUE_X1)
  NEW_LINE (2);
  Y := X1 + X2;
  PUT ("X1 + X2 = ");
  PUT (Y);
  NEW_LINE;
end NESTED_IF;
```

Listing 3.3 This illustrates the use of the NESTED 'if' action.

the operator determines the resulting course of events. For instance, a message out to the screen might read as follows:

```
**************************************
*                                     *
*   Customer List - Set-up Procedure  *
*   Select customer location by number *
*                                     *
*      1. London                      *
*      2. North East                  *
*      3. North West                  *
*      4. South East                  *
*      5. South West                  *
*      6. Midlands                    *
*                                     *
**************************************
```

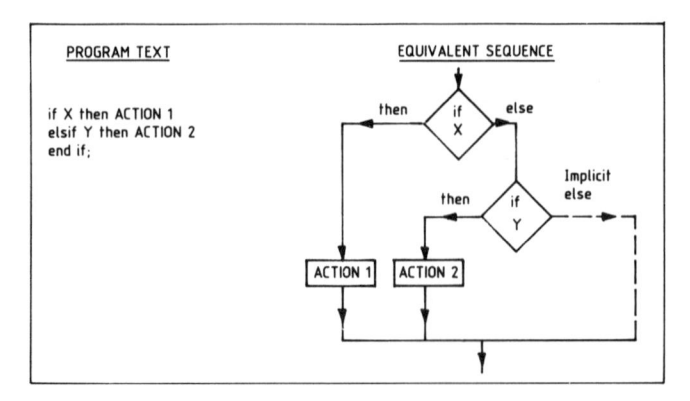

```
                PROGRAM TEXT                    EQUIVALENT SEQUENCE

          if X then ACTION 1              then      if      else
          elsif Y then ACTION 2                     X
          end if;
                                                                       Implicit
                                                  then    if           else
                                                          Y

                                              ACTION 1   ACTION 2
```

Fig.3.6 The basic 'else–if' sequence.

The next programmed action would be to read in the response from the operator and begin the set-up sequence for the selected group. Such decision making could be handled either by a sequence of statements as follows

```
if <1> then <action W> end if;
if <2> then <action X> end if;
etc.
```

or by a series of if–then–else actions. However, the first case, although it will work, does not by itself ensure that the operations are mutually exclusive. A little bit of creative programming will soon put an end to such good intentions. In the second case use of multiple if–then–else's soon gives rise to a complicated program structure which is difficult to read and understand. Two methods of dealing with situations such as these are provided in Ada by the **elsif** and **case** structures.

(a) elsif

The basic functioning of the **elsif** statement is shown in Fig.3.6.
When applied to the message handling problem outlined above it would be used as follows:

```
if    1 then <London>
elsif 2 then <North East>
elsif 3 then <North West>
elsif 4 then <South East>
elsif 5 then <South West>
elsif 6 then <Midlands>
end if;
```

Selection 51

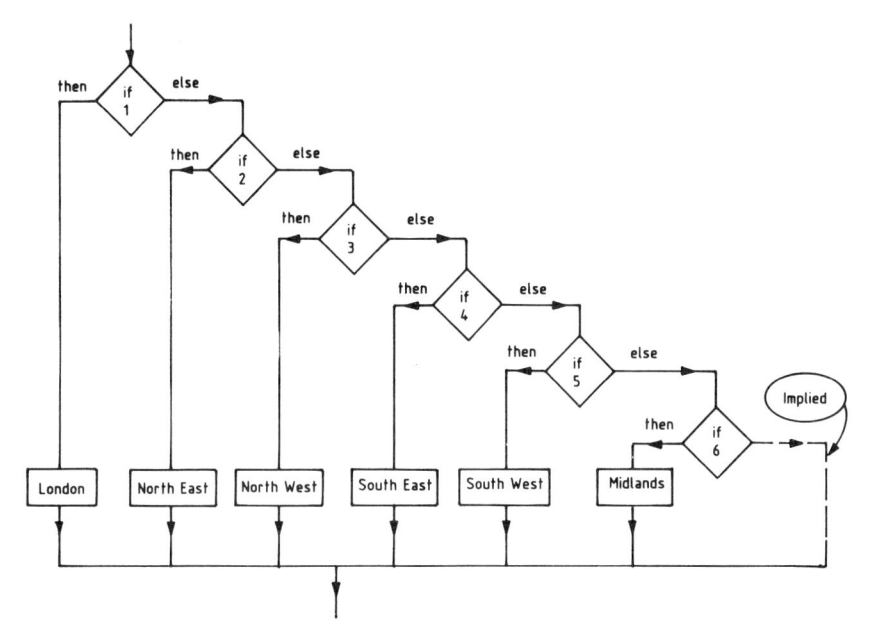

Fig.3.7 A more general 'else–if' sequence.

The flow of operations is shown in Fig.3.7.

That's fine as far as it goes. However, in the situation above only numbers 1 to 6 are valid inputs; what if a 7 is entered by mistake? What will happen is that the program will pass control on to the statement following the elsif construct. This could, if the software is carefully designed, indicate that an invalid number has been received. You may believe that programmers always incorporate such defensive programming methods as a matter of course. In that case you probably still believe in Santa Claus.

A much safer technique is to combine the **elsif** with an **else**; this ensures that some action is always carried out when the sequence is encountered, for instance

```
if    1 then <London>
elsif 2 then <North East>
elsif 3 then <North West>
elsif 4 then <South East>
elsif 5 then <South West>
elsif 6 then <Midlands>
else <Warning Message to Operator>
end if;
```

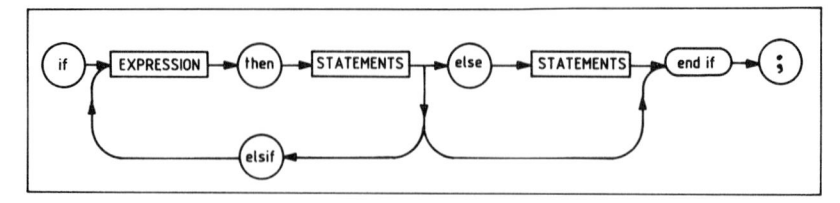

Fig.3.8 Syntax for the 'if' construct.

```
with TEXT_IO;              use TEXT_IO;
procedure CHOOSE_ONE is
  package INT_IO is new INTEGER_IO (INTEGER);
  use INT_IO;
  ANSWER          :       INTEGER;
begin
  NEW_LINE (2);
  PUT_LINE ("Customer list - Set-up procedure ");
  PUT_LINE ("Select customer location by number");
  PUT_LINE ("1. London");
  PUT_LINE ("2. North East");
  PUT_LINE ("3. North West");
  PUT_LINE ("4. South East");
  PUT_LINE ("5. South West");
  PUT_LINE ("6. Midlands");
  PUT ("Enter selection => ");
  GET (ANSWER);
  SKIP_LINE;
  NEW_LINE;
  if ANSWER = 1 then
    PUT_LINE ("London area selected");
  elsif ANSWER = 2 then
    PUT_LINE ("North East area selected");
  elsif ANSWER = 3 then
    PUT_LINE ("North West area selected");
  elsif ANSWER = 4 then
    PUT_LINE ("South East area selected");
  elsif ANSWER = 5 then
    PUT_LINE ("South West area selected");
  elsif ANSWER = 6 then
    PUT_LINE ("Midlands area selected");
  else
    PUT_LINE ("Invalid entry");
  end if;
  NEW_LINE;
  PUT_LINE ("Program finished");
end CHOOSE_ONE;
```

Listing 3.4 Here the use of the 'else-if' construct is demonstrated. It handles multiple branches in a program.

The complete syntax for the **if** statements is defined in Fig.3.8.

An example showing how to deal with multiple branches in a program is given in Listing 3.4. In the example here only one statement follows each **elsif**; it is quite permissible to have multiple statements in such places.

Note that **elsif** is a reserved word.

Selection   53

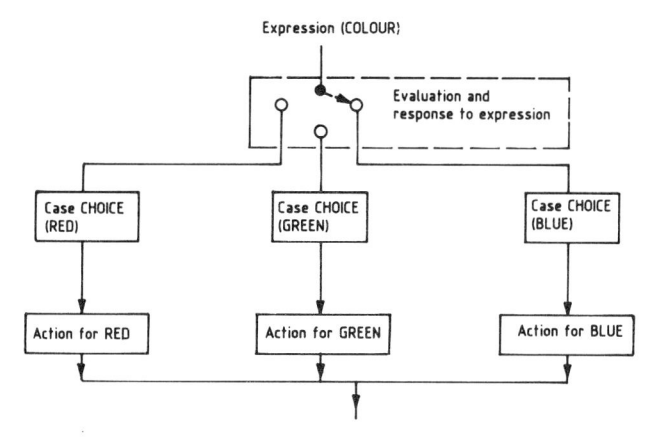

[Figure: diagram showing Expression (COLOUR) feeding into Case CHOICE (RED), Case CHOICE (GREEN), Case CHOICE (BLUE), each leading to Action for RED, Action for GREEN, Action for BLUE, with "Evaluation and response to expression" annotation]

Fig.3.9 'case' logical control structure.

(b) case

Ada gives us an easier way of handling these multiple choice problems, called the **case** statement. It acts as a selector switch (Fig.3.9), selecting one course of action from a number of choices. For instance, to select an action depending on a colour we would write

```
case COLOUR is
    when RED   => STATEMENTS_FOR_RED
    when GREEN => STATEMENTS_FOR_GREEN
    when BLUE  => STATEMENTS_FOR_BLUE
end case;
```

The route selected for use is determined by the value of the expression 'COLOUR'. This is demonstrated in Listing 3.5. In this example the expression between **case** and **is** (i.e. COLOUR) is first evaluated. Then the caselist is scanned to find a match between this and the listed 'choices' of COLOUR (i.e. RED, GREEN, BLUE). Where this occurs the corresponding statements are carried out. On completion of these statements, program control passes to the one following the case operation.

Note the use of a 'when others' choice. It acts as a safety net when the expression value – which is evaluated at run time – doesn't match any of the choices. This feature is required when certain expression types are used. We strongly recommend that it should always be included within **case** statements. Its position in the case construct must be the final alternative selection, as shown in Listing 3.5.

Now let's redo the earlier **elsif** example using the case feature (Listing 3.6).

Program control structures

```
with TEXT_IO;              use TEXT_IO;
procedure CASES is
  COLOUR           :       CHARACTER;
begin
  PUT_LINE ("Select colour");
  PUT_LINE ("Red = R,  Green = G,  Blue = B");
  PUT ("Enter selection => ");
  GET (COLOUR);
  SKIP_LINE;
  case COLOUR is
    when 'R' =>
      PUT_LINE ("Red scores one point");
    when 'G' =>
      PUT_LINE ("Green scores two points");
    when 'B' =>
      PUT_LINE ("Blue scores five points");
    when others =>
      PUT_LINE ("Only R, G, B allowed");
  end case;
  -- (end of the case statement)
  PUT_LINE ("Program finished");
end CASES;
```

Listing 3.5 This is an introduction to the 'case' feature for handling multiple branches in a program.

Even in this simple example the clarity and ease of the **case** statement, compared with multiple 'if's, is obvious.

In the example given so far, each choice is unique. There are situations, though, where we might want to carry out the same course of action for a number of choices, as for instance:

```
case MONTH is
   when JANUARY   => USE_ELSPEEDY_DELIVERY_SERVICE;
   when FEBRUARY  => USE_ELSPEEDY_DELIVERY_SERVICE;
   when MARCH     => USE_ELCHEEPO_DELIVERY_SERVICE;
   when APRIL     => USE_ELSPEEDY_DELIVERY_SERVICE;
   when MAY       => USE_ELCHEEPO_DELIVERY_SERVICE;
```

Ada gives us a way to show this in a clearer and more easily understood form:

```
case MONTH is
   when JANUARY | FEBRUARY | APRIL => USE_ELSPEEDY_DELIVERY_SERVICE;
   when MARCH | MAY                => USE_ELCHEEPO_DELIVERY_SERVICE;
```

```
with TEXT_IO;                use TEXT_IO;
procedure CHOOSE_TWO is
  package INT_IO is new INTEGER_IO (INTEGER);
  use INT_IO;
  ANSWER              :       INTEGER;
begin
  NEW_LINE (2);
  PUT_LINE ("Customer list - Set-up procedure ");
  PUT_LINE ("Select customer location by number");
  PUT_LINE ("1. London");
  PUT_LINE ("2. North East");
  PUT_LINE ("3. North West");
  PUT_LINE ("4. South East");
  PUT_LINE ("5. South West");
  PUT_LINE ("6. Midlands");
  PUT ("Enter selection => ");
  GET (ANSWER);
  SKIP_LINE;
  NEW_LINE;
  case ANSWER is
    when 1 =>
      PUT_LINE ("London area selected");
    when 2 =>
      PUT_LINE ("North East area selected");
    when 3 =>
      PUT_LINE ("North West area selected");
    when 4 =>
      PUT_LINE ("South East area selected");
    when 5 =>
      PUT_LINE ("South West area selected");
    when 6 =>
      PUT_LINE ("Midlands area selected");
    when others =>
      PUT_LINE ("Invalid entry");
  end case;
  NEW_LINE;
  PUT_LINE ("Program finished");
end CHOOSE_TWO;
```

Listing 3.6 This is another example of the 'case' construct. Compare it with the 'elsif' solution of Listing 3.4.

Now the single choice used in earlier examples is replaced by a more complex construct. Here each **when** is followed by a number of choices, a vertical bar being used to separate the alternatives within this list. However, each choice within a list produces the same resulting action (Listing 3.7).

Here, for program simplicity, numbers instead of names are used as choice labels.

One final point concerns the reserved word **null**. We use it whenever we want nothing to happen. This, at first sight, may seem odd: why bother? In fact, the reason for using it is quite logical; it shows clearly that we intend that nothing should happen.

It can be used with the **case** statement, as follows:

```
with TEXT_IO;                    use TEXT_IO;
procedure CHOICES is
   package INT_IO is new INTEGER_IO (INTEGER);
   use INT_IO;
   ANSWER              :       INTEGER;
begin
   NEW_LINE (2);
   PUT_LINE ("Delivery schedules - Set-up procedure ");
   PUT_LINE ("Select month by number");
   PUT_LINE ("1. January");
   PUT_LINE ("2. February");
   PUT_LINE ("3. March");
   PUT_LINE ("4. April");
   PUT_LINE ("5. May");
   PUT ("Enter selection => ");
   GET (ANSWER);
   SKIP_LINE;
   NEW_LINE;
   case ANSWER is
     when 1 | 2 | 4 =>
       PUT_LINE ("USE_ELSPEEDY_SERVICE");
     when 3 | 5 =>
       PUT_LINE ("USE_ELCHEEPO_SERVICE");
     when others =>
       PUT_LINE ("Invalid entry");
   end case;
   NEW_LINE;
   PUT_LINE ("Program finished - Goodbye");
end CHOICES;
```

Listing 3.7 This is another example of the 'case' construct where a number of case choices require the same action.

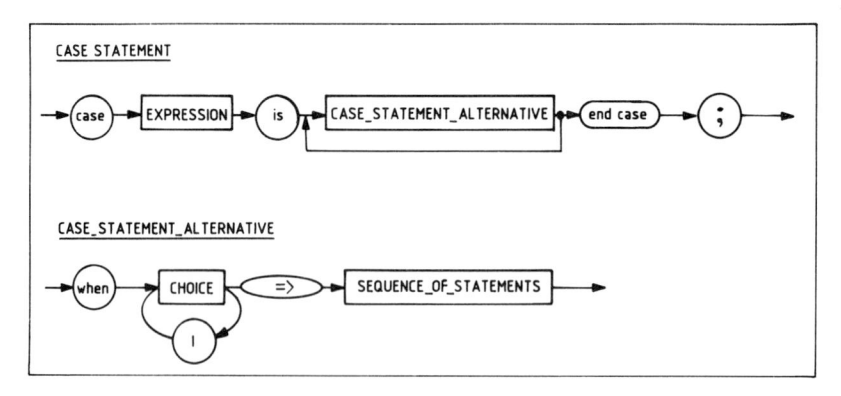

Fig.3.10 The 'case' syntax diagram.

```
case MONTH is
    when JANUARY | FEBRUARY | APRIL => USE_ELSPEEDY_SERVICE;
    when MARCH | MAY                => USE_ELCHEEPO_SERVICE;
    when others                     => null;
end case;
```

The general case syntax is shown in Fig.3.10.

The compiler must be able to determine the values of the case choices in a **when** clause. That is, they must be static values. We cannot use a choice value which is computed during execution of the program.

Note that **case, when, others** and **null** are reserved words.

3.3 REPETITION OR 'LOOP CONTROL'

3.3.1 Introduction

Repetition occurs frequently in real-life applications (Fig.3.11).

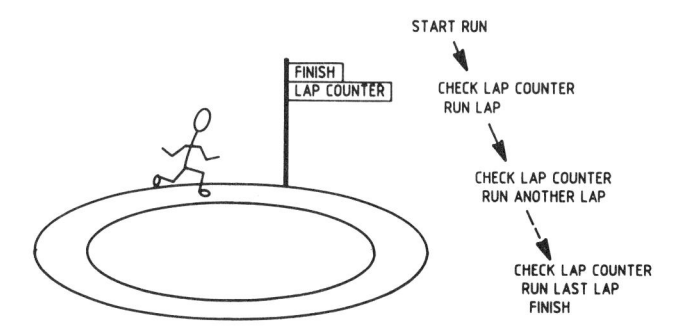

Fig.3.11 Repetition or 'here we go round again'.

It is no surprise then that we meet similar requirements within programs. For instance, we may want to input characters from a keyboard until the carriage return key is pressed, or to drive a pump motor while a pressure transducer shows low pressure. Very broadly these repetitive program sequences can be split into two groups (Fig.3.12). Within the first set repetition is defined by the program code; termination takes place only after the correct number of iterations has been carried out. In contrast, repetition may depend on program conditions, the number of loops being set by the state of a control variable. It is also possible that the program may never loop.

Thus the four basic iterative control structures are (Fig.3.12):

58 Program control structures

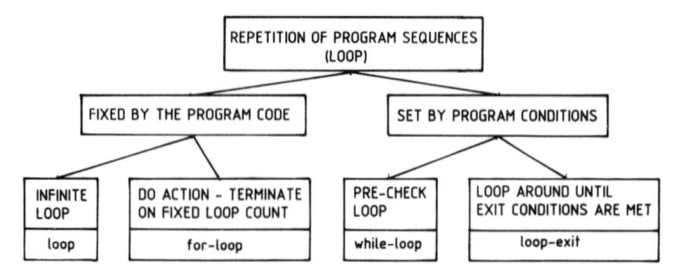

Fig.3.12 Repetition (loop) control structures of Ada.

- Infinite loop (the basic 'loop' construct);
- Fixed looping conditions (the 'for–loop' construct);
- Pre-check loop ('while–loop' construct);
- Check within loop (the general 'loop' construct, which includes the post-check operation).

3.3.2 The basic **loop** statements

The **loop** statement means exactly what it says, that is loop round this set of statements indefinitely (Fig.3.13).

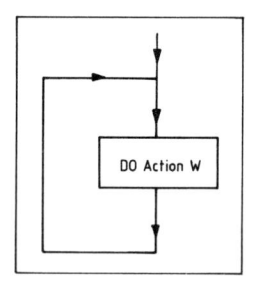

Fig.3.13 Infinite loop.

Syntactically it is expressed as defined in Fig.3.14.

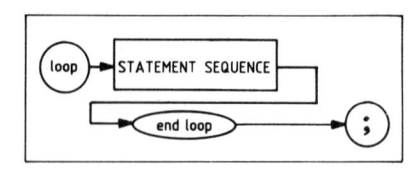

Fig.3.14 Basic 'loop' statement syntax.

Where would this be useful? Well, in many real-time applications the

```
with TEXT_IO;                   use TEXT_IO;
procedure SIMPLE_LOOP is
  package REAL_IO is new FLOAT_IO (FLOAT);
  use REAL_IO;
  X1, Y              :      FLOAT;
begin
  -- WARNING: this program never exits
  loop
    PUT ("Enter data (real value only) => ");
    GET (X1);
    SKIP_LINE;
    Y := 0.707 * X1;
    PUT ("The rms value is ");
    PUT (Y);
    NEW_LINE (2);
  end loop;
  -- (end of the simple loop)
end SIMPLE_LOOP;
```

Listing 3.8 This is the simple 'loop' operation.

complete software consists of a background program and a number of interrupt-driven foreground tasks. This background program runs as an infinite loop, waiting for the next interrupt.

In our case it is very useful to run programs repeatedly at the console without having to restart them each time. This can be done very simply using the loop operation as shown in the program of Listing 3.8.

3.3.3 **Loop** and **exit** statements

Loop operations are much more useful if somehow we can break out from the loop (if you ran the last example you'll know exactly why). This feature is implemented in Ada by using an **exit** statement. During loop execution, when conditions are met which satisfy the exit requirements, the loop is immediately terminated. Program control then passes to the statement which directly follows the loop sequence. The basic program structure when using the **exit** statement is

```
begin
  loop
    <PROGRAM_STATEMENTS>
    if <EXIT_REQUIREMENTS_SATISFIED> then exit;
    end if;
    <MORE_PROGRAM_STATEMENTS_IF_NEEDED>
  end loop;
end PROGRAM;
```

```ada
with TEXT_IO;                   use TEXT_IO;
procedure LOOP_EXIT is
  package INT_IO is new INTEGER_IO (INTEGER);
  use INT_IO;
  ANSWER          :       INTEGER;
  REPLY           :       CHARACTER;
begin
  loop
    NEW_LINE (2);
    PUT_LINE ("Customer list - Set-up procedure ");
    PUT_LINE ("Select customer location by number");
    PUT_LINE ("1. London");
    PUT_LINE ("2. North East");
    PUT_LINE ("3. North West");
    PUT_LINE ("4. South East");
    PUT_LINE ("5. South West");
    PUT_LINE ("6. Midlands");
    PUT ("Enter selection => ");
    GET (ANSWER);
    SKIP_LINE;
    NEW_LINE (2);
    case ANSWER is
      when 1 =>
        PUT_LINE ("London area selected");
      when 2 =>
        PUT_LINE ("North East area selected");
      when 3 =>
        PUT_LINE ("North West area selected");
      when 4 =>
        PUT_LINE ("South East area selected");
      when 5 =>
        PUT_LINE ("South West area selected");
      when 6 =>
        PUT_LINE ("Midlands area selected");
      when others =>
        PUT_LINE ("Invalid entry");
    end case;
    NEW_LINE;
    PUT ("Are you finished (Answer y or n)? ");
    GET (REPLY);
    SKIP_LINE;
    if REPLY = 'y' then
      exit;
    end if;
  end loop;
  PUT_LINE ("Program finished");
end LOOP_EXIT;
```

Listing 3.9 This demonstrates the 'loop' statement which has an 'exit' condition.

This can be demonstrated by returning to the earlier man–machine interface (MMI) interactions involving the case structure (program Listing 3.6). From a practical point of view the operator must always be allowed to correct any data entry mistakes – but as the program stands this isn't so. However, by using the loop structure with an exit (Listing 3.9), we can easily include this requirement.

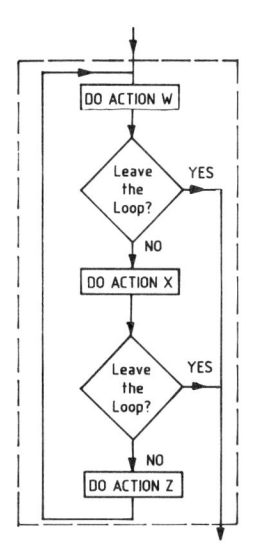

```
                    ┌──────────┐
                    │DO ACTION W│
                    └──────────┘
                          │
                       ╱Leave╲     YES
                      ╱  the  ╲ ──────→
                      ╲ Loop? ╱
                       ╲     ╱
                         NO
                          │
                    ┌──────────┐
                    │DO ACTION X│
                    └──────────┘
                          │
                       ╱Leave╲     YES
                      ╱  the  ╲ ──────→
                      ╲ Loop? ╱
                       ╲     ╱
                         NO
                          │
                    ┌──────────┐
                    │DO ACTION Z│
                    └──────────┘
```

Fig.3.15 Loop with multiple exits.

A clearer way of using the **exit** statement is to combine it with **when**, as shown below:

```
<PROGRAM_STATEMENTS>
exit when <EXIT_REQUIREMENTS_SATISFIED>
<MORE_PROGRAM_STATEMENTS_IF_NEEDED>
```

A major feature of the loop operation is to have multiple exit points in a loop (Fig.3.15), this being extremely useful in MMI software (Listing 3.10).

3.3.4 The **for** statement

Often we want to carry out an action a fixed number of times irrespective of the state of the program being actioned. This can be done in Ada using the 'for–loop'; this is expressed in very general terms in the diagram of Fig.3.16. Suppose, for instance, we wish to read in six analogue values to a digital controller. We could write

```
for ANALOG in 1..6 loop
   <statements>
end loop;
```

62 Program control structures

```
with TEXT_IO;                  use TEXT_IO;
procedure LOOP_EX2 is
  package REAL_IO is new FLOAT_IO (FLOAT);
  use REAL_IO;
  X1, Y              :       FLOAT;
  REPLY              :       CHARACTER;
begin
  loop
    PUT ("Enter a real value => ");
    GET (X1);
    SKIP_LINE;
    Y := 0.707 * X1;
    PUT ("The rms value is ");
    PUT (Y);
    NEW_LINE (2);
    PUT ("OK to calculate the average value (y/n)? ");
    GET (REPLY);
    SKIP_LINE;
    NEW_LINE;
    exit when REPLY /= 'y';
 -- the first exit statement
    Y := 0.637 * X1;
    PUT ("The average value is ");
    PUT (Y);
    NEW_LINE (2);
    PUT ("Calculations finished (y/n)? ");
    GET (REPLY);
    SKIP_LINE;
    NEW_LINE;
    exit when REPLY = 'y';
 -- the second exit statement
  end loop;
 -- (end of the two-exit loop)
  PUT_LINE ("Program finished");
end LOOP_EX2;
```

Listing 3.10 This demonstrates the 'loop' operation which has two 'exit' conditions.

The **for–loop** statement starts off by setting the identifier ANALOG (the loop control variable or 'counter') to 1. It then tests to see if this control variable exceeds the final value (6). If it doesn't then the statement body is executed and the control variable in incremented by 1. The sequence is repeated until the terminating condition is reached, at which point the statement is concluded. Observe that we must use a discrete range of values as the counting function.

Fig.3.17 gives the syntax of this statement while Listing 3.11 shows it in use.

From the syntax diagram it is clear that both range bounds must be the same type. Further, the bounds must be assignment compatible with the loop counter (the identifier). The counter does not have to be declared in the normal way; writing it within the iteration clause as shown acts as its declaration. This is a case of implicit declaration. Question: How can the compiler determine the type of the loop counter? Answer: It is defined by the type of the range (counting) function.

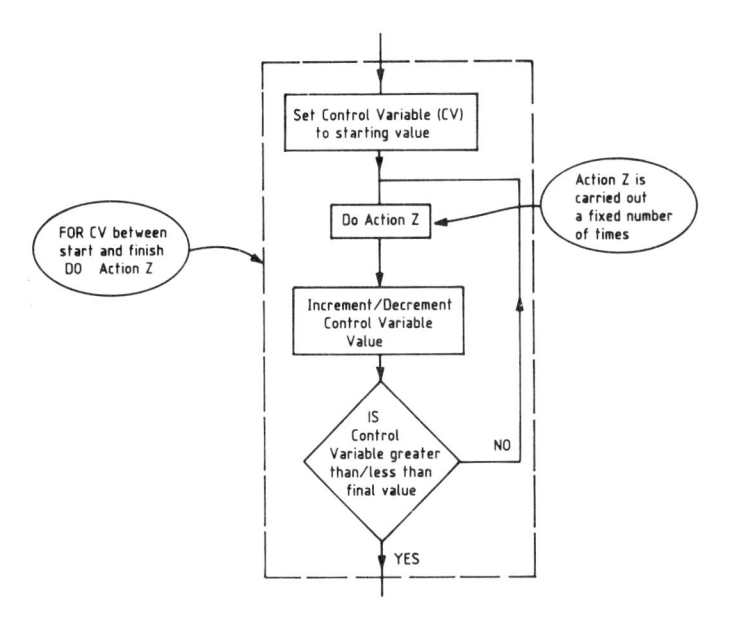

Fig.3.16 Fixed number of loop operations – 'for–loop' structure.

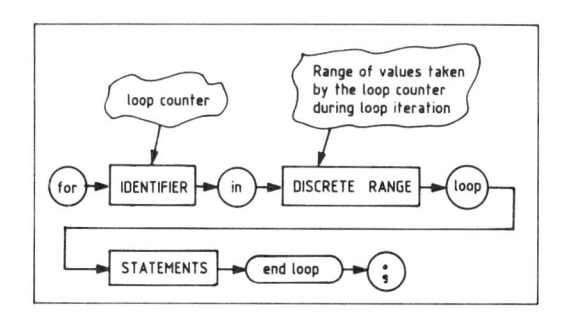

Fig.3.17 Basic syntax of the 'for' statement.

```
with TEXT_IO;            use TEXT_IO;
procedure FOR_LOOP is
begin
   for NUM in 1..70 loop
      PUT ("*");
   end loop;
   -- (end of for loop)
   NEW_LINE;
end FOR_LOOP;
```

Listing 3.11 This is a trivial use of the 'for' statement. This results in 70 * signs being printed across the screen.

64 Program control structures

```
with TEXT_IO;             use TEXT_IO;
procedure SECOND_FOR_LOOP is
begin
  for CHANNEL in 'A'..'E' loop
    PUT ("Now setting channel ");
    PUT (CHANNEL);
    NEW_LINE;
    PUT ("Channel ");
    PUT (CHANNEL);
    PUT_LINE (" switches set safe");
    NEW_LINE (2);
  end loop;
  -- (end of for loop)
  NEW_LINE;
end SECOND_FOR_LOOP;
```

Listing 3.12 This is another example using the 'for' statement.

The starting and terminating conditions of the discrete range are clearly stated. The incremental (step) value is NOT shown; in fact, by default it is 1 (one). In some instances it may be desirable to step in increments other than 1. This cannot be done using a for-loop.

We may also count down from a larger to a smaller value using the for-loop construct. In this case the **reverse** statement must be used, as in

```
for NUM in reverse 1..70 loop
   <statements>
end loop;
```

The for-loop control structure is used mainly when the number of operations to be performed is known in advance, when particular items in a complete group are to be accessed, and in similar situations. Very often this is met when handling arrays (see later), though the following is a simple application of the for-loop action.

Suppose a microprocessor controller has ten output switch channels which, during system initialization, must be set to a safe condition. A statement of the form

```
for SWITCHES in 1..10 loop
   SET_SAFE;
end loop;
```

is a compact way of carrying this out. An operation similar to this is given in Listing 3.12.

Repetition or 'loop control' 65

You can see that the range function is still a discrete value, although now it is of type CHARACTER.

Note that **for, in, reverse** and **loop** are reserved words.

3.3.5 The **while–loop**

In this operation the test condition is evaluated before the action is carried out – a pre-check loop (Fig.3.18). If it is FALSE then no action is performed and control passes on as usual to the next program statement. Otherwise the defined action is implemented and the test condition is once more evaluated.

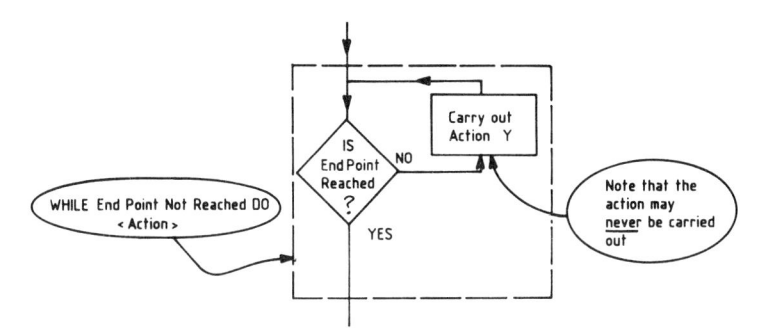

Fig.3.18 Pre-check loop – 'while–loop' structure.

In Ada the pre-check or 'while' operation is syntactically defined as in Fig.3.19.

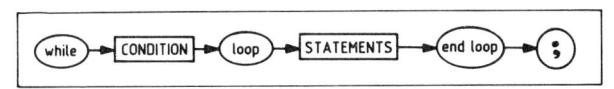

Fig.3.19 'while–loop' statement syntax.

Note that **while** is a reserved word. Below is a program (Listing 3.13) which uses the **while** construct.

3.3.6 Nested loops

In practical programs there are many occasions when we need to form loops within loops, that is nested loops. Consider the situation shown in Fig.3.20.

Here, loop 2 is an inner loop within loop 1. When an exit is made from loop 2, what is the resulting program control flow?. Well, following the rules laid down so far, the structure of Fig.3.21 is produced.

From this it can be seen that the normal (or 'simple') exit returns program

66 Program control structures

```
with TEXT_IO;                     use TEXT_IO;
procedure WHILE_DO is
  package REAL_IO is new TEXT_IO.FLOAT_IO (FLOAT);
  use REAL_IO;
  X1                  :      FLOAT;
  X2                  :      FLOAT;
begin
  X1 := 0.0;
  X2 := 0.0;
  while X1 < 10.0 loop
 --(this is the pre-check condition)
    PUT ("Enter a real number X1 => ");
    GET (X1);
    SKIP_LINE;
    X2 := X2 + X1;
    PUT ("The value of X2 is ");
    PUT (X2, 10);
    NEW_LINE;
  end loop;
  -- (end of the while loop)
  PUT_LINE ("Program finished");
end WHILE_DO;
```

Listing 3.13 This is the 'while' statement in action.

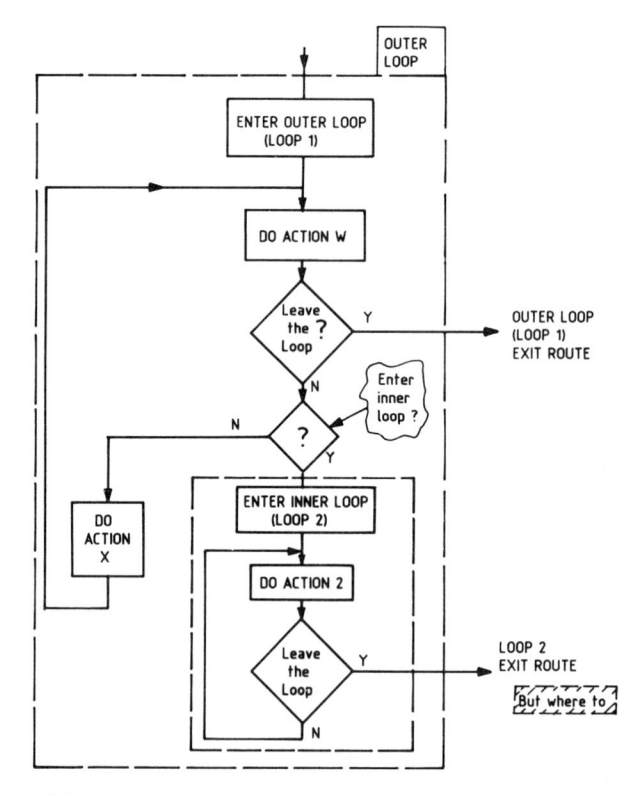

Fig.3.20 Nested loops – the basic issue.

Repetition or 'loop control' 67

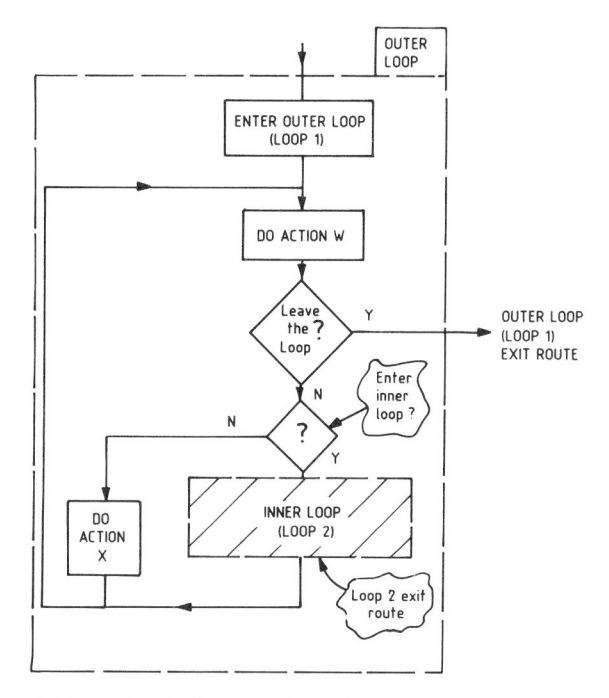

[Flowchart showing nested loop structure with OUTER LOOP containing: ENTER OUTER LOOP (LOOP 1), DO ACTION W, decision "Leave the Loop?" with Y exit to OUTER LOOP (LOOP 1) EXIT ROUTE, decision "Enter inner loop?" with N going to DO ACTION X and Y going to INNER LOOP (LOOP 2), with Loop 2 exit route]

Fig.3.21 Normal (simple) exit from an inner loop.

control to the higher-level loop. Now this is fine and, whenever possible, it should be used because the resulting programs are well structured, visible and safe. However, when deep nesting is used, fall-back level by level is time consuming and inefficient. We can overcome this in Ada by first naming loops, and then exiting to the required loop level. Fig.3.22 shows the program control structure which this produces for a single nested loop.

Listing 3.14 shows how this is done. Here the outer loop has a name given to it using a loop naming 'identifier' GET_DIVIDEND. Then, at the **exit** statement within the inner loop, this identifier is appended to the **exit** statement; it denotes which outer loop is to be exited from.

Note that the syntax is

```
    IDENTIFIER_NAME:
loop (it may be used with any of the loop constructs)
    <STATEMENT>
    <STATEMENT>
    loop (inner loop – any loop construct)
        <INNER_LOOP_STATEMENT>
        <INNER_LOOP_STATEMENT>
        exit IDENTIFIER_NAME;
    end loop (end of inner loop)
end IDENTIFIER_NAME;
```

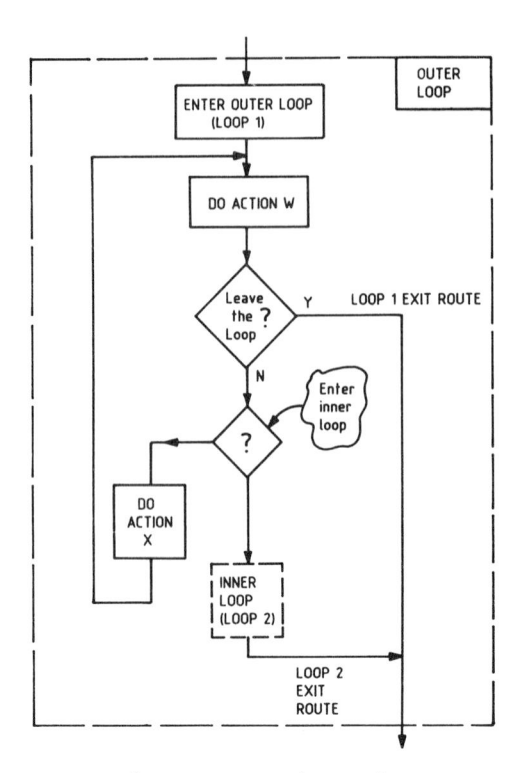

Fig.3.22 Exit from an inner loop to a named outer loop.

The point in the program marked by the loop identifier can only be reached from within the loop construct. That is, it cannot be accessed from other points within the program; it is not a label in the conventional language sense.

In summary, the exit constructs of Ada are:

1. exit – Unconditional exit to the enclosing loop.
2. exit IDENTIFIER_NAME – Unconditional exit from the named loop.
3. exit when CONDITION_IS_TRUE – Conditional exit to the enclosing loop.
4. exit IDENTIFIER_NAME when CONDITION_IS_TRUE – Conditional exit from the named loop.

3.4 THE **goto**

There is no good reason for using the **goto** instead of the other control structures of Ada. In fact there are many reasons for avoiding it, all of them

```
with TEXT_IO;              use TEXT_IO;
procedure EXIT_FROM_INNER is
  DIVIDEND         :     INTEGER;
  DIVISOR          :     INTEGER;
  REMAINDER        :     INTEGER;
  SELECTOR         :     INTEGER;
  package INT_IO is new INTEGER_IO (INTEGER);
  use INT_IO;
begin
  GET_DIVIDEND:loop
    PUT ("Please enter an INTEGER dividend : ");
    GET (DIVIDEND);
    SKIP_LINE;
    GET_DIVISOR:loop
      PUT ("Please enter an INTEGER divisor for the dividend ");
      PUT (DIVIDEND, 0);
      PUT (" : ");
      GET (DIVISOR);
      SKIP_LINE;
      NEW_LINE;
      REMAINDER := DIVIDEND rem DIVISOR;
      if REMAINDER = 0 then
        PUT (DIVISOR, 0);
        PUT (" is a factor of ");
        PUT (DIVIDEND, 0);
        NEW_LINE;
      else
        PUT (DIVISOR, 0);
        PUT (" is NOT a factor of ");
        PUT (DIVIDEND, 0);
        NEW_LINE;
      end if;
      NEW_LINE;
      PUT_LINE ("1. Select another divisor");
      PUT_LINE ("2. Select another dividend");
      PUT_LINE ("3. Exit program");
      PUT ("Please enter the number of your choice : ");
      GET (SELECTOR);
      SKIP_LINE;
   -- If 2 has been selected then exit the nested loop into
   -- the outer loop.
      exit GET_DIVISOR when (SELECTOR = 2);
   -- if 3 has been selected exit the outer loop
      exit GET_DIVIDEND when (SELECTOR = 3);
    end loop GET_DIVISOR;
    PUT_LINE ("Selecting another divisor...");
  end loop GET_DIVIDEND;
  PUT_LINE ("Exiting program - Thankyou");
end EXIT_FROM_INNER;
```

Listing 3.14 This shows exiting an outer loop from an inner (nested) loop.

to do with program correctness, reliability, maintainability and readability. Why, then, does Ada have the goto construct? John Barnes, one of the original Ada design team, justifies it on three grounds. First, it aids the task of translating programs from other languages into Ada. Second, it simplifies the automatic generation of programs from design specifications. Third, it may provide the neatest way of moving around the program structure (but then he becomes equivocal on this point). However, YOU, at this stage, are not going to get involved with automatically generated programs. So don't use the **goto** in your work.

NOTE on the **goto**:

- Setting a label: <<LABEL_IDENTIFIER>>;
- Using the **goto**: **goto** LABEL_IDENTIFIER;
- You cannot jump into an **if, case** or **loop** statement using the **goto**;
- You cannot jump between alternative choices in the **if** and **case** constructs.

REVIEW

Having got to this point you should have achieved the aims of the chapter; that is, to:

- Define the basic control structures of sequence, selection and repetition used in Ada;
- Understand how and why they are used;
- Write simple programs using these structures.

Chapter Four

Subprograms in Ada – procedures and functions

We are now ready to tackle one of the most important and useful aspects of high-level languages, the use of subprograms. These are fundamental in the design of good, clear and reliable software. Moreover, if structured programming techniques are to be put into practice these constructs must be used.

After studying this chapter you will:

- Understand the reason for and the use of subprograms in high-level languages;
- Understand the structure and use of procedures and functions;
- Know the reason for and use of formal and actual parameters in procedures and functions;
- Appreciate the difference between local and global objects and grasp the concept of scope and visibility;
- Recognize the structuring of subprograms in terms of interfacing and implementation aspects;
- Realize that a subprogram definition consists of a body and an (optional) declaration;
- Perceive the essential difference between a specification and a declaration;
- Know how to structure an Ada program using blocks.

4.1 HOW TO HANDLE LARGE JOBS

4.1.1 The background

Small programs are easy to understand. We can see and appreciate both the detail and the overall idea simultaneously (well, almost). New programs can be turned out fast and efficiently. Any mistakes quickly show, and equally quickly they can be rectified. So, is control and management of software a simple task? Unfortunately, no. In reality most programs are much, much larger than those shown so far. Moreover, they're usually much more complex and difficult to understand. Such programs often display the idiosyncrasies (a polite way of saying 'quirky peculiarities') of the authors.

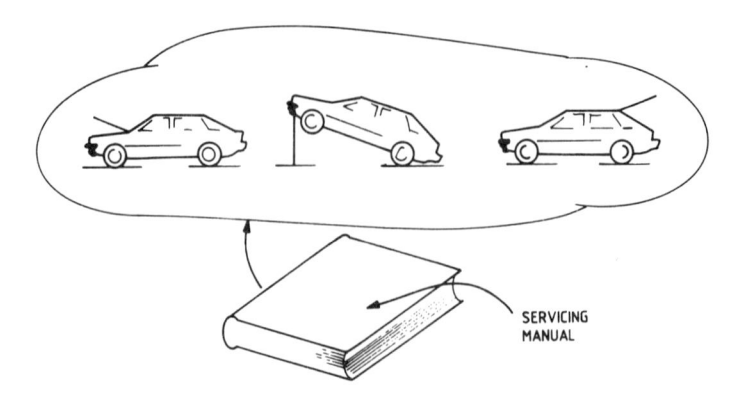

Fig.4.1 Unstructured document.

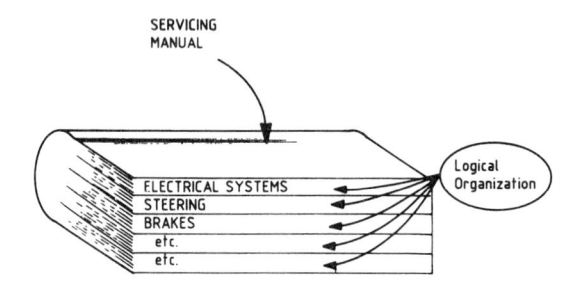

Fig.4.2 Structured document.

How, then, do we go about handling program development for the larger job? Is it just an extension of our ways of dealing with small ones? Or do we need to change completely our working methods? These are the questions we're going to try to answer here.

4.1.2 An organizational problem

The problems we're faced with are nothing new. Thor the Viking probably got just as frustrated in trying to organize his rape and pillage detail as did the software managers of the Nimrod project. So let's look at the problems, and their solutions, in the context of something we can all understand.

Imagine we've taken over the running of a small garage workshop. Through neglect the servicing manual has degenerated into a great mass of oil-stained paper (like computer print-outs, though these are usually treated with coffee) (Fig.4.1). As the first step towards changing this chaos into some semblance of order we reorganize the paperwork (Fig.4.2). Now it's properly bound, with related items being grouped together; we've probably also put in con-

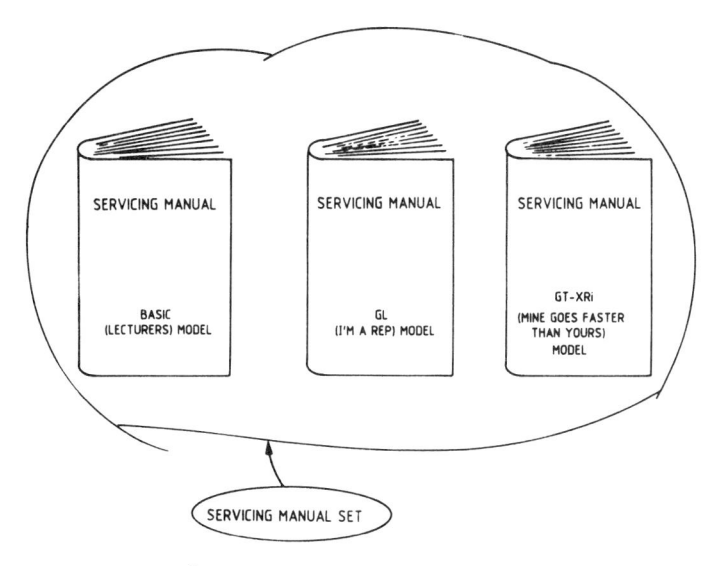

Fig.4.3 Variations on a theme.

tents and index lists. No great effort of imagination is needed to see that this is quite an improvement.

Having just one manual now creates an obvious bottleneck. We could buy one for each mechanic, but this might well be an expensive and unnecessary step. The situation is complicated by the need to deal with minor variations on a theme (Fig.4.3). Does this mean that each worker has to be given a manual for each individual model? On top of this, does it really make sense for the electrician to carry information on engine maintenance and repair? Clearly a better solution is needed.

What if we were to make up a set of procedure manuals, each one based on specific topics within the servicing manual? This would simplify the use of the manuals. For instance, the electrician would normally only use the electrical procedure manual; this would hardly upset the engine mechanic. Further, servicing job cards could be simplified by calling up the appropriate procedures (Fig.4.4). The contents of a procedure manual describe in detail what has to be done; this is then given a particular task name (Fig.4.5). By writing this name on the job card we define the action which is to be carried out; note that no task details are included.

We started out to simplify the documentation system and keep costs down. But, without really appreciating it, we've given ourselves a whole host of benefits. Lets look at exactly what these are.

In the first case, documents may be customized simply and easily (Fig.4.6). Each individual service can have its own specific job card. These can be put together without too much effort by the front office; after all they aren't exactly going to be tomes of information. By limiting the information on the

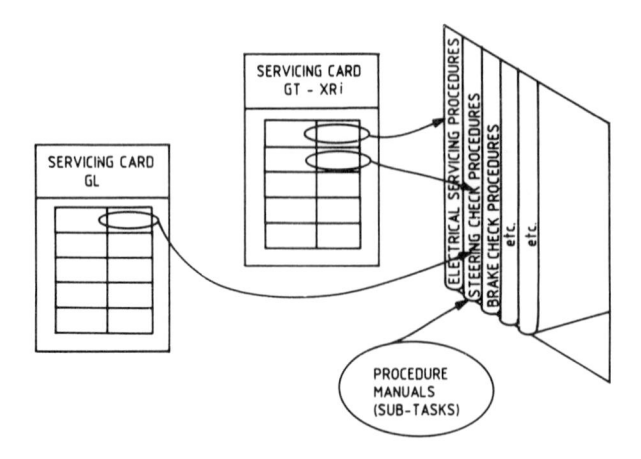

Fig.4.4 Card reference system.

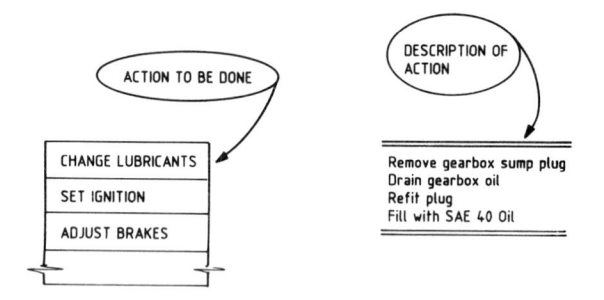

Fig.4.5 What and how.

Fig.4.6 Customizing documents (using building blocks).

Fig.4.7 Job sharing.

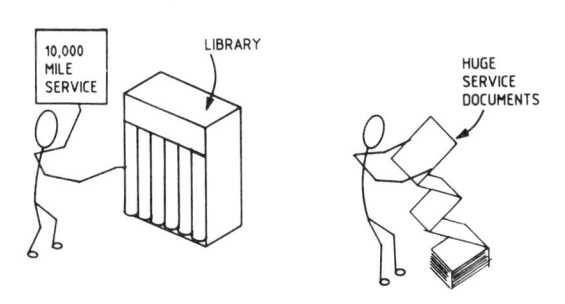

Fig.4.8 Simplifying documentation maintenance.

document we can see what the job is all about (the 'is this really what I'm supposed to be doing?' question).

The second issue is job sharing (Fig.4.7). Splitting up the document makes it easier for a team to work simultaneously on a task. Moreover, we've effectively 'hidden' details within the procedure manuals. If you don't need to know about a topic you don't have to read about it (this may seem a revolutionary idea to some people).

Finally, it's much easier to maintain the documentation (Fig.4.8). After the lubrication change manual has attained the texture of greaseproof paper it can be consigned to the boiler and be replaced by a new version. But note that the rest of the manual set is unaffected; there is no 'ripple through' effect. Our documentation set has 'stability'. In the same way, individual manuals can be amended with the minimum of fuss and disruption. If the change merely affects HOW a task is performed nobody else needs to know about it; we can view it as a 'private' item. Only when the actual task affects other items does the change have to made public.

Finally we're unlikely to make many mistakes when dealing with a small amount of information. That is, we're building reliability into our working processes.

So, in conclusion, we are, in one sense, putting the qualities of small jobs into a much larger one. It is based on the very simple approach of 'divide and conquer' (now that's an original phrase).

4.1.3 Program design – the Ada approach

The problems discussed above are directly applicable to software development. So too are the solutions. In essence we are looking for techniques which will:

- Enable us to split up a complete program into sensible-sized parts;
- Associate these with logically related activities;
- Develop program building blocks;
- Allow a number of programmers to work simultaneously on the project;
- Hide information;
- Provide program stability.

The structures provided in Ada to enable us to attain these ends are defined to be program units. In this chapter we are going to look – in great detail – at one particular type of program unit, the subprogram. This comes in two forms, the procedure and the function.

We've been using subprograms all along without having had them described in a formal way. 'PUT', 'SKIP_LINE' and 'GET' are examples of these subprograms, being held in library units. Yet we haven't had to know any details of their construction or implementation to be able to use them. Just re-read the list given above defining desirable qualities for software construction. Surely our experience from earlier chapters shows that subprograms go a long way to meet these needs.

4.2 INTRODUCTION TO THE PROCEDURE

A standard Ada procedure may be defined as a textually complete (and usually compact) program construct. It is stored away for use until it is called into action (invoked). The calling may be done by the main program OR by another procedure. Therefore it has to be identified; so we give it a name. The compiler must be made aware of its existence; hence at some point it must be declared in the program.

For the moment we'll restrict ourselves to using procedures within main program units. Their general format and structure is shown in Fig.4.9.

In such cases the procedure is written before the 'begin' statement which opens the program code. By writing the procedure we also define its existence to the compiler. That is, no separate declaration is needed (we'll see later in chapter 7 that it is quite permissible for a program unit to hold nothing but procedures; for the moment consider them to be part of the main program unit).

Listing 4.1 is a very simple example of using procedures, the major points being identified in Fig.4.9. It can be seen that the procedure structure is

Introduction to the procedure 77

```
                          with _____
                          procedure A_MAIN_PROGRAM is
                          Main_Program_Declarations                  THE PROCEDURE ITSELF

                                                                     THIS IS ALSO THE
  DECLARATIVE                                                        DECLARATION OF
  PART OF                 procedure      CHANGE_LUBRICANTS   is      THE PROCEDURE
  A_MAIN_PROGRAM          begin

                                                                     THE NAME OF THE PROCEDURE

                          end CHANGE_LUBRICANTS ;

                          begin                                      USING (INVOKING)
                                                                     THE PROCEDURE
                             CHANGE_LUBRICANTS

                          end A_MAIN_PROGRAM ;
```

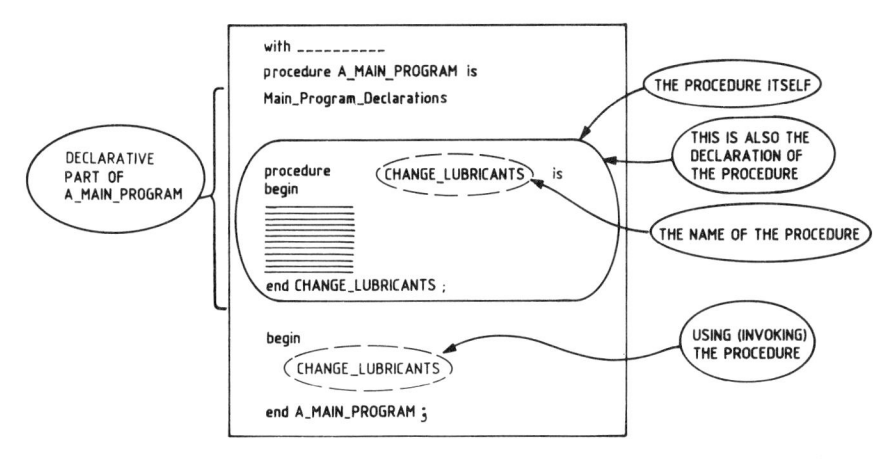

Fig.4.9 Main program format incorporating a procedure.

```
with TEXT_IO;              use TEXT_IO;
procedure MAIN is
  -- The actual procedure is written here.
  -- This also acts as its declaration.
  procedure CHANGE_LUBRICANTS is
  begin
    PUT_LINE ("Lubricants have been changed");
  end CHANGE_LUBRICANTS;
begin
  -- this is the main procedure
  PUT_LINE ("This is the first demo using procedures");
  CHANGE_LUBRICANTS;
  -- the procedure is called here.
  PUT_LINE ("This is a repeat printout");
  CHANGE_LUBRICANTS;
  -- and again here.
end MAIN;
```

Listing 4.1 This illustrates the use of a simple procedure in a program.

similar to that of a main program unit. Likewise, it is optional to use the procedure name (the *identifier*) after the final '**end**' and before the ';' delimiter. We recommend that you always include this name. Then, in a program which uses many procedures, you can clearly see which **end** belongs to which procedure.

In Listing 4.1 the procedure 'CHANGE_LUBRICANTS' is called twice, yet the procedure code is written once only. The net result is a saving on the amount of computer memory needed to execute this program. Originally, saving on memory space was a prime reason for using procedures. Now it is used mainly as a basic structuring tool for program design.

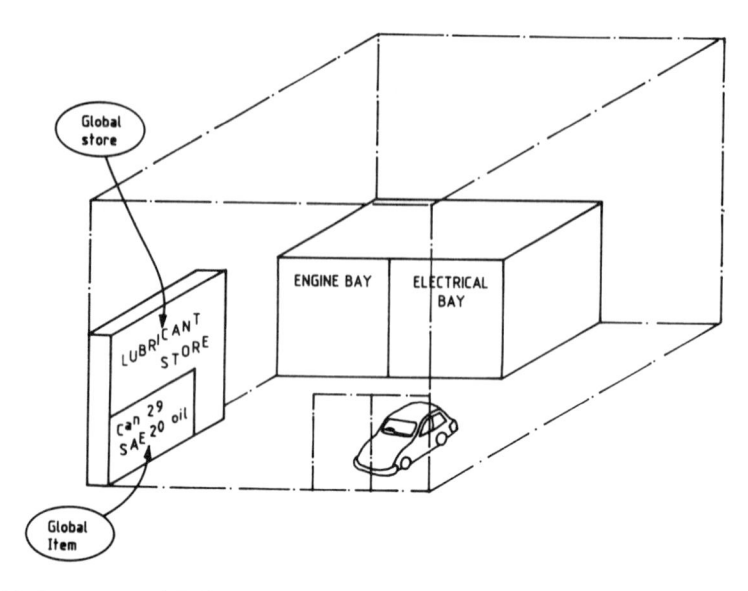

Fig.4.10 Concept – global storage (Listing 4.2).

4.3 USING VARIABLES IN PROCEDURES – SCOPE AND LOCALITY

The procedure above was kept deliberately simple; even variables were omitted from the program unit. As you can guess, this is the exception rather than the norm. Variables haven't exactly caused us problems up to now. So why pay them special attention just because of procedures? The reason is that the rules governing their use within procedures often cause confusion to the first-time user. So let's look at some simple analogies, using our garage workshop to illustrate these rules.

We've now reorganized our workshop into a general garage space and two special work bays, the engine and electrical service areas (Fig.4.10). Inside the general area is a lubricant store; this may be used by all workers in the garage. One particular item, CAN_29, holds SAE 20 oil. Any worker, in any part of the garage, who receives an instruction to use CAN_29 goes to the lubricant store; the resulting lubricant is SAE 20. We can view this store item as being a 'global' one. That is, its name is known throughout all parts of the garage; further, it means the same thing to all users. Now let's place this in the context of an Ada program. Listing 4.2 is an extended version of 4.1, now using two procedures. In addition, a string constant 'CAN_29' has been introduced; this is declared in the usual place. It is used both within the procedures AND the main program to generate screen printing text. We can therefore infer that the data item is visible throughout the whole program unit, i.e. it is 'global'.

Using variables in procedures – scope and locality   79

```
with TEXT_IO;              use TEXT_IO;
procedure GLOBAL_DATA is
  CAN_29             :     constant STRING := "SAE 20 oil";
  -- the global item
  procedure CHANGE_LUBRICANTS is
  begin
    PUT_LINE ("Lubricants have been changed");
    PUT_LINE (CAN_29);
  end CHANGE_LUBRICANTS;
  -- end of procedure code.
  procedure SERVICE_ELECTRICALS is
  begin
    PUT_LINE ("Electrics have been serviced");
    PUT_LINE (CAN_29);
  end SERVICE_ELECTRICALS;
  -- end of procedure code.
begin
  -- this is the main procedure
  PUT_LINE ("This is the first procedure");
  CHANGE_LUBRICANTS;
  PUT_LINE ("This is the second procedure");
  SERVICE_ELECTRICALS;
  PUT ("The global item is ");
  PUT_LINE (CAN_29);
end GLOBAL_DATA;

------------------------------------------------------------------
-- When the program is run the following print-out results
-- This is the first procedure
-- Lubricants have been changed
-- SAE 20 oil
-- This is the second procedure
-- Electrics have been serviced
-- SAE 20 oil
-- The global item is SAE 20 oil
------------------------------------------------------------------
```

Listing 4.2 This illustrates the use of a global item in a program which contains procedures.

All is now running smoothly in our garage. However, we realize that it would be both efficient and effective if our servicing bays had their own local stores (Fig.4.11). We'll identify individual items by can numbers. But then it's essential to make sure that no confusion arises over the numbering system. One solution would be to give every store location a unique identifier. Certainly this would work; but then somebody would have to be given the job of controlling the number system. An alternative, and much simpler, method is to allow each bay manager to control his or her own numbering system. Thus local items belong to a local store. Even if another store uses exactly the same number it doesn't matter; only those defined to belong to the local store can be used.

These ideas, applied to Ada, are shown in Listing 4.3. Having declarations within a procedure is analogous to building your own local store; local

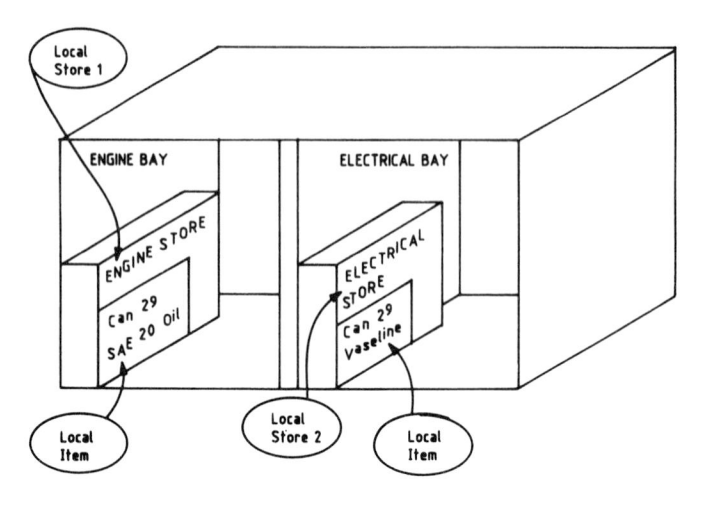

Fig.4.11 Concept – local storage (Listing 4.3).

```
with TEXT_IO;              use TEXT_IO;
procedure LOCAL_DATA is
  procedure CHANGE_LUBRICANTS is
    CAN_29          :    constant STRING := "SAE 20 oil";
  -- local item
  begin
    PUT_LINE ("Lubricants have been changed");
    PUT (CAN_29);
    PUT_LINE (" used");
  end CHANGE_LUBRICANTS;
  -- end of procedure code.
  procedure SERVICE_ELECTRICALS is
    CAN_29          :    constant STRING := "Vaseline";
  -- local item
  begin
    PUT_LINE ("Electrics have been serviced");
    PUT (CAN_29);
    PUT_LINE (" used");
  end SERVICE_ELECTRICALS;
  -- end of procedure code.
begin
  -- this is the main procedure
  PUT_LINE ("This is the first procedure");
  CHANGE_LUBRICANTS;
  PUT_LINE ("This is the second procedure");
  SERVICE_ELECTRICALS;
end LOCAL_DATA;
------------------------------------------------------------
-- When the program is run the following print-out results:
-- This is the first procedure
-- Lubricants have been changed
-- SAE 20 oil used
-- This is the second procedure
-- Electrics have been serviced
-- Vaseline used
------------------------------------------------------------
```

Listing 4.3 This illustrates the use of local items in a program which contains procedures.

variables and constants correspond to local items. In this listing both procedures have a declarations section; in fact each one has declared a string constant 'CAN_29'. Although they have the same name they are not the same. Now we have to be able to distinguish between the two. The rules for use are very simple: only the one defined within the procedure, the 'local' object, is actually used when the procedure is called. The area of a program for which an identifier is declared is called its 'scope'. Thus the scope of "CAN_29 := 'SAE 20 Oil'" is that of the procedure 'CHANGE_LUBRICANTS'.

What are the advantages of using local variables? The major one is that it helps us to produce reliable error-free programs which are maintainable. An identifier is bound to its procedure; therefore it cannot be accessed from other parts of the program. The programmer doesn't have to check through a name list to avoid clashes; by limiting scope, identifiers become easily visible and hence controllable. Accidental access to, and modification of, such items is eliminated.

The second advantage is that we can save on computer storage space by using local variables. Such variables are brought into being only while the procedure is active; their storage space is disposed of once the procedure has finished (obviously this would be an advantage when dealing with very large quantities of data). It is very important that you realize that variables disappear between procedure calls – they are said to be dynamic. Also note well that the values of such local variables are undefined each time a procedure is called. Therefore you must assign them a value before using them.

It's very unlikely that we'll write real programs which don't use global variables (for variables also read constants in this context). So what are the rules for handling the combination of local and global items? These are illustrated by the program in Listing 4.4.

'CAN_29' and 'GLOBAL_MESSAGE' are globals; observe that we also have local items identified as 'CAN_29'. The rules for handling clashing names have already been covered (Listing 4.3). The use of a non-clashing global item was demonstrated in Listing 4.2. Listing 4.4 merely reinforces these points.

The terms visibility and scope are often used interchangeably, and, in fact, for several computer languages this is the case. For Ada, however, we need to make a subtle distinction between them (why will become clear in a moment). In simple terms, if we can access a program object using its declared name, then it is visible. If an object is *potentially* visible, then it is said to be in scope.

As a final example consider the highest level of complexity, namely procedures nested within procedures (Listing 4.5).

The structure of the main program unit NEST_PROC is shown in Fig.4.12; the nesting of procedures is clearly visible.

The various global and local items are shown in the figure, together with

82 Subprograms in Ada – procedures and functions

```
with TEXT_IO;              use TEXT_IO;
procedure GLOBAL_AND_LOCAL is
   CAN_29           :    constant STRING := "Diesel Oil";
   GLOBAL_MESSAGE   :    constant STRING := "Service Information";
   procedure CHANGE_LUBRICANTS is
      CAN_29        :    constant STRING := "SAE 20 oil";
   -- First local item
   begin
      PUT_LINE (GLOBAL_MESSAGE);
      PUT_LINE ("Lubricants have been changed");
      PUT (CAN_29);
      PUT_LINE (" used");
   end CHANGE_LUBRICANTS;
   -- end of procedure code.
   procedure SERVICE_ELECTRICALS is
      CAN_29        :    constant STRING := "Vaseline";
   -- Second local item
   begin
      PUT_LINE (GLOBAL_MESSAGE);
      PUT_LINE ("Electrics have been serviced");
      PUT (CAN_29);
      PUT_LINE (" used");
   end SERVICE_ELECTRICALS;
   -- end of procedure code.
begin
   -- this is the main procedure
   PUT_LINE (GLOBAL_MESSAGE);
   PUT ("The boiler fuel supply is ");
   PUT_LINE (CAN_29);
   PUT_LINE ("This is the first procedure");
   CHANGE_LUBRICANTS;
   PUT_LINE ("This is the second procedure");
   SERVICE_ELECTRICALS;
end GLOBAL_AND_LOCAL;
-----------------------------------------------------------------
-- When the program is run the following print-out results:
-- Service Information
-- The boiler fuel supply is Diesel Oil
-- This is the first procedure
-- Service Information
-- Lubricants have been changed
-- SAE 20 oil used
-- This is the second procedure
-- Service Information
-- Electrics have been serviced
-- Vaseline used
-----------------------------------------------------------------
```

Listing 4.4 This illustrates the use of global and local items in a program which contains procedures.

their areas of visibility. After studying this figure the following rules should be appreciated and understood:

(a) Main program global identifiers are visible everywhere within the unit unless new (inner) redeclarations are made.
(b) If a global identifier X is redeclared in a procedure within the main program then the LOCAL identifier replaces the GLOBAL identifier.

Using variables in procedures – scope and locality 83

```
with TEXT_IO;          use TEXT_IO;
procedure NEST_PROC is
  CAN_29            :   constant STRING := "Diesel oil";
  BANNER_MESSAGE    :   constant STRING := "This is a procedure start point";
  procedure DO_FIRST_STAGE_SERVICE is
    LOCAL_MESSAGE   :   constant STRING := "This is a nested procedure";
    procedure CHANGE_LUBRICANTS is
      CAN_29          :   constant STRING := "SAE 20 Oil";
  -- First local item
    begin
      PUT_LINE (BANNER_MESSAGE);
      PUT_LINE (LOCAL_MESSAGE);
      PUT_LINE ("Lubricants have been changed");
      PUT (CAN_29);
      PUT_LINE (" used");
    end CHANGE_LUBRICANTS;
  -- end of procedure code.
    procedure SERVICE_ELECTRICALS is
      CAN_29          :   constant STRING := "Vaseline";
  -- Second local item
    begin
      PUT_LINE (BANNER_MESSAGE);
      PUT_LINE (LOCAL_MESSAGE);
      PUT_LINE ("Electrics have been serviced");
      PUT (CAN_29);
      PUT_LINE (" used");
    end SERVICE_ELECTRICALS;
  -- end of procedure code.
  begin
  -- program of outermost procedure
    PUT_LINE (BANNER_MESSAGE);
    CHANGE_LUBRICANTS;
    SERVICE_ELECTRICALS;
  end DO_FIRST_STAGE_SERVICE;
  -- end of outermost procedure
begin
  -- main procedure
  PUT ("The boiler fuel supply is ");
  PUT_LINE (CAN_29);
  DO_FIRST_STAGE_SERVICE;
end NEST_PROC;
```

Listing 4.5 This illustrates the use of local and global items with nested procedures.

(c) If a procedure (say 'BETA') encloses other procedures then any variables declared in BETA are visible throughout all parts of the procedure. Naturally enough this includes the procedures enclosed within BETA unless inner redeclarations are made.

(d) Assume an identifier Y is declared in a procedure BETA. Let us refer to this as Y(BETA). The same identifier is later redeclared in a procedure 'DELTA' which is inner to BETA. Call this Y(DELTA). In these circumstances Y(BETA) is not visible in DELTA. When DELTA is invoked the most local identifier – that is, Y(DELTA) – is visible.

Consider Listing 4.5 again. Here the global constant 'CAN_29' is in scope throughout the complete program. But, because there are inner redeclarations

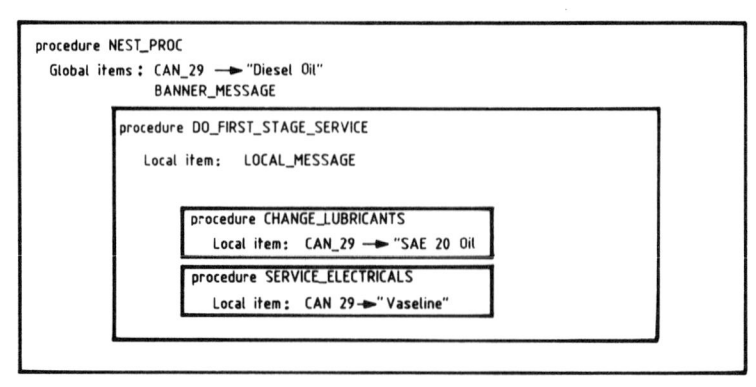

84 Subprograms in Ada – procedures and functions

```
procedure NEST_PROC
    Global items :  CAN_29 ⟶ "Diesel Oil"
                    BANNER_MESSAGE

    procedure DO_FIRST_STAGE_SERVICE
        Local item :  LOCAL_MESSAGE

        procedure CHANGE_LUBRICANTS
            Local item :  CAN_29 ⟶ "SAE 20 Oil"

        procedure SERVICE_ELECTRICALS
            Local item :  CAN_29 ⟶ "Vaseline"
```

ITEM	WHERE VISIBLE	SCOPE
CAN_29 ⟶ "Diesel Oil"	Everywhere except the two innermost procedures	Everywhere
BANNER_MESSAGE	Everywhere	Everywhere
LOCAL_MESSAGE	within all three inner procedures	within all three inner procedures
CAN_29 ⟶ "SAE 20 Oil"	Procedure CHANGE_LUBRICANTS	Procedure CHANGE_LUBRICANTS
CAN_29 ⟶ "Vaseline"	Procedure SERVICE_ELECTRICALS	Procedure SERVICE_ELECTRICALS

Fig.4.12 Scope and visibility of program items.

using the same name, it is made invisible within these inner sections. The question then is: does this make it impossible to access this global item from WITHIN the inner sections? The answer is NO – provided we use a special form of notation (variously called 'selected component notation', 'dot notation' or 'qualified notation'). For procedures and functions this is done by prefixing identifiers with the name of their enclosing program unit. Once more consider Listing 4.5. Here we can access the global 'CAN_29' from inner sections by writing 'NEST_PROC.CAN_29' within these inner sections. To see this in action add the following statements to the procedure 'CHANGE LUBRICANTS' of Listing 4.5:

```
TEXT_IO.PUT_LINE ("The global lubricants are");
TEXT_IO.PUT_LINE (NEST_PROC.CAN_29);
```

We believe that qualified notation leads to poorer programs in terms of clarity, comprehension and maintenance. Hence it should be avoided wherever possible.

4.4 PROCEDURES WITH PARAMETERS

4.4.1 An introduction

Looking back at our procedure examples, you should be able to see that they have one thing in common: each one carries out a specific task. True, they can be called within a program as many times as needed, but how often in life do we need to carry out, on a repetitive basis, jobs which are identical? Not very often. Much more likely is the need to do jobs which are almost, but not quite, alike. The present procedure construct is thus quite limiting; so we've got to find a way to improve it.

Let's once more use an example from our mythical garage to see what can be done. Each month a check is made on the fuel consumption of the hire cars (business has boomed as a result of the reorganizations described earlier). There's no reason why special forms shouldn't be produced for each vehicle, describing exactly what has to be done. Then, every month, the front office issues the appropriate paperwork. This gives instructions to the shop floor to fill in the monthly fuel figures, on the special forms, for the vehicles concerned.

As described, this is analogous to the use of a procedure operation. It works, yes, but is very clumsy. Imagine the need to store, order and control all these different forms. At best it just generates paperwork; at its worst chaos ensues. Now let's consider the method shown in Fig.4.13. Here a standard 'Consumption Calculation Form' is supplied to the shop floor. This can be used with any car as the details are expressed in general terms. These generalized items of information may be defined as 'formal' details. When the instruction sheet is produced by the front office it asks for fuel consumption figures to be calculated. On this sheet it specifies the actual details of mileage and fuel used. By replacing the formal details with the actual details, consumption figures can be produced for specific vehicles. Now we don't need a variety of consumption calculation forms; one is sufficient.

The formal details on our garage form denote items to be supplied when the form is used. In exactly the same way we can devise procedures, using formal data items in our procedure program. These are defined as the 'formal parameters' of the procedure. It, the procedure, is written as if these formal parameters are the actual items used. So, as far as procedure writing is concerned, nothing has really changed. However, when the procedure is invoked, the actual information must be supplied at the time of call. Such items of data are called the 'actual parameters'. Take, for instance, the procedure 'INT_IO.PUT'. When we write 'INT_IO.PUT (Y, 4)' the actual

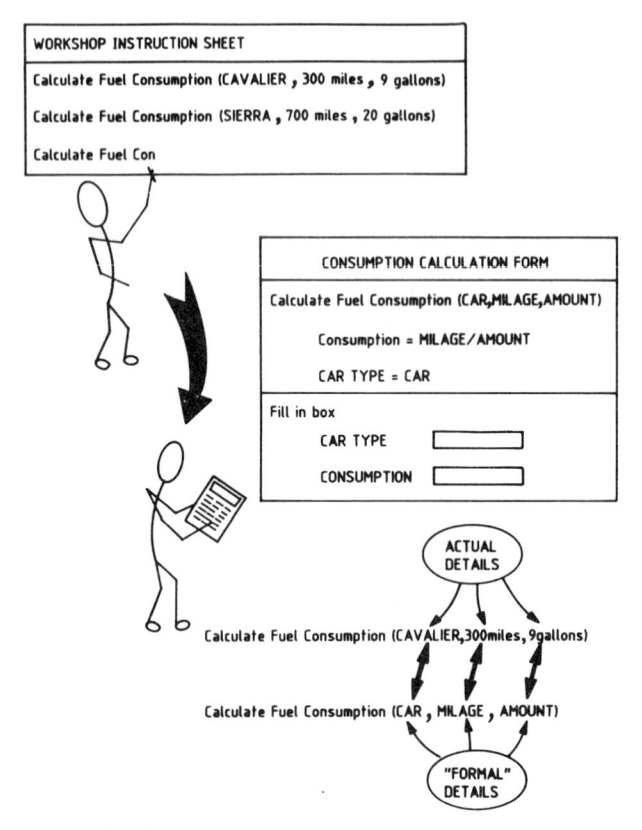

Fig.4.13 Using generalized sets of instructions.

parameters are 'Y' and '4'. These replace the formal parameters at execution time.

Now, what about the order and type of formal and actual parameters? Fundamentally, there is no reason to write these in any particular order or to restrict the types which can be used. But, in the simplest declaration method (as described here), the actual parameter list must coincide with the formal one, otherwise the procedure results will be nonsense. Fortunately, most errors are likely to be picked up by the compiler. This checks that the formal–actual pairing is correct at compile time. More will be said later on this topic.

The parameters can be regarded as the interface between the calling program and the procedure itself (Fig.4.14). By having parameters we can pass information between the two without using global variables. The safety, security and visibility aspects of this cannot be overstated.

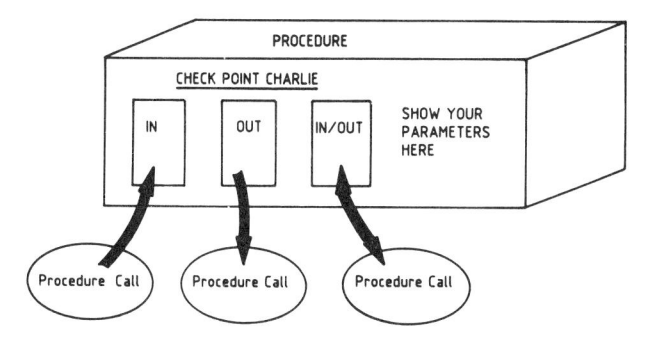

Fig.4.14 Information passing using parameters.

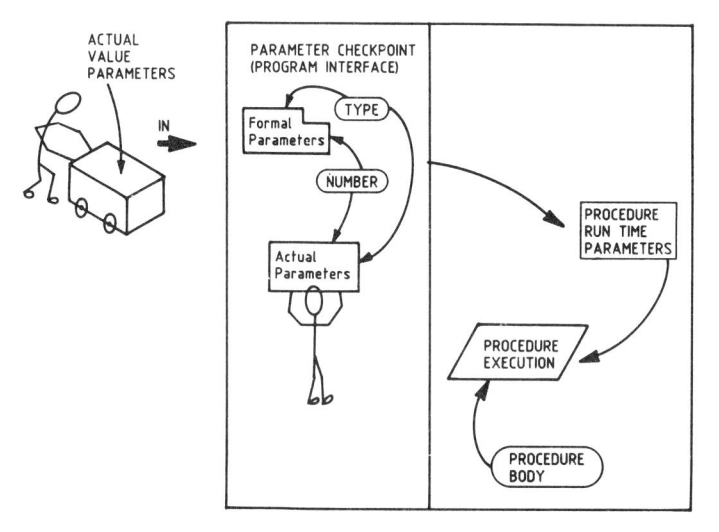

Fig.4.15 Using 'in' parameters.

4.4.2 Using parameters to input data – *in* mode

In our example above we used parameters to pass information into the fuel consumption calculation. This was a one-way process; no reply was asked for. When we do this with Ada procedures the parameter configuration (or *mode*) is defined to be 'in'. For simplicity they are called in parameters. The concept is illustrated in Fig.4.15, a simple program example being that of Listing 4.6. It can be seen that the procedure 'CHANGE_LUBRICANTS' has one formal parameter only. Its name is 'OIL_TYPE', and is of type CHARACTER. When the procedure is called the actual parameter used is 'OIL'; this also is a CHARACTER type.

88   Subprograms in Ada – procedures and functions

```
with TEXT_IO;               use TEXT_IO;
procedure IN_PARAM is
  OIL        :        CHARACTER;
  procedure CHANGE_LUBRICANTS (OIL_TYPE  : in      CHARACTER) is
  begin
    if OIL_TYPE = 'A' then
       PUT_LINE ("Oil is SAE 20");
    elsif OIL_TYPE = 'B' then
       PUT_LINE ("Oil is SAE 30-50");
    else
       PUT_LINE ("Bad entry");
    end if;
  end CHANGE_LUBRICANTS;
  -- end of procedure code.
begin
  -- this is the main procedure
  PUT_LINE ("What is the lubricant type?");
  PUT_LINE ("Enter A for SAE 20, B for SAE 30-50 oil");
  PUT ("=>   ");
  GET (OIL);
  SKIP_LINE;
  NEW_LINE;
  CHANGE_LUBRICANTS (OIL);
end IN_PARAM;
```

Listing 4.6 This illustrates the use of a parameter to pass information to a procedure.

You will see that, within the procedure, there is no declaration for the variable 'OIL_TYPE'. This comes about because the formal parameter listing is also used as a variable declaration listing (Fig.4.16).

Now for one very important point. Actual parameters are read-only items and cannot be changed within the procedure itself. That is, they are treated as constant values. This may be demonstrated by trying to compile the program of Listing 4.7. From this, it can be seen that assigning values to an in parameter is regarded as a source code error.

Suppose now that we have a number of formal parameters to be listed; further, assume there is a mix of types. How is this done? As an example consider parameters as follows:

```
FLOAT – K1 K2 K3
INTEGER – X1 X2
CHARACTER – ERROR
```

Then the procedure heading could read:

```
procedure COMPUTE (X1,X2    : in INTEGER;
                   K1,K2,K3 : in FLOAT;
                   ERROR    : in CHARACTER) is
```

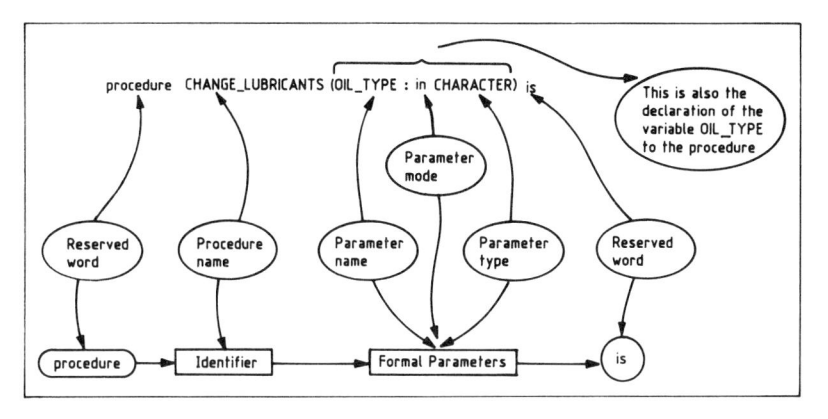

Fig.4.16 Procedure heading incorporating an 'in' parameter.

```
with TEXT_IO;           use TEXT_IO;
procedure IN_PARAM_ERR is
  OIL            :    CHARACTER;
  procedure CHANGE_LUBRICANTS (OIL_TYPE  : in     CHARACTER) is
  begin
    if OIL_TYPE = 'A' then
      PUT_LINE ("Oil is SAE 20");
    elsif OIL_TYPE = 'B' then
      PUT_LINE ("Oil is SAE 30-50");
    else
      PUT_LINE ("Bad entry");
    end if;
 -- The next line is illegal
    OIL_TYPE := 'Z';
  end CHANGE_LUBRICANTS;
  -- end of procedure code.
begin
  -- this is the main procedure
  PUT_LINE ("What is the lubricant type?");
  PUT_LINE ("Enter A for SAE 20, B for SAE 30-50 oil");
  PUT ("=>  ");
  GET (OIL);
  SKIP_LINE;
  NEW_LINE;
  CHANGE_LUBRICANTS (OIL);
end IN_PARAM_ERR;
```

Listing 4.7 This illustrates that 'in' mode parameters become constants when passed into a procedure.

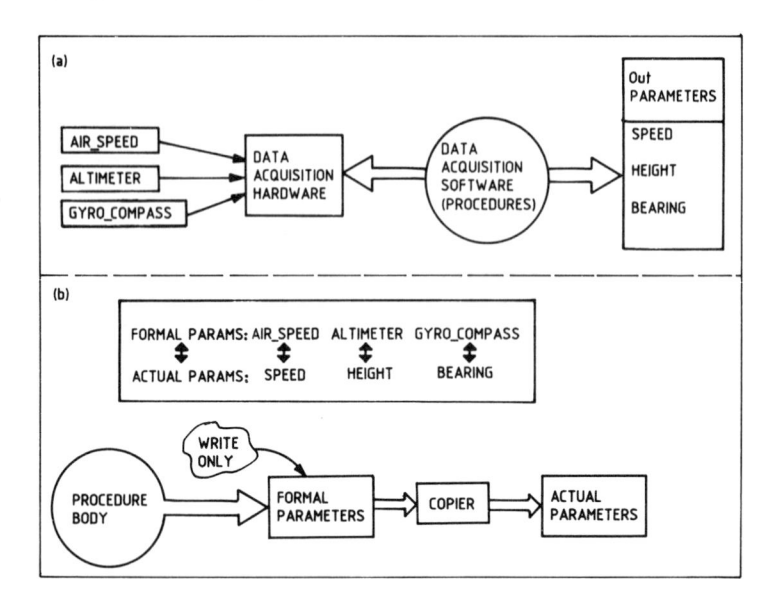

90 Subprograms in Ada – procedures and functions

Fig.4.17 'out' parameter application and concept.

The order of writing the formal parameters is unimportant. But make it as readable and understandable as possible.

When **in** parameters are listed it is legal to omit the mode identifier. Thus the example above could have been written

```
procedure COMPUTE (X1, X2  : INTEGER;
                   K1,K2,K3 : FLOAT;
                   ERROR    : CHARACTER) is
```

We regard this as bad programming practice, for two reasons. First, programs should always be explicit, not implicit. Be as clear as possible. Second, if the programmer makes a mistake and leaves out the mode identifier, the parameter will default to **in** – which may be wrong.

4.4.3 **out** parameters

out parameters are the reverse of **in**. They are used to transmit information from within the procedure to the calling program. Consider, for instance, the situation shown in Fig.4.17a.

This depicts part of an aircraft air data system, representing a data acquisition task. The data itself is collected from a set of sensors (airspeed, altimeter

```
with TEXT_IO;                use TEXT_IO;
procedure OUT_ONLY_PARAMS is
  package INT_IO is new INTEGER_IO (INTEGER);
  use INT_IO;
  SPEED           :       INTEGER;
  HEIGHT          :       INTEGER;
  BEARING         :       INTEGER;
  procedure MEASURE_AIR_DATA (AIR_SPEED    :      out INTEGER;
                              ALTIMETER    :      out INTEGER;
                              GYRO_COMPASS :      out INTEGER) is
  begin
    PUT ("Enter current air speed (max 250 mph)         => ");
    GET (AIR_SPEED);
    SKIP_LINE;
    PUT ("Enter current altimeter reading (max 30,000 ft) => ");
    GET (ALTIMETER);
    SKIP_LINE;
    PUT ("Enter current giro compass reading (0-360 deg) => ");
    GET (GYRO_COMPASS);
    SKIP_LINE;
  end MEASURE_AIR_DATA;
begin
  -- this is the main procedure
  PUT_LINE ("Reading current Air Data status");
  MEASURE_AIR_DATA (SPEED, HEIGHT, BEARING);
  NEW_LINE;
  PUT ("Our current air speed is ");
  PUT (SPEED, 0);
  PUT_LINE (" miles per hour");
  PUT ("Our current height   is ");
  PUT (HEIGHT, 0);
  PUT_LINE (" feet above sea level");
  PUT ("Our current bearing  is ");
  PUT (BEARING, 0);
  PUT_LINE (" degrees");
end OUT_ONLY_PARAMS;
```

Listing 4.8 This example uses 'out' parameters only.

and gyro compass), digitized, and fed into the main body of the software. Here the data acquisition task software could be implemented using a procedure with **out** parameters only. This function is simulated in Listing 4.8.

Values assigned to formal **out** parameters within the procedure are copied to the corresponding actual parameters of the procedure call (Fig.4.17b). The important point here is that, as far as the procedure is concerned, **out** parameters are meant to be treated as write-only items. The basic reason for using the procedure is to update the value of the actual parameter. This has two important consequences. First, if you try to read the value of a formal **out** parameter your compiler will give an error message. Second, the procedure must assign values to formal **out** parameters. If this isn't done then, after the procedure is executed, the values of the actual parameters are undefined. You should also expect to receive a compiler warning message if you make this mistake.

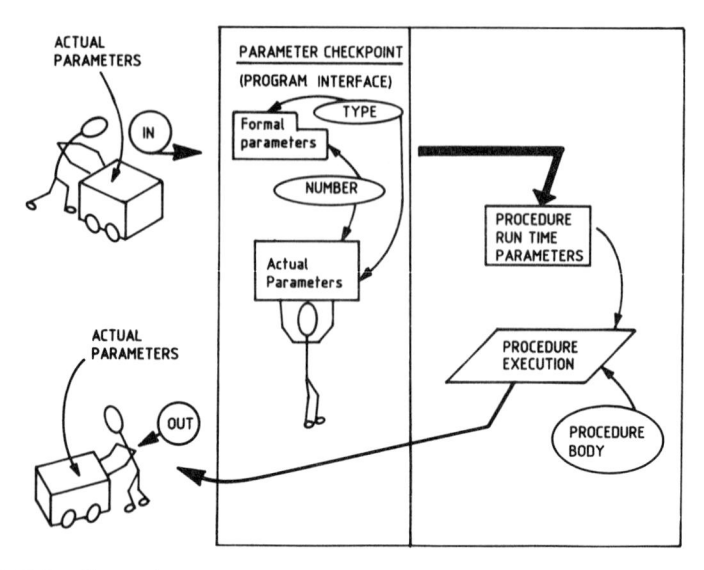

Fig.4.18 Using 'in out' parameters.

We aren't likely to meet many procedures which use only **out** parameters for general programming tasks. Generally they are used in conjunction with the other parameter modes.

4.4.4 **in out** parameters

The primary function of the **in out** mode is to support two-way transfer of data when using parameters. Figure 4.18 defines the ideas behind the use of such parameters, which are quite simple and sound. The essentials are shown in Listing 4.9.

Observe also the change in the declaration format (Fig.4.19).

What about a formal listing of **in, out** and **in out** parameters then? There is nothing surprising here; we maintain consistency of our rules. In each case the formal parameters must be listed as follows:

- Parameters of different types must be shown separately.
- **in, out** and **in out** modes must be separated.

As an example, consider the need to declare:

> in parameters:
> REAL – K1
> INTEGER – X1

```
with TEXT_IO;              use TEXT_IO;
procedure IN_OUT_PARAM is
  OIL            :        CHARACTER;
  procedure CHANGE_LUBRICANTS (OIL_TYPE   : in out CHARACTER) is
  begin
    if OIL_TYPE = 'A' then
      PUT_LINE ("Oil is SAE 20");
      OIL_TYPE := 'B';
    elsif OIL_TYPE = 'B' then
      PUT_LINE ("Oil is SAE 30-50");
      OIL_TYPE := 'A';
    end if;
  end CHANGE_LUBRICANTS;
 -- end of procedure code.
begin
 -- this is the main procedure
  OIL := 'A';
  CHANGE_LUBRICANTS (OIL);
  CHANGE_LUBRICANTS (OIL);
  CHANGE_LUBRICANTS (OIL);
end IN_OUT_PARAM;
```

Listing 4.9 This illustrates the use of an 'in out' mode parameter to pass information to/from a procedure.

```
procedure   CHANGE_LUBRICANTS  (OIL_TYPE : in out CHARACTER) is
```
- Parameter name
- Parameter mode
- Parameter type

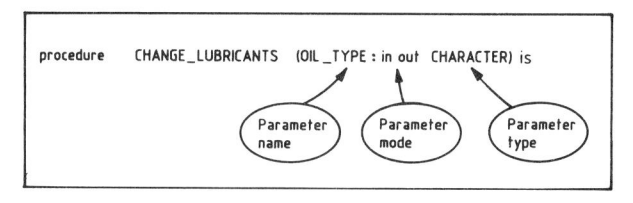

Fig.4.19 Procedure heading incorporating an 'in out' parameter.

out parameters:
REAL – Y1

in out parameters:
CHARACTER – MESSAGE
INTEGER – W1

The procedure heading has the following form:

```
procedure COMPUTE_AGAIN (K1        : in REAL;
                         X1        : in INTEGER;
                         MESSAGE   : in out CHARACTER;
                         W1        : in out INTEGER;
                         Y1        : out REAL) is
```

Again, the ordering of the formal parameters is not important.

You may well ask why we bother to use **in** parameters at all. After all, we could do exactly the same job using **in out** ones. That's true, so there must be more to it than just a matter of moving information about. In fact it's the way the parameters are handled that's important. Running the program of Listing 4.9 proves that the information held by variable 'OIL_TYPE' is changed by the procedure itself. But when we use **in** parameters (Listing 4.7) the original value cannot be changed by the procedure. Thus **in** parameters are intrinsically safer than **in out** ones; we are prevented from accidentally changing what we started with. *Ergo*, use **in** parameters unless there is a good reason not to.

4.5 FUNCTIONS

4.5.1 Introduction

We often find that the primary purpose of a procedure is to produce a particular result, as, say, in mathematical calculations. Consider, for instance, that we want to write a procedure to calculate fuel consumption according to the equation:

> Average fuel consumption = Distance ÷ Fuel used

Ada gives us a neat way to deal with this by providing another type of subprogram – the 'function'. This should not be seen as a replacement for the standard procedure. Normally it would only be used when the subprogram is designed to give a result. In rather simple terms we can say that a procedure causes something to happen while a function causes a computation to be carried out.

4.5.2 Using functions

The underlying ideas of the function are shown in Fig.4.20. In most cases input information is needed by the function. We supply this, as with the procedure, using parameters. However, only **in** mode is permitted with the function. Once it has been invoked it begins executing, processing its data. Finally a result is generated; its value is then returned to a designated variable in the calling program. The item to be returned is appended to the reserved word **return**, forming a **return** statement.

Like procedures, there are two major points concerning functions. The first is the way in which they are written, and the second is the method of call.

Functions 95

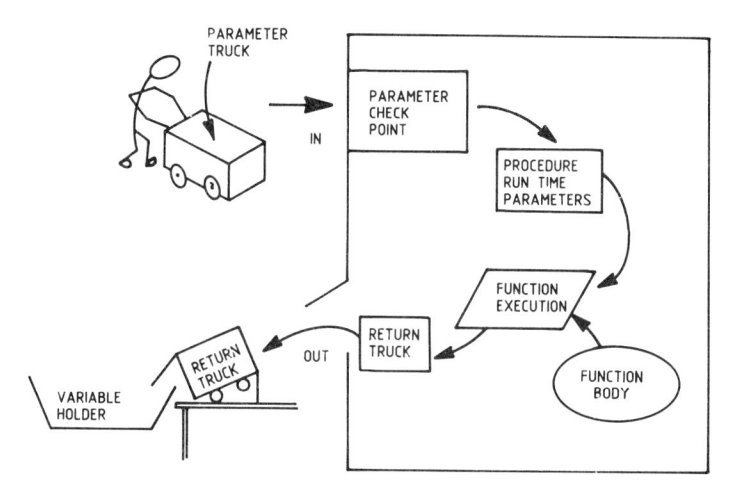

Fig.4.20 The function concept.

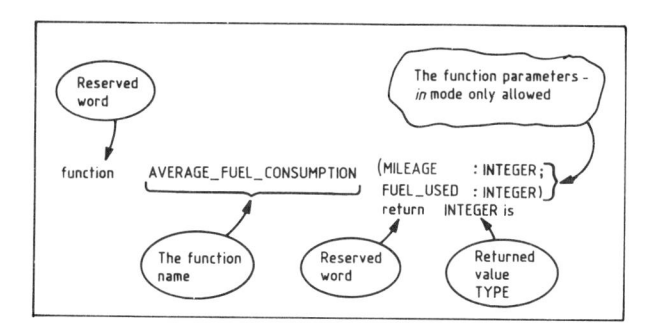

Fig.4.21 Function details.

The essentials are illustrated in Figs.4.21 and 4.22. Here we have a function 'AVERAGE_FUEL_CONSUMPTION' (Fig.4.21) which has two parameters – which must be of mode **in**. It performs a calculation, returning the computed value of the locally declared variable 'AVG_CONSUMPTION' (Listing 4.10). This is an INTEGER value, the type being defined in the function heading. When the function is called we actually assign the result to some variable: in this case 'FUEL_CONSUMPTION' (Fig.4.22).

Read through Listing 4.10 to see how to write and use the function.
In summary then:

- Only one result is returned (here being AVG_CONSUMPTION);
- Its type is defined in the function heading (INTEGER);
- The result is given to any desired variable using the assignment statement (FUEL_CONSUMPTION). The returned value and the program variable must be of the same type.

96 Subprograms in Ada – procedures and functions

```
with TEXT_IO;              use TEXT_IO;
procedure SHOW_FUNCTION is
  package INT_IO is new INTEGER_IO (INTEGER);
  use INT_IO;
  MILES              :      INTEGER;
  GALLONS            :      INTEGER;
  FUEL_CONSUMPTION   :      INTEGER;
  function AVERAGE_FUEL_CONSUMPTION (MILEAGE    :       INTEGER;
                                     FUEL_USED  :       INTEGER )
     return INTEGER is
     AVG_CONSUMPTION :      INTEGER;
  begin
     PUT_LINE ("Calculation running");
     AVG_CONSUMPTION := MILEAGE / FUEL_USED;
     return AVG_CONSUMPTION;
  end AVERAGE_FUEL_CONSUMPTION;
  -- end of function code.
begin
  -- this is the main procedure
  PUT ("What is the mileage (integer value)? ");
  GET (MILES);
  SKIP_LINE;
  PUT ("How many gallons have been used (integer value)? ");
  GET (GALLONS);
  SKIP_LINE;
  FUEL_CONSUMPTION := AVERAGE_FUEL_CONSUMPTION (MILES, GALLONS);
  PUT ("The average fuel consumption is ");
  PUT (FUEL_CONSUMPTION, 0);
  PUT_LINE (" miles per gallon");
end SHOW_FUNCTION;
```

Listing 4.10 This illustrates the use of a function subprogram to obtain results from a calculation.

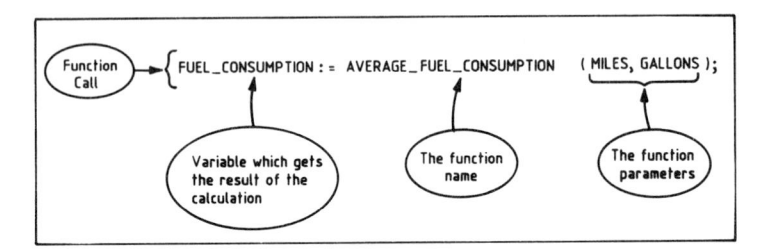

Fig.4.22 Function call.

Listing 4.11 is a further example of the use of functions.

The **return** statement may also be used within a procedure. In this case the statement consists only of '**return;**' – no value is returned to the calling program. The effect of executing this is to return control back to the point

```
with TEXT_IO;              use TEXT_IO;
procedure BOOL_RETURN is
  LETTER      :    CHARACTER;
  function IS_CAPITAL (CHAR  :        CHARACTER)
    return BOOLEAN is
    CAPITAL_LETTER  :    BOOLEAN;
  begin
    if CHAR >= 'A' then
      if CHAR <= 'Z' then
        CAPITAL_LETTER := TRUE;
      else
        CAPITAL_LETTER := FALSE;
      end if;
    else
      CAPITAL_LETTER := FALSE;
    end if;
    return CAPITAL_LETTER;
  end IS_CAPITAL;
begin
  -- this is the main procedure
  TEXT_IO.PUT ("Enter any character => ");
  TEXT_IO.GET (LETTER);
  TEXT_IO.SKIP_LINE;
  if IS_CAPITAL (LETTER) then
    TEXT_IO.PUT_LINE ("This is a capital letter");
  else
    TEXT_IO.PUT_LINE ("This is not a capital letter");
  end if;
  TEXT_IO.NEW_LINE;
end BOOL_RETURN;
```

Listing 4.11 This illustrates the use of a function that returns a BOOLEAN value. This can then be used in an expression.

at which the procedure was called. We recommend that this should not be used. In effect it simulates a **goto,** and can lead to sloppy programming.

Note that this form of return is illegal in a function, which must always return a value.

4.5.3 Functions vs. procedures

Is it necessary to use functions? Well, consider Listing 4.12, which is a procedurized equivalent of the function in Listing 4.10. Any program implemented as a function can also be written using procedures. Therefore we don't actually need the function. But it is a valuable program construct, from two aspects. First, the way we use it can make programs clearer, easier to read, and more meaningful. Second, because a function is an expression (the procedure being a statement), we can use it to form more complex constructs, as, for instance,

98 Subprograms in Ada – procedures and functions

```
with TEXT_IO;              use TEXT_IO;
procedure PROC_OUT is
  package INT_IO is new INTEGER_IO (INTEGER);
  use INT_IO;
  MILES               :    INTEGER;
  GALLONS             :    INTEGER;
  FUEL_CONSUMPTION    :    INTEGER;
  procedure COMPUTE_AVERAGE_FUEL_CONSUMPTION
                              (MILEAGE         : in       INTEGER;
                               FUEL_USED       : in       INTEGER;
                               AVG_CONSUMPTION :   out INTEGER) is
  begin
    PUT_LINE ("Calculation running");
    AVG_CONSUMPTION := MILEAGE / FUEL_USED;
  end COMPUTE_AVERAGE_FUEL_CONSUMPTION;
begin
 -- this is the main procedure
  PUT ("What is the mileage (integer value)? ");
  GET (MILES);
  SKIP_LINE;
  PUT ("How many gallons have been used (integer value)? ");
  GET (GALLONS);
  SKIP_LINE;
  COMPUTE_AVERAGE_FUEL_CONSUMPTION (MILES, GALLONS, FUEL_CONSUMPTION);
  PUT ("The average fuel consumption is ");
  PUT (FUEL_CONSUMPTION, 0);
  PUT_LINE (" miles per gallon");
  NEW_LINE;
end PROC_OUT;
```

Listing 4.12 This illustrates the use of a procedure with a single 'out' parameter to obtain the result from calculation.

```
CONSUMPTION := (CONSUMPTION + AVG_FUEL_CONSUMPTION (MILES, GALLONS))/2;
```

That is, the function may be called and used within an expression (or a statement). A further example is

```
Tan X = (SIN X)/(COS X)
```

where both SIN and COS are functions. In this way we can produce compact source code which is also readable and meaningful.

Can we always use functions rather than procedures? If the subprogram has to produce a number of results – and not just a single value – the answer is obviously no. Here we have to use the procedure in conjunction with **out** parameters. This point will be raised again when we meet structured variables in chapters 8 and 9.

On a final point, never use global variables to transfer information between

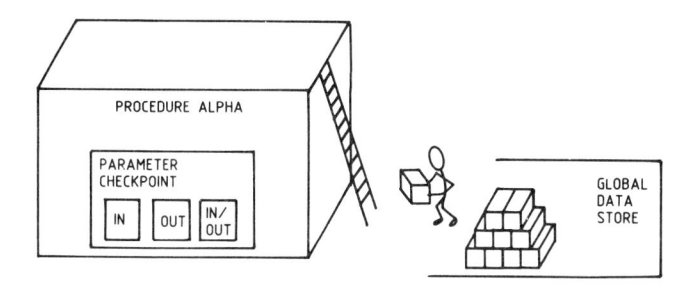

Fig.4.23 Uncontrolled access using global variables.

subprograms and their surrounding environment (Fig.4.23). It is a form of uncontrolled access which bypasses all the checks introduced by parameter passing. Almost certainly it will lead to major run-time problems in anything but the smallest of programs.

4.6 NESTING AND RECURSION

In this chapter some example subprograms have themselves invoked other subprograms. Such a construct is called 'nesting'. It is also permissible for a subprogram to invoke itself. This is defined as 'recursion'. Many mathematical operations involve recursion; in such situations recursive subprograms may provide a more elegant solution than alternative methods.

As an example, consider the problem of estimating the number of direct point-to-point signal links in a data communication network. For a system consisting of N nodes, the corresponding number of links is Ln, calculated as follows:

$$Ln = (N - 1) + (N - 2) + (N - 3) + \ldots + (1 - 1)$$

i.e. for four nodes,

$$L4 = (4 - 1) + (3 - 1) + (2 - 1) + (1 - 1) = 3 + 2 + 1 = 6$$

But this is the same as

$$L4 = (4 - 1) + L3$$

Hence the expression for the number of links involves the calculation for the number of links. This is an example of a recursive action. Generalizing:

$$Ln = (N - 1) + L(n - 1)$$

The program to run this is given in Listing 4.13.

Here the recursive function is 'LINK_POINTS'. Note that this is called

100 Subprograms in Ada – procedures and functions

```
with TEXT_IO;              use TEXT_IO;
procedure RECURSION is
  package INT_IO is new INTEGER_IO ( INTEGER );
  use INT_IO;
  NODE_POINTS      :     INTEGER;
  function LINK_POINTS (NODES    :        INTEGER)
    return INTEGER is
    DIRECT_LINKS   :     INTEGER;
  begin
    if NODES <= 0 then
      PUT_LINE ("Error in value, program aborted");
      DIRECT_LINKS := -1;
    elsif NODES = 1 then
      DIRECT_LINKS := 0;
    else
      DIRECT_LINKS := (NODES - 1) + LINK_POINTS (NODES - 1);
    end if;
    return DIRECT_LINKS;
  end LINK_POINTS;
begin
  -- this is the main procedure
  PUT ("Enter the number of communication nodes => ");
  GET (NODE_POINTS);
  SKIP_LINE;
  PUT ("The number of direct links is ");
  PUT (LINK_POINTS (NODE_POINTS), 0);
end RECURSION;
```

Listing 4.13 This illustrates the use of recursion in functions.

up in the body of the function itself, thus invoking recursive action. It is vital that recursive functions (procedures) have definite terminating conditions, otherwise it would be impossible to break out from them.

Some readers may find the idea of recursion difficult to grasp at first. If you simply consider that each time the subprogram is invoked it behaves like a new subprogram, the process is easy to follow. Naturally, on each invocation, new parameters are passed and new local variables are created.

Generally, problems solved using recursion can also be handled using iteration. Which method is used depends on individual circumstances.

4.7 A RETURN TO PARAMETERS – NAMED AND DEFAULT TYPES

4.7.1 Named parameters

So far when we've used parameters, the positions of the actual and formal parameters have had to match up. This is called 'positional notation'. Ada

```
with TEXT_IO;              use TEXT_IO;
procedure NAMED_PARAM is
  package INT_IO is new INTEGER_IO (INTEGER);
  use INT_IO;
  MILES             :       INTEGER;
  GALLONS           :       INTEGER;
  FUEL_CONSUMPTION  :       INTEGER;
  function AVERAGE_FUEL_CONSUMPTION (MILEAGE   :         INTEGER;
                                     FUEL_USED :         INTEGER )
    return INTEGER is
    AVG_CONSUMPTION :       INTEGER;
  begin
    PUT_LINE ("Calculation running");
    AVG_CONSUMPTION := MILEAGE / FUEL_USED;
    return AVG_CONSUMPTION;
  end AVERAGE_FUEL_CONSUMPTION;
  -- end of function code.
begin
  -- this is the main procedure
  PUT ("What is the mileage (integer value)? ");
  GET (MILES);
  SKIP_LINE;
  PUT ("How many gallons have been used (integer value)? ");
  GET (GALLONS);
  SKIP_LINE;
  FUEL_CONSUMPTION := AVERAGE_FUEL_CONSUMPTION (MILEAGE   => MILES,
                                                FUEL_USED => GALLONS);
  PUT ("The average fuel consumption is ");
  PUT (FUEL_CONSUMPTION, 0);
  PUT_LINE (" miles per gallon");
end NAMED_PARAM;
```

Listing 4.14 This illustrates the use of named parameters in an Ada subprogram.

gives us more flexibility here by letting us use named pairing of the parameters. This is shown in Listing 4.14, a redone version of Listing 4.10.

The important statement line is

```
FUEL_CONSUMPTION := AVERAGE_FUEL_CONSUMPTION (MILEAGE   => MILES,
                                              FUEL_USED => GALLONS);
```

Here we've made the actual/formal pairing using names.

It is good practice to use similar, clear and meaningful names for both the actual and formal parameters. In such cases named parameters are really a luxury item. In other circumstances, though, they can make the software much easier to read and understand. For instance, consider the situation shown in Fig.4.17. Assume that the data acquisition hardware of the computer system is a standard device. In this case we'd probably develop a standard procedure to read in the data values, the 'device driver' software. Also assume that we identify the data acquisition channels as 'channel 1', 'channel 2', etc.

102 Subprograms in Ada – procedures and functions

```
with TEXT_IO;                    use TEXT_IO;
procedure DEFAULT_PARAM is
  package INT_IO is new INTEGER_IO (INTEGER);
  use INT_IO;
  procedure MOVE_CURSOR (ROW        : in     INTEGER := 0;
                         COL        : in     INTEGER := 0) is
  begin
    PUT ("Row number is    => ");
    PUT (ROW, 0);
    NEW_LINE;
    PUT ("Column number is => ");
    PUT (COL, 0);
    NEW_LINE;
  end MOVE_CURSOR;
  -- end of procedure code.
begin
  -- this is the main procedure
  PUT_LINE ("The default values of the row and column are ");
  MOVE_CURSOR;
  NEW_LINE;
  PUT ("Here the row and column values are supplied ");
  PUT_LINE ("as positional parameters ");
  MOVE_CURSOR (1, 10);
  NEW_LINE;
  PUT ("Here the row and column values are supplied ");
  PUT_LINE ("as named parameters");
  MOVE_CURSOR (COL       => 10,
               ROW       =>  2);
  NEW_LINE;
  PUT ("Here the column value only is given ");
  PUT_LINE ("as a named parameter");
  MOVE_CURSOR (COL       => 730);
  NEW_LINE;
  PUT ("Here the row value only is given ");
  PUT_LINE ("as a positional parameter ");
  MOVE_CURSOR (5);
  NEW_LINE;
end DEFAULT_PARAM;
```

Listing 4.15 This illustrates the use of default parameters in an Ada subprogram.

(i.e. using general purpose names in a general purpose application). Now if we write

```
MEASURE_AIR_DATA_PARAMETERS (CHANNEL_1 => TIME,
                             CHANNEL_2 => ALTITUDE,
                             CHANNEL_3 => BEARING);
```

it is much easier to see where our information is derived from.

Positional and named parameters may be mixed. But, if we do this, positional parameters must precede named ones. So, for Listing 4.15 we could use

A return to parameters – named and default types 103

```
FUEL_CONSUMPTION := AVERAGE_FUEL_CONSUMPTION (MILES,
                                             FUEL_USED => GALLONS);
```

but NOT

```
FUEL_CONSUMPTION := AVERAGE_FUEL_CONSUMPTION (MILEAGE => MILES,
                                              GALLONS);
```

To reinforce this point: once a named parameter has been used the rest of the call must consist only of named parameters.

Named parameters also allow us to list the actual parameters in whatever order suits us. It doesn't have to match that of the formal parameter listing. For instance, the call for the example above could have been written as

```
FUEL_CONSUMPTION := AVERAGE_FUEL_CONSUMPTION (FUEL_USED => GALLONS,
                                              MILEAGE   => MILES);
```

4.7.2 Default parameters

There are many instances where the **in** parameters of a procedure usually have the same value. That is, for a specific procedure, we normally supply the same parameter values on each and every call. In this case we can, if we want to, supply this information as a 'default' value when writing the formal parameters. In Listing 4.15 for instance, the procedure in question is MOVE_CURSOR, its parameters being ROW and COL. We set their default values (in this particular case, to zero) by an assignment operation in the formal parameter listing, as

>   ROW : **in** INTEGER := 0;
>   COL : **in** INTEGER := 0

Then, when we invoke the procedure, we don't need to supply actual parameters; the default values are automatically inserted.

NOTE WELL that this applies only to **in** parameters.

Thus, on each call the same default value is used. However, we can mix default notation with positional and with named notations, as shown in Listing 4.15. Here the first call uses default values for both parameters, the second involves positional notation, and the third uses named notation. In the fourth call a named value is used for one parameter only. Finally, a single positional parameter only is supplied. In these examples note carefully where the default values are used.

When the program of Listing 4.15 is run the following screen print-out results:

The default values of the row and column are
Row number is   => 0
Column number is => 0

Here the row and column values are supplied
as positional parameters
Row number is   => 1
Column number is => 10

Here the row and column values are supplied
as named parameters
Row number is   => 2
Column number is => 10

Here the column value only is given
as a named parameter
Row number is   => 0
Column number is => 730

Here the row value only is given
as a positional parameter
Row number is   => 5
Column number is => 0

Treat default parameters with great care. Major problems can arise if formal parameters are accidentally omitted from procedure calls when default parameters are used. In such cases programs compile correctly; whether they run properly is quite another matter.

4.8 PROCEDURES AND FUNCTIONS – BODY, SPECIFICATION AND DECLARATION

As stated earlier, writing the code for a procedure or function subprogram acts as its program definition. In the examples covered so far this definition consists of two quite distinct parts: an interface and an implementation. Taken

Procedures and functions – body, specification and declaration   105

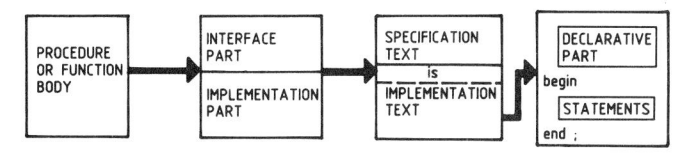

Fig.4.24 Subprogram – structure.

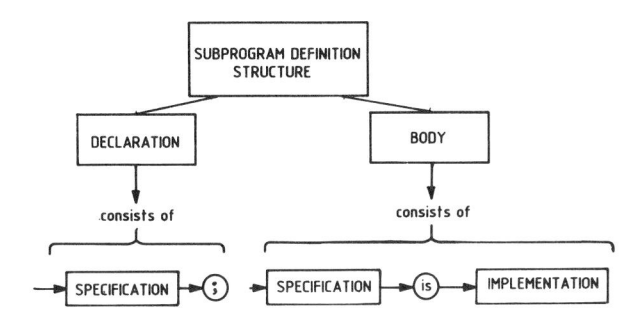

Fig.4.25 Subprogram definition.

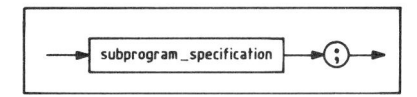

Fig.4.26 Subprogram declaration syntax diagram.

together these form the subprogram body, Fig.4.24 (you will find that *body* is often – mistakenly – used to describe the implementation part).

The purpose of the interface – the *specification* – is to define HOW the subprogram interfaces to the rest of the software. WHAT it actually does is defined in the implementation part. The dividing line between specification and implementation is the word 'is'; this acts as the opening item of the implementation.

In some situations it can be useful to list the specification (i.e. the interface) and the body as two separate items. In such a case the specification forms the major part of the subprogram declaration, Fig.4.25.

The syntax diagram for the subprogram declaration is given in Fig.4.26.

Note that the construct consists of the specification followed by a semicolon delimiter. By way of example, consider the procedure MOVE_CURSOR (Listing 4.15). Its specification (see Fig.4.27) is

procedure MOVE_CURSOR (ROW : **in** INTEGER := 0;
                        COL : **in** INTEGER := 0)

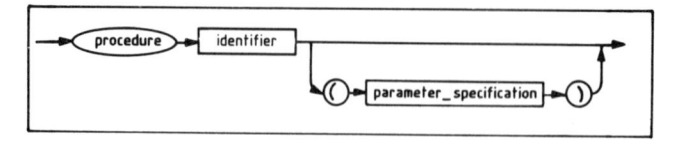

```
                  ┌──────────────────────────────────────────────────┐
                  │                ┌───────────┐                     │
                  │──▶( procedure )─▶│ identifier │────────────────────▶│
                  │                └───────────┘      ┌──────────────────────┐     │
                  │                       └─▶(─▶│ parameter_specification │─▶)┘│
                  │                                  └──────────────────────┘     │
                  └──────────────────────────────────────────────────┘
```

Fig.4.27 Syntax of the procedure specification.

whilst its declaration is

```
procedure MOVE_CURSOR (ROW : in INTEGER := 0;
                       COL : in INTEGER := 0);
```

An important factor must be considered when the specification is listed separately from the body. The specification syntax of the declaration and the body must match exactly, even if they convey the same information. For instance, the following will cause an error to be flagged up at compilation time:

THE DECLARATION

```
procedure FAIL (X : in INTEGER;
                Y : in INTEGER);
```

THE BODY

```
procedure FAIL (X, Y : in INTEGER) is
   etc.
   etc.
```

This, the separation of specification and body, is demonstrated in Listing 4.16.

We will return to this topic later to show why separation of the WHAT from the HOW is important in software design.

4.9 THE BLOCK CONTROL STRUCTURE OF ADA

This topic, the block control structure of Ada, has little to do with subprograms as such. It is, though, an item which straddles a number of important points in the language. As such it is difficult to cover it totally in one place. Moreover,

```
with TEXT_IO;              use TEXT_IO;
procedure SEPARATE_DEC is
  -- The next line declares the function
  function IS_CAPITAL (CHAR      :         CHARACTER)
    return BOOLEAN;
  -- other declarations can go here
  LETTER          :         CHARACTER;
  -- Here is the function body. It begins with the function specification
  function IS_CAPITAL (CHAR      :         CHARACTER)
    return BOOLEAN is
    CAPITAL_LETTER  :     BOOLEAN;
  begin
    if CHAR >= 'A' then
      if CHAR <= 'Z' then
        CAPITAL_LETTER := TRUE;
      else
      ' CAPITAL_LETTER := FALSE;
      end if;
    else
      CAPITAL_LETTER := FALSE;
    end if;
    return CAPITAL_LETTER;
  end IS_CAPITAL;
begin
  -- this is the main procedure
  TEXT_IO.PUT ("Enter any character => ");
  TEXT_IO.GET (LETTER);
  TEXT_IO.SKIP_LINE;
  if IS_CAPITAL (LETTER) then
    TEXT_IO.PUT_LINE ("This is a capital letter");
  else
    TEXT_IO.PUT_LINE ("This is not a capital letter");
  end if;
  TEXT_IO.NEW_LINE;
end SEPARATE_DEC;
```

Listing 4.16 This shows a function with a separate declaration. It is functionally the same as Listing 4.11.

its function only makes sense when the concepts of program structuring and object visibility and scope are understood. That's why it hasn't been introduced earlier in this text.

First, though, what IS a block? In its simplest form it is a sequence of statements delineated by the reserved words **begin** and **end**, Fig.4.28a (using this definition a main program unit can be considered to be a block).

Each single program may, if required, be subdivided into:

- A number of sequential blocks (Fig.4.28b).
- A nested block structure (Fig.4.28c).
- A combination of sequential and nested block structures.

More generally, a block consists of statements and associated declarations. This leads to the following general block structure within a program:

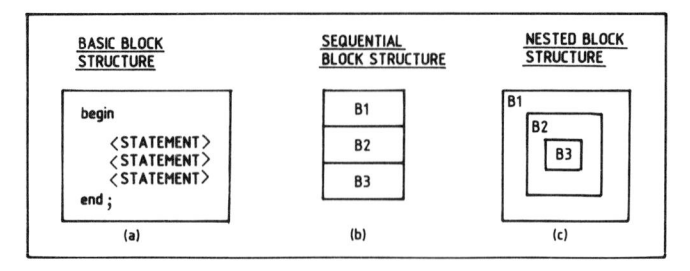

108 Subprograms in Ada – procedures and functions

BASIC BLOCK STRUCTURE	SEQUENTIAL BLOCK STRUCTURE	NESTED BLOCK STRUCTURE

begin
  <STATEMENT>
  <STATEMENT>
  <STATEMENT>
end ;
(a)
	B1
	B2
	B3
	(b)
		B1 / B2 / B3 (nested)
		(c)

Fig.4.28 Program block structures.

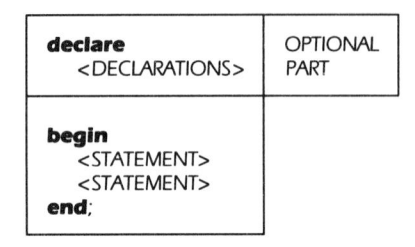

declare <DECLARATIONS>	OPTIONAL PART

begin
  <STATEMENT>
  <STATEMENT>
end;	

Objects declared at the head of the block are visible in this block and in any block nested within it. They are NOT visible elsewhere in the program. Further, they are dynamic, not static.

Note that **declare** is a reserved word.

An example of a sequential block structure is given in Listing 4.17.

When this program is executed, the following is produced on the display screen:

```
This is a block start point
Lubricants have been changed
SAE 20 Oil used
This is a block start point
Electrics have been serviced
Vaseline used
This is a block start point
The boiler fuel supply is Diesel Oil
```

We can also identify blocks using labels, as follows:

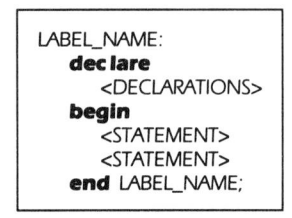

```
LABEL_NAME:
    declare
        <DECLARATIONS>
    begin
        <STATEMENT>
        <STATEMENT>
    end LABEL_NAME;
```

```
with TEXT_IO;            use TEXT_IO;
procedure BLOCK is
  CAN_29          :      constant STRING := "Diesel Oil";
  BANNER_MESSAGE  :      constant STRING := "This is a block start point";
begin
  -- main procedure
  declare
  -- this is the start of the first block
     CAN_29          :      constant STRING := "SAE 20 Oil";
  -- local item
  begin
    PUT_LINE (BANNER_MESSAGE);
    PUT_LINE ("Lubricants have been changed");
    PUT (CAN_29);
    PUT_LINE (" used");
  end;
  -- of the first block
  declare
  -- this is the start of the second block
     CAN_29          :      constant STRING := "Vaseline";
  -- local item
  begin
    PUT_LINE (BANNER_MESSAGE);
    PUT_LINE ("Electrics have been serviced");
    PUT (CAN_29);
    PUT_LINE (" used");
  end;
  -- of the second block
  -- the following statements do not need a 'begin'
  -- they are within the scope of the opening 'begin'
  PUT_LINE (BANNER_MESSAGE);
  PUT ("The boiler fuel supply is ");
  PUT_LINE (CAN_29);
end BLOCK;
```

Listing 4.17 This illustrates the use of the sequential block structure.

The label name must be repeated at the end of the block. It is recommended that blocks should always be labelled, especially where nesting is used, Listing 4.18.

This program, when executed, generates the following screen text:

> This is a block start point
> Lubricants have been changed
> SAE 20 Oil used
> This is a block start point
> Electrics have been serviced
> Vaseline used
> Have now returned to the outer block
> This is a block start point
> The boiler fuel supply is Diesel Oil

Read through this carefully and make sure you understand exactly how it works and how its scoping rules apply.

110 Subprograms in Ada – procedures and functions

```
with TEXT_IO;             use TEXT_IO;
procedure NESTED_BLOCK is
   CAN_29          :      constant STRING := "Diesel Oil";
   BANNER_MESSAGE  :      constant STRING := "This is a block start point";
begin
 -- main procedure
   OUTERMOST_BLOCK:
 -- this is the start of the outer block
   declare
     CAN_29        :      constant STRING := "SAE 20 Oil";
 -- local item
   begin
     PUT_LINE (BANNER_MESSAGE);
     PUT_LINE ("Lubricants have been changed");
     PUT (CAN_29);
     PUT_LINE (" used");
     INNER:
 -- this is the start of the inner block
     declare
 -- this is the start of the second block
       CAN_29      :      constant STRING := "Vaseline";
 -- local item
     begin
       PUT_LINE (BANNER_MESSAGE);
       PUT_LINE ("Electrics have been serviced");
       PUT (CAN_29);
       PUT_LINE (" used");
     end INNER;
 -- end of the inner block
     PUT_LINE ("Have now returned to the outer block");
   end OUTERMOST_BLOCK;
 -- end of the outer block
 -- the following statements do not need a 'begin'
 -- they are within the scope of the opening 'begin'
   PUT_LINE (BANNER_MESSAGE);
   PUT ("The boiler fuel supply is ");
   PUT_LINE (CAN_29);
end NESTED_BLOCK;
```

Listing 4.18 This illustrates the use of a nested block structure.

What does the block structure do? Fundamentally, it confines a set of program statements (and associated declarations) within a specific section of text. Why should we want to do this?

- First, to prevent other parts of the program from using particular objects (the locally declared items);
- Second, to provide a local exception handler.

This first item is concerned with program design methods, the second with error handling facilities. These will be covered in detail in later chapters.

On a final note, consider the major difference between procedures and blocks. A procedure is written once, but can be invoked as often as necessary (within the program structure, of course). The block is also written once only. However, it has a fixed position in the program, and cannot be called by any other section of the software.

4.10 OVERLOADING OF SUBPROGRAMS

4.10.1 General

Overloading is, in essence, using one name to mean different things. For instance, PUT ("hello") means 'output the text string within the brackets'. But PUT (55) means 'output the integer value 55, and use the default fieldwidth setting'. Similar operations can be found in Pascal, for instance.

Why use overloading? The intention is to simplify things for the programmer. For example, a single name PUT can be used to output characters, strings, integers and real numbers. By contrast, to do the same in Modula-2, we have to use four separate procedures – Write, WriteString, WriteInt and WriteReal. You will now realize that many of the subprograms used so far are overloaded ones. These, of course, come as part of the predefined language facilities. Where Ada is different to most other languages is that the programmer can also implement overloaded subprograms. Let us see why and how we do this.

Suppose we produce a function for carrying out alarm checks:

> **function** LOW_ALARM (A, B : INTEGER) **return** BOOLEAN;

We later find a need to carry out exactly the same operation, but on FLOAT types. So we devise another function:

> **function** LOW_ALARM_1 (C, D : FLOAT) **return** BOOLEAN;

These two do exactly the same job, although they operate on different types. Wouldn't life be easier if, for any particular operation, we use just a single name, one that always has the same meaning, even if the mechanics involved are different? In other words, overload the subprogram name. So, how do we achieve it in practice? First, rewrite the declaration for the two functions above as

> **function** LOW_ALARM (A, B : INTEGER) **return** BOOLEAN;   ... function (1)
> **function** LOW_ALARM (C, D : FLOAT) **return** BOOLEAN;   ... function (2)

112　Subprograms in Ada – procedures and functions

Implement the bodies as appropriate. Then, to use these in a program unit, we could have:

```
declare
    STEAM_PRESSURE       : INTEGER;
    LO_PRESS_LIMIT       : INTEGER;
    TURBINE_SPEED        : FLOAT;
    LO_SPEED_LIMIT       : FLOAT;
    LOW_STEAM_PRESSURE   : BOOLEAN;
    LOW_TURBINE_SPEED    : BOOLEAN
begin
    LOW_STEAM_PRESSURE   := LOW_ALARM (STEAM_PRESSURE, LO_PRESS_LIMIT);
    LOW_TURBINE_SPEED    := LOW_ALARM (TURBINE_SPEED, LO_SPEED_LIMIT);
end;
```

This does raise one important question: how does the compiler know which version of function LOW_ALARM it should use?

The technique is quite simple. Identification is achieved using the type information of the actual parameters. For the example above, the first call of the procedure LOW_ALARM clearly requires function (1). Function (2) is invoked on the second call. Listing 4.19 shows this as a complete program.

A subprogram profile consists of the parameter type profile and, for a function, a result type profile. We say that two subprograms have the same parameter type profile if:

- They have the same number of parameters;
- Corresponding parameters have the same type (i.e. parameter 1 in subprogram 1 has the same type as parameter 1 in subprogram 2, etc.).

As long as the various parameter profiles differ, then we can always tell which subprogram is being called.

4.10.2　Overloading of operators

First, a brief detour. By now you should be used to the 'conventional' use of functions. That is, we declare the function, giving it a name, relevant parameters, and a return type:

```
function AVERAGE_FUEL_CONSUMPTION (MILEAGE    : INTEGER,
                                  FUEL_USED  : INTEGER)
                                  return INTEGER;
```

We then apply it, for example, as follows:

```ada
with TEXT_IO;              use TEXT_IO;
procedure OVERLOADING is
  package INT_IO is new INTEGER_IO (INTEGER);
  use INT_IO;
  package REAL_IO is new FLOAT_IO (FLOAT);
  use REAL_IO;
  -- two overloaded functions
  function LOW_ALARM (A, B   :          INTEGER)
    return BOOLEAN;
  function LOW_ALARM (C, D   :          FLOAT)
    return BOOLEAN;
  STEAM_PRESSURE     :    INTEGER;
  LO_PRESS_LIMIT     :    INTEGER;
  TURBINE_SPEED      :    FLOAT;
  LO_SPEED_LIMIT     :    FLOAT;
  LOW_STEAM_PRESSURE :    BOOLEAN;
  LOW_TURBINE_SPEED  :    BOOLEAN;
  function LOW_ALARM (A, B   :          INTEGER)
    return BOOLEAN is
  begin
    return (A < B);
  end LOW_ALARM;
  function LOW_ALARM (C, D   :          FLOAT)
    return BOOLEAN is
  begin
    return (C < D);
  end LOW_ALARM;
begin
  PUT ("Enter the LOW steam pressure limit (integer value) => ");
  GET (LO_PRESS_LIMIT);
  SKIP_LINE;
  PUT ("Enter the steam pressure value (integer)          => ");
  GET (STEAM_PRESSURE);
  SKIP_LINE;
  PUT ("Enter the LOW turbine speed limit (real value)    => ");
  GET (LO_SPEED_LIMIT);
  SKIP_LINE;
  PUT ("Enter the turbine speed value (real)              => ");
  GET (TURBINE_SPEED);
  SKIP_LINE;
  LOW_STEAM_PRESSURE := LOW_ALARM (STEAM_PRESSURE, LO_PRESS_LIMIT);
  LOW_TURBINE_SPEED  := LOW_ALARM (TURBINE_SPEED, LO_SPEED_LIMIT);
  if LOW_STEAM_PRESSURE then
    PUT_LINE ("ALARM -  steam pressure too low");
  else
    PUT_LINE ("Steam pressure OK");
  end if;
  if LOW_TURBINE_SPEED then
    PUT_LINE ("ALARM -  turbine speed too low");
  else
    PUT_LINE ("Turbine speed OK");
  end if;
end OVERLOADING;
```

Listing 4.19 Overloading of subprograms.

```
FUEL_CONSUMPTION := AVERAGE_FUEL_CONSUMPTION (MILES, GALLONS);
```

That is, the conventional method is to write the name of the function followed (if applicable) by the actual parameters. This format is similar to *prefix* or Polish notation.

You probably won't have realized it but, in Ada, the operator '+' represents a function (as does =, >, **and**, etc.). This can be interpreted as 'the function + has two **in** parameters and a single result; it takes in the two actual values, adds them together, and assigns this to the returned value'. If this was applied using prefix notation the result would be

```
Y := + (A, B);
```

Clearly this is very unnatural, and, for long maths expressions, cumbersome and confusing. Hence we write the function using a conventional mathematical layout:

```
Y := A + B;
```

Infix notation is the name given to this format. Here the operators appear between their operands.

What has this got to do with overloading? Ada, as delivered to us, has a whole range of predefined operators. But they can't be applied indiscriminately. The +, for instance, can only be used with types INTEGER and FLOAT. Suppose, though, we wanted to add together two items which are neither INTEGER nor FLOAT (call these SPECIAL_TYPEs). How would this be tackled? A first approach is to develop a function called ADD_SPECIAL_TYPE:

```
function ADD_SPECIAL_TYPE (LEFT, RIGHT : SPECIAL_TYPE)
                   return SPECIAL_TYPE;
```

But, as overloading is permitted, we can instead use

```
function "+" (LEFT, RIGHT : SPECIAL_TYPE)
         return SPECIAL_TYPE;
```

(the rules of Ada insist that the operator symbol is enclosed in quote marks). Then, assuming that SPECIAL_Y, SPECIAL_A and SPECIAL_B are of type SPECIAL_TYPE, the following statements are all equivalent:

PREFIX_NOTATION
    SPECIAL_Y := "+" (SPECIAL_A, SPECIAL_B); -- a conventional call,
                                              -- positional association.
    SPECIAL_Y := "+" (LEFT => SPECIAL_A,
                      RIGHT => SPECIAL_B);   -- named
                                              -- association.

INFIX_NOTATION
    SPECIAL_Y := SPECIAL_A + SPECIAL_B;

The compiler identifies the required function from the type of the operands.

We will demonstrate the use of infix notation and operator overloading later, applied to matrix manipulation (chapter 8).

4.11 A LAST COMMENT

Now is the time to settle down with your system manual and have a good look at the range of subprograms provided with the compiler package. In particular, those contained in the package 'TEXT_IO' should be recognizable.

REVIEW

To finish this chapter off ensure that you:

- Understand the reason for and the use of subprograms in high-level languages;
- Understand the structure and use of procedures and functions;
- Know the reason for and use of formal and actual parameters in procedures and functions;
- Appreciate the difference between local and global objects and grasp the concept of scope and visibility;
- Recognize the structuring of subprograms in terms of interfacing and implementation aspects;
- Realize that a subprogram definition consists of a body and an (optional) declaration;
- Perceive the essential difference between a specification and a declaration;
- Know how to structure an Ada program using blocks;
- Understand the concept and application of overloading;
- Appreciate what is meant by prefix and infix notation.

Chapter Five
Types revisited

Up to the present we've worked with data objects of various types, such as INTEGER, real, and so on. In general it has been a fairly painless experience, made easier by our knowledge of conventional mathematics. What we intend to do here is to extend our understanding and use of data typing. This will show us why strong typing is such an important part of modern high-level computer languages. After having studied this chapter you should:

- Appreciate how typing allows us to take a conceptual view of our problems;
- Understand what strong typing is and how it helps the compiler to pick up mistakes in the software;
- See why good typing is an essential part of program security;
- Understand the ideas of cardinality, ordinality and enumeration;
- Realize that Ada supports both predefined and user-defined types;
- Be able to create your own data types;
- Be conversant with enumeration types, subtypes and derived types;
- Know how to carry out type mixing using type conversion.

You will also extend your work on both CHARACTER and BOOLEAN types. The attributes and uses of numeric types will be covered in the next chapter.

5.1 SETTING THE SCENE

If your objective is to produce software which is complex, obscure and bug ridden (in short, a kludge) then miss out this chapter. Data typing is a powerful tool for the development of good, understandable and reliable programs; in which case it won't interest you. On the other hand, if your objective is to produce quality software, read on.

The use of types is an abstraction process, being a fundamental instrument of high-level language working. Typing is rarely applied to assembly languages. Now, it is well known that such low-level programming frequently produces very poor software. Yet often these programs have been produced by conscientious professionals for use in critical applications. So it's interesting to start off the discussion on types by looking at the difficulties of working in assembly language.

Fig.5.1 The basic idea of abstraction.

In developing assembler software what are the main considerations for the programmer? They are, basically, how to represent the data in the computer store system (memory), where to store it and what operations to carry out on it:

- Is it possible to examine the contents of a data store and define its meaning? Yes, but only as a binary number value.
- What happens if you try to store a data word in the wrong location? The system will do exactly what you tell it to do.
- By examining operations carried out on the data can you deduce what is supposed to happen? Only if the text is heavily commented and you have a good understanding of the processor instruction set.

It is no surprise that assembly language is very time consuming. It is also a fact that it is very easy to make mistakes, the most serious being the so-called algorithmic and logical ones. That is, from the machine's point of view the code runs. Unfortunately it just doesn't do what was intended by the designer.

This situation arises because we spend most time concentrating on machine details and data handling features, and much less on the problem itself. Data typing, however, helps us to focus on what we're trying to do (i.e. to solve a particular problem) instead of getting trapped in the mire of machine detail.

5.2 DATA TYPES – BASIC CONCEPTS REVIEWED

5.2.1 Background

Show Fig.5.1 to an electrical engineering student and ask him or her what it is. He or she will probably reply 'Oh, that's a capacitor.' Well, of course, it is nothing of the sort, it is merely marks on a piece of paper. What the student really means is that it 'represents' a capacitor in his or her mind. Not

118   Types revisited

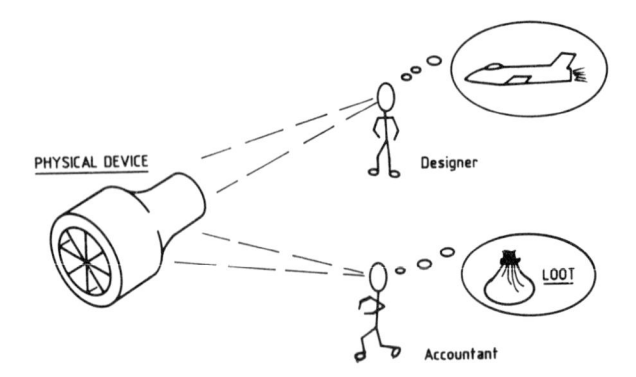

Fig.5.2 Reality and concepts.

that it has a particular shape and size, etc., but that it has the electrical circuit properties that we define as being capacitance. Now, at this stage, you may consider this to be pretty irrelevant stuff. Not so. In reality it is an extremely important point. What it does is to demonstrate our ability to separate concepts from implementations.

Dealing with abstract ideas affects the way in which we interact with the real world. How, for instance, do we view the jet engine of an aircraft? To the aircraft designer it's a power unit, the driving force of the vehicle (Fig.5.2). To the company accountant it's a profit centre (we hope), existing only on the balance books. Yet we're talking about the same physical device.

Let's put this in the context of Ada. Suppose we want to print out the value 100 000 as a real number in floating point format. We can express it either as 100 000.0 or as 1.0E + 5, two ways of viewing the same quantity. The difference exists only in our mind.

5.2.2 Concepts of data types

A data type is essentially a conceptual idea. Each type defined within a programming language has two characteristics:

(a) A set of values.
(b) A set of operations which can be carried out on these values.

Consider, for instance, type INTEGER. This has a set of values consisting of whole numbers. These typically lie in the range −32 768 to +32 767, with a step size of 1 (one). We are allowed to carry out the following operations on these values:

- addition (+)
- subtraction (−)
- multiplication (∗)
- division (/, rem, mod)
- modulus (abs)
- negation (−)
- exponentiation (∗∗)

Note that we haven't said anything about how INTEGER values are held in the machine itself. Thus at the programming level we work with the abstract concept of a type. Particular implementations only become important when we load and run a program into a target machine.

It is fundamental to high-level language design that data objects should be named and not accessed using memory addresses (this, of course, can't hold in all situations, a point covered in low-level programming). However, naming objects is one of the simplest aspects of Ada programming. There are many rules and constraints concerning types, the major points being that:

- Every data object must belong to one (unique) type;
- Associated with each type is a set of values and operations;
- Every operator used with a data type must belong to the set defined for that type;
- Where assignments are carried out, data objects must be of the same type.

This last point shows why explicit type assignments have to be made from INTEGER to FLOAT and vice versa. For instance, given the declaration

```
X1 : INTEGER;
Y1 : FLOAT;
```

then the statement

```
Y1 := X1;
```

would be rejected by the compiler as the types are incompatible. However, writing

```
Y1 := FLOAT (X1);
```

is perfectly valid as this is a 'type conversion' action.

It should be clear now why we say that Ada is a 'strongly typed' language.

120 Types revisited

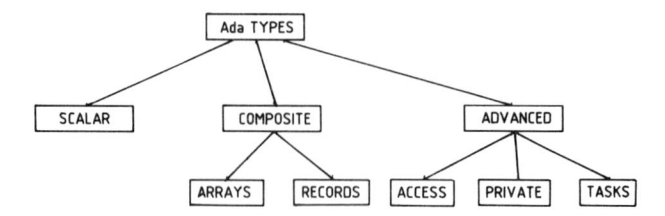

Fig.5.3 Ada types – a high-level view.

5.2.3 A few more qualities we've taken for granted

Let's consider our old friend type INTEGER again, and look more closely at its qualities.

First, as implemented in a real computer system, it has a finite range, say −32 768 to 32 767. The number of elements contained within the range is defined to be its *cardinality*. Thus here the cardinality is 65 536.

Second, there is a defined order for the elements, for example 10 precedes 11 but follows 9. The type is said to have *ordinality*.

Third, following from these first two qualities, not only can we list all elements of type INTEGER, but also we can place them in order in the list. Listing items in order is defined as *enumeration*.

Therefore, by definition, an enumeration type must have both cardinality and ordinality.

What has also been demonstrated here are the practical aspects of constraints and range. The type INTEGER is *constrained* by the practicalities of the computer hardware to lie within a specific range of values. Shortly we shall see how we ourselves can introduce range constraints on data types.

5.3 A BRIEF REVIEW OF ADA TYPES

Ada is complex. This really becomes obvious when you list all the data types provided in the language. There is only one sensible way to handle this complexity: tackle it from the top down, a piece at a time, as shown in Fig.5.3.

Scalar types are the subject of this chapter. Composite types are discussed in chapters 8 and 9, and advanced types are covered in chapters 10 (access), 11 (private) and 14 (tasks).

What is the one factor that marks out a scalar type? It is that such types are simple, not structured. That is, they are not made up of subcomponents. Fig.5.4 shows the major scalar groups of Ada, the numeric and the discrete

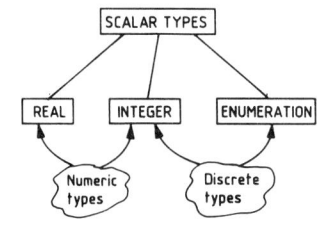

Fig.5.4 Ada scalar types.

types. Unfortunately, to confuse the issue, type INTEGER falls into both categories.

In this chapter we'll concentrate on scalar discrete types, leaving the details of real types to chapter 6.

5.4 PREDEFINED TYPES

5.4.1 Type INTEGER

We have used type INTEGER extensively in the first four chapters. By now its features and uses should be well understood. To recap:

- INTEGER is a predefined type. No declarations are needed to establish the type.
- An integer variable is an object whose value can be changed as the program runs.
- An integer constant is a program object which has a fixed value.

Typical declaration formats are:

(a)

```
MAX_AIRSPEED : INTEGER;
```

Here the program object MAX_AIRSPEED is defined to be a variable of type INTEGER. It is not given any initial value.
Comment: a program variable should always be assigned a value before being used in a program.

(b)

```
MAX_ALTITUDE : INTEGER := 30_000;
```

Here the object MAX_ALTITUDE is defined to be an integer variable. It is assigned an initial value of 30000.

Comment: the underscore character in a number is ignored by the compiler. Thus '60_000' and '60000' mean exactly the same thing in an Ada program. Use the underscore to improve readability.

(c)
```
OIL_LEVEL, FLOW_RATE : INTEGER := 0;
```

Here two objects are defined to be integer variables, each one being assigned an initial value of zero.

Comment: This means exactly the same as the declaration

OIL_LEVEL : INTEGER := 0;
FLOW_RATE : INTEGER := 0;

From a style point of view it is recommended that only one item is listed per line.

(d)
```
MAX_ALTITUDE   : INTEGER := 30_000;
MIN_ALTITUDE   : INTEGER := 500;
ALTITUDE_RANGE : INTEGER := MAX_ALTITUDE - MIN_ALTITUDE;
```

This declaration defines three integer variables. The first is initialized to 30 000, the second to 500, and the third to 29 500 (30 000 − 500). This third line is a valid construct only because MAX_ALTITUDE and MIN_ALTITUDE have already been declared.

(e)
```
MIN_AIRSPEED : constant INTEGER := 100;
```

This declaration defines object MIN_AIRSPEED to be an integer constant, its value being 100.

(f)
```
BOTTLE_WEIGHT   : constant := 2;
BOTTLES_PER_BOX : constant := 12;
TOTAL_WEIGHT    : constant := BOTTLE_WEIGHT * BOTTLES_PER_BOX;
```

The meaning of this should be self-explanatory.

Comment: The expression BOTTLE_WEIGHT * BOTTLES_PER_BOX is one form of a static expression. A static expression is one whose value can be computed by the compiler (or the programmer) from the program code. It does not depend on what happens when the program is executed.

Predefined types   123

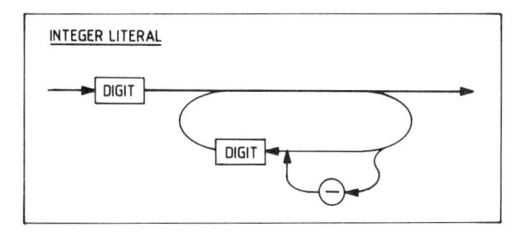

Fig.5.5 Syntax of the integer literal.

In these examples the numbers 30_000, 0, 500, etc., are defined – using Ada terminology – as 'integer literals'. We can formally define a literal to be 'a word, symbol or number that defines itself; it does not represent anything else'. Thus integer literals are whole numbers that do not have a decimal point, see the syntax diagram of Fig.5.5.

5.4.2 Attributes of type INTEGER

Attribute has a formal meaning in Ada. Its definition is confusingly presented, so it is best to think of it as defined in the *Oxford Reference Dictionary*: Attribute, noun, 'a quality ascribed to or a characteristic of ...'. Thus the attributes of type INTEGER define its characteristic. For instance, type INTEGER has the following characteristics or attributes:

- A minimum value, defined as FIRST;
- A maximum value, LAST;
- A successor to each number (except the max. one), SUCC;
- A predecessor to each number (except the min. one), PRED.

Where can we find this information? For most languages we'd have to consult their reference manuals. Ada, however, allows us to extract this data using program statements. The simplest way to refer to the attributes of a type is shown in Fig.5.6.

Two items are needed to identify the type attribute: the name of the type and the characteristic of interest. For instance, to print out the lowest bound of type INTEGER in our system we use the statement

```
PUT (INTEGER'FIRST);
```

Conversely, to print the upper bound value, the LAST attribute is used, as in

```
PUT (INTEGER'LAST);
```

124   Types revisited

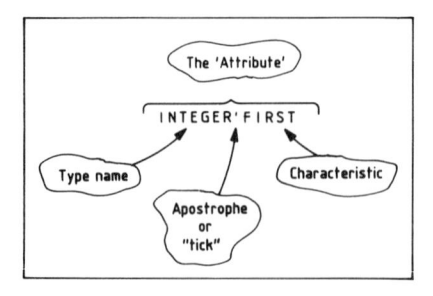

Fig.5.6 Identifying an attribute.

As a further example, consider how we'd find the successor to an integer number. As before the type has to be defined, together with the characteristic of interest. However, we now also need to specify the number whose successor is wanted. The format in this case is

INTEGER'SUCC (N)

where N is the integer number in question.

These points are illustrated in Listing 5.1.

5.4.3 Type CHARACTER

So far the character type has been used extensively to support programmer interaction with running programs via a display/keyboard unit (Fig.5.7). Very roughly then, we can say that character types are needed to support communications between the computer and the outside world. The external devices include not only visual display units (VDUs), but printers, plotters and other computer systems.

How many elements do we need within our data type CHARACTER, and what should they contain? If we include all the symbols found on a typewriter keyboard then we're a long way towards a solution. Added to this is the need to emulate typewriter functions (carriage return, line feed, etc.) and to control the actual communications activities (end-of-text message, acknowledge message, etc.). Thus we have a set of printable characters plus the control (non-printing) ones.

One major obstacle still lies ahead. How can we be sure that the recipient of our message (say) is using the same character set? Without having an agreed set of ground rules, we can't. Therefore we enforce standardization on our communications system. The most widely used coding methods are those

```
with TEXT_IO;                    use TEXT_IO;
procedure INT_ATTRIBUTES is
  package INT_IO is new INTEGER_IO (INTEGER);
  use INT_IO;
  N                   :        INTEGER;
begin
  PUT ("The lowest value for type INTEGER is ");
  PUT (INTEGER'FIRST, 0);
  NEW_LINE;
  PUT ("The highest value for type INTEGER is ");
  PUT (INTEGER'LAST, 0);
  NEW_LINE;
  -- read in an integer value and print out its successor
  PUT ("Please enter an integer value within this range ");
  GET (N);
  SKIP_LINE;
  NEW_LINE;
  PUT ("The successor of this integer is ");
  PUT (INTEGER'SUCC (N), 0);
  NEW_LINE;
end INT_ATTRIBUTES;
```

Listing 5.1 This illustrates three attributes of the type INTEGER.

Fig.5.7 Use of the character type.

of ASCII (American Standard Code for Information Interchange) and EBCDIC (Extended Binary Coded Decimal Interchange Code). ASCII actually defines 128 characters, as shown in Table 5.1. The Ada predefined type CHARACTER consists of these (and only these) characters.

Hence it should be realized that CHARACTER is an enumeration type. It has a cardinality of 128, the order defined in Table 5.1. Type CHARACTER constants, if they were defined explicitly, would be written as

> **type** CHARACTER **is** (nul, soh, ..., ... 'a', 'b', 'c', ..., del);

No arithmetic operations are defined on CHARACTER but we can work with the ordinal numbers of the type. Note that each printable character (also

Table 5.1 ASCII character set

Decimal no.	Hex. no.	Character no.	Decimal no.	Hex. no.	Character no.	Decimal no.	Hex. no.	Character no.	Decimal no.	Hex. no.	Character no.
0	00	nul	32	20	sp	64	40	@	96	60	`
1	01	soh	33	21	!	65	41	A	97	61	a
2	02	stx	34	22	"	66	42	B	98	62	b
3	03	etx	35	23	£	67	43	C	99	63	c
4	04	eot	36	24	$	68	44	D	100	64	d
5	05	enq	37	25	%	69	45	E	101	65	e
6	06	ack	38	26	&	70	46	F	102	66	f
7	07	bel	39	27	'	71	47	G	103	67	g
8	08	bs	40	28	(	72	48	H	104	68	h
9	09	tab	41	29	)	73	49	I	105	69	i
10	0A	lf	42	2A	*	74	4A	J	106	6A	j
11	0B	vt	43	2B	+	75	4B	K	107	6B	k
12	0C	ff	44	2C	,	76	4C	L	108	6C	l
13	0D	cr	45	2D	-	77	4D	M	109	6D	m
14	0E	so	46	2E	.	78	4E	N	110	6E	n
15	0F	si	47	2F	/	79	4F	O	111	6F	o
16	10	dle	48	30	0	80	50	P	112	70	p
17	11	dc1	49	31	1	81	51	Q	113	71	q
18	12	dc2	50	32	2	82	52	R	114	72	r
19	13	dc3	51	33	3	83	53	S	115	73	s
20	14	dc4	52	34	4	84	54	T	116	74	t
21	15	nak	53	35	5	85	55	U	117	75	u
22	16	syn	54	36	6	86	56	V	118	76	v
23	17	etb	55	37	7	87	57	W	119	77	w
24	18	can	56	38	8	88	58	X	120	78	x
25	19	em	57	39	9	89	59	Y	121	79	y
26	1A	sub	58	3A	:	90	5A	Z	122	7A	z
27	1B	esc	59	3B	;	91	5B	[	123	7B	{
28	1C	fs	60	3C	<	92	5C	\	124	7C	|
29	1D	gs	61	3D	=	93	5D	]	125	7D	}
30	1E	rs	62	3E	>	94	5E	^	126	7E	~
31	1F	us	63	3F	?	95	5F	_	127	7F	del

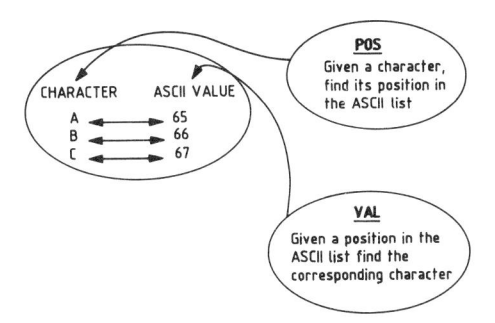

Fig.5.8 POS and VAL attributes.

called a 'graphic' character) is defined to be a character literal when it is enclosed in single quote marks. So, for example:

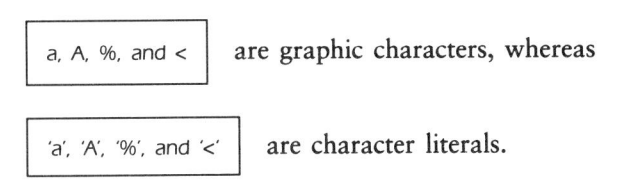

> a, A, %, and <

are graphic characters, whereas

> 'a', 'A', '%', and '<'

are character literals.

Two Ada attributes which may be used with characters are POS and VAL (Fig.5.8). POS enables us to obtain the position number, that is the ordinal value, of a character. For instance

> CHARACTER'POS ('B') gives the result 66, i.e. the position of B
> CHARACTER'POS ('C') gives 67
> CHARACTER'POS ('0') gives 48
> CHARACTER'POS ('1') gives 49

Thus, for example,

> C_POS := CHARACTER'POS ('C');

results in the variable C_POS being assigned the value 67. A further example is

> BC_DIFF := CHARACTER'POS ('C') - CHARACTER'POS ('B');

After the statement is executed the variable BC_DIFF holds the value 1, the result of subtracting 66 from 67.

128   Types revisited

```
with TEXT_IO;                    use TEXT_IO;
procedure USE_OF_POS is
  package INT_IO is new INTEGER_IO(INTEGER);
  use INT_IO;
  CHAR_LITERAL     :   CHARACTER;
  POSITION         :   INTEGER;
begin
  PUT_LINE ("Enter X to finish");
  loop
    PUT ("Enter any character => ");
    GET (CHAR_LITERAL);
    SKIP_LINE;
    PUT ("The ASCII position of ");
    PUT (CHAR_LITERAL);
    PUT (" is ");
    POSITION := CHARACTER'POS (CHAR_LITERAL);
    PUT (POSITION, 0);
    NEW_LINE;
    exit when POSITION = CHARACTER'POS ('X');
  end loop;
end USE_OF_POS;
```

Listing 5.2 This demonstrates the use of the POS attribute.

VAL, the other attribute, allows us to obtain a character from its ordinal number, as follows:

```
CHARACTER'VAL (66)
```

gives the result 'B'. Hence

```
ALPHA := CHARACTER'VAL (66);
```

results in the letter B being assigned to the variable ALPHA (assumed to be a CHARACTER type).

EXAMPLE: The program of Listing 5.2 takes in a character from the keyboard, extracts its position number, and outputs the result to the screen.

EXAMPLE: Listing 5.3 gives a program which takes in a numeric character from the keyboard, computes its actual numeric value, and outputs the result to the screen.

EXAMPLE: The example given in Listing 5.4 takes in characters from the keyboard until the CR key is pressed. It then computes the value of the input number and outputs the result to the screen. During the data entry process

```
with TEXT_IO;                use TEXT_IO;
procedure FURTHER_USE_OF_POS is
  package INT_IO is new INTEGER_IO (INTEGER);
  use INT_IO;
  CHAR_LITERAL    :      CHARACTER;
  VALUE           :      INTEGER;
begin
  PUT_LINE ("Enter X to finish");
  loop
    PUT ("Enter a number 0..9 => ");
    GET (CHAR_LITERAL);
    SKIP_LINE;
    exit when CHAR_LITERAL = 'X';
    VALUE := CHARACTER'POS (CHAR_LITERAL) - CHARACTER'POS ('0');
    PUT ("The INTEGER value is ");
    PUT (VALUE, 0);
    NEW_LINE;
  end loop;
end FURTHER_USE_OF_POS;
```

Listing 5.3 Further use of the POS attribute.

```
with TEXT_IO;              use TEXT_IO;
procedure CHAR_CONVERSION is
  package INT_IO is new INTEGER_IO (INTEGER);
  use INT_IO;
  DIGIT           :      CHARACTER;
  NUM             :      INTEGER;
  TOTAL           :      INTEGER;
begin
  TOTAL := 0;
  PUT ("Enter a 3 digit number => ");
  for COUNT in 1..3 loop
    GET (DIGIT);
    if (DIGIT >= '0') and (DIGIT <= '9') then
      NUM := CHARACTER'POS (DIGIT) - CHARACTER'POS ('0');
      TOTAL := (TOTAL * 10) + NUM;
    end if;
  end loop;
  SKIP_LINE;
  PUT ("The number was => ");
  PUT (TOTAL, 0);
  NEW_LINE;
end CHAR_CONVERSION;
```

Listing 5.4 Extending Listing 5.3 to convert a series of characters.

```
with TEXT_IO;                    use TEXT_IO;
procedure CHARACTER_VAL is
begin
  for CAPS in 65..90 loop
  -- ASCII 'A' through 'Z'
    PUT (CHARACTER'VAL (CAPS));
    PUT (',');
  end loop;
  NEW_LINE;
  for LOWER in 97..122 loop
  -- ASCII 'a' through 'z'
    PUT (CHARACTER'VAL (LOWER));
    PUT (',');
  end loop;
  NEW_LINE;
end CHARACTER_VAL;
```

Listing 5.5 The use of VAL to output ASCII characters.

it rejects non-numeric characters. For simplicity it works within the INTEGER number range.

EXAMPLE: Listing 5.5 uses the CHARACTER attribute VAL to print out:

- first, the upper case letters of the alphabet, followed by
- the lower case letters.

Why should we ever need to use the POS and VAL attributes for handling characters? We've managed without them up to now, but only because the necessary conversion work has been done by the standard functions such as GET, PUT, etc. Moreover, our programs have been very simple with the keyboard types (e.g. INTEGER or FLOAT, etc.) being clearly defined. Further, these only work correctly if the coding scheme is ASCII. Now this is fine – as long as we work in this very limited way. For more general programming, however, we do need the features provided by POS and VAL.

The attributes SUCC and PRED can also be applied to character types, as in Listing 5.6.

Read through this carefully, decide what should happen, and then test your understanding by running the program.

One last point needs mentioning, a matter of definition only. In many of our examples so far we have used strings of printable characters. Formally, a string literal is defined to be a sequence of graphic characters enclosed in double quote marks. Note again that a string literal must fit on one line in the source program.

```
with TEXT_IO;                    use TEXT_IO;
procedure SUCC_AND_PRED is
  CHAR_LITERAL      :     CHARACTER;
  PRED_OF_CHAR      :     CHARACTER;
  SUCC_OF_CHAR      :     CHARACTER;
begin
  PUT_LINE ("Enter X to finish");
  loop
    PUT ("Enter any character => ");
    GET (CHAR_LITERAL);
    SKIP_LINE;
    PRED_OF_CHAR := CHARACTER'PRED (CHAR_LITERAL);
    SUCC_OF_CHAR := CHARACTER'SUCC (CHAR_LITERAL);
    PUT ("The character before ");
    PUT (CHAR_LITERAL);
    PUT (" is ");
    PUT (PRED_OF_CHAR);
    PUT (" and the character after is ");
    PUT (SUCC_OF_CHAR);
    NEW_LINE;
    exit when CHAR_LITERAL = 'X';
  end loop;
end SUCC_AND_PRED;
```

Listing 5.6 Simple example of the use of SUCC and PRED.

5.4.4 Boolean operations

The basis and use of a Boolean type has already been covered in chapter 2. Now let's re-evaluate this in more formal terms:

(a) It is an enumeration type;
(b) It consists of two elements, FALSE and TRUE;
(c) The order is FALSE, TRUE. Thus FALSE = 0, TRUE = 1;
(d) The basic set of operations which can be carried out on it are:

      Logical **not** (Unary logical negation) – highest precedence;
      Logical **and** (Conjunction);
      Logical **or**   (Disjunction);
      Logical **xor** (Exclusive disjunction).

If you are familiar with Boolean logic, be careful; the operators **and, or, xor** have equal precedence in Ada. Moreover, they have the lowest precedence of all the Ada operators. The truth tables for these are given in Table 5.2, while Table 5.3 defines the Boolean relational operators.

The order of precedence of the Boolean and associated conditional operators must be taken into account when writing logical expressions. For instance:

132   Types revisited

Table 5.2 Truth tables for Boolean operations

C = not A	
A	C
T	F
F	T

T = TRUE
F = FALSE

C = A and B		
A	B	C
T	T	T
T	F	F
F	T	F
F	F	F

C = A or B		
A	B	C
T	T	T
T	F	T
F	T	T
F	F	F

C = A xor B		
A	B	C
T	T	F
T	F	T
F	T	T
F	F	F

Table 5.3 The Boolean relational operators

SYMBOL	OPERATION	OPERAND TYPE	RESULT TYPE
=	equal to	Any	Boolean
/=	not equal to	Any	Boolean
<	less than	Any scalar or discrete array type	Boolean
<=	less than or equal to	as above	Boolean
>	greater than	as above	Boolean
>=	greater than or equal to	as above	Boolean

> X > W **and** C < D   is interpreted logically as   (X > W) **and** C < D

But what can we make of the following?

> A **and** B **or** C **and** D

In fact it is impossible to evaluate it – all operators have equal precedence. Because of this such a construct is not allowed. The compiler should flag it up as an error. Just the same, to be safe, we strongly recommend that parentheses (brackets) should always be used to enforce correct logic operations. For the case above the use of brackets would give

> (A **and** B) **or** (C **and** D)   or   A **and** (B **or** C) **and** D

Predefined types   133

```
with TEXT_IO;                       use TEXT_IO;
procedure FIRST_BOOLEAN is
  X                :         BOOLEAN;
begin
  X := TRUE;
  if X then
    PUT_LINE ("X is TRUE");
  end if;
end FIRST_BOOLEAN;
```

Listing 5.7 Simple BOOLEAN example.

```
with TEXT_IO;              use TEXT_IO;
procedure FURTHER_BOOLEAN is
  package INT_IO is new INTEGER_IO (INTEGER);
  use INT_IO;
  X                :         BOOLEAN;
  I1               :         INTEGER;
  I2               :         INTEGER;
begin
  PUT ("Enter first Integer => ");
  GET (I1);
  SKIP_LINE;
  PUT ("Enter next Integer => ");
  GET (I2);
  SKIP_LINE;
  X := I2 > I1;
  if X then
    PUT_LINE ("X is TRUE. The second number is greater than the first");
  end if;
  if not X then
    PUT_LINE ("X is FALSE. The second number is not greater than the first");
  end if;
end FURTHER_BOOLEAN;
```

Listing 5.8 Example showing an INTEGER test producing a BOOLEAN result.

depending on the desired operation.

Now let's clarify a few more points using the example given below (Listing 5.7). When this program is run it first assigns the condition (or value) TRUE to the variable X. The statement 'if X' really means 'if X is true'. Hence, as X has been set to be true, the text string 'X is TRUE' is printed out on the screen.

Expanding on this, Listing 5.8 illustrates a few more aspects of Boolean operations.

In the seventh line after 'begin' we evaluate the statement (relationship) 'I2 is greater than I1'. The result of this evaluation (TRUE or FALSE) is assigned to the Boolean variable X. If X is TRUE (i.e. I2 is greater than I1), the first

134   Types revisited

```
with TEXT_IO;              use TEXT_IO;
procedure NEXT_BOOLEAN is
  package INT_IO is new INTEGER_IO (INTEGER);
  use INT_IO;
  RUNNING                :    BOOLEAN;
  LOW_OIL_PRESSURE       :    BOOLEAN;
  ALARM                  :    BOOLEAN;
  OIL_PRESSURE           :    INTEGER;
  STATUS                 :    CHARACTER;
  FINISHED               :    CHARACTER;
  LOW_PRESSURE_POINT :        constant      := 20;
begin
  loop
    PUT ("Low oil pressure alarm point is ");
    PUT (LOW_PRESSURE_POINT, 3);
    PUT_LINE (" psi");
    PUT ("Enter actual oil pressure - psi => ");
    GET (OIL_PRESSURE);
    SKIP_LINE;
    PUT ("What is the engine status - ");
    PUT ("R = Running  S = Stopped (R/S) ? ");
    GET (STATUS);
    SKIP_LINE;
    NEW_LINE;
    RUNNING := (STATUS = 'R') or (STATUS = 'r');
    LOW_OIL_PRESSURE := (OIL_PRESSURE < LOW_PRESSURE_POINT);
    ALARM := LOW_OIL_PRESSURE and RUNNING;
    if ALARM then
      PUT_LINE ("Engine fault !");
    else
      PUT_LINE ("System OK");
    end if;
    PUT ("Test finished   (Y/N) ? ");
    GET (FINISHED);
    SKIP_LINE;
    exit when (FINISHED = 'Y') or (FINISHED = 'y');
  end loop;
end NEXT_BOOLEAN;
```

Listing 5.9 Further example showing Boolean tests.

text string is printed out. Should X turn out to be FALSE, then '**not** X' is TRUE. Hence the second text string is printed out on the screen.

As a final example read and run Listing 5.9. In this example more statements have been used than are necessary, to make it easier to follow the program. Therefore as an exercise compress

```
RUNNING            := (STATUS = 'R') or (STATUS = 'r');
LOW_OIL_PRESSURE   := (OIL_PRESSURE < LOW_PRESSURE_POINT);
ALARM              := LOW_PRESSURE and RUNNING;
```

into a single-line statement.

Now for an important point relating to the evaluation of operands in an Ada expression. Consider, for example, the following logical statement:

Table 5.4 Truth tables for short-circuit Boolean operations

C = A and then B		
A	B	C
T	T	T
T	F	F
F	X	F
F	X	F

C = A or else B		
A	B	C
T	X	T
T	X	T
F	T	T
F	F	F

NOTE
X denotes a 'don't care' condition

```
Y := (A > B) and (C > D);
```

Do we first evaluate (A > B), then (C > D), and then define the Boolean value of Y? The answer is – we don't know. In Ada the order of evaluation is not defined. Now, for the example above it doesn't matter. But consider the following – classic – example:

```
if (COUNT /= 0) and (X / COUNT > Y)
then
    .
    statements
    .
and if;
```

This presents no difficulty provided the first (leftmost) operand is evaluated first. But should the second operand be evaluated first, and COUNT is zero, there is a problem: we would attempt to divide by zero (which has no mathematical answer). How can we overcome this? Simply by forcing evaluation to take place in a defined order – and then terminating the evaluation once the result is known. To do this we use the so-called short-circuit operators, **and then** and **or else**. With these constructs (Table 5.4) the left-hand operand is evaluated first. If the result defines the logical outcome of the expression, the right-hand one is not evaluated. Consider the **and then** operation. If the first operand is FALSE then the expression must be FALSE. Likewise, with the **or else** operator, if the first operand is TRUE the expression must be TRUE.

Using the short-circuit operation to guard against the type of problem given above is not so important nowadays. Most modern computers have built-in hardware checks to trap divide-by-zero operations. Further, most modern compilers provide both compile-time and run-time checks on the validity of numerical operations. There are, though, situations where short-circuiting operations can be useful – to be described later.

We can also use Boolean operations to test whether a value lies within a particular range. Alternatively we can check that a value does not lie within a specific range. These are called the set membership tests, defined as **in** and **not in**. An example of a membership test is the part expression

> "HOURS **in** 0..24"

This can be read as "if the object HOURS has a value in the range 0 to 24 then return a BOOLEAN result TRUE. Otherwise return FALSE". Writing

> "PM_HOURS **not in** 0..12"

means "if the object PM_HOURS has a value which is not in the range 0 to 12 then return a BOOLEAN result TRUE. Otherwise return FALSE". A more general use of membership tests is shown in Listing 5.10.

5.5 INVENTING YOUR OWN DATA TYPES

5.5.1 Why new data types?

Let's open with a very reasonable question. Why should we bother to devise new data types in the first place? After all, this feature isn't available in older languages. True, but the issue of concern here is one of program design and maintenance. Remember that the whole object of typing is to help us to produce reliable programs. By using type information the compiler can pick up many errors which otherwise would go through to the run-time code (as we're sure you've discovered by now). However, the number of types supplied in Ada – the 'predefined' ones – are relatively small. As a result any individual type (e.g. INTEGER) will probably represent a wide range of variables. Many of these will be logically quite different (from the programmer's point of view). Thus the compiler isn't able to find logical errors where types are compatible. Consider the following simple example, Listing 5.11, for computing the average of four measurements.

Here the programmer has used an integer variable 'NEXT' to control the counting loop for the inputs. The rules of the for–loop construct declare it to be of type INTEGER ('NEXT in 1..4'). Now this is a perfectly valid and reasonable (if tiny) program. Why should we have problems here? Well, suppose that the programmer had accidently written

```
with TEXT_IO;              use TEXT_IO;
procedure USE_OF_IN is
  package INT_IO is new INTEGER_IO (INTEGER);
  use INT_IO;
  DIGIT            :      CHARACTER;
  NUM              :      INTEGER;
  TOTAL            :      INTEGER;
begin
  TOTAL := 0;
  PUT ("Enter 3 digit number => ");
  for COUNT in 1..3 loop
    GET (DIGIT);
    if (DIGIT in '0'..'9') then
      NUM := CHARACTER'POS (DIGIT) - CHARACTER'POS ('0');
      TOTAL := (TOTAL * 10) + NUM;
    end if;
  end loop;
  SKIP_LINE;
  PUT ("The number was => ");
  PUT (TOTAL);
  NEW_LINE;
end USE_OF_IN;
```

Listing 5.10 Use of 'in' for Boolean expressions. Extension of Listing 5.4.

```
with TEXT_IO;              use TEXT_IO;
procedure POSSIBLE_ERROR is
  package INT_IO is new INTEGER_IO (INTEGER);
  use INT_IO;
  NEXT_VALUE       :      INTEGER;
  TOTAL_VALUE      :      INTEGER;
  AVERAGE_VALUE    :      INTEGER;
begin
  TOTAL_VALUE := 0;
  for NEXT in 1..4 loop
    PUT ("Enter number => ");
    GET (NEXT_VALUE);
    SKIP_LINE;
    TOTAL_VALUE := TOTAL_VALUE + NEXT_VALUE;
  end loop;
  AVERAGE_VALUE := TOTAL_VALUE / 4;
  PUT ("The average value is ");
  PUT (AVERAGE_VALUE);
  NEW_LINE;
end POSSIBLE_ERROR;
```

Listing 5.11 Averaging of four numbers with possible error condition.

138   Types revisited

> TOTAL_VALUE := TOTAL_VALUE + NEXT;

instead of

> TOTAL_VALUE := TOTAL_VALUE + NEXT_VALUE;

The compiler would accept it as a valid statement, yet logically it is completely wrong. Unfortunately the program will appear to run correctly, but the results will be nonsensical. What can be done to help the compiler stop us implementing such code? There is no way that it can spot the flaws in program logic. After all, each program is unique. What is needed is another mechanism which, while not being foolproof, significantly improves the situation. It's rather like putting up 'stop' signs at dangerous junctions. They don't prevent motorists driving dangerously, yet they certainly reduce the accident rate. By analogy, our contribution to software safety is first to invent new data types, and then use this information to distinguish between logically different items. In effect, we force the compiler to check for name equivalence. Until now it's been looking for structural compatibility.

We can devise new data types in Ada in three ways: enumeration, subtypes and derived types. These are discussed in the following sections.

5.5.2 Defining new types – enumeration types

Let's modify the averaging program of Listing 5.11 by introducing a new type which is enumerated. That is, we have to list the elements or values of the type, the ordinality of the values being given by the listing order. The ideas behind defining and using your own enumeration types are given in Fig.5.9. These concepts will become clearer as we go along.

Let us demonstrate the basic ideas using a new type, 'COUNTER'. It consists of four elements, ONE, TWO, THREE and FOUR. These are called the *enumeration literals*. Thus its cardinality is four, the ordinality being defined (by us, the programmer) as

> ONE = 0   TWO = 1   THREE = 2   FOUR = 3

The declaration form is

> **type** COUNTER **is** (ONE, TWO, THREE, FOUR);

Inventing your own data types 139

STANDARD TYPE CHARACTER		USER-DEFINED TYPE	
TYPE DECLARATION	None needed	TYPE DECLARATION	type DIGITAL_1_STATUS is (OFF, ON, TRIPPED) ;
SET OF VALUES (PRE-DEFINED)	• • 'A' 'B' 'C' • • 'W' 'X' •	SET OF VALUES (USER DEFINED)	OFF ON TRIPPED
VARIABLE DECLARATION FORMAT	ALPHA : CHARACTER	VARIABLE DECLARATION FORMAT	CPP_PUMP_MOTOR : DIGITAL_1_STATUS;
TYPICAL USAGE	ALPHA : = 'W';	TYPICAL USAGE	CPP_PUMP_MOTOR : = ON ;

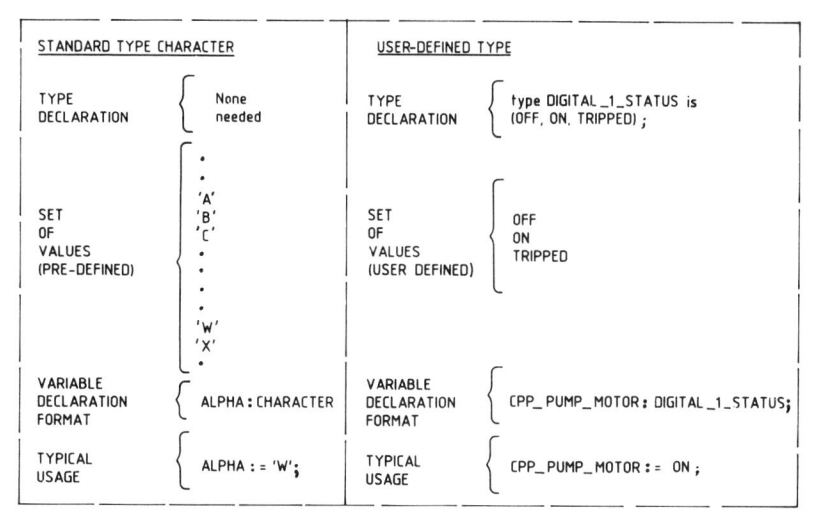

Fig.5.9 Comparison of standard and user-defined enumeration types.

Now let's use this in the averaging program (Listing 5.12). Here NEXT has been declared as being of type 'COUNTER'; hence it cannot be mixed with INTEGER values in an expression. Just to prove this alter the code to read

> TOTAL_VALUE := TOTAL_VALUE + NEXT;

and verify that the compiler generates a type incompatibility message.

The syntax diagram for the enumeration type declaration is shown in Fig.5.10. Note that only assignment and relational operations apply to such types.

In general then, how do we benefit from using programmer-defined types? Examine the program of Listing 5.13. First, for the two user-defined types DIGITAL_1_STATUS, DIGITAL_2_STATUS we've clearly and unambiguously spelt out all possible conditions. The reader doesn't have to interpret the meaning of the source code. Second, we've used names which are logically associated with the type attributes. This makes the program easier to read, understand and maintain. Third, we've built in extra safety factors. Suppose that, by accident, we write

> BEARING_TEMP := OFF;

```
with TEXT_IO;              use TEXT_IO;
procedure USER_ENUM_TYPE is
  package INT_IO is new INTEGER_IO (INTEGER);
  use INT_IO;
  type COUNTER is (ONE, TWO, THREE, FOUR);
  NEXT_VALUE      :      INTEGER;
  TOTAL_VALUE     :      INTEGER;
  AVERAGE_VALUE   :      INTEGER;
begin
  TOTAL_VALUE := 0;
  for NEXT in ONE..FOUR loop
    PUT ("Enter number => ");
    GET (NEXT_VALUE);
    SKIP_LINE;
    TOTAL_VALUE := TOTAL_VALUE + NEXT_VALUE;
  end loop;
  AVERAGE_VALUE := TOTAL_VALUE / 4;
  PUT ("The average value is ");
  PUT (AVERAGE_VALUE);
  NEW_LINE;
end USER_ENUM_TYPE;
```

Listing 5.12 Introduction to user-defined enumeration types.

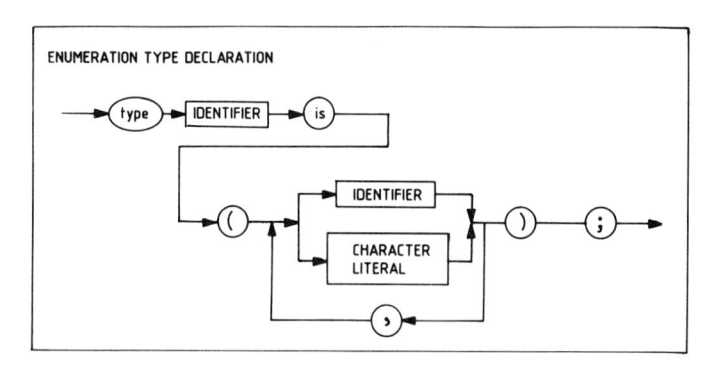

Fig.5.10 Syntax diagram – enumeration type declaration.

```
procedure TWO_ENUM_TYPES is
  type DIGITAL_1_STATUS is (OFF, ON, TRIPPED);
  type DIGITAL_2_STATUS is (LOW, HIGH);
  OIL_PURIFIER_MOTOR :     DIGITAL_1_STATUS;
  CPP_PUMP_MOTOR     :     DIGITAL_1_STATUS;
  BEARING_TEMP       :     DIGITAL_2_STATUS;
begin
  CPP_PUMP_MOTOR      := ON;
  OIL_PURIFIER_MOTOR  := TRIPPED;
  BEARING_TEMP        := HIGH;
end TWO_ENUM_TYPES;
```

Listing 5.13 Extending enumeration types.

When the program is compiled a 'type incompatibility' error message will be flagged up.

For the small number of variables shown in this example such a mistake is unlikely. Visualize, though, the job of developing software for the machinery control systems on a modern warship. The number of items to be monitored and controlled runs into thousands. Do you still think that mistakes like this are unimaginable?

5.5.3 Overloading of enumeration types

We use enumeration types for a number of reasons. In particular, we want to produce programs that are easy to read, clear and meaningful. Therefore it is common sense to use clear and meaningful names for the elements of the type. This, though, can bring problems with it. Consider the situation where we invent a type 'WASHING_MACHINE', having elements 'OFF', 'PREWASH', 'WASH' and 'RINSE'. We then devise another enumeration type 'DISHWASHER'. Following the recommendations for clarity, etc., we name the elements 'OFF', 'RINSE' and 'WASH'. This leads to the following part declarations:

```
type WASHING_MACHINE is (OFF, PREWASH, WASH, RINSE);
type DISHWASHER      is (OFF, RINSE, WASH);

HOOVER_MODEL_100 : WASHING_MACHINE;
AEG_MODEL_420    : DISHWASHER;
```

Here we have a case of overloading. In this case it means that two data types share the same values, as with OFF, RINSE and WASH above. Now, the enumeration literal WASH of type WASHING_MACHINE is not the same as the WASH of type DISHWASHER. We, as the programmer, know what we mean. But will the compiler be able to do the same? Look at the program of Listing 5.14, in particular the statements

```
HOOVER_MODEL_100 := OFF;
HOOVER_MODEL_100 := WASH;
AEG_MODEL_420    := WASH;
```

Compile this program. Even though there are two values called WASH, the program will compile correctly. Possible confusions are removed by the type information supplied in the declarations. The compiler can work out which WASH belongs to which variable.

142   Types revisited

```
procedure ENUM_OVERLOAD is
  type WASHING_MACHINE is (OFF, PREWASH, WASH, RINSE);
  type DISHWASHER is (OFF, RINSE, WASH);
  HOOVER_MODEL_100 :    WASHING_MACHINE;
  AEG_MODEL_420    :    DISHWASHER;
begin
  HOOVER_MODEL_100 := OFF;
  HOOVER_MODEL_100 := WASH;
  AEG_MODEL_420    := WASH;
end ENUM_OVERLOAD;
```

Listing 5.14 This illustrates the compiler's ability to resolve overloading of enumeration literals.

```
procedure ENUM_ERROR is
  type WASHING_MACHINE is (OFF, PREWASH, WASH, RINSE);
  type DISHWASHER is (OFF, RINSE, WASH);
begin
  for WASH_CYCLE_STEP in OFF..WASH loop
    null;
  end loop;
end ENUM_ERROR;
```

Listing 5.15 This illustrates where the compiler cannot resolve the overloading of enumeration literals.

Unfortunately, situations do arise which are ambivalent. Review the program of Listing 5.15.

Here the for-loop control variable WASH_CYCLE_STEP is declared in the usual way, its type defined by the loop range values. The range limits are OFF and WASH. So, the variable is of type WASHING_MACHINE. Or is it type DISHWASHER? It could be either, and there's no way of working it out.

Clearly then, extra information must be supplied to state precisely what we mean. The name given to this action is overload resolution. In Ada we do this by specifying the data type to which the enumeration literal belongs, as follows:

| WASHING_MACHINE' (WASH); | or | DISHWASHER' (WASH); |

More formally, we qualify the enumeration literal by the name of the enumeration type, that is:

| TYPE_NAME' (ENUMERATION_LITERAL); |

As an exercise, modify Listing 5.15 in line with these rules and verify that it now compiles correctly.

5.5.4 Subtypes

What we are going to look at here are almost, but not quite, new types – the *subtypes*. As with enumeration types they are defined by the programmer. So in one way this makes them 'new'. However, unlike enumeration types, they don't bring a new type into existence. Subtypes are not new types. They are based on existing types – the *base* type. Note that the base type may be a predefined type such as CHARACTER or INTEGER. But equally well it could also be a user-defined enumeration type.

You could reasonably ask: 'Why bother with subtypes? Just use the base type instead.' A good question. The answer is that there are some situations where we want to limit ('constrain') the range of values that a variable can take. Usually this is done for reasons of safety. For example, suppose we wish to record information relating to days of the month. To do this we could declare a variable:

```
DATE_IN_MONTH : INTEGER;
```

If we made the assignment statement

```
DATE_IN_MONTH := 32;
```

it would be valid, but wrong. In many languages the only way to prevent this is to check positively for out-of-range conditions. Thus the responsibility for eliminating invalid or dangerous conditions rests with the programmer. As a result, one single program mistake made on an off-day could produce a catastrophe.

In Ada the problem could be handled by defining a new type having the required cardinality and ordinality. This, however, may not be necessary or even desirable. Moreover, in many cases our program variables, although of a standard type, don't use the full range of values available to us.

This leads us to the idea of a 'subset' of a data type, the subtype. This is defined to be a contiguous subset of a given data type, and is described conceptually in Fig.5.11.

We can extend this as shown in Fig.5.12, with subtypes having subtypes.

Further, by redrawing Fig.5.12 as in Fig.5.13, it can be seen that subtypes fit in naturally with hierarchical relationships.

144   Types revisited

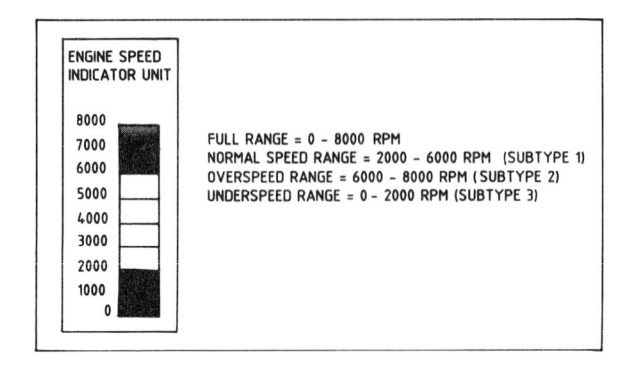

```
┌─────────────────────────────────────────────────────────┐
│  ┌─────────────────┐                                    │
│  │ ENGINE SPEED    │                                    │
│  │ INDICATOR UNIT  │                                    │
│  │                 │                                    │
│  │ 8000            │                                    │
│  │ 7000  ▓▓        │  FULL RANGE = 0 - 8000 RPM         │
│  │ 6000            │  NORMAL SPEED RANGE = 2000 - 6000 RPM  (SUBTYPE 1) │
│  │ 5000            │  OVERSPEED RANGE = 6000 - 8000 RPM (SUBTYPE 2)     │
│  │ 4000            │  UNDERSPEED RANGE = 0 - 2000 RPM (SUBTYPE 3)       │
│  │ 3000            │                                    │
│  │ 2000            │                                    │
│  │ 1000            │                                    │
│  │ 0               │                                    │
│  └─────────────────┘                                    │
└─────────────────────────────────────────────────────────┘
```

Fig.5.11 Subtype concept.

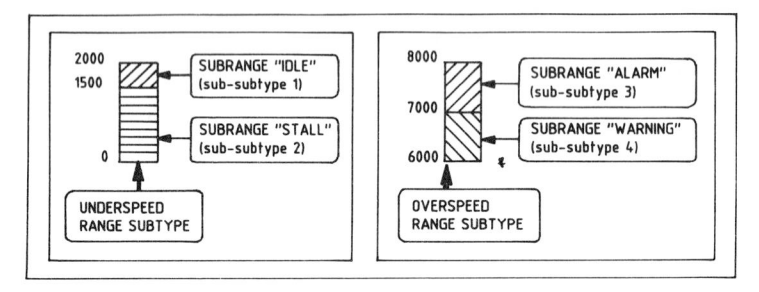

```
┌──────────────────────────────────┐  ┌──────────────────────────────────┐
│ 2000 ┌──┐  ┌─────────────────┐   │  │ 8000 ┌──┐  ┌─────────────────┐   │
│ 1500 │▓▓│◄─┤ SUBRANGE "IDLE" │   │  │      │▓▓│◄─┤ SUBRANGE "ALARM"│   │
│      │══│  │ (sub-subtype 1) │   │  │ 7000 │══│  │ (sub-subtype 3) │   │
│      │══│  └─────────────────┘   │  │      │══│  └─────────────────┘   │
│      │══│  ┌─────────────────┐   │  │      │▒▒│  ┌─────────────────┐   │
│      │══│◄─┤ SUBRANGE "STALL"│   │  │ 6000 │▒▒│◄─┤ SUBRANGE "WARNING"│ │
│   0  └──┘  │ (sub-subtype 2) │   │  │      └──┘  │ (sub-subtype 4) │   │
│        ▲   └─────────────────┘   │  │        ▲   └─────────────────┘   │
│   ┌────┴─────┐                   │  │   ┌────┴─────┐                   │
│   │UNDERSPEED│                   │  │   │OVERSPEED │                   │
│   │RANGE SUBTYPE│                │  │   │RANGE SUBTYPE│                │
│   └──────────┘                   │  │   └──────────┘                   │
└──────────────────────────────────┘  └──────────────────────────────────┘
```

Fig.5.12 Subtypes of subtypes.

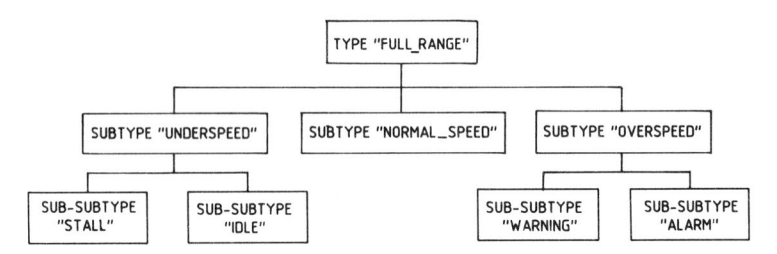

```
                    ┌─────────────────────┐
                    │ TYPE "FULL_RANGE"   │
                    └──────────┬──────────┘
             ┌─────────────────┼─────────────────┐
   ┌─────────┴──────────┐ ┌────┴────────────┐ ┌──┴──────────────────┐
   │ SUBTYPE "UNDERSPEED"│ │SUBTYPE "NORMAL_SPEED"│ │ SUBTYPE "OVERSPEED"│
   └──────┬──────┬───────┘ └─────────────────┘ └──────┬──────┬───────┘
   ┌──────┴──┐┌──┴──────┐                      ┌──────┴──┐┌──┴──────┐
   │SUB-SUBTYPE││SUB-SUBTYPE│                  │SUB-SUBTYPE││SUB-SUBTYPE│
   │ "STALL"   ││ "IDLE"    │                  │ "WARNING" ││ "ALARM"   │
   └───────────┘└───────────┘                  └───────────┘└───────────┘
```

Fig.5.13 Hierarchical relationships of subtypes.

The subrange syntax for scalar types is given in Fig.5.14.

Here the **range** construct is used to specify a subset of values of a scalar type. The example of Listing 5.16 shows this construct being applied to the days of the month problem.

Formally, a subtype is defined to be 'a type together with a range constraint'. Note how subtypes and their base types are compatible. That is, values and variables can be freely interchanged, as shown in Listing 5.17.

It is implicit in Fig.5.11 that the range constraints of a subtype cannot

Inventing your own data types   145

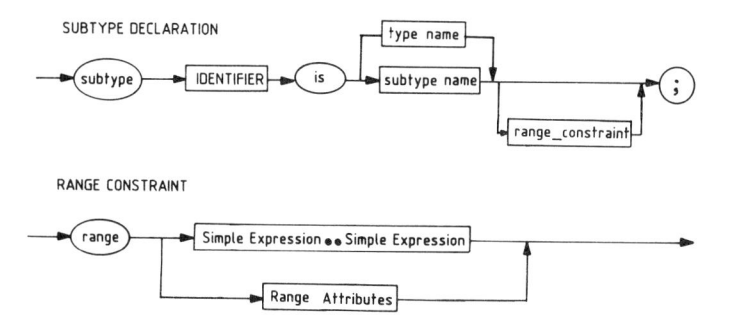

Fig.5.14 Syntax of the scalar subtype.

```
procedure SUB_TYPES is
  -- Declare a subtype for the day, month and year
  subtype YEAR_TYPE is INTEGER range 1990..1999;
  subtype MONTH_TYPE is INTEGER range 1..12;
  subtype DAY_TYPE is INTEGER range 1..31;
  SAMPLE_YEAR     :    YEAR_TYPE;
  SAMPLE_MONTH    :    MONTH_TYPE;
  SAMPLE_DAY      :    DAY_TYPE;
begin
  SAMPLE_DAY   := 4;
  SAMPLE_MONTH := 1;
  SAMPLE_YEAR  := 1991;
end SUB_TYPES;
```

Listing 5.16 This illustrates the use of a subtype to validate a date.

contradict those of its base type. For instance, the subrange *overspeed range* could not have an upper bound of 8100 RPM as the base upper bound is 8000 RPM.

We could also have expressed the range constraint using the range attribute form, as shown in Listing 5.18.

How does the compiler recognize the parent or 'base' type? Simply by checking the type of the two bounds. These are fairly self-explanatory for INTEGERs, but what of other base types? Consider the example of Listing 5.19, Fig.5.15.

Here we've first defined (declared) an enumeration type DIGITAL_1_STATUS and then declared a subtype of this, DIGITAL_2_STATUS. DIGITAL_2_STATUS has a lower bound of OFF, an upper bound of STANDBY, its cardinality is three and the ordinality is OFF, ON, STANDBY. As a result the OIL_PURIFIER_MOTOR can be defined to be in one of five conditions, but the CPP_PUMP_MOTOR in only three.

One point is well worth repeating here. Subtypes of an enumeration type

```ada
with TEXT_IO;
procedure TYPE_INTERCHANGE is
  -- Declare an enumeration type to represent the months of a year
  type MONTH is (JANUARY, FEBRUARY, MARCH, APRIL, MAY, JUNE, JULY, AUGUST,
                 SEPTEMBER, OCTOBER, NOVEMBER, DECEMBER);
  -- Declare a subtype for the months in each quarter
  subtype FIRST_QUARTER is MONTH range JANUARY..MARCH;
  subtype SECOND_QUARTER is MONTH range APRIL..JUNE;
  subtype THIRD_QUARTER is MONTH range JULY..SEPTEMBER;
  subtype FINAL_QUARTER is MONTH range OCTOBER..DECEMBER;
  package MONTH_IO is new TEXT_IO.ENUMERATION_IO (MONTH);
  EXAMPLE_MONTH      :    MONTH;
  LAST_MONTH         :    MONTH;
  FIRST_MONTH        :    MONTH;
  MONTH_Q1           :    FIRST_QUARTER;
  MONTH_Q2           :    SECOND_QUARTER;
  MONTH_Q3           :    THIRD_QUARTER;
  MONTH_Q4           :    FINAL_QUARTER;
begin
  TEXT_IO.PUT ( "Please Enter a Month (JANUARY-DECEMBER) " );
  MONTH_IO.GET (EXAMPLE_MONTH);
  TEXT_IO.SKIP_LINE;
  -- determine which quarter this month is in
  if EXAMPLE_MONTH in FIRST_QUARTER then
  -- Assignment of a base type variable to a subtype.
  -- The assignment will be valid as we have checked that
  -- the value of the base type variable is within the
  -- range of the subtype
    MONTH_Q1 := EXAMPLE_MONTH;
  -- In the next statement a variable of subtype FIRST_QUARTER
  -- is passed as a parameter to a procedure requiring a
  -- parameter of type MONTH
    MONTH_IO.PUT (MONTH_Q1);
    TEXT_IO.PUT_LINE (" is in the first quarter");
  -- Here a variable of type Month is assigned to one of the
  -- attributes of a subtype of MONTH. This attribute has
  -- the type of the subtype, so the assignment is of a
  -- subtype to its base type
    FIRST_MONTH := FIRST_QUARTER'FIRST;
    LAST_MONTH := FIRST_QUARTER'LAST;
  elsif EXAMPLE_MONTH in SECOND_QUARTER then
    MONTH_Q2 := EXAMPLE_MONTH;
    MONTH_IO.PUT (MONTH_Q2);
    TEXT_IO.PUT_LINE (" is in the second quarter");
    FIRST_MONTH := SECOND_QUARTER'FIRST;
    LAST_MONTH := SECOND_QUARTER'LAST;
  elsif EXAMPLE_MONTH in THIRD_QUARTER then
    MONTH_Q3 := EXAMPLE_MONTH;
    MONTH_IO.PUT (MONTH_Q3);
    TEXT_IO.PUT_LINE (" is in the third quarter");
    FIRST_MONTH := THIRD_QUARTER'FIRST;
    LAST_MONTH := THIRD_QUARTER'LAST;
  else
  -- month must be in the final quarter
    MONTH_IO.PUT (MONTH_Q4);
    TEXT_IO.PUT_LINE (" is in the final quarter");
    FIRST_MONTH := FINAL_QUARTER'FIRST;
    LAST_MONTH := FINAL_QUARTER'LAST;
  end if;
  TEXT_IO.PUT ("This quarter runs from ");
  MONTH_IO.PUT (FIRST_MONTH);
  TEXT_IO.PUT (" to ");
  MONTH_IO.PUT (LAST_MONTH);
  TEXT_IO.NEW_LINE;
end TYPE_INTERCHANGE;
```

Listing 5.17 This illustrates how variables of subtypes and their base types may be interchanged, as long as the range constraints are met.

```
with TEXT_IO;                use TEXT_IO;
procedure USE_RANGE_ATTRIB is
  package INT_IO is new INTEGER_IO (INTEGER);
  use INT_IO;
  subtype RPM is INTEGER range 0..8000;
  -- declare subtypes of this. Use the FIRST and LAST attributes of the
  -- subtype RPM.
  subtype UNDERSPEED is RPM range RPM'FIRST..2000;
  subtype OVERSPEED is RPM range 6000..RPM'LAST;
  -- The final subtype lies between UNDERSPEED and OVERSPEED. Use attributes
  -- of these subtypes.
  subtype NORMAL_SPEED is RPM range UNDERSPEED'LAST..OVERSPEED'FIRST;
  TEST_NUMBER     :       INTEGER;
begin
  PUT ("Please enter an INTEGER : ");
  GET (TEST_NUMBER);
  SKIP_LINE;
  if not (TEST_NUMBER in RPM) then
    PUT_LINE ("Sorry, the number is outside the defined range for rpm");
  elsif TEST_NUMBER in NORMAL_SPEED then
    PUT_LINE ("The number entered is in the NORMAL_SPEED range");
  elsif TEST_NUMBER in UNDERSPEED then
    PUT_LINE ("The number entered in in the UNDERSPEED range");
  elsif TEST_NUMBER in OVERSPEED then
    PUT_LINE ("The number entered is in the OVERSPEED range");
  end if;
end USE_RANGE_ATTRIB;
```

Listing 5.18 Using range attributes when declaring subtypes.

```
procedure ENUM_SUBTYPE is
  type DIGITAL_1_STATUS is (PRIMED, OFF, ON, STANDBY, TRIPPED);
  subtype DIGITAL_2_STATUS is DIGITAL_1_STATUS range OFF..STANDBY;
  OIL_PURIFIER_MOTOR :     DIGITAL_1_STATUS;
  CPP_PUMP_MOTOR     :     DIGITAL_2_STATUS;
begin
  OIL_PURIFIER_MOTOR := OFF;
  CPP_PUMP_MOTOR     := STANDBY;
end ENUM_SUBTYPE;
      MONTH_Q4 := EXAMPLE_MONTH;
      MONTH_IO.PUT (MONTH_Q4);
      TEXT_IO.PUT_LINE (" is in the final quarter");
      FIRST_MONTH := FINAL_QUARTER'FIRST;
      LAST_MONTH := FINAL_QUARTER'LAST;
    end if;
    TEXT_IO.PUT ("This quarter runs from ");
    MONTH_IO.PUT (FIRST_MONTH);
    TEXT_IO.PUT (" to ");
    MONTH_IO.PUT (LAST_MONTH);
    TEXT_IO.NEW_LINE;
  end TYPE_INTERCHANGE;
```

Listing 5.19 Subtype of an enumeration type.

148   Types revisited

```
type DIGITAL_1_STATUS is (PRIMED, OFF, ON, STANDBY, TRIPPED);
subtype DIGITAL_2_STATUS is DIGITAL_1_STATUS range OFF..STANDBY;
```

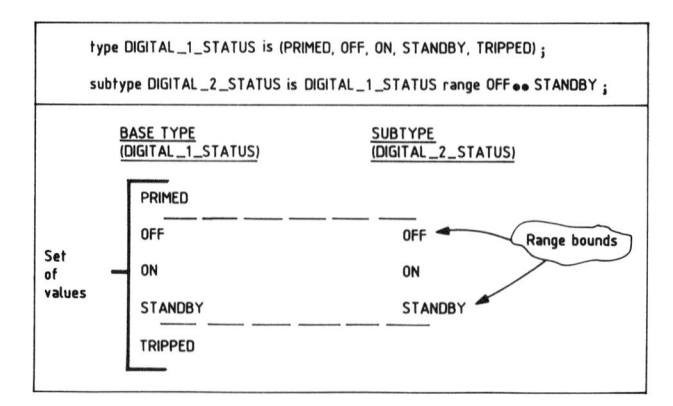

	BASE TYPE (DIGITAL_1_STATUS)	SUBTYPE (DIGITAL_2_STATUS)
	PRIMED	
Set of values	OFF	OFF ← Range bounds
	ON	ON
	STANDBY	STANDBY
	TRIPPED	

Fig.5.15 Subtype of an enumeration type.

```
type DIGITAL_1_STATUS is (PRIMED, OFF, ON, STANDBY, TRIPPED);
subtype DIGITAL_2_STATUS is DIGITAL_1_STATUS range OFF..STANDBY;
subtype DIGITAL_3_STATUS is DIGITAL_2_STATUS range OFF..ON;
```

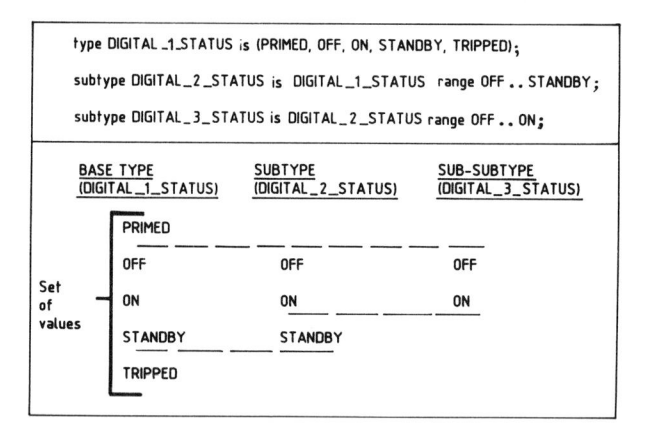

	BASE TYPE (DIGITAL_1_STATUS)	SUBTYPE (DIGITAL_2_STATUS)	SUB-SUBTYPE (DIGITAL_3_STATUS)
	PRIMED		
Set of values	OFF	OFF	OFF
	ON	ON	ON
	STANDBY	STANDBY	
	TRIPPED		

Fig.5.16 Subtypes and sub-subtypes.

must have contiguous (consecutive) enumerated values from the base type. It would be impossible to create a subtype of DIGITAL_1_STATUS which contains PRIMED, STANDBY and TRIPPED only.

It has already been mentioned that we can have subtypes of subtypes. This point is illustrated in Fig.5.16. and Listing 5.20.

When a number of subtypes are formed from a single base, their bounds may overlap, as shown in Fig.5.17 and Listing 5.21.

It has already been pointed out that subtypes and their base types are type compatible. So too are subtypes and their sub-subtypes. However, problems will arise if we try to work outside the range bounds of subtypes. The rules governing this are demonstrated in Listing 5.22, which should be self-explanatory.

```
with TEXT_IO;              use TEXT_IO;
procedure SUB_SUBTYPE_1 is
   type DIGITAL_1_STATUS is (PRIMED, OFF, ON, STANDBY, TRIPPED);
   subtype DIGITAL_2_STATUS is DIGITAL_1_STATUS range OFF..STANDBY;
   subtype DIGITAL_3_STATUS is DIGITAL_2_STATUS range OFF..ON;
   package STATUS_IO is new ENUMERATION_IO (DIGITAL_1_STATUS);
   use STATUS_IO;
   OIL_PURIFIER_MOTOR :      DIGITAL_1_STATUS;
   CPP_PUMP_MOTOR     :      DIGITAL_2_STATUS;
   PUMP_MONITOR       :      DIGITAL_3_STATUS;
begin
   OIL_PURIFIER_MOTOR := OFF;
   CPP_PUMP_MOTOR     := OFF;
   PUMP_MONITOR       := OFF;
end SUB_SUBTYPE_1;
```

Listing 5.20 Subtype of a subtype.

```
type DIGITAL_1_STATUS is (PRIMED, OFF, STANDBY, TRIPPED);

subtype DIGITAL_2_STATUS is DIGITAL_1_STATUS range OFF..STANDBY;

subtype DIGITAL_4_STATUS is DIGITAL_1_STATUS range OFF..TRIPPED;

          BASE TYPE          SUBTYPE            SUBTYPE
          DIGITAL_1_STATUS   (DIGITAL_2_STATUS) DIGITAL_4_STATUS

          PRIMED
   set
   of     OFF                OFF                OFF
   values
          ON                 ON                 ON

          STANDBY            STANDBY            STANDBY

          TRIPPED                               TRIPPED
```

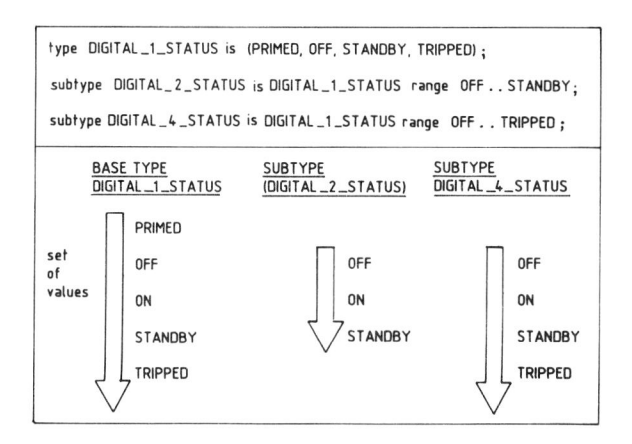

Fig.5.17 Overlapping subtypes.

```
procedure OVERLAPPING_SUBTYPES is
   type DIGITAL_1_STATUS is (PRIMED, OFF, ON, STANDBY, TRIPPED);
   subtype DIGITAL_2_STATUS is DIGITAL_1_STATUS range OFF..STANDBY;
   subtype DIGITAL_4_STATUS is DIGITAL_1_STATUS range OFF..TRIPPED;
   OIL_PURIFIER_MOTOR :      DIGITAL_1_STATUS;
   CPP_PUMP_MOTOR     :      DIGITAL_2_STATUS;
   MOTOR_MONITOR      :      DIGITAL_4_STATUS;
begin
   OIL_PURIFIER_MOTOR := OFF;
   CPP_PUMP_MOTOR     := OFF;
   MOTOR_MONITOR      := OFF;
end OVERLAPPING_SUBTYPES;
```

Listing 5.21 Subtypes with overlapping ranges.

150   Types revisited

```
with TEXT_IO;                use TEXT_IO;
procedure SUB_SUBTYPE_2 is
  type DIGITAL_1_STATUS is (PRIMED, OFF, ON, STANDBY, TRIPPED);
  subtype DIGITAL_2_STATUS is DIGITAL_1_STATUS range OFF..STANDBY;
  subtype DIGITAL_3_STATUS is DIGITAL_2_STATUS range OFF..ON;
  package STATUS_IO is new ENUMERATION_IO (DIGITAL_1_STATUS);
  use STATUS_IO;
  OIL_PURIFIER_MOTOR :       DIGITAL_1_STATUS;
  CPP_PUMP_MOTOR     :       DIGITAL_2_STATUS;
  PUMP_MONITOR       :       DIGITAL_3_STATUS;
begin
  OIL_PURIFIER_MOTOR := OFF;
  CPP_PUMP_MOTOR := OIL_PURIFIER_MOTOR;
  PUMP_MONITOR := CPP_PUMP_MOTOR;
  loop
    PUT ("Enter Oil purifier motor status...");
    GET (OIL_PURIFIER_MOTOR);
    SKIP_LINE;
    NEW_LINE;
    PUT ("Enter CPP pump motor status...");
    GET (CPP_PUMP_MOTOR);
    SKIP_LINE;
    NEW_LINE;
    if (CPP_PUMP_MOTOR /= STANDBY) then
      PUMP_MONITOR := CPP_PUMP_MOTOR;
    else
      PUT_LINE ("PUMP_MONITOR := CPP_PUMP_MOTOR ");
      PUT ("would generate an error, as CPP_PUMP_MOTOR = STANDBY");
    end if;
    if (CPP_PUMP_MOTOR = ON) and (OIL_PURIFIER_MOTOR = TRIPPED) then
      NEW_LINE;
      PUT_LINE ("Shutting down CPP...");
      exit;
    else
      NEW_LINE (2);
    end if;
  end loop;
  PUT_LINE ("CPP shut down...");
end SUB_SUBTYPE_2;
```

Listing 5.22 Assignment between subtypes and subtypes of subtypes.

Subtypes can make it easier to read and understand programs, examples being given later when arrays are discussed.

It can be seen from Fig.5.14 that a subtype declaration does not have to specify range constraints. Thus we could have the declarations

```
type     ALARMS is (EXTRA_LOW, LOW, HIGH, EXTRA_HIGH);
subtype  PRESSURE_ALARMS is ALARMS;
subtype  FLOW_ALARMS is ALARMS;
```

In this case both PRESSURE_ALARMS and FLOW_ALARMS are exactly the same as the base type. What we have done is merely rename the base type.

Inventing your own data types

```
procedure SUBTYPE_WITHOUT_RANGE is
  type ALARMS is (EXTRA_LOW, LOW, HIGH, EXTRA_HIGH);
  subtype PRESSURE_ALARMS is ALARMS;
  subtype FLOW_ALARMS is ALARMS;
  HYDRALICS_PRESSURE_ALARM :      PRESSURE_ALARMS;
  HYDRALICS_FLOW_ALARM     :      FLOW_ALARMS;
begin
  HYDRALICS_PRESSURE_ALARM := HIGH;
  HYDRALICS_FLOW_ALARM     := LOW;
end SUBTYPE_WITHOUT_RANGE;
```

Listing 5.23 Enumeration subtypes without range.

The reason for using this is to make programs more readable, see Listing 5.23.

On a closing point, consider the following declarations:

(a)

```
subtype PRESSURE_ALARMS is INTEGER range 0..200;
OXYGEN_PRESSURE    : PRESSURE_ALARMS;
HYDROGEN_PRESSURE  : PRESSURE_ALARMS;
```

(b)

```
OXYGEN_PRESSURE    : INTEGER range 0..200;
HYDROGEN_PRESSURE  : INTEGER range 0..200;
```

These, in essence, are equivalent – but there is a subtle difference. In (a) the subtype PRESSURE_ALARMS is said to be an *explicit* subtype. That is, it has a name. Variables OXYGEN_PRESSURE and HYDROGEN_PRESSURE clearly belong to subtype PRESSURE_ALARMS. In the second declaration form (b) the variables belong to unnamed or *implicit* subtypes. The explicit or named form gives us a better view of the structure of our system. It also makes it easier to control our software. For instance, suppose that we decide to change the alarm range to 0..400. Using the explicit form a single change only is needed, namely:

```
subtype PRESSURE_ALARMS is INTEGER range 0..400;
```

But with the implicit form all variables have to be updated.

5.5.5 Derived types

Study the scenario shown in Fig.5.18. This illustrates a simple chemical plant which produces oxygen and hydrogen, and stores these at high pressure in liquid form. Each storage tank is fitted with a vent valve as a safety device, together with a pressure sensor. To control these valves we could produce a program such as that of Listing 5.24 (subtypes have been used only to improve program readability and security).

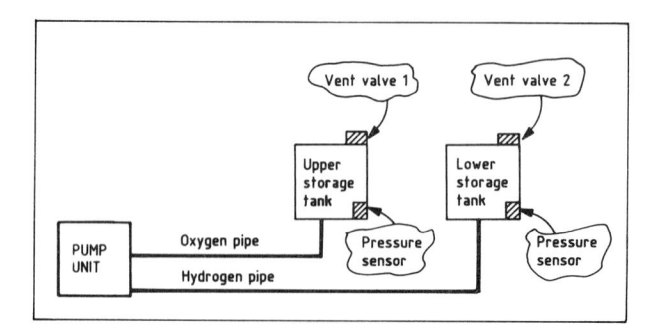

Fig.5.18 Simple chemical plant system.

Unfortunately, if by mistake we write

```
if (PH > UPPER_TANK_P_TRIP) then OPEN (VENT_VALVE_1); end if;
if (PO > LOWER_TANK_P_TRIP) then OPEN (VENT_VALVE_2); end if;
```

this will be accepted by the compiler. Yet in a real system this very simple slip could produce a disastrous situation. You could reasonably argue that better naming would avert such problems. True, but there are cases where we have to work with established notation, which may limit our freedom of action. What, then, can we do to improve the safety of our software? This is where the derived type comes in.

A derived type is one which is created from an existing parent type to form a new type. Objects of this new type are not compatible with any other object types. This includes the parent type and any other types derived from the parent. However, it inherits all the attributes of the parent type. Fig.5.19 defines the syntax for the derived type, so allowing us to implement the following declaration:

```
type OXYGEN_PRESSURE    is new INTEGER range 0..200;
type HYDROGEN_PRESSURE  is new INTEGER range 0..250;
```

```ada
with TEXT_IO;                use TEXT_IO;
procedure CHEMICAL_PLANT_SIMULATION is
  package INT_IO is new INTEGER_IO (INTEGER);
  use INT_IO;
  type VENT_VALVE is (OPEN, CLOSED);
  subtype OXYGEN_PRESSURE is INTEGER range 0..200;
  subtype HYDROGEN_PRESSURE is INTEGER range 0..250;
  VENT_VALVE_1         :    VENT_VALVE       := CLOSED;
  VENT_VALVE_2         :    VENT_VALVE       := CLOSED;
  PO                   :    OXYGEN_PRESSURE  := 0;
  PH                   :    HYDROGEN_PRESSURE := 0;
  UPPER_TANK_P_TRIP    :    constant OXYGEN_PRESSURE := 180;
  UPPER_TANK_P_RESTART :    constant OXYGEN_PRESSURE := 25;
  LOWER_TANK_P_TRIP    :    constant HYDROGEN_PRESSURE := 230;
  LOWER_TANK_P_RESTART :    constant HYDROGEN_PRESSURE := 25;
  procedure OPEN (VALVE      : in out VENT_VALVE) is
  begin
    VALVE := OPEN;
  end OPEN;
  procedure CLOSE (VALVE     : in out VENT_VALVE) is
  begin
    VALVE := CLOSED;
  end CLOSE;
  procedure CALCULATE is
  begin
    if VENT_VALVE_1 = OPEN then
      PO := PO - 10;
    else
      PO := PO + 10;
    end if;
    if VENT_VALVE_2 = OPEN then
      PH := PH - 10;
    else
      PH := PH + 10;
    end if;
  end CALCULATE;
begin
  loop
    CALCULATE;
    if (PO > UPPER_TANK_P_TRIP) then
      OPEN (VENT_VALVE_1);
    end if;
    if (PH > LOWER_TANK_P_TRIP) then
      OPEN (VENT_VALVE_2);
    end if;
    if (PO < UPPER_TANK_P_RESTART) then
      CLOSE (VENT_VALVE_1);
    end if;
    if (PH < LOWER_TANK_P_RESTART) then
      CLOSE (VENT_VALVE_2);
    end if;
    PUT(" PO => ");
    PUT(PO);
    PUT(" PH => ");
    PUT(PH);
    NEW_LINE;
    for WASTE_TIME in 1..10000 loop
      null;
    end loop;
  end loop;
end CHEMICAL_PLANT_SIMULATION;
    PUT (" PH => ");
    PUT (PH);
    NEW_LINE;
    for WASTE_TIME in 1..10000 loop
      null;
    end loop;
  end loop;
end CHEMICAL_PLANT_SIMULATION;
```

Listing 5.24 Using subtypes in a chemical plant simulation.

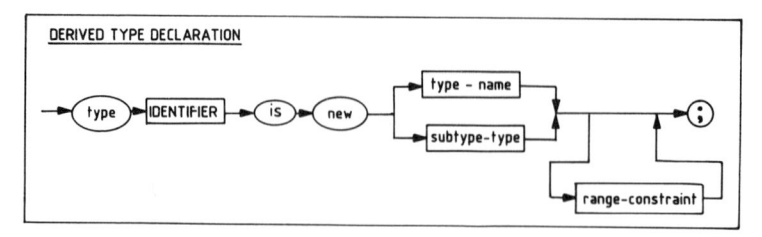

Fig.5.19 Syntax of the derived type.

Listing 5.25 is a revised version of Listing 5.24, using derived types instead of subtypes. With this form the types OXYGEN_PRESSURE and HYDROGEN _PRESSURE are considered to be different, even though they share the same parent (INTEGER). Thus the program statements

> **if** (PH > UPPER_TANK_P_TRIP) **then** OPEN (VENT_VALVE_1); **end if**;
> **if** (PO > LOWER_TANK_P_TRIP) **then** OPEN (VENT_VALVE_2); **end if**;

will be rejected by the compiler. Modify the program of Listing 5.25 and prove to yourself that this is the case.

NOTE 1: Ada defines that a subtype is acquired from a *base* type, whereas a derived type originates from a *parent* type.

NOTE 2: From the syntax definition of Fig.5.19, the following declarations are legal:

> **type** ALARMS **is** (EXTRA_LOW, LOW, HIGH, EXTRA_HIGH);
> **type** PRESSURE_ALARMS **is new** ALARMS;
> **type** FLOW_ALARMS **is new** ALARMS;

Here the parent type is ALARMS. The two derived types have exactly the same elements as their parent, yet all three are considered to be unique. Contrast this with the example given in the section on subtypes.

5.5.6 More on derived types – integer type definitions

Our earlier work with integer numbers was based on the predefined Ada type INTEGER (or one of its subtypes). But, as pointed out in chapter 1, we are not necessarily restricted to this. It is possible that SHORT_INTEGER and/ or LONG_INTEGER types are also provided by our compiler. To use these

```ada
with TEXT_IO;                 use TEXT_IO;
procedure CHEMICAL_PLANT_SIMULATION is
  type VENT_VALVE is (OPEN, CLOSED);
  type OXYGEN_PRESSURE is new INTEGER range 0..200;
  type HYDROGEN_PRESSURE is new INTEGER range 0..250;
  package OP_IO is new INTEGER_IO (OXYGEN_PRESSURE);
  use OP_IO;
  package HP_IO is new INTEGER_IO (HYDROGEN_PRESSURE);
  use HP_IO;
  VENT_VALVE_1            :   VENT_VALVE          := CLOSED;
  VENT_VALVE_2            :   VENT_VALVE          := CLOSED;
  PO                      :   OXYGEN_PRESSURE     := 0;
  PH                      :   HYDROGEN_PRESSURE   := 0;
  UPPER_TANK_P_TRIP       :   constant OXYGEN_PRESSURE := 180;
  UPPER_TANK_P_RESTART    :   constant OXYGEN_PRESSURE := 25;
  LOWER_TANK_P_TRIP       :   constant HYDROGEN_PRESSURE := 230;
  LOWER_TANK_P_RESTART    :   constant HYDROGEN_PRESSURE := 25;
  procedure OPEN (VALVE   : in out VENT_VALVE) is
  begin
    VALVE := OPEN;
  end OPEN;
  procedure CLOSE (VALVE  : in out VENT_VALVE) is
  begin
    VALVE := CLOSED;
  end CLOSE;
  procedure CALCULATE is
  begin
    if VENT_VALVE_1 = OPEN then
      PO := PO - 10;
    else
      PO := PO + 10;
    end if;
    if VENT_VALVE_2 = OPEN then
      PH := PH - 10;
    else
      PH := PH + 10;
    end if;
  end CALCULATE;
begin
  loop
    CALCULATE;
    if (PO > UPPER_TANK_P_TRIP) then
      OPEN (VENT_VALVE_1);
    end if;
    if (PH > LOWER_TANK_P_TRIP) then
      OPEN (VENT_VALVE_2);
    end if;
    if (PO < UPPER_TANK_P_RESTART) then
      CLOSE (VENT_VALVE_1);
    end if;
    if (PH < LOWER_TANK_P_RESTART) then
      CLOSE (VENT_VALVE_2);
    end if;
    PUT (" PO => ");
    PUT (PO);
    PUT (" PH => ");
    PUT (PH);
    NEW_LINE;
    for WASTE_TIME in 1..10000 loop
      null;
    end loop;
  end loop;
end CHEMICAL_PLANT_SIMULATION;
```

Listing 5.25 A revised version of Listing 5.24 using derived types instead of subtypes.

effectively it is necessary to know what number ranges these types represent. Unfortunately, this can vary from implementation to implementation – the actual number range for these types is not defined in the language standard.

Suppose the target computer is a 16 bit machine. In this case INTEGER will probably have 16 bits, LONG_INTEGER 32 bits and SHORT_INTEGER 8. However, on moving to a 32 bit machine, this is almost certain to change. Most likely INTEGER would be represented using 32 bits, LONG_INTEGER with 64 bits and SHORT_INTEGER with 16. Clearly, this may well lead to portability problems, specifically involving constraint errors and code inefficiency.

Suppose our program is first implemented on a 32 bit machine. Suppose also that, within this program, we assign a value of 100 000 to an INTEGER variable. As this is within the 32 bit number range, it is perfectly legal. But, should this be recompiled for a 16 bit machine, it would produce a constraint error. We would have to declare the variable as LONG_INTEGER to overcome this.

Now consider a change of scenario – the program is first implemented on a 16 bit machine. To assign a value of 100 000 to a variable, it must be declared as type LONG_INTEGER. At the machine level this will be represented using 32 bits. Assume that, for some reason, the program is recompiled for a 32 bit computer. Consequently the variable will be represented using 64 bits. In this situation there is no problem with the number range. But the variable could have been implemented using type INTEGER on the second machine. Clearly it is a waste of 32 bits of storage space (it may also degrade performance).

What is needed here is a method by which the compiler can choose the best representation. In Ada this is done by using a particular form of the derived type declaration – the 'integer type definition'. The general format is

> **type** TYPE_NAME **is range** LOWER_BOUND..UPPER_BOUND;

as in

> **type** OXYGEN_PRESSURE **is range** 0..200;

Here the type OXYGEN_PRESSURE is regarded as a derived type. But note that the programmer does not define its parent type. This is automatically selected by the compiler to suit the situation. For instance, suppose the following declarations are made:

```
type ALTITUDE is range 0..50000;
CURRENT_ALTITUDE : ALTITUDE;
```

We could find that CURRENT_ALTITUDE is implemented on one machine as LONG_INTEGER and on a second one as INTEGER.

5.6 CONVERSION OF DATA TYPES

It might look as if we're painting ourselves into a corner by insisting on strong typing rules. Situations do arise where variables have to be handled as different types. Yet Ada appears to forbid the mixing of such types – a case, perhaps, of the immovable object and the irresistible force. Well, not quite. After all, if this were true the language would become unusable. Ada does provide us with the means to deal with type mixing operations, called type conversion.

When a type is converted its representation within the computer is changed from the old type to the new type. We have, in fact, done this in some earlier examples without highlighting the fact. For instance, in Listing 2.1 the following statements were written:

```
X1R := FLOAT (X1);
X1  := INTEGER (X1R);
```

where X1R is of type FLOAT and X1 is an INTEGER. These examples show how to convert the type of a program item. Simply write the name of the destination type followed by the name (in parentheses) of the item to be converted.

WARNING: Do not confuse the syntax of type conversion with that of qualification for overloading.

REVIEW

Do you now:

- See why good typing is an essential part of program security?
- Understand what strong typing is and how it helps the compiler to pick up mistakes in the software?
- Appreciate how typing allows us to take a conceptual view of our problems?

158 Types revisited

- Understand the ideas of cardinality, ordinality and enumeration?
- Appreciate how to create your own data types?
- Understand the use of programmer-defined enumeration types?
- Perceive the need for and the use of subtypes and derived types?
- Grasp the ideas behind, and the use of, type mixing using the type conversion mechanism?

Chapter Six
Number crunching in Ada

Ada was primarily designed for the programming of real-time systems. And a central aspect of almost all real-time working is the use of numerical calculations. We've already looked at this topic (see chapter 2) in a fair amount of detail. For many programmers the level of information presented there is all that they'll ever need. But others must attain a much deeper understanding of this subject if they are to construct efficient, correct and safe programs. The actual programming of maths operations in Ada is quite straightforward. Unfortunately, when such programs are executed, the results can be most unexpected. The reason for this is simple – a yawning gulf between our concept of the situation and the reality of computer operations. We forget (or don't even realize) that we are dealing with finite number systems. And, furthermore, we don't understand their limitations.

The purpose of this chapter is to describe the way in which numbers are represented and manipulated – both theoretically and practically. Type INTEGER has been fully discussed in chapter 2; hence here we will concentrate on real number types only. After studying this chapter you will:

- Understand the extent and severity of errors in numerical operations;
- Understand the basics of positional number systems, together with fixed point and floating point notation;
- Appreciate the difference between the infinite and the model number set;
- Realize why errors are generated by calculations involving floating or fixed point operations;
- Comprehend the methods for handling real numbers within computers;
- Know how to write Ada programs to manipulate both fixed and floating point numbers.

6.1 SETTING THE SCENE

6.1.1 Problems in disguise

Do we really need to understand how mathematical operations are carried out within a computer? Well, consider the situations depicted in Fig.6.1.

In (a), we use the calculation $(0 - X)$ to determine if X has a negative value.

160 Number crunching in Ada

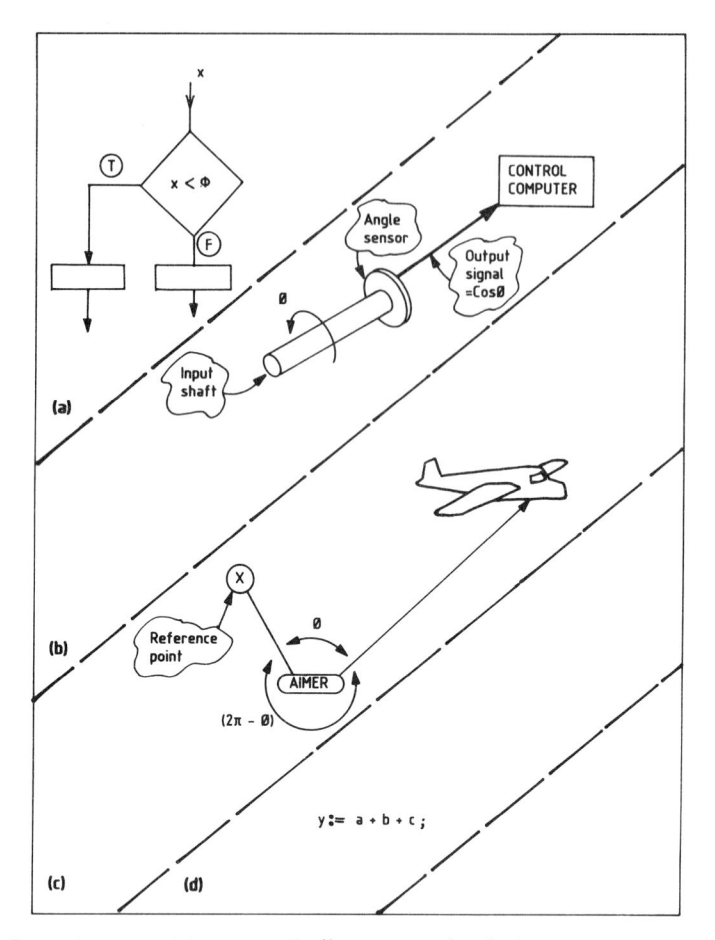

Fig.6.1 Operations requiring numerically computed solutions.

The next example, (b), shows the output from a shaft angle sensor being fed to a control computer, to provide monitoring data. In (c) a missile aimer measures the angle between a fixed reference point and a target aircraft in order to engage at the optimal launch angle. The final item, (d), is a simple mathematical statement in source code form. If you are likely to work with these or similar applications, then you do need to know what happens during the number-crunching process, because there are disguised problems in all these examples. For instance, in (a) the calculation may give a FALSE result (indicating that X is not negative), when it actually is negative. In (b), working with the cosine of the angle may well give different results to those obtained by using the angle itself. With the situation shown in (c), the aimer should be able to use either ϕ or $(2\pi - \phi)$, yet these may not produce identical

Setting the scene   161

results. Finally, for example (d), if the programmer changes the order of calculation (say to y := a + c + b;), the computed result may also change. There is a common reason for all these problems: the limits of computers in the handling of numbers. And what disguises the size and nature of this problem? It is that we fail to recognize or remember that computers have these definite limits.

6.1.2 Making measurements

When we make measurements there are two distinct points to consider: measurement type and result representation (Fig.6.2).

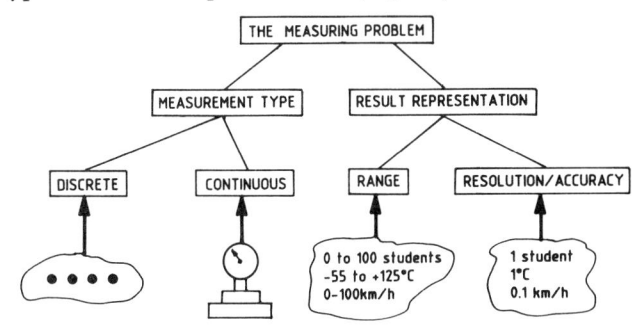

Fig.6.2 The measuring problem.

Measurements that we carry out in the real world fall into two categories, discrete and continuous. Counting the number of students in a class is clearly a case of dealing with discrete values. In contrast, measuring the amount of liquid in a container involves a continuously varying quantity. Now consider how we would show the results of such measurements using written digits. Listing the student total is simple and direct; further, the problem itself defines the number range needed in the calculation. For the second example, writing down the volume isn't a problem. The question is: how many digits should we use? In theory, an infinite number; in practice, a limited amount. Thus the practical answer is less precise than the theoretical one. We say that the theoretical value has infinite precision whilst practical numbers have finite precision. How, though, is the degree of precision defined? Consider the following:

(a) Number range 0 to 999 with a step size of 1.
    The precision (or *resolution*) is 1 in 1000 (i.e. 1/1000).
(b) Number range 0 to 10^6 with a step size of 1.
    The precision is 1/1 000 000.
(c) Number range 0.001 to 0.999 with a step size of 0.001.
    The precision is 1/1000.

162   Number crunching in Ada

Now consider the accuracy of measurements and calculations. First, what is accuracy? Second, how do accuracy and precision interact?

Accuracy is defined to be the 'degree of correctness' of the measurement or calculation. In the next section we'll look at accuracy/precision aspects in terms of finite number systems. For the moment, though, consider that we can display a quantity using as many digits as we desire. Suppose that we weigh items using a sensor which, we are told, 'has a range of 0 to 100 kg with an accuracy of ±0.1 kg'. Further suppose that the weight display is a six-digit readout. When a sack of potatoes is put on the measuring scales the readout shows '25.7941 kg'. The precision of this number is impressive – and can easily fool us into forgetting the accuracy limits of the result. The last digit '1' (the *least significant*) has little meaning; it represents only 0.5% of the total error band of 0.2 kg. We really need to match the number of digits used to the inherent accuracy of the problem. It's pointless using meaningless digits. This leads to the definition of the significant figures of a number – those digits which make a contribution to its value.

In summary, three parameters have to be considered in numerical operations: precision, accuracy and range.

6.1.3 Basic number representation and arithmetic

The basic numeric operations of arithmetic are addition, subtraction, multiplication and division. But how we do the arithmetic is related to the way in which numbers are represented. For us, two particular methods are very important: fixed point and floating point representation.

First, though, let us review some basics of number systems, starting with positional notation. Take, for instance, the number '256'. This really means '200 + 50 + 6', provided we are using decimal values, of course. Thus:

$$256 = 200 + 50 + 6$$
$$\equiv (2 \times 10^2) + (5 \times 10^1) + (6 \times 10^0) = (256)_{10}$$

and

$$0.147 = 0.1 + 0.04 + 0.007$$
$$\equiv (1 \times 10^{-1}) + (4 \times 10^{-2}) + (7 \times 10^{-3}) = (.147)_{10}$$

We can see that these are particular examples of the general rule for positional notation, namely:

$$(X_2 X_1 X_0 \cdot X_{-1} X_{-2} X_{-3})_{10} = X_2 10^2 + X_1 10^1 + X_0 10^0 + X_{-1} 10^{-1} + X_{-2} 10^{-2} + X_{-3} 10^{-3}$$

Setting the scene 163

[Figure showing positional numbering notation with $(X_2 X_1 X_0 . X_{-1} X_{-2} X_{-3})_b$ labeled with "most significant digit", "least significant digit", "radix point", "radix or base", and meaning $X_2 b^2 + X_1 b^1 + X_0 b^0 + X_{-1} b^{-1} + X_{-2} b^{-2} + X_{-3} b^{-3}$]

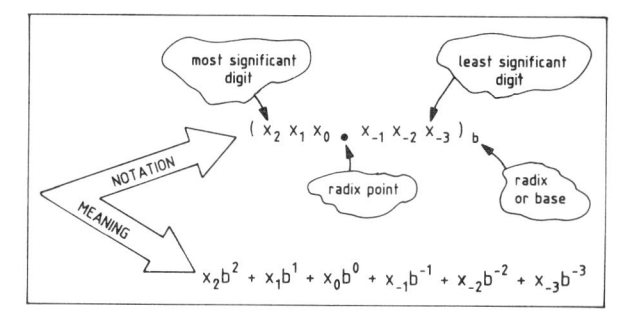

Fig.6.3 Positional numbering system – definition.

Here the X is the digit of representation, the leftmost one being the most significant, whilst the rightmost is the least significant (see also Fig.6.3).

The dot between X_0 and X_{-1} is called the radix point. In this example it is called the decimal point as the number base (or radix) is 10. More generally:

$$(\ldots X_2 X_1 X_0 . X_{-1} X_{-2} X_{-3} \ldots)_b \equiv \ldots X_2 b^2 + X_1 b^1 + X_0 b^0 + X_{-1} b^{-1} + X_{-2} b^{-2} + X_{-3} b^{-3} \ldots$$

When b = 2 we have binary notation. Therefore:

$$(\ldots X_2 X_1 X_0 . X_{-1} X_{-2} X_{-3} \ldots)_2 \equiv \ldots X_2 2^2 + X_1 2^1 + X_0 2^0 + X_{-1} 2^{-1} + X_{-2} 2^{-2} + X_{-3} 2^{-3} \ldots$$

The radix point is called the binary point in this instance.

Fixed point numbers are those expressed using the positional notation outlined above, but subject to certain restrictions. First, a number is represented by a fixed set of digits. Second, the radix point has a predetermined location. Thus 127.5, 0.779, 4095, etc., are examples of four-digit fixed point numbers. Observe that whole numbers can be considered to be a special case of fixed point representation – the radix point is at the rightmost part of the number. Extending this idea, we could use representations where the radix point is somewhere to the left or the right of the digits, as in

Digits		Representing	Digits		Representing
1024	≡	10 240	1025	≡	10 250
1024	≡	102 400	1025	≡	102 500
1024	≡	0.010 24	1025	≡	0.010 25
1024	≡	0.001 024	1025	≡	0.001 025

164   Number crunching in Ada

In normal circumstances we wouldn't write numbers down in this format. However, when we have only a limited number of digits available (see later), it can be useful.

At this stage there is little more to be said concerning fixed point numbers. Everyone should be familiar with their arithmetic operations. They are, after all, the staple diet of elementary school mathematics.

Now let's move on to floating point numbers. These have the following representation:

$$M \times b^e \qquad \begin{array}{l} M \text{ is the mantissa} \\ b \text{ is the radix} \\ e \text{ is the exponent} \end{array}$$

The following are examples of floating point representation:

Floating point value	5×10^2	5.4×10^2	$1 \times 10^{2.5}$	$5.4 \times 10^{2.5}$
Fixed point equivalent	500	540	316.228*	1707.63*

* – approximate values

When doing arithmetic on floating point numbers, the following rules must be followed.

(a) Addition and subtraction

$$(M_1 \times b^{e1}) \pm (M_2 \times b^{e1}) = (M_1 \pm M_2) \times b^{e1}$$

Note that the exponents must be equal. If they aren't, then the numbers must first be adjusted until they are equal. Only then can addition or subtraction be carried out.

EXAMPLE: $(5 \times 10^2) + (5.4 \times 10^2) = 10.4 \times 10^2$
$(5 \times 10^2) + (5.4 \times 10^1) = (50 \times 10^1) + (5.4 \times 10^1) = 55.4 \times 10^1$
OR $= (5 \times 10^2) + (.54 \times 10^2) = 5.54 \times 10^2$

(b) Multiplication and division

$$\text{(i)} \quad (M_1 \times b^{e1}) \times (M_2 \times b^{e2}) = (M_1 \times M_2) \times b^{(e1+e2)}$$

EXAMPLE: $(5 \times 10^2) \times (5.4 \times 10^1) = 27 \times 10^3$

(ii) $(M_1 \times b^{e1}) + (M_2 \times b^{e2}) = (M_1 + M_2) \times b^{(e1-e2)}$

EXAMPLE: $(5 \times 10^1) \div (8 \times 10^2) = 0.625 \times 10^{-1}$

Observe that we manipulate only the mantissa and the exponents. The radix itself plays no part in these operations. What it does, though, is allow us to put the radix point in the correct place. For instance:

$$55.4 \times 10^1 \equiv 554.00$$
$$27 \times 10^3 \equiv 27\,000.00$$
$$0.625 \times 10^{-1} \equiv 0.0625$$

Floating point notation is widely applied in scientific and engineering work. It is used mainly for the representation of very large and very small quantities in preference to fixed point notation. Examples of this include:

- Mean earth–sun distance: 1.49×10^8 km;
- Elementary charge: 1.6×10^{-19} coulombs;
- Mass of earth: 5.98×10^{24} kg.

Do not, however, conclude from this that we use exactly the same reasoning when choosing number representation within computer systems.

6.2 THE LIMITATIONS OF FINITE NUMBER SYSTEMS

6.2.1 General points

There are a number of practical reasons for limiting the size of numbers in our calculations. One, as pointed out above, involves the accuracy of information. If we aren't careful we can spend much time producing meaningless results. The second reason concerns the time taken to perform numerical operations. It is generally true to say that bigger numbers result in longer calculation times. Where we want fast calculation we must limit the number of digits used. The drawback, though, is that this limits precision. And we find that many problems arise exactly because of this limited precision.

We need a good understanding of these problems if we are safely to program numerical functions. Moreover, we also need to recognize system limitations if we wish to trade off time for precision. This is an extremely important factor in hard real-time systems, that is those with deadlines which must not be missed.

6.2.2 Infinite numbers, model numbers and error bounds

Our theoretical number scale is an infinite one, having infinite range and infinite resolution, Fig.6.4(a).

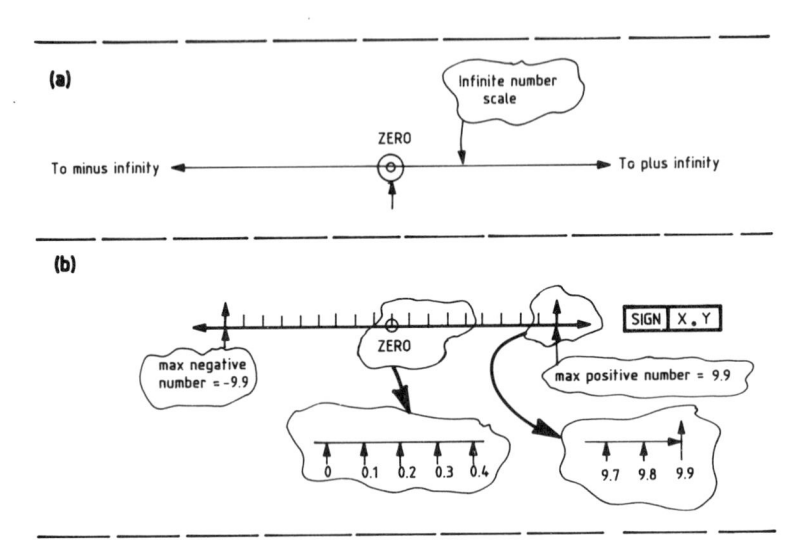

Fig.6.4 Number scale – theoretical and fixed point values.

However, in practical situations, we have to limit the number of digits used. Therefore we can represent only a small portion of this infinite scale. Take, for instance, the situation shown in Fig.6.4(b). This is the number scale for the fixed point format

$$\pm X.Y$$

where X and Y are single decimal digits. The maximum values are ±9.9, giving a range of −9.9 to +9.9. The resolution is 0.1. Thus all numbers which fall within this range have to be represented by a number system which has 199 discrete values. So when is the representation error free? Only if a true value coincides with one of these predefined (or *model*) numbers. Now, in practice, we never know what values are going to emerge from our calculations. Therefore the only safe approach is to assume that the maximum possible error will always occur. The next question is: what is the size of this error? This depends on whether we truncate numbers or round them off. Truncation cuts off the less significant digits of the true number to give us a model number. In contrast, rounding adjusts the true value to be equal to the nearest model number. For example, using the fixed point representation of Fig.6.4, we could have:

The limitations of finite number systems 167

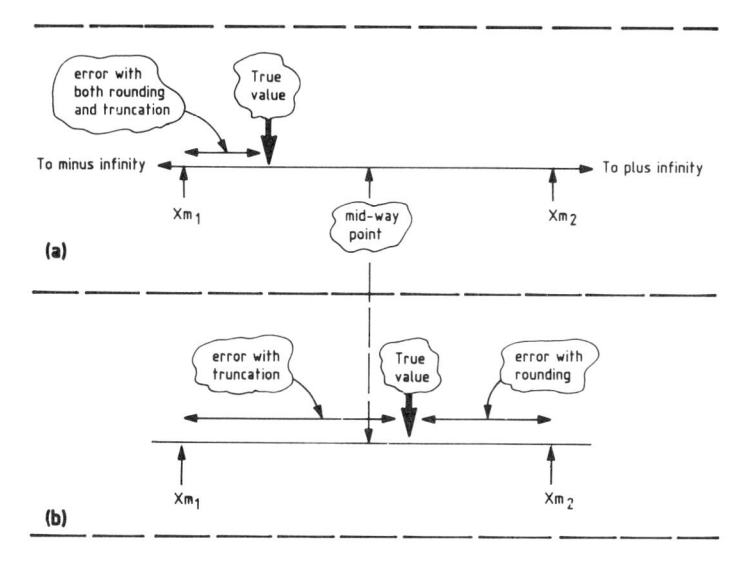

Fig.6.5 Errors due to rounding and truncation.

Original number	Operation	True result	Truncated	Rounded
5.8	÷ 5	1.16	1.1	1.2
5.4	÷ 5	1.08	1.0	1.1
5.6	÷ 5	1.12	1.1	1.1
5.75	÷ 5	1.15	1.1	1.2

These points are illustrated in Fig.6.5.

It should be clear that truncation can generate an error as great (almost) as one least significant digit. For the example above this value is 0.1, giving an error range of 0 to 0.1. With rounding this maximum is reduced by one-half, giving an error range of 0 to ±0.05.

Note that if we can control the resolution (the *step* or *delta*) value then we also control the error size. This example also demonstrates another point: once the resolution is defined the maximum error has a fixed, absolute, value. It is always the same, no matter where we are on our number scale.

Now let's examine floating point numbers. Take the very simple two-digit representation

$$X \times 10^y$$

where X is a single-digit mantissa and y is a single-digit exponent. Fig.6.6 shows three number scales corresponding to y = 0, 1 and −1.

168 Number crunching in Ada

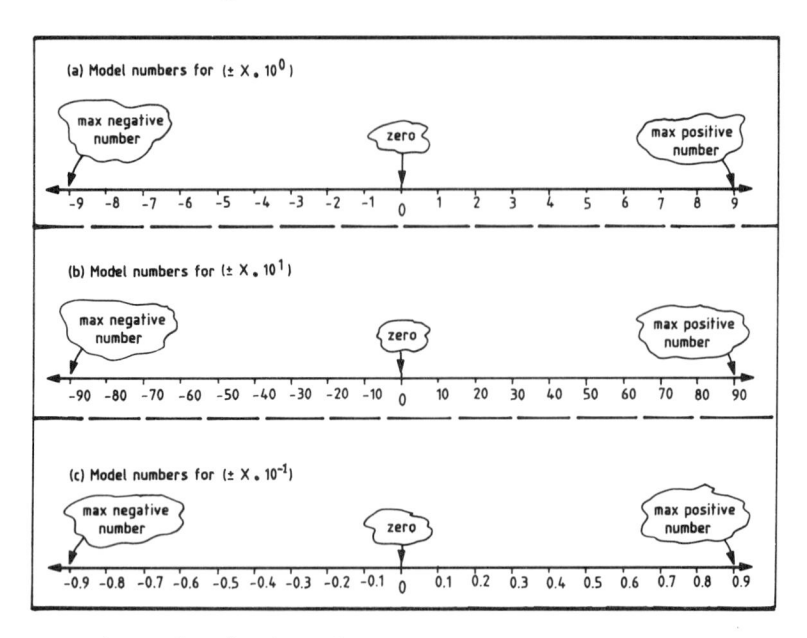

Fig.6.6 Number scale – floating point.

Each one has a defined number range with a defined resolution. However, both factors depend on the value of exponent. The resolution on any one scale is fixed, being proportional to one least significant digit (LSD). But the absolute value of this depends on the exponent, given by

$$\text{Precision} = (\text{least\_significant\_digit\_value}) \times 10^y$$

and the maximum error (assuming rounding) is half this value. For the example of Fig.6.6:

Representation	LSD = 1 × 10^y	Max. error = $\frac{1}{2}$ LSD
(a) X × 10^0	1 × 10^0 = 1	±0.5
(b) X × 10^1	1 × 10^1 = 10	±5
(c) X × 10^{-1}	1 × 10^{-1} = 0.1	±0.05

What is the meaning of this in terms of numerical errors? If numbers used in a calculation have equal exponents, the maximum possible error is the same for each number. That is, in relative terms, they are fixed. However, the absolute value of this error depends on the exponent. It can be seen clearly from the above example that the absolute error size increases as the exponent gets larger.

The limitations of finite number systems 169

How does this affect us in terms of precision and error bounds? Assume that the number of digits allocated to the mantissa is fixed (the usual practical situation). Then the model number range is defined by the size of the exponent. If our problem requires a large number range we need to use a large exponent. But the absolute precision reduces as the exponent increases – and the absolute error band increases. So, for floating point operations, we can have large number ranges and high precision – but not simultaneously.

The essential differences between practical fixed and floating point number representation are that:

- Fixed point arithmetic gives us fixed precision of working. However, it requires many digits to represent both very small and very large numbers. In general, as we increase the degree of precision of computer numbers, calculation times become longer.
- Floating point arithmetic enables us to express large number ranges using few digits. In such situations calculations can be made considerably faster than the equivalent fixed point operations. However, the degree of precision obtained varies with the size of the number being manipulated.

6.2.3 Problems in floating point working

The purpose of this section is to alert the reader to some major issues relating to floating point arithmetic. It does not set out to give a detailed, mathematically rigorous, description of such issues. That is beyond the scope of this text.

Two particular factors are at the bottom of most floating point numerical problems: loss of information and violation of basic mathematical laws. These are illustrated in the numeric operations outlined below.

(a) Changing the exponent value

Suppose that our computer allows us to represent floating point numbers using four digits for the mantissa and one for the exponent. Thus the value 1200 would be represented as

| 1200×10^0 | in written form and | 1 2 0 0 | 0 | within the machine.

Now let's consider what happens when we change the exponent value. As shown in Fig.6.7, each time we increase the exponent by 1 we shift the mantissa number one place to the right. Let us assume that we merely discard the rightmost digit after this shift. In the example here there is no problem until the exponent is increased from 2 to 3. Now the number held in the

170 Number crunching in Ada

TRUE VALUE	COMPUTER REPRESENTATION		COMPUTER VALUE
	MANTISSA	EXPONENT	
1200×10^0	1 2 0 0	0	1200
120×10^1	0 1 2 0	1	1200
12×10^2	0 0 1 2	2	1200
1.2×10^3	0 0 0 1	3	1000
0.12×10^4	0 0 0 0	4	0
12000×10^{-1}	2 0 0 0	-1	200

Fig.6.7 Mantissa–exponent relationship.

computer has changed from 1200 to 1000, a considerable loss of information. But even more dramatic is the last shift: the computer internal value drops to zero.

This shows how we can lose information even without performing mathematical calculations. Moreover, in this example, decreasing the exponent (to −1) produces a major error in the number. We lose the most significant digit. By contrast, shifting the mantissa rightwards results in a loss of the least significant digit.

In practice, most computer systems use the same general method for representing floating point values. The rule used for writing the mantissa is to present the radix (in this case decimal) point to the extreme left of the mantissa. Thus:

$$1200 \equiv 0.1200 \times 10^4 \quad \text{giving}$$
$$\text{Mantissa} = 1200, \quad \text{Exponent} = 4$$

With such representations the mantissa is often called the fractional part of the floating point number. The following text assumes the use of this notation.

(b) **Adding and subtracting numbers**

It was pointed out earlier that to add/subtract floating point numbers, their exponents must be equal (aligned). But, if we have to adjust exponents, should one or both be changed? To simplify computing software or hardware we leave one fixed. The other exponents are aligned with the selected one. But which one? The example above gives the answer to this – the one with the largest exponent. Then, when the other exponents are aligned (increasing their exponents), only least significant digits will be lost. This effect is illustrated in Fig.6.8.

The limitations of finite number systems   171

TRUE VALUE	COMPUTER REPRESENTATION	ALIGNED VALUES	COMPUTER VALUE
$x_1 = 1200$	[1|2|0|0] [4]	[1|2|0|0] [4]	
$x_2 = 162$	[1|6|2|0] [3]	[0|1|6|2] [4]	
$x_1 + x_2 = 1362$		[1|3|6|2] [4]	→ 1362
$x_1 = 1200$	[1|2|0|0] [4]	[1|2|0|0] [4]	
$x_2 = 1.62$	[1|6|2|0] [1]	[0|0|0|1] [4]	
$x_1 + x_2 = 1201.62$		[1|2|0|1] [4]	→ 1201

Fig.6.8 Errors in floating point addition.

TRUE VALUE	COMPUTER REPRESENTATION	COMPUTER VALUE	% ERROR
$x_1 = 12054$	[1|2|0|5] [5]	12050	0.0332
$x_2 = 12040$	[1|2|0|4] [5]	12040	0
$(x_1 - x_2) = 14$	[0|0|0|1] [5]	→ 10	≃ 30%

Fig.6.9 Errors when subtracting similar values.

In the first part of the example – adding 1200 to 162 – the computed result is correct. However, in the second part, data has been lost due to the rightward shift of the smaller mantissa. This illustrates an important feature of floating point numbers – error build-up when adding or subtracting very large and very small numbers.

It might seem that we are on safe ground when dealing with similar-sized numbers. Unfortunately, no. Major errors can occur when subtracting numbers which are close together, as shown in Fig.6.9. The problem is caused by the limited resolution of the mantissa.

One of the basic laws of arithmetic is the associative law. This says that, when we perform calculations, the order doesn't matter. For instance:

$$(A - B) + C = (-B + C) + A$$

With limited precision arithmetic this law may break down, as shown in Fig.6.10.

This example assumes that only four digits are available to hold the mantissa value, as in the previous cases. In (a), the result is correct. In (b), the first

172   Number crunching in Ada

	(a)	(b)
INITIAL STATE	(1113 − 1111) + (2.423)	1113 + (−1111 + 2.423)
STEP 1	2 + 2.423	1113 − 1109
STEP 2	4.423	4

Fig.6.10 Breakdown of the associative law of arithmetic.

	(a) FRACTION OVERFLOW	(b) NUMBER OVERFLOW
x_1	9 0 0 0 8	9 0 0 0 9
x_2	6 0 0 0 8	6 0 0 0 9
$x_1 + x_2$	1 5 0 0 0 8	1 5 0 0 0 9
Normalized	1 5 0 0 9	OVERFLOW (error condition)

Fig.6.11 Overflow during addition.

operation, calculating (−1111 + 2.423), produces an error. At this stage it appears to be negligible: 0.423 in 1109, or 0.038%. However, when the next calculation is made, it gives an error of almost 10% in the final result.

When adding numbers together it is possible to produce a result which is too large to be represented, called overflow. Fig.6.11 demonstrates two aspects of this, fraction overflow and number overflow.

In (a), the mantissa addition generates an overflow or carry digit. This isn't a problem as the situation can be corrected by adjusting (or *normalizing*) the exponent. However, part (b) shows addition producing a value which is too large for the defined number system. This overflow must be treated as an error condition.

(c) **Multiplying and dividing numbers**

Multiplication and division are generally easier to deal with than addition/subtraction. We still, though, have to be on our guard for the build-up of errors and the failure of the associative law. The most significant errors are likely to be those of overflow (which we've already dealt with), and *underflow*, illustrated in Fig.6.12.

Here the result of a calculation is too small to be represented within the floating point number system. Although an underflow value is tiny, its effect can be out of all proportion to its size, as shown in Fig.6.13.

This is a rather artificial example. Nevertheless it does highlight the signifi-

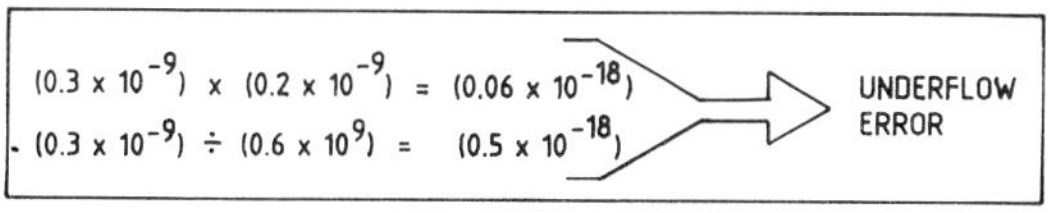

Fig.6.12 Underflow during multiplication and division.

CALCULATION:	$(0.3 \times 10^{-9}) \times (0.2 \times 10^{-9}) \times 10^9 \div 10^{-9} \times 10^9$	
STEP 1	$(0.06 \times 10^{-18}) \times 10^9 \div 10^{-9} \times 10^9$	$(0) \times 10^9 \div 10^{-9} \times 10^9$
FINAL RESULT	$0.06 \times 10^9 = 6 \times 10^7$	0
	RESULT WITH INFINITE PRECISION	RESULT WITH LIMITED PRECISION

Fig.6.13 Error due to underflow.

cance of underflow, especially when it occurs in a chain of calculations. You should now see why this is regarded as a major error, and should be flagged up as such.

6.2.4 Problems in fixed point working

Many of the potential problems of fixed point working are similar to those found in floating point arithmetic. In practice few occur, because fixed point operations are highly visible. Moreover, if we ourselves define number range and precision – instead of leaving it to specific machines – the situation is further improved. For instance, suppose we define a pressure signal to lie in the range 0 to 10 bars with a precision of 0.1 bar. From this we can immediately define our model numbers, and, if required, perform error analysis on numerical operations. When we come to carry out calculations we can define the range and precision of the computations to be used. This also allows us to flag up out-of-range results.

6.2.5 Internal representation and binary notation

(a) Binary–decimal equivalence

All numeric processing in computers is carried out in binary format. Unfortunately this doesn't fit in well with our normal thinking processes – these are geared to decimal (base 10) notation. So it is useful to develop a feel for the relationship between binary and decimal digits. We can arrive at a rough figure surprisingly easily, as follows. A single decimal digit can represent the values 0 to 9. Three binary digits can represent the values 0 to 7. Thus it takes between three and four binary digits to replace one decimal digit (the correct figure is 3.32).

(b) Floating point representation

In floating point notation a relatively small exponent gives us a very large number range. On the other hand we need as many digits as possible for the mantissa – to increase precision and minimize errors. Two particular number ranges are in common use, often defined as short real and long real. Short real uses 24 bits for the fraction and 8 for the exponent. This gives a precision of seven decimal digits or, in fractional terms, seven decimal places. The exponent has the equivalent of two decimal digits, with a range of $10^{\pm 38}$. Long real has a 64 bit mantissa, the precision being 19 decimal digits. The number of bits in the exponent is 11, its range being $10^{\pm 1023}$.

It was pointed out earlier that in floating point operations, the binary point normally lies to the left of the mantissa. Suppose that we have four digits available to hold mantissa values. Further suppose that the true value of a binary number is 0.011011×2^3 (3.375 decimal). We could put this into floating point form in a number of ways, including:

| 0110 | 3 | representing decimal 3.0 (error is 0.375)

| 1101 | 2 | representing decimal 3.25 (error is 0.125)

Observe that by shifting the mantissa as far left as possible we have achieved maximum precision. This is defined to be a normalized floating point number – the standard method in use. Consequently the mantissa values always lie in the range

$0.1 \leq$ mantissa < 1.0 binary, that is
$0.5 \leq$ mantissa < 1.0 decimal

(c) Fixed point representation

It is common practice to make fixed point representation independent of computer architecture. Moreover, positioning of the binary point is usually left to the compiler. This simplifies arithmetic operations and leads to efficient use of data storage space. In such circumstances how does the compiler deduce the required word size and set the binary point? From information supplied by the programmer. One technique is to define the total number of bits needed together with the size of the fractional part. For instance, suppose we decide to use a single word (16 bits) to hold our fixed point variables. We further decide that 5 bits should be allocated to the fractional part. Then a declaration of the form 'FIXED(16,5)' would be used in the source code. The following examples show how this word is used:

Decimal value	Binary value
1.0	00000000001.00000
1.5	00000000001.10000
0.5	00000000000.10000
1023.986 75	01111111111.11111

We could also use a declaration of the form 'FIXED(16, −2)'. This implies that the binary point is two places to the right of the least significant bit. The following is an example in the use of this definition:

Binary value	Decimal value
0000000000000000	0
0000000000000001	4
0000000000000010	8

Similarly, the declaration 'FIXED(16,17)' implies that the binary point is to the left of the most significant digit. This gives, for example,

Binary value	Decimal value
1000000000000000	0.25
1100000000000000	0.375

This technique is quite satisfactory, but it has one deficiency. That is, the details of the number structure must be defined by the programmer. It is much better – and safer – to leave this to the compiler. Further, we should be able to define it in terms of our problem, not the underlying bit representation. Two factors are sufficient to determine the required binary format: range and precision. Consider the following examples:

Range	Precision	Binary format	
0–1	0.5	X.Y	(2 bits)
0–1	0.125	X.YYY	(4 bits)
0–7	0.125	XXX.YYY	(6 bits)
0–6	2.0	XX	(2 bits)

In the first example, to represent decimal numbers in the range 0 to 1 with a precision of 0.5, two binary digits are needed. This, in fact, allows us to cover the range 0 to 1.5 decimal. Similar comments apply to the other items. Note that in the last example the binary point is implied to be one place to the right of the least significant digit.

6.3 HANDLING REAL NUMBER TYPES IN Ada

6.3.1 Introductory comments

'Real' numbers are defined in mathematics as consisting of all rational and irrational numbers. Rational numbers are those which can be expressed as the ratio of two integers, e.g. $\frac{1}{2}$, $\frac{4}{3}$, etc. Irrational numbers (or surds) are those such as $\sqrt{2}$ which cannot be defined in such a way. In Ada we have a 'real type' to represent such numbers. However, this real type can only represent a limited set of the infinite set of real numbers – the so-called model numbers (see section 6.2.2). Real types can be defined using either floating point or fixed point notation. Thus we have two sets of model numbers, one for each notation. Further, model numbers are represented exactly – that is, without error – within the computer. (You may, at this point, be developing a glazed expression, wondering what on earth this is all about. Have patience, there is a good reason for this digression.)

Who, or what, defines the set of model numbers in Ada? First, they may be predefined (strictly this applies only to the floating point type, see section 6.3.2). Second, they can be defined by the programmer. Now this has important implications for the portability of source code. The model numbers of a predefined type may vary from compiler to compiler – they are implementation dependent. Thus a mathematical routine produced using different compilers could actually generate different results at run time. By contrast, a programmer-defined type always contains the same set of model numbers; it doesn't depend on the compiler. Therefore mathematical routines written using such types should be fully transportable between machines (note that if a compiler cannot meet the requirements of a type declaration it should flag up an error).

A last note: in Ada, real numbers contain a radix (usually decimal) point.

6.3.2 Floating point types

(a) General note

As discussed earlier (chapter 2), floating point representation is given by

$$\text{sign.mantissa.radix}^{\text{exponent}}$$

In Ada the mantissa has the range

$$0.5 \leq \text{mantissa} < 1.0$$

Its precision is normally specified in terms of the required number of decimal digits D. Within the computer this is held as a binary number of B bits. The relationship between D and B is given as

$$B \geq [(3.32 \times D) + 1] \geq (B - 1)$$

where B is a whole number. The exponent range is defined in terms of B as

$$-4B \leq \text{exponent} \leq +4B$$

For example, suppose we require a mantissa precision of six decimal digits. Then

$$B \geq [(3.32 \times 6) + 1] \geq (B - 1)$$
$$B \geq 20.92 \geq (B - 1), \text{ giving } B = 21$$

The corresponding exponent range is ±4B, that is ±84.

Note that this needs eight binary digits for its representation (sign plus value).

(b) Predefined type FLOAT

It can be useful and instructive to obtain the numerical qualities of your own specific predefined type FLOAT. The following information relating to the model numbers can be obtained:

- The number of decimal digits in the mantissa (DIGITS);
- The number of binary digits in the mantissa (MANTISSA);
- The largest exponent value (EMAX);
- The smallest positive number (SMALL);
- The largest positive number (LARGE);
- The value of the difference between the number '1' and the next number above it (EPSILON).

We obtain these using the predefined language attributes as shown in Listing 6.1.

(c) Defining our own precision

In Ada we define the required precision of floating point types in a very simple way. The declaration format is

178   Number crunching in Ada

```
with TEXT_IO;                 use TEXT_IO;
procedure PREDEFINED is
  package INT_IO is new INTEGER_IO (INTEGER);
  package REAL_IO is new FLOAT_IO (FLOAT);
begin
  PUT ("Mantissa - number of decimal digits => ");
  INT_IO.PUT (FLOAT'DIGITS);
  NEW_LINE;
  PUT_LINE ("This is the :");
  PUT ("Mantissa - number of binary digits  => ");
  INT_IO.PUT (FLOAT'MANTISSA);
  NEW_LINE;
  PUT ("Largest exponent value              => ");
  INT_IO.PUT (FLOAT'EMAX);
  NEW_LINE;
  PUT ("Smallest positive model number      => ");
  REAL_IO.PUT (FLOAT'SMALL);
  NEW_LINE;
  PUT ("Largest positive model number       => ");
  REAL_IO.PUT (FLOAT'LARGE);
  NEW_LINE;
  PUT ("Epsilon value                       => ");
  REAL_IO.PUT (FLOAT'EPSILON);
  NEW_LINE;
end PREDEFINED;
```

Listing 6.1 Information relating to the model numbers using the predefined language attributes.

> **type** TYPE_NAME **is digits** NUMBER_OF_DIGITS_REQUIRED;

as, for example,

> **type** VELOCITY **is digits** 4;

The model numbers for this type are guaranteed to have at least a precision of four decimal places. But be aware that, in practice, you may well get more than this.

In this example the type VELOCITY is really a derived type of the predefined type FLOAT. Clearly we cannot get a precision greater than the predefined type. Listing 6.2 illustrates the points raised here.

(d) **Introducing range constraints**

In addition to defining a required precision for a number we can also limit its range of values. The declaration format is

> **type** T **is digits** D **range** L..R;

Handling real number types in Ada   179

```
with TEXT_IO;                   use TEXT_IO;
procedure IS_DIGITS_4 is
  type VELOCITY is digits 4;
  package VELOCITY_IO is new FLOAT_IO (VELOCITY);
  use VELOCITY_IO;
  CURRENT_VELOCITY :    VELOCITY;
begin
  CURRENT_VELOCITY := 322.120034;
  PUT ("CURRENT_VELOCITY (322.120034)     => ");
  PUT (CURRENT_VELOCITY);
  NEW_LINE;
  CURRENT_VELOCITY := 3221200.34;
  PUT ("CURRENT_VELOCITY (3,221,200.34)   => ");
  PUT (CURRENT_VELOCITY);
  NEW_LINE;
  CURRENT_VELOCITY := 0.00322120034;
  PUT ("CURRENT_VELOCITY (0.00322120034) => ");
  PUT (CURRENT_VELOCITY);
  NEW_LINE;
end IS_DIGITS_4;
```

Listing 6.2 First example showing floating point representation and how defining precision works.

as in

> **type** VELOCITY **is digits** 6 **range** 0.0..1000.0;

Listing 6.3 uses floating point types having range constraints.

(e) **Using subtypes**

We are allowed to define subtypes of a floating point type, so gaining the advantages of using subtypes. Consider the following type declaration:

> **type** ANGLES **is digits** 7 **range** 0.0..360.0;

From this the following subtypes could be formed:

(a) to limit the range:

> **subtype** QUADRANT_1_ANGLES **is** ANGLES **range** 0.0..90.0;

(b) to reduce the precision:

> **subtype** AZIMUTH **is** ANGLES **digits** 4;

180 Number crunching in Ada

```
with TEXT_IO;              use TEXT_IO;
procedure USING_RANGE is
   type VELOCITY is digits 6 range 0.0 .. 1000.0;
   package VELOCITY_IO is new FLOAT_IO (VELOCITY);
   use VELOCITY_IO;
   CURRENT_VELOCITY :    VELOCITY;
begin
   CURRENT_VELOCITY := 0.0000322120034;
   PUT ("CURRENT_VELOCITY (0.0000322120034) => ");
   PUT (CURRENT_VELOCITY);
   NEW_LINE;
   CURRENT_VELOCITY := 555.5555;
   PUT ("CURRENT_VELOCITY (555.5555)          => ");
   PUT (CURRENT_VELOCITY);
   NEW_LINE;
   CURRENT_VELOCITY := 1000.0;
   PUT ("CURRENT_VELOCITY (1000.0)            => ");
   PUT (CURRENT_VELOCITY);
   NEW_LINE;
end USING_RANGE;
```

Listing 6.3 Example showing precision and range.

(c) to modify range and precision attributes:

> **subtype** ELEVATION **is** ANGLES **digits** 4 **range** 0.0..90.0;

These aspects are illustrated in Listing 6.4.

Note that when carrying out floating point arithmetic all operands must be the same type.

6.3.3 Fixed point types

From the user's point of view Ada doesn't have predefined fixed point types. Thus before using fixed point operations appropriate types have to be declared. The first attribute to be defined is the maximum allowable error in the number – the accuracy requirement. For instance, suppose that we can tolerate a maximum error of ±0.1° in an angle measurement. You might think that, for this case, a suitable declaration would be

> **type** ELEVATION_ANGLE **is delta** 0.1;

The delta value is used to define the maximum allowable error in variables of type ELEVATION_ANGLE. In other words, all numbers will be precise to ±0.1 units. However, this is not sufficient to specify the set of model

```
with TEXT_IO;                use TEXT_IO;
procedure FLOAT_TEST is
  type ANGLES is digits 7 range 0.0 .. 360.0;
  subtype QUADRANT_1_ANGLES is ANGLES range 0.0 .. 90.0;
  subtype AZIMUTH is ANGLES digits 4;
  subtype ELEVATION is ANGLES digits 4 range 0.0 .. 90.0 ;
  package ANGLE_IO is new FLOAT_IO (ANGLES);
  package ELEVATION_IO is new FLOAT_IO (ELEVATION);
  TRACK_ANGLE        :    ANGLES;
  CURRENT_ELEVATION :    ELEVATION;
begin
  TRACK_ANGLE := 3.1213;
  PUT ("TRACK_ANGLE       => ");
  ANGLE_IO.PUT (TRACK_ANGLE);
  NEW_LINE;
  TRACK_ANGLE := TRACK_ANGLE + TRACK_ANGLE;
  PUT ("TRACK_ANGLE       => ");
  ANGLE_IO.PUT (TRACK_ANGLE);
  NEW_LINE;
  TRACK_ANGLE := TRACK_ANGLE * 14.0;
  PUT ("TRACK_ANGLE       => ");
  ANGLE_IO.PUT (TRACK_ANGLE);
  NEW_LINE (2);
  CURRENT_ELEVATION := 3.1213;
  PUT ("CURRENT_ELEVATION => ");
  ELEVATION_IO.PUT (CURRENT_ELEVATION);
  NEW_LINE;
  CURRENT_ELEVATION := CURRENT_ELEVATION + CURRENT_ELEVATION;
  PUT ("CURRENT_ELEVATION => ");
  ELEVATION_IO.PUT (CURRENT_ELEVATION);
  NEW_LINE;
  CURRENT_ELEVATION := CURRENT_ELEVATION * 14.0;
  PUT ("CURRENT_ELEVATION => ");
  ELEVATION_IO.PUT (CURRENT_ELEVATION);
  NEW_LINE (2);
end FLOAT_TEST;
```

Listing 6.4 Showing subtypes and range attributes.

numbers. More information is needed. We also have to supply the range of numbers to be represented by the type. Combining precision and range factors gives us the general declaration form:

type TYPE_NAME **is delta** ACCURACY_DEFINITION **range** Lower..Upper;

A typical declaration example is

type ELEVATION_ANGLE **is delta** 0.1 **range** 0.0..90.0;

Thus all variables of type ELEVATION_ANGLE must lie in the range 0 to 90 units, having a maximum error in the number of 0.1 units.

182 Number crunching in Ada

```ada
with TEXT_IO;              use TEXT_IO;
procedure FIXED_POINT is
  type DISTANCE is delta 0.1 range 0.0 .. 200.0;
  type SPEED is delta 0.01 range 0.0 .. 200.0;
  package DIST_IO is new FIXED_IO ( DISTANCE );
  use DIST_IO;
  package SPEED_IO is new FIXED_IO ( SPEED );
  use SPEED_IO;
  CURRENT_DISTANCE :    DISTANCE;
  CURRENT_SPEED    :    SPEED;
begin
  CURRENT_DISTANCE := 0.0;
  PUT ("CURRENT_DISTANCE => ");
  PUT (CURRENT_DISTANCE);
  NEW_LINE;
  CURRENT_SPEED := 0.0;
  PUT ("CURRENT_SPEED    => ");
  PUT (CURRENT_SPEED);
  NEW_LINE;
  CURRENT_DISTANCE := 56.472;
  PUT ("CURRENT_DISTANCE => ");
  PUT (CURRENT_DISTANCE);
  NEW_LINE;
  CURRENT_SPEED := 56.472;
  PUT ("CURRENT_SPEED    => ");
  PUT (CURRENT_SPEED);
  NEW_LINE;
  CURRENT_DISTANCE := 56.478;
  PUT ("CURRENT_DISTANCE => ");
  PUT (CURRENT_DISTANCE);
  NEW_LINE;
  CURRENT_SPEED := 56.478;
  PUT ("CURRENT_SPEED    => ");
  PUT (CURRENT_SPEED);
  NEW_LINE;
  CURRENT_DISTANCE := 150.0;
  PUT ("CURRENT_DISTANCE => ");
  PUT (CURRENT_DISTANCE);
  NEW_LINE;
  CURRENT_SPEED := 150.0;
  PUT ("CURRENT_SPEED    => ");
  PUT (CURRENT_SPEED);
  NEW_LINE;
end FIXED_POINT;
```

Listing 6.5 Fixed point declarations.

Listing 6.5 is one example of the use of fixed point variables.

This is fairly straightforward, but consider where we declare a number of fixed point types – and wish to mix them. Can this be done? And if so, what are the limitations? First let us consider addition and subtraction, using the unary adding operators + and –. Here, as illustrated in Listing 6.6, all types must be identical.

When it comes to multiplication and division the situation is different. Here we have the rare situation where implicit type mixing is allowed. This is summarized for the operations A∗B and A/B:

Handling real number types in Ada 183

```
with TEXT_IO;                 use TEXT_IO;
procedure FIXED_ARITHMETIC is
  type DISTANCE is delta 0.1 range 0.0 .. 200.0;
  type SPEED is delta 0.01 range 0.0 .. 200.0;
  package DISTANCE_IO is new FIXED_IO (DISTANCE);
  use DISTANCE_IO;
  CURRENT_DISTANCE         :    DISTANCE;
  DISTANCE_LAST_READING    :    DISTANCE      :=  54.397;
  CURRENT_SPEED            :    SPEED         :=  29.5788;
begin
  CURRENT_DISTANCE := 0.0;
  PUT (CURRENT_DISTANCE);
  NEW_LINE;
  -- literal arithmetic
  CURRENT_DISTANCE := 54.3 + 29.1;
  PUT (CURRENT_DISTANCE);
  NEW_LINE;
  --   arithmetic
  CURRENT_DISTANCE := CURRENT_DISTANCE + 5.8356;
  PUT (CURRENT_DISTANCE);
  NEW_LINE;
  --   arithmetic
  CURRENT_DISTANCE := CURRENT_DISTANCE + DISTANCE_LAST_READING;
  PUT (CURRENT_DISTANCE);
  NEW_LINE;
  --   arithmetic
  CURRENT_DISTANCE := DISTANCE_LAST_READING - 20.01;
  PUT (CURRENT_DISTANCE);
  NEW_LINE;
  -- The following line is not allowed due to normal typing rules
  --     CURRENT_DISTANCE := CURRENT_DISTANCE + CURRENT_SPEED;
  --     PUT (CURRENT_DISTANCE);
  --     NEW_LINE;
  -- Type conversion solves the problem
  CURRENT_DISTANCE := CURRENT_DISTANCE + DISTANCE(CURRENT_SPEED);
  PUT (CURRENT_DISTANCE);
  NEW_LINE;
end FIXED_ARITHMETIC;
```

Listing 6.6 Fixed point arithmetic (addition and subtraction).

Op.	Type A	Type B	Result type
A*B	Any fixed point type	INTEGER	Same as A
A*B	INTEGER	Any fixed point type	Same as B
A*B	Any fixed point type	Any fixed point type	Universal fixed
A/B	Any fixed point type	INTEGER	Same as A
A/B	Any fixed point type	Any fixed point type	Universal fixed

Note that where both operands are fixed point types, the result type is *universal fixed*. This is an Ada predefined fixed point type which has infinite accuracy. However, such a value does not exist in the computer. Therefore it must be converted to an actual numeric type before it can be used in further calculations. Listing 6.7 demonstrates type mixing of fixed point operands.

```ada
with TEXT_IO;              use TEXT_IO;
procedure FIXED_FURTHER_ARITHMETIC is
  type DISTANCE is delta 0.1 range 0.0 .. 200.0;
  type SPEED is delta 0.01 range 0.0 .. 200.0;
  package DISTANCE_IO is new FIXED_IO (DISTANCE);
  use DISTANCE_IO;
  CURRENT_DISTANCE       :    DISTANCE;
  DISTANCE_LAST_READING  :    DISTANCE       := 1.0;
  CURRENT_SPEED          :    SPEED          := 1.0;
  INT_VALUE              :    INTEGER        := 1;
begin
  CURRENT_DISTANCE := 54.3;
-------------------------------------------------------------------------------
  -- Multiplication Section
-------------------------------------------------------------------------------
  --  Fixed * Int Literal = Fixed
  CURRENT_DISTANCE := CURRENT_DISTANCE * 3;
  --  Fixed * Int variable = Fixed
  CURRENT_DISTANCE := CURRENT_DISTANCE * INT_VALUE;
  --  Int variable * Fixed = Fixed
  CURRENT_DISTANCE := INT_VALUE * DISTANCE_LAST_READING;
  -- The following line is not allowed as the result is universal_fixed
  --    CURRENT_DISTANCE := CURRENT_DISTANCE * CURRENT_SPEED;
  -- This works
  CURRENT_DISTANCE := DISTANCE (CURRENT_DISTANCE * CURRENT_SPEED);
  -- This will fail at compilation time as 2.0 is a universal real
  -- CURRENT_DISTANCE := DISTANCE (CURRENT_DISTANCE * 2.0);
  -- This will compile and work by using type conversion
  CURRENT_DISTANCE := DISTANCE (CURRENT_DISTANCE * DISTANCE (2.0));
  -- and even this will fail (both same type!), as result is still universal
  -- fixed
  -- CURRENT_DISTANCE := CURRENT_DISTANCE * DISTANCE_LAST_READING
  -- But this is okay
  CURRENT_DISTANCE := DISTANCE (CURRENT_DISTANCE * DISTANCE_LAST_READING);
-------------------------------------------------------------------------------
  -- Division Section
-------------------------------------------------------------------------------
  --  Fixed / Int Literal = Fixed
  CURRENT_DISTANCE := CURRENT_DISTANCE / 3;
  --  Fixed / Int variable = Fixed
  CURRENT_DISTANCE := CURRENT_DISTANCE / INT_VALUE;
  --  Int variable / Fixed = Not allowed in fixed point arithmetic
  -- CURRENT_DISTANCE := INT_VALUE / DISTANCE_LAST_READING;
  -- The following line is not allowed as the result is universal_fixed
  --    CURRENT_DISTANCE := CURRENT_DISTANCE / CURRENT_SPEED;
  -- This works
  CURRENT_DISTANCE := DISTANCE (CURRENT_DISTANCE / CURRENT_SPEED);
  -- This will not compile as 2.0 is a universal real
  -- CURRENT_DISTANCE := DISTANCE (CURRENT_DISTANCE / 2.0);
  -- But this will
  CURRENT_DISTANCE := DISTANCE (CURRENT_DISTANCE / DISTANCE (2.0));
  -- and even this will fail due to result being universal fixed
  -- CURRENT_DISTANCE := CURRENT_DISTANCE / DISTANCE_LAST_READING
  -- But this is okay
  CURRENT_DISTANCE := DISTANCE (CURRENT_DISTANCE / DISTANCE_LAST_READING);
end FIXED_FURTHER_ARITHMETIC;
```

Listing 6.7 Fixed point arithmetic (multiplication and division).

This may seem to be confusing on a first read-through. We suggest that you refer back to the rules outlined above whilst digesting the listing information.

REVIEW

If you now:

- understand the extent and severity of errors in numerical operations;
- understand the basics of positional number systems, together with fixed point and floating point notation;
- appreciate the difference between the infinite and the model number set;
- realize why errors are generated by calculations involving floating or fixed point operations;
- comprehend the methods for handling real numbers within computers;
- know how to write Ada programs to manipulate both fixed and floating point numbers;

then you will understand why the problems described in section 6.1.1 arose:

(a) The logical test 'is X negative?' can give the wrong result if X is a very small negative number. In such an instance the actual value is converted to the nearest model number – which in this instance is zero. Thus the answer to the test is no.
(b) When the value of an angle changes, its cosine value also changes – but not by the same ratio. For instance, if there is a 1° change in angle, the change in the cosine value depends on the angle itself:

θ	Cos θ	$\Delta\theta$	$\Delta\cos\theta$
45°	0.7071		
		1.0	0.0124
46°	0.6947		

θ°	Cos θ	$\Delta\theta$	$\Delta\cos\theta$
0°	1.0000		
		1.0	0.0001
1°	0.9999		

The values given here are accurate to four decimal places. So we may be able to represent the difference between two angle values in our model number system, but not the difference between their cosines. In such a case the two actual cosine values are represented by the same model number.

(c) Suppose the value of ϕ is 0.000 124 6 radians. Then $(2\pi - \phi)$ is 3.141 468 1. The question is: can we represent both numbers with the same degree of precision? If not, numerical accuracy suffers.
(d) Any difference produced by changing the order of the operands is clearly a case of failure of the associative law.

Chapter Seven
Modular construction, information hiding and the package

We now come to what probably makes Ada different to most earlier programming languages, the 'package'. Through the use of the package we can divide a total program into a number of smaller segments, the objective being to enhance reliability and productivity. Earlier we saw how subprograms help us to attain such goals; the package takes us many more steps along this road.

After studying this chapter you will:

- Understand the need for modularity to achieve reliable programming;
- Appreciate the difference between monolithic, modular and independent compilation techniques;
- Perceive the design formality and control introduced by Ada through the use of packages and related **with** and **use** clauses;
- Know which package types are provided in Ada, what their functions are, how they communicate with each other and how they are structured;
- Understand the difference between static and dynamic variables;
- Be able to write and compile package specifications, package bodies and combined specification/body units;
- Know how to deal with chained sets of packages and program units;
- Understand the concept of package elaboration and initialization.

7.1 FUNDAMENTAL IDEAS

7.1.1 Introduction

The work we've carried out so far shows that an Ada program consists of a series of major building blocks called subprograms. Every specimen program has been put together to conform with the modular structure of the language in two ways. First, each main program has been structured as a single unit, defined to be a procedure. Second, various library facilities (e.g. TEXT_IO) have been called into use within the programs via the **with** clause. Fine. So why do we need to study the topic of modularity? Why is it considered to be such an important topic in modern software engineering? After all, people have (apparently) managed quite all right with Basic for years now.

This question goes right to the heart of good software design and is much broader than the simple 'Basic vs. Ada' type of duel. In essence it questions the whole design approach of the block-structured languages (the grandaddy of them all being Algol 60). Ada has taken these ideas much further than earlier languages such as Pascal, Coral 66 and RTL2, the purpose being to support implicitly reliable software design. Hence the key question is 'what are we trying to do?', the 'how' actually being much less important. In this chapter we're going to answer both questions, at the same time showing how Ada's structure forces us into good design techniques.

7.1.2 Fundamental design methods

Software design techniques can be split into three major groups: monolithic, independent and modular. These, in reality, are not mutually exclusive approaches. Many programmers use combinations of these when writing source code – which probably says more about the rigour and discipline of software design as practised rather than preached. The concepts behind these methods can be grasped fairly easily by looking at a simple DIY task, the design and build of a kit-car.

Method 1, 'monolithic', is illustrated in Fig.7.1.

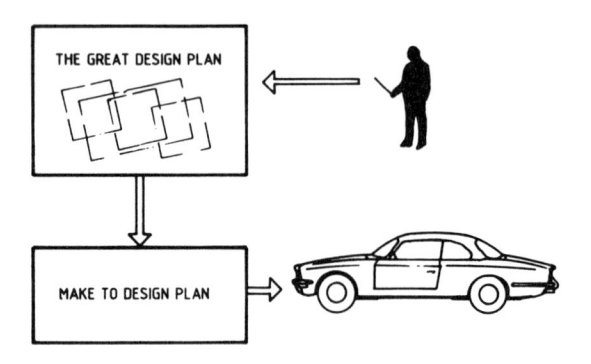

Fig.7.1 Monolithic design and make.

Work begins by producing an all-embracing design plan. That is, the problem is considered as consisting of a single design task. Once the design is complete the car can be built to the plan's specifications and instructions.

Fundamental ideas 189

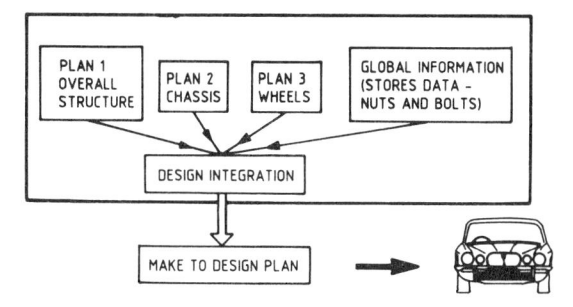

Fig.7.2 Modular design.

Method 2, 'modular', tackles the problem in a different way at the design stage (Fig.7.2).

An overall design plan is produced together with individual designs for major subsystems such as chassis, wheels, etc. The design can be carried out either by one individual, as in method 1, or else by a number of designers who can work on the job simultaneously. When design work is finished, the various subsystem designs are integrated to produce a manufacturing workplan. Manufacture takes place as in method 1.

Note a significant difference between these two methods. In the first one, as the design is monolithic, all information relating to the system is implicitly available at all times. However, in the second method this may not be the case. Some information just doesn't need sharing; it's private or 'local' to that particular design activity. However, other information does have to be made generally available. For instance, both the wheel and the suspension system designers need to know the wheel/drive shaft coupling arrangement. Otherwise there's no guarantee that the items will fit together correctly. Question: How are these details made known throughout the design team? Simply by explicitly defining design data which is to be made available to all parties, the so-called 'global' information.

In the third design method the idea of splitting the total task into a number of 'independent' subtasks is taken one stage further. Not only is the design compartmentalized, the same ideas are applied to manufacturing as well (Fig.7.3). It is at the final production stage that all parts come together in what is basically an assembly operation. Only the interfacing details of the subsystems are important, assuming, of course, that the design itself is satisfactory.

Note also that the final assembly is essentially divorced from the detailed design process. This means that we can develop optional designs and choose the most appropriate one at assembly stage (compare this with selecting either a 1.3 or 1.6 litre engine in a standard production car).

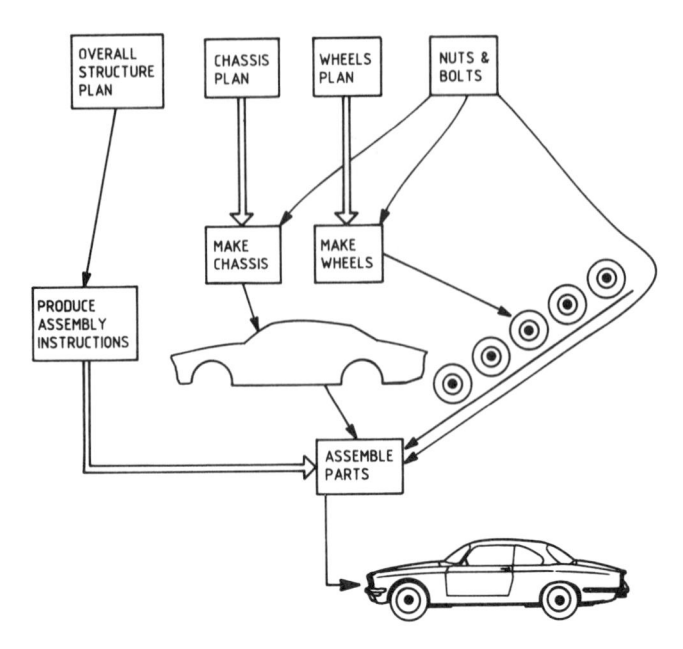

190 Modular construction, information hiding and the package

Fig.7.3 Independent design.

7.1.3 Monolithic, modular and independent operations – an evaluation

(a) Monolithic operation

The monolithic method will clearly work best where one person only is concerned with the design and build programme. For simple tasks it works quite well. As the project becomes more complex, though, the design document itself becomes equally complex. In the end only one person may be capable of understanding it, the original designer. Further, the technique inherently makes it very difficult to split the job amongst a number of designers.

Now consider what happens when a revision to the operation of a unit is requested. The complete design plan has to be assessed in the light of any changes, a time-consuming and costly effort. Once changes are made a full rebuild is necessary before we can even begin to evaluate the resulting effects. And this is where many problems really start. In a complex system the introduction of just a single revision may very well produce a 'knock-on' effect, leading to totally undesirable (and unpredicted) side effects. As a result it can be extremely difficult to maintain such designs once they are in service.

Fundamental ideas 191

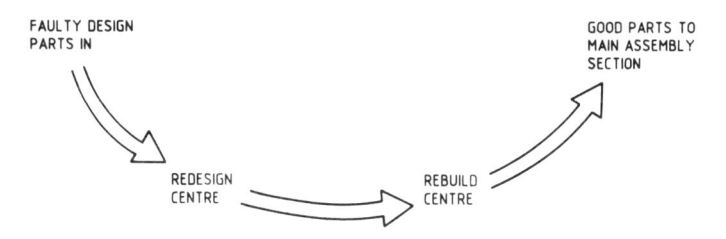

Fig.7.4 Design modification procedure – independent operation.

(b) Modular operation

By breaking up the complete problem into a series of smaller ones even quite complex designs can be managed comfortably. Moreover, individual subtasks may be handled simultaneously by different designers. This assumes, of course, that the job is properly co-ordinated. As a result, designs become more understandable and can be completed more quickly.

What about introducing modifications to an existing program? Here significant advantages have been gained over the monolithic approach. Individual changes are likely to be quite localized, possibly affecting only one subtask. Hence the effects of such changes can be quickly evaluated. Further, they are far less likely to lead to unwanted side effects. The disadvantage, though, is that a complete rebuild is needed to carry out any change in a production unit.

Apart from this last point, does the modular approach have any other major drawback? Unfortunately, yes. Global information, by definition, is available to all design sections. Consequently it may also be modified by any individual as work progresses. Where only one designer is involved this probably won't be a problem. Where the design is a team effort global information falls into the category of 'accidents waiting to happen'. Without rigorous project control, changes to the global values (especially undocumented ones) can produce design chaos.

(c) Independent operation

This sets out to minimize the shortcomings of the modular method of working. All of the advantages gained at the design stage are retained but are now extended into manufacture as well. This has a tremendous impact on product development and maintenance. For instance, suppose a fault shows up in a gearbox which calls for redesign action. Now we can limit the design and build operations to the gearbox and its interfacing components (Fig.7.4). This minimizes the time taken to implement and test the change. It also reduces the likelihood of side effects.

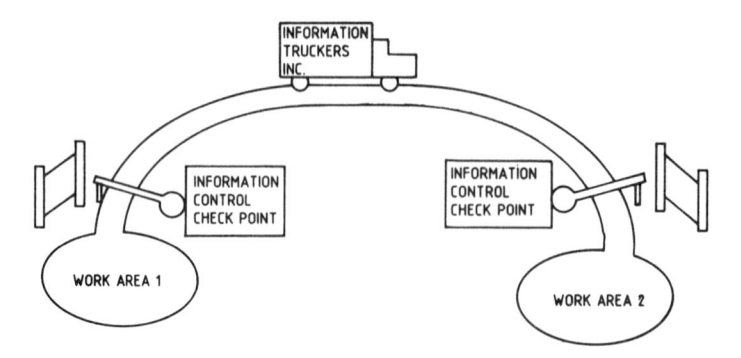

192 Modular construction, information hiding and the package

Fig.7.5 Controlling information flow.

What about global information? Clearly, when designs are carried out as described here, information has to be passed between individual subtasks – which brings us back to the use of a 'global bin' of information. The only way to prevent (in reality, minimize) errors caused by the abuse of global values is NOT to use globals. This means that information interchange must be handled in a more controlled (and probably more complex) way, Fig.7.5.

7.2 SOFTWARE CONSTRUCTION METHODS

From the previous section you should have grasped the basic concepts of the three different constructional methods. Now let's put them in the context of software design and compilation (Fig.7.6).

Monolithic program development is directly analogous to the first method outlined above in Fig.7.1. Standard Basic forces us to use this approach, the language essentially being simple and straightforward. Here the source program is written out in its entirety as a series of successive statements, that is one large block. Compilation to object code may then be carried out.

Standard Pascal allows us to use a 'building-block' approach in the design of the software. The blocks are realized as a series of subtasks (or subprograms) based on the use of procedures and functions. But compilation of the source code is, like Basic, still carried out on the complete program.

Ada, various extended Pascals, and Modula-2 use the independent design method. In Ada the major program building blocks are those of the main program unit and supporting software units. These individual blocks are written separately and compiled as complete items. They come together only at the final stage of 'linkage', equivalent to the assembly operation of vehicle component parts. One of the most important single supporting blocks is the package, the subject of this chapter.

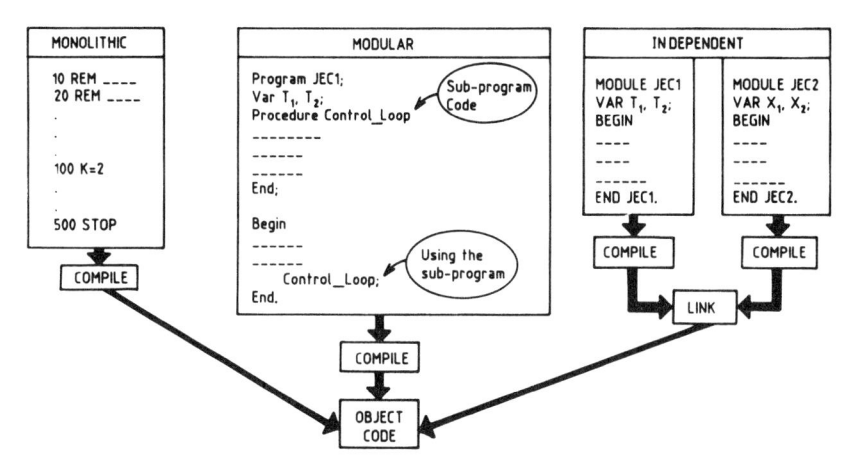

Fig.7.6 Alternative software construction methods.

Table 7.1 compares the advantages and weaknesses of the three compilation methods discussed above.

What we have been discussing here is a highly emotive issue, so don't expect these conclusions to be accepted without question. Program writing reflects very much the attitudes and intellectual attributes of the programmer. Criticize the method and, by implication, you are attacking the designer. Try getting sensible discussions in such a situation. What is generally agreed, though, is that programming, in the past, has lacked the formality and rigour of engineering design. This has resulted in some pretty awful software (if you don't believe this we recommend that you read *The Mythical Man-Month* by F.P. Brooks). Nowadays the emphasis is on getting it right at the design stage, so consigning 'hacking' to a place in history. Ada is a language intended to support these laudable aims.

7.3 BUILDING SOFTWARE THE ADA WAY – THE PACKAGE CONCEPT

7.3.1 Introduction

So far, all program examples have consisted of a single main program unit. But this is not the way that Ada is meant to be used. Ada is designed to enable teams of programmers to build **large** programs, consisting of many program units, Fig.7.7 (the word program unit is used here as a general term to avoid nit picking and confusing detail).

194 Modular construction, information hiding and the package

Table 7.1 Comparison of compilation methods

Compilation method	For	Against
Monolithic	Simple to use Suitable for small programs	Large programs are difficult to handle Program document soon becomes complex Difficult for more than one designer to work on the job Revisions can be costly and time consuming Unwanted effects may easily be inserted when doing changes
Modular	Overall structure can be made highly 'visible' using modularity of design Design can be split amongst a number of programmers, giving faster program development Changes are easier to implement Side effects are reduced Standard program building blocks can be developed (e.g. I/O to console).	Any change means a complete program recompilation Global variables are a source of potential danger
Independent	As for the modular compilation method	More complex cross-referencing needed

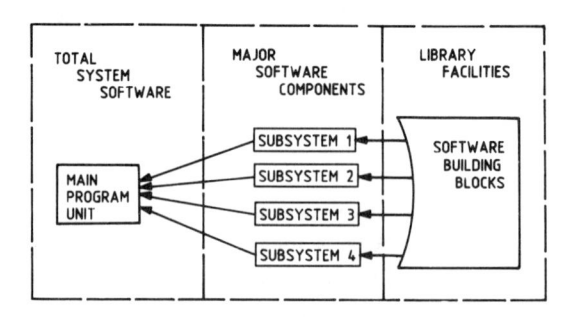

Fig.7.7 Ada program structure.

Building software the Ada way – the package concept   195

The program structure of Fig.7.7 arises from the use of good, modern software design principles. Here the total problem is decomposed into smaller, manageable units, using two techniques: hierarchical decomposition and what is defined here as service decomposition.

Hierarchical decomposition is the process of decomposing the overall system operation into a set of subsystems. These are called into use by the main program unit to implement the desired software task.

Service decomposition is the method of defining and devising standard software 'building bricks' for use in our programs (the software equivalent of integrated circuits). These we usually refer to as library facilities (though for a more precise discussion of the Ada library, see chapter 17). By now this should seem a familiar idea. We have, in fact, been using many of these (such as PUT, GET and SKIP_LINE from TEXT_IO) in our specimen programs right from the beginning of the book. Of course, we may find that a building block is required that cannot be found in the program library. In this case we have identified an obvious need to develop a new library unit.

Hierarchical decomposition falls in quite naturally with the structured programming concepts of top-down design and stepwise refinement. Service decomposition supports a 'bottom-up' design approach – it generates component parts from which we can build our software (now commonly referred to as an object-oriented methodology). The Ada package enables us to implement both strategies. In this chapter the emphasis is placed on developing libraries of useful software routines for general use. Here the usual design approach is to develop, compile and test individual library units. Once proven they can be used immediately by a client unit. No further detailed development or compilation needs to be carried out. This approach can produce major improvements in software productivity, correctness and reliability.

7.3.2 The role and structure of the package

The basic purpose of the package is to act as a 'holder' for software facilities which may then be used by 'client' programs. Such facilities consist of:

- Program items (or objects), such as types, constants and variables.
- Executable code, including program units such as procedures and functions.
- Combinations of the above.

Each individual package consists of two distinct parts, a specification and a body, Fig.7.8. The specification defines what the package does and what it provides. The body describes how it achieves its objectives.

At first sight this may not appear to be exactly a radical move. In fact, the separation of definition and implementation is one of the most important

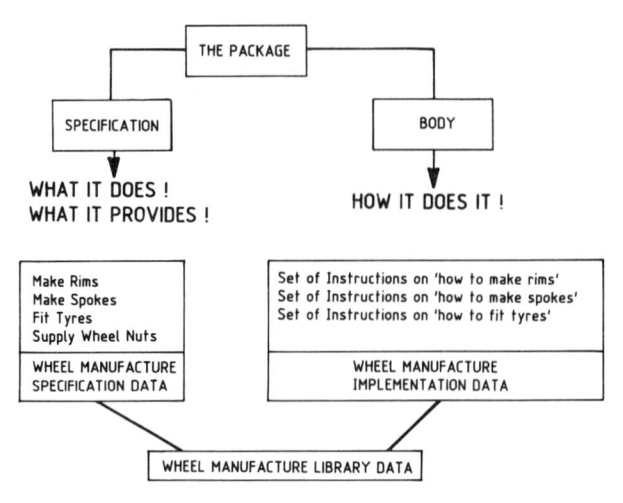

196   Modular construction, information hiding and the package

Fig.7.8 The package structure concept.

features of modern software design. At this stage you will probably not appreciate this. By the end of this book, however, it will seem to be a self-evident truth.

The relationship between a package and its client may conceptually be described as in Fig.7.9. Here a client unit 'MAKE WHEEL' makes use of the facilities provided by the package 'WHEEL MANUFACTURE'. This diagram brings out the basic function of the specification – to act as the package interface. To use the features provided by the package the client only needs to know how to interface to it. Its internal workings are of no concern provided it does the job correctly. Here we have a prime example of 'information hiding'. The designer only makes essential information visible to the client in the specification or 'public' part of the package. The rest – the implementation – is hidden away in the body.

So far we've seen that the package provides us with a 'software building block' for program construction. It also presents us with a means to hide information. But that's not all it does. By using this construct we can have different implementations for one specification. That is, it allows us to implement the same function in quite different computing environments. This has an important bearing on program portability.

7.3.3 Communication between packages

Any practical program will contain several packages. Moreover, these normally have to exchange information. This could be done using global vari-

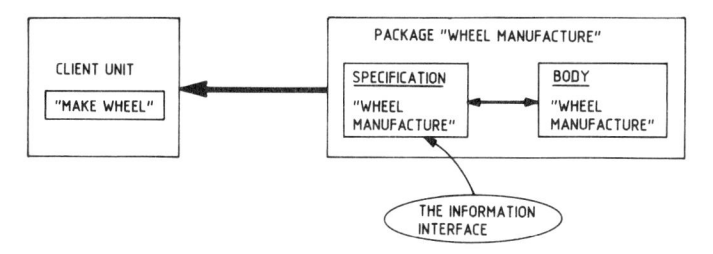

Building software the Ada way – the package concept 197

Fig.7.9 Packages and their clients.

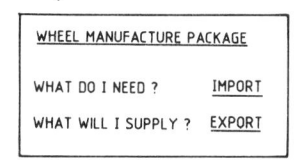

Fig.7.10 Packages – the import–export concept.

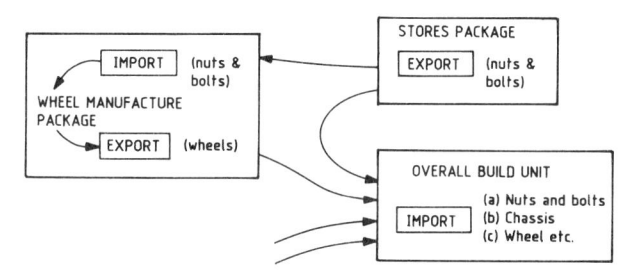

Fig.7.11 Use of imports and exports.

ables; but, as pointed out earlier, this is a potentially dangerous method. How then can we provide a communication method which is well defined and controlled, yet avoids global information?

Let's go back to our kit-car again. Consider the manufacture of a wheel followed by the overall assembly operation. Nuts and bolts are just two of the items needed by the WHEEL MANUFACTURE package for the construction of a wheel. These items can be considered to be 'imported' into the package. On completion of wheel manufacture the finished unit is sent off to the final assembly stage, that is it is 'exported' to the overall build module. This import–export feature (Fig.7.10) is an essential aspect of package operation.

Now let's turn to (part of) the complete manufacture and assembly process, Fig.7.11. The overall build unit imports wheels from the WHEEL

MANUFACTURE package. But it also imports nuts and bolts from the STORES package to fix units together. Nuts and bolts come from the stores module, forming export items. This simple example thus illustrates the concept of import only, export only, and both import and export.

So far, so good. But how do we control the exchange of the parts (information) flow to minimize unwanted changes to this information? Simply by DEFINING what is to be imported or exported, the rules being:

- Items are made available by using an explicit listing;
- A package can only use items located in another package by importing that package in the first place.

Two further points worth noting are that:

- Program units which import packages are known as 'clients' (of the exporting packages);
- Strictly speaking, we use package contents, not the package itself.

7.3.4 Comments on library packages

We've already discussed the reason for using library features. Now let us review their structure and implementation in an Ada program.

The primary function of a library package is to provide facilities for use by other program units. For instance, the example program GET_AND_COMMENT of Listing 1.4 uses resources held in the library package TEXT_IO. Specifically it uses procedures PUT, GET and SKIP_LINE. Observe that we don't need to know exactly how these procedures are implemented. In most cases we really don't care as long as they work properly. What is important is that the procedures are used correctly, and that any parameters used are also of the correct type.

In well-designed software, program units derived using hierarchical structuring are relatively small. Frequently these are formed as a sequence of procedure calls. With such designs the ratio of library to program units may well be 10:1 (or even more). What is the significance of this? Well, it's all related to what happens when we modify the software – either in library packages or their clients.

First consider a change to a package procedure which is purely an internal one. That is, as far as the client is concerned, the library operation appears to be unchanged. In this case only the library package itself has to be modified and recompiled.

Second, what if we need to modify only the client? It is clear that, in this case, only the client needs recompiling. Imported items are unaffected.

Third, look at the case where changes to a library package affect a client. To be more specific, these are changes made to the library package interface.

Building and using the package   199

The way to handle this is to alter the clients in line with these revisions, and then to recompile them.

What are the advantages of selective recompilation? A major benefit is the time saving over that needed to recompile the whole program. As program sizes grow this becomes an important development factor, especially at test and integration time. A second significant factor is the stability this approach brings to the software. That is, changes made in one area do not ripple through the complete program.

7.4 BUILDING AND USING THE PACKAGE

7.4.1 The package specification

In general a package consists of both a specification and a body. The purpose of the specification is to define WHAT is provided by the package to the outside world. Not all provided items come from the body; they may be defined only within the specification itself. Such items include program types, constants and variables. Where the provided items are declared only in the specification then only a specification needs to be built. There is no corresponding body.

This section deals with such a situation. Its purpose is to show:

- How a package specification is formed and compiled;
- How it is used, involving both **with** and **use** clauses;
- Its ability to encapsulate information.

The template structure for a package specification is as follows:

```
package EXAMPLE is
    DECLARED ITEMS
end EXAMPLE;
```

Note that we start with the reserved word **package**, followed by the package name, and then the reserved word **is**. After this come the 'declared items' – those items defined in the specification and made available to clients. In Ada terminology, these are 'visible entities'.

Listing 7.1 gives an example of a package consisting only of a specification.

This package may now be compiled as an individual program unit. Once compiled it is available for use by clients, as demonstrated in Listing 7.2.

Observe that the **with** clause is used in the client program. There isn't anything new here, this construct having appeared in all our specimen programs so far. However, its concept, as shown in Fig.7.12, should now be clear.

```
package TEMPERATURE is
  -- Declare constants for safe working values
    SAFE_MAXIMUM     :    constant        := 150;
    SAFE_MINIMUM     :    constant        := -5;
end TEMPERATURE;
```

Listing 7.1 Package specification only.

```
with TEXT_IO;
with TEMPERATURE;
procedure IMPORTED_PACKAGE is
  CURRENT_TEMPERATURE : INTEGER;
begin
  CURRENT_TEMPERATURE := 50;
  if (CURRENT_TEMPERATURE > TEMPERATURE.SAFE_MAXIMUM) then
    TEXT_IO.PUT_LINE ("Critical High temperatue condition");
  elsif (CURRENT_TEMPERATURE < TEMPERATURE.SAFE_MINIMUM) then
    TEXT_IO.PUT_LINE ("Critical low temperature condition");
  else
    TEXT_IO.PUT_LINE ("Safe working conditions");
  end if;
end IMPORTED_PACKAGE;
```

Listing 7.2 Importing the package from Listing 7.1.

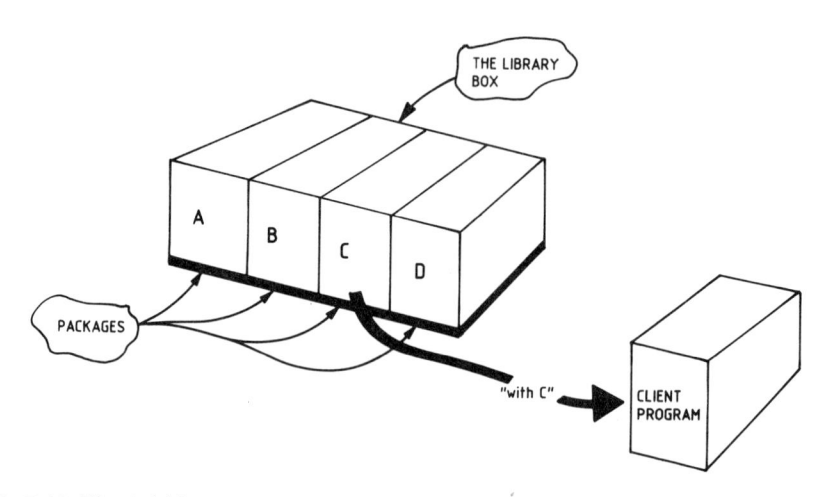

Fig.7.12 The 'with' concept.

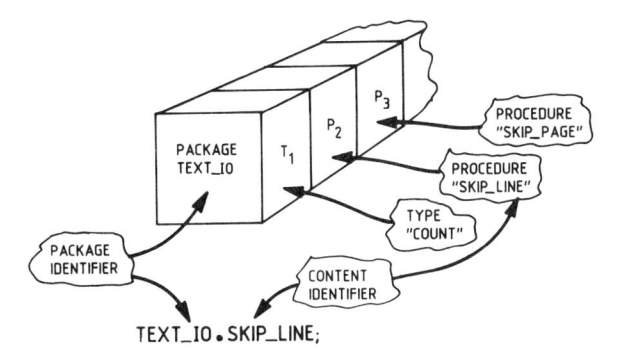

Fig.7.13 Using package items.

```
with TEXT_IO;
with TEMPERATURE;         use TEMPERATURE;
procedure IMPORTED_PACKAGE is
  CURRENT_TEMPERATURE : INTEGER;
begin
  CURRENT_TEMPERATURE := 50;
  if (CURRENT_TEMPERATURE > SAFE_MAXIMUM) then
    TEXT_IO.PUT_LINE ("Critical High temperatue condition");
  elsif (CURRENT_TEMPERATURE < SAFE_MINIMUM) then
    TEXT_IO.PUT_LINE ("Critical low temperature condition");
  else
    TEXT_IO.PUT_LINE ("Safe working conditions");
  end if;
end IMPORTED_PACKAGE;
```

Listing 7.3 As per Listing 7.2 but including a 'use' clause.

To obtain access to a package in the library we have to use the **with** construct. Thus we 'import' the package into the client program. Bear in mind, though, that we use the contents of the package, not the package itself. To extract these from their 'software container', we have to define two factors: the item of interest and the package in which it is housed. This is the reason for using dot notation, as illustrated in Fig.7.13.

As an analogy, consider that **with** gets us the package. The dot qualifier – as in TEMPERATURE.SAFE_MAXIMUM – removes a particular item from its container.

Now consider Listing 7.3.

This performs exactly the same function as Listing 7.2, but here the **use** clause has been invoked. Visualize this as shaking out all items from the package container. We can now pick these up for use simply by naming them; there is no need to use dot notation. In some cases this can lead to clearer program code.

```
package TEMPERATURE is
  -- Declare constants for safe working values
    SAFE_MAXIMUM    :    constant        := 150;
    SAFE_MINIMUM    :    constant        := -5;
end TEMPERATURE;
package PRESSURE is
  -- Declare constants for safe working values
    SAFE_MAXIMUM    :    constant        := 80;
    SAFE_MINIMUM    :    constant        := 30;
end PRESSURE;
```

Listing 7.4 Example of two package specifications which declare constants of the same name.

```
with TEXT_IO;
with TEMPERATURE;         use TEMPERATURE;
with PRESSURE;            use PRESSURE;
procedure TWO_IMPORTED_PACKAGES is
  CURRENT_TEMPERATURE : INTEGER;
  CURRENT_PRESSURE :    INTEGER;
begin
  CURRENT_TEMPERATURE := 50;
  CURRENT_PRESSURE := 50;
  if (CURRENT_TEMPERATURE > SAFE_MAXIMUM) and (CURRENT_PRESSURE > SAFE_MAXIMUM)
    then
      TEXT_IO.PUT_LINE ("Critical High temperatue/pressure condition");
    elsif (CURRENT_TEMPERATURE < SAFE_MINIMUM) and (CURRENT_PRESSURE <
    SAFE_MINIMUM) then
      TEXT_IO.PUT_LINE ("Critical low temperature/pressure condition");
    else
      TEXT_IO.PUT_LINE ("Safe working conditions");
  end if;
end TWO_IMPORTED_PACKAGES;
```

Listing 7.5 Example procedure showing the need for dot notation. This example will fail at compilation time.

Unfortunately, we can't always avoid dot notation. The reason is that in practice (especially in large systems), the same names may appear in different packages, as illustrated in Listing 7.4.

If we now **with** and **use** both packages in a client program (Listing 7.5) the compiler will get very confused. How can it tell which package holds the item being referred to? The answer, of course, is that it can't. So we have to supply the missing information by using dot notation, as shown in Listing 7.6.

It is recommended that dot notation should be used whenever possible to minimize errors and improve reader comprehension.

What exactly have we achieved in the examples above by using packages? Two things: encapsulation and control of information. The package, in this application, can be seen as a storage place for information. Further, this

```
with TEXT_IO;
with TEMPERATURE;          use TEMPERATURE;
with PRESSURE;             use PRESSURE;
procedure TWO_IMPORTED_PACKAGES is
  CURRENT_TEMPERATURE : INTEGER;
  CURRENT_PRESSURE :    INTEGER;
begin
  CURRENT_TEMPERATURE := 50;
  CURRENT_PRESSURE := 50;
  if (CURRENT_TEMPERATURE > TEMPERATURE.SAFE_MAXIMUM) and (CURRENT_PRESSURE >
  PRESSURE.SAFE_MAXIMUM) then
    TEXT_IO.PUT_LINE ("Critical High temperature/pressure condition");
  elsif (CURRENT_TEMPERATURE < TEMPERATURE.SAFE_MINIMUM) and (CURRENT_PRESSURE
   < PRESSURE.SAFE_MINIMUM) then
    TEXT_IO.PUT_LINE ("Critical low temperature/pressure condition");
  else
    TEXT_IO.PUT_LINE ("Safe working conditions");
  end if;
end TWO_IMPORTED_PACKAGES;
```

Listing 7.6 Example showing how to overcome the problem in Listing 7.5.

information can only be used by accessing the package in a well-defined, visible manner. You might, at this stage, say 'So what? The information contained within the package could have been located in the client program, saving effort and complexity.' Very true – but it applies where only one client is involved. Now this isn't the way we use libraries. Each library unit commonly has many client units. In such systems information encapsulation and control improve the structure, clarity, reliability and maintainability of the resulting software.

7.4.2 Package specification and body – a combined item

Now let's put our minds to building packages which actually do something. This is where the body, the part that holds executable code, comes into use. In the following example the package specification and body are combined into a single text file. The template for this is shown in Fig.7.14.

```
package NAME is
    DECLARED ITEMS            SPECIFICATION PART
end NAME;

package body NAME is
    DECLARED ITEMS            BODY
begin
    EXECUTABLE STATEMENTS
end NAME ;
```

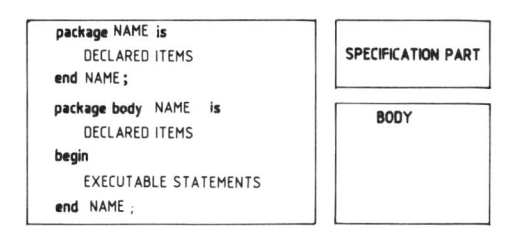

Fig.7.14 Package template.

The completed file can be compiled quite separately from all other program units.

NOTE 1: The two parts of the file – specification and body – are actually two individual compilable units.

NOTE 2: Repeating the package name after **end** is optional, but strongly recommended.

Now for two important points. First, items declared in the specification part of the package are visible outside the package – exactly as before. But they are also visible inside the package, that is within the body. In contrast, items declared within the body are visible only within the body – they cannot be accessed by clients (in fact, all items contained within a package body are invisible to the outside world). Second, it is perfectly correct to produce a package which does not have any code in the 'executable statements' section. This may seem surprising, and is an aspect which we'll return to shortly. For the moment, though, let us concentrate on using the package as a holder for subprograms.

We stressed earlier that a most important software building block of Ada is the subprogram. Therefore it seems logical to build package facilities using procedures and functions. That is what we're going to do now. Remember, though, our objective is to provide facilities for use by clients – yet to prevent clients getting at the details of such facilities.

Some points need to be clearly understood before we proceed any further. When using the subprogram in a package we need to:

- Define its existence – declare it (as detailed below);
- Keep its implementation invisible – write the subprogram body within the package body;
- Make it available for use by clients – write its declaration in the package specification.

All these points are illustrated in Listings 7.7 and 7.8.

The rationale for placing the **with** clause in the opening line of the client should now be apparent. It shows clearly that the client depends on facilities provided by a separate program unit – and specifies the name of that unit.

7.4.3 Package specification and body – separate items

In the previous section the package specification and body were treated as a single program file. This, as you will discover, is the exception rather than the rule. The usual approach is to separate the two, building them as distinct items. This is shown in Listings 7.9 and 7.10.

```
package TEMPERATURE is
  -- Declare constant values for safe working values
  SAFE_MAXIMUM   :   constant      := 150;
  SAFE_MINIMUM   :   constant      := -5;
  -- Declare a procedure
  procedure ERROR_CONDITION;
end TEMPERATURE;
with TEXT_IO;
package body TEMPERATURE is
  procedure ERROR_CONDITION is
  begin
    TEXT_IO.PUT_LINE ("ERROR CONDITION: Shut down system");
  end ERROR_CONDITION;
end TEMPERATURE;
```

Listing 7.7 Package specification and body within one file.

```
with TEXT_IO;
with TEMPERATURE;
procedure IMPORTED_PACKAGE is
  CURRENT_TEMPERATURE : INTEGER;
begin
  CURRENT_TEMPERATURE := 170;
  if (CURRENT_TEMPERATURE > TEMPERATURE.SAFE_MAXIMUM) or
     (CURRENT_TEMPERATURE < TEMPERATURE.SAFE_MINIMUM) then
  -- Use imported procedure to handle the error condition
    TEMPERATURE.ERROR_CONDITION;
  else
    TEXT_IO.PUT_LINE ("Safe working conditions");
  end if;
end IMPORTED_PACKAGE;
```

Listing 7.8 Using the subprogram from the imported package of Listing 7.7.

```
package TEMPERATURE is
  -- Declare constant values for safe working values
  SAFE_MAXIMUM   :   constant      := 150;
  SAFE_MINIMUM   :   constant      := -5;
  -- Declare a procedure to handle error conditions
  procedure ERROR_CONDITION;
end TEMPERATURE;
```

Listing 7.9 Example of package specification only. The body is in another file.

```
with TEXT_IO;
package body TEMPERATURE is
  procedure ERROR_CONDITION is
  begin
    TEXT_IO.PUT_LINE ("ERROR CONDITION: Shut down system");
  end ERROR_CONDITION;
end TEMPERATURE;
```

Listing 7.10 Package body for specification given in Listing 7.9.

The package specification must be compiled before either the body or clients can be compiled. A client program can, in fact, be compiled without the package body being present in the system. Compilation issues is an important topic, one that we will return to later.

What exactly have we achieved by separating out these two parts of the package? The direct effect is to change the way we handle program compilation and software control aspects. As a result the task of developing and maintaining the software is very much simplified. The indirect effects are also quite significant. Provided we design our software in a professional manner, major gains can be made in terms of productivity and portability.

The specification gives us the outside (client) view of a package function – the WHAT aspect. During the process of developing the total software for a system, package specifications are generally stable. Few changes are required (provided the design was well thought out in the first place). In contrast we find that the implementation parts are usually subject to regular – sometimes extensive – changes.

Consider when the body and specification are combined into a single file. If any change is made to the package then both must be recompiled. When they are separated only the affected part needs to be recompiled. The difference in compilation times is not usually significant – but the consequential effects are. When a specification is recompiled all clients must be recompiled (this is not a mandatory feature of Ada, but is, to our knowledge, enforced by all Ada compilers). This applies even if no change is made to the specification. And, as pointed out, changes are most likely to be in the body rather than the specification. So, by keeping the two parts separate, we minimize the 'knock-on' effects of changes. The saving in time and effort in a large project cannot be stressed too highly. This point, together with that of portability, is discussed in the next section.

One very important point to be noted concerns the syntax of specifications and their associated bodies. Consider the following:

(a) Package specification:

```
package SYNTAX_EXAMPLE is
    procedure TEST_DATE (X, Y : in INTEGER);
```

(b) Corresponding body (part):

```
package body SYNTAX_EXAMPLE is
    procedure TEST_DATE (X, Y : INTEGER) is
```

Both comply with the rules of Ada. The procedure TEST_DATE has, in each case, exactly the same parameters. Yet the compiler will flag up an error because the two are not identical. Specifications and bodies must match in every detail.

7.4.4 Portability issues

Ada was specifically designed with real-time systems in mind. In such systems we frequently develop our software on one machine (the host) but install it on another (the target). If this host software can be installed in (ported to) the target without modification, then it is fully portable. Normally this can be done only when both machines are exactly the same – a rare event. How can we minimize the amount of change needed to the software in such a situation? Here the package helps, in two ways. We can develop different package bodies for the same specification. Host development is carried out with the 'host' package body linked in to the application software. Once completed, the 'host' body is replaced by the 'target' body, and the software ported to the target. This point is illustrated by Listings 7.11–7.14.

```
package TEMPERATURE is
  -- Declare constant values for safe working values
  SAFE_MAXIMUM   :    constant     := 150;
  SAFE_MINIMUM   :    constant     := -5;
  -- Declare a procedure to handle error conditions
  procedure ERROR_CONDITION;
  -- Declare a function that will prompt for the current temperature
  function GET_CURRENT_TEMPERATURE
     return INTEGER;
end TEMPERATURE;
```

Listing 7.11 Specification of package TEMPERATURE, with a new function, GET_CURRENT_TEMPERATURE.

First compile Listings 7.11, 7.12 and 7.13. Then build and run the program for Listing 7.13 and observe the results. Now compile 7.14. This will automatically replace 7.12 in your system. Rebuild and rerun your program. Observe the effects by the use of 7.14 in place of 7.12. From this you should be able to deduce the rule that the last compiled body is used.

7.4.5 Information hiding – again

In the examples above, the package body has been used to hide details of a procedure from the outside world. The procedure itself was made available for use by the client. However, the hiding properties of packages are much more extensive, as displayed by Listings 7.15a and 7.15b.

Here the exported functions GET_CURRENT_MPH and GET_CURRENT_KPH themselves use a function GET_CURRENT_SPEED to achieve their

```
with TEXT_IO;
package body TEMPERATURE is
  procedure ERROR_CONDITION is
  begin
    TEXT_IO.PUT_LINE ("ERROR CONDITION: Shut down system");
  end ERROR_CONDITION;
  -- A simple implementation of the function GET_CURRENT_TEMPERATURE which always
  -- returns the same value.
  function GET_CURRENT_TEMPERATURE
    return INTEGER is
  begin
    return 170;
  end GET_CURRENT_TEMPERATURE;
end TEMPERATURE;
```

Listing 7.12 Body of package TEMPERATURE as defined in Listing 7.11.

```
with TEXT_IO;
with TEMPERATURE;         use TEMPERATURE;
procedure USE_DIFFERENT_BODIES is
  CURRENT_TEMPERATURE : INTEGER;
begin
  -- Use the function from TEMPERATURE to get the current working value
  CURRENT_TEMPERATURE := GET_CURRENT_TEMPERATURE;
  if (CURRENT_TEMPERATURE > SAFE_MAXIMUM) or
     (CURRENT_TEMPERATURE < SAFE_MINIMUM) then
    ERROR_CONDITION;
  else
    TEXT_IO.PUT_LINE ("Safe working conditions");
  end if;
end USE_DIFFERENT_BODIES;
```

Listing 7.13 Main program using package TEMPERATURE.

```
with TEXT_IO;
package body TEMPERATURE is
  package INT_IO is new TEXT_IO.INTEGER_IO (INTEGER);
  procedure ERROR_CONDITION is
  begin
    TEXT_IO.PUT_LINE ("ERROR CONDITION: Shut down system");
  end ERROR_CONDITION;
  function GET_CURRENT_TEMPERATURE
    return INTEGER is
    CURRENT_TEMPERATURE : INTEGER;
  begin
    TEXT_IO.PUT ("Enter the current working temperature (-40..220 deg/C) => ");
    INT_IO.GET (CURRENT_TEMPERATURE);
    TEXT_IO.SKIP_LINE;
    return CURRENT_TEMPERATURE;
  end GET_CURRENT_TEMPERATURE;
end TEMPERATURE;
```

Listing 7.14 This shows a different version of the body of package TEMPERATURE. The function GET_CURRENT_TEMPERATURE has changed.

```ada
package MEASUREMENT is
  MAX_VELOCITY    :     constant    :=  200.0;
  MAX_MPH         :     constant    :=  70.0;
  MPH_TO_KPH      :     constant    :=  1.61;
  MAX_KPH         :     constant    :=  MAX_MPH * MPH_TO_KPH;
  type VELOCITY is delta 0.01 range 0.0 .. MAX_VELOCITY;
  subtype MPH is VELOCITY range 0.0 .. MAX_MPH;
  subtype KPH is VELOCITY range 0.0 .. MAX_KPH;
  function GET_CURRENT_MPH
    return MPH;
  function GET_CURRENT_KPH
    return KPH;
end MEASUREMENT;
with TEXT_IO;              use TEXT_IO;
package body MEASUREMENT is
  package VELOCITY_IO is new FIXED_IO (VELOCITY);
  CURRENT_SPEED   :     VELOCITY          :=  0.0;
  function GET_CURRENT_SPEED
    return VELOCITY is
    NEW_SPEED     :     VELOCITY;
  begin
    PUT ("The current speed is (in MPH) => ");
    VELOCITY_IO.PUT (CURRENT_SPEED);
    NEW_LINE;
    PUT ("Enter the new speed (in MPH) => ");
    VELOCITY_IO.GET(CURRENT_SPEED);
    return CURRENT_SPEED;
  end GET_CURRENT_SPEED;
  function GET_CURRENT_MPH
    return MPH is
    CURRENT_MPH   :     MPH;
  begin
    CURRENT_MPH := GET_CURRENT_SPEED;
    return CURRENT_MPH;
  end GET_CURRENT_MPH;
  function GET_CURRENT_KPH
    return KPH is
    CURRENT_MPH   :     MPH;
    CURRENT_KPH   :     KPH;
  begin
    CURRENT_MPH := GET_CURRENT_SPEED;
    CURRENT_KPH := KPH (KPH (CURRENT_MPH) * KPH (MPH_TO_KPH));
    return CURRENT_KPH;
  end GET_CURRENT_KPH;
end MEASUREMENT;
```

Listing 7.15a Package spec. and body showing hidden procedure.

210 Modular construction, information hiding and the package

```
with TEXT_IO;              use TEXT_IO;
with MEASUREMENT;          use MEASUREMENT;
procedure DISPLAY is
   type OPTION is (MILES, KILOMETRES, QUIT);
   package OPTION_IO is new ENUMERATION_IO (OPTION);
   package VELOCITY_IO is new FIXED_IO (VELOCITY);
   CURRENT_DISPLAY_VELOCITY :     VELOCITY;
   NEW_OPTION               :     OPTION;
begin
  loop
    PUT ("Enter display option (MILES, KILOMETRES) or QUIT => ");
    OPTION_IO.GET (NEW_OPTION);
    SKIP_LINE;
    case NEW_OPTION is
      when MILES =>
        CURRENT_DISPLAY_VELOCITY := GET_CURRENT_MPH;
        PUT ("Current speed => ");
        VELOCITY_IO.PUT (CURRENT_DISPLAY_VELOCITY);
        PUT_LINE (" Miles per Hour");
      when KILOMETRES =>
        CURRENT_DISPLAY_VELOCITY := GET_CURRENT_KPH;
        PUT ("Current speed => ");
        VELOCITY_IO.PUT (CURRENT_DISPLAY_VELOCITY);
        PUT_LINE (" Kilometers per Hour");
      when QUIT =>
        exit;
    end case;
  end loop;
end DISPLAY;
```

Listing 7.15b Using the package MEASUREMENT.

aims. GET_CURRENT_SPEED is located in the package body, and is thus totally invisible to external software. Thus we can build packages safely and securely – using constructs and entities of our own choice – with minimum concern for the rest of the software.

7.4.6 Executable statements in the package body

Let us now expand the concept of the package body. So far our examples have shown package bodies which consist of data items and subprograms. Some of these are destined to be exported by the package; others are used only within the package. Nevertheless, in both cases, they are written out in the declarative region of the package. However, the package body template (Fig.7.14) shows that there is a second section – the executable statements. This section (or block) is optional. Further, the code it contains is executed only once. This raises two interesting questions. Why do we have this feature? And when is the code executed?

Consider the very common situation of interacting with a VDU from an embedded processor system. Suppose that we develop a library package

Building and using the package 211

```
package FIRST_IMPORT is
end FIRST_IMPORT;
 -- Nothing declared in the specification
with TEXT_IO;
package body FIRST_IMPORT is
 -- empty body except for elaboration text
begin
  TEXT_IO.PUT_LINE ("This is the elaboration of the package FIRST_IMPORT");
end FIRST_IMPORT;
```

Listing 7.16 This shows elaboration code for a package.

```
with FIRST_IMPORT;
with TEXT_IO;
procedure MAIN is
begin
   TEXT_IO.PUT_LINE ("This is the main program body running");
end MAIN;
```

Listing 7.17 This demonstrates elaboration order when importing packages.

'COMMUNICATIONS' to handle detailed aspects of such interactions. When the application software uses the package we assume that the communications hardware has been set up correctly. But has it? We can't really be sure without carefully checking through the program code – a tedious and error-prone task. Fortunately there is a solution to this problem. Insert the set-up code, as executable statements, within the communications package.

In this situation, when is the set-up code actually executed? This can be demonstrated using the example of Listings 7.16 and 7.17.

Here a main program unit MAIN (Listing 7.17) has '**with FIRST_IMPORT**' as its opening clause. That is, the facilities of package FIRST_IMPORT can be used by MAIN. However, for this demonstration, note the following:

(a) Package FIRST_IMPORT specification does not have any declared items.
(b) Package FIRST_IMPORT body does not have any declared items.
(c) The main program MAIN merely imports FIRST_IMPORT.

Compile FIRST_IMPORT and MAIN, then build and run MAIN. You will find that the following screen print-out is produced:

```
This is the elaboration of the package body FIRST_IMPORT
This is the main program body running
```

212 Modular construction, information hiding and the package

```
package SECOND_IMPORT is
end SECOND_IMPORT;
with TEXT_IO;
package body SECOND_IMPORT is
  -- empty body except for elaboration text
begin
  TEXT_IO.PUT_LINE ("This is the elaboration of the package SECOND_IMPORT");
end SECOND_IMPORT;
```

Listing 7.18 This shows elaboration code for another package.

```
with FIRST_IMPORT;
with SECOND_IMPORT;
with TEXT_IO;
procedure IMPORT_TWO is
begin
  TEXT_IO.PUT_LINE ("This is the main program body running");
end IMPORT_TWO;
```

Listing 7.19 Elaboration order when importing two packages.

```
with SECOND_IMPORT;
with FIRST_IMPORT;
with TEXT_IO;
procedure CHANGE_IMPORT_ORDERING is
begin
  TEXT_IO.PUT_LINE ("This is the main program body running");
end CHANGE_IMPORT_ORDERING;
```

Listing 7.20 Second example showing elaboration order when importing two packages.

This shows that the code statements of the package body are executed when the program reaches the **with** clause. More precisely, the package is elaborated. We can demonstrate this point further by importing two packages into a client, Listings 7.18, 7.19 and 7.20.

When the program in Listing 7.19 is run the following screen print-out results:

```
This is the elaboration of the package SECOND_IMPORT
This is the elaboration of the package FIRST_IMPORT
This is the main program body running
```

However, when Listing 7.20 is executed the screen display shows:

Building and using the package 213

> This is the elaboration of the package FIRST_IMPORT
> This is the elaboration of the package SECOND_IMPORT
> This is the main program body running

However, do not be surprised if the second screen display comes up when 7.19 is executed. In that case running 7.20 will produce the first display. These demonstrate clearly the point at which elaboration occurs.

Elaboration can be a mystifying subject. To quote the Ada LRM:

The process by which a declaration achieves its effect is called the elaboration of the declaration; this process happens during program execution (section 3.1).... For the elaboration of a package body its declarative part is first elaborated, and its sequence of statements (if any) is then executed (section 7.3).

This is a somewhat complex topic, so we will return to it later. For the moment, though, think of elaboration simply as bringing a declared item into being. In this example, the package – as far as the main program is concerned – is just another declared item.

7.4.7 Controlling and hiding information – embedded packages

Up to this point we have stressed the use of packages to build 'software machines'. The primary purpose is to make it easy for us to develop programs in a structured manner. But the package can also be put to good use for the control and hiding of information. This is one of its minor but useful roles. To do this it is 'embedded' within another program unit, providing services to that unit. Now this can be a complex issue. So here we will limit ourselves to a relatively simple case – a package embedded (named EMBEDDED) within another package (named SERVICE), Listing 7.21.

```
package SERVICE is
   X              :    INTEGER      := 0;
   package EMBEDDED is
      Y           :    INTEGER      := 1;
   end EMBEDDED;
end SERVICE;
```

Listing 7.21 This listing shows an embedded package.

Now we come to the use of the packages SERVICE and EMBEDDED by a main program unit. Four examples are given, starting with Listing 7.22a.

Because package SERVICE is 'withed' (imported) by MAIN, we can access all resources contained within the package. And this includes the embedded package. The meaning and use of the first executable statement

214 *Modular construction, information hiding and the package*

```
with SERVICE;
procedure WITH_ONLY is
  Z            :       INTEGER;
begin
  Z := SERVICE.X;
  Z := SERVICE.EMBEDDED.Y;
end WITH_ONLY;
```

Listing 7.22a First of four examples showing the use of an embedded package.

```
with SERVICE;                  use SERVICE;
procedure USE_OUTER_ONLY is
  Z            :       INTEGER;
begin
  Z := X;
  Z := EMBEDDED.Y;
end USE_OUTER_ONLY;
```

Listing 7.22b This shows visibility of the outer package only.

```
with SERVICE;                  use SERVICE;
procedure USE_BOTH_PACKAGES is
  use EMBEDDED;
  Z            :       INTEGER;
begin
  Z := X;
  Z := Y;
end USE_BOTH_PACKAGES;
```

Listing 7.22c This shows making both packages visible.

```
Z := SERVICE.X;
```

should be obvious. The second line, however,

```
Z := SERVICE.EMBEDDED.Y;
```

has a new construct. Its meaning is clear enough: EMBEDDED.Y is within SERVICE, and Y is within EMBEDDED.

Listings 7.22b, 7.22c and 7.22d extend this example to show variations in using the **use** clause.

```
with SERVICE;
procedure USE_INNER_ONLY is
  use SERVICE.EMBEDDED;
  Z              :        INTEGER;
begin
  Z := SERVICE.X;
  Z := Y;
end USE_INNER_ONLY;
```

Listing 7.22d This shows the 'use' clause on the embedded package only.

As mentioned earlier, this is not a simple topic. Packages can also be embedded within subprograms and within program blocks. Extending this, one can visualize a subprogram containing a package which in turn contains a subprogram carrying an embedded package which.... Enough said. We strongly recommend that, where packages are to be embedded, a simple approach be taken.

7.4.8 Compilation order and visibility of objects

In this section we will have another brief look at compilation and visibility issues. Specifically, these are concerned with the relationship between packages and client program units. Further, the context is that of separate, and not embedded, packages.

How do we arrive at the order of compilation? Client programs import library functions. Then clearly a library package must exist before the client can use it. However, to insist that implementation (body) code must be generated at this stage may create serious bottlenecks in the design process. And it isn't even necessary. The client, remember, only needs to know what the library package does, not how it does it. In Ada the package specification acts as the interface between the client and its resource provider (the package body). This structure enables us to compile both client and body as quite separate items. It also means that these can be modified separately and independently.

Thus the basic rules are (Fig.7.15):

- Package specifications must be compiled first.
- Package bodies and client programs can then be compiled in any order.

Note that a package body can itself be a client, that is it uses smaller building blocks from the library. What is the compilation order in this case? Well, the rules given above still apply. The body (of the importing package) can be compiled only when its own specification and those of imported packages have been compiled.

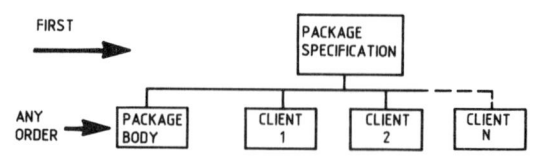

216 Modular construction, information hiding and the package

Fig.7.15 Order of compilation.

```
package COMPUTE is
   type MEASUREMENT is delta 0.1 range 0.0 .. 100.0;
   procedure CHECK_LIMITS (INPUT     : in      MEASUREMENT);
end COMPUTE;
```

Listing 7.23a Set of four listings showing order of compilation.

```
with COMPUTE;               use COMPUTE;
package CONTROL_ALGORITHM is
   function INTEGRAL (SIGNAL    :              MEASUREMENT)
      return MEASUREMENT;
end CONTROL_ALGORITHM;
```

Listing 7.23b

If a package body is revised and recompiled, does this affect clients? The answer is no. After all, the client essentially calls on the library to perform its defined task, passing parameters as necessary. It is not concerned with the way in which the task is performed.

What is the situation concerning package specifications? Suppose, for instance, we change the number of parameters used in a procedure. This means that the corresponding specification must be altered in line with the change. So we recompile the specification. Fine. But what about clients which use this library procedure? Even more complex, what about library packages which use library packages which use further library packages – which have just been changed? Grim!

So we have to maintain a strict code of conduct when dealing with changes like this. There is only one safe way to handle this situation. The specification, remember, forms the interface between the client and the implementation. Therefore, always recompile client units whenever the specification of an imported package is changed.

Is there a unique order of compilation? Consider the situation in Listings 7.23a–d, where a program calls up three separate library packages.

However, observe that all packages are themselves interrelated by just

Building and using the package 217

```
with COMPUTE;                use COMPUTE;
package FILTER is
  function MOVING_AVERAGE (VALUE   :    MEASUREMENT)
    return MEASUREMENT;
end FILTER;
```

Listing 7.23c

```
with COMPUTE;                 use COMPUTE;
with CONTROL_ALGORITHM;       use CONTROL_ALGORITHM;
with FILTER;                  use FILTER;
procedure PROCESS_SIGNAL is
  MEASURED_VALUE    :   MEASUREMENT;
  SMOOTHED_VALUE    :   MEASUREMENT;
  INTEGRATED_VALUE  :   MEASUREMENT;
begin
  -- MEASURED_VALUE is assigned some value
  SMOOTHED_VALUE := MOVING_AVERAGE (MEASURED_VALUE);
  INTEGRATED_VALUE := INTEGRAL (SMOOTHED_VALUE);
  CHECK_LIMITS (INTEGRATED_VALUE);
end PROCESS_SIGNAL;
```

Listing 7.23d

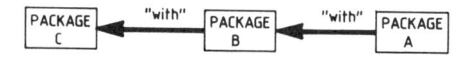

```
PACKAGE  <--"with"--  PACKAGE  <--"with"--  PACKAGE
   C                     B                     A
```

Fig.7.16 Use of resources.

one package – 'COMPUTE'. This is used by the library packages 'CONTROL_ALGORITHM' and 'FILTER' as well as the main program unit. To comply with the rules given earlier, package 'COMPUTE' must be compiled first and the main program 'PROCESS_SIGNAL' last. The others are done in-between. The order is not important; that is, it doesn't matter whether 'CONTROL_ALGORITHM' is compiled before 'FILTER' or vice versa. For detailed discussions relating to compilation issues, see Chapter 17.

Now let us consider visibility issues when we have the situation shown in Fig.7.16.

Here package C uses the resources of package B which uses resources supplied by package A. Clearly package C can access the resources of B. Likewise, B can access those of A. But, given this chain of packages, can C directly access the resources of A? The answer is NO, as demonstrated in Listings 7.24a (package MILES), 7.24b (package KILOMETRES) and 7.24c (package ACCESS) below.

A final point relating to chained program units concerns the order of

```
package MILES is
  MAX_MPH        :     constant      := 130.0;
  type MPH is delta 0.01 range 0.0 .. MAX_MPH;
  -- use sensors to read current speed in MPH
  function GET_CURRENT_MPH
    return MPH;
end MILES;
```

Listing 7.24a A package that gets the current road speed in Miles-Per-Hour.

```
with MILES;
package KILOMETRES is
  MPH_TO_KPH    :    constant       := 1.61;
  MAX_KPH       :    constant       := MILES.MAX_MPH * MPH_TO_KPH;
  type KPH is delta 0.01 range 0.0 .. MAX_KPH;
  function GET_CURRENT_KPH
    return KPH;
end KILOMETRES;
```

Listing 7.24b A package that gets the current road speed in Kilometres-Per-Hour. The package makes use of package MILES.

```
with KILOMETRES;            use KILOMETRES;
procedure PACKAGE_ACCESS is
  CURRENT_SPEED   :    KPH;
  MPH_SPEED       :    MPH;
  -- this will fail as the type MPH cannot be seen.
begin
  CURRENT_SPEED := GET_CURRENT_KPH;
  -- okay !
  MPH_SPEED := MAX_MPH;
  -- cannot see this without "withing" MILES!
end PACKAGE_ACCESS;
```

Listing 7.24c The main program that uses package KILOMETRES. The example shows valid and invalid access of package resources. As only package KILOMETRES has been imported, resources from MILES cannot be accessed.

elaboration of their declarations. This is demonstrated in Listings 7.25a and 7.25b.

When these are compiled and run, the following screen print-out may be produced:

```
This is the elaboration of package body AAA
This is the elaboration of package body AAB
This is the elaboration of package body AA
This is the elaboration of package body ABA
This is the elaboration of package body ABB
This is the elaboration of package body AB
This is the elaboration of package body A
This is the main program
```

What you will get in practice is dependent on your compiler. All that we can guarantee is that:

- The main program will be the last one elaborated.
- Package A will elaborate before the main program but after packages AA and AB. However, we do not know whether AA elaborates before AB, or vice versa.
- Package AA will elaborate after packages AAA and AAB, etc.

At this point, a small but important aspect of Ada needs revisiting – declaration order. In general, the order of declaration will not cause you problems – until a body is declared (this includes both subprogram and package bodies). You will then find that certain restrictions are encountered. For instance, you will not be allowed to declare any more program objects. The rules aren't obvious or intuitive; see Chapter 17 for further details. Further, you will see there that the arrows showing compilation dependencies are reversed compared with Fig.7.16. This has been done to conform with the notation used by the majority of Ada diagramming toolsets.

7.5 GLOBAL ITEMS – A WARNING

The subject of global items has been discussed on a number of occasions earlier in the text. Our advice has always been the same – avoid using them if at all possible. But, if globals are necessary, be very careful. The following example shows how very easy it is to get into trouble in this situation.

Listing 7.26 is a package GLOBAL_DATA which defines an integer variable GLOBAL_ITEM.

Because this is a global item, it is available to all clients. As shown below, it is used by package CORRUPT (Listing 7.27) and by the main program MAIN (Listing 7.28).

```
--                           +--> AAA
--                           |
--            +--> AA --+
--            |              |
--            |              +--> AAB
--    A --+
--            |              +--> ABA
--            |              |
--            +--> AB --+
--                           |
--                           + -->ABB
```
```ada
package AAA is
end AAA;
with TEXT_IO;         use TEXT_IO;
package body AAA is
begin
  PUT_LINE ("This is the elaboration of package body AAA");
end AAA;
package AAB is
end AAB;
with TEXT_IO;         use TEXT_IO;
package body AAB is
begin
  PUT_LINE ("This is the elaboration of package body AAB");
end AAB;
------------------------------------------------------------------------
package ABA is
end ABA;
with TEXT_IO;         use TEXT_IO;
package body ABA is
begin
  PUT_LINE ("This is the elaboration of package body ABA");
end ABA;
------------------------------------------------------------------------
package ABB is
end ABB;
with TEXT_IO;         use TEXT_IO;
package body ABB is
begin
  PUT_LINE ("This is the elaboration of package body ABB");
end ABB;
------------------------------------------------------------------------
with AAA;
with AAB;
package AA is
end AA;
with TEXT_IO;         use TEXT_IO;
package body AA is
begin
  PUT_LINE ("This is the elaboration of package body AA");
end AA;
------------------------------------------------------------------------
with ABA;
with ABB;
package AB is
end AB;
with TEXT_IO;         use TEXT_IO;
package body AB is
begin
  PUT_LINE ("This is the elaboration of package body AB");
end AB;
------------------------------------------------------------------------
with AA;
with AB;
package A is
end A;
with TEXT_IO;         use TEXT_IO;
package body A is
begin
  PUT_LINE ("This is the elaboration of package body A");
end A;
------------------------------------------------------------------------
```

Listing 7.25a This shows elaboration order for a number of packages.

```
with TEXT_IO;              use TEXT_IO;
with A;
procedure MAIN is
begin
  PUT_LINE ("This is the main program");
end MAIN;
```

Listing 7.25b This is the main program that elaborates package A, which in turn elaborates AA and AB, which in turn ... etc.

```
package GLOBAL_DATA is
  GLOBAL_ITEM               :      INTEGER;
end GLOBAL_DATA;
```

Listing 7.26 Package specification with globally accessible data.

```
package CORRUPT is
  procedure DO_SOMETHING;
end CORRUPT;
with GLOBAL_DATA;
package body CORRUPT is
  procedure DO_SOMETHING is
  begin
    GLOBAL_DATA.GLOBAL_ITEM := 200;
  end DO_SOMETHING;
end CORRUPT;
```

Listing 7.27 Package spec. and body with procedure that alters the global data GLOBAL_DATA. GLOBAL_ITEM.

```
with TEXT_IO;           use TEXT_IO;
with GLOBAL_DATA;
with CORRUPT;
procedure MAIN is
  package INT_IO is new INTEGER_IO (INTEGER);
begin
  GLOBAL_DATA.GLOBAL_ITEM := 1;
  PUT ("The value of GLOBAL_DATA.GLOBAL_ITEM is => ");
  INT_IO.PUT (GLOBAL_DATA.GLOBAL_ITEM);
  NEW_LINE;
  -- Here the global data is changed
  CORRUPT.DO_SOMETHING;
  -- Global data should be 1!
  GLOBAL_DATA.GLOBAL_ITEM := GLOBAL_DATA.GLOBAL_ITEM + 1;
  PUT_LINE ("The value of GLOBAL_DATA.GLOBAL_ITEM should be incremented by 1");
  PUT ("The real value of GLOBAL_DATA.GLOBAL_ITEM is => ");
  INT_IO.PUT (GLOBAL_DATA.GLOBAL_ITEM);
  NEW_LINE;
end MAIN;
```

Listing 7.28 Main program that unknowingly corrupts the global data.

When MAIN is executed it uses packages GLOBAL_DATA and CORRUPT. In each instance the variable GLOBAL_ITEM is affected. Read through this listing carefully. Deduce precisely what happens to the value of GLOBAL_ITEM as the program executes. This should bring home to you how easy it is to make mistakes when handling globals. Learn from this.

REVIEW

Do you now:

- Understand the need for modularity to achieve reliable programming?
- Appreciate the difference between monolithic, modular and independent compilation techniques?
- Perceive the design formality and control introduced by Ada through the use of packages and related **with** and **use** clauses?
- Feel confident to write and compile package specifications and package bodies?
- Know how to deal with chained sets of packages and program units?
- Understand the concept of package elaboration and initialization?

Chapter Eight

Composite data types – the array

Up to this point we have dealt with only a single data item at a time. In previous examples, for instance, we had NUM, D1, D2, etc., each name representing a single variable of a particular type. These are called 'simple' variables. There are many cases, though, where we work with variables which are related to each other. It may be the set of computation coefficients for a digital filter, the collection of all monitored parameters on a diesel engine, or the set of exam marks for a course. All of these can be organized as a grouping of simple variables of course, but in many cases significant benefits are gained by arranging these in a defined structure. This organization is called a data structure, variables used within the structure being structured data types.

On completing this chapter you will:

- Understand the use of structured data types;
- Appreciate the need for a variety of structures;
- Understand the concept and use of arrays;
- Be able to work with their contents as single entities or as a collection of components.

8.1 INTRODUCTION TO STRUCTURED VARIABLES

Why should we want to structure, that is arrange or order, our information in the first place? Or, if we don't use structured types, are certain jobs beyond our capabilities as programmers?

In answering the second question we also give the reply to the first one. No, we don't need to use structured types in programming. It is just that they make life much easier for many tasks. After all, you don't need to use a mechanical digger to dig a hole for a swimming pool, it could be done by hand.

There are a number of reasons for structuring. In each and every case we will be dealing with a collection of data items; more importantly these items are somehow related to each other. The nature of the relationships varies; as a result a number of different data structures have been produced, each having particular features and uses.

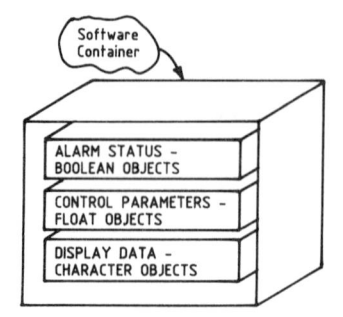

Fig.8.1 Data structure requirement 1 – grouping of data objects.

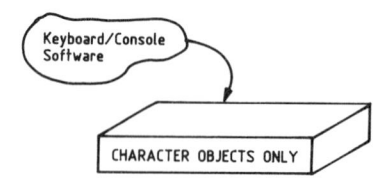

Fig.8.2 Grouping of homogeneous objects.

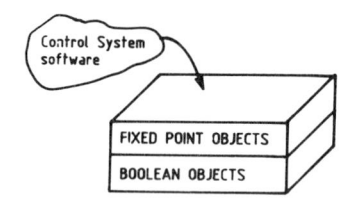

Fig.8.3 Grouping of heterogeneous objects.

Let's consider what we want from the data structure:

(a) It must first allow us to group data objects together (Fig.8.1).
(b) It must support the grouping of objects of the same type ('homogeneous') and those of different types ('heterogeneous') (Figs 8.2 and 8.3).
(c) It must let us handle individual objects within the group as well as manipulating the group (or parts of the group) as a single entity (Figs 8.4 and 8.5).
(d) In some cases it must enable single items to be accessed at random. In others it should allow us to work with large quantities of data using sequential accessing methods (Figs 8.6 and 8.7).
(e) Accessing the information should be both simple and efficient.

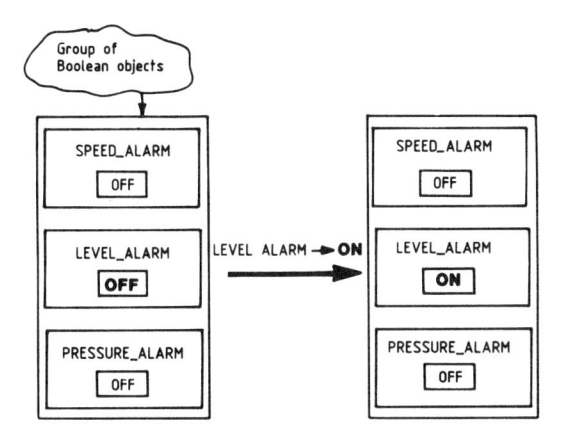

Fig.8.4 Handling individual objects.

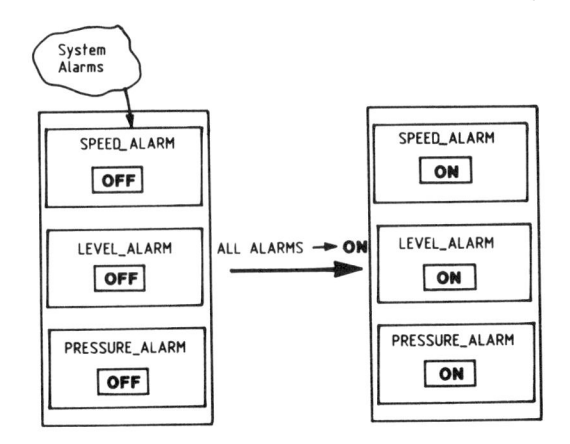

Fig.8.5 Group manipulation.

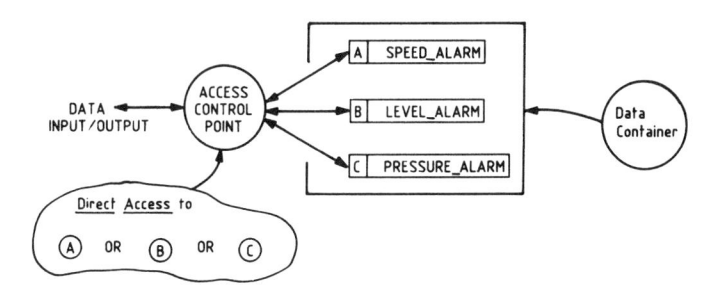

Fig.8.6 Random selection.

226 Composite data types – the array

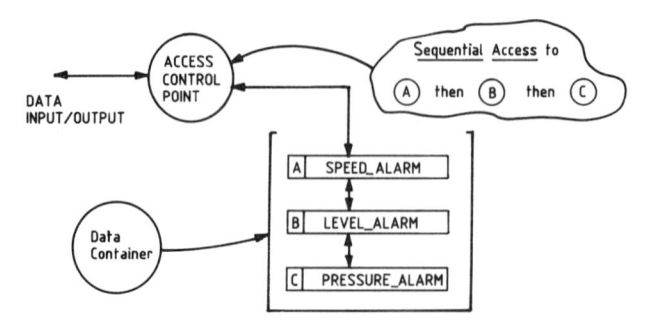

Fig.8.7 Sequential selection.

In this and the following chapter we'll see what the various data structures of Ada do for us.

8.2 ARRAYS

8.2.1 Overview

The array structure is provided in virtually all high-level programming languages, being used with homogeneous data objects (Fig.8.8).

As an example of its use consider the following digital control algorithm:

$$Ynew = (A0) \times (Xnew) + (A1) \times (Xold) - (A2) \times (Yold)$$

Here the A's are algorithm coefficients of the same data type. Our objective now is to form a data type which:

- Holds the values of the algorithm coefficients;
- Is uniquely identified by a single name;
- Enables us to handle the whole set of coefficients as if it is a single variable;
- Enables us to manipulate each coefficient separately;
- Is easy to manage.

First, group the coefficients into a single compound type (the 'Array'), identifying the unit so formed as a named variable (Fig.8.9).

In this case we'll identify the coefficient grouping as 'Accel', having three individual components ('elements').

Now we need to implement an efficient and simple way of identifying the elements. Each element in the array is unique; hence it needs a unique reference or identifier. Obviously this identifier must also carry the array name.

Arrays 227

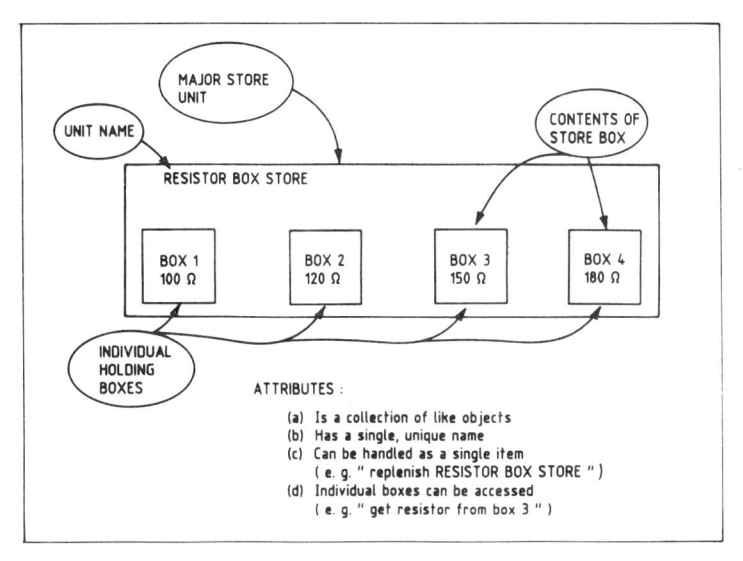

Fig.8.8 Array structure – concept.

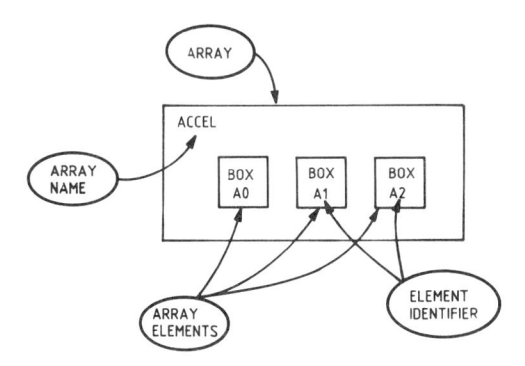

Fig.8.9 Array structure of algorithm coefficients.

So for the example above we could have a set of array elements called Accel(A0), Accel(A1) and Accel(A2).

The fact that all elements belong to the variable 'Accel' means that we don't have to use names as individual identifiers. Tagging numbers to each element is a simple and effective technique. This would allow us to use element identifiers such as Accel(0), Accel(1) and Accel(2).

Whichever system is used, elements are always arranged in a contiguous sequence. Each one is then identified by a suffix attached to the array identifier. Note that we use a similar method for numbering houses; this makes it easy to find houses and organize postal deliveries. This structure is called a one-dimensional array.

8.2.2 Declaring and using arrays – a first introduction

For the above example let us suppose that we are calculating the acceleration (Y_NEW) of an engine from speed measurements (X). The array could be identified as ACCEL, having three elements named as ACCEL(1), ACCEL(2) and ACCEL(3). Four factors have to be declared to the compiler:

- The presence of the array variable ('ACCEL');
- The fact that it is an array;
- The number of elements in the array;
- The type of its elements.

As all elements are organized in a contiguous sequence we can specify the array size using only two values. These are the numbers of the first and last element positions. Thus the most basic array declaration format is

> ACCEL : **array** (1..3) **of** INTEGER;

Here the variable ACCEL is declared to be an array, having three elements (Fig.8.10).

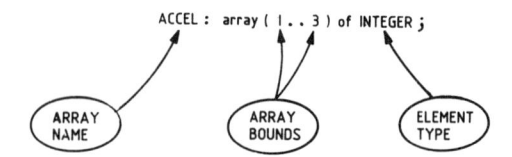

Fig.8.10 Array declaration format.

The first element is identified as number 1, the last being 3. These are defined to be the array bounds. All elements are of type INTEGER, the component type.

A simple example of the use of arrays is given in Listing 8.1 where it can be seen that:

- Arrays are declared, as per normal, in the declarations section;
- The declaration starts with the identifier name;
- It is followed by the word **array**;
- The array bounds are placed in brackets (parentheses), lower and upper limits being separated by '..';
- The word **of** comes next;

```ada
with TEXT_IO;              use TEXT_IO;
procedure CALC_ACCELERATION is
  package INT_IO is new INTEGER_IO (INTEGER);
  use INT_IO;
  ACCEL           :    array (1..3) of INTEGER;
  XNEW            :    INTEGER;
  XOLD            :    INTEGER;
  YNEW            :    INTEGER;
  YOLD            :    INTEGER;
begin
  ACCEL (1) := 2;
  ACCEL (2) := 1;
  ACCEL (3) := 1;
  PUT ("Input XNEW => ");
  GET (XNEW);
  SKIP_LINE;
  PUT ("Input XOLD => ");
  GET (XOLD);
  SKIP_LINE;
  PUT ("Input YOLD => ");
  GET (YOLD);
  SKIP_LINE;
  YNEW := ACCEL (1) * XNEW + ACCEL (2) * XOLD + ACCEL (3) * YOLD;
  PUT ("The value of Ynew is ");
  PUT (YNEW, 0);
  NEW_LINE;
end CALC_ACCELERATION;
```

Listing 8.1 This is a very simple use of arrays.

- The declaration is finished off with the type of the array elements;
- Within the program, array elements are accessed using a 'subscript' or 'array index' enclosed in brackets (Fig.8.11).

The subscript must be a discrete type, for example INTEGER, BOOLEAN, CHARACTER, etc. Examples of such index types will be given later.

8.2.3 Why arrays are powerful constructs

Up to this time we don't seem to have gained very much by using the array construct. In fact in the above example we've probably created more work for ourselves. So, in some situations, such as:

- where only a few variables are involved;
- where the number of variables is fixed,

arrays are of limited use. However, if the converse is true, then arrays come into their own. This is best shown by example, using simple array operations, including:

230 Composite data types – the array

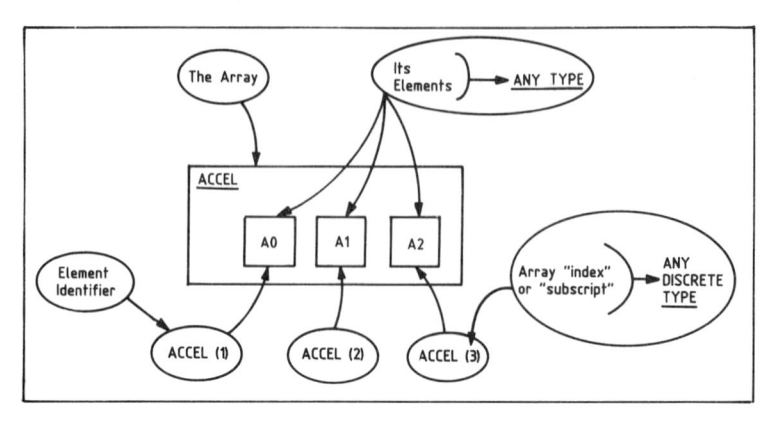

Fig.8.11 Array elements.

- Presetting values;
- Transferring data between related variables;
- Handling information of varying size;
- Transferring data between arrays.

(a) Presetting values

Consider that we have a set of variables which must be preset before they can be used (this particular operation is often needed during program initialization). We could, of course, handle each variable individually. However, if we can form them into an array our work is very much reduced. Consider the simplicity of the following statement:

```
for J in 1..3 loop
   ACCEL (J) := 0;
end loop;
```

When this statement is executed all elements of the array ACCEL are set to zero (Fig.8.12).

Now, for three elements this may seem elaborate. However, when the number of elements becomes large (say a few hundred) this construct is tremendously useful.

(b) Transferring values between related variables

Suppose that we have to carry out the following computation:

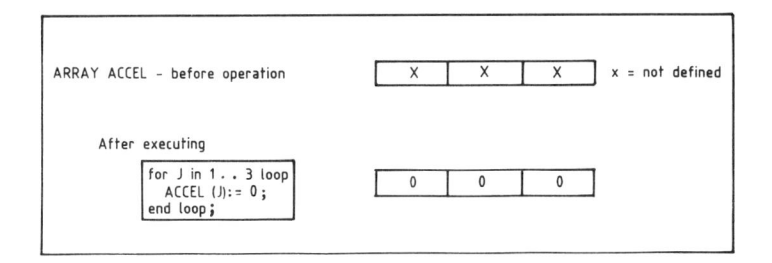

```
┌─────────────────────────────────────────────────────────────────┐
│                                                                 │
│   ARRAY ACCEL - before operation    ┌───┬───┬───┐  x = not defined │
│                                     │ x │ x │ x │               │
│                                     └───┴───┴───┘               │
│       After executing                                           │
│         ┌─────────────────┐                                     │
│         │ for J in 1..3 loop│       ┌───┬───┬───┐               │
│         │   ACCEL (J):= 0; │        │ 0 │ 0 │ 0 │               │
│         │ end loop;        │        └───┴───┴───┘               │
│         └─────────────────┘                                     │
└─────────────────────────────────────────────────────────────────┘
```

Fig.8.12 Presetting an array.

$$Y_i := X_i + X_{i-1} + X_{i-2} + X_{i-3}$$

where X is the sampled value of the input parameter (say Speed). X_i is the most recent sample, X_{i-1} the last value, etc. Each time the calculation is carried out a new value of X is obtained whilst the past values all 'slip' back one sample time (i.e. the value in location X_{i-1} is replaced by the value that was in location X_i, etc.). By forming an 'X' or Speed array, this can be done in a neat, simple, way. First of all form the array 'SPEED' as shown above so that

$$\text{SPEED}(0) \text{ holds the value of } X_i$$
$$\text{SPEED}(1) \text{ holds the value of } X_{i-1}$$
$$\text{SPEED}(2) \text{ holds the value of } X_{i-2}$$
$$\text{SPEED}(3) \text{ holds the value of } X_{i-3}$$

Then the values can be slipped back as follows:

```
for J in reverse 0..2 loop
  SPEED (J+1) := SPEED (J);
end loop;
```

Finally, the new measured input can be placed into SPEED(0) using (Fig.8.13):

```
SPEED (0) := Xi;
```

(c) Handling information of varying size

Assume that we have the task of modelling a real plant or system using its input and output signal values. This technique is used extensively in simulation and self-tuning control systems, where signal processing is normally

232 Composite data types – the array

Source Code	STAGE ITEM	BEFORE LOOP OPERATION	END LOOP 1	2	3	4	5
for J in reverse 0..2 loop	SPEED (0)	0	5	4	2	3	7
SPEED (J + 1) := SPEED (J);	SPEED (1)	0	0	5	4	2	3
end loop ;	SPEED (2)	0	0	0	5	4	2
SPEED (0) := Xi ;	SPEED (3)	0	0	0	0	5	4
	Xi	5	4	2	3	7	

Fig.8.13 Shifting values within an array.

carried out in software. The measured signal values can be formed into an array within the computer; subsequently these are manipulated mathematically to extract model information. One parameter will almost certainly change during system analysis: the number of data samples taken by the measurement process. But if the array size is fixed how do we deal with this requirement?

The answer is to use named values as bounds, adjusting these as needed. In the example of Listing 8.2 two named bounds are given. The first one ('MAX_NUMBER') is used to set the maximum size of the array. Note that this is declared as a constant value. The second, 'ACTUAL_NUMBER', is used to select the number of elements accessed when the program is run.

It is important to realize that the array size is set by the program declaration. Thus it cannot change during a program run. What we have here is an example of a *static* array. Such arrays can lead to inefficient use of computer storage space, particularly with large structures. To overcome this we can use *dynamic* bounds, giving us the dynamic array structure (described later).

(d) **Transferring data between arrays**

Suppose that we have data contained in an array ('INPUT)' which we wish to copy but still retain the original data. Then by forming a second array ('INPUT_COPY') we can very simply transfer data between the two arrays. For instance, the statement

```
INPUT_COPY (15) := INPUT (15);
```

will assign the value of element 15 of INPUT to element 15 of INPUT_COPY.

The following statement (Fig.8.14) will cause the entire array to be copied

```
with TEXT_IO;                use TEXT_IO;
procedure ARRAY_BOUNDS is
  package INT_IO is new INTEGER_IO (INTEGER);
  use INT_IO;
  MAX_NUMBER       :   constant        := 100;
  ACTUAL_NUMBER    :   INTEGER;
  SPEED            :   array (1..MAX_NUMBER) of INTEGER;
begin
  for J in 1..MAX_NUMBER loop
    SPEED (J) := 10;
  end loop;
  PUT ("Please enter the number of data points ");
  GET (ACTUAL_NUMBER);
  SKIP_LINE;
  for J in 1..ACTUAL_NUMBER loop
    SPEED (J) := 0;
    PUT ("speed reading " );
    PUT (J, 4);
    PUT (" => ");
    PUT (SPEED (J), 0);
    NEW_LINE;
  end loop;
end ARRAY_BOUNDS;
```

Listing 8.2 This shows the basic use of named array bounds.

Source Code	ELEMENT No	BEFORE		AFTER	
for I in 1.. MAX_NUMBER loop		INPUT_COPY	INPUT	INPUT_COPY	INPUT
INPUT_COPY (I):= INPUT (I);	1	X	6	6	6
end loop;	2	X	3	3	3
	3	X	2	2	2
	4	X	8	8	8
X = not defined here	5	X	1	1	1

Fig.8.14 Copying array values.

(assuming that MAX_NUMBER is the maximum element number of the array):

```
for I in 1..MAX_NUMBER loop
  INPUT_COPY (I) := INPUT (I);
end loop;
```

Here INPUT_COPY and INPUT can be different types. However, the array elements must be the same type.

234   Composite data types – the array

8.2.4 Array types – anonymous, constrained and unconstrained

(a) Anonymous types

In Listing 8.1 we made the following declaration:

```
ACCEL : array (1..3) of INTEGER;
```

This is actually the declaration of the program object called ACCEL. But observe that we haven't explicitly declared an array type. INTEGER only defines the type of the array elements. What we have here is an *implicit* type declaration, the type being *anonymous*. By anonymous we mean that the type is not named. Further, each and every anonymous type is considered to be unique. This construct can lead to unforeseen problems, which we will discuss shortly.

(b) Constrained types

In the above example we could have made an *explicit* type declaration as, for instance,

```
type COEFFICIENTS is array (1..3) of INTEGER;
ACCEL : COEFFICIENTS;
```

From this it is clear that the object ACCEL is of type COEFFICIENTS. What we also have here is an example of a constrained type definition, Fig.8.15.

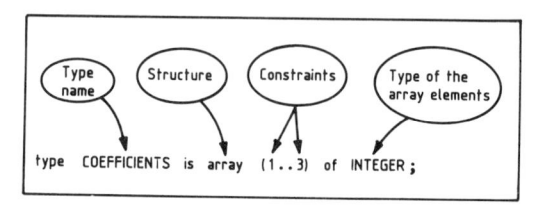

Fig.8.15 Constrained array declaration format.

The array is constrained by the array bounds to have a specific discrete range. More formally, the type declaration syntax is

```
type NAME is array Index_Constraint of Component_Subtype;
```

Thus Ada enables us to declare an array structure as a data type. Subsequently we can declare variables as belonging to that type, as follows:

```
type VECTOR is array (0..100) of INTEGER;
SPEED, DELTA : VECTOR;
```

This layout is easy to follow and understand. By using this the programmer, when working with arrays, is much less likely to make mistakes. Such mistakes occur most often when using procedures or when mixing arrays from different packages. In fact this declaration form forces the compiler to check for name, rather than structural, equivalence.

With constrained arrays we can use a different approach for copying whole arrays. The assignment operation can be applied, as follows:

```
INPUT_COPY := INPUT;
```

Clearly to use this construct the arrays themselves must be the same type. Even so, the **for-loop** is a very useful technique for handling selective parts of the array structure, as shown in Listing 8.3.

(c) **Unconstrained arrays**

For many applications the constrained form poses no problems or difficulties. In certain instances, though it can be very restrictive. Consider the need to solve linear equations of the form:

$$a_1 X_1 + a_2 X_2 + a_3 X_3 = Y$$

This can be written in matrix form as

$$[a_1\ a_2\ a_3] \begin{bmatrix} X_1 \\ X_2 \\ X_3 \end{bmatrix} = Y$$

The program of Listing 8.4 performs the mathematical operations of multiplying these two vectors (the 'a' array and the 'X' array) together.

Suppose now that we have to calculate

$$b_1 X_1 + b_2 X_2 + b_3 X_3 + b_4 X_4 + b_5 X_5 = Y$$

```
with TEXT_IO;                 use TEXT_IO;
procedure ARRAY_COPY is
  package INT_IO is new INTEGER_IO (INTEGER);
  use INT_IO;
  type INTEGER_LIST is array (1..10) of INTEGER;
  INPUT_LIST         :        INTEGER_LIST;
  COPY_LIST          :        INTEGER_LIST;
  REVERSE_LIST       :        INTEGER_LIST;
  INPUT_INDEX        :        INTEGER;
begin
  -- read in the input_array
  PUT_LINE ("Please Enter 10 integer values");
  for I in 1..10 loop
    PUT (I, 0);
    PUT (" => ");
    GET (INPUT_LIST (I));
    SKIP_LINE;
  end loop;
  -- copy the elements into another array
  COPY_LIST := INPUT_LIST;
  -- copy the elements, in reverse, into the output array
  for REVERSE_INDEX in 1..10 loop
    INPUT_INDEX := 11 - REVERSE_INDEX;
    REVERSE_LIST (REVERSE_INDEX) := INPUT_LIST (INPUT_INDEX);
  end loop;
  -- print out the copied array
  PUT_LINE ("The numbers you have entered are");
  for COPY_INDEX in 1..10 loop
    PUT (COPY_INDEX, 0);
    PUT (" => ");
    GET (COPY_LIST (COPY_INDEX));
    SKIP_LINE;
  end loop;
  -- print out the reversed array
  PUT_LINE ("The numbers you have, in reverse, entered are");
  for REVERSE_INDEX in 1..10 loop
    PUT (REVERSE_INDEX, 0);
    PUT (" => ");
    GET (REVERSE_LIST (REVERSE_INDEX));
    SKIP_LINE;
  end loop;
end ARRAY_COPY;
```

Listing 8.3 Copying between arrays.

We would be forced to form a new array type, say

```
type VECTOR_2 is array (1..5) of INTEGER;
```

And yet the only difference between array types VECTOR and VECTOR_2 is their size. Can we avoid having to create new array types just to handle size variations? For Ada, the answer is yes, using the unconstrained array type.

Arrays 237

```
procedure VECTOR_MULTIPLICATION is
   type VECTOR is array (1..3) of INTEGER;
   ALPHA         :     VECTOR;
   X             :     VECTOR;
   RESULT        :     INTEGER      := 0;
begin
   -- put data in the vectors
   ALPHA (1) := 1;
   ALPHA (2) := 2;
   ALPHA (3) := 3;
   X (1) := 2;
   X (2) := 4;
   X (3) := 6;
   for I in 1..3 loop
      RESULT := RESULT + (ALPHA (I) * X (I));
   end loop;
end VECTOR_MULTIPLICATION;
```

Listing 8.4 This is a part program showing the use of arrays for multiplying two vectors.

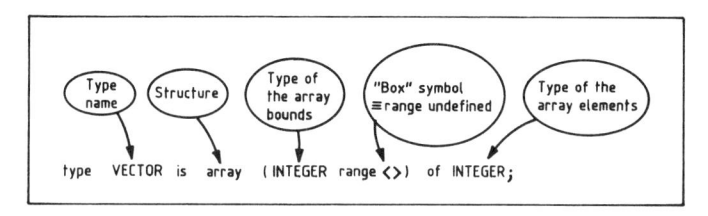

```
type VECTOR is array ( INTEGER range <>) of INTEGER;
```
Type name / Structure / Type of the array bounds / "Box" symbol ≡ range undefined / Type of the array elements

Fig.8.16 Unconstrained array declaration format.

In this type the size of the array is not constrained in size when it is declared. Instead the index bounds are replaced by a subtype definition, as for example (Fig.8.16):

```
type VECTOR is array (INTEGER range <>) of INTEGER;
```

Here we have replaced '(1..3)' with 'INTEGER **range** < >'. Thus the bounds of the array are unspecified – but they are of type INTEGER. The '< >' symbol, called a box, means 'the range is undefined'.

We can regard this type as being a template. When we use the template we merely fill in the missing information – the array bounds. There are two ways of using this unconstrained type. First, we can declare objects, specifying that they belong to the type, as in:

238   Composite data types – the array

```
procedure UNCONSTRAINED is
  type VECTOR is array (INTEGER range <>) of INTEGER;
  A_ROW     :  VECTOR (1..3);
  RESULT_A  :  INTEGER       := 0;
  B_ROW     :  VECTOR (1..5);
  X         :  VECTOR (1..5);
  RESULT_B  :  INTEGER       := 0;
begin
  -- put data in the vectors
  A_ROW (1) := 1;
  A_ROW (2) := 2;
  A_ROW (3) := 3;
  B_ROW (1) := 5;
  B_ROW (2) := 4;
  B_ROW (3) := 3;
  B_ROW (4) := 2;
  B_ROW (5) := 1;
  X (1) := 10;
  X (2) := 8;
  X (3) := 6;
  X (4) := 4;
  X (5) := 2;
  for INDEX in 1..3 loop
    RESULT_A := RESULT_A + (A_ROW (INDEX) * X (INDEX));
  end loop;
  for INDEX in 1..5 loop
    RESULT_B := RESULT_B + (B_ROW (INDEX) * X (INDEX));
  end loop;
end UNCONSTRAINED;
```

Listing 8.5 Unconstrained arrays.

```
type VECTOR is array (INTEGER range <>) of INTEGER;
A_ROW : VECTOR (1..3);
B_ROW : VECTOR (1..5);
```

Thus the array variable (object) A_ROW contains three elements, whilst B_ROW contains five. Even though the number of elements is different they are both the same type, VECTOR. Listing 8.5 shows this construct in use.

The second method is to declare a subtype of the unconstrained type, as, for instance,

```
type VECTOR is array (INTEGER range <>) of INTEGER;
subtype THREE_ELEMENT_ARRAY is VECTOR (1..3);
subtype FIVE_ELEMENT_ARRAY is VECTOR (1..5);
A_ROW : THREE_ELEMENT_ARRAY;
B_ROW : FIVE_ELEMENT_ARRAY;
```

These points are demonstrated in Listing 8.6.

Arrays 239

```
procedure ARRAY_SUBTYPE is
  type VECTOR is array (INTEGER range <>) of INTEGER;
  subtype THREE_ELEMENT_ARRAY is VECTOR (1..3);
  subtype FIVE_ELEMENT_ARRAY is VECTOR (1..5);
  A_ROW          :     THREE_ELEMENT_ARRAY;
  RESULT_A       :     INTEGER           := 0;
  B_ROW          :     FIVE_ELEMENT_ARRAY;
  X              :     FIVE_ELEMENT_ARRAY;
  RESULT_B       :     INTEGER           := 0;
begin
  -- put data in the vectors
  A_ROW (1) := 1;
  A_ROW (2) := 2;
  A_ROW (3) := 3;
  B_ROW (1) := 5;
  B_ROW (2) := 4;
  B_ROW (3) := 3;
  B_ROW (4) := 2;
  B_ROW (5) := 1;
  X (1) := 10;
  X (2) := 8;
  X (3) := 6;
  X (4) := 4;
  X (5) := 2;
  for INDEX in 1..3 loop
    RESULT_A := RESULT_A + (A_ROW (INDEX) * X (INDEX));
  end loop;
  for INDEX in 1..5 loop
    RESULT_B := RESULT_B + (B_ROW (INDEX) * X (INDEX));
  end loop;
end ARRAY_SUBTYPE;
```

Listing 8.6 Array subtype – declaration and use.

NOTE: The type of the bounds and the type of the elements are not in any way related, as demonstrated by the declaration

```
type GENERAL_ALARMS is array (INTEGER range <>) of BOOLEAN;
```

Here the array index is of type INTEGER, whilst the array element values are BOOLEANs.

8.2.5 Array aggregates

To aggregate is 'to unite'; an aggregate is 'a total' (*Oxford English Dictionary*). In Ada, an aggregate is 'a basic operation that combines component values into a composite value ...'. Using aggregates we can set up the value of an entire array, as in

240 Composite data types – the array

```
with TEXT_IO;              use TEXT_IO;
procedure SIMPLE_AGGREGATE is
----------------------------
  LOGIC           :    array (1..3) of BOOLEAN;
  package INT_IO is new INTEGER_IO (INTEGER);
  package BOOLEAN_IO is new ENUMERATION_IO (BOOLEAN);
  use INT_IO;
  use BOOLEAN_IO;
begin
  LOGIC := (TRUE, FALSE, TRUE);
  for I in 1..3 loop
    PUT ("Logic ");
    PUT (I, 0);
    PUT (" => ");
    PUT (LOGIC (I));
    NEW_LINE;
  end loop;
end SIMPLE_AGGREGATE;
```

Listing 8.7 This is a simple example of the use of aggregates.

```
ACCEL : array (1..3) of INTEGER;
begin
      .
  ACCEL := (105, 2016, 5);
      .
end ...
```

After executing this statement the following values are held by the array elements:

$$ACCEL(1) \longrightarrow 105$$
$$ACCEL(2) \longrightarrow 2016$$
$$ACCEL(3) \longrightarrow 5$$

These points are shown in Listing 8.7.

We can define an array aggregate as 'a particular set of values applied to the whole array'. In the example here the aggregate is

$$(105, 2016, 5)$$

Each value in the array aggregate '(105, 2016, 5)' is assigned to the array element in the corresponding position. From this it should be plain that the aggregate must contain values for all elements – it must be complete. Otherwise the compiler won't be able to work out the allocation details.

Assignment using the aggregate can be used at any point in a program. However, it is frequently used to initialize arrays, when it may be used in the declarations section, namely:

```
procedure INIT_AND_CONST is
  type VECTOR is array (1..3) of INTEGER;
  X       :  constant VECTOR := (2, 4, 6);
  ALPHA   :  VECTOR           := (1, 2, 3);
  RESULT  :  INTEGER          := 0;
begin
  for I in 1..3 loop
    RESULT := RESULT + (ALPHA (I) * X (I));
  end loop;
end INIT_AND_CONST;
```

Listing 8.8 Using array aggregates – initialization and constants.

```
ACCEL : array (1..3) of INTEGER := (0, 1, 0);
```

The aggregate is essential when we form a constant array, as, for instance,

```
LINEARIZATION_TABLE : constant array (0..3) of FLOAT
                    := (0.0, 5.0, 12.5 20.9);
```

Listing 8.8 illustrates these aspects.

8.2.6 Array slices

To slice is 'to cut from a larger piece'. In the case of Ada, a slice is an array of the components of another array. That is, we slice the original array to form the new one. Suppose we have

```
type VECTOR is array (0..100) of BOOLEAN;
DELTA : VECTOR
```

Then the following are slices of DELTA:

```
DELTA (0..9);
DELTA (10..90);
DELTA (91..100);
```

A simple use of slicing is given in Listing 8.9.
  We will return to slices when we discuss the string type.

```
with TEXT_IO;                    use TEXT_IO;
procedure BASIC_SLICE is
  type VECTOR is array (0..100) of BOOLEAN;
  DELTA      :      VECTOR;
begin
  -- set the first ten elements of DELTA as a slice
  DELTA (0..9)    := (TRUE, TRUE, FALSE, FALSE, TRUE,
                      TRUE, TRUE, TRUE, FALSE, FALSE);
  -- copy the first ten elements to the last ten elements as a slice
  DELTA (91..100) := DELTA (0..9);
NULL;
end BASIC_SLICE;
```

Listing 8.9 A basic example of the use of slices.

8.2.7 String arrays

A string array is a one-dimensional array of characters. The elements are of type CHARACTER, and indices are of type POSITIVE (integer numbers lying between one and the highest integer value in the computer system). We have, in fact, been using strings from the very beginning – without any consideration for (or even any knowledge of) arrays. We have been able to do this because strings are predefined in Ada, in the package STANDARD. So far the applications have been very restrictive. Their major use has been as parameters of PUT-like statements. Here we will extend their use.

The declaration in STANDARD is

> **type** STRING **is array** (POSITIVE **range** <>) **of** CHARACTER

Thus it can be seen to be an unconstrained type. Hence constraints must be applied when we declare objects to be of type string, as in

> ENGINE_FIRE_ALARM : STRING (1..44);

Now we can assign characters to the object ENGINE_FIRE_ALARM. The most common method is to put the entire string in quotes, as follows:

> ENGINE_FIRE_ALARM := "Jet pipe temperature monitors - FIRE WARNING";

Listing 8.10 is a simple example of string operations.

Note that the size of the string (number of characters) must match the size constraints – even if we need fewer characters. If, for instance, we wrote

```
with TEXT_IO;              use TEXT_IO;
procedure SIMPLE_STRING is
  ENGINE_FIRE_ALARM :      STRING (1..39);
  TEMPERATURE       :      INTEGER;
  package INT_IO is new INTEGER_IO (INTEGER);
  use INT_IO;
begin
  PUT ("Please enter the jet pipe temperature : ");
  GET (TEMPERATURE);
  SKIP_LINE;
  if TEMPERATURE > 100 then
    ENGINE_FIRE_ALARM := "Jet pipe temperature monitor - TOO HIGH";
  else
    ENGINE_FIRE_ALARM := "Jet pipe temperature monitor - NORMAL  ";
  end if;
  PUT_LINE (ENGINE_FIRE_ALARM);
end SIMPLE_STRING;
```

Listing 8.10 This is a simple example of string operations.

```
with TEXT_IO;              use TEXT_IO;
procedure STRING_INIT_AND_SLICE is
  ENGINE_FIRE_ALARM_NORMAL :   STRING (1..39) :=
                               "Jet pipe temperature monitor - NORMAL  ";
  ENGINE_FIRE_ALARM_HIGH   :   STRING (1..39) :=
                               "Jet pipe temperature monitor - TOO HIGH";
  ALARM_MESSAGE            :   STRING (1..15);
  TEMPERATURE              :   INTEGER;
  package INT_IO is new INTEGER_IO (INTEGER);
  use INT_IO;
begin
  PUT ("Please enter the jet pipe temperature : ");
  GET (TEMPERATURE);
  SKIP_LINE;
  if TEMPERATURE > 100 then
    PUT_LINE (ENGINE_FIRE_ALARM_HIGH);
    ALARM_MESSAGE := "SYSTEM SHUTDOWN";
    PUT_LINE (ALARM_MESSAGE);
  else
    PUT_LINE (ENGINE_FIRE_ALARM_NORMAL);
    ALARM_MESSAGE (1..9) := "SYSTEM OK";
    PUT_LINE (ALARM_MESSAGE (1..9));
  end if;
end STRING_INIT_AND_SLICE;
```

Listing 8.11 This demonstrates string aggregates and slices.

```
ENGINE_FIRE_ALARM := "Deactivated";
```

the compiler will give a warning message as it contains 11 characters only. To implement this we have to increase the number of characters by padding out, using blanks.

We can both aggregate and slice arrays, Listing 8.11.

8.2.8 More on indexing and bounds

(a) Recap

A one-dimensional array is a collection of homogeneous, distinct components. Each component is identified (located) using an index value. These indices must form a contiguous sequence, the lowest and highest values being the bounds. Once we define the bounds for an array we also define all possible values for the index. This range of values is called the index range. It is clear from this description that this range MUST be a discrete type. Thus, for an array of five elements using index values 1, 2, 3, 4, 5 we define the range as (1..5). Look back to the section on subtypes; it can be seen that subtype bound definitions 'X .. Y' are identical to those of array bounds. Therefore we can view the array bound type as being a subtype of some existing type, either predefined or userdefined. In the declaration

> **type** VECTOR **is array** (1..5) **of** FLOAT;

the array index is a subtype of type INTEGER. Note again that each index value denotes a placeholder for a program object. It says nothing about the type of such objects.

As an aid to program clarity we can also declare the bounds to be a subtype, associating a name with this type, as follows:

> **subtype** MEASUREMENTS **is** INTEGER **range** 1..100;
> **type** VECTOR **is array** (MEASUREMENTS) **of** FLOAT;

Its use is demonstrated in Listing 8.12.

(b) User-defined index types

There is no reason why we can't form our own index type, provided we conform to the basic rules set out above. So, for example, we could first form an enumerated type DATA_POINTS, and then use this for the index values:

> **type** DATA_POINTS **is** (I0, I1, I2, I3, I4);
> **type** SPEED_ARRAY **is array** (DATA_POINTS) **of** INTEGER;
> SPEED : SPEED_ARRAY;

The use of this is shown in Listing 8.13.

```
with TEXT_IO;            use TEXT_IO;
procedure USE_SUBTYPE is
  subtype LIST_LENGTH is INTEGER range 1..10;
  type NUMBERS_LIST is array (LIST_LENGTH) of INTEGER;
  PRIME_NUMBER    :    NUMBERS_LIST    := (1, 3, 5, 7, 11, 13, 17, 19, 23, 29);
  PRIME_INDEX     :    LIST_LENGTH;
  package INT_IO is new INTEGER_IO(INTEGER);
  use INT_IO;
begin
  PUT ("Which Prime number do you require? ");
  GET (PRIME_INDEX);
  SKIP_LINE;
  PUT ("Prime Number ");
  PUT (PRIME_INDEX, 0);
  PUT (" => " );
  PUT (PRIME_NUMBER (PRIME_INDEX), 0);
  NEW_LINE;
end USE_SUBTYPE;
```

Listing 8.12 Here a subtype is defined and used to set array bounds.

```
with TEXT_IO;            use TEXT_IO;
procedure ENUMERATION_BOUNDS is
  type DATA_POINTS is (I0, I1, I2, I3, I4);
  type SPEED_ARRAY is array (DATA_POINTS) of INTEGER;
  SPEED           :    SPEED_ARRAY;
  package INT_IO is new INTEGER_IO (INTEGER);
  package DATA_POINTS_IO is new ENUMERATION_IO (DATA_POINTS);
  use INT_IO;
  use DATA_POINTS_IO;
begin
  for SPEED_DATA in I0..I4 loop
    PUT ("Please enter speed value ");
    PUT (SPEED_DATA, 0);
    PUT (" : ");
    GET (SPEED (SPEED_DATA));
    SKIP_LINE;
  end loop;
  PUT_LINE ("The speed values are");
  NEW_LINE;
  for SPEED_DATA in I0..I4 loop
    PUT ("Speed value ");
    PUT (SPEED_DATA, 0);
    PUT (" => ");
    PUT (SPEED (SPEED_DATA), 0);
    if SPEED (SPEED_DATA) > 100 then
      PUT (" - Please check this value");
    end if;
    NEW_LINE;
  end loop;
end ENUMERATION_BOUNDS;
```

Listing 8.13 This uses an enumeration type as array bounds.

246 Composite data types – the array

8.2.9 Dynamic arrays

Earlier we looked at some of the limitations of arrays of fixed size. We've also seen that the unconstrained array is a great help in many instances. Unfortunately the resulting arrays are still fixed in size, and cannot be changed at run time. Yet often it would be quite useful to change array sizes as we run the program.

According to the Ada language definition array bounds can have the form

> simple_expression .. simple_expression

Now this means that the bounds could be evaluated at run time. But, an array declared in the usual way is a static object, and according to the rules of Ada we cannot go around changing its structure after its declaration. There is only one way to change its size during run time – turn the array itself into a dynamic object. Then each time we want to alter its size we invoke it as a new object.

To make it dynamic we declare it within a program block, as for instance:

```
declare -- start of block
   VECTOR : array (LOWER_BOUND..UPPER_BOUND) of FLOAT;
begin
   .
   Program statements, including use of VECTOR
end; -- end of block
```

Both LOWER_BOUND and UPPER_BOUND are declared prior to the block. They are static variables.

Thus the array VECTOR comes into existence only when the block is entered. Its size is set by the values of the two bounds – which have been evaluated prior to entry to the block. When the block is exited the array is disposed of – it ceases to exist. These basic features are demonstrated in Listing 8.14.

Be very careful when using dynamic arrays. It is very easy to forget that we are dealing with transient objects, see Listing 8.15.

8.2.10 Multidimensional arrays and the array-of-arrays

(a) **Conceptual points**

Suppose that we are operating a numerically controlled drilling machine. How do we specify the points at which drilling is to be carried out? The usual

```ada
with TEXT_IO;                 use TEXT_IO;
procedure DYNAMIC_ARRAY is
   type MONTH is (JAN, FEB, MAR, APR, MAY, JUN, JUL, AUG, SEP, OCT, NOV, DEC);
   type RAIN_DEPTH is delta 0.01 range 0.00..100.00;
   type MEASUREMENTS_LIST is array (MONTH range <>) of RAIN_DEPTH;
   FIRST_MONTH        :      MONTH;
   LAST_MONTH         :      MONTH;
   TOTAL_RAIN_FALL    :      RAIN_DEPTH    := 0.0;
   AVERAGE_RAIN_FALL  :      RAIN_DEPTH;
   NO_OF_MONTHS       :      INTEGER range 0..12 := 0;
   package RAIN_DEPTH_IO is new FIXED_IO (RAIN_DEPTH);
   package MONTH_IO is new ENUMERATION_IO (MONTH);
   use RAIN_DEPTH_IO;
   use MONTH_IO;
begin
   PUT ("Which is the first month for which you have rain data ? ");
   GET (FIRST_MONTH);
   SKIP_LINE;
   PUT ("Which is the last month for which you have rain data ? ");
   GET (LAST_MONTH);
   SKIP_LINE;
   declare
      RAIN_FALL       :       MEASUREMENTS_LIST (FIRST_MONTH..LAST_MONTH);
      begin
         for M in FIRST_MONTH..LAST_MONTH loop
            PUT ("Enter the rain fall in centimetres for ");
            PUT (M);
            PUT (" : ");
            GET (RAIN_FALL (M));
            SKIP_LINE;
            TOTAL_RAIN_FALL := TOTAL_RAIN_FALL + RAIN_FALL (M);
            NO_OF_MONTHS := NO_OF_MONTHS + 1;
         end loop;
         AVERAGE_RAIN_FALL := RAIN_DEPTH (TOTAL_RAIN_FALL / NO_OF_MONTHS);
         PUT ("The average rain fall over this period is ");
         PUT (AVERAGE_RAIN_FALL, 0);
         PUT (" cm");
         NEW_LINE;
      end;
end DYNAMIC_ARRAY;
```

Listing 8.14 Demonstrating the use of dynamic arrays.

way is to describe its drilling area using a two-dimensional co-ordinate system (Fig.8.17) and then identify locations using an X–Y number pairing.

Now take something quite different – identifying seat locations in a theatre. For the most part seats are grouped in lettered rows, each seat being numbered within its row (Fig.8.18).

Thus we have seats at, for instance, Row A/Seat 1, Row B/Seat 1, Row C/Seat 1, etc.

Both these examples show how to define a location in two dimensions. But there is a subtle difference between them. In the second case we can clearly separate out rows and seats, treating them as entities in their own right. For instance, we could give an order for the removal of a complete row of seats.

```ada
with TEXT_IO;              use TEXT_IO;
procedure MISUSE_DYNAMIC_ARRAY is
  type MONTH is (JAN, FEB, MAR, APR, MAY, JUN, JUL, AUG, SEP, OCT, NOV, DEC);
  type RAIN_DEPTH is delta 0.01 range 0.00..100.00;
  type MEASUREMENTS_LIST is array (MONTH range <>) of RAIN_DEPTH;
  FIRST_MONTH        :     MONTH;
  LAST_MONTH         :     MONTH;
  TOTAL_RAIN_FALL    :     RAIN_DEPTH      := 0.0;
  AVERAGE_RAIN_FALL  :     RAIN_DEPTH;
  NO_OF_MONTHS       :     INTEGER range 0..12 := 0;
  FIRST_QUARTER_FALL : MEASUREMENTS_LIST (JAN..MAR);
  package RAIN_DEPTH_IO is new FIXED_IO (RAIN_DEPTH);
  package MONTH_IO is new ENUMERATION_IO (MONTH);
  use RAIN_DEPTH_IO;
  use MONTH_IO;
begin
  PUT ("Which is the first month for which you have rain data ? ");
  GET (FIRST_MONTH);
  SKIP_LINE;
  PUT ("Which is the last month for which you have rain data ? ");
  GET (LAST_MONTH);
  SKIP_LINE;
  declare
    RAIN_FALL         :       MEASUREMENTS_LIST (FIRST_MONTH..LAST_MONTH);
    begin
      for M in FIRST_MONTH..LAST_MONTH loop
        PUT ("Enter the rain fall in centimetres for ");
        PUT (M);
        PUT (" : ");
        GET (RAIN_FALL (M));
        SKIP_LINE;
        TOTAL_RAIN_FALL := TOTAL_RAIN_FALL + RAIN_FALL (M);
        NO_OF_MONTHS := NO_OF_MONTHS + 1;
      end loop;
      AVERAGE_RAIN_FALL := RAIN_DEPTH (TOTAL_RAIN_FALL / NO_OF_MONTHS);
      PUT ("The average rain fall over this period is ");
      PUT (AVERAGE_RAIN_FALL, 0);
      PUT (" cm");
      NEW_LINE;
      FIRST_QUARTER_FALL := RAIN_FALL (JAN..MAR);
 -- !!!! The above statement will only be legal if FIRST_MONTH
 -- !!!! is JAN and LAST_MONTH is in the range MAR to DEC
    end;
    PUT_LINE ("The rain fall in the first quarter was :");
    for EARLY_MONTH in JAN..MAR loop
      PUT (EARLY_MONTH);
      PUT (" => ");
      PUT (FIRST_QUARTER_FALL (EARLY_MONTH));
      PUT (" cm");
      NEW_LINE;
    end loop;
  end MISUSE_DYNAMIC_ARRAY;
```

Listing 8.15 Dynamic arrays – demonstrating their dynamic properties.

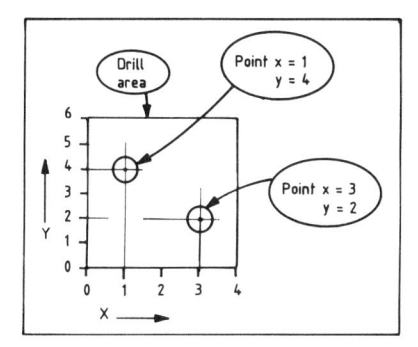

Fig.8.17 Two-dimensional co-ordinate system.

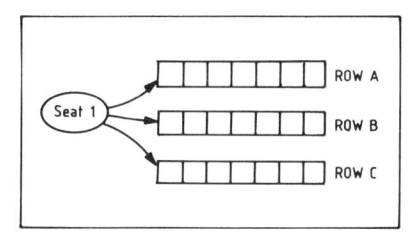

Fig.8.18 Row/seat identification.

Or we could demand that individual seats within specific rows should not be allocated by the booking office. By contrast, when we describe drilling operations, we really are working within a two-dimensional space. There is no sense of the X and Y axes being compartmentalized as individual 'things'.

How would we develop programs to deal with such situations? From our previous work it would seem that a modified or extended array mechanism could be appropriate. And that is exactly what is used. Two forms are provided in Ada: multidimensional arrays and the array-of-arrays. The multidimensional array is appropriate for problems such as programming the drill machine. For a theatre seat reservation program we'd use the array-of-arrays construct.

(b) Multidimensional arrays

What we've dealt with so far are so-called 'one-dimensional' arrays. These are directly analogous to vectors in matrix algebra. For instance, as we saw earlier the linear equation

$$a_1X_1 + a_2X_2 + a_3X_3 = Y$$

can be written in matrix form as

$$[a_1 \ a_2 \ a_3]\begin{bmatrix} X_1 \\ X_2 \\ X_3 \end{bmatrix} = Y$$

The programming to implement this was given in Listing 8.4. So far, so good. But how do we go about calculating matrix operations, typified by the need to solve equations of the following form?

$$a_{11}X_1 + a_{12}X_2 + a_{13}X_3 = Y_1$$
$$a_{21}X_1 + a_{22}X_2 + a_{23}X_3 = Y_2$$

In matrix notation this is

$$\begin{bmatrix} a_{11} & a_{12} & a_{13} \\ a_{21} & a_{22} & a_{23} \end{bmatrix} \begin{bmatrix} X_1 \\ X_2 \\ X_3 \end{bmatrix} = \begin{bmatrix} Y_1 \\ Y_2 \end{bmatrix}$$

We can regard the A matrix components as existing within a two-dimensional structure. By contrast the X and Y components exist within a one-dimensional array (vector) construct. To handle the A matrix requirement we use the Ada multidimensional array organization.

For the matrix example above the declaration would be

```
ALPHA : array (1..2, 1..3) of FLOAT;
```

or

```
type MATRIX is array (1..2, 1..3) of FLOAT;
ALPHA : MATRIX;
```

Nowhere in Ada are array structures defined in mathematical form as 'rows' and 'columns'. However, these are very widely used in engineering calculations. Therefore it is useful to think in such terms when handling arrays (Fig.8.19).

For the situation described here the elements of the A matrix are accessed as follows:

Arrays 251

```
type MATRIX is array (1..2, 1..3) of FLOAT;
ALPHA : MATRIX;
```
(Double Subscript → Dimension 1, Dimension 2)

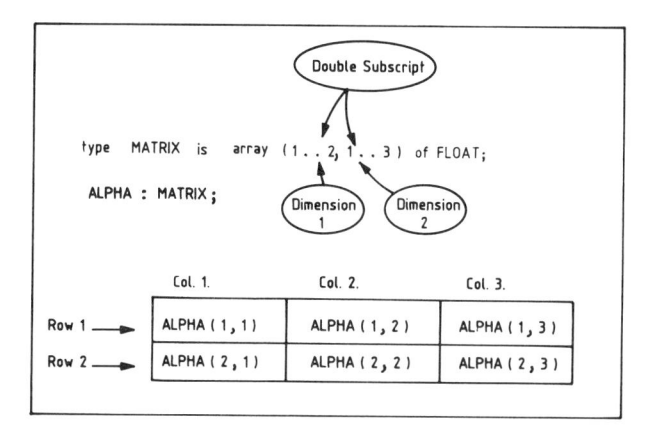

	Col. 1.	Col. 2.	Col. 3.
Row 1	ALPHA(1,1)	ALPHA(1,2)	ALPHA(1,3)
Row 2	ALPHA(2,1)	ALPHA(2,2)	ALPHA(2,3)

Fig.8.19 Two-dimensional array – row/column interpretation.

a_{11} ... ALPHA(1,1) (interpreted as row1/column1 intersection)
a_{13} ... ALPHA(1,3) (interpreted as row1/column3 intersection)
a_{21} ... ALPHA(2,1) (interpreted as row2/column1 intersection)

Listing 8.16 illustrates the use of two-dimensional arrays, using the notation described above for the ALPHA matrix.

So far the examples have been limited to two-dimensional problems. To handle three-dimensional operations we merely add a third set of array components (Fig.8.20).

Note that each location is uniquely identified and contains a FLOAT value. These points are demonstrated in Listing 8.17.

Note also that, in Ada, each location in a multi-dimensional array is defined to be a component of that array.

(c) **Array-of-arrays**

The concept of the array-of-arrays construct is shown in Fig.8.21.

As described here this is an array of one-dimensional arrays. Note how we access individual components of the structure, as, for example,

SEAT_NUMBER ('A')(1)   denotes the first component of 'A'.

This is quite different to that used with multi-dimensional arrays.

Listing 8.18 is a simple illustration of the use of the array-of-arrays construct.

Each one-dimensional array is regarded as a component of the array-of-arrays. Each item within a one-dimensional array is considered to be a component of that array. Thus,

```
procedure MATRIX_VECTOR_MULT is
   type MATRIX is array (1..2, 1..3) of FLOAT;
   type VECTOR is array (1..2) of FLOAT;
   ALPHA              :    MATRIX;
   X                  :    VECTOR;
   RESULT             :    VECTOR;
begin
   -- put data in alpha and X
   ALPHA (1, 1) := 1.0;
   ALPHA (1, 2) := 2.0;
   ALPHA (1, 3) := 3.0;
   ALPHA (2, 1) := 4.0;
   ALPHA (2, 2) := 5.0;
   ALPHA (2, 3) := 6.0;
   X (1) := 2.5;
   X (2) := 4.6;
   -- initialize the result
   for I in 1..2 loop
      RESULT (I) := 0.0;
   end loop;
   -- perform the multiplication
   for I in 1..2 loop
      for J in 1..3 loop
         RESULT (I) := RESULT (I) + (ALPHA (I, J) * X (J));
      end loop;
   end loop;
end MATRIX_VECTOR_MULT;
```

Listing 8.16 This part program shows the use of two-dimensional arrays for multiplying a matrix by a vector.

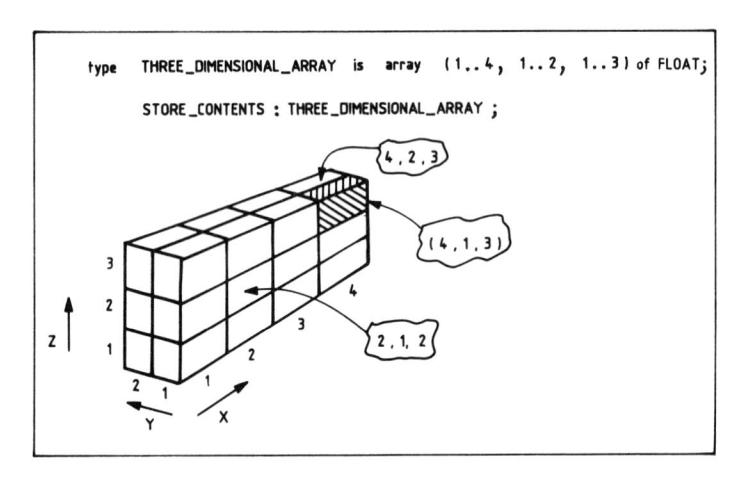

Fig.8.20 Three-dimensional array.

```ada
with TEXT_IO;              use TEXT_IO;
procedure THREE_D_ARRAY is
  type TV_MAKE is (HITACHI, SONY, PHILLIPS);
  type TV_FEATURE is (NICAM_STEREO, TELETEXT, STEREO_AND_TELETEXT);
  subtype YEAR_OF_MANUFACTURE is INTEGER range 1990..1992;
  type SERIAL_NO_ARRAY is array ( TV_MAKE, TV_FEATURE,
                                  YEAR_OF_MANUFACTURE) of INTEGER;
  TV_SERIAL_NO         :    SERIAL_NO_ARRAY;
  NEXT_SERIAL_NUMBER   :    INTEGER         := 1000;
  SERIAL_NUMBER        :    INTEGER;
  TV_FOUND             :    BOOLEAN         := FALSE;
  package MAKE_IO is new ENUMERATION_IO (TV_MAKE);
  package FEATURE_IO is new ENUMERATION_IO (TV_FEATURE);
  package INT_IO is new INTEGER_IO (INTEGER);
  use MAKE_IO;
  use FEATURE_IO;
  use INT_IO;
begin
  -- set up TV_STOCK
  for MAKE in HITACHI..PHILLIPS loop
    for FEATURE in NICAM_STEREO..STEREO_AND_TELETEXT loop
      for YEAR in 1990..1992 loop
        TV_SERIAL_NO (MAKE, FEATURE, YEAR) := NEXT_SERIAL_NUMBER;
        NEXT_SERIAL_NUMBER := NEXT_SERIAL_NUMBER + 1;
      end loop;
    end loop;
  end loop;
  PUT ("Please enter the TV Serial Number : ");
  GET (SERIAL_NUMBER);
  SKIP_LINE;
  TV_FOUND := FALSE;
  for MAKE in HITACHI..PHILLIPS loop
    for FEATURE in NICAM_STEREO..STEREO_AND_TELETEXT loop
      for YEAR in 1990..1992 loop
        if TV_SERIAL_NO (MAKE, FEATURE, YEAR) = SERIAL_NUMBER then
          PUT ("The TV is a ");
          PUT (MAKE);
          PUT (" with ");
          PUT (FEATURE);
          PUT (" made in ");
          PUT (YEAR, 0);
          NEW_LINE;
          TV_FOUND := TRUE;
        end if;
      end loop;
    end loop;
  end loop;
  if not TV_FOUND then
    PUT_LINE ("Sorry that TV is not in our stock");
  end if;
end THREE_D_ARRAY;
```

Listing 8.17 Applying three-dimensional arrays.

254 *Composite data types – the array*

One-dimensional array

  type   SEAT_ROW is array (1..5) of INTEGER ;

Array-of-arrays

  type   AUDIENCE_SEATING is array ('A'..'C') of SEAT_ROW ;

Variable array-of-arrays structure

  SEAT_NUMBER : AUDIENCE_SEATING ;

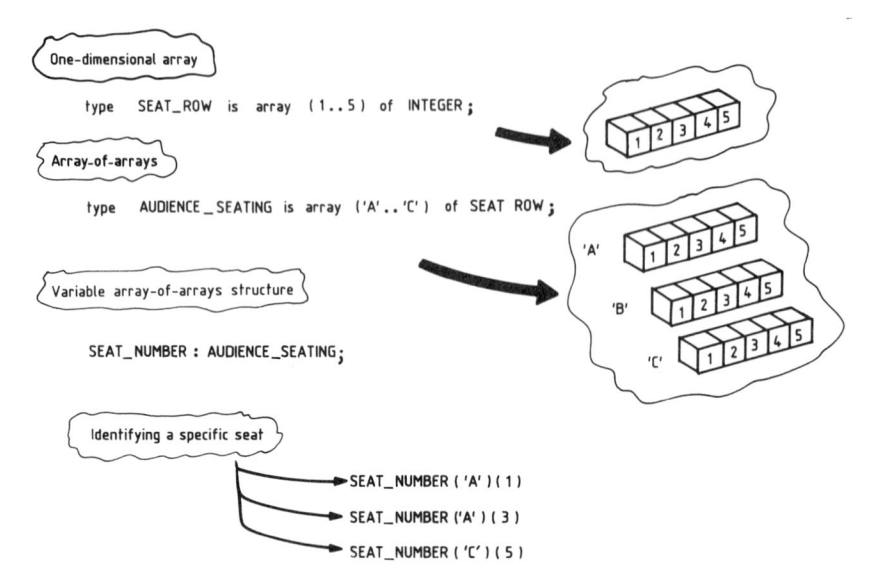

Identifying a specific seat

      → SEAT_NUMBER ('A') (1)
      → SEAT_NUMBER ('A') (3)
      → SEAT_NUMBER ('C') (5)

Fig.8.21 The array-of-arrays construct.

```
SEAT_NUMBER ('A')(1)
```

denotes, in more formal terms, the first component of component 'A' of the array-of-arrays AUDIENCE_SEATING.

There is another significant difference between the two constructs described above. In the multi-dimensional array structure we have one type. By contrast, with the array-of-array approach we have, in this example, two types: SEAT_ROW and AUDIENCE_SEATING. Therefore it is permissible to treat objects of these types as quite separate items. This point can be seen more clearly in the following text:

```
type SEAT_ROW is array (1..5) of INTEGER;
type AUDIENCE_SEATING is array ('A'..'C') of SEAT_ROW;
BALCONY_FIRST_ROW_SEATS : SEAT_ROW;
SEAT_NUMBER              : AUDIENCE_SEATING;
   .
   -- working with type SEAT_ROW only
   BALCONY_FIRST_ROW_SEATS (1) := 207;  -- Ticket no. 207
   -- working with type AUDIENCE_SEATING
   SEAT_NUMBER ('A')(2) := 350;  -- Ticket no. 350
```

The array-of-arrays framework can be used to build quite complex structures, as for example:

```
with TEXT_IO;              use TEXT_IO;
procedure BOOKING_PLAN is
  type SEAT_ROW is array (1..5) of INTEGER;
  type AUDIENCE_SEATING is array ('A'..'C') of SEAT_ROW;
  SEAT_NUMBER      :   AUDIENCE_SEATING;
  SELECTED_SEAT    :   INTEGER;
  SELECTED_ROW     :   CHARACTER;
  SELECT_AGAIN     :   CHARACTER;
  SEAT_FREE        :   constant      := 0;
  TICKET_NUM       :   INTEGER       := 1;
  package SEAT_NO_IO is new INTEGER_IO (integer);
  use SEAT_NO_IO;
begin
  -- initialize SEAT_NUMBER
  for SEAT in 1..5 loop
    for ROW in 'A'..'C' loop
      SEAT_NUMBER (ROW)(SEAT) := SEAT_FREE;
    end loop;
  end loop;
  loop
    PUT ("Which ROW do you require (A - C) : ");
    GET (SELECTED_ROW);
    SKIP_LINE;
    PUT ("Which seat NUMBER (1 - 5)? ");
    GET (SELECTED_SEAT);
    SKIP_LINE;
    if SEAT_NUMBER (SELECTED_ROW)(SELECTED_SEAT) = SEAT_FREE then
      SEAT_NUMBER (SELECTED_ROW)(SELECTED_SEAT) := TICKET_NUM;
      TICKET_NUM := TICKET_NUM + 1;
      PUT_LINE ("The seat has been reserved");
    else
      PUT_LINE ("Sorry, this seat is already reserved");
    end if;
    PUT ("Do you wish to select another seat? ");
    GET (SELECT_AGAIN);
    exit when (SELECT_AGAIN = 'N') or (SELECT_AGAIN = 'n');
  end loop;
end BOOKING_PLAN;
```

Listing 8.18 Applying the array-of-arrays construct.

```
type WORDS is array (1..20) of CHARACTER;
type LINES is array (1..10) of WORDS;
type PAGES is array (1..50) of LINES;
type BOOK  is array (1..500) of PAGES;
CATCH_22 : BOOK;
```

Then an individual character can be accessed by writing, for instance,

```
Y := CATCH_22 (68)(5)(2)(1);
```

that is page 68, line 5, word 2, character 1.

We can also use a multi-dimensional array as the basic array component

256 Composite data types – the array

in the array-of-arrays construct. In fact extremely complex and convoluted structures can be formed, if we are so minded. Common sense needs to prevail – always try to keep things simple.

8.2.11 Using arrays in procedures and functions

It should be no surprise that arrays can be used in subprograms, this being straightforward when the array is confined within the procedure. However, when the array is used as a formal parameter of the subprogram, the situation is more complicated. Remember that the declaration format for a procedure using an 'in' parameter is

> **procedure** PROCEDURE_NAME (PARAMETER_NAME : **in** TYPE_NAME) **is**

typified by

> **procedure** CHECK (X1 : **in** INTEGER) **is**

From this it should be clear that, when using array parameters, the array type must also be declared. The following format may be used in Ada:

> **procedure** VECTOR (ALPHA : **in** ROW_VECTOR) **is**

where ROW_VECTOR is a previously declared array type. Listing 8.19 gives an example which uses arrays as a function parameter.

That's all right as far as it goes, but have a close look at this example. Although the function carries out array multiplication perfectly well it is quite limited in use. Why? The reason is tied up with the rules of formal and actual parameter pairing. When using subprograms, formal and actual parameters must be the same type. Consequently, formal and actual array bounds must also be the same (Fig.8.22).

Thus the function VECTOR_MULT_VECTOR can only be used for a specific fixed-size array. In other words, every time we change the size of the vector (or matrix) we need to develop a different function. Clearly this is unacceptable in a modern language, especially one that places so much stress on the use of library functions. This is where we can put the unconstrained array declaration to good use – to build subprograms containing dynamic, not static, arrays.

For the previous example, let us first declare the type ROW_VECTOR as an unconstrained one:

```
procedure ARRAY_PARAM is
  type ROW_VECTOR is array (1..3) of FLOAT;
  WORK_DONE          :       FLOAT;
  FORCE              :       ROW_VECTOR;
  DISTANCE           :       ROW_VECTOR;
  function VECTOR_MULT_VECTOR (ALPHA, X :          ROW_VECTOR)
    return FLOAT is
    RESULT           :       FLOAT      := 0.0;
  begin
    for I in 1..3 loop
      RESULT := RESULT + (ALPHA (I) * X (I));
    end loop;
    return RESULT;
  end VECTOR_MULT_VECTOR;
begin
  --
  -- statements giving values for FORCE and DISTANCE
  --
  WORK_DONE := VECTOR_MULT_VECTOR (ALPHA    => FORCE,
                                   X        => DISTANCE);
  --
  -- rest of program statements
  --
end ARRAY_PARAM;
```

Listing 8.19 This is a part program showing the use of arrays as a subprogram parameter. The function VECTOR_MULT_VECTOR calculates the multiplication of two vectors, returning a scalar.

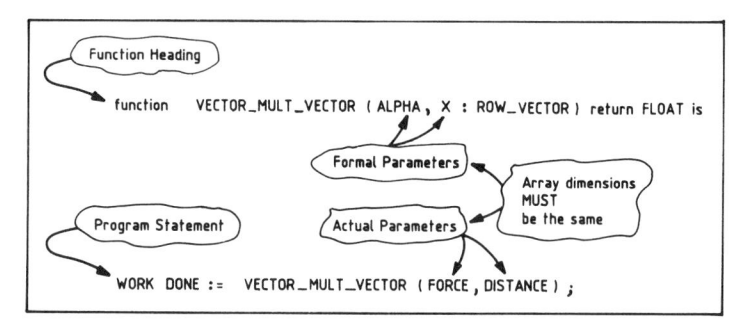

Fig.8.22 Basic use of array parameters.

```
type ROW_VECTOR is array (INTEGER range <>) of FLOAT;
```

Declare the function exactly the same as before. Now, however, the formal parameters are not assigned bounds. Instead they are set by those of the actual parameters at the time of call. Using this, we can pass an array of any size into a procedure (Fig.8.23).

258 Composite data types – the array

```
type ROW_VECTOR is array (1..10) of FLOAT;
function VECTOR_MULT_VECTOR ( ALPHA, X : ROW VECTOR ) return FLOAT is
```

ALPHA → | 1 | 2 | 3 | 4 | 5 | 6 | 7 | 8 | 9 | 10 |

Fixed array size

```
type ROW_VECTOR is array ( INTEGER range <> ) of FLOAT;
function VECTOR_MULT_VECTOR ( ALPHA, X : ROW_VECTOR ) return FLOAT is
```

ALPHA

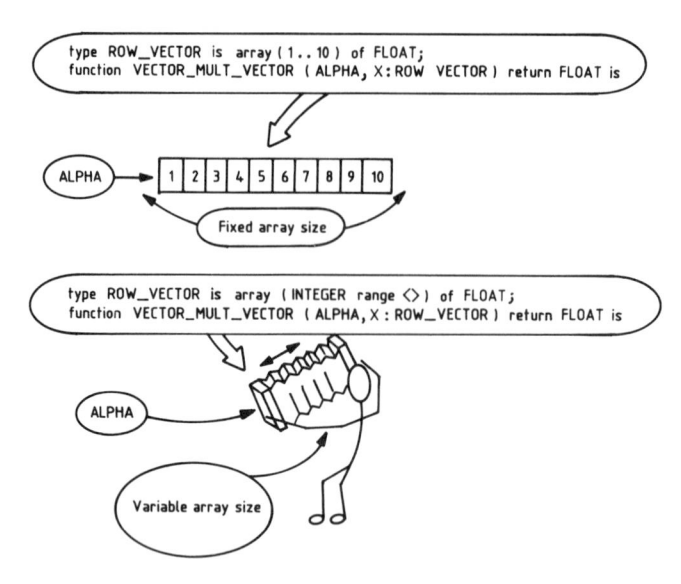

Variable array size

Fig.8.23 Comparing constrained with unconstrained array parameters.

In this way the array size becomes dynamic. Listing 8.20 shows how to use this feature.

8.2.12 Aggregates revisited

We've already met array aggregates and seen how they can be used to set up array values. The operation described was a simple one; now we'll look at aggregates in more detail.

(a) Positional association

Consider the following:

```
COEFFICIENTS : array (1..5) of INTEGER;
.
COEFFICIENTS := (4, 3, 2, 1, 0);
```

Here the array aggregate is (4, 3, 2, 1, 0). Using it like this assigns values to the elements of the array COEFFICIENTS, as follows:

Element 1 is assigned the value 4
Element 2 is assigned the value 3

```
procedure UNCONSTRAINED_PARAM is
  type ROW_VECTOR is array (INTEGER range <>) of FLOAT;
  subtype MECH_VECTOR is ROW_VECTOR (1..20);
  subtype ELEC_VECTOR is ROW_VECTOR (1..10);
  FORCE           :    MECH_VECTOR;
  DISTANCE        :    MECH_VECTOR;
  VOLTAGE         :    ELEC_VECTOR;
  CURRENT         :    ELEC_VECTOR;
  WORK_DONE       :    FLOAT;
  function VECTOR_MULT_VECTOR (ALPHA    :       ROW_VECTOR;
                               X        :       ROW_VECTOR)
     return FLOAT is
     RESULT          :    FLOAT        := 0.0;
  begin
    for I in ALPHA'FIRST..ALPHA'LAST loop
      RESULT := RESULT + (ALPHA (I) * X (I));
    end loop;
    return RESULT;
  end VECTOR_MULT_VECTOR;
begin
  --
  -- statements giving values for FORCE and DISTANCE
  --
    WORK_DONE := VECTOR_MULT_VECTOR (ALPHA     => FORCE,
                                     X         => DISTANCE);
  --
  -- statements giving values for VOLTAGE and CURRENT
  --
    WORK_DONE := VECTOR_MULT_VECTOR (ALPHA     => VOLTAGE,
                                     X         => CURRENT);
  --
  -- rest of program statements
  --
end UNCONSTRAINED_PARAM;
```

Listing 8.20 This is a part program showing the use of dynamic array bounds within subprograms. The procedure calculates the multiplication of two vectors returning a scalar.

Element 3 is assigned the value 2
Element 4 is assigned the value 1
Element 5 is assigned the value 0

This is called positional association. The first value in the aggregate gets assigned to the first element (component) of the array, the second value to the second component, and so on.

(b) **Positional association, aggregate qualification and using others**

Suppose in the example above we want to set the first component value to 25 and the other component values to 1. We can do this by using an **others** construct in the aggregate, as follows:

260 Composite data types – the array

```
(25, others => 1)
```

Now, when the compiler meets this it is faced with the task of working out exactly how many **others** there are. To simplify this process we explicitly define which data type the aggregate refers to. This is done using aggregate qualification, as, for instance,

```
type MATRIX_ELEMENTS is array (1..5) of INTEGER;
COEFFICIENTS : MATRIX_ELEMENTS;
.
.
.
COEFFICIENTS := MATRIX_ELEMENTS'(25, others => 1);
```

Here the aggregate qualification MATRIX_ELEMENTS spells out precisely the data type involved. Using the aggregate qualification is quite simple. Unfortunately, the rules governing its use are not so simple. The safest approach is 'if in doubt, use it'.

Note that, as shown above, the **others** association must appear last. Moreover, it can only have a single value. The others choice can also be used as a single item in the aggregate. Suppose we wish to set all the elements of the array to the same value (particularly useful for initialization). We could write out the same value for each element, namely:

```
COEFFICIENTS := (0, 0, 0, 0, 0);
```

or produce a loop operation. However, this is made simpler in Ada by the others choice:

```
COEFFICIENTS := (others => 0);
```

This sets all the elements of COEFFICIENTS to zero. Observe that there is no need to use the aggregate qualification.

(c) **Named association**

Positional notation is useful but fairly inflexible. Would it be helpful if we could shuffle the order of listing the values of an aggregate? The answer is yes, demonstrated in later examples. But to do this we need to supply extra information in the aggregate. That is, which array components should the values be assigned to? We do this by including the component name and its assigned value as part of the aggregate, as follows:

```
COEFFICIENTS := (1 => 5, 2 => 4, 3 => 2, 4 => 1, 5 => 0);
```

This is called named association.

Any listing order can be used, for example:

```
COEFFICIENTS := (2 => 4, 1 => 5, 3 => 2, 5 => 0, 4 => 1);
```

In the example given, named association doesn't appear to offer much (in fact it is rather confusing). Consider, though, the following example:

```
type STATUS is (NORMAL, LOW, HIGH);
type ENGINE_DATA is (N1, P1, P3, T6);
type ENGINE_STATUS is array (ENGINE_DATA) of STATUS;
PORT_ENGINE : ENGINE_STATUS;

PORT_ENGINE := (LOW, LOW, NORMAL, HIGH);
```

Now consider the added readability of the following:

```
PORT_ENGINE := (N1 => LOW, P1 => LOW, P3 => NORMAL, T6 => HIGH);
```

We can, at a glance, see exactly what is intended by the program writer. Moreover, we eliminate the possibility of making ordering mistakes.

We can also use the others choice with named association, as, for instance,

```
PORT_ENGINE := ENGINE_DATA' (N1     => LOW,
                             P1     => LOW,
                             others => NORMAL);
```

Listing 8.21 demonstrates the application of these particular aspects of aggregates.

(d) Mixing positional and named associations

We are not allowed to use both positional and named associations in the same aggregate, with one exception – when the name is others (in one sense

262 Composite data types – the array

```
with TEXT_IO;                 use TEXT_IO;
procedure AGGREGATE_1 is
  type NEWSPAPER is (TIMES, GUARDIAN, EXPRESS, MAIL);
  subtype WEEKDAY is INTEGER range 1..5;
  type WEEKDAY_PAPER is array (WEEKDAY) cf NEWSPAPER;
  subtype PRICE is INTEGER range 20..60;
  type PAPER_PRICE is array (NEWSPAPER) of PRICE;
  CUSTOMER_1       :      WEEKDAY_PAPER := (MAIL, EXPRESS, MAIL, GUARDIAN, TIMES);
  CURRENT_PRICE    :      constant PAPER_PRICE := (TIMES    => 50,
                                                   GUARDIAN => 45,
                                                   EXPRESS  => 30,
                                                   MAIL     => 30);
  DAYS_PAPER       :      NEWSPAPER;
  CUSTOMER_1_BILL  :      INTEGER        := 0;
begin
  for DAY in 1..5 loop
    DAYS_PAPER := CUSTOMER_1 (DAY);
    CUSTOMER_1_BILL := CUSTOMER_1_BILL + CURRENT_PRICE (DAYS_PAPER);
  end loop;
end AGGREGATE_1;
```

Listing 8.21 This demonstrates simple applications of positional and named association of aggregates.

others has a named relationship with the array components, although this may be stretching semantics somewhat). The rules governing its use have already been discussed.

(e) Contiguous and non-contiguous index values

Suppose that we wish to set N1, P1 and P3 to NORMAL and T6 to HIGH. Because N1 to P3 are contiguous values the following aggregate can be used:

```
(N1..P3 => NORMAL, T6 => HIGH)
```

That is, we can define a range of elements and then assign them a particular value. In accordance with range rules the element numbering (indices) must be contiguous. However, because we are using named association, the index grouping does not have to be ordered. So we could equally well have written:

```
(T6 => HIGH, N1..P3 => NORMAL)
```

Suppose now that we want to set N1 and P3 to NORMAL, P1 to LOW and T6 to HIGH. As N1 and P3 aren't contiguous we cannot use the range construct. We do, though, have the choice construct, similar to the vertical bar of the case construct (chapter 3). So, for this example we would use the aggregate as follows:

```
with TEXT_IO;                  use TEXT_IO;
procedure AGGREGATE_2 is
  type NEWSPAPER is (TIMES, GUARDIAN, EXPRESS, MAIL);
  subtype WEEKDAY is INTEGER range 1..5;
  type WEEKDAY_PAPER is array (WEEKDAY) of NEWSPAPER;
  subtype PRICE is INTEGER range 20..60;
  type PAPER_PRICE is array (NEWSPAPER) of PRICE;
  CUSTOMER_1        :      WEEKDAY_PAPER   := (1 | 2 => MAIL,
                                                3      => EXPRESS,
                                                4      => GUARDIAN,
                                                5      => TIMES);
  CURRENT_PRICE     :  constant PAPER_PRICE := (TIMES         =>  50,
                                                GUARDIAN      =>  45,
                                                EXPRESS..MAIL =>  30);
  DAYS_PAPER        :    NEWSPAPER;
  CUSTOMER_1_BILL   :    INTEGER         :=  0;
begin
  for DAY in 1..5 loop
    DAYS_PAPER := CUSTOMER_1 (DAY);
    CUSTOMER_1_BILL := CUSTOMER_1_BILL + CURRENT_PRICE (DAYS_PAPER);
  end loop;
end AGGREGATE_2;
```

Listing 8.22 This demonstrates the use of contiguous and non-contiguous index values in aggregates.

```
PORT_ENGINE := ENGINE_DATA' (N1 | P3 => NORMAL,
                             T6 => HIGH,
                             P1 => LOW);
```

These aspects are demonstrated in Listing 8.22.

We can, of course, have combinations of single values, discrete ranges and choices, including **others**. Note, though, that **others** cannot be combined with another index value, that is

```
Illegal -----> (P3 => LOW,  N1 | others => NORMAL) <----- Illegal
```

If you think about it, it's a nonsensical operation. However, different index values can be used in aggregates, as shown in Listing 8.23.

8.2.13 Aggregates – multidimensional arrays and array-of-arrays

Let us, for simplicity, consider only two-dimensional structures here. Further, we can regard a structure made up of a linear arrangement of one-dimensional arrays as being similar to a two-dimensional array. Each can be viewed as consisting of rows and columns (although the component access methods are different).

264 Composite data types – the array

```
with TEXT_IO;                 use TEXT_IO;
procedure MIXED_AGGREGATE is
  type NEWSPAPER is (TIMES, GUARDIAN, EXPRESS, MAIL);
  subtype WEEKDAY is INTEGER range 1..5;
  type WEEKDAY_PAPER is array (WEEKDAY) of NEWSPAPER;
  subtype PRICE is INTEGER range 20..60;
  type PAPER_PRICE is array (NEWSPAPER) of PRICE;
  JONES_PAPER      :    WEEKDAY_PAPER  := (1 | 5 => MAIL, 2..4 => EXPRESS);
  GREEN_PAPER      :    WEEKDAY_PAPER  := (GUARDIAN, others => TIMES);
  CURRENT_PRICE    :    constant PAPER_PRICE := (TIMES          => 50,
                                                 GUARDIAN       => 45,
                                                 EXPRESS..MAIL  => 30);
  begin
  --
  -- statements using JONES_PAPER, GREEN_PAPER, CURRENT_PRICE
  --
    null;
  end MIXED_AGGREGATE;
```

Listing 8.23 This is an example showing how different index values can be used in aggregates.

From this point of view, we can form aggregates for the rows and columns in a number of different ways:

1. Positional notation for both rows and columns;
2. Positional notation for the rows, named notation for the columns;
3. Named notation for the rows, positional notation for the columns;
4. Named notation for both rows and columns.

In general it is not a good idea to use mixed association (notation). Confusion rather than clarity results from this. Thus positional or named association is the better approach. But how do we go about selecting the most appropriate notation? In the end it comes down to specific applications. If the arrays consist fundamentally of numbered indices, then positional association may be acceptable. But if the index values use names (especially meaningful names), then use named association (these comments also apply to one-dimensional arrays). Our view is that named association is the preferred technique, for reasons of clarity, readability and error reduction.

In the examples below we will use positional association (for demonstration purposes) for two-dimensional arrays and named association for array-of-arrays.

(a) **Two-dimensional array aggregates**

Two-dimensional arrays are widely used in mathematics, particularly for matrix algebra and vector calculus. Here the index values are usually numbered, as shown in Fig.8.24.

```
type MATRIX is array (1..2, 1..3) of FLOAT;
ALPHA : MATRIX
```

ROW/COLUMN INTERPRETATION

	Col. 1	Col. 2	Col. 3
Row 1	ALPHA (1, 1)	ALPHA (1, 2)	ALPHA (1, 3)
Row 2	ALPHA (2, 1)	ALPHA (2, 2)	ALPHA (2, 3)

MATRIX INTERPRETATION

	Col. 1	Col. 2	Col. 3
Row 1	ALPHA 11	ALPHA 12	ALPHA 13
Row 2	ALPHA 21	ALPHA 22	ALPHA 23

AGGREGATE SYNTAX AND POSITIONAL ASSOCIATION

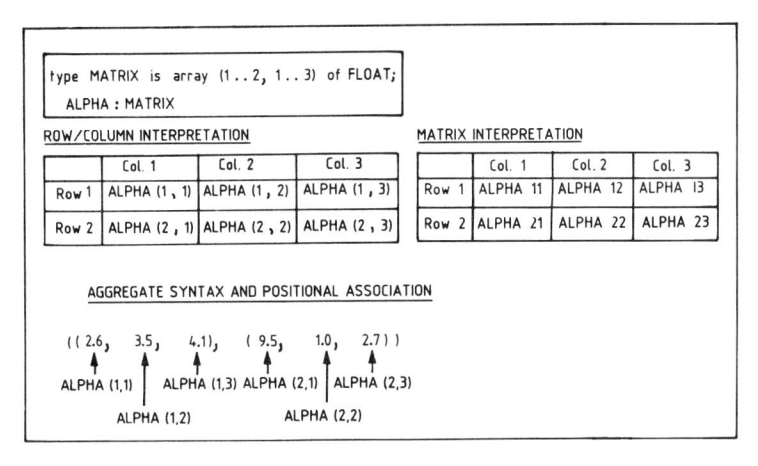

```
(( 2.6,  3.5,  4.1),  ( 9.5,  1.0,  2.7 ))
   ↑     ↑     ↑        ↑     ↑     ↑
ALPHA(1,1)  ALPHA(1,3) ALPHA(2,1)  ALPHA(2,3)
      ALPHA(1,2)           ALPHA(2,2)
```

Fig.8.24 Aggregates for two-dimensional arrays.

```
procedure MULTI_DIM_AGGREGATE is
   type MATRIX is array (1..2, 1..3) of FLOAT;
   type VECTOR is array (1..2) of FLOAT;
   ALPHA       :     MATRIX      := (1 => (1.0, 2.0, 3.0),
                                     2 => (4.0, 5.0, 6.0));
   X           :     VECTOR      := (2.5, 4.8);
   RESULT      :     VECTOR      := (others => 0.0);
begin
   -- perform the multiplication
   for I in 1..2 loop
      for J in 1..3 loop
         RESULT (I) := RESULT (I) + (ALPHA (I, J) * X (I));
      end loop;
   end loop;
end MULTI_DIM_AGGREGATE;
```

Listing 8.24 A simple example – applying aggregates to two-dimensional arrays.

The aggregate syntax is also shown on this diagram. Observe how we list the aggregates for this – study this carefully. Now, provided we are used to working with matrix notation (and that's likely to be the case in this application), a new layout of the aggregate can be very useful, namely:

```
ALPHA := ( (2.6, 3.5, 4.1),
           (9.5, 1.0, 2.7) );
```

Note the close similarity between this and the conventional layout for a matrix.

Listing 8.24 illustrates the use of aggregates in two-dimensional arrays.

266   Composite data types – the array

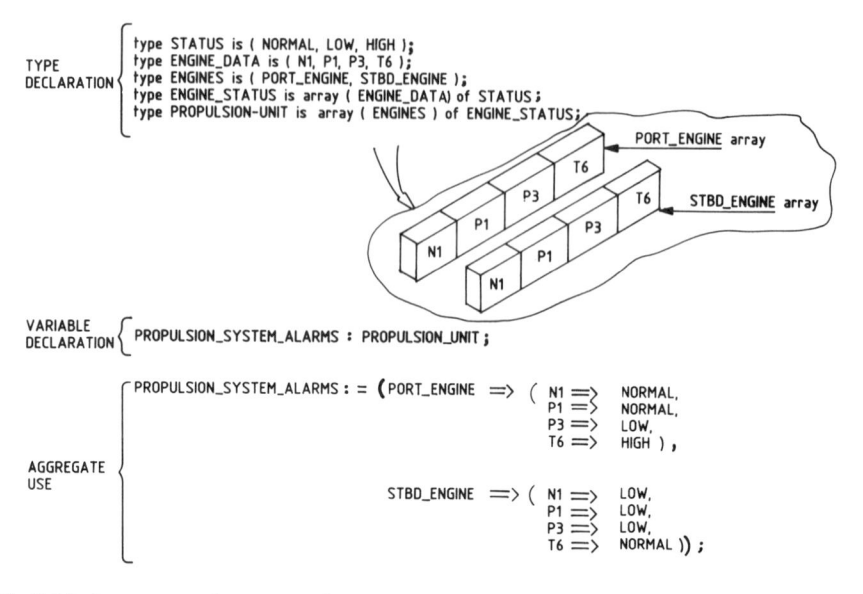

TYPE DECLARATION
```
type STATUS is ( NORMAL, LOW, HIGH );
type ENGINE_DATA is ( N1, P1, P3, T6 );
type ENGINES is ( PORT_ENGINE, STBD_ENGINE );
type ENGINE_STATUS is array ( ENGINE_DATA) of STATUS;
type PROPULSION-UNIT is array ( ENGINES ) of ENGINE_STATUS;
```

PORT_ENGINE array

STBD_ENGINE array

VARIABLE DECLARATION
PROPULSION_SYSTEM_ALARMS : PROPULSION_UNIT ;

AGGREGATE USE
```
PROPULSION_SYSTEM_ALARMS : = (PORT_ENGINE  => ( N1 => NORMAL,
                                                 P1 => NORMAL,
                                                 P3 => LOW,
                                                 T6 => HIGH ) ,

                              STBD_ENGINE  => ( N1 => LOW,
                                                 P1 => LOW,
                                                 P3 => LOW,
                                                 T6 => NORMAL )) ;
```

Fig.8.25 Aggregates for array-of-arrays.

(b) Array-of-arrays

The array-of-arrays is more likely to be used with named items. Thus the example here, Fig.8.25, is based on this approach.

Study this in detail. The use and syntax for aggregates should become clear from the application shown in the figure. Note that the layout is not a unique one. As noted earlier, named association gives us great flexibility when writing out aggregates; see Listing 8.25.

8.2.14 Array attributes

Arrays are defined to have four attributes (characteristics):

- LENGTH
- RANGE
- FIRST
- LAST

Examine the array variable ROW_VECTOR defined by the declaration

```
type VECTOR is array (2..7) of INTEGER;
ROW_VECTOR : VECTOR;
```

```
with TEXT_IO;              use TEXT_IO;
procedure ARRAY_OF_ARRAY_AGG is
  subtype SEAT_NO is INTEGER range 1..5;
  type SEAT_ROW is array (SEAT_NO) of BOOLEAN;
  subtype ROW_LETTER is CHARACTER range 'A'..'C';
  type AUDIENCE_SEATING is array (ROW_LETTER) of SEAT_ROW;
  SEAT_AVAILABLE   :    AUDIENCE_SEATING := ( 'A' => (1..2 => FALSE,
                                                      3..5 => TRUE),
                                              'B' => (others => FALSE),
                                              'C' => (1 | 3 | 5 => TRUE,
                                                      2 | 4     => FALSE) );
  SELECTED_SEAT    :    SEAT_NO;
  SELECTED_ROW     :    ROW_LETTER;
  SELECT_AGAIN     :    CHARACTER;
  package SEAT_NO_IO is new INTEGER_IO (SEAT_NO);
  use SEAT_NO_IO;
begin
  loop
    PUT ("Which ROW do you require (A - C) : ");
    GET (SELECTED_ROW);
    SKIP_LINE;
    PUT ("Which seat NUMBER (1 - 5)? ");
    GET (SELECTED_SEAT);
    SKIP_LINE;
    if SEAT_AVAILABLE (SELECTED_ROW)(SELECTED_SEAT) then
      SEAT_AVAILABLE (SELECTED_ROW)(SELECTED_SEAT) := FALSE;
      PUT_LINE ("The seat has been reserved");
    else
      PUT_LINE ("Sorry, this seat is already reserved");
    end if;
    PUT ("Do you wish to select another seat? ");
    GET (SELECT_AGAIN);
    exit when (SELECT_AGAIN = 'N') or (SELECT_AGAIN = 'n');
  end loop;
end ARRAY_OF_ARRAY_AGG;
```

Listing 8.25 A simple example – applying aggregates to the array-of-arrays structure.

Then, ROW_VECTOR'LENGTH   gives the value   6 (i.e. six elements)
       ROW_VECTOR'RANGE   gives the value   2..7
       ROW_VECTOR'FIRST   gives the value   2
       ROW_VECTOR'LAST   gives the value   7

Now take the two-dimensional array variable described below, ALPHA:

```
type COEFFICIENTS is array (1..4, 5..7) of FLOAT;
ALPHA : COEFFICIENTS;
```

Here, when we use the attributes, we need to specify which dimension we're referring to. The first set of elements define the first dimension, the second set the second dimension (and so on for a multidimensional array). We can pick out the attributes, as follows:

268 Composite data types – the array

```
with TEXT_IO;                use TEXT_IO;
procedure ARRAY_ATTRIBUTES is
  subtype LIST_LENGTH is INTEGER range 1..10;
  type NUMBERS_LIST is array (LIST_LENGTH) of INTEGER;
  PRIME_NUMBER   :    NUMBERS_LIST   := (1, 3, 5, 7, 11, 13, 17, 19, 23, 29);
  PRIME_INDEX    :    LIST_LENGTH;
  package INT_IO is new INTEGER_IO(INTEGER);
  use INT_IO;
begin
  PUT ("The first prime number is ");
  PUT (PRIME_NUMBER (PRIME_NUMBER'FIRST), 0);
  NEW_LINE;
  PUT ("The last prime number in the range 1 to 30 is ");
  PUT (PRIME_NUMBER (PRIME_NUMBER'LAST), 0);
  NEW_LINE;
  PUT ("Between 1 and 30 there are ");
  PUT (PRIME_NUMBER'LENGTH, 0);
  PUT_LINE (" prime numbers");
  PUT ("These are");
  for COUNT in PRIME_NUMBER'range loop
    PUT (PRIME_NUMBER (COUNT), 3);
  end loop;
  NEW_LINE;
end ARRAY_ATTRIBUTES;
```

Listing 8.26 A simple example – array attributes.

ALPHA'LENGTH(1)	gives the value	4
ALPHA'LENGTH(2)	gives the value	3
ALPHA'RANGE(1)	gives the value	1..4
ALPHA'RANGE(2)	gives the value	5..7
ALPHA'FIRST(1)	gives the value	1
ALPHA'FIRST(2)	gives the value	5
ALPHA'LAST(1)	gives the value	4
ALPHA'LAST(2)	gives the value	7

The advantage of using attributes will be shown shortly. For the moment a simple example is given in Listing 8.26.

8.2.15 Compatibility issues

And now for something really confusing. What's the difference between the following two declarations?

```
type COEFFICIENTS is array (1..50) of INTEGER;
DELTA, SPEED : COEFFICIENTS;
```

and

```
DELTA, SPEED : array (1..50) of INTEGER;
```

For the first case the following two sets of statements are valid:

```
(i)   SPEED (25) := DELTA (30);
(ii)  SPEED := DELTA;
```

However, when the second declaration format is used, statement (ii) will be rejected by the compiler (different!). This comes about because, in the first declaration, Ada considers the two arrays to belong to the same data type – COEFFICIENTS. But, when the second form is used, they are defined to be *anonymous* types. And, in Ada, each anonymous type is considered to be unique. Therefore in case (ii) the

```
SPEED := DELTA;
```

statement fails on type compatibility grounds. Nevertheless, statement (i)

```
SPEED (25) := DELTA (30);
```

is valid because all elements of the two arrays are the same type, that is INTEGER. Remember that the assignment action relates individual elements; thus type compatibility rules are still obeyed.

8.2.16 Operations on arrays

The operations which can be carried out on array types are given in Table 8.1.

Note that this includes unconstrained arrays. Objects declared to belong to this type may well have different bounds (i.e. be of different size). Note also that we are concerned with the array object, not an array element.

8.2.17 Array declarations and usage – some final comments

We've seen that array types and array objects can be declared in many different ways. And, confusingly, these are usually acceptable alternatives. Why this variation? And which one(s) should we use? The answer to the first

270 Composite data types – the array

Table 8.1 Operations of array types

Operation	Array types
Array attributes	All
Equality/inequality comparisons: =, =/	Same type
Assignment	Same type, same size
Type conversion	Same size, same component type, same index type
Slicing	One dimensional
Relational operations (<, <=, >=, >) Concatenation (&)	One dimensional, discrete component values, same type
Logical operations (**not, and, or, xor**)	One dimensional, Boolean component values, same type, same length

question – why variations – is that different applications are best expressed in different ways. But for the second one, there really isn't a simple cookbook solution. Our aims are to produce:

1. Readable code;
2. Meaningful code;
3. General purpose code;
4. Minimal disturbance when changes are made to the code (localization of change);
5. Minimization of unforeseen errors.

Let's start with the simplest form of array declaration:

```
ACCEL : array (1..10) of FLOAT;
```

This anonymous array declaration would be quite acceptable in a small, localized, section of code. Generally it is better to avoid anonymous types to minimize type compatibility problems. Use the declaration form

```
type SPEED_VALUES is array (1..10) of FLOAT;
ACCEL : SPEED_VALUES;
```

We can make the bounds more meaningful and readable by using the form

```
LOW_LIMIT  : constant := 1;
HIGH_LIMIT : constant := 10;
type SPEED_VALUES is array (LOW_LIMIT .. HIGH_LIMIT) of FLOAT;
```

In some circumstances the following construct is better for readability:

```
LOW_LIMIT  : constant := 1;
HIGH_LIMIT : constant := 10;
type MEASUREMENTS is range LOW_LIMIT .. HIGH_LIMIT;
type SPEED_VALUES is array (MEASUREMENTS) of FLOAT;
```

For high program reliability in multidimensional arrays, the following form is useful:

```
LOW_1  : constant := 1;
HIGH_1 : constant := 10;
LOW_2  : constant := 2;
HIGH_2 : constant := 6;

type ROW_ELEMENTS is range LOW_1 .. HIGH_1;
type COLUMN_ELEMENTS is range LOW_2 .. HIGH_2;
type MATRIX_1 is array (ROW_ELEMENTS, COLUMN_ELEMENTS) of FLOAT;
COEFFICIENTS : MATRIX_1;
```

Suppose we wish to design an array type to form the basic structure for a number of objects which differ only in size. Here the unconstrained array is a natural solution, as:

```
type GENERAL_MEASUREMENTS is array (INTEGER range <>) of FLOAT;
ACCEL : GENERAL_MEASUREMENTS (1..10);
DECEL : GENERAL_MEASUREMENTS (0..50);
```

Attributes are important from the point of view of code stability (localization of change) and portability. Consider the following:

```
ACCEL : array (1..10) of FLOAT;
.
.
   for I in ACCEL'RANGE loop
      ACCEL(I) := 0.0;
   end loop;
.
.
```

If for any reason we change the size of the array there is no need to change the for–loop code. It is taken into account automatically. Contrast this with using

```
for I in 1..10 loop
    ACCEL(I) := 0.0;
end loop;
```

REVIEW

You should now:

1. Understand the use of structured data types;
2. Appreciate the need for a variety of structures;
3. Understand the concept and use of arrays;
4. Be conversant with the ideas of anonymous, constrained and unconstrained arrays, array aggregates and slices, and array indexing and bounds;
5. Be able to work with dynamic, multidimensional and array-of-arrays structures.

Chapter Nine
Composite data types – records

As shown previously, all individual data elements within array data structures are the same type. Thus we can have an array of INTEGER components, or an array of BOOLEANs – but not an array which is a mixture of INTEGERs and BOOLEANs. In the past this was good enough to satisfy most engineering and scientific computing needs. Unfortunately these constructs are unsuited for handling large amounts of data, especially data involving different types. We find that data structures are needed which allow different types to be mixed together. We also need to be able to manipulate the contents of such data structures both collectively and individually. Moreover, it must also be possible to work with large quantities of data. To meet these needs the record data structure has been devised.

On completing this chapter you will:

1. Understand the concept and use of records;
2. Be able to work with their contents as single entities or as a collection of components;
3. Know how to build and manipulate complex data structures;
4. Understand the reason for, and use of, discriminants;
5. Understand the role and application of variant records.

9.1   RECORDS – BASIC TYPES

9.1.1   The whats and whys of records

In the real world we often work with items which are related to each other, yet are of different types. For instance, the specification of a ship's propulsion control system states (in part):

> Group warnings will be given on the Visual Display Unit for the following units:
>   Port Gas Turbine
>   Stbd. Gas Turbine
>   Port Cruise Diesel
>   Stbd. Cruise Diesel
>
> For the Gas Turbines the following alarms will be provided:
>   PT fire
>   GG overspeed
>   GG vibration

274 Composite data types – records

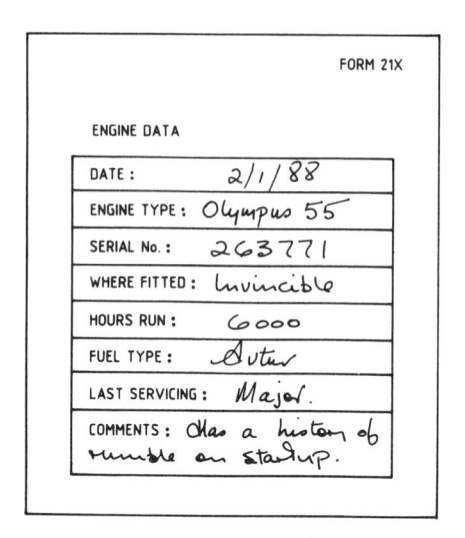

```
                                         FORM 21X

        ENGINE DATA

        DATE:           2/1/88
        ENGINE TYPE:    Olympus 55
        SERIAL No.:     263771
        WHERE FITTED:   Invincible
        HOURS RUN:      6000
        FUEL TYPE:      Avtur
        LAST SERVICING: Major.
        COMMENTS: Has a history of
                  rumble on startup.
```

Fig.9.1 A conventional manual record.

It is more natural for a user to relate individual alarms to a specific propulsion unit rather than to a group of, say, fire alarms. Moreover, it is much more useful to use names instead of cryptic identifiers. After all, 'Port Gas Turbine, Fire' is slightly more attention getting than 'Alarm 27'.

Consider now how we deal with such information. We may talk, for instance, about the 'Port Gas Turbine alarms' as if they are a single object or entity. In other cases we are concerned with an individual item within the group, as with the fire alarm.

Now look at this in the context of developing a program for such a system. If we have a data structure which matches our view of the real world then we are likely to produce programs which are:

1. Meaningful;
2. Readable;
3. Understandable;
4. Maintainable.

Unfortunately the array is not particularly suitable to hold data structures like that described above. What we use instead is a new construct, the RECORD. Actually, there is nothing new about the record concept. Consider how we'd keep data relating to an engine fitted to a ship, Fig.9.1.

Here we've made up a form which defines all information to be recorded. For identification, it's given a reference number. When it is used, appropriate data is entered into the boxes concerned. So, in informal terms, we could

Records – basic types   275

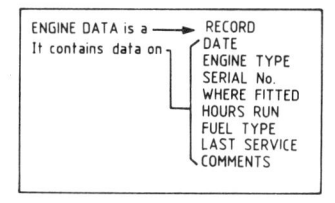

```
ENGINE DATA is a ──▶ RECORD
It contains data on ┐  ┌DATE
                    │  │ENGINE TYPE
                    │  │SERIAL No.
                    │  │WHERE FITTED
                    └──┤HOURS RUN
                       │FUEL TYPE
                       │LAST SERVICE
                       └COMMENTS
```

Fig.9.2 Informal description of the record form.

describe it as in Fig.9.2. And really that's all there is to the record. Now for the software equivalent of our pencil and paper system.

In programming terms a record is defined as a direct access, heterogeneous, fixed-size data structure. It has the following features:

1. It allows a mix of data types;
2. The complete data structure can be handled as if it is a single object;
3. Each component (element) within the structure can be accessed and manipulated individually;
4. Names are used to identify the complete structure and its elements.

These points, together with the formal construct of RECORDS, are illustrated in the following example programs.

9.1.2 Declaring and using records – an introduction

Let us build up a record for the Port Gas Turbine, at this stage including only three alarms. Four items have to be declared to the compiler:

1. The name of the record structure ('PROPULSION_ENGINE');
2. The fact that it is a record;
3. The individual components of the record;
4. The type of each component.

Consider the requirements to form a record for the alarms of the propulsion engines (Fig.9.3).

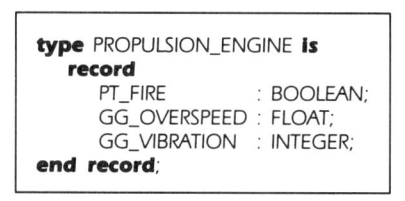

In this case the declaration format is

```
type PROPULSION_ENGINE is
   record
      PT_FIRE        : BOOLEAN;
      GG_OVERSPEED   : FLOAT;
      GG_VIBRATION   : INTEGER;
   end record;
```

276 Composite data types – records

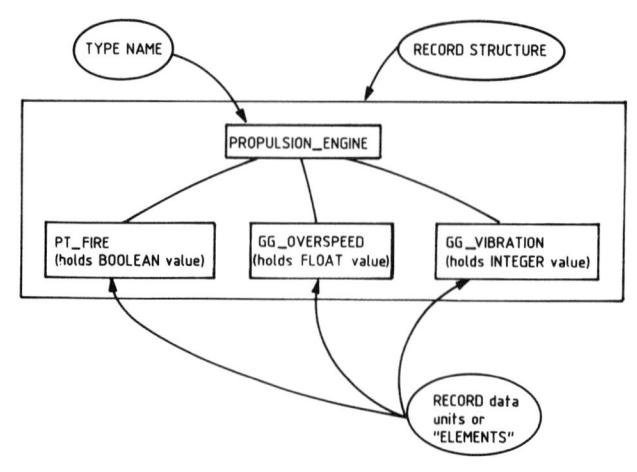

```
                    TYPE NAME                    RECORD STRUCTURE

                              PROPULSION_ENGINE

      PT_FIRE              GG_OVERSPEED           GG_VIBRATION
  (holds BOOLEAN value)   (holds FLOAT value)   (holds INTEGER value)

                                                    RECORD data
                                                    units or
                                                    "ELEMENTS"
```

Fig.9.3 Structure of record type 'PROPULSION_ENGINE'.

Variables belonging to this record type are declared in the usual way, as follows:

```
PORT_GAS_TURBINE : PROPULSION_ENGINE;
STBD_GAS_TURBINE : PROPULSION_ENGINE;
```

Thus we have two record objects, PORT_GAS_TURBINE and STBD_GAS_TURBINE (Fig.9.4).

It should be realized that record type declarations (as with all other type declarations) do not reserve computer storage. This takes place only when variables are declared to belong to that type. Each variable has a set of individual components, these being PT_FIRE, GG_OVERSPEED and GG_VIBRATION. When used in the program they are accessed by name, as follows:

```
PORT_GAS_TURBINE.PT_FIRE
STBD_GAS_TURBINE.PT_FIRE
PORT_GAS_TURBINE.GG_VIBRATION
```

Their use is demonstrated in the simple example of Listing 9.1.

Now for a few definitions. In the above example the grouping

```
PT_FIRE        : BOOLEAN;
GG_OVERSPEED   : FLOAT;
GG_VIBRATION   : INTEGER;
```

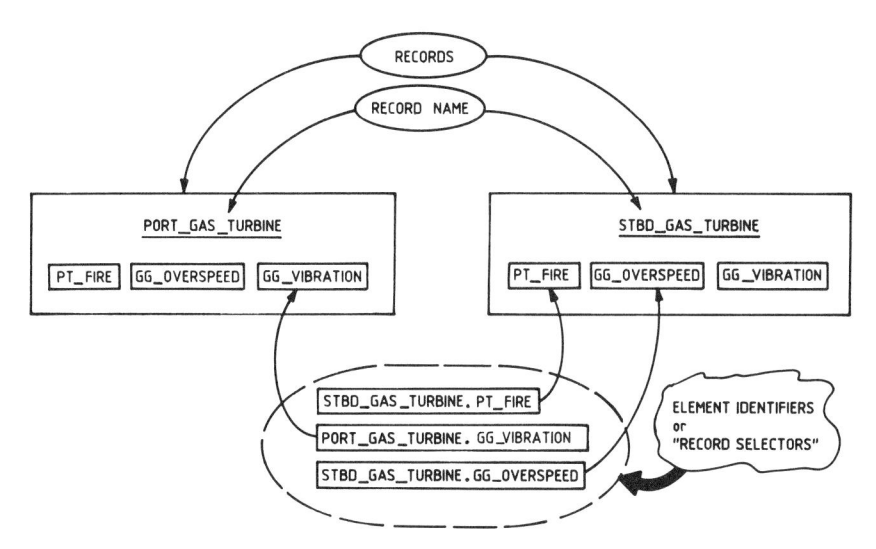

Fig.9.4 Identifying variables of type record.

```
with TEXT_IO;                use TEXT_IO;
procedure SIMPLE_RECORD is
  package INT_IO is new INTEGER_IO (INTEGER);
  use INT_IO;
  type PROPULSION_ENGINE is
    record
      PT_FIRE          :      BOOLEAN;
      GG_OVERSPEED     :      FLOAT;
      GG_VIBRATION     :      INTEGER;
    end record;
  PORT_GAS_TURBINE :    PROPULSION_ENGINE;
  STBD_GAS_TURBINE :    PROPULSION_ENGINE;
  INPUT_VALUE      :    INTEGER;
begin
  PORT_GAS_TURBINE.PT_FIRE := TRUE;
  PORT_GAS_TURBINE.GG_OVERSPEED := 7100.6;
  PUT ("Enter the Port Turbine vibration trip level - mm => ");
  GET (INPUT_VALUE);
  SKIP_LINE;
  PORT_GAS_TURBINE.GG_VIBRATION := INPUT_VALUE;
  STBD_GAS_TURBINE.PT_FIRE := FALSE;
  STBD_GAS_TURBINE.GG_OVERSPEED := 6591.7;
  PUT ("Enter the Stbd Turbine vibration trip level - mm => ");
  GET (INPUT_VALUE);
  SKIP_LINE;
  STBD_GAS_TURBINE.GG_VIBRATION := INPUT_VALUE;
  -- This shows that the trip levels have been set
  PUT ("The Port Turbine vibration alarm tip level is ");
  PUT (PORT_GAS_TURBINE.GG_VIBRATION, 0);
  NEW_LINE;
  PUT ("The Stbd Turbine vibration alarm tip level is ");
  PUT (STBD_GAS_TURBINE.GG_VIBRATION, 0);
  NEW_LINE;
end SIMPLE_RECORD;
```

Listing 9.1 This is a simple demonstration of the declaration and use of the 'record' construct.

278 Composite data types – records

```
type PROPULSION_ENGINE is
   record
      PT_FIRE: BOOLEAN;
      GG_OVERSPEED: FLOAT;
      GG_VIBRATION: INTEGER;
   end record;
```

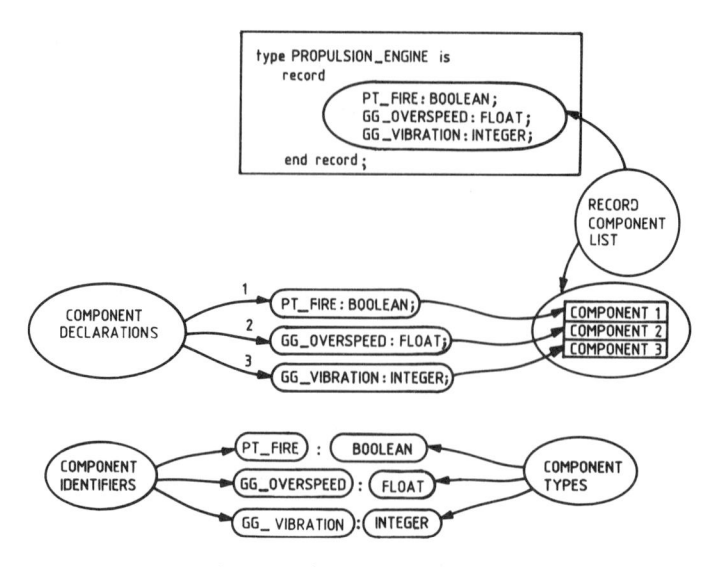

Fig.9.5 Defining the parts of a record.

is called the 'record component list' or the 'record component list sequence' (Fig.9.5).

We can regard 'PT_FIRE : BOOLEAN;' as being 'component number 1' or 'component declaration number 1', 'GG_OVERSPEED : FLOAT' as component 2, etc.

The name 'PT_FIRE' is called the 'component identifier' whilst the type designator 'BOOLEAN' is called the 'component type'. It can be seen that individual components within a record are accessed using their component identifiers attached to the variable name, as, for instance,

```
PORT_GAS_TURBINE.GG_VIBRATION
```

This individual element identifier is called the 'record variable designator'.

The order in which component lists are written is not important. Note well that the variables are those declared in the variable listing, for example 'STBD_GAS_TURBINE', having individual components such as 'STBD_GAS_TURBINE.PT_FIRE', etc. The record component names by themselves (e.g. PT_FIRE, etc.) are not variables.

The syntax diagram for the record type is shown in Fig.9.6.

Just to recap, when using records the normal format is

Records – basic types 279

[Diagram: Record type syntax - showing flow from 'type' → IDENTIFIER → 'is' → 'record' → COMPONENT LIST (IDENTIFIER : TYPE_NAME with ',' and ';' loops) → 'end record' → ';']

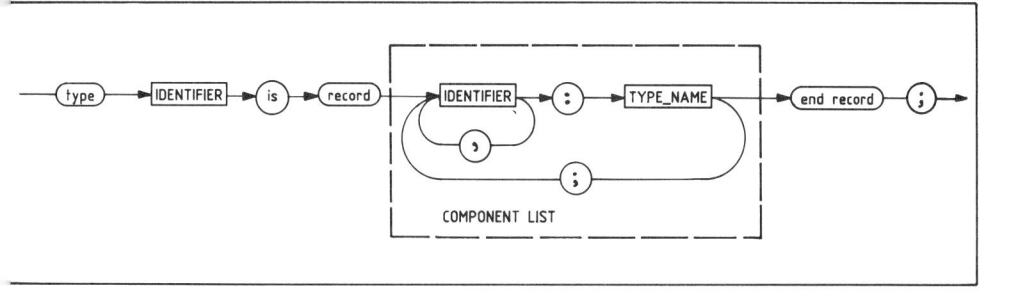

Fig.9.6 Record type – basic syntax.

```
type STRUCTURE is      -- STRUCTURE is the name of the type
   record
      ALARM : INTEGER;  -- This is the
      FILTER : FLOAT;   -- component list
   end record;
```

Both ALARM and FILTER are component names; INTEGER and FLOAT are component types. It should also be mentioned that the word 'field' (used widely in programming language descriptions) has the same meaning as 'component'.

One final point needs to be mentioned here. We are not allowed to have anonymous records; they must belong to some explicitly defined type.

9.1.3 Record aggregates – a comment

Earlier we met the array aggregate. Now comes its close cousin, the record aggregate. In concept, function and application these have much in common with array aggregates, so there should be no surprises here. Basically the record aggregate enables us to assign values to the whole structure (or parts of the structure) in a relatively simple manner. Positional, named and mixed association may be used, together with multiple value assignment (**others**) and the choice construct. The use of aggregates will be demonstrated in the following two sections.

9.1.4 Working with records – handling component parts

The example of Listing 9.1 shows how to work with individual record components. This is described in conceptual terms in Fig.9.7.

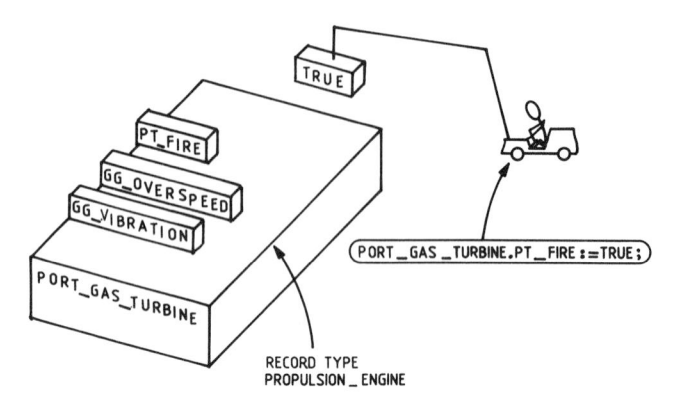

Fig.9.7 Handling individual record components.

Little more needs to be said as the process is straightforward. Record elements are declared in exactly the same way as program variables (go back and look). The only difference is that they are located in the RECORD section. So it isn't surprising that the following constructs can be used with record types and variables.

(a) **Declaring several identifiers of one component type**

We could declare each component identifier individually with its associated component type, as in

```
type GENERATING_UNIT is
   record
      GG_VIBRATION : INTEGER;
      BEARING_TEMP : INTEGER;
   end record;
```

A more compact method is

```
type GENERATING_UNIT is
   record
      GG_VIBRATION, BEARING_TEMP : INTEGER;
end record;
```

We recommend, however, that this style isn't used. List all items individually as shown in the previous layout.

Records – basic types   281

(b) Initializing record variables – aggregate positional association

Consider the following declaration:

```
type GENERATING_UNIT is
   record
      GG_VIBRATION              : INTEGER;
      BEARING_TEMP              : INTEGER;
      GG_PRESSURE_TRIP_LIMIT    : FLOAT;
   end record;
```

One way to initialize variables of this type is to use the following declaration form:

```
PORT_GAS_TURBINE : GENERATING_UNIT := (100, 25, 1.5);
```

The record type GENERATING_UNIT has three component parts. Thus the aggregate, when using positional association, must define three values. As a result of using the above declaration, the record components are initialized to the following values:

```
PORT_GAS_TURBINE.GG_VIBRATION --------------->>    100   (first component)
PORT_GAS_TURBINE.BEARING_TEMP --------------->>     25   (second component)
PORT_GAS_TURBINE.GG_PRESSURE_TRIP_LEVEL--->>       1.5   (third component)
```

(c) Initializing record variables – aggregate named association

An alternative to positional association is the named association aggregate form, as, for example,

```
PORT_GAS_TURBINE : GENERATING_UNIT := (GG_VIBRATION => 100,
                                       BEARING_TEMP => 25,
                                       GG_PRESSURE_TRIP_LEVEL => 1.5);
```

The order of the components is not important.

(d) Initializing record variables – aggregate mixed association

A further option when using aggregates is to mix positional and named associations, as for instance:

282 Composite data types – records

```
procedure RECORD_HANDLING is
  type GENERATING_UNIT is
    record
      GG_VIBRATION            :      INTEGER;
      BEARING_TEMP            :      INTEGER;
      GG_PRESSURE_TRIP_LIMIT  :      FLOAT;
    end record;
  PORT_GAS_TURBINE :  GENERATING_UNIT := (66, 100, 7100.6);
  STBD_GAS_TURBINE :  GENERATING_UNIT := (GG_VIBRATION            => 28,
                                          BEARING_TEMP            => 112,
                                          GG_PRESSURE_TRIP_LIMIT  => 6034.98);
begin
  PORT_GAS_TURBINE := (26, 78, GG_PRESSURE_TRIP_LIMIT => 2600.0);
  STBD_GAS_TURBINE := (88, 99, 3789.9);
end RECORD_HANDLING;
```

Listing 9.2 This demonstrates various techniques for handling record component parts, including initialization and assignment methods incorporating the aggregate construct.

```
PORT_GAS_TURBINE : GENERATING_UNIT := (100
                                       25,
                                       GG_PRESSURE_TRIP_LEVEL => 1.5);
```

Two important points should be noted. First, positional association must precede named association. Second, once we start to use named association we cannot revert to the positional form.

(e) Normal assignment operations using aggregates

Record aggregates can be used in normal assignment statements. The statement

```
PORT_GAS_TURBINE := (100, 25, 1.5);
```

assigns values to the individual record components as in (b) above. All other aggregate forms are also valid in assignment operations.

Listing 9.2 illustrates all these points.

(f) Aggregates – choice and others construct

The choice and others constructs are used in the same way as in arrays. For example, the assignment statement

```
PORT_GAS_TURBINE := (GG_VIBRATION | BEARING_TEMP => 50,
                     GG_PRESSURE_TRIP_LEVEL => 1.5);
```

causes the value 50 to be assigned to components GG_VIBRATION and BEARING_TEMP of record variable PORT_GAS_TURBINE. The third component is given the value 1.5. We could also have written:

> PORT_GAS_TURBINE := (GG_PRESSURE_TRIP_LEVEL => 1.5,
>   **others** => 50);

We are not likely to use these particular constructs extensively in record handling. They really aren't all that flexible for dealing with record component parts. Generally, components tend to be of different types. Thus, in the example here, if we wrote

> PORT_GAS_TURBINE := (GG_VIBRATION => 50,
>   **others** => 10);

the compiler would reject it. The reason? BEARING_TEMP is of type INTEGER, having no decimal part. By contrast, GG_PRESSURE_TRIP_LEVEL is a real number, and thus must include a decimal point. Clearly, no matter what we put after **others**, it is impossible to satisfy both requirements. And even when they are the same type, they frequently use quite different ranges within the type.

If **others** is used, it must be the last item in the aggregate. Note also that it can be used by itself to set all record components to the same value, as in

> SOME_INTEGER_SET := (**others** => 0);

We suggest that you do not use **others** in the record structure.

(g) **Setting type default values**

Here we set the initial values for the components of the type, the format being:

> **type** GENERATING_UNIT **is**
>   **record**
>   GG_VIBRATION   : INTEGER := 20;
>   BEARING_TEMP   : INTEGER := 25;
>   GG_PRESSURE_TRIP_LIMIT : FLOAT   := 1.0;
>   **end record**;

284   Composite data types – records

As a result any variable declared to belong to this type takes on these as initial default values. They can, of course, be changed by using variable initialization and assignment statements.

NOTE: The following construct is legal:

```
GG_VIBRATION, BEARING_TEMP: INTEGER := (20, 25);
```

(h) Read-only records – constants

We can also set up records to hold constant (read-only) values. The declaration form is

```
REFERENCE_ENGINE : constant GENERATING_UNIT := (15, 20, 0.5);
```

When using this construct we must treat all component parts as constants. Listing 9.3 demonstrates the use of default and constant values.

(j) Setting range constraints

We can, when declaring records, set constraints on the range of values which can be taken by components. The declaration format follows the usual style. That is:

```
type PROPULSION_ENGINE is
   record
      PT_FIRE       : BOOLEAN;
      GG_VIBRATION  : INTEGER range 0..50;
      GG_OVERSPEED  : FLOAT range 0.0..2.0;
   end record;
```

9.1.5 Handling the complete data structure as a single unit

What operations can we carry out on the record when it is considered to be a composite unit? The answer is – very little. Only assignment and tests for equality/inequality are permitted. These are described below.

(a) Assignment operations

Suppose in our propulsion system all gas turbines are set up for the same conditions. By using the approach shown above every individual item has to

```
with TEXT_IO;              use TEXT_IO;
procedure FURTHER_RECORD_HANDLING is
  type GENERATING_UNIT is
    record
      GG_VIBRATION           :      INTEGER      := 20;
      BEARING_TEMP           :      INTEGER      := 25;
      GG_PRESSURE_TRIP_LIMIT :      FLOAT        := 1.0;
    end record;
  PORT_GAS_TURBINE :    GENERATING_UNIT;
  STBD_GAS_TURBINE :    GENERATING_UNIT;
 -- constant elements still need defining
  STANDARD_ENGINE  :    constant GENERATING_UNIT :=
                                          (GG_VIBRATION             => 20,
                                           BEARING_TEMP             => 25,
                                           GG_PRESSURE_TRIP_LIMIT   => 1.0);
  REFERENCE_ENGINE :    constant GENERATING_UNIT :=
                                          (GG_VIBRATION             => 15,
                                           BEARING_TEMP             => 20,
                                           GG_PRESSURE_TRIP_LIMIT   => 0.5);
  package INT_IO is new INTEGER_IO (INTEGER);
  use INT_IO;
  package PRESSURE_IO is new FLOAT_IO (FLOAT);
  use PRESSURE_IO;
begin
  PORT_GAS_TURBINE.GG_VIBRATION := STANDARD_ENGINE.GG_VIBRATION;
  STBD_GAS_TURBINE.BEARING_TEMP := REFERENCE_ENGINE.BEARING_TEMP;
 -- print the contents of the two variables
  PUT_LINE ("PORT_GAS_TURBINE :");
  PUT ("GG_VIBRATION          => ");
  PUT (PORT_GAS_TURBINE.GG_VIBRATION, 0);
  NEW_LINE;
  PUT ("BEARING_TEMP          => ");
  PUT (PORT_GAS_TURBINE.BEARING_TEMP, 0);
  NEW_LINE;
  PUT ("GG_PRESSURE_TRIP_LIMIT =>");
  PUT (PORT_GAS_TURBINE.GG_PRESSURE_TRIP_LIMIT);
  NEW_LINE;
  PUT_LINE ("STBD_GAS_TURBINE :");
  PUT ("GG_VIBRATION          => ");
  PUT (STBD_GAS_TURBINE.GG_VIBRATION, 0);
  NEW_LINE;
  PUT ("BEARING_TEMP          => ");
  PUT (STBD_GAS_TURBINE.BEARING_TEMP, 0);
  NEW_LINE;
  PUT ("GG_PRESSURE_TRIP_LIMIT =>");
  PUT (STBD_GAS_TURBINE.GG_PRESSURE_TRIP_LIMIT);
  NEW_LINE;
end FURTHER_RECORD_HANDLING;
```

Listing 9.3 This demonstrates the use of default and constant values in records.

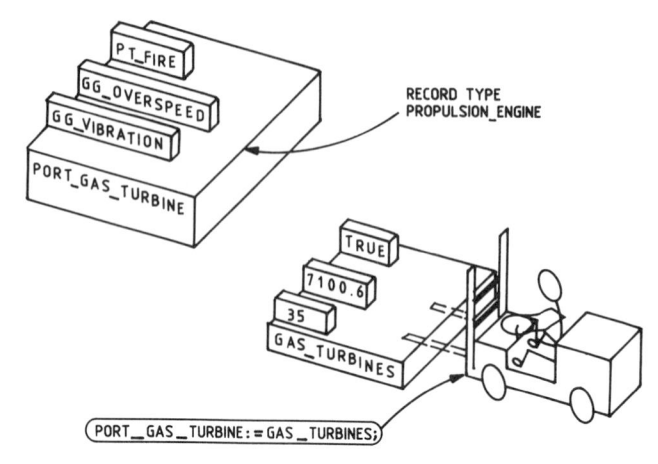

Fig.9.8 Handling complete records.

be set up separately, a fairly tedious process. Furthermore, there is always the chance of making mistakes. What can be done about this? Here the ability to handle complete records as a single unit is useful. Start by doing a record declaration, as follows:

```
type PROPULSION_ENGINE is
   record
      PT_FIRE         : BOOLEAN;
      GG_VIBRATION    : INTEGER;
      GG_OVERSPEED    : FLOAT;
   end record;

PORT_GAS_TURBINE  : PROPULSION_ENGINE;
STBD_GAS_TURBINE  : PROPULSION_ENGINE;
GAS_TURBINES      : PROPULSION_ENGINE;
```

Within the program, we can set up all values in the record variable GAS_TURBINES, a once-only activity. Then we can proceed to copy them (assign them) *en bloc* to the other records (Fig.9.8).

This eliminates the need to enter up the component values for these other records. The program below (Listing 9.4) illustrates this point.

(b) **Testing records for equality/inequality**

A moment's thought will make it clear why we can apply very limited tests to records structures. For instance, what would be the meaning of saying that one record variable is greater than another one? However, checking to see if

Records – basic types   287

```
with TEXT_IO;                 use TEXT_IO;
procedure COMPLETE_RECORD_HANDLING is
  package INT_IO is new INTEGER_IO (INTEGER);
  use INT_IO;
  type PROPULSION_ENGINE is
    record
       PT_FIRE            :      BOOLEAN;
       GG_VIBRATION       :      INTEGER;
       GG_OVERSPEED       :      FLOAT;
    end record;
  PORT_GAS_TURBINE :    PROPULSION_ENGINE;
  STBD_GAS_TURBINE :    PROPULSION_ENGINE;
  GAS_TURBINES     :    PROPULSION_ENGINE ;
begin
  GAS_TURBINES :=  (PT_FIRE       => FALSE,
                    GG_VIBRATION => 15,
                    GG_OVERSPEED => 1.0);
  -- complete record copying
  PORT_GAS_TURBINE := GAS_TURBINES;
  STBD_GAS_TURBINE := GAS_TURBINES;
  -- just print out the GG_vibration of each record
  PUT ("The Port Turbine vibration alarm trip level is now set to ");
  PUT (PORT_GAS_TURBINE.GG_VIBRATION, 0);
  NEW_LINE;
  PUT ("The Stbd Turbine vibration alarm trip level is now set to ");
  PUT (STBD_GAS_TURBINE.GG_VIBRATION, 0);
  NEW_LINE;
end COMPLETE_RECORD_HANDLING;
```

Listing 9.4 This is a demonstration showing how to manipulate records as single units (entities).

two (or more) such records contain the same values is a sensible operation. So it isn't a surprise that, in Ada, we are limited to checking records for equality (=) or inequality (/=). These operations are shown below in Listing 9.5.

```
procedure EQUALITY_INEQUALITY is
  type PROPULSION_ENGINE is
    record
       PT_FIRE         :    BOOLEAN       := FALSE;
       GG_VIBRATION    :    INTEGER       := 20;
       GG_OVERSPEED    :    FLOAT         := 0.5;
    end record;
  PORT_GAS_TURBINE :    PROPULSION_ENGINE;
  STBD_GAS_TURBINE :    PROPULSION_ENGINE;
  REFERENCE_ENGINE :    constant PROPULSION_ENGINE := (PT_FIRE      => FALSE,
                                                      GG_VIBRATION => 15,
                                                      GG_OVERSPEED => 1.0);
begin
  PORT_GAS_TURBINE := REFERENCE_ENGINE;
  if STBD_GAS_TURBINE /= PORT_GAS_TURBINE then
     STBD_GAS_TURBINE := PORT_GAS_TURBINE;
  end if;
end EQUALITY_INEQUALITY;
```

Listing 9.5 Testing records for equality/inequality.

288 Composite data types – records

9.1.6 Building complex records

Any record can itself be made up of other structured data types such as arrays and records, and also enumerated types. Further, we can form arrays of records (or, if you're feeling really masochistic, arrays of records which are themselves made up of structured types...). Let's look at a few examples, starting with the use of arrays (Listing 9.6).

A more complex structure still is given below in Listing 9.7.

Here two records are declared, ENGINE_DATA and PROPULSION_UNIT. The first one, ENGINE_DATA, contains two components. The second, PROPULSION_UNIT, also has two components. Observe, though, that its second component, ENGINE, is declared to be of type ENGINE_DATA – which has just been declared as a record. This gives rise to a nested record

```
with TEXT_IO;              use TEXT_IO;
procedure ARRAYS_IN_RECORDS is
  package INT_IO is new INTEGER_IO (INTEGER);
  use INT_IO;
  type VIBRATION_LOG is array (1..10) of INTEGER;
  type PROPULSION_ENGINE is
    record
      PT_FIRE               :    BOOLEAN        :=  FALSE;
      GG_OVERSPEED          :    FLOAT          :=  0.0;
      GG_VIBRATION          :    INTEGER        :=  0;
      GG_VIBRATION_HISTORY  :    VIBRATION_LOG  :=  ( others => 0);
    end record;
  PORT_GAS_TURBINE :    PROPULSION_ENGINE;
  STBD_GAS_TURBINE :    PROPULSION_ENGINE;
  VALUE            :    INTEGER;
  VARIATION        :    INTEGER;
begin
  PORT_GAS_TURBINE.PT_FIRE := TRUE;
  PORT_GAS_TURBINE.GG_OVERSPEED := 7100.6;
  PORT_GAS_TURBINE.GG_VIBRATION := 35;
  for HISTORY in reverse VIBRATION_LOG'FIRST..VIBRATION_LOG'LAST loop
    PUT ("Enter variation on previous reading (+/-) => ");
    GET (VARIATION);
    PORT_GAS_TURBINE.GG_VIBRATION_HISTORY (HISTORY) := VARIATION;
    SKIP_LINE;
  end loop;
  NEW_LINE;
  PUT_LINE ("The history of readings are :");
  VALUE := PORT_GAS_TURBINE.GG_VIBRATION;
  for HISTORY in VIBRATION_LOG'FIRST..VIBRATION_LOG'LAST loop
    VALUE := VALUE + PORT_GAS_TURBINE.GG_VIBRATION_HISTORY (HISTORY);
    PUT (VALUE, 0);
    NEW_LINE;
  end loop;
end ARRAYS_IN_RECORDS;
```

Listing 9.6 Using arrays in records.

```ada
with TEXT_IO;                use TEXT_IO;
procedure NESTED_RECORDS is
   package INT_IO is new INTEGER_IO (INTEGER);
   use INT_IO;
   subtype RUNNING_HOURS is INTEGER range 0..10000;
   type ENGINE_DATA is
      record
         FUEL            :    STRING (1..5)   :=  (others => ' ');
         HOURS           :    RUNNING_HOURS   :=  0;
      end record;
   type PROPULSION_UNIT is
      record
         SHIP            :    STRING (1..10) :=  (others => ' ');
         ENGINES         :    ENGINE_DATA;
      end record;
   OLYMPUS_55          :    PROPULSION_UNIT;
begin
   OLYMPUS_55.ENGINES.HOURS := 2075;
   OLYMPUS_55.ENGINES.FUEL  := "Avtur";
   OLYMPUS_55.SHIP (1..9)   := "Andromeda";
   PUT ("The engine is fitted to ");
   PUT_LINE (OLYMPUS_55.SHIP);
   PUT ("The running hours are ");
   PUT (OLYMPUS_55.ENGINES.HOURS, 0);
   NEW_LINE;
   PUT ("The fuel type is ");
   PUT_LINE (OLYMPUS_55.ENGINES.FUEL);
end NESTED_RECORDS;
```

Listing 9.7 A more complex record example – using components which are themselves records (nested records).

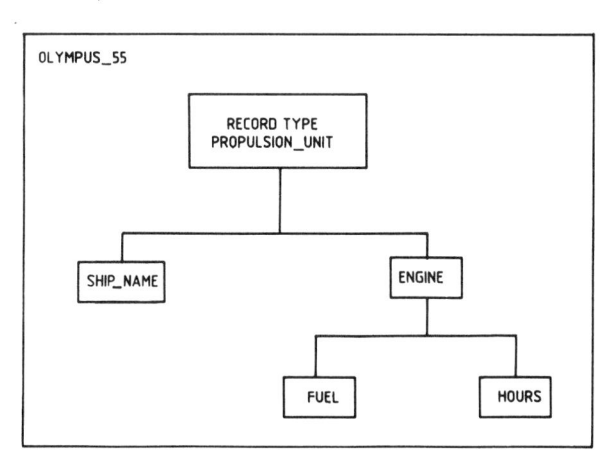

Fig.9.9 Structure of the record variable OLYMPUS_55.

structure. Following this, a variable, OLYMPUS_55, is declared to be of type PROPULSION_UNIT. Consequently, OLYMPUS_55 is structured as shown in Fig.9.9.

The method of component (element) selection is shown in Fig.9.10.

The next example here (Listing 9.8) includes an array of records.

290 Composite data types – records

```
                    ┌─────────────────┐
                    │ PROPULSION_UNIT │
                    └─────────────────┘
                     ╱        │       ╲
           ┌───────────┐      │      ┌────────┐
           │ SHIP_NAME │      │      │ ENGINE │
           └───────────┘      │      └────────┘
          ╱                   │       ╱      ╲
  (OLYMPUS_55.SHIP)           │   ┌──────┐ ┌───────┐
                              │   │ FUEL │ │ HOURS │
                              │   └──────┘ └───────┘
                              │                  ╲
                     (OLYMPUS_55.ENGINE.HOURS)
```

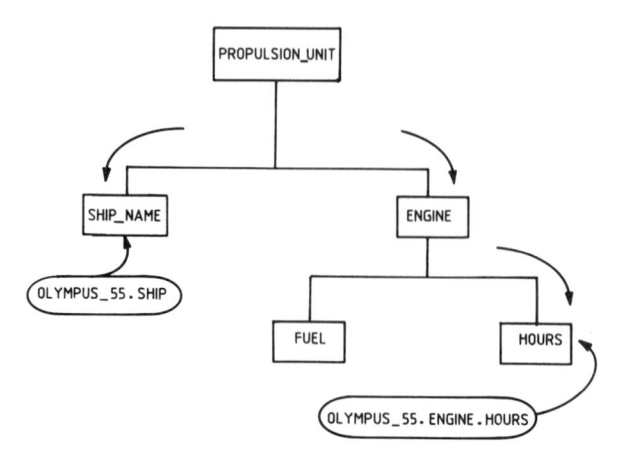

Fig.9.10 Element selection in a complex record structure.

Structurally the array appears as in Fig.9.11. Note that in such constructs the array must be a constrained one.

The next example consists of an array of records which themselves have records as component parts. A modified version of Listing 9.7 is given below (Listing 9.9).

9.1.7 Nested records and aggregates

Suppose the following declarations are made:

```
subtype RUNNING_HOURS is INTEGER range 0..10000;
type ENGINE_DATA is
   record
      FUEL  : STRING (1..5);
      HOURS : RUNNING_HOURS :=0;
end record;
type PROPULSION_UNIT is
   record
      SHIP_NAME : STRING (1..10) := (others => ' ');
      ENGINE    : ENGINE_DATA;
end record;
OLYMPUS_55 : PROPULSION_UNIT;
```

We can use aggregates with the variable OLYMPUS_55 in the usual way, as for instance:

```ada
with TEXT_IO;              use TEXT_IO;
procedure ARRAY_OF_RECORDS is
  package INT_IO is new INTEGER_IO (INTEGER);
  use INT_IO;
  type PROPULSION_ENGINE is
    record
      PT_FIRE           :   BOOLEAN      :=  FALSE;
      GG_OVERSPEED      :   FLOAT        :=  6700.1;
      GG_VIBRATION      :   INTEGER      :=  35;
    end record;
  type GAS_TURBINES is array (1..4) of PROPULSION_ENGINE;
  SHIP_TURBINES  :   GAS_TURBINES;
  INPUT_VALUE    :   INTEGER;
begin
  PUT ("Enter the Engine No.1 Turbine vibration trip level - mm => ");
  GET (INPUT_VALUE);
  SKIP_LINE;
  SHIP_TURBINES (1).GG_VIBRATION := INPUT_VALUE;
  PUT ("Enter the Engine No.2 Turbine vibration trip level - mm => ");
  GET (INPUT_VALUE);
  SKIP_LINE;
  SHIP_TURBINES (2).GG_VIBRATION := INPUT_VALUE;
  PUT ("Enter the Engine No.3 Turbine vibration trip level - mm => ");
  GET (INPUT_VALUE);
  SKIP_LINE;
  SHIP_TURBINES (3).GG_VIBRATION := INPUT_VALUE;
  PUT ("Enter the Engine No.4 Turbine vibration trip level - mm => ");
  GET (INPUT_VALUE);
  SKIP_LINE;
  SHIP_TURBINES (4).GG_VIBRATION := INPUT_VALUE;
  -- This shows that the trip levels have been set
  PUT_LINE ("The Turbine vibration alarm tip level is ");
  for ENGINE_NUMBER in 1..4 loop
    PUT ("Engine Number ");
    PUT (ENGINE_NUMBER, 0);
    PUT (" => ");
    PUT (SHIP_TURBINES (ENGINE_NUMBER).GG_VIBRATION, 0);
    NEW_LINE;
  end loop;
end ARRAY_OF_RECORDS;
```

Listing 9.8 Using an array of records.

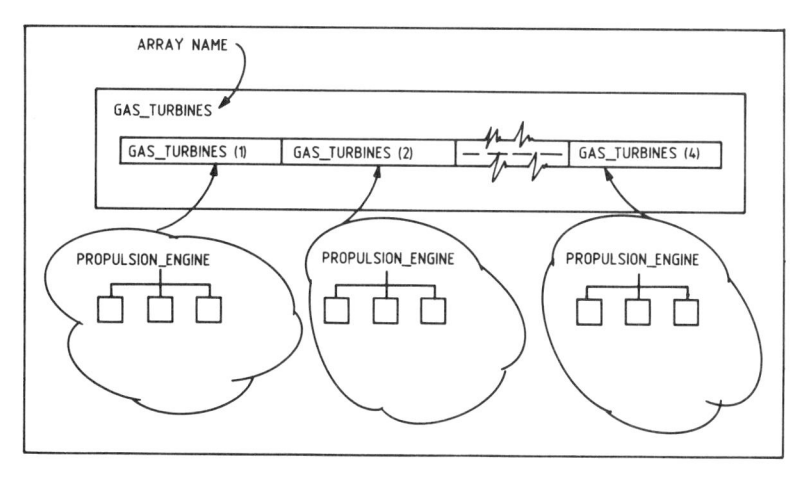

Fig.9.11 Example – array of records.

292 Composite data types – records

```ada
with TEXT_IO;                use TEXT_IO;
procedure ARRAY_OF_NESTED_RECORDS is
  package INT_IO is new INTEGER_IO (INTEGER);
  use INT_IO;
  subtype RUNNING_HOURS is INTEGER range 0..10000;
  type ENGINE_DATA is
    record
      FUEL            :      STRING (1..5) := (others => ' ');
      HOURS           :      RUNNING_HOURS := 0;
    end record;
  type PROPULSION_UNIT is
    record
      SHIP_NAME       :      STRING (1..10) := (others => ' ');
      ENGINE          :      ENGINE_DATA;
    end record;
  type SERVICE_REFERENCE is array (1..100) of PROPULSION_UNIT;
  OLYMPUS_55           :      PROPULSION_UNIT;
  GAS_TURBINE_MAINTENCE_RECORD : SERVICE_REFERENCE;
begin
  OLYMPUS_55.SHIP_NAME (1..9) := "Andromeda";
  OLYMPUS_55.ENGINE.HOURS := 2075;
  OLYMPUS_55.ENGINE.FUEL  := "Avtur";
  GAS_TURBINE_MAINTENCE_RECORD (1) := OLYMPUS_55;
  PUT_LINE ("Maintenance record No. 1");
  PUT_LINE ("Unit type : Olympus ");
  PUT ("This engine is fitted to ");
  PUT_LINE (GAS_TURBINE_MAINTENCE_RECORD (1).SHIP_NAME);
  PUT ("The running hours are ");
  PUT (GAS_TURBINE_MAINTENCE_RECORD (1).ENGINE.HOURS, 0);
  NEW_LINE;
  PUT ("The fuel type is ");
  PUT_LINE (GAS_TURBINE_MAINTENCE_RECORD (1).ENGINE.FUEL);
end ARRAY_OF_NESTED_RECORDS;
```

Listing 9.9 Using an array of nested records.

```
OLYMPUS_55.ENGINE := (FUEL => "Avtur",
                      HOURS => 2075);
```

and

```
OLYMPUS_55.SHIP_NAME := ("Andromeda");
```

However, we can also assign aggregates to nested records at the outer record level, as follows:

```
OLYMPUS_55 := (SHIP_NAME => "Andromeda",
               ENGINE    => (FUEL  => "Avtur",
                             HOURS => 2075));
```

Observe that the nested aggregate (for ENGINE) is bracketed within the brackets of the complete aggregate. We have used named association here for clarity; positional association is equally valid. Moreover, the association method used within the nested aggregate does not have to be the same as that used for the overall record. Thus, if we desired, we could have the following:

```
OLYMPUS_55 := (SHIP_NAME => "Andromeda",
               ENGINE    => ("Avtur", 2075));
```

These points are demonstrated in Listing 9.10.

```
with TEXT_IO;              use TEXT_IO;
procedure NESTED_RECORD_AGGREGATES is
  package INT_IO is new INTEGER_IO (INTEGER);
  use INT_IO;
  subtype RUNNING_HOURS is INTEGER range 0..10000;
  type ENGINE_DATA is
    record
      FUEL            :    STRING (1..5);
      HOURS           :    RUNNING_HOURS  :=  0;
    end record;
  type PROPULSION_UNIT is
    record
      SHIP            :    STRING (1..10) := (others => ' ');
      ENGINES         :    ENGINE_DATA;
    end record;
  OLYMPUS_55        :    PROPULSION_UNIT := (SHIP    => "Andromeda ",
                                             ENGINES => (FUEL  => "Avtur",
                                                         HOURS => 2075));
  OLYMPUS_56        :    PROPULSION_UNIT;
begin
  OLYMPUS_56 := (SHIP    => "Nottingham",
                 ENGINES => ("Avtur" , 1509));
  OLYMPUS_55.ENGINES := ("Avtur", 3072);
  PUT ("The Olympus 55 engine is fitted to ");
  PUT_LINE (OLYMPUS_55.SHIP);
  PUT ("The running hours are ");
  PUT (OLYMPUS_55.ENGINES.HOURS,0);
  NEW_LINE;
  PUT ("The fuel type is ");
  PUT_LINE (OLYMPUS_55.ENGINES.FUEL);
  PUT ("The Olympus 56 engine is fitted to ");
  PUT_LINE (OLYMPUS_56.SHIP);
  PUT ("The running hours are ");
  PUT (OLYMPUS_56.ENGINES.HOURS,0);
  NEW_LINE;
  PUT ("The fuel type is ");
  PUT_LINE (OLYMPUS_56.ENGINES.FUEL);
end NESTED_RECORD_AGGREGATES;
```

Listing 9.10 Aggregates of nested records.

9.2 INTRODUCTION TO DISCRIMINANTS

Very loosely we can say that Ada language features are either 'fixed' or 'programmable'. By programmable we mean that some basic feature is tailored to meet particular needs. Two examples illustrate this clearly: subprogram parameters and unconstrained arrays. Here, in this section, the idea of 'tailored' records is introduced. Using these we can produce record objects where their components differ in:

- Size;
- Number;
- Type.

Yet these objects can be viewed (conceptually) as being of the same type. However, before going into this in detail, certain ideas and definitions need to be established.

Any component of a record structure which can be adapted to suit specific needs is called a *discriminated component* (Fig.9.12).

Record types fall into two categories, non-discriminated ('normal') and discriminated ('with discriminants'). Normal records have a fixed structure. Objects of such types always contain the components defined for that type. By contrast, record objects based on a discriminated type do not necessarily have the same structure. Any variation relates to the discriminated components only. The actual structure of such objects is defined by the value of a 'parameter' called the *discriminant* (confusingly, the LRM calls this a component). And, to reiterate a point, these objects are considered to be of the same type.

How are discriminants declared? By using a discriminant part within the type description, as shown in Fig.9.13.

The discriminant part is written between the name of the record type (here, GROUP_ALARMS) and the keyword is. It consists of a discriminant

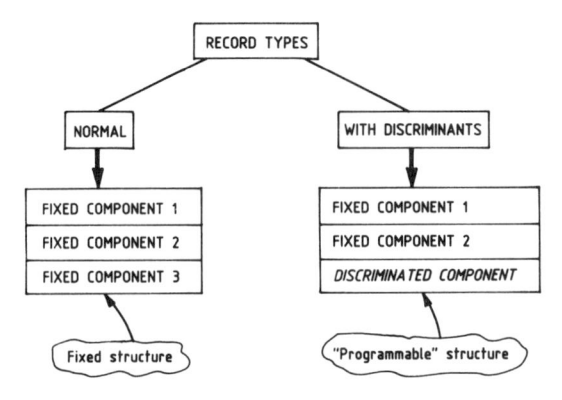

Fig.9.12 Record types – discriminated and non-discriminated.

```
type GROUP_ALARMS (ALARM_NUMBER : INTEGER) is
  record
    FIXED COMPONENT
    DISCRIMINATED COMPONENT
  end record;
```

(ALARM_NUMBER : INTEGER) → The discriminant part

ALARM_NUMBER : INTEGER → The discriminant specification

The discriminant identifier / The discriminant type

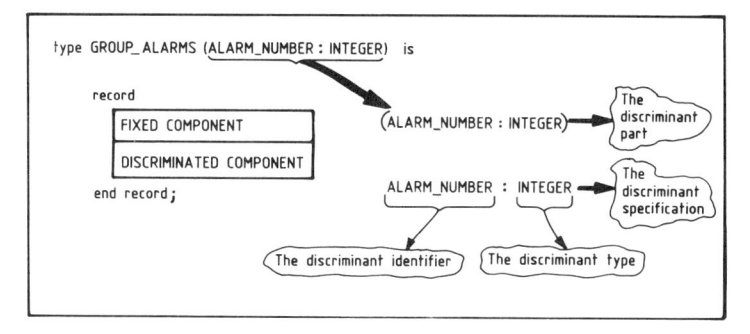

Fig.9.13 Specifying discriminant components.

specification contained within parentheses. This specifies the identifier of the discriminant and its type. For instance, in the example of Fig.9.13, the discriminant name is ALARM_NUMBER and its type is INTEGER.

We are now in a position to explore the use of discriminated records.

9.3 RECORD COMPONENTS – SETTING THEIR SIZE

A first application of record discriminants is to set the size of components within the record. There is one limitation though; it applies only to unconstrained array types (these, remember, are arrays whose bounds are not defined until objects of the type are declared).

Suppose that we wish to form a record of vectors. Further suppose that all vectors should have the same number of elements. There is nothing new so far – the standard record structure can be used. Now for a change. We further specify that:

- we wish to build objects of this record type where the actual number of elements used can vary from object to object; and
- the objects are type compatible.

We cannot meet these requirements with the normal record – thus the need for discriminated records.

First we have to declare an unconstrained array type, as below (this has, in itself, little to do with discriminants). Then the discriminated record type is declared.

```
-- declaring the unconstrained array type
type LINEAR_VECTOR is array (INTEGER range <>) of FLOAT;
-- declaring the discriminated record
type TWO_D_RECORD (SIZE : INTEGER) is
  record
    VECTOR_1 : LINEAR_VECTOR (1..SIZE);
    VECTOR_2 : LINEAR_VECTOR (1..SIZE);
  end record;
```

296 Composite data types – records

The discriminant here is SIZE, its type being INTEGER.

Objects of this type can now be declared. This is much the same as before – except here the discriminant value must be stated. For instance, to declare two record objects having array sizes of 10 and 20, we have

```
POWER_1 : TWO_D_RECORD (10);
POWER_2 : TWO_D_RECORD (20);
```

In each case the discriminant value sets the size of the arrays within the record. That is, it acts as an array constraint. On a matter of terminology, the items '(10)' and '(20)' are defined to be discriminant constraints. In this case we are said to have defined 'explicit discriminant values'. With such declarations the value of the constraint is now fixed. We are not allowed to change it later during program execution. Listing 9.11 expands on the points raised here.

9.4 MORE ON DISCRIMINANTS

9.4.1 Multiple discriminants – named and positional notation

In the previous example one discriminant only was used. For the following example, although it is a very different application, the same situation occurs. Here we have designed a record for storing veterinary details, specifically a pet name and an owner name:

```
type PET_RECORD (NAME_LENGTH : POSITIVE) is
   record
      OWNER_NAME : STRING (1..NAME_LENGTH);
      PET_NAME   : STRING (1..NAME_LENGTH);
   end record;
```

The discriminant NAME_LENGTH defines the length of the string used to hold each of these names. However, this means that both strings are the same size – not a very flexible solution. What is needed is a means of setting each string length individually. The solution is to use two discriminants, as in

```
type PET_RECORD (NAME_LENGTH     : POSITIVE;
                 PET_NAME_LENGTH : POSITIVE) is
   record
      OWNER_NAME : STRING (1..NAME_LENGTH);
      PET_NAME   : STRING (1..PET_NAME_LENGTH);
   end record;
```

More on discriminants

```
procedure DISCRIM_FOR_SIZE is
   type LINEAR_VECTOR is array (INTEGER range <>) of FLOAT;
   type TWO_D_RECORD (SIZE : INTEGER) is
      record
         VECTOR_1          :       LINEAR_VECTOR (1..SIZE);
         VECTOR_2          :       LINEAR_VECTOR (1..SIZE);
      end record;
   POWER_1               :       TWO_D_RECORD (10);
   POWER_2               :       TWO_D_RECORD (20);
begin
 -- give POWER_1 and POWER_2 some values
   POWER_1.VECTOR_1 := (others => 5.8);
   POWER_1.VECTOR_2 := (others => 77.678);
   POWER_2.VECTOR_1 := (others => 67.89);
   POWER_2.VECTOR_2 := (others => 100.0);
 -- change certain elements of POWER_1
   POWER_1.VECTOR_1 (5) := POWER_1.VECTOR_1 (5) + 10.0;
   POWER_1.VECTOR_2 (1..5) := POWER_1.VECTOR_2 (6..10);
 -- copy between POWER_1 and POWER_2
   POWER_1.VECTOR_1 (1) := POWER_2.VECTOR_1 (1);
   POWER_2.VECTOR_2 (11..20) := POWER_1.VECTOR_2 (1..10);
end DISCRIM_FOR_SIZE;
```

Listing 9.11 Using a discriminant to set the size of a record.

When objects of the type are declared, two discriminant values have to be supplied. Either named or positional association can be used, giving:

(a) Named association:

```
PATIENT_1 : PET_RECORD (NAME_LENGTH    => 7,
                       PET_NAME_LENGTH => 8);
```

Any order can be used for named associations.

(b) Positional association:

```
PATIENT_1 : PET_RECORD (7, 8);
```

Here we have to match up the values with the discriminant positions.

Both named and positional association can be mixed. However, once named association is used you must continue to use it. It is not permitted to revert to positional notation.

These aspects are demonstrated in Listing 9.12.

So far the record examples have used discriminated components only. It is, though, more common to find that normal components are also present. For example:

298 Composite data types – records

```
with TEXT_IO;            use TEXT_IO;
procedure MULTI_DISCRIM is
  type PET_RECORD (NAME_LENGTH     :    POSITIVE;
                   PET_NAME_LENGTH :    POSITIVE) is
    record
      OWNER_NAME      :    STRING (1..NAME_LENGTH);
      PET_NAME        :    STRING (1..PET_NAME_LENGTH);
    end record;
  PATIENT_1 : PET_RECORD (NAME_LENGTH     => 7,
                          PET_NAME_LENGTH => 8);
  PATIENT_2 : PET_RECORD (6, 4);
begin
  PATIENT_1.OWNER_NAME := "Cooling";
  PATIENT_1.PET_NAME   := "Guinness";
  PATIENT_2.OWNER_NAME := "Dennis";
  PATIENT_2.PET_NAME   := "Smut";
  PUT ("OWNER'S NAME : ");
  PUT_LINE (PATIENT_1.OWNER_NAME);
  PUT ("PET'S NAME   : ");
  PUT_LINE (PATIENT_1.PET_NAME);
  NEW_LINE;
  PUT ("OWNER'S NAME : ");
  PUT_LINE (PATIENT_2.OWNER_NAME);
  PUT ("PET'S NAME   : ");
  PUT_LINE (PATIENT_2.PET_NAME);
end MULTI_DISCRIM;
```

Listing 9.12 Using named and positional association with multiple discriminants.

```
type PET_RECORD (NAME_LENGTH     : POSITIVE;
                 PET_NAME_LENGTH : POSITIVE) is
  record
    OWNER_NAME : STRING (1..NAME_LENGTH);
    PET_NAME   : STRING (1..PET_NAME_LENGTH);
    PEDIGREE   : BOOLEAN;
  end record;
```

9.4.2 Default discriminant values

Discriminants can be given a default value at declaration time. Normally this would be used to set their initial condition. To illustrate this we define the initial value of the discriminant NAME_LENGTH (below) to be 10:

```
type PET_RECORD (NAME_LENGTH : POSITIVE := 10) is
  record
    OWNER_NAME : STRING (1..NAME_LENGTH);
  end record;
```

When objects of this record type are declared, we can omit their constraints, as in

More on discriminants

```
with TEXT_IO;              use TEXT_IO;
procedure DEFAULT_DISCRIM is
  type PET_RECORD (NAME_LENGTH     :  POSITIVE := 10;
                   PET_NAME_LENGTH :  POSITIVE := 10) is
    record
      OWNER_NAME       :    STRING (1..NAME_LENGTH );
      PET_NAME         :    STRING (1..PET_NAME_LENGTH);
      PEDIGREE         :    BOOLEAN;
    end record;
  STANDARD_PATIENT    : PET_RECORD;
  LONG_NAMED_PATIENT  : PET_RECORD (NAME_LENGTH     => 12,
                                    PET_NAME_LENGTH => 18);
begin
  STANDARD_PATIENT.OWNER_NAME := "Cooling     ";
  STANDARD_PATIENT.PET_NAME   := "Guinness    ";
  STANDARD_PATIENT.PEDIGREE   := FALSE;
  LONG_NAMED_PATIENT.OWNER_NAME := "Higgenbottom";
  LONG_NAMED_PATIENT.PET_NAME   := "Ruthus II of Hoton";
  LONG_NAMED_PATIENT.PEDIGREE   := TRUE;
end DEFAULT_DISCRIM;
```

Listing 9.13 Using default discriminant values.

```
NEW_PATIENT : PET_RECORD;
```

For the two-discriminant case we could have:

```
type PET_RECORD (NAME_LENGTH     : POSITIVE := 10;
                 PET_NAME_LENGTH : POSITIVE := 10) is
```

A point to note when using default values: they must be supplied for all discriminants of the declaration. In the example here it would be illegal to write

```
type PET_RECORD (NAME_LENGTH     : POSITIVE := 10;
                 PET_NAME_LENGTH : POSITIVE ) is
```

Listing 9.13 shows the use of default discriminant values.

One small but important point is worth raising here. In the examples above the discriminant NAME_LENGTH was defined to be type POSITIVE. Frequently this corresponds to the range 1 to 32 767. Given this, the result of declaring

```
OWNER_NAME : STRING (1..NAME_LENGTH);
```

is that the compiler may assume that the maximum string length will be 32 767, and reserves storage space for 32 767 characters for each object of this record type. If this happens it won't be long before the computer store becomes exhausted, giving rise to an error condition. It is recommended that in situations like this a constrained subtype be used, for example:

```
subtype STRING_LENGTH is POSITIVE range 1..20;
type PET_RECORD (NAME_LENGTH : STRING_LENGTH := 10) is
   record
      OWNER_NAME : STRING (1..NAME_LENGTH);
   end record;
```

9.4.3 Using aggregates with discriminated records

Values of a discriminated record can be set using aggregates. Two situations have to be taken into account: record types with and without default discriminant values.

Take the following declaration which includes a default:

```
subtype VECTOR_SIZE is POSITIVE range 1..200;
type LINEAR_VECTOR is array (VECTOR_SIZE range <>) of FLOAT;
type DATA_RECORD (SIZE : VECTOR_SIZE := 2) is
   record
      VALID_DATA : BOOLEAN;
      VECTOR_1 : LINEAR VECTOR (1..SIZE);
   end record;
```

Then, when declaring an object of this type, we can assign values using the aggregate construction. Both named and positional notation may be used. First, named association:

```
CONTROL_LAW_COEFFICIENTS : DATA_RECORD := (SIZE => 2,
                                           VALID_DATA => TRUE,
                                           VECTOR_1 => (1 => 0.9,
                                                        2 => 0.09));
```

Here we have a free choice in the ordering of components. However, for positional notation the discriminant values must appear first. Thus, for this example, we have

```
CONTROL_LAW_COEFFICIENTS : DATA_RECORD (2, TRUE, (0.9, 0.09));
```

We can, of course, use aggregates to change the value of the components at any later time.

Now consider the use of a discriminant which is declared without a default value:

```
subtype VECTOR_SIZE is POSITIVE range 1..200;
type LINEAR_VECTOR is array (VECTOR_SIZE range <>) of FLOAT;
type DATA_RECORD_X (SIZE : VECTOR_SIZE) is
    record
        VALID_DATA : BOOLEAN;
        VECTOR     : LINEAR_VECTOR (1..SIZE);
    end record;
```

When we declare an object of this type we have to supply the discriminant constraint:

```
INPUT_VECTORS : DATA_RECORD_X (3);
```

To set up the whole record at declaration time, we use an aggregate as follows:

```
INPUT_VECTORS : DATA_RECORD_X (3) := (SIZE       => 3,
                                      VALID_DATA => TRUE,
                                      VECTOR     => (1 => 0.8,
                                                     2 => 0.08,
                                                     3 => 0.008));
```

Note that, as shown earlier, the discriminant constraint has to be written after the type name. But now its value must also be repeated as the first item in the aggregate. And remember, we cannot change this value. Positional association may, of course, also be used here.

Various aspects involving aggregates in discriminated records are illustrated in Listing 9.14.

9.4.4 Changing discriminant values

The discriminant value of a record object can be changed – but only if it is declared without a constraint. Such declarations were demonstrated earlier, as for example:

```
NEW_PATIENT : PET_RECORD;
```

302 Composite data types – records

```
procedure AGG_DISCRIM is
  subtype VECTOR_SIZE is POSITIVE range 1..200;
  type LINEAR_VECTOR is array (VECTOR_SIZE range <>) of FLOAT;
  type DATA_RECORD_X (SIZE : VECTOR_SIZE) is
    record
       VALID_DATA        :    BOOLEAN;
       VECTOR            :    LINEAR_VECTOR (1..SIZE);
    end record;
  NAMED_AGG_RECORD        :   DATA_RECORD_X (3);
  POSITIONAL_AGG_RECORD   :   DATA_RECORD_X (3);
  MIXED_AGG_RECORD_1      :   DATA_RECORD_X (3);
  MIXED_AGG_RECORD_2      :   DATA_RECORD_X (3);
  MIXED_AGG_RECORD_3      :   DATA_RECORD_X (3);
  MIXED_AGG_RECORD_4      :   DATA_RECORD_X (3) := (SIZE       =>  3,
                                                    VALID_DATA => TRUE,
                                                    VECTOR     => (1 => 0.8,
                                                                   2 => 0.08,
                                                                   3 => 0.008));
begin
-- The following statements make all the records declared
-- hold the same values
-- named association
   NAMED_AGG_RECORD := (SIZE       => 3,
                        VALID_DATA => TRUE,
                        VECTOR     => (1 => 0.8, 2 => 0.08, 3 => 0.008));
-- positional association
   POSITIONAL_AGG_RECORD := (3, TRUE, (0.8, 0.08, 0.008));
-- mixed association
   MIXED_AGG_RECORD_1 := (SIZE       => 3,
                          VALID_DATA => TRUE,
                          VECTOR     => ( 0.8, 0.08, 0.008));
   MIXED_AGG_RECORD_2 := (3, TRUE, VECTOR   => (0.8, 0.08, 0.008));
   MIXED_AGG_RECORD_3 := (3, TRUE, (1 => 0.8, 2 => 0.08, 3 => 0.008));
end AGG_DISCRIM;
```

Listing 9.14 Using aggregates with discriminated records.

Furthermore, this applies just to record types which have default discriminant values. Suppose we decide to change the value of the discriminant NAME_LENGTH of the record type PET_RECORD. The logical move would be to assign a new value to NAME_LENGTH and leave it at that. To do this we might be tempted to write

```
NEW_PATIENT.NAME_LENGTH := 20;   (assuming we want to change
                                  NAME_LENGTH to 20)
```

Unfortunately, something that simple is not allowed. We have to change the value of the complete record. This is illustrated in Listing 9.15.

To sum up, discriminant values can be changed only when:

- record types are declared having default discriminant values; and
- objects of such types are declared without constraints.

```
procedure CHANGE_DISCRIM is
   type PET_RECORD (NAME_LENGTH     :     POSITIVE :=  10;
                    PET_NAME_LENGTH :     POSITIVE :=  10) is
      record
         OWNER_NAME       :     STRING (1..NAME_LENGTH );
         PET_NAME         :     STRING (1..PET_NAME_LENGTH);
         PEDIGREE         :     BOOLEAN;
      end record;
   NEW_PATIENT            :     PET_RECORD;
begin
   NEW_PATIENT := (NAME_LENGTH      => 20,
                   PET_NAME_LENGTH  => 10,
                   OWNER_NAME       => "J. Baker-Smith-Jones",
                   PET_NAME         => "JASPER III",
                   PEDIGREE         => TRUE);
end CHANGE_DISCRIM;
```

Listing 9.15 Changing discriminant values.

9.4.5 Using discriminants to initialize record components

One further feature of discriminants is their use for initializing record components:

```
type DATA_POINTS (STATUS : BOOLEAN) is
   record
      DATA_VALID         : BOOLEAN := STATUS;
      ACTUAL_DATA_POINTS : INTEGER;
   end record;
```

Here the component DATA_VALID has been assigned an initial 'formal' value STATUS. Observe that this is the discriminant of the record, and is of type BOOLEAN. When we declare an object of this type we supply the actual value to be used. For example:

```
YAW_RATE  : DATA_POINTS (FALSE);
ELEVATION : DATA_POINTS (TRUE);
```

As a result YAW_RATE.DATA_VALID is FALSE and ELEVATION.DATA_VALID is TRUE.

9.4.6 Nesting discriminated records within records

Suppose we intend to build a record where one of its components is a discriminant record type (Fig.9.14).

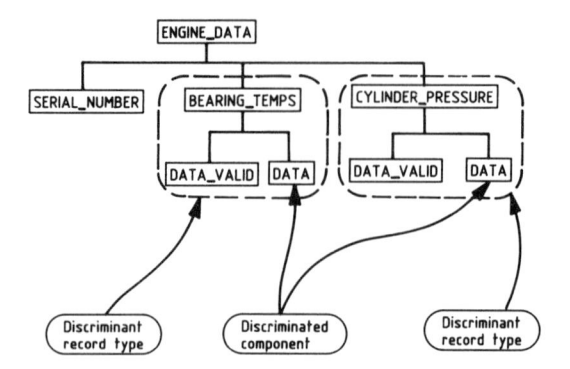

Fig.9.14 Nesting of discriminated records – example structure.

How is this done? The approach follows on from that described earlier for nested records. First, declare the inner record, for example

```
type DATA_POINTS is array (INTEGER range < >) of INTEGER;
type DATA_SAMPLE (NO_OF_DATA_POINTS : INTEGER) is
   record
      DATA_VALID          : BOOLEAN := FALSE;
      DATA                : DATA_POINTS (1..NO_OF_DATA_POINTS);
   end record;
```

Now declare the outer record, and supply the discriminant value:

```
type ENGINE_DATA is
   record
      SERIAL_NUMBER      : INTEGER;
      BEARING_TEMPS      : DATA_SAMPLE (NO_OF_DATA_POINTS => 4);
      CYLINDER_PRESSURE  : DATA_SAMPLE (NO_OF_DATA_POINTS => 8);
   end record;
```

Finally, declare an object of type ENGINE_DATA:

```
PORT_TURBINE : ENGINE_DATA;
```

An example of this construction is given in Listing 9.16.

```
with TEXT_IO;              use TEXT_IO;
procedure NESTED_DISCRIM is
  type DATA_POINTS is array (INTEGER range <>) of INTEGER;
  type DATA_SAMPLE (NO_OF_DATA_POINTS : INTEGER) is
    record
      DATA_VALID         :    BOOLEAN         := FALSE;
      DATA               :    DATA_POINTS (1..NO_OF_DATA_POINTS);
    end record;
  type ENGINE_DATA is
    record
      SERIAL_NUMBER      :    INTEGER;
      BEARING_TEMPS      :    DATA_SAMPLE (NO_OF_DATA_POINTS => 4);
      CYLINDER_PRESSURE  :    DATA_SAMPLE (NO_OF_DATA_POINTS => 8);
    end record;
  PORT_TURBINE      :    ENGINE_DATA;
  package INT_IO is new INTEGER_IO (INTEGER);
  use INT_IO;
begin
  PORT_TURBINE.SERIAL_NUMBER := 1234;
  PORT_TURBINE.BEARING_TEMPS.DATA := (30, 29, 29, 31);
  PORT_TURBINE.BEARING_TEMPS.DATA_VALID := TRUE;
  PORT_TURBINE.CYLINDER_PRESSURE.DATA := (100, 100, 100, 101, 99, 98, 98, 99);
  PUT ("Port Turbine Serial Number ");
  PUT (PORT_TURBINE.SERIAL_NUMBER, 0);
  NEW_LINE;
  if PORT_TURBINE.BEARING_TEMPS.DATA_VALID then
    PUT ("Bearing Temperature readings : ");
    for I in 1..PORT_TURBINE.BEARING_TEMPS.NO_OF_DATA_POINTS loop
      PUT (PORT_TURBINE.BEARING_TEMPS.DATA (I), 4);
    end loop;
    NEW_LINE;
  else
    PUT_LINE ("No valid Bearing Temperature data");
  end if;
  if PORT_TURBINE.CYLINDER_PRESSURE.DATA_VALID then
    PUT ("Cylinder Pressure readings : ");
    for I in 1.. PORT_TURBINE.CYLINDER_PRESSURE.NO_OF_DATA_POINTS loop
      PUT (PORT_TURBINE.CYLINDER_PRESSURE.DATA (I), 0);
    end loop;
    NEW_LINE;
  else
    PUT_LINE ("No valid Cylinder Pressure data");
  end if;
end NESTED_DISCRIM;
```

Listing 9.16 Using a discriminated record type as a component of a record.

9.4.7 Using discriminants to constrain discriminated records

The topic here follows on directly from the previous section. There we supplied the value of the discriminant for the inner record when declaring the outer record type. It would, though, be more flexible if we could define this when declaring objects of the outer record type. It turns out that this can be done by using a discriminant with the outer record. First, as before, declare the inner record:

```
type DATA_POINTS is array (INTEGER range < >) of INTEGER;
type DATA_SAMPLE (NO_OF_DATA_POINTS : INTEGER) is
   record
      DATA_VALID           : BOOLEAN := FALSE;
      DATA                 : DATA_POINTS (1..NO_OF_DATA_POINTS);
   end record;
```

Now declare the outer record. Use the discriminant of the outer record to define the discriminant 'formal' value for the inner record:

```
type ENGINE_DATA (TEMP_PNTS     : INTEGER;
                  PRESSURE_PNTS : INTEGER ) is
   record
      SERIAL_NUMBER     : INTEGER;
      BEARING_TEMPS     : DATA_SAMPLE (NO_OF_DATA_POINTS => TEMP_PNTS);
      CYLINDER_PRESSURE : DATA_SAMPLE (NO_OF_DATA_POINTS => PRESSURE_PNTS);
   end record;
```

Finally, declare an object of type ENGINE_DATA:

```
PORT_TURBINE : ENGINE_DATA (TEMP_PNTS => 4, PRESSURE_PNTS => 8);
```

As a result, the discriminant TEMP_PNTS is assigned the value 4. It, in turn, is used in the declaration of BEARING_TEMPS to set the discriminant NO_OF_DATA_POINTS to 4. These features are elaborated in Listing 9.17.

An aggregate is used to set up the values of the record.

9.4.8 Applying the CONSTRAINED attribute

We said earlier that it is forbidden to change the discriminant value of a constrained record. If you try to do this your system will regard it as an error condition and take appropriate action. Most likely the program will stop and you will see a screen message 'CONSTRAINT ERROR'. This can be a very frustrating experience. You can, though, check to see if record objects are constrained or not – before accessing the discriminant. To do this we apply the attribute 'CONSTRAINED', see Listing 9.18 below.

9.5 RECORDS WITH VARIANT PARTS – 'VARIANT RECORDS'

9.5.1 Introduction – the case for variant records

Up to now we've considered records to have a fixed size, that is a fixed number of fields. Let us see why, in some circumstances, this can be inefficient.

```
procedure NESTED_AND_OUTER_DISCRIM is
  type DATA_POINTS is array (INTEGER range <>) of INTEGER;
  type DATA_SAMPLE (NO_OF_DATA_POINTS : INTEGER) is
    record
      DATA_VALID      :    BOOLEAN        := FALSE;
      DATA            :    DATA_POINTS (1..NO_OF_DATA_POINTS);
    end record;
  type ENGINE_DATA (TEMP_PNTS     :    INTEGER;
                    PRESSURE_PNTS :    INTEGER) is
    record
      SERIAL_NUMBER     : INTEGER;
      BEARING_TEMPS     : DATA_SAMPLE (NO_OF_DATA_POINTS => TEMP_PNTS);
      CYLINDER_PRESSURE : DATA_SAMPLE (NO_OF_DATA_POINTS => PRESSURE_PNTS);
    end record;
PORT_TURBINE : ENGINE_DATA (TEMP_PNTS =>  4,
                            PRESSURE_PNTS => 8);
MAIN_ENGINE  : ENGINE_DATA (TEMP_PNTS => 10,
                            PRESSURE_PNTS => 16);
begin
  PORT_TURBINE.SERIAL_NUMBER := 1234;
  PORT_TURBINE.BEARING_TEMPS.DATA := (30, 29, 29, 31);
  PORT_TURBINE.BEARING_TEMPS.DATA_VALID := TRUE;
  PORT_TURBINE.CYLINDER_PRESSURE.DATA := (100, 100, 100, 101, 99, 98, 98, 99);
  PORT_TURBINE.CYLINDER_PRESSURE.DATA_VALID := TRUE;
  MAIN_ENGINE.SERIAL_NUMBER := 5623;
  MAIN_ENGINE.BEARING_TEMPS.DATA := (40, 57, 89, 12, 22, 0, 0, 12, 12, 190);
  MAIN_ENGINE.CYLINDER_PRESSURE.DATA := (102, 103, 102, 104, 101, 101, 101,
                                         101, 103, 108, 109, 107, 100, 100,
                                         100, 99);
  MAIN_ENGINE.CYLINDER_PRESSURE.DATA_VALID := TRUE;
end NESTED_AND_OUTER_DISCRIM;
```

Listing 9.17 Nested records – constraining a record component which is itself a discriminated record type.

```
with TEXT_IO;            use TEXT_IO;
procedure CONSTRAINED_ATTRIB is
  type PET_RECORD (NAME_LENGTH      :    POSITIVE    := 10;
                   PET_NAME_LENGTH  :    POSITIVE    := 10) is
    record
      OWNER_NAME    :    STRING (1.. NAME_LENGTH )    := (others => ' ');
      PET_NAME      :    STRING (1..PET_NAME_LENGTH)  := (others => ' ');
      PEDIGREE      :    BOOLEAN;
end record;
STANDARD_PATIENT   : PET_RECORD;
LONG_NAMED_PATIENT : PET_RECORD (NAME_LENGTH => 12,
                                 PET_NAME_LENGTH => 18);
begin
  if STANDARD_PATIENT'CONSTRAINED then
    PUT_LINE ("STANDARD_PATIENT is constrained");
  else
    PUT_LINE ("STANDARD_PATIENT is NOT constrained");
  end if;
  if LONG_NAMED_PATIENT'CONSTRAINED then
    PUT_LINE ("LONG_NAMED_PATIENT is constrained");
  else
    PUT_LINE ("LONG_NAMED_PATIENT is NOT constrained");
  end if;
end CONSTRAINED_ATTRIB;
```

Listing 9.18 Applying the CONSTRAINED attribute.

Suppose that we have set up records to define the operational state of missile systems on a number of warships, as follows:

Ship name	Missile systems
Nottingham	Seadart
Andromeda	Seaslug
Broadsword	Seawolf, Ikara

Using our current knowledge of records we could tackle this in two ways. First, form three distinct record types:

```
type SYSTEM_1 is
   record
      SEADART : BOOLEAN;
   end record;
```

```
type SYSTEM_2 is
   record
      SEASLUG : BOOLEAN;
   end record;
```

```
type SYSTEM_3 is
   record
      SEAWOLF : BOOLEAN;
      IKARA   : BOOLEAN;
   end record;
```

Alternatively, for simplicity, have only one record type, as in:

```
type MISSILE_SYSTEM is
   record
      SEADART : BOOLEAN;
      SEASLUG : BOOLEAN;
      SEAWOLF : BOOLEAN;
      IKARA   : BOOLEAN;
   end record;
```

We merely fill in the record details as appropriate to the ships Nottingham, Broadsword and Andromeda, as shown in Listing 9.19.

What we have done is to create three objects which are identical. However, we are only using certain fields within each record. The unused fields constitute wasted computer storage space and possible cause for error. What we really want is a record structure that varies depending on its use (after all, it is highly unlikely that an individual ship will have all missile types fitted). In Ada this is provided by a record which has alternative parts, the 'variant' parts (these are often referred to as variant records). Using this feature we can vary the number of fields, and their type, for a record variable. We do not, note, declare a new record type.

Note that a discriminant, as applied earlier, allowed us to vary details of discriminated components. It did not enable us to include or exclude such components.

Records with variant parts – 'variant records' 309

```
procedure FIXED_RECORD is
  type MISSILE_SYSTEM is
    record
      SEADART        :     BOOLEAN;
      SEASLUG        :     BOOLEAN;
      SEAWOLF        :     BOOLEAN;
      IKARA          :     BOOLEAN;
    end record;
  NOTTINGHAM       :   MISSILE_SYSTEM;
  ANDROMEDA        :   MISSILE_SYSTEM;
  BROADSWORD       :   MISSILE_SYSTEM;
begin
  -- Nottingham has a SEADART missile system. It is operational.
  NOTTINGHAM.SEADART := TRUE;
  -- Andromeda has a SEASLUG missile system. It is operational.
  ANDROMEDA.SEASLUG := TRUE;
  -- Broadsword has a SEAWOLF and a IKARA missile system. SEAWOLF
  -- is operational here, IKARA is not.
  BROADSWORD.SEAWOLF := TRUE;
  BROADSWORD.IKARA := FALSE;
end FIXED_RECORD;
```

Listing 9.19 This demonstrates the inefficiency of the fixed record structure.

9.5.2 Variant parts – declaration and application

In the record declaration we denote the fields that are conditional using the CASE statement. Taking the above example we could declare the record as

```
type SHIP_CLASS is (F21, F22, D42);
type MISSILE_SYSTEM (CLASS : SHIP_CLASS) is  --CLASS is the discriminant
  record
    case CLASS is
      when D42 => SEADART : BOOLEAN;
      when F22 => SEAWOLF : BOOLEAN;
                  IKARA   : BOOLEAN;
      when F21 => SEASLUG : BOOLEAN;
    end case;
  end record;
```

In the record type MISSILE_SYSTEM, the fields which can vary (the variants) lie within the case construction. Fig.9.15 formally describes the variant record structure in detail.

Each variant consists of the keyword **when**, followed by a selector (or choice). 'CLASS' is a discriminant; D42, F22 and F21 are 'choices'.

The value of the discriminant defines which choice is to be used, that is which variant is included in the record. Each field is associated with a specific value of the discriminant. For instance, when the value F21 is assigned to 'CLASS'

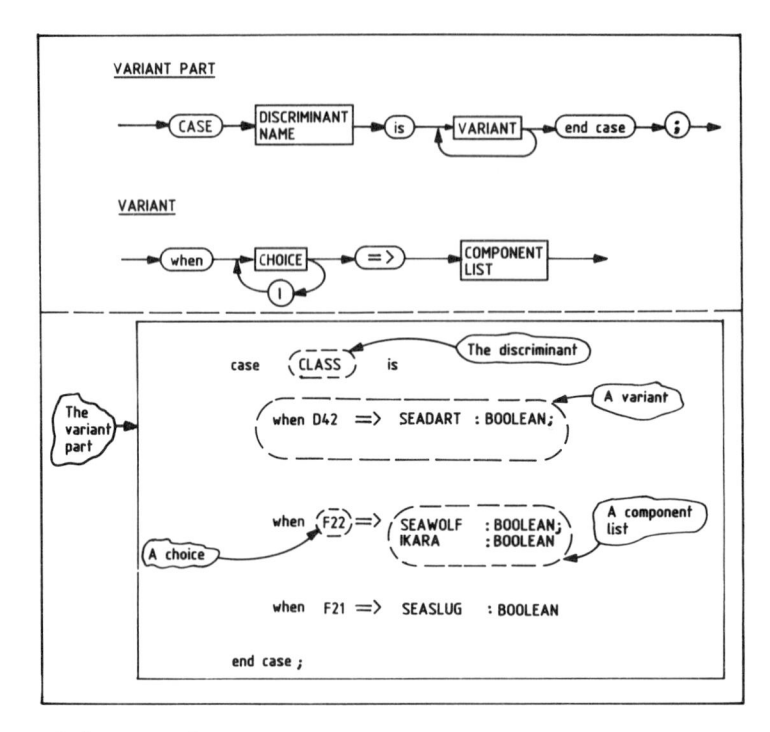

Fig.9.15 Variant record structure.

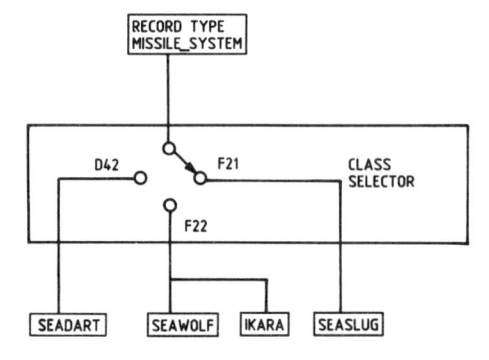

Fig.9.16 Variant records – the selection concept.

only the field labelled with F21 ('SEASLUG') is selected. Fig.9.16 shows the conceptual use of the selection process.

How does this work in practice? Suppose we set up a record for the variable 'ANDROMEDA'. In doing this we assign a value to the discriminant. Here we'll use F21:

Records with variant parts – 'variant records' 311

```
procedure SIMPLE_VAR_REC is
  type SHIP_CLASS is (F21, F22, D42);
  type MISSILE_SYSTEM (CLASS : SHIP_CLASS) is
    record
      case CLASS is
        when D42 => SEADART : BOOLEAN;
        when F22 => SEAWOLF : BOOLEAN;
                    IKARA   : BOOLEAN;
        when F21 => SEASLUG : BOOLEAN;
      end case;
    end record;
  NOTTINGHAM    :     MISSILE_SYSTEM (CLASS    => D42);
  ANDROMEDA     :     MISSILE_SYSTEM (CLASS    => F21);
  BROADSWORD    :     MISSILE_SYSTEM (CLASS    => F22);
  begin
  -- Nottingham's missile system is operational.
    NOTTINGHAM.SEADART := TRUE;
  -- Andromeda's missile system is operational.
    ANDROMEDA.SEASLUG := TRUE;
  -- Broadsword only has SEAWOLF operational.
    BROADSWORD.SEAWOLF := TRUE;
    BROADSWORD.IKARA   := FALSE;
  end SIMPLE_VAR_REC;
```

Listing 9.20 This is a simple example of the use of variant records.

```
ANDROMEDA : MISSILE_SYSTEM (F21);
```

Once we've done this only the field named 'SEASLUG' is associated with the record for ANDROMEDA.

To show a simple example of variant records, modify the previous program to that of Listing 9.20.

This record has variant parts only. In practice we are much more likely to use fixed (invariant) as well as variant components, Listing 9.21.

The variant part must be placed after the invariant components.

In the example above each variant had a single choice associated with it. We are not restricted to one only; a number can be used. For instance,

```
when F22 | F23 => SEAWOLF : BOOLEAN;
                  IKARA   : BOOLEAN;
```

means that either F22 or F23 will select this variant.

Up to now we have assumed that one of the components is always selected. Unfortunately, this may not be the case. Therefore, to cater for the use of a discriminant which does not select any component, we have the **others** choice. This is demonstrated in Listing 9.22.

```
procedure VAR_AND_INVAR is
  type SHIP_CLASS is (F21, F22, D42);
  type MISSILE_SYSTEM (CLASS : SHIP_CLASS) is
    record
      SYSTEM_TESTED    :       BOOLEAN;
      case CLASS is
        when D42 => SEADART : BOOLEAN;
        when F22 => SEAWOLF : BOOLEAN;
                    IKARA   : BOOLEAN;
        when F21 => SEASLUG : BOOLEAN;
      end case;
    end record;
  NOTTINGHAM      :       MISSILE_SYSTEM (CLASS     =>  D42);
  ANDROMEDA       :       MISSILE_SYSTEM (CLASS     =>  F21);
  BROADSWORD      :       MISSILE_SYSTEM (CLASS     =>  F22);
  begin
-- Nottingham's missile system is operational and has been tested
    NOTTINGHAM.SYSTEM_TESTED := TRUE;
    NOTTINGHAM.SEADART := TRUE;
-- Andromeda's missile system is operational, but has not been tested
    ANDROMEDA.SYSTEM_TESTED := FALSE;
    ANDROMEDA.SEASLUG := TRUE;
-- Broadsword only has SEAWOLF operational. It has been tested.
    BROADSWORD.SYSTEM_TESTED := TRUE;
    BROADSWORD.SEAWOLF := TRUE;
    BROADSWORD.IKARA := FALSE;
  end VAR_AND_INVAR;
```

Listing 9.21 A record structure consisting of invariant and variant components.

```
procedure OTHER_VARIANTS is
  type TRANSACTION_TYPE is (BALANCE_ENQUIRY, DEPOSIT, WITHDRAWAL);
  type TRANSACTION_RECORD (ACTION : TRANSACTION_TYPE) is
    record
      case ACTION is
        when BALANCE_ENQUIRY => BALANCE_AVAILABLE  : BOOLEAN;
        when others          => TRANSACTION_AMOUNT : INTEGER;
--in pence
      end case;
    end record;
  TRANSACTION_1   :    TRANSACTION_RECORD (ACTION   =>  BALANCE_ENQUIRY);
  TRANSACTION_2   :    TRANSACTION_RECORD (ACTION   =>  WITHDRAWAL);
  begin
    TRANSACTION_1.BALANCE_AVAILABLE := FALSE;
    TRANSACTION_2.TRANSACTION_AMOUNT := 5000;
  end OTHER_VARIANTS;
```

Listing 9.22 Variants, the others choice.

The **others** choice must be the final variant, and it cannot be combined with any other choices. Note that if we don't want anything to happen we can use the **null** clause.

Summarizing, a record can contain both variant and invariant parts. Only one variant part is allowed, and it must follow the invariant part. The variant part consists of a set of variants within the case construction. Each variant begins with the keyword **when**, and is selected using one or more choices. All choices must be distinct. The choice **others** can be used. If it is, it must be the last one, and by itself. The choice to be used is determined by the record discriminant.

9.5.3 Variant parts and aggregates

We have had many examples in the use of aggregates with normal records. It turns out that these can also be used with variant records. We have, though, to be careful in their application – a value can be supplied only to a valid variant field. Thus the discriminant value and the component value must be consistent, as demonstrated in Listing 9.23.

In this the discriminant name is ACTION. Assigning this a value of DEPOSIT or WITHDRAWAL causes the variant choice **when others** to be selected. Thus an object like this (as in TRANSACTION_2) has the structure equivalent to

```
record
    TRANSACTION_AMOUNT : INTEGER;
end record;
```

Values supplied must be valid for, and applicable to, these fields.

9.5.4 Variant parts and default discriminant values

We showed earlier how to change discriminant values when using discriminated records. This could be done only when default values were assigned to the discriminant at declaration time. In the same way we can apply this to records having variant parts. What we do is assign a default value to the discriminant. This therefore sets the value of the choice used for the case selector. Listing 9.24 illustrates this point.

As before, an aggregate must be used. From the listing you can see that the discriminant name is ACTION. It is assigned a default value DEPOSIT.

A COMMENT: Variables declared to be a record type having variant parts may cause us trouble. The compiler will treat them as being type compatible,

314 Composite data types – records

```
procedure VARIANT_AGG is
   type TRANSACTION_TYPE is (BALANCE_ENQUIRY, DEPOSIT, WITHDRAWAL);
   type TRANSACTION_RECORD (ACTION : TRANSACTION_TYPE) is
      record
         case ACTION is
            when BALANCE_ENQUIRY => BALANCE_AVAILABLE : BOOLEAN;
            when others          => TRANSACTION_AMOUNT : INTEGER;
   --in pence
         end case;
      end record;
   TRANSACTION_1 :    TRANSACTION_RECORD (ACTION   => BALANCE_ENQUIRY);
   TRANSACTION_2 :    TRANSACTION_RECORD (ACTION   => WITHDRAWAL);
   begin
      TRANSACTION_1 := (ACTION            => BALANCE_ENQUIRY,
                        BALANCE_AVAILABLE => FALSE);
      TRANSACTION_2 := (ACTION             => WITHDRAWAL,
                        TRANSACTION_AMOUNT => 5000);
   end VARIANT_AGG;
      PUT (ELEMENT.VALUE_STORED);
      ELEMENT := ELEMENT.NEXT_ELEMENT;
   end loop;
end ELEMENT_REMOVAL;
-- remember element_to_be_removed.next_element is an element in itself
   ELEMENT_TO_BE_REMOVED.NEXT_ELEMENT.PREVIOUS_ELEMENT := LAST_LOOKED_AT;
-- alternatively
-- ELEMENT := ELEMENT_TO_BE_REMOVED.NEXT_ELEMENT;
-- ELEMENT.PREVIOUS_ELEMENT := LAST_LOOKED_AT;
-- completely take us out of the loop
   ELEMENT_TO_BE_REMOVED.PREVIOUS_ELEMENT := null;
   ELEMENT_TO_BE_REMOVED.NEXT_ELEMENT := null;
   end if;
-- now print the list
-- skip first element as never used.
   ELEMENT := HEAD_OF_LIST.NEXT_ELEMENT;
   PUT_LINE ("The values left are => ");
   while (ELEMENT /= HEAD_OF_LIST)
-- bottom of list
   loop
      PUT (ELEMENT.VALUE_STORED);
      ELEMENT := ELEMENT.NEXT_ELEMENT;
   end loop;
end DOUBLE_LINK;
```

Listing 9.23 Assigning variant records by aggregates.

yet they may actually differ in their structure because the variant parts are used differently. Such a situation may easily lead to programming errors. Be warned.

REVIEW

Do you now:

- Understand the concept and use of records?
- Know how to work with their contents as single entities or as a collection of components?

```
procedure VAR_DEFAULT is
  type TRANSACTION_TYPE is (BALANCE_ENQUIRY, DEPOSIT, WITHDRAWAL);
  type TRANSACTION_RECORD (ACTION : TRANSACTION_TYPE := DEPOSIT) is
    record
      case ACTION is
        when BALANCE_ENQUIRY => BALANCE_AVAILABLE  : BOOLEAN;
        when others          => TRANSACTION_AMOUNT : INTEGER;
 --in pence
      end case;
    end record;
  CURRENT_TRANSACTION : TRANSACTION_RECORD;
begin
  for TRANSACTION in TRANSACTION_TYPE loop
    case TRANSACTION is
      when BALANCE_ENQUIRY =>
        CURRENT_TRANSACTION := (ACTION             =>  BALANCE_ENQUIRY,
                                BALANCE_AVAILABLE => TRUE);
      when DEPOSIT =>
        CURRENT_TRANSACTION := (ACTION              =>  DEPOSIT,
                                TRANSACTION_AMOUNT => 23456);
      when WITHDRAWAL =>
        CURRENT_TRANSACTION := (ACTION              =>  WITHDRAWAL,
                                TRANSACTION_AMOUNT => 2000);
    end case;
  end loop;
end VAR_DEFAULT;
```

Listing 9.24 Changing variant records with default values.

- See how aggregates are used with records?
- Feel confident to build and work with complex record structures?
- Appreciate the basic idea of the discriminant parameter and the discriminant component of a record?
- Understand how discriminants are used to vary the structure of a record?
- Know how to use multiple discriminants, and to incorporate named and positional notation?
- Appreciate the need for, and the structure of, records with variant parts?
- See how to apply aggregates and discriminants to variant records?

Chapter Ten
Dynamic data types

In the previous chapter we dealt with data structures which are essentially fixed in size. If such structures are used for handling very large amounts of data then computer storage space is soon exhausted. Data like this is usually dynamic, that is in a constant state of change. Consequently the amount of storage space needed during a program run can change considerably. What is the best way to deal with this? The solution is to employ data structures which match our needs. In other words, items should only be brought into being when we want to use them. Once in use we must be able to expand and contract their number as our requirements change. Finally, we must be able to dispose of them when they are no longer required. These we define to be dynamic data objects (variables).

In this chapter you'll meet data structures which have been devised to match the needs outlined above. After having studied it you will:

- Understand the concepts of dynamic data structures;
- Understand the concept and use of access types (pointers);
- Understand how to construct simple linked-list files;
- Appreciate that dynamic data structures are potent sources of software unreliability.

10.1 INTRODUCTION TO DYNAMIC DATA STRUCTURES

Let's return to the subject of storing and accessing data in our system. In simple terms we can visualize data storage locations as being much the same as a set of 'pigeon holes' for letters, Fig.10.1.

Each hole has a unique identifier number or 'address'. By using this address we can obtain the information contained within the hole. Only one item of information is held within each location. Therefore, for one of our earlier specimen programs we might well have the situation shown in Fig.10.2.

Here the first data item is X_NEW, the next X_OLD, and so on. To get the value contained within the first 'box' we only need to refer to the item by its name, actual addressing being handled by the compiler.

What we have here is a 'static' data storage structure, that is the data store size is fixed. By defining our system data we also define the amount of memory space needed to support it. Implicit is the assumption that we'll always know how much storage is needed when the program runs. Do we,

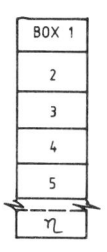

Fig.10.1 Data storage – concept.

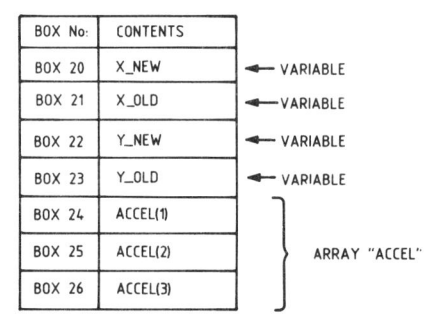

Fig.10.2 Static data storage.

though? Consider the requirement to monitor production line machinery, maintaining a log of equipment status. We would like to know those systems which are running, those defective, those shut down, etc. This is going to be a dynamic log; after all, in the real world, equipment states continually change. Therefore we cannot say exactly how much data storage is needed at any one instant. This presents us with a problem if our data structures are fixed. The data store must be large enough to cope with the worst case situation, that is a maximum amount of data needing to be stored. And yet most of the time we won't actually have a full set of data. Hence we end up wasting memory space.

Looking at a totally different aspect of the problem, suppose we are asked to generate a maintenance log for the machinery. This should show when maintenance is required, and its nature. Now, not only will this be dynamic (we can't predict when equipment will fail) but the order of items within the log will change. Certain items must be given high priority, even if they've just arrived in the log. So here we have to store data which not only changes its size but is also subject to constant reorganization.

It is in response to such needs that dynamic data structures have been devised. Their main use is for handling large quantities of information; sensibly then we have to be talking about structured as opposed to simple data types.

318 Dynamic data types

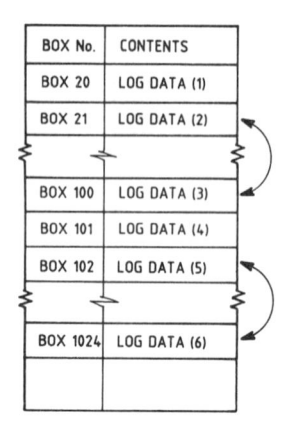

BOX No.	CONTENTS
BOX 20	LOG DATA (1)
BOX 21	LOG DATA (2)
BOX 100	LOG DATA (3)
BOX 101	LOG DATA (4)
BOX 102	LOG DATA (5)
BOX 1024	LOG DATA (6)

Fig.10.3 Dynamic data structure – basic concept.

10.2 DYNAMIC VARIABLES AND POINTERS

From a practical point of view our store size cannot be infinite. After all, there's only a certain amount of memory available in our computers. But, within this constraint, we can use it to its maximum if each and every memory location is available for use. Hence the first 'must' for a dynamic data structure is that it can use storage locations wherever they happen to be available. Such a case is shown in Fig.10.3.

Here the items belonging to the maintenance log are located as shown, using memory storage as and when available. From this it can be seen that its size can be changed to meet differing situations.

Now this raises some interesting questions. How, as the amount of data changes, do we add and delete information? Further, how do we find individual storage locations (called 'nodes') within the structure? These are fundamental points, requiring an efficient solution to minimize store requirements. The answers define the nature of dynamic data structures. In practice this has led to the widespread use of sequential data storage techniques for dynamic objects (other methods are also used, but are beyond the scope of this text). Note, however, that this does not restrict the data types which can be used as dynamic variables.

Fig.10.4 is a redrawn version of Fig.10.3, defined as a linked list. Each element or node now holds two pieces of information. The first is the data itself, the second the address of the next node in the list. This address has traditionally been called a 'pointer'. We access data through the use of the pointer, not by name. Two final pieces of information are still needed: the start and the finish of the list. The first item added to a list automatically defines the start; the last needs to be identified as such. This is done by pointing to a predefined object, the so-called 'null' item.

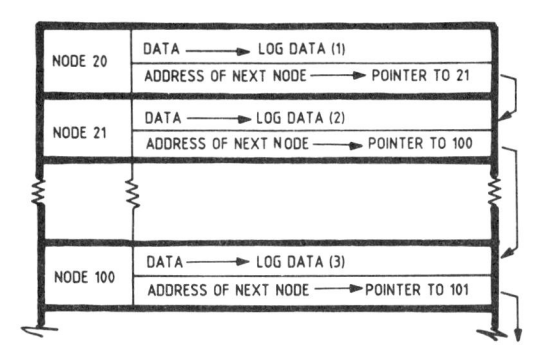

```
┌─────────┬──────────────────────────────────────────────┐
│         │ DATA ─────────► LOG DATA (1)                 │
│ NODE 20 ├──────────────────────────────────────────────┤
│         │ ADDRESS OF NEXT NODE ─────► POINTER TO 21    │
├─────────┼──────────────────────────────────────────────┤
│         │ DATA ─────────► LOG DATA (2)                 │
│ NODE 21 ├──────────────────────────────────────────────┤
│         │ ADDRESS OF NEXT NODE ─────► POINTER TO 100   │
└─────────┴──────────────────────────────────────────────┘

┌─────────┬──────────────────────────────────────────────┐
│         │ DATA ─────────► LOG DATA (3)                 │
│NODE 100 ├──────────────────────────────────────────────┤
│         │ ADDRESS OF NEXT NODE ─────► POINTER TO 101   │
└─────────┴──────────────────────────────────────────────┘
```

Fig.10.4 Linked-list construct.

Dynamic variables are not generated by the compiler. They come into being as a result of program execution. In such a situation it is natural that the number of variables produced will vary from time to time, including the case where none are present. This underlines the fact that we only have as many variables as are actually needed at that time.

When the program runs there are really only three actions which we want to carry out on the data structure:

- Add variables;
- Delete variables;
- Manipulate variables;

Specific statements are used to add and delete variables, as shown later. However, the technique for accessing variables is conceptually quite different to those described earlier; we do it through the use of pointers, not names. Variables stored within a dynamic structure do not have individual names, only data values and locations.

In Ada, pointers are defined to be 'access types'. These words are used interchangeably in the rest of this chapter.

10.3 WORKING WITH DYNAMIC VARIABLES

The starting point here is to look at the declarations which must be made before working with dynamic variables. In the first case we need to define the required access types. Then, for each one, we must specify which variable type a pointer points to. As a result the defined access type is then 'bound' to that particular data type. It cannot point to any other.

The basic operations used with access types are as follows:

- Create an access type;
- Create an access object (the pointer);

320   Dynamic data types

```
┌─────────────────────────────────────────────────────────────────┐
│ (a) Create an access type.                  The pointer   'null'│
│      type INTEGER_POINTER is access INTEGER;                    │
│                                          NEW_VAL →  INTEGER     │
│ (b) Create an access object ("the pointer").         Associated │
│      NEW_VAL : INTEGER_POINTER ;        pointer name  data type │
├─────────────────────────────────────────────────────────────────┤
│ (c) Reserve memory storage space and associate the pointer with │
│     that space.                                                 │
│      NEW_VAL := new INTEGER ;          NEW_VAL →  INTEGER       │
│                                                   Associated    │
│                                         Pointer   storage space │
├─────────────────────────────────────────────────────────────────┤
│ (d) Insert a value into the storage space.                      │
│      NEW_VAL.all := 25 ;               NEW_VAL →  25            │
├─────────────────────────────────────────────────────────────────┤
│ (e) Change value held in the storage space                      │
│      NEW_VAL.all := 50 ;               NEW_VAL →  50            │
├─────────────────────────────────────────────────────────────────┤
│ (f) Dispose of the storage space                                │
│      use UNCHECKED_DEALLOCATION        NEW_VAL → ┆NULL┆         │
└─────────────────────────────────────────────────────────────────┘
```

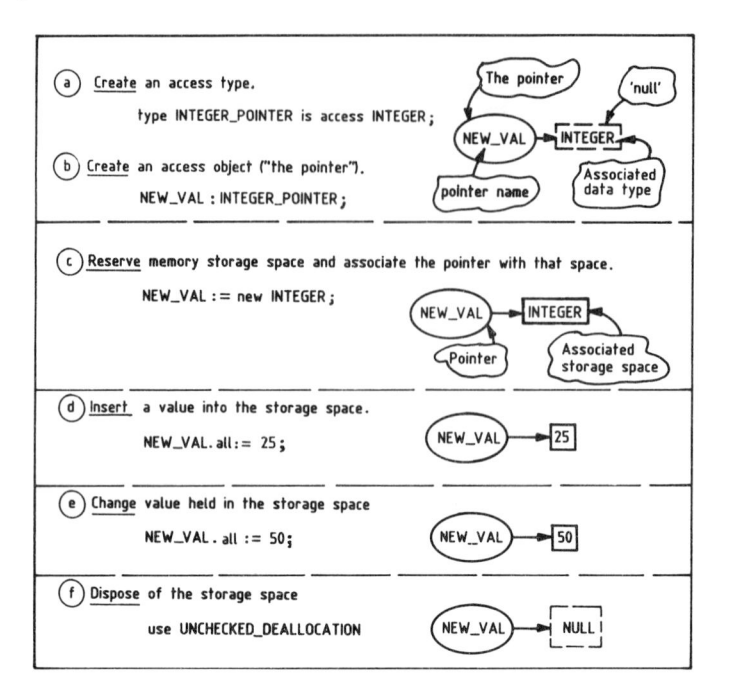

Fig.10.5 Creating and using a dynamic variable – basic operations.

- Reserve memory storage space and associate the pointer with that space;
- Insert a value into this storage space;
- Read out and then change the value in the store;
- Dispose of the storage space.

These are illustrated in Fig.10.5.
Let's consider these in turn.

(a) **Creating the access type**

To create an access type, the general construct is

> **type** NAME_OF_TYPE **is access** TYPE_POINTED_TO;

Suppose that we need an access type to access items of type INTEGER. We therefore make the declaration:

> **type** INTEGER_POINTER **is access** INTEGER;

Note one very important point here: any object of type INTEGER_POINTER can access type INTEGER only.

(b) Create the access object

There is nothing new here. Assume that we wish to define an object called NEW_VAL; then we declare

> NEW_VAL : INTEGER_POINTER;

Thus the access object NEW_VAL may be used to point to INTEGERs (but only to INTEGERs). However, we have not yet introduced the item to be pointed to by NEW_VAL. Ada enforces security of operations by automatically making the pointer point at a default item (object), called null. This ensures that pointers always point to some designated item – thus avoiding the 'pointing at nothing' problem. Another name for this is the 'dangling pointer'.

A minor comment: null, strictly speaking, is not really an object, but in everyday use we tend to treat it in that way.

(c) Reserve memory storage space and associate the pointer with that space

The statement format is

> NEW_VAL := **new** INTEGER;

new is a reserved word, and 'new INTEGER' is defined to be an allocator. The allocator creates an object in memory (here type INTEGER) which can be accessed only by an access object. The statement

> NEW_VAL := **new** INTEGER;

couples the memory object so created to the access object NEW_VAL. Observe that the object in memory does not have a name (for brevity, we will use the word node instead of memory object or object pointed to).

(d) Insert a value into the storage space

Here we are going to assign a value to the node. Now, as just mentioned, nodes do not have names – they are designated by pointers. But we have to be able to distinguish between a pointer itself and the object (node) to which it points. We do this quite simply by using dot notation, as follows:

> The pointer name: NEW_VAL
> The object pointed to: NEW_VAL.**all**

Thus to assign a value to the node we write:

> NEW_VAL.**all** := 25;

(e) **Change the value held in the storage space**

This is the same as above:

> NEW_VAL.**all** :=50;

(f) **Dispose of the storage space**

There are two basic ways of disposing of unwanted storage space. First, we can use special programs called garbage collectors. These are supplied with, and applicable to, specific Ada implementations. Otherwise we implement the disposal action using the library procedure UNCHECKED_DEALLOCATION. For the moment accept its use in the specimen programs. We will return to this issue in chapter 15, in 'Unchecked storage deallocation', section 15.5.2.

Listing 10.1 is a very simple example of the use of access types.

Observe that here we define the stored data items as being of type RUNNING_HOURS, that is

> **type** RUNNING_HOURS **is new** INTEGER **range** 0..9000;

The access type is defined to be RUNNING_HOURS_POINTER, as follows:

> **type** RUNNING_HOURS_POINTER **is access** RUNNING_HOURS;

The access object CURRENT_RUNNING_HOURS is created as

> CURRENT_RUNNING_HOURS : RUNNING_HOURS_POINTER;

Working with dynamic variables

```
with TEXT_IO;                use TEXT_IO;
with UNCHECKED_DEALLOCATION;
procedure ACCESS_TYPES is
  type RUNNING_HOURS is new INTEGER range 0..9000;
  type RUNNING_HOURS_POINTER is access RUNNING_HOURS;
  procedure DISPOSE is new UNCHECKED_DEALLOCATION(RUNNING_HOURS,
                                            RUNNING_HOURS_POINTER);
  package RUNNING_HOURS_IO is new INTEGER_IO (RUNNING_HOURS);
  use RUNNING_HOURS_IO;
  CURRENT_RUNNING_HOURS :    RUNNING_HOURS_POINTER;   -- A
  TEMP                  :    RUNNING_HOURS := 0;
  HOURS                 :    RUNNING_HOURS := 0;
begin
  -- Reserve storage space for the pointer
  CURRENT_RUNNING_HOURS := new  RUNNING_HOURS;        -- B
  PUT ("Enter running hours => ");
  GET (HOURS);                                        -- C
  SKIP_LINE;
  -- Insert a value into the storage space
  CURRENT_RUNNING_HOURS.all := HOURS;                 -- D
  -- Read it out into a variable of type INTEGER
  TEMP := CURRENT_RUNNING_HOURS.all;                  -- E
  PUT ("You entered => ");
  PUT (TEMP);
  NEW_LINE;
  -- deallocate the memory reserved. Alternatively, the program
  -- termination will deallocate the memory
  DISPOSE (CURRENT_RUNNING_HOURS);                    -- F
end ACCESS_TYPES;
```

Listing 10.1 This is an ultra-simple demonstration of the use of dynamic variables and pointers.

Reserving storage space and associating the pointer with that space is implemented by the statement

```
CURRENT_RUNNING_HOURS := new RUNNING_HOURS;
```

Fig.10.6 shows what happens as we progress through the program.

This figure also demonstrates clearly the difference between static and dynamic variables. From this it should be clear that CURRENT_ RUNNING_ HOURS is a *static* variable – its type being INTEGER_POINTER – which points to a *dynamic* variable. It is not a dynamic variable.

The above example has been produced to show the basics of pointer operations and dynamic variables. Normally the data structures involved are much larger, typically being records. The program of Listing 10.2 shows the use of the record structure in such an application.

Note how the individual record components are accessed using dot notation, as in LOG.RUNNING_TIME, LOG.FUEL_CONSUMPTION, etc.

PROGRAM STAGE	STATIC VARIABLE 'HOURS'	STATIC ACCESS VARIABLE	DYNAMIC ACCESSED OBJECT	STATIC VARIABLE 'TEMP'
A	0	CURRENT RUNNING HOURS	NOT IN EXISTENCE	0
B	0	CURRENT RUNNING HOURS	CREATED - DATA AREA RESERVED	0
C	KEYBOARD INPUT VALUE (KIV)	CURRENT RUNNING HOURS	DATA AREA RESERVED	0
D	KIV	CURRENT RUNNING HOURS	KIV	0
E	KIV	CURRENT RUNNING HOURS	KIV	KIV
F	KIV	CURRENT RUNNING HOURS	DISPOSED OF	KIV

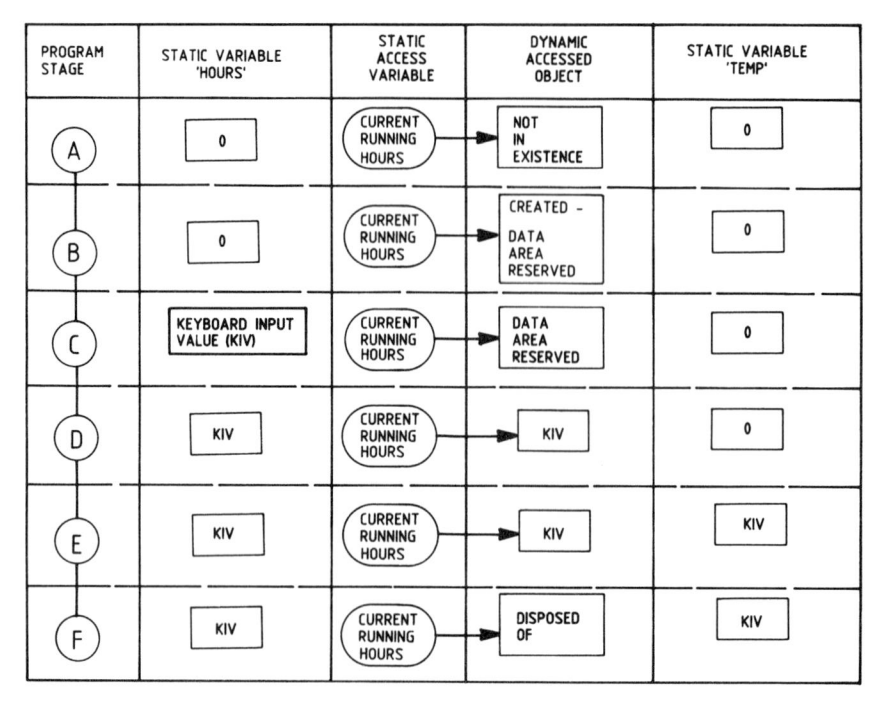

Fig.10.6 Operating with static and dynamic variables.

```
with TEXT_IO;                    use TEXT_IO;
procedure RECORD_ACCESS is
   type RUNNING_HOURS is new INTEGER range 0..9000;
   type LOG_ITEMS is
      record
         RUNNING_TIME      :    RUNNING_HOURS;
         LAST_SERVICE      :    STRING(1..20);
         FUEL_CONSUMPTION  :    FLOAT;
      end record;
   type LOG_POINTER is access LOG_ITEMS;
   package RUNNING_HOURS_IO is new INTEGER_IO (RUNNING_HOURS);
   use RUNNING_HOURS_IO;
   LOG           :    LOG_POINTER;
   TEMP          :    RUNNING_HOURS;
   HOURS         :    RUNNING_HOURS;
begin
   LOG := new  LOG_ITEMS;
   PUT ("Enter running hours => ");
   GET (HOURS);
   SKIP_LINE;
   LOG.RUNNING_TIME := HOURS;
   TEMP := LOG.RUNNING_TIME;
   PUT ("You entered => ");
   PUT (TEMP, 0);
   NEW_LINE;
   -- the memory will be deallocated upon program termination
end RECORD_ACCESS;
```

Listing 10.2 This is a further example of the use of dynamic variables, involving a record structure.

Working with dynamic variables 325

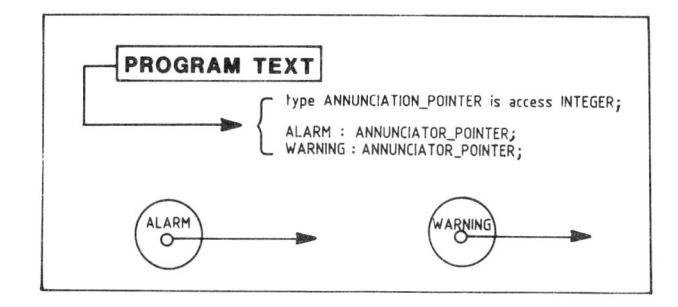

```
┌─ PROGRAM TEXT ─────────────────────────────────┐
│   type ANNUNCIATION_POINTER is access INTEGER; │
│   ALARM   : ANNUNCIATOR_POINTER;               │
│   WARNING : ANNUNCIATOR_POINTER;               │
│                                                │
│      (ALARM) →              (WARNING) →        │
└────────────────────────────────────────────────┘
```

Fig.10.7 Creating access types and access objects (pointers).

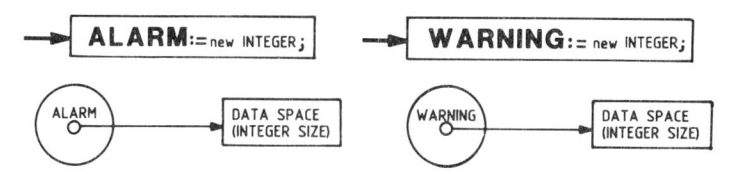

→ | ALARM := new INTEGER; | → | WARNING := new INTEGER; |

(ALARM) → [DATA SPACE (INTEGER SIZE)]   (WARNING) → [DATA SPACE (INTEGER SIZE)]

Fig.10.8 Allocating data storage space.

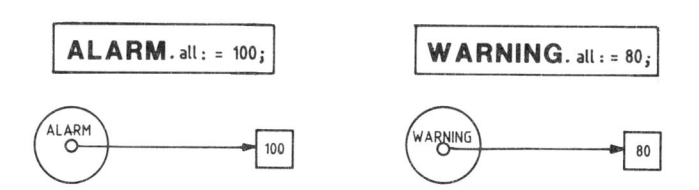

| ALARM.all := 100; | | WARNING.all := 80; |

(ALARM) → [100]   (WARNING) → [80]

Fig.10.9 Putting data into the data stores.

At this stage let's review and extend the basic operations involved when using pointers. First, access types must be created; then pointers are brought into existence (Fig.10.7).

Now data storage space can be established for the node (Fig.10.8).

Only then can data be loaded into this space (Fig.10.9).

Copying of data is carried out as shown in Fig.10.10.

Observe that we change the value of the data pointed to, not the pointers themselves. If we need to alter pointer values then the construct of Fig.10.11 is used.

Finally, the data space can be disposed of if it is no longer required, Fig.10.12.

We can also define that a pointer does NOT point to an object (Fig.10.13) using the **null** literal. This, remember, is also the default initial value pointed to by an access object.

This feature is used to establish the end of a linked set of data stores.

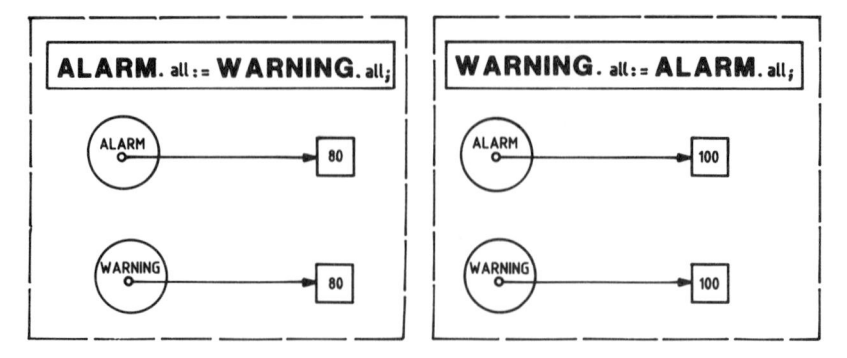

Fig.10.10 Copying data.

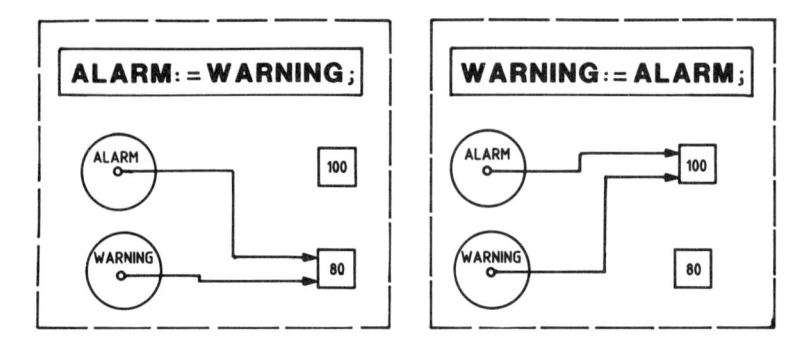

Fig.10.11 Changing pointer values.

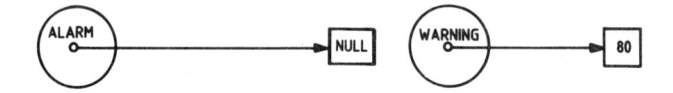

Fig.10.12 Disposing of storage space.

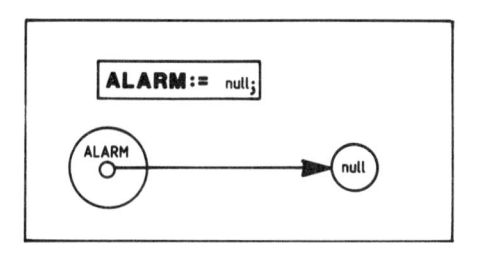

Fig.10.13 Pointing the pointer at no object.

10.4 ACCESS TYPES AND OBJECTS – SOME FEATURES

(a) Initializing a node value at declaration time

We can, if we want to, create an access object, reserve storage space and point the pointer at that space at declaration time. The construct is

> POINTER_NAME : ACCESS_TYPE := **new** qualified_expression;

as, for instance,

> NEW_VAL : INTEGER_POINTER := **new** INTEGER'(25);

In the case of a record we can set all values using the aggregate construct. For the items defined in Listing 10.2 we could have written:

> LOG : LOG_POINTER := **new** LOG_ITEM' (1500,
> "July 17th 1991 @0700",
> 35.62);

or used name association:

> LOG: LOG_POINTER := **new** LOG_ITEM'
> (RUNNING_HOURS   => 1500,
> LAST_SERVICE   => "July 17th 1991 @0700",
> FUEL_CONSUMPTION => 35.62);

(b) Constructing a new node

The result of evaluating the declaration

> NEW_VAL : INTEGER_POINTER := **new** INTEGER'(25);

is to produce the situation shown in Fig.10.14a.

Now, suppose we wish to construct a new node, allocate it a value and point NEW_VAL at it, Fig.10.14b. This can be done simply by writing the statement

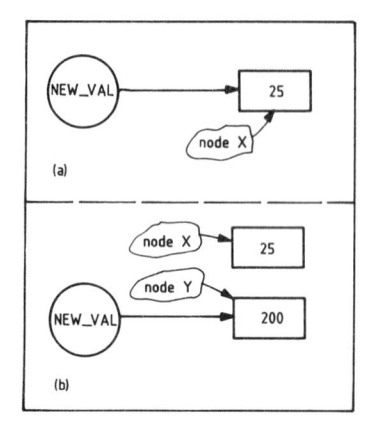

Fig.10.14 Constructing a new node.

```
NEW_VAL := new INTEGER'(200);
```

in the source code. Note, however, that the memory location holding the value '25' cannot now be accessed – it is not available for use.

(c) Defining a constant pointer

There are cases where we always want a specific pointer to access a specific store location. Or we want to guarantee that we can't accidentally change the value of the pointer. To do this we can make the pointer a constant object, using the declaration format

```
type POINTER_TO_UART is access INTEGER;
DATA_BUS_DEVICE : constant POINTER_TO_UART := new INTEGER;
```

Initial values can be allocated to the dynamic object when it is created, as for instance:

```
DATA_BUS_DEVICE : constant POINTER_TO_UART := new INTEGER'(4095);
```

That is, the item pointed to by DATA_BUS_DEVICE is given the initial value of 4095. Of course, even though the pointer is fixed (constant), the value contained within the node can be changed. Thus the following statement is legal:

```
with TEXT_IO;            use TEXT_IO;
procedure ACCESS_INITIALISATION is
  subtype RUNNING_HOURS is INTEGER range 0..9000;
  type RUNNING_HOURS_POINTER is access RUNNING_HOURS;
  type LOG_ITEMS is
    record
      RUNNING_TIME      :    RUNNING_HOURS;
      LAST_SERVICE      :    STRING(1..20);
      FUEL_CONSUMPTION  :    FLOAT;
    end record;
  type LOG_POINTER is access LOG_ITEMS;
  package RUNNING_HOURS_IO is new INTEGER_IO (RUNNING_HOURS);
  use RUNNING_HOURS_IO;
  TIME_NOT_INITIALISED :   RUNNING_HOURS_POINTER;
  LOG_NOT_INITIALISED  :   LOG_POINTER;
  TIME_INITIALISED     :   RUNNING_HOURS_POINTER := new  RUNNING_HOURS'(25);
  LOG_INITIALISED      :   LOG_POINTER :=  new LOG_ITEMS'
                                  (RUNNING_TIME      => 1500,
                                   LAST_SERVICE      => "July 17th 1991 @0700",
                                   FUEL_CONSUMPTION  => 35.62 );
  CONSTANT_LOG         :   constant LOG_POINTER := new LOG_ITEMS;
  CONSTANT_TIME        :   constant RUNNING_HOURS_POINTER := new RUNNING_HOURS;
begin
  TIME_NOT_INITIALISED := new RUNNING_HOURS'(25);
  LOG_NOT_INITIALISED  := new LOG_ITEMS'
                                  (RUNNING_TIME      => 1500,
                                   LAST_SERVICE      => "June  8th 1991 @1535",
                                   FUEL_CONSUMPTION  => 32.87 );
  CONSTANT_LOG.all     := LOG_INITIALISED.all;
  CONSTANT_TIME.all    := TIME_INITIALISED.all;
end ACCESS_INITIALISATION;
```

Listing 10.3 This demonstrates manipulation of pointers and nodes.

```
DATA_BUS_DEVICE.all := 250;
```

Assume that we have made the following declaration:

```
DATA_BUS_DEVICE : POINTER_TO_UART;
```

Then a statement of the form

```
DATA_BUS_DEVICE := DIFFERENT_BUS_DEVICE;
```

attempts to change the value of the pointer DATA_BUS_DEVICE – which is a constant. This is not allowed, and so would be rejected by the compiler.

Listing 10.3 illustrates the aspects raised in subsections (a), (b) and (c) above.

(d) Miscellaneous items

(i) Type compatibility   Given the declaration

```
type INTEGER_POINTER_1 is access INTEGER;
type INTEGER_POINTER_2 is access INTEGER;
RUNNING_HOURS_1 : INTEGER_POINTER_1;
RUNNING_HOURS_2 : INTEGER_POINTER_2;
```

then RUNNING_HOURS_1 and RUNNING_HOURS_2 belong to different types. The assignment statement

```
RUNNING_HOURS_1 := RUNNING_HOURS_2;
```

is therefore illegal on type compatibility grounds. However,

```
RUNNING_HOURS_1.all := RUNNING_HOURS_2.all;
```

is all right as the data held in the nodes is of type INTEGER.

(ii) Range constraints   At declaration time we can impose a range constraint on the node values, as, for instance,

```
type INTEGER_POINTER_1 is access INTEGER range 0..255;
type INTEGER_POINTER_2 is access INTEGER range 256..512;
```

(iii) Arrays of pointers   Pointer arrays can be formed using a construct of the form

```
type INTEGER_POINTER is access INTEGER;
SET_OF_INTEGER_POINTERS : array (1..20) of INTEGER_POINTER;
```

10.5   LINKING DATA ITEMS – DECLARATION ISSUES

So far we've successfully managed to create a store space for a data item, put data into the store, move data, change pointer values, and finally dispose of the space. Good. But that is only the first step. What we want to do is to

Linking data items – declaration issues 331

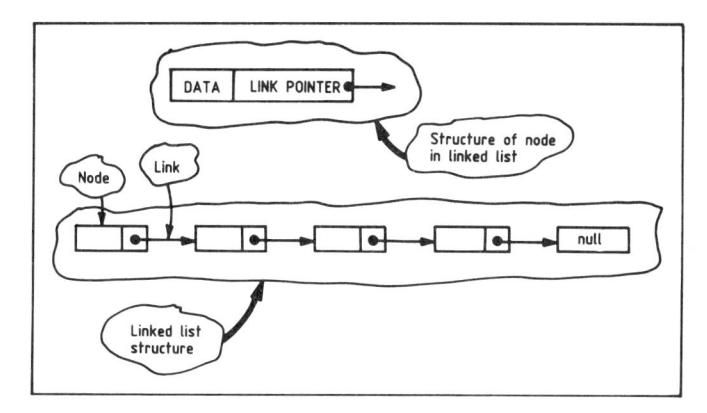

Fig.10.15 Basic features of the linked list.

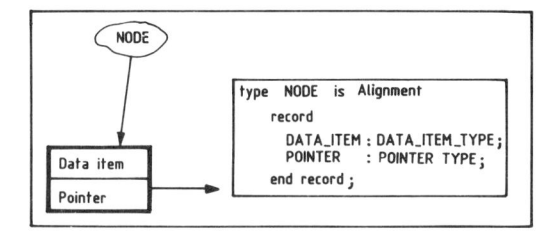

```
type NODE is Alignment
    record
        DATA_ITEM : DATA_ITEM_TYPE;
        POINTER   : POINTER TYPE;
    end record;
```

Fig.10.16 Node structure incorporating a pointer.

form a dynamically varying data space based on the linked-list construct. This consists of a whole grouping of store locations, linked together as illustrated in Fig.10.3. What is missing in the present arrangement is a mechanism for pointing to the next item in the list – the 'link' of Fig.10.15.

It would seem that we can solve this problem in a simple way. Just form the node as a record structure, and then incorporate a pointer into this structure, Fig.10.16.

It should be noted that the pointer can be located anywhere in the record structure. However, conventionally we put it as the final item – which also increases its visibility.

Now this apparently simple move raises a conundrum. We've already said that an access type is bound to one specific node type; it cannot point to any other. Let us call this SERVICE_LIST. Remember, also, that all nodes must be the same type. Thus the pointer carried within the data structure of SERVICE_LIST – which points to the next store location – must point to a data item of SERVICE_LIST. Therefore it itself must be a specific access type. Let's see what happens when we try to declare the structure of the node:

332 Dynamic data types

```
type SERVICE_LIST is
   record
      SERVICE_PRIORITY   : INTEGER;
      MACHINE            : MESSAGE;
      NEXT_NODE          : ???????; -- the pointer
   end record;
type SERVICE_LIST_POINTER is access SERVICE_LIST;
SERVICE_LOG : SERVICE_LIST_POINTER;
```

Our problem here is that the pointer NEXT_NODE must be an access type which can point to SERVICE_LIST. But such a type isn't defined until we reach the next declaration – SERVICE_LIST_POINTER. This puts us in a position of trying to define a pointer without an associated type. Such a move is not permissible. You might be tempted to attack this problem by trying to define type SERVICE_LIST_POINTER before SERVICE_LIST. This is also doomed to fail; the problem is exactly the same.

Ada gives us a way to handle this issue, called an *incomplete type declaration*. We use the construct

```
type NAME_OF_TYPE;
```

This tells the compiler that the type NAME_OF_TYPE exists, and that details will be supplied later. For the example above we would have

```
type SERVICE_LIST; -- The incomplete type declaration
type SERVICE_LIST_POINTER is access SERVICE_LIST;
type SERVICE_LIST is
   record
      SERVICE_PRIORITY   : INTEGER;
      MACHINE            : MESSAGE;
      NEXT_NODE          : SERVICE_LIST_POINTER;
   end record;
SERVICE_LOG : SERVICE_LIST_POINTER;
```

10.6 BUILDING AND MANIPULATING LINKED LISTS

Linked lists can be built in a number of ways, but we will concentrate on the most common technique. In this we first define the head of the list, and then build from that towards the end or tail. Such a construction is demonstrated in Listing 10.4.

For simplicity it involves the creation and use of two data stores only. The

```ada
with TEXT_IO;               use TEXT_IO;
procedure HEAD_TO_TAIL is
  type MESSAGE is new STRING (1..10);
  type SERVICE_LIST;
  type SERVICE_LIST_POINTER is access SERVICE_LIST;
  type SERVICE_LIST is
    record
      SERVICE_PRIORITY :    INTEGER;
      MACHINE          :    MESSAGE           := (others => ' ');
      NEXT_NODE        :    SERVICE_LIST_POINTER;
    end record;
  SERVICE_LOG      :    SERVICE_LIST_POINTER;
begin
  -- create our first record element
  SERVICE_LOG := new  SERVICE_LIST;
  -- set the elements details
  SERVICE_LOG.MACHINE (1..5)    := "Brown";
  SERVICE_LOG.SERVICE_PRIORITY := 3;
  -- create a new service log and point the current on to it
  SERVICE_LOG.NEXT_NODE := new  SERVICE_LIST;
  -- set the new elements details
  SERVICE_LOG.NEXT_NODE.MACHINE (1..9)    := "Red No. 1";
  SERVICE_LOG.NEXT_NODE.SERVICE_PRIORITY := 2;
end HEAD_TO_TAIL;
```

Listing 10.4 This shows how linked lists can be constructed head to tail.

example is straightforward but has been written out explicitly so that the reader can follow the sequence of events. These are further depicted graphically in Fig.10.17.

The approach adopted here has one major shortcoming, which shows as we add more elements to the list. The statements required to access the last (final) node in the list become longer and less readable. For example, to add another node, we write

```
SERVICE_LOG.NEXT_NODE.NEXT_NODE := new SERVICE_LIST;
```

Putting data into this new node is accomplished by the statements

```
SERVICE_LOG.NEXT_NODE.NEXT_NODE.MACHINE (1..4)   := "Blue";
SERVICE_LOG.NEXT_NODE.NEXT_NODE.SERVICE_PRIORITY := 10;
```

Fortunately, things can be simplified by introducing two new variables, as demonstrated in Listing 10.5.

One variable is used to point to the first node, the head of the list (HEAD_OF_LIST), and the other points to the last node, the tail of the list

334 Dynamic data types

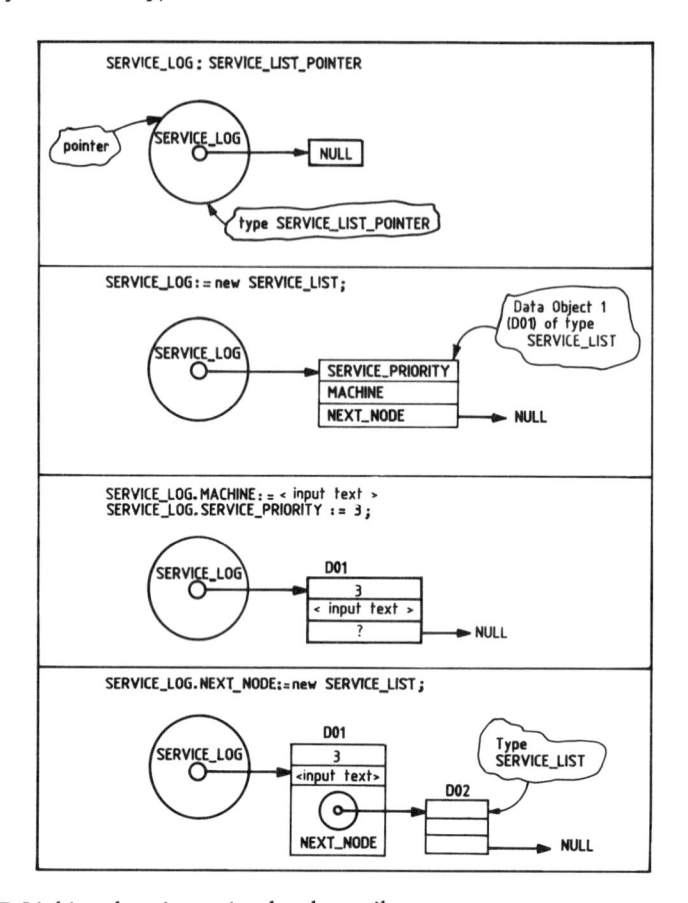

Fig.10.17 Linking data items 1 – head-to-tail construct.

(TAIL_OF_LIST). The behaviour of this program is shown diagrammatically in Fig.10.18.

The program example:

- Takes in data from the keyboard;
- Dynamically allocates storage for each entry;
- Appends each new entry to the data list;
- Links this to the previous data store location;
- Terminates data entry when 0 is entered as the service priority;
- Writes out the stored information, with the first entry shown first.

This is the action of a first-in first-out (FIFO) data store.

There are instances where we may have to build a list in a defined order. Suppose, for instance, that we are directed to:

```
with TEXT_IO;              use TEXT_IO;
procedure LINKED_LIST is
  package NATURAL_IO is new INTEGER_IO (NATURAL);
  use NATURAL_IO;
  type LIST_ELEMENT;
  type LIST_POINTER is access LIST_ELEMENT;
  type LIST_ELEMENT is
    record
       VALUE_STORED     :     NATURAL;
       NEXT_ELEMENT     :     LIST_POINTER;
    end record;
  HEAD_OF_LIST    :    LIST_POINTER;
  TAIL_OF_LIST    :    LIST_POINTER;
  ELEMENT         :    LIST_POINTER;
  VALUE           :    NATURAL;
begin
-- create our first record element
  ELEMENT := new   LIST_ELEMENT'(VALUE_STORED    => 0,
                                 NEXT_ELEMENT    => null);
-- set element and head_of_list to point at the same record
  HEAD_OF_LIST := ELEMENT;
  TAIL_OF_LIST := HEAD_OF_LIST;                                     -- A
  loop
    PUT ("Enter a positive value (0 to finish) => ");
    GET (VALUE);                                                    -- B
    SKIP_LINE;
    exit when VALUE = 0;
-- create our new element and tag it onto the list
    ELEMENT := new   LIST_ELEMENT'(VALUE_STORED    => VALUE,
                                   NEXT_ELEMENT    => null);    -- C
-- point previous end_of_list to new element, and set new element
-- to bottom of list
    TAIL_OF_LIST.NEXT_ELEMENT := ELEMENT;                           -- D
    TAIL_OF_LIST := ELEMENT;                                        -- E
  end loop;
-- now print the list in the order entered
-- skip first element as never used.
  ELEMENT := HEAD_OF_LIST.NEXT_ELEMENT;
  PUT_LINE ("The values entered were => ");
  while (ELEMENT /= null)
-- bottom of list
  loop
    PUT (ELEMENT.VALUE_STORED);
    ELEMENT := ELEMENT.NEXT_ELEMENT;
  end loop;
end LINKED_LIST;
```

Listing 10.5 Building a linked list head to tail, a more general form.

- take in a series of numbers from the keyboard, and;
- store them in ascending order of their numerical values.

If this is handled using a simple linked-list method, numbers are stored in entry – not numerical – order. Unfortunately, we haven't specified a connection between the entry order and the associated number value. Thus '210' could be entered before '3', etc. – we have no way of knowing what the entry

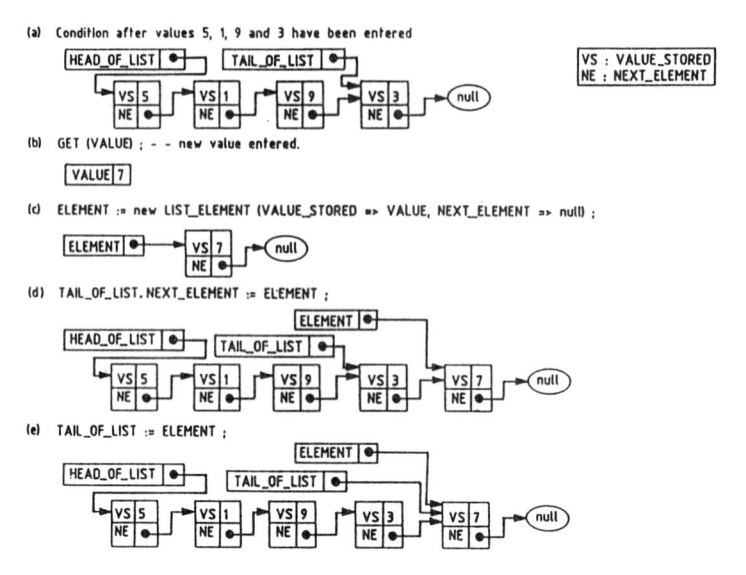

Fig.10.18 Constructing a generalized head-to-tail linked list.

sequence is. Therefore a more sophisticated technique is required – a search and insert operation. When a new value is entered, we first search the current list to determine where it should be placed. It is then inserted at this point. This, of course, may be at the head, at the tail, or somewhere within the list. The program solution to this requirement is shown in Listing 10.6. It illustrates how to search down (traverse) a list and append or insert nodes as required by the problem statement.

That is, the value entered at the keyboard must define the position of the item in the list. The example shows two operations. First, how the list is traversed to find the correct position. Second, how the item is inserted into the list at that point. The behaviour of the program in its initial stages is shown diagrammatically in Fig.10.19.

We may also have to remove a node(s) from a linked list. As discussed above, this may be the head node, the tail node, or a node within the list. Such actions are illustrated in Listing 10.7 and Fig.10.20.

10.7 IMPLICATIONS FOR REAL-TIME SYSTEMS

By now it should be clear that dynamic data structures are really useful (or necessary) for handling large amounts of data. Consequently they are used extensively in data-strong systems such as databases, accounting systems and similar applications. Their application in real-time systems is – relatively

```ada
with TEXT_IO;                 use TEXT_IO;
procedure ORDERED_LINKED_LIST is
  package NATURAL_IO is new INTEGER_IO (NATURAL);
  use NATURAL_IO;
  type LIST_ELEMENT;
  type LIST_POINTER is access LIST_ELEMENT;
  type LIST_ELEMENT is
    record
       VALUE_STORED     :     NATURAL;
       NEXT_ELEMENT     :     LIST_POINTER;
    end record;
  HEAD_OF_LIST       :     LIST_POINTER;
  CURRENT_IN_LIST    :     LIST_POINTER;
  LAST_LOOKED_AT     :     LIST_POINTER;
  ELEMENT            :     LIST_POINTER;
  VALUE              :     NATURAL;
begin
 -- create our first record element
 ELEMENT := new  LIST_ELEMENT'(VALUE_STORED     =>  0,
                               NEXT_ELEMENT     =>  null);
 -- set element and head_of_list to point at the same record
 HEAD_OF_LIST := ELEMENT;
 loop
    PUT ("Enter a positive value (0 to finish) => ");
    GET (VALUE);
    SKIP_LINE;
    exit when VALUE = 0;
 -- create our new element
    ELEMENT := new   LIST_ELEMENT'(VALUE_STORED    =>   VALUE,
                                   NEXT_ELEMENT    =>   null);
 -- Traverse the list, starting at the head, searching for the correct place
    CURRENT_IN_LIST := HEAD_OF_LIST;
 -- search until end of list or position in list found
    while ((CURRENT_IN_LIST /= null) and then
           (CURRENT_IN_LIST.VALUE_STORED <= ELEMENT.VALUE_STORED)) loop
 -- move down the list one element, keeping a track of the last element
 -- looked at
       LAST_LOOKED_AT  := CURRENT_IN_LIST;
       CURRENT_IN_LIST := CURRENT_IN_LIST.NEXT_ELEMENT;
    end loop;
 -- insert into list, between last_looked_at and current_element
    LAST_LOOKED_AT.NEXT_ELEMENT := ELEMENT;
    ELEMENT.NEXT_ELEMENT        := CURRENT_IN_LIST;
 end loop;
 -- now print the list in numerical order
 -- notice this loop hasn't changed from listing 10.5
 -- skip first element as never used.
 ELEMENT := HEAD_OF_LIST.NEXT_ELEMENT;
 PUT_LINE ("The values entered, in numerical order, were => ");
 while (ELEMENT /= null)
 -- bottom of list
 loop
    PUT (ELEMENT.VALUE_STORED);
    ELEMENT := ELEMENT.NEXT_ELEMENT;
 end loop;
end ORDERED_LINKED_LIST;
```

Listing 10.6 Building an ordered linked list, i.e. the values are stored in numerical order.

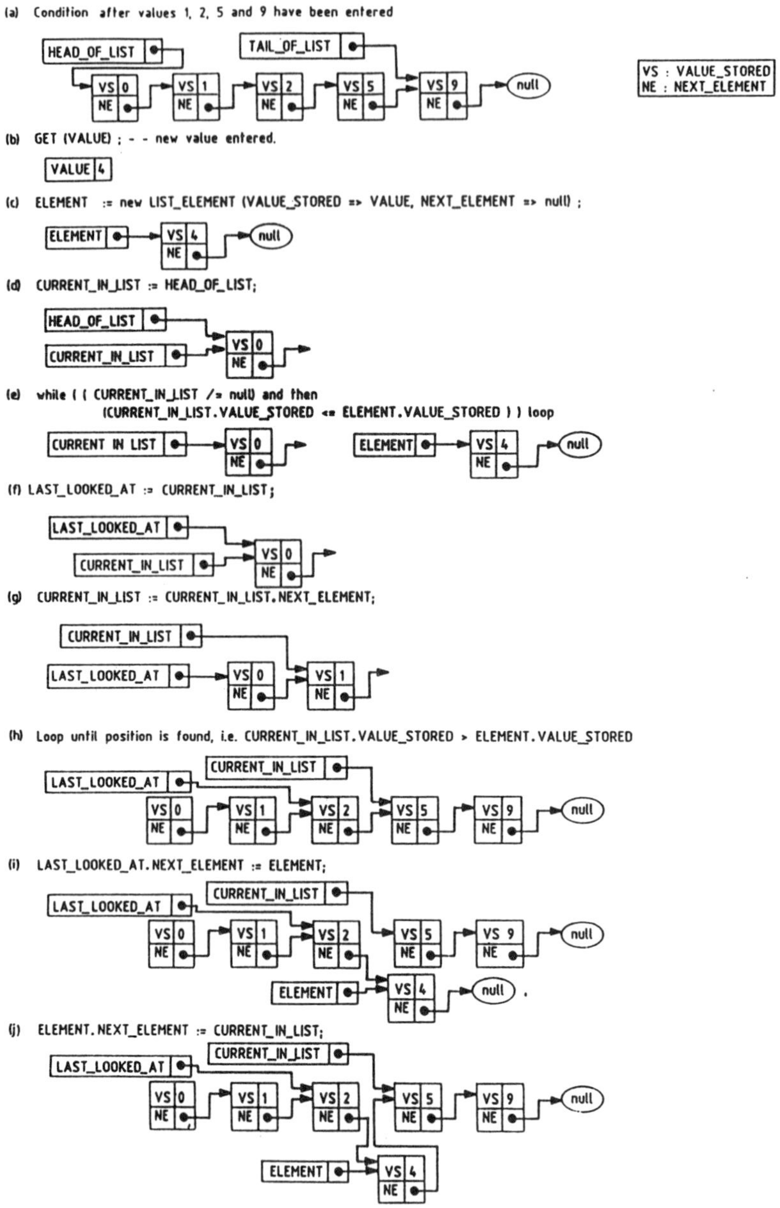

(a) Condition after values 1, 2, 5 and 9 have been entered

VS : VALUE_STORED
NE : NEXT_ELEMENT

(b) GET (VALUE) ; - - new value entered.

(c) ELEMENT := new LIST_ELEMENT (VALUE_STORED => VALUE, NEXT_ELEMENT => null) ;

(d) CURRENT_IN_LIST := HEAD_OF_LIST;

(e) while ((CURRENT_IN_LIST /= null) and then
            (CURRENT_IN_LIST.VALUE_STORED <= ELEMENT.VALUE_STORED)) loop

(f) LAST_LOOKED_AT := CURRENT_IN_LIST;

(g) CURRENT_IN_LIST := CURRENT_IN_LIST.NEXT_ELEMENT;

(h) Loop until position is found, i.e. CURRENT_IN_LIST.VALUE_STORED > ELEMENT.VALUE_STORED

(i) LAST_LOOKED_AT.NEXT_ELEMENT := ELEMENT;

(j) ELEMENT.NEXT_ELEMENT := CURRENT_IN_LIST;

Fig.10.19 Inserting an element into a linked list.

```ada
with TEXT_IO;               use TEXT_IO;
procedure ELEMENT_REMOVAL is
  package NATURAL_IO is new INTEGER_IO (NATURAL);
  use NATURAL_IO;
  type LIST_ELEMENT;
  type LIST_POINTER is access LIST_ELEMENT;
  type LIST_ELEMENT is
    record
       VALUE_STORED       :    NATURAL;
       NEXT_ELEMENT       :    LIST_POINTER;
    end record;
  HEAD_OF_LIST             :    LIST_POINTER;
  TAIL_OF_LIST             :    LIST_POINTER;
  ELEMENT_TO_BE_REMOVED    :    LIST_POINTER;
  LAST_LOOKED_AT           :    LIST_POINTER;
  ELEMENT                  :    LIST_POINTER;
  VALUE                    :    NATURAL;
begin
 -- create our first record element
  ELEMENT := new  LIST_ELEMENT'(VALUE_STORED       =>  0,
                                NEXT_ELEMENT       =>  null);
 -- set element and head_of_list to point at the same record
  HEAD_OF_LIST := ELEMENT;
  TAIL_OF_LIST := HEAD_OF_LIST;
 -- create an ordered list holding the values 1 to 10
  for INDEX in 1..10 loop
 -- create our new element and tag it onto the list
    ELEMENT := new   LIST_ELEMENT'(VALUE_STORED      =>  INDEX,
                                   NEXT_ELEMENT      =>  null);
 -- link onto bottom of list
    TAIL_OF_LIST.NEXT_ELEMENT := ELEMENT;
    TAIL_OF_LIST              := ELEMENT;
  end loop;
 -- remove an element
  PUT ("Select an element to remove (1..10) => ");
  GET (VALUE);
  SKIP_LINE;
  ELEMENT_TO_BE_REMOVED := HEAD_OF_LIST;
  while ((ELEMENT_TO_BE_REMOVED /= null) and then
           (ELEMENT_TO_BE_REMOVED.VALUE_STORED /= VALUE)) loop
     LAST_LOOKED_AT        := ELEMENT_TO_BE_REMOVED;
     ELEMENT_TO_BE_REMOVED := ELEMENT_TO_BE_REMOVED.NEXT_ELEMENT;
  end loop;
  if (ELEMENT_TO_BE_REMOVED = null) then
    PUT_LINE ("Value out of range");
  else
    LAST_LOOKED_AT.NEXT_ELEMENT            := ELEMENT_TO_BE_REMOVED.NEXT_ELEMENT;
    ELEMENT_TO_BE_REMOVED.NEXT_ELEMENT := null;
  end if;
 -- now print the list
 -- skip first element as never used.
  ELEMENT := HEAD_OF_LIST.NEXT_ELEMENT;
  PUT_LINE ("The values left are => ");
  while (ELEMENT /= null)
 -- bottom of list
  loop
    PUT (ELEMENT.VALUE_STORED);
    ELEMENT := ELEMENT.NEXT_ELEMENT;
  end loop;
end ELEMENT_REMOVAL;
```

Listing 10.7 Building an ordered linked list, and then removing an element.

Fig.10.20 Removing an element from a linked list.

speaking – limited. Even then their use must be carefully controlled. We have always to bear in mind that the information is built up in a dynamic manner. If for any reason the pointer or link connections become corrupted we can completely – and irretrievably – lose information. The consequences of this cannot be underestimated. To minimize the effects of such breakages the double linked-list structure has been devised. Each node points to two items: the next node in the list and the previous node in the list. This applies also to the head and the tail nodes. In this structure the predecessor of the head node is the tail node. Similarly, the successor to the tail node is the head node. Thus the list is circular, as demonstrated in Listing 10.8.

```ada
with TEXT_IO;              use TEXT_IO;
procedure DOUBLE_LINK is
  package NATURAL_IO is new INTEGER_IO (NATURAL);
  use NATURAL_IO;
  type LIST_ELEMENT;
  type LIST_POINTER is access LIST_ELEMENT;
  type LIST_ELEMENT is
    record
      VALUE_STORED     :   NATURAL;
      PREVIOUS_ELEMENT :   LIST_POINTER;
      NEXT_ELEMENT     :   LIST_POINTER;
    end record;
  HEAD_OF_LIST    :   LIST_POINTER;
  TAIL_OF_LIST    :   LIST_POINTER;
  ELEMENT_TO_BE_REMOVED : LIST_POINTER;
  LAST_LOOKED_AT  :   LIST_POINTER;
  ELEMENT         :   LIST_POINTER;
  VALUE           :   NATURAL;
begin
-- create our first record element, not used, only created for simplicity
  ELEMENT := new  LIST_ELEMENT'(VALUE_STORED     => 0,
                                PREVIOUS_ELEMENT => null,
                                NEXT_ELEMENT     => null);
-- set tail and head to point at the same record
  HEAD_OF_LIST := ELEMENT;
  TAIL_OF_LIST := HEAD_OF_LIST;
-- create an ordered list holding values 1..10 in ascending order
  for INDEX in 1..10 loop
-- create our new element and tag it onto the list
    ELEMENT := new  LIST_ELEMENT'(VALUE_STORED     => INDEX,
                                  PREVIOUS_ELEMENT => TAIL_OF_LIST,
                                  NEXT_ELEMENT     => HEAD_OF_LIST);
-- insert onto the end of the list
    TAIL_OF_LIST.NEXT_ELEMENT := ELEMENT;
    TAIL_OF_LIST := ELEMENT;
    HEAD_OF_LIST.PREVIOUS_ELEMENT := TAIL_OF_LIST;
  end loop;
-- remove an element
  PUT ("Select an element to remove (1..10) => ");
  GET (VALUE);
-- set up initial conditions in case value = 1 and loop bypassed
  ELEMENT_TO_BE_REMOVED := HEAD_OF_LIST.NEXT_ELEMENT;
  LAST_LOOKED_AT := HEAD_OF_LIST;
  while ((ELEMENT_TO_BE_REMOVED /= HEAD_OF_LIST) and then
         (ELEMENT_TO_BE_REMOVED.VALUE_STORED /= VALUE)) loop
-- traverse list
    LAST_LOOKED_AT        := ELEMENT_TO_BE_REMOVED;
    ELEMENT_TO_BE_REMOVED := ELEMENT_TO_BE_REMOVED.NEXT_ELEMENT;
  end loop;
  if (ELEMENT_TO_BE_REMOVED = HEAD_OF_LIST) then
    PUT_LINE("Value out of range");
  else
-- bypass the element to be removed
    LAST_LOOKED_AT.NEXT_ELEMENT := ELEMENT_TO_BE_REMOVED.NEXT_ELEMENT;
-- use list to re-point next in list to our predecessor
-- remember element_to_be_removed.next_element is an element in itself
    ELEMENT_TO_BE_REMOVED.NEXT_ELEMENT.PREVIOUS_ELEMENT := LAST_LOOKED_AT;
-- alternatively
-- ELEMENT := ELEMENT_TO_BE_REMOVED.NEXT_ELEMENT;
-- ELEMENT.PREVIOUS_ELEMENT := LAST_LOOKED_AT;
-- completely take us out of the loop
    ELEMENT_TO_BE_REMOVED.PREVIOUS_ELEMENT := null;
    ELEMENT_TO_BE_REMOVED.NEXT_ELEMENT := null;
  end if;
-- now print the list
-- skip first element as never used.
  ELEMENT := HEAD_OF_LIST.NEXT_ELEMENT;
  PUT_LINE ("The values left are => ");
  while (ELEMENT /= HEAD_OF_LIST)
-- bottom of list
  loop
    PUT (ELEMENT.VALUE_STORED);
    ELEMENT := ELEMENT.NEXT_ELEMENT;
  end loop;
end DOUBLE_LINK;
```

Listing 10.8 Building a double-linked list and then removing an element.

342 Dynamic data types

(a) Condition after values 1 and 2 have been inserted into the list

(b) INDEX is currently set to 3

INDEX 3

PE : PREVIOUS ELEMENT
VS : VALUE_STORED
NE : NEXT_ELEMENT

(c) ELEMENT := new LIST_ELEMENT (VALUE_STORED => INDEX
PREVIOUS_ELEMENT => TAIL_OF_LIST
NEXT_ELEMENT => HEAD_OF_LIST);

(d) TAIL_OF_LIST.NEXT_ELEMENT := ELEMENT ;

(e) TAIL_OF_LIST := ELEMENT ;

(f) HEAD_OF_LIST.PREVIOUS_ELEMENT := TAIL OF LIST;

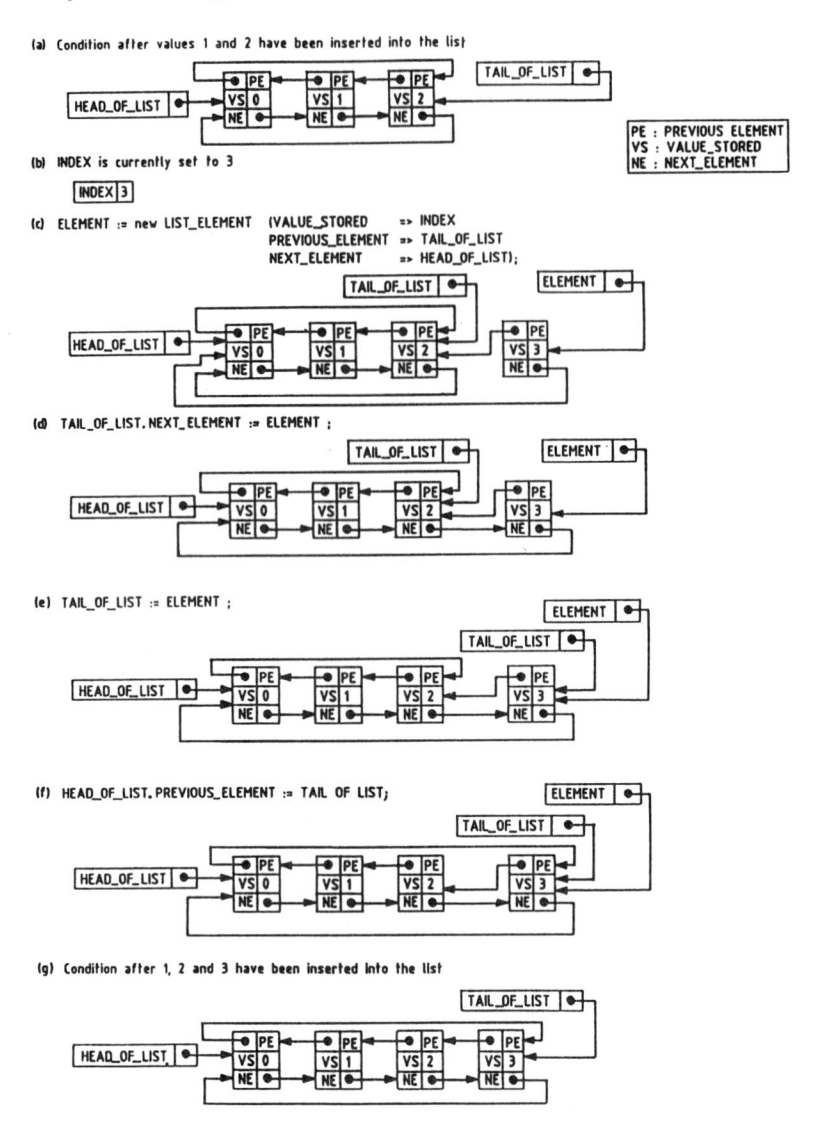

(g) Condition after 1, 2 and 3 have been inserted into the list

Fig 10.21 A doubly linked-list structure.

Various aspects of this are shown in Fig.10.21. This is quite a complex structure and should be studied carefully until it is understood.

Problems also arise from errors made at the programming stage. Experience has shown that program reliability is reduced when dynamic data techniques are applied carelessly. Three particular points need to be considered:

- The use of pointers;
- Confusion between pointers and objects which are referred to by pointers;
- The need to dispose of dynamic data objects.

In general purpose computing, program failures aren't usually catastrophic. The same is not true for real-time engineering applications. Software errors may well produce dangerous situations, sometimes leading to injury or death. For such applications dynamic data structures should be used with great care (if at all).

REVIEW

You should now:

- Understand the concepts of dynamic data structures;
- Understand the concept and use of access types (pointers);
- Be able to create and manipulate access types and access objects;
- Be able to construct a simple linked-list file, head to tail;
- Be able to construct a simple ordered linked-list file;
- Be able to search across lists and insert/remove objects into/from simple and doubly linked lists;
- Appreciate that dynamic data structures are potential sources of software unreliability.

Chapter Eleven

Information hiding, data abstraction and private types

Earlier, in chapter 7, we discussed the importance of information hiding in software engineering and program design. We saw how the package was used to provide facilities whilst hiding the underlying implementation of such facilities. The procedure and the function are the main building blocks of such implementations.

We set out to make the programmer consider the resources as a set of abstract machines – by having clear distinctions between what is done and how it is achieved. These machines are primarily concerned with the operations which are carried out in a system. But what of the things (data, objects, entities, thingys, call them what you will) that we manipulate using these operations? Up to this point we have clearly and completely defined the structure of such objects – concrete data. Now we want to extend the ideas of information hiding and abstraction into the realms of program objects – data abstraction.

By hiding the structure of objects we force the user to concentrate on their characteristics and use. Further, it becomes impossible to manipulate the internals of such objects – we can't even see how they are built. So, in this chapter you will:

- See what problems can arise through using detailed knowledge of the structure of program objects;
- Meet the Ada private types;
- Understand the role of public and private declarations for types;
- See how the private type construct enables the programmer to control the use of objects;
- Perceive how private types can be used in practical situations.

11.1 SETTING THE SCENE

Consider the linked-list structure depicted in Fig.11.1.

It is decided to locate list manipulation facilities within a single package, SERVICE_PACKAGE (Listing 11.1).

Setting the scene

```
                    ┌─────────────────────────────────────────────────┐
                    │  HEAD             ●                              │
                    │  CURRENT_SERVICE  ●──────────────┐               │
                    └──────────────────────────────────┼───────────────┘
      │              │                │                │
      ↓              ↓                ↓                ↓
┌──────────────┐ ┌──────────────┐ ┌──────────────┐ ┌──────────────┐
│ NEXT_SERVICE●├→│ NEXT_SERVICE●├→│ NEXT_SERVICE●├→│ NEXT_SERVICE●├→ null
│ SERVICE_CODE │ │ SERVICE_CODE │ │ SERVICE_CODE │ │ SERVICE_CODE │
│    1000      │ │    1001      │ │    1002      │ │    1003      │
└──────────────┘ └──────────────┘ └──────────────┘ └──────────────┘

          SERVICE RECORD                    SERVICE LIST
   ┌─────────────────────────────┐   ┌──────────────────────────────────┐
   │ NEXT_SERVICE : SERVICE_POINTER │ │ HEAD            : SERVICE_POINTER │
   │ SERVICE_CODE : INTEGER         │ │ CURRENT_SERVICE : SERVICE_POINTER │
   └─────────────────────────────┘   └──────────────────────────────────┘
```

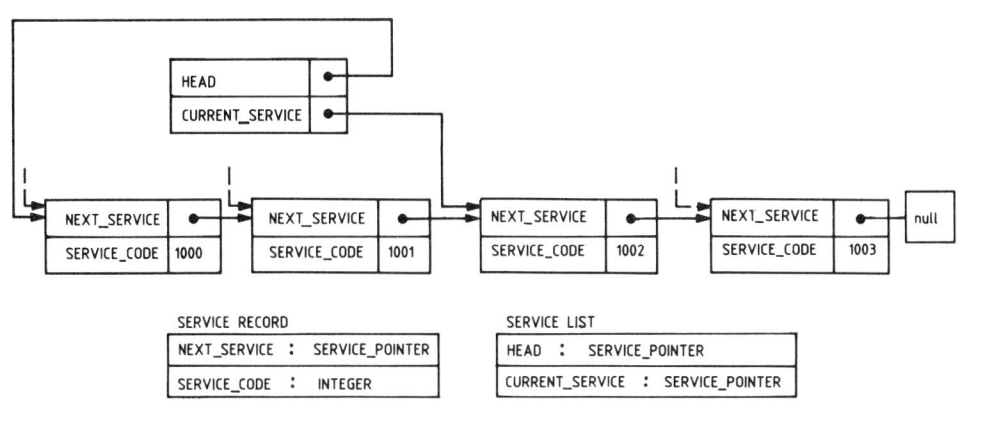

Fig.11.1 The linked list.

```
package SERVICE_PACKAGE is
  type SERVICE_RECORD;
  type SERVICE_POINTER is access SERVICE_RECORD;
  type SERVICE_RECORD is
    record
      NEXT_SERVICE       :   SERVICE_POINTER;
      SERVICE_CODE       :   INTEGER;
    end record;
  type SERVICE_LIST is
    record
      HEAD             :   SERVICE_POINTER := new SERVICE_RECORD;
      CURRENT_SERVICE  :   SERVICE_POINTER;
    end record;
  -- This procedure returns the first service code in the list and resets
  -- SERVICE_DATA to the top of the list
  procedure GET_FIRST_SERVICE (SERVICE_DATA : in out SERVICE_LIST;
                               SERVICE_CODE :    out INTEGER);
  -- This procedure returns the service code for the next service
  -- and a Boolean to show if another sevice code exists in the list.
  -- It moves one service down the list in SERVICE_DATA
  procedure GET_NEXT_SERVICE (SERVICE_DATA    : in out SERVICE_LIST;
                              SERVICE_CODE    :    out INTEGER;
                              ANOTHER_SERVICE :    out BOOLEAN);
end SERVICE_PACKAGE;
```

Listing 11.1 This is a part package specification defining the structure of a linked list and facilities needed to traverse the list.

Here we have adopted good software techniques, using the package for information hiding and program building. Unfortunately, this is not as foolproof as it seems (fools can be quite creative in their use of software). Problems may well arise later when using this package. These fall into two categories, compilation and run-time errors. Now, the package itself isn't the source of such potential problems. It is, in fact, due to the way its

346 Information hiding, data abstraction and private types

```
with SERVICE_PACKAGE;
procedure TRAVERSE_SERVICE_LIST is
   TODAYS_SERVICES            :   SERVICE_PACKAGE.SERVICE_LIST;
   FIRST_SERVICE_CODE         :   INTEGER;
   NEXT_SERVICE_CODE          :   INTEGER;
   ANOTHER_SERVICE_AVAILABLE  :   BOOLEAN;
begin
  --
  -- code setting up TODAYS_SERVICES
  --
  -- Now traverse TODAYS_SERVICES using the facilities provided by
  -- SERVICE_PACKAGE.
  SERVICE_PACKAGE.GET_FIRST_SERVICE (SERVICE_DATA => TODAYS_SERVICES,
                                    SERVICE_CODE => FIRST_SERVICE_CODE);
  while ANOTHER_SERVICE_AVAILABLE loop
    SERVICE_PACKAGE.GET_NEXT_SERVICE
                            (SERVICE_DATA    => TODAYS_SERVICES,
                             SERVICE_CODE    => NEXT_SERVICE_CODE,
                             ANOTHER_SERVICE => ANOTHER_SERVICE_AVAILABLE);
  end loop;
  -- However we could use our knowledge of the structure of TODAYS_SERVICES
  -- to access the data within it. Access the first service code in the list
  -- in this way.
  FIRST_SERVICE_CODE := TODAYS_SERVICES.HEAD.SERVICE_CODE;
end TRAVERSE_SERVICE_LIST;
```

Listing 11.2 This is a simple main program using SERVICE_PACKAGE of Listing 11.1.

information is used. We will demonstrate these two types of error by program example.

(a) **Compilation error**

Observe that, to make type SERVICE_RECORD of Listing 11.1 visible, we've also had to make its structure visible. It may be that, when implementing tasks, designers make use of the structure to simplify operations. For instance, to get the current value of some data we could use the program of Listing 11.2.

Notice how this software makes use of the structure of type SERVICE_LIST from package SERVICE_PACKAGE. Suppose we now change the structure of SERVICE_LIST as shown in Listing 11.3.

We have to recompile all modules affected by this change. Unfortunately, procedure TRAVERSE_SERVICE_LIST will now fail to compile. Thus we are forced to revise this program. A similar situation may well apply to the other users of package SERVICE_PACKAGE – in which case recompilation becomes a major operation.

Our problems came about because we based the design of Listing 11.2 around the structure of the object SERVICE_LIST. There is nothing unusual

```
package SERVICE_PACKAGE is
  type SERVICE_CODE_ARRAY is array (INTEGER range 1..10) of INTEGER;
  type SERVICE_LIST is
    record
    -- The first field holds the index into the second field to access
    -- the next service_code in the list.
      NEXT_CODE        :    INTEGER           := SERVICE_CODE_ARRAY'FIRST;
      SERVICE_CODES    :    SERVICE_CODE_ARRAY;
    end record;
  -- This procedure returns the first service code in the list and resets
  -- SERVICE_DATA to the top of the list
  procedure GET_FIRST_SERVICE (SERVICE_DATA : in out SERVICE_LIST;
                               SERVICE_CODE :    out INTEGER);
  -- This procedure returns the service code for the next service
  -- and a Boolean to show if another service code exists in the list.
  -- It moves one service down the list in SERVICE_DATA
  procedure GET_NEXT_SERVICE (SERVICE_DATA    : in out SERVICE_LIST;
                              SERVICE_CODE    :    out INTEGER;
                              ANOTHER_SERVICE :    out BOOLEAN);
end SERVICE_PACKAGE;
```

Listing 11.3 This is a revised version of Listing 11.1. We have changed the data structure of SERVICE_LIST.

in this; it is a common programming technique. However, during software development, we frequently find that information is in a state of change. Data structures are always likely to be altered. In cases like this, users should not directly control structural details. That, though, is asking a lot of human nature. Perhaps the only workable solution is not to provide details of the structure – hide such information and allow users to work only with the object itself in its entirety.

(b) Run-time error

Once more assume that the programmer imports the package of Listing 11.1 for use in his or her particular application. Part of the resulting code is shown in Listing 11.4.

The programmer's error, given as the last line of the code, is a 'fatal' one. There is no recovery from it – a very undesirable effect.

Once again problems arise because the programmer works with the internal details of the package. Mistakes like this are easily made. And, unfortunately, the program error is missed by the compiler because it is a perfectly legal operation. In situations like this we rely on the programmer's skill to keep us out of trouble. A better solution is to make it impossible to produce such mistakes. We can do this by hiding the package data and its structure from users. But then, of course, we must also supply the means for the user to handle this object.

What has been shown here is how problems can arise due to:

348 Information hiding, data abstraction and private types

```
with SERVICE_PACKAGE;
procedure CORRUPT_SERVICE_LIST is
   TODAYS_SERVICES           :    SERVICE_PACKAGE.SERVICE_LIST;
   FIRST_SERVICE_CODE        :    INTEGER;
   NEXT_SERVICE_CODE         :    INTEGER;
   ANOTHER_SERVICE_AVAILABLE :    BOOLEAN;
begin
   --
   -- code setting up TODAYS_SERVICES
   --
   -- Now traverse TODAYS_SERVICES using the facilities provided by
   -- SERVICE_PACKAGE.
   SERVICE_PACKAGE.GET_FIRST_SERVICE (SERVICE_DATA => TODAYS_SERVICES,
                                     SERVICE_CODE => FIRST_SERVICE_CODE);
   while ANOTHER_SERVICE_AVAILABLE loop
      SERVICE_PACKAGE.GET_NEXT_SERVICE
                             (SERVICE_DATA    => TODAYS_SERVICES,
                              SERVICE_CODE    => NEXT_SERVICE_CODE,
                              ANOTHER_SERVICE => ANOTHER_SERVICE_AVAILABLE);
   end loop;
   -- We have traversed the whole service list. TODAYS_SERVICES.CURRENT_SERVICE
   -- now points to the last service in the list. The next line passes
   -- compiler checks but will corrupt the list.
   TODAYS_SERVICES.HEAD := TODAYS_SERVICES.CURRENT_SERVICE;
   -- We have lost the whole list! If we tried to process TODAYS_SERVICES again
   -- we would have no list to work on!
end CORRUPT_SERVICE_LIST;
```

Listing 11.4 This code uses the package of Listing 11.1. It illustrates a programmer error which passes all compiler checks.

- Changes in data structures;
- Accessing detailed parts of data structures.

This leads us into the topic of private types. Using these we can hide object structures, yet provide facilities to manipulate such objects. Thus errors as described above should be eliminated.

11.2 INTRODUCTION TO THE PRIVATE TYPE

The first important point is that private types can be located only within packages, Fig.11.2.

As we've already seen, a primary function of the package is to hide information. Strictly speaking it hides internal objects and operations carried out within the package. The private type is also used to hide information. However, in this case, the objective is to hide the structure of types and values associated with types.

The package consists of a specification and a body. From our earlier work we know that the location of declarations determines whether items are

Introduction to the private type 349

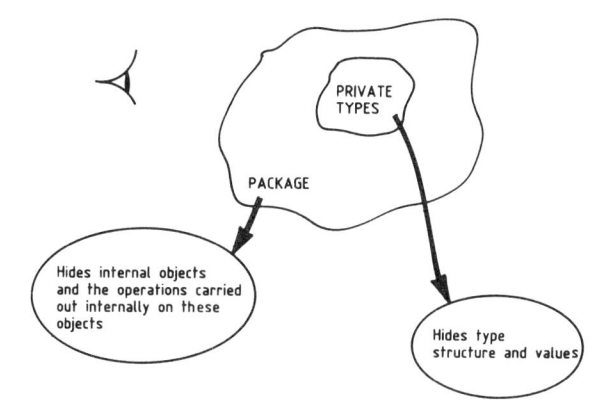

Fig.11.2 Location and role of the private type.

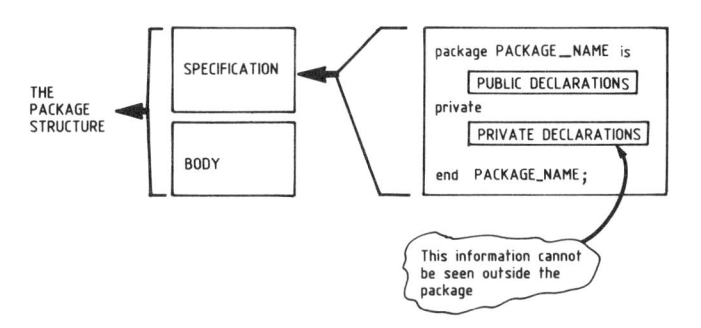

Fig.11.3 Location of public and private declarations.

visible (public) or hidden. Public items are declared in the package specification; they are freely available for use by clients. In contrast, items declared only within the body cannot be accessed from outside the package. With private types we have a more complex situation. For a given item some information is to be made available to clients; the rest is to be kept private. To meet these needs we modify the framework of the specification as shown in Fig.11.3.

Note how the keyword **private** splits the package specification into two parts. Above this we have items which are visible to potential clients – public declarations – and below this we define the details which we wish to hide. So, to make a type available to clients, we declare it in the public part – without divulging its structure. The structure is then defined in the private part, Fig.11.4. We will return to this in more detail in a moment.

Ada provides us with two forms of private type, the 'normal' or 'standard' one and the 'limited private' one, Fig.11.5. More correctly, they are defined

350 Information hiding, data abstraction and private types

```
package SENSOR_DATA is
    type ATTITUDE_COORDINATES is private;   ← making the type visible
private
    type ATTITUDES_COORDINATES is           ← Hiding the details of the type structure
        record
            AZIMUTH : FLOAT;
            ELEVATION : FLOAT;
        end record;
end SENSOR_DATA;
```

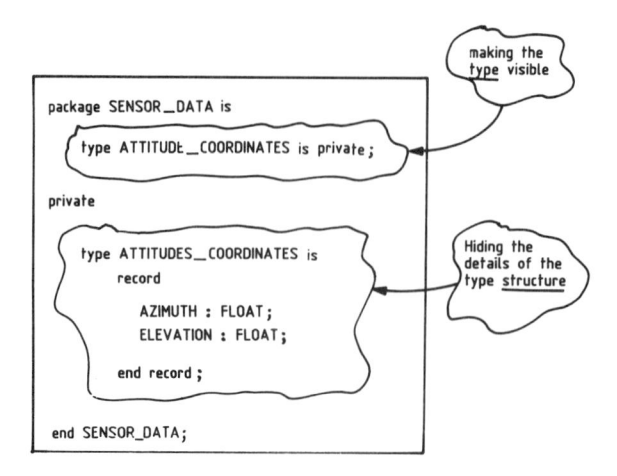

Fig.11.4 Visible and hidden features of private types.

```
                    PRIVATE TYPES
                   /             \
           "NORMAL"              LIMITED
           PRIVATE               PRIVATE
           TYPES                 TYPES

    Standard Operations        Standard Operations
         :=                         none
         =
         /=
                    Non-Standard Operations
                    "Explicit" - user defined
```

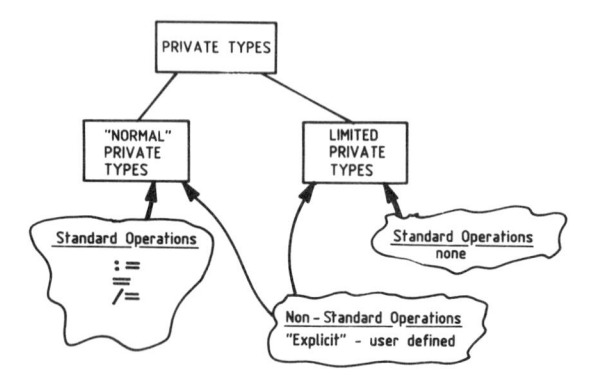

Fig.11.5 Private types – general information.

in the LRM as *private* and *limited private* types. To avoid confusion we will use the terms normal and limited.

We identify a private type as being normal or limited by the form of the type declaration (see later). When we use either type outside the package (i.e. as a client), we are quite limited in what we can do to it. The normal private type can use only a restricted number of standard operations (standard operations are those provided as part of the Ada language). Assignment, equality and inequality testing (Fig.11.5) are – at the moment – the most important ones for us. Even more surprising, we cannot apply any standard operations to the limited private type. However, the programmer can define a set of operations to be used on private types, the so-called *explicit* operations.

It is clear that we really can't do anything with a limited private type unless we provide explicit operations. Even with the normal private type we won't get very far using the standard operators. Why these restrictions? And what is the rationale for this approach? The answer is quite simple. It enables the designer to control fully operations which can be applied to objects of such types. We'll see by example how this helps us in the building of reliable programs.

11.3 THE 'NORMAL' PRIVATE TYPE

Fig.11.4 shows the declaration format used with normal private types. Here we define the type ATTITUDE_COORDINATES to be a private type. By locating its declaration in the public part of the package specification we make it available to clients. Note, however, at this point that we don't give any details of its construction. Such information is subsequently defined in the private part of the specification (Listing 11.5).

```
package SENSOR_DATA is
   type ATTITUDE_COORDINATES is private;
   private
   type ATTITUDE_COORDINATES is
      record
         AZIMUTH      :     FLOAT           := 0.0;
         ELEVATION    :     FLOAT           := 0.0;
      end record;
end SENSOR_DATA;
```

Listing 11.5 This is a package which declares a private data type.

What can we do with this type (more precisely, objects of this type)? First let us look at usage by clients, Listing 11.6.

This example brings out clearly that, in a client module, you cannot access the component parts of private objects (using standard operations, that is). Values cannot be assigned to these, nor can they be manipulated in any way. The need to provide explicit operations should now be very clear.

Consider now the use of the type within the package, that is in the body. Here it is treated as a normally declared type – so there is nothing new here. Thus all standard operations applicable to this type are valid.

We are now in a position to use private types sensibly in client modules. Remember, our purpose in using private types is:

- To hide as much information as possible.
- To provide any special facilities needed for the manipulation of such data (note that three standard operations only can be applied).

352 Information hiding, data abstraction and private types

```
with TEXT_IO;                use TEXT_IO;
with SENSOR_DATA;            use SENSOR_DATA;
procedure USE_PRIVATE_SENSOR_DATA is
  FIRST_SET          :     ATTITUDE_COORDINATES;
  SECOND_SET         :     ATTITUDE_COORDINATES;
  EQUAL_AZIMUTH      :     BOOLEAN;
begin
 -- we can use the '=' function
  if (FIRST_SET = SECOND_SET) then
    PUT_LINE ("FIRST_SET = SECOND_SET");
  end if;
 -- we can use the '/=' function
  if (FIRST_SET /= SECOND_SET) then
    PUT_LINE ("FIRST_SET /= SECOND_SET");
  end if;
 -- we can assign whole objects of the private type
  FIRST_SET := SECOND_SET;
 -- We cannot access the components of the private type.
 -- The following lines would not compile
 -- FIRST_SET.AZIMUTH := 582.7;
 -- EQUAL_AZIMUTH        := FIRST_SET.AZIMUTH = SECOND_SET.AZIMUTH;
 -- FIRST_SET.AZIMUTH := FIRST_SET.AZIMUTH + SECOND_SET.AZIMUTH;
end USE_PRIVATE_SENSOR_DATA;
```

Listing 11.6 This is a user of the private data type of Listing 11.5.

Again, to reiterate a point, we define these special facilities, not the user of the package. How, though, do we do this? This answer is (Fig.11.6):

- First, declare the provided operations as subprograms in the public part of the package. Here the provided operation is the function RESET_ATTITUDE_COORDINATES;
- Now build the provided operations in the body of the package;
- With these subprograms, use parameters or results which belong to the private type (here the type is ATTITUDE_COORDINATES).

The application of these principles is shown in Listings 11.7 and 11.8.

11.4 CONSTANTS AS PRIVATE TYPES

Consider the requirement to define a system constant which will be used by several client programs. The usual solution is to use a package specification as a 'placeholder' for such constants. Now consider that we wish to define a system constant – yet keep its type private. The obvious solution is first to declare the constant object in the public declarations section. Then we define its structure as part of the private declarations. Sadly, there is a fatal flaw with this approach. It is a requirement that constants must be initialized at

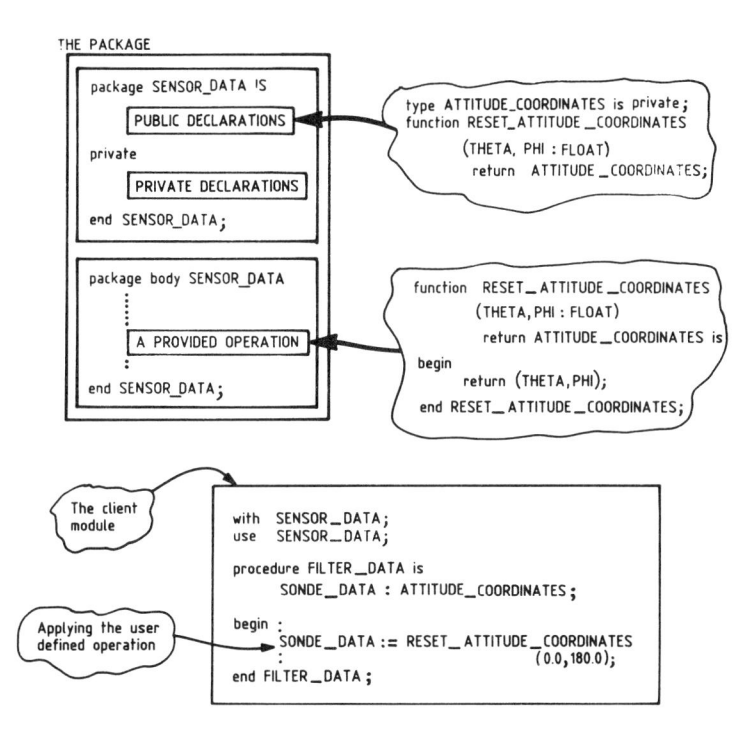

Fig.11.6 Providing and applying user-defined operations to private types.

```
package SENSOR_DATA is
  type ATTITUDE_COORDINATES is private;
  function RESET_ATTITUDE_COORDINATES (THETA      :      FLOAT;
                                       PHI        :      FLOAT)
    return ATTITUDE_COORDINATES;
  function GET_ELEVATION_VALUE (COORDINATES :     ATTITUDE_COORDINATES)
    return FLOAT;
private
  type ATTITUDE_COORDINATES is
    record
      AZIMUTH       :   FLOAT        := 0.0;
      ELEVATION     :   FLOAT        := 0.0;
    end record;
end SENSOR_DATA;
--
-- Package Body
--
package body SENSOR_DATA is
  function RESET_ATTITUDE_COORDINATES (THETA      :      FLOAT;
                                       PHI        :      FLOAT)
    return ATTITUDE_COORDINATES is
  begin
    return (AZIMUTH => THETA, ELEVATION => PHI);
  end RESET_ATTITUDE_COORDINATES;
  function GET_ELEVATION_VALUE (COORDINATES :     ATTITUDE_COORDINATES)
    return FLOAT is
  begin
    return COORDINATES.ELEVATION;
  end GET_ELEVATION_VALUE;
end SENSOR_DATA;
```

Listing 11.7 This example demonstrates how to provide user-defined operations relating to private types.

354 Information hiding, data abstraction and private types

```
with TEXT_IO;              use TEXT_IO;
with SENSOR_DATA;          use SENSOR_DATA;
procedure OPERATIONS_ON_PRIVATE is
  CURRENT_COORDS    :    ATTITUDE_COORDINATES;
  CURRENT_ELEVATION :    FLOAT;
  package ELEVATION_IO is new FLOAT_IO (FLOAT);
  use ELEVATION_IO;
begin
  CURRENT_COORDS := RESET_ATTITUDE_COORDINATES (THETA    => 10.9,
                                                PHI      => 12.9);
  CURRENT_ELEVATION := GET_ELEVATION_VALUE (COORDINATES => CURRENT_COORDS);
  PUT ("The current elevation is => ");
  PUT (CURRENT_ELEVATION);
  NEW_LINE;
end OPERATIONS_ON_PRIVATE;
```

Listing 11.8 This example demonstrates how a client applies user-defined operations relating to private types.

declaration time. But, when the constant object is declared, we haven't yet defined its structure – so we can't assign initial values to the object.

We earlier met a similar problem with linked-list structures – trying to define pointers prior to their type declaration. The solution there was to use the incomplete type declaration. Here we handle our problem in much the same way. Declare the constant twice, first in the visible part of the specification, and then in the private part, as shown below:

```
package MACHINE_PARAMETERS is
    type ALARM_LIMITS is private;
    SHAFT SPEEDS: constant ALARM_LIMITS; -- This is the first
                                          -- declaration of the constant
private
    type ALARM LIMITS is
        record
            LP_SHAFT : INTEGER;
            HP_SHAFT : INTEGER;
        end record;
    SHAFT_SPEEDS: constant  ALARM_LIMITS := (9000, 6000);  -- Here is
                                                            -- the second
end MACHINE_PARAMETERS;
```

A constant declared in this way is called a deferred constant within the visible section of the package. Note that we follow up the restricted declaration with a full declaration in the private part of the package.

11.5 A PRACTICAL APPLICATION EXAMPLE OF PRIVATE TYPES

In this section we will look at the use of the private type in a practical application. Our intent is to show that we can minimize change effects through the use of this type.

Consider the scenario of Fig.11.7.

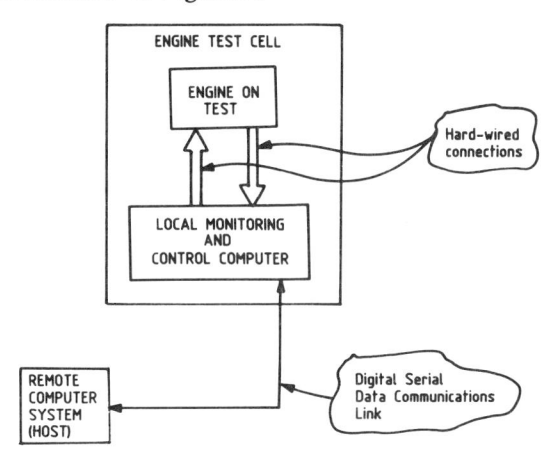

Fig.11.7 Engine test installation.

Here we have an engine test and development facility. It, the facility, consists of a test cell and a remote computer system. The test cell houses the engine on test and a local monitoring and control computer. Engine sensors and actuators are hard wired to the local computer. Two of the primary functions of this computer are to:

- Monitor and control the engine status;
- Pre-process data for onward transmission to the host (remote) computer system.

At the host this information is used for remote data alarming functions.

Now let us review part of the data collection software in the local computer. Engine status information consists of three items: power, fuel and air supply. Each one has two states, on or off. We build a package ENGINE_STATUS_PARAMETERS to house the data, part of it being shown in Listing 11.9.

The data is structured as an array – ENGINE_STATUS_DATA – within the package ENGINE_STATUS_PARAMETERS (observe that the array elements are an enumeration type). It is transmitted to the host, where it is used as input for the alarm monitoring and display function. Assume that procedure ENGINE_MONITORING (Listing 11.10) performs one of these tasks.

```ada
package ENGINE_STATUS_PARAMETERS is
  type ENGINE_STATUS_DATA is private;
  type SUPPLY_STATE is (ON, OFF);
  -- procedures for storing values
  procedure WRITE_POWER_SUPPLY_STATE
                             (ENGINE_STATUS      : in out ENGINE_STATUS_DATA;
                              POWER_SUPPLY_STATE : in     SUPPLY_STATE);
  procedure WRITE_FUEL_SUPPLY_STATE
                             (ENGINE_STATUS      : in out ENGINE_STATUS_DATA;
                              FUEL_SUPPLY_STATE  : in     SUPPLY_STATE);
  procedure WRITE_AIR_SUPPLY_STATE
                             (ENGINE_STATUS      : in out ENGINE_STATUS_DATA;
                              AIR_SUPPLY_STATE   : in.    SUPPLY_STATE);
  -- A procedure for displaying current values
  procedure PUT_ENGINE_STATUS (ENGINE_STATUS : in ENGINE_STATUS_DATA);
private
  type SUPPLY is (POWER, FUEL, AIR_SUPPLY);
  type ENGINE_STATUS_DATA is array (SUPPLY) of SUPPLY_STATE;
end ENGINE_STATUS_PARAMETERS;
            case BOOK_CHOICE is
              when 1 =>
                RETURN_BOOK (TITLE    => GONE_WITH_THE_WIND,
                             RETURNED => REQUEST_ACTIONED);
              when 2 =>
                RETURN_BOOK (TITLE    => GREAT_EXPECTATIONS,
                             RETURNED => REQUEST_ACTIONED);
              when others =>
                null;
            end case;
            if REQUEST_ACTIONED then
              PUT_LINE ("The book has been returned");
            else
              PUT_LINE ("Sorry, The book is already in the Library");
            end if;
          when 3 =>
            case BOOK_CHOICE is
              when 1 =>
                DISPLAY_CURRENT_STATE (TITLE    => GONE_WITH_THE_WIND);
              when 2 =>
                DISPLAY_CURRENT_STATE (TITLE    => GREAT_EXPECTATIONS);
              when others =>
                null;
            end case;
          when 4 =>
            exit ACTION_BOOK;
          when 5 =>
            exit OUTER_MOST;
          when others =>
            PUT_LINE ("Please enter a number in the range 1 to 5");
        end case;
      end loop ACTION_BOOK;
  end loop OUTER_MOST;
end LIBRARY;
```

Listing 11.9 This is a part package listing, showing the data structure used with a set of collected data from a test installation.

```
with ENGINE_STATUS_PARAMETERS; use ENGINE_STATUS_PARAMETERS;
procedure ENGINE_MONITORING is
   ENGINE_DATA       :       ENGINE_STATUS_DATA;
begin
   WRITE_POWER_SUPPLY_STATE (ENGINE_STATUS       => ENGINE_DATA,
                             POWER_SUPPLY_STATE => ON);
   WRITE_FUEL_SUPPLY_STATE (ENGINE_STATUS        => ENGINE_DATA,
                            FUEL_SUPPLY_STATE => ON);
   WRITE_AIR_SUPPLY_STATE (ENGINE_STATUS      => ENGINE_DATA,
                           AIR_SUPPLY_STATE => ON);
   PUT_ENGINE_STATUS (ENGINE_STATUS => ENGINE_DATA);
end ENGINE_MONITORING;
```

Listing 11.10 This is a simple main program using the package ENGINE_STATUS_PARAMETERS of Listing 11.9.

Its function (in part) is to print out engine status information.

What we have here, remember, is a prototype development activity. In such situations things always change. Suppose we now decide to monitor speed (RPM), fuel rack position and oil pressure. How does this affect our software?

The new items are subtypes of type INTEGER. We therefore decide to change type ENGINE_STATUS_DATA to a record to incorporate these extra parameters. The revised package ENGINE_STATUS_PARAMETERS is shown in Listing 11.11.

The consequence of this change is that package ENGINE_STATUS_PARAMETERS and all its clients have to be recompiled. Included with these is procedure ENGINE_MONITORING. But now we should have no problems with the recompilation, even though we changed ENGINE_STATUS_DATA from an array to a record.

11.6 LIMITED PRIVATE TYPES

Earlier in this chapter we met the limited private type. Types, and objects of this type, cannot use any of the implicit Ada operations. Only explicit – programmer-defined – operations may be used. These, remember, are:

- Implemented in the package body.
- Defined in the package specification.

To define a type as being limited private we use the declaration format

> **type** TYPE_NAME **is limited private**;

For example:

```
package ENGINE_STATUS_PARAMETERS is
  type ENGINE_STATUS_DATA is private;
  type SUPPLY_STATE is (ON, OFF);
  -- declare new subtypes
  subtype REVS_PER_MIN is INTEGER range 0..8500;
  subtype DEGREES is INTEGER range 0..360;
  subtype OIL_PRESSURE_RANGE is INTEGER range 0..400;
  -- procedures for storing values
  procedure WRITE_POWER_SUPPLY_STATE
                           (ENGINE_STATUS      : in out ENGINE_STATUS_DATA;
                            POWER_SUPPLY_STATE : in      SUPPLY_STATE);
  procedure WRITE_FUEL_SUPPLY_STATE
                           (ENGINE_STATUS      : in out ENGINE_STATUS_DATA;
                            FUEL_SUPPLY_STATE  : in      SUPPLY_STATE);
  procedure WRITE_AIR_SUPPLY_STATE
                           (ENGINE_STATUS      : in out ENGINE_STATUS_DATA;
                            AIR_SUPPLY_STATE   : in      SUPPLY_STATE);
  -- new procedure for storing the new engine parameters
  procedure WRITE_RPM (ENGINE_STATUS : in out ENGINE_STATUS_DATA;
                       RPM           : in     REVS_PER_MIN);
  procedure WRITE_FUEL_RACK_POSITION
                           (ENGINE_STATUS      : in out ENGINE_STATUS_DATA;
                            FUEL_RACK_POSITION : in      DEGREES);
  procedure WRITE_OIL_PRESSURE (ENGINE_STATUS : in out ENGINE_STATUS_DATA;
                                OIL_PRESSURE  : in     OIL_PRESSURE_RANGE);
  -- A procedure for displaying current values
  procedure PUT_ENGINE_STATUS (ENGINE_STATUS : in    ENGINE_STATUS_DATA);
private
  type ENGINE_STATUS_DATA is
    record
      POWER_SUPPLY_STATE  :    SUPPLY_STATE;
      FUEL_SUPPLY_STATE   :    SUPPLY_STATE;
      AIR_SUPPLY_STATE    :    SUPPLY_STATE;
      RPM                 :    REVS_PER_MIN;
      FUEL_RACK_POSITION  :    DEGREES;
      OIL_PRESSURE        :    OIL_PRESSURE_RANGE;
    end record;
end ENGINE_STATUS_PARAMETERS;
```

Listing 11.11 This is a revised version of Listing 11.9. Three new items have been added to the data monitoring system.

```
package MACHINE_PARAMETERS is
    type ALARM_LIMITS is limited private;
private
    type ALARM_LIMITS is
      record
        LP_SHAFT : INTEGER;
        HP_SHAFT : INTEGER;
      end record;
end MACHINE_PARAMETERS;
```

In this example we haven't defined any explicit operations. So what can we do with the type ALARM_LIMITS? In a nutshell, nothing.

The reason for making this apparently pointless statement is to emphasize strongly why we have limited private types. It is so that the programmer can completely define what can be done to objects of such types.

11.7 A PRACTICAL APPLICATION EXAMPLE OF THE LIMITED PRIVATE TYPE

Limited private types are widely used in one particular application – the management of shared resources. Its concept and implementation can be described using a very simple analogy – managing book loans in a library, Fig.11.8.

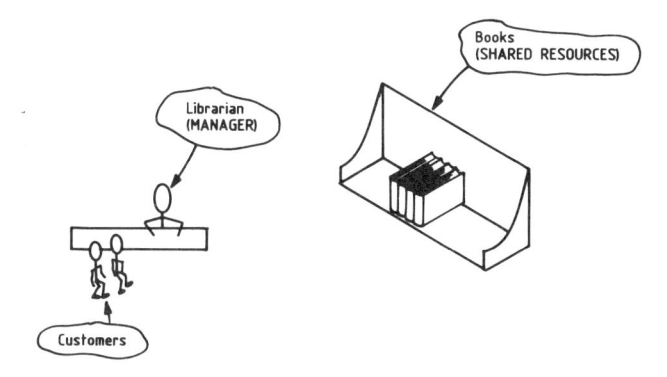

Fig.11.8 Essential elements of the library.

First we have the shared resources, the books. Then we have the manager of such resources, the librarian. Finally we have prospective users of the resources, the customers. Assume that, in our case, the librarian is an 'electronic' one. Operations relating to the books are made using a data terminal unit. These operations are:

- Check if a book is available (DISPLAY_STATE);
- Borrow a book (REMOVE_BOOK);
- Return a book (RETURN_BOOK).

Take the following scenario. A customer uses his or her data terminal to make a book enquiry. Assuming the title is available, the customer then asks to borrow it. As a result the book is delivered to the customer collection point (we will assume that he or she is entitled to borrow the book). Further, its state is automatically marked by the librarian as 'Not Available'. At this stage another customer enters the library... and so on.

What are the important points here? First, accesses to the shared resources are controlled by the librarian. Second, only the librarian can change the state of a book; it is impossible for a customer to do this. If customers were able to alter book status, we would probably end up with chaos. Third, we would also like it to be impossible for customers to copy books.

Now put this into program terms. We will show how the limited private type is applied in such a situation. First, build the librarian and its facilities in a package. We will call this BOOK_MANAGER (Listing 11.12).

This includes three procedures which implement the operations described above: DISPLAY_STATE, REMOVE_BOOK and RETURN_BOOK. The type BOOK is defined to be limited private. Here it is structured as a record for one reason only: so that it can be assigned an initial value.

Interaction between customer and librarian is demonstrated in procedure LIBRARY of Listing 11.13.

This example is fairly straightforward – but what precisely have we gained by making BOOK limited private? Suppose, for instance, we had made type BOOK visible in the normal way. Then, in procedure LIBRARY, we could have written:

```
GREAT_EXPECTATIONS.CURRENT_STATE := NOT_AVAILABLE;
```

In other words, a user sets the status of a book – which is not supposed to happen. This can be overcome by turning BOOK into a normal private type. But then we could still do something like:

```
MY_OWN_BOOK : BOOK;
begin
    MY_OWN_BOOK := GREAT_EXPECTATIONS;
```

Another requirement is broken – copying is meant to be forbidden. However, with limited private types, it is impossible to copy objects of the type. Assignment is not allowed (in fact, no standard operations can be applied to limited private types). Don't go on. Re-read these last few sentences. Make sure that you clearly understand what they say, because this is the essence of limited private types.

What does this mean in terms of software design? It is that we (the resource managers) can make objects available to many users – and yet define precisely what can be done to such objects. Thus we can guarantee to maintain the integrity of our software.

The basic reason for using resource management in programs is a simple one. It is to prevent abuse of data where a number of tasks need to access a shared resource(s) – and where such accesses may occur simultaneously. You will only truly appreciate the use of a resource manager after studying

A practical application example of the limited private type 361

```ada
with TEXT_IO;            use TEXT_IO;
package BOOK_MANAGER is
  type BOOK is limited private;
  procedure REMOVE_BOOK (TITLE    : in out BOOK;
                         REMOVED  :     out BOOLEAN);
  procedure RETURN_BOOK (TITLE    : in out BOOK;
                         RETURNED :     out BOOLEAN);
  procedure DISPLAY_CURRENT_STATE (TITLE   : in      BOOK);
private
  type BOOK_STATE is (AVAILABLE, NOT_AVAILABLE);
  type BOOK is
    record
      CURRENT_STATE   :    BOOK_STATE    := AVAILABLE;
    end record;
end BOOK_MANAGER;
package body BOOK_MANAGER is
  procedure REMOVE_BOOK (TITLE    : in out BOOK;
                         REMOVED  :     out BOOLEAN) is
  begin
    if TITLE.CURRENT_STATE = AVAILABLE then
      TITLE.CURRENT_STATE := NOT_AVAILABLE;
      REMOVED := TRUE;
    else
      REMOVED := FALSE;
    end if;
  end REMOVE_BOOK;
  procedure RETURN_BOOK (TITLE    : in out BOOK;
                         RETURNED :     out BOOLEAN) is
  begin
    if TITLE.CURRENT_STATE = NOT_AVAILABLE then
      TITLE.CURRENT_STATE := AVAILABLE;
      RETURNED := TRUE;
    else
      RETURNED := FALSE;
    end if;
  end RETURN_BOOK;
  procedure DISPLAY_CURRENT_STATE (TITLE   : in      BOOK) is
  begin
    if TITLE.CURRENT_STATE = AVAILABLE then
      PUT_LINE ("The book is in the Library");
    else
      PUT_LINE ("The book is currently not available");
    end if;
  end DISPLAY_CURRENT_STATE;
end BOOK_MANAGER;
```

Listing 11.12 This package BOOK_MANAGER uses the limited private type for resource management.

concurrency in Chapter 14. It doesn't make much sense in the context of sequential programs.

```ada
with BOOK_MANAGER;          use BOOK_MANAGER;
with TEXT_IO;               use TEXT_IO;
procedure LIBRARY is
  GONE_WITH_THE_WIND :      BOOK;
  GREAT_EXPECTATIONS :      BOOK;
  BOOK_CHOICE        :      INTEGER;
  ACTION_CHOICE      :      INTEGER;
  REQUEST_ACTIONED   :      BOOLEAN;
  package INT_IO is new INTEGER_IO (INTEGER);
  use INT_IO;
begin
  OUTER_MOST:loop
    CHOOSE_BOOK:loop
      NEW_LINE;
      PUT_LINE ("1. Gone With The Wind");
      PUT_LINE ("2. Great Expectations");
      NEW_LINE;
      PUT ("Please enter book number : ");
      GET (BOOK_CHOICE);
      SKIP_LINE;
      NEW_LINE;
      if (BOOK_CHOICE > 2) or (BOOK_CHOICE < 1) then
        PUT_LINE ("Please enter a number in the range 1 to 2");
      else
        exit CHOOSE_BOOK;
      end if;
    end loop CHOOSE_BOOK;
    ACTION_BOOK:loop
      NEW_LINE;
      PUT_LINE ("1. Take out book");
      PUT_LINE ("2. Return book");
      PUT_LINE ("3. Display book state");
      PUT_LINE ("4. Choose another book");
      PUT_LINE ("5. EXIT program");
      NEW_LINE;
      PUT ("Please enter choice : ");
      GET (ACTION_CHOICE);
      SKIP_LINE;
      NEW_LINE;
      case ACTION_CHOICE is
        when 1 =>
          case BOOK_CHOICE is
          when 1 =>
            REMOVE_BOOK (TITLE    => GONE_WITH_THE_WIND,
                         REMOVED  => REQUEST_ACTIONED);
          when 2 =>
            REMOVE_BOOK (TITLE    => GREAT_EXPECTATIONS,
                         REMOVED  => REQUEST_ACTIONED);
          when others =>
            null;
          end case;
          if REQUEST_ACTIONED then
            PUT_LINE ("The book has been taken out");
          else
            PUT_LINE ("Sorry, The book is currently not available");
          end if;
        when 2 =>
          case BOOK_CHOICE is
          when 1 =>
            RETURN_BOOK (TITLE    => GONE_WITH_THE_WIND,
                         RETURNED => REQUEST_ACTIONED);
          when 2 =>
            RETURN_BOOK (TITLE    => GREAT_EXPECTATIONS,
                         RETURNED => REQUEST_ACTIONED);
```

```
                when others =>
                  null;
              end case;
              if REQUEST_ACTIONED then
                PUT_LINE ("The book has been returned");
              else
                PUT_LINE ("Sorry, The book is already in the Library");
              end if;
            when 3 =>
              case BOOK_CHOICE is
                when 1 =>
                  DISPLAY_CURRENT_STATE (TITLE     => GONE_WITH_THE_WIND);
                when 2 =>
                  DISPLAY_CURRENT_STATE (TITLE     => GREAT_EXPECTATIONS);
                when others =>
                  null;
              end case;
            when 4 =>
              exit ACTION_BOOK;
            when 5 =>
              exit OUTER_MOST;
            when others =>
              PUT_LINE ("Please enter a number in the range 1 to 5");
          end case;
        end loop ACTION_BOOK;
      end loop OUTER_MOST;
end LIBRARY;
```

Listing 11.13 This shows the package BOOK_MANAGER in use.

11.8 MISCELLANEOUS POINTS

(a) For limited private types

- When we declare a variable (object) of a limited private type we cannot initialize it in the declaration.
- As a consequence, constants of such types cannot be declared by a package user (i.e. outside the defining package).
- Parameters cannot have default values.
- The equality operator '=' can be overloaded for limited private types.
- The inequality operator '/=' is automatically provided when '=' is defined. It is not explicitly declared.

(b) General

- The private declarations section is not restricted to declarations of private types. You can declare what you like in this section (though it is good practice to limit it to private types and associated entities).

364 Information hiding, data abstraction and private types

- A limited number of predefined attributes apply to private types (see the LRM, section 7.4.2).

REVIEW

You should now:

- See what problems can arise through using detailed knowledge of the structure of program objects;
- Understand the structure and application of Ada private types;
- Understand the role of public and private declarations for types;
- Be able to work with normal and limited private types;
- Be able to use the private type construct to control the use of objects;
- Perceive how private and limited private types can be used in practical situations.

Chapter Twelve
Exceptions

Ada is primarily intended for use in real-time systems. Such systems, particularly the embedded ones, are designed to operate continuously for long periods – and frequently unattended. Probably the most demanding application is that of fire detection. But it's not only a matter of longevity, or of unattended operation; it also involves speed of response and reliable behaviour. For instance, modern fighter aircraft are uncontrollable without assistance from the flight control computer. Our major concern for such systems is what to do when things go wrong – loosely, when exceptions occur. Briefly, we:

- Need to detect fault conditions;
- Determine the appropriate response;
- Institute this response.

In this chapter we will look at how Ada deals with exceptions as a standard feature of the language. After studying this you will:

- Understand the concepts and principles of detecting, raising and handling exceptions;
- Appreciate the difference between predefined and user-defined exceptions;
- Know how to implement exception handling strategies in blocks, subprograms and packages;
- Understand the basics of scope and visibility rules for exceptions;
- Perceive how exceptions are propagated from inner (enclosed) program units to outer (enclosing) ones;
- Recognize the difference between exception raising during statement execution and during declaration elaboration;
- Realize that exceptions can be suppressed.

12.1 EXCEPTIONS – WHAT AND WHY?

Exceptions are defined to be 'errors or fault conditions that make further execution of a program meaningless' (*Oxford Dictionary of Computing*). Note that this definition concerns what happens when a program is executed – a run-time issue. Problems at compilation time are not exceptions.

Programmers of real-time software should accept that it is impossible to guarantee error-free systems. The problems are not necessarily within the software; other factors must be taken into account. So how, when, why and where do these problems arise? Generally they are due to:

- The human factor;
- Computational problems;
- Hardware failure.

(a) The human factor

The problem can originate outside the system due to the behaviour of people (assuming they can interact with the software). For instance, consider using a processor as a controller for a closed loop control system. Normally the controller is expected to carry out tasks additional to that of controlling the loop. So, under normal conditions, the control task runs at regular and preset times; other tasks are executed in the remaining time. Assume that the operator can set the system sampling rate as desired. If the operator sets this too fast the processor will execute nothing but the loop control algorithm; all other tasks are ignored. Despite the fact the software may be faultless, the system fails to work correctly.

(b) Computational problems

One of the well-known mistakes here is not allowing for invalid mathematical operations. These, such as dividing by zero, produce indeterminate results. Other items, such as going outside the correct limits of array bounds, also fall into this category.

(c) Hardware failure

The following example typifies the problems of hardware failure. A control program instructs an analogue-to-digital converter to begin conversion. It then polls the converter, looking for the end of conversion signal. But for some reason the converter fails to generate this signal. The result is that the program sits there *ad infinitum* (or until the power is switched off); control of the system is completely lost.

Recapping, when we design any software system we aim to guarantee that it will always behave properly. This is true for all programming, but is especially important for real-time applications. It is, though, a fact of life that errors will arise from time to time, some trivial, some catastrophic. Therefore our design objectives change. We cannot guarantee that a system will always perform its desired function. Instead we strive to maintain control of the situation – even if we can provide only a degraded level of service.

The technique used to handle situations like these is called *defensive programming*. Part of any defensive programming strategy is to:

- Detect faults (exceptions) if they do occur;
- Report the presence of such faults;
- Control the resulting response of the system.

These operations are defined to be exception detection, reporting (raising) and handling. The software used to implement the handling operations is called an exception handler.

In this chapter we'll look at how Ada provides mechanisms for dealing with exceptions as a standard, inbuilt, feature.

12.2 DEALING WITH EXCEPTIONS – THE ADA WAY

12.2.1 General aspects

The fundamental aspects of exceptions within the Ada language are detailed in Fig.12.1.

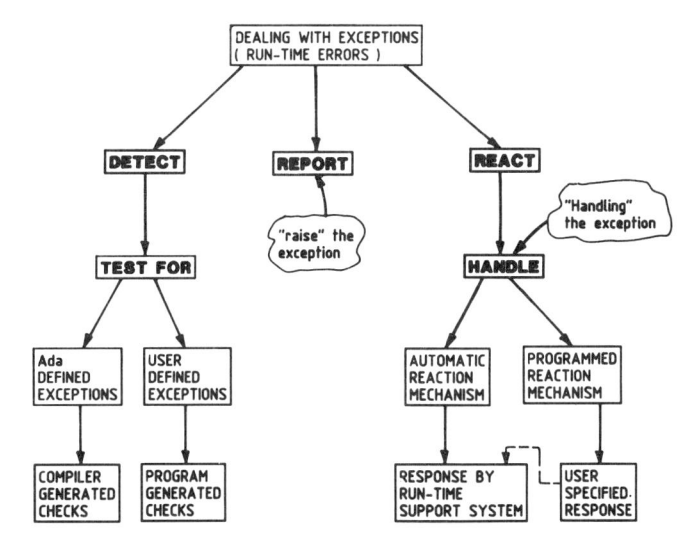

Fig.12.1 Fundamental aspects of exceptions.

When an exception occurs the first requirement is to detect it and then transfer control to a reaction mechanism (this transfer is defined to be the reporting or raising of the exception). We then have to respond to the problem – handling the exception.

368   Exceptions

Detectable errors fall into two categories: Ada-defined and user-defined exceptions. Those defined by the Ada language are usually called the predefined exceptions. Conditions which can lead to predefined exceptions are always checked out, the test code being generated automatically by the compiler. By contrast, user-defined exceptions are specified explicitly – in source code – by the programmer.

Exception handling comes in a number of flavours. First, the response may be a completely automatic one, carried out under the control of the Ada runtime support system. Second, it may be a programmer-defined one. Third, the response may be a combination of the above. The initial handling is defined by the programmer, who finally transfers control to the support system. All three will be demonstrated in this chapter.

12.2.2 Predefined exceptions

In Ada there are five predefined exceptions:

- CONSTRAINT_ERROR
- NUMERIC_ERROR
- PROGRAM_ERROR
- STORAGE_ERROR
- TASKING_ERROR

A brief description of these is given below. For fuller details see section 11.1 of the LRM.

(a) CONSTRAINT_ERROR

A constraint error occurs if, for example, a value goes out of its defined range. An attempt to access an array index which is not within the set bounds is also a constraint error. This is demonstrated in Listing 12.1, where illegal values can be entered from the keyboard.

```
with TEXT_IO;
procedure FIRST_EXCEPTION is
  package INT_IO is new TEXT_IO.INTEGER_IO (INTEGER);
  X1              :       INTEGER range 0..50;
begin
  TEXT_IO.PUT ("Enter X1 => ");
  INT_IO.GET (X1);
  -- if value < 0 or > 50 then exception raised here!
  TEXT_IO.SKIP_LINE;
  TEXT_IO.PUT_LINE ("Program finished");
end FIRST_EXCEPTION;
```

Listing 12.1 This demonstrates the effect of a CONSTRAINT_ERROR.

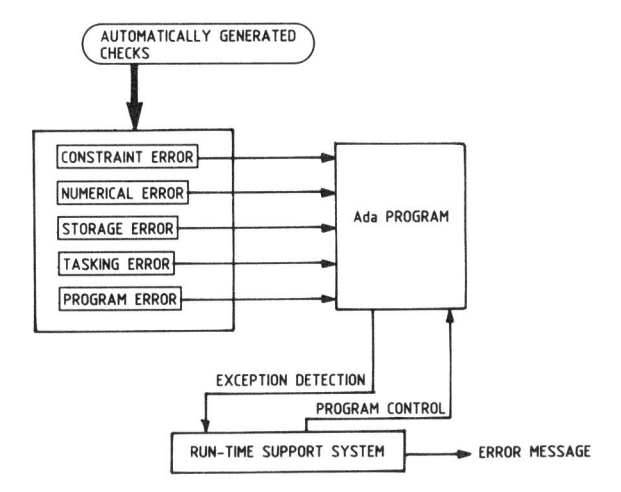

Fig.12.2 Operations involving predefined exceptions.

(b) NUMERIC_ERROR

The results of mathematical operations are the source of the exception NUMERIC_ERROR. One of the most often-quoted examples is the divide-by-zero problem. Be aware that it isn't always easy to differentiate between constraint and numeric errors.

(c) PROGRAM_ERROR

PROGRAM_ERROR exceptions are concerned essentially with attempts to run programs which have not been correctly implemented. For instance, this exception is raised if a call is made to a subprogram whose body has not been elaborated. Consider this to be a do-all exception.

(d) STORAGE_ERROR

If the computer system runs out of available memory at any time it generates a STORAGE_ERROR exception. This is particularly important when using dynamic variables.

(e) TASKING_ERROR

This will be discussed when tasks are covered, see chapter 14.

When an Ada program is compiled the compiler automatically generates checks for these exceptions, as and when required (Fig.12.2).

If one of these exceptions is detected, control is transferred to the run-time support system. Information relating to the type of exception is also passed to this system. What the support system does with this varies from implementation to implementation. The most usual response is that the system:

- Halts the program which is being executed;
- Generates an appropriate screen text message;
- Returns control of the computer to the keyboard operator.

In more sophisticated development environments logging of the error conditions may take place. These logs can be used for post-mortem analysis of the error conditions (and possibly conditions leading up to the raising of the exception).

There is one important point to be gleaned from this section. You, the programmer, have no control over system exception handling in these circumstances.

12.2.3 Introducing the exception handler

If you haven't already done so, run the program of Listing 12.1 and enter an out-of-range number. You will probably end up with a message similar to

CONSTRAINT_ERROR raised

All we can glean from this is that a constraint error occurred; we have no information detailing the source of the problem. For the example here it's pretty obvious what caused the exception. But practical programs are very much larger than this, and the sources of errors in such software can be extremely difficult to pinpoint. Thus, when an exception does occur, it can be very helpful if information specific to that exception is generated. That is where the exception handler comes into use. Using this construct, the programmer, not the system, defines the response to exception conditions.

The exception handler is the last section of code in a program unit, Fig.12.3.

It is located after the reserved word **exception**. After this, opening with **when**, we specify the exception that will be handled. Then the desired response is programmed, its beginning denoted by the symbol => (assume, for the moment, that only one exception is managed). Everything between **exception** and **end**; is defined to be the exception handler. An important point is that exception handling operations apply only to the unit in which the handler is located.

Let us now consider a few examples which illustrate these basic points (we strongly recommend that all these examples be compiled and run).

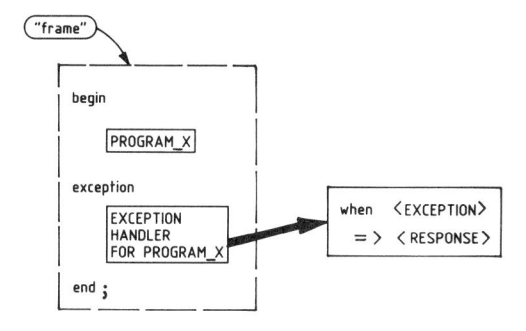

Fig.12.3 The exception handler.

```
with TEXT_IO;
procedure HANDLED_EXCEPTION is
   package INT_IO is new TEXT_IO.INTEGER_IO (INTEGER);
   X1            :     INTEGER range 0..50;
begin
   TEXT_IO.PUT ("Enter X1 => ");
   INT_IO.GET (X1);
   -- if value < 0 or > 50 then exception raised here !
   TEXT_IO.SKIP_LINE;
   TEXT_IO.PUT_LINE ("Program finished");
exception
   when CONSTRAINT_ERROR =>
      TEXT_IO.PUT_LINE ("The value entered for X1 was not in the range 0..50");
end HANDLED_EXCEPTION;
```

Listing 12.2 This demonstrates the detection of CONSTRAINT_ERRORs and their handling by an exception handler.

(a) Single exception

Listing 12.2 is a simplified version of Listing 12.1, used to demonstrate CONSTRAINT_ERROR exceptions. This version, however, includes an exception handler.

To generate a CONSTRAINT_ERROR enter a value for X1 outside its defined range, and observe the resulting response. The sequence of events looks like:

```
Enter X1 => 60
The value entered for X1 was not in the range 0..50
```

372 Exceptions

```
with TEXT_IO;
procedure BLOCK_EXCEPTION is
  package INT_IO is new TEXT_IO.INTEGER_IO (INTEGER);
  X1              :      INTEGER range 0..50;
begin
  begin
    TEXT_IO.PUT ("Enter X1 => ");
    INT_IO.GET (X1);
 -- if value < 0 or > 50 then exception raised here!
    TEXT_IO.SKIP_LINE;
    TEXT_IO.PUT_LINE ("This line is never reached if the exception is raised");
  exception
    when CONSTRAINT_ERROR =>
       TEXT_IO.PUT_LINE ("The value entered for X1 was not in the range 0..50");
  end;
  -- of block
  TEXT_IO.PUT_LINE ("Program finished");
end BLOCK_EXCEPTION;
```

Listing 12.3 This shows exception handling within a block structure.

(b) Exceptions within a block structure

Let us extend this example by changing the frame from that of a main program to that of a block structure, Listing 12.3.

Compile and run this program. When an exception occurs the following text should be written to the screen:

```
The value entered for X1 was not in the range 0..50
Program finished
```

This clearly demonstrates that once an exception has been raised program control passes to the exception handler for that block. Control then passes to the outer (surrounding) unit as though the block had completed as normal. The outer unit then runs to completion.

(c) Two exception possibilities – same type

Listing 12.4 is based on Listing 12.1 in that it allows us to enter two values from the keyboard.

Either entry can generate a CONSTRAINT_ERROR exception. The resulting screen displays in the event of such errors are:

```
X1 in error ---> CONSTRAINT ERROR raised when entering that number
X2 in error ---> CONSTRAINT ERROR raised when entering that number
```

Dealing with exceptions – the Ada way   373

```
with TEXT_IO;
procedure TWO_EXCEPTIONS_GLOBAL_HANDLER is
  package INT_IO is new TEXT_IO.INTEGER_IO (INTEGER);
  X1           :       INTEGER range 0..50;
  X2           :       INTEGER range 50..100;
begin
  TEXT_IO.PUT ("Enter X1 => ");
  INT_IO.GET (X1);
  -- if value < 0 or > 50 then exception raised here!
  TEXT_IO.SKIP_LINE;
  TEXT_IO.PUT ("Enter X2 => ");
  INT_IO.GET (X2);
  -- if value < 50 or > 100 then exception raised here!
  TEXT_IO.SKIP_LINE;
  TEXT_IO.PUT_LINE ("Program finished");
exception
  when CONSTRAINT_ERROR =>
    TEXT_IO.PUT_LINE ("CONSTRAINT_ERROR raised when entering that number");
end TWO_EXCEPTIONS_GLOBAL_HANDLER;
```

Listing 12.4 This demonstrates the detection of a CONSTRAINT_ERROR at more than one point in a program.

There are two reasons for using this example. First, it shows that a single handler is used for any specific error type – no matter how many times it occurs in a program. Second, it demonstrates that you may be able to handle errors but you can't always tell where they occurred.

(d) Two different predefined exceptions

Listing 12.5 shows how we deal with, say, both a CONSTRAINT_ERROR and a NUMERIC_ERROR.

Here we have introduced two exception handlers, one for each error. Should a specific exception arise it activates its associated handler, printing out the relevant text message.

Now run this program and instigate errors. You will find that only one of these text messages is ever printed out, followed by the system message. Note this well. Only one handler in the list is ever activated. On its completion, control transfers out of the program unit.

It is possible to have one handler activated by either exception – without having to repeat the code. We use the construct

> **when** CONSTRAINT_ERROR | NUMERIC_ERROR =>

Here we've used the vertical bar (like that of the **case** statement) to mean OR. It therefore seems logical that we should be able to use the **when others**

374 Exceptions

```
with TEXT_IO;              use TEXT_IO;
procedure TWO_DIFFERENT_EXCEPTIONS is
  package INT_IO is new INTEGER_IO (INTEGER);
  X1              :    INTEGER range 0..50;
  X2              :    INTEGER;
begin
  X2 := INTEGER'LAST;
  PUT ("Enter X1 => ");
  INT_IO.GET (X1);
  -- if value < 0 or > 50 then constraint exception
  -- raised here!
  SKIP_LINE;
  X2 := X2 + X1;
  -- if X1 > 0 the numeric error raised here as the
  -- result is outside the physical bounds of the type
  PUT_LINE ("Program finished");
exception
  when CONSTRAINT_ERROR =>
    PUT_LINE ("CONSTRAINT_ERROR raised");
    PUT_LINE ("Number entered did not fall in the range 0..50");
  when NUMERIC_ERROR =>
    PUT_LINE ("NUMERIC_ERROR from addition of X1 and X2");
end TWO_DIFFERENT_EXCEPTIONS;
```

Listing 12.5 This demonstrates the detection and handling of a CONSTRAINT_ERROR and a NUMERIC_ERROR using two exception handlers.

clause. This is demonstrated in Listing 12.6. Observe that, as in previous usage, it must be the last one, and on its own (i.e. not combined with others using the ';' symbol).

This example also demonstrates a very useful feature of exception handling. Because the **when others** clause is included, any exception will be handled. That is, all exception responses are controlled by the programmer. Using this we can avoid what, in other circumstances, would result in program abortion.

Six important points to note are that:

- An exception handler can only be located within specific program units (called frames, LRM section 11.2);
- It responds only to exceptions raised within this frame (but a frame may have nested items – see later);
- It must be the last construct within the frame;
- When an exception occurs control immediately passes to the exception handler (this assumes, of course, that the exception can be handled);
- When the handler has finished executing, control is passed beyond the frame;
- If an exception hasn't got a related handler, it (the exception) is propagated to the enclosing unit. This point is dealt with in detail later.

Dealing with exceptions – the Ada way   375

```
with TEXT_IO;              use TEXT_IO;
procedure WHEN_OTHERS is
  package INT_IO is new INTEGER_IO (INTEGER);
  X1             :     INTEGER range 0..50;
  X2             :     INTEGER;
begin
  X2 := INTEGER'LAST;
  PUT ("Enter X1 => ");
  INT_IO.GET (X1);
  -- if value < 0 or > 50 then constraint exception
  -- raised here!
  SKIP_LINE;
  X2 := X2 + X1;
  -- if X1 > 0 the numeric error raised here as the
  -- result is outside the physical bounds of the type
  PUT_LINE ("Program finished");
exception
  when CONSTRAINT_ERROR =>
    PUT_LINE ("CONSTRAINT_ERROR raised");
    PUT_LINE ("Number entered did not fall in the range 0..50");
  when others =>
    PUT_LINE ("An exception has been raised that has no explicit handler");
end WHEN_OTHERS;
```

Listing 12.6 This demonstrates the use of the 'when others' clause in an exception handler.

12.2.4 User-defined exceptions

Now let us devise our own exception mechanisms. There is nothing new to be said concerning the exception handler; its structure and use is unchanged. However, the raising of the exception is now our responsibility. After all, how can we expect the program to detect exceptions about which it knows nothing? Also, we need to inform the compiler of the existence of the exception. Taking all this into account, we end up with the general structure shown in Fig.12.4.

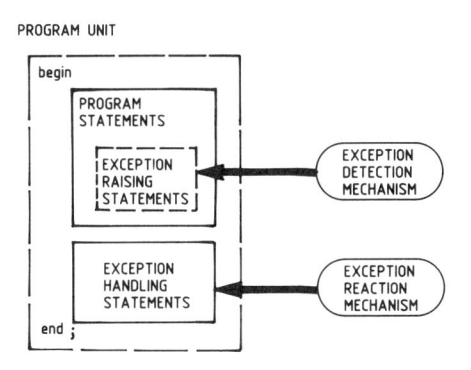

Fig.12.4 Programmed exception mechanism.

```
┌─────────────────────────┐
│  ┌─────────────────┐    │
│  │ DECLARATION OF  │───▶ <NAME_OF_EXCEPTION>: exception ;
│  │ EXCEPTION       │    │
│  └─────────────────┘    │
│  begin                  │
│    ┌───────────────┐    │
│    │TEST FOR EXCEPTION│─▶ if <CONDITION> then
│    │RAISE EXCEPTION│───▶ raise <NAME_OF_EXCEPTION>
│    └───────────────┘    │
│  exception              │
│    ┌───────────────┐    │
│    │HANDLE EXCEPTION│──▶ when <NAME OF EXCEPTION>
│    └───────────────┘      => <RESPONSE>
│  end ;                  │
└─────────────────────────┘
```

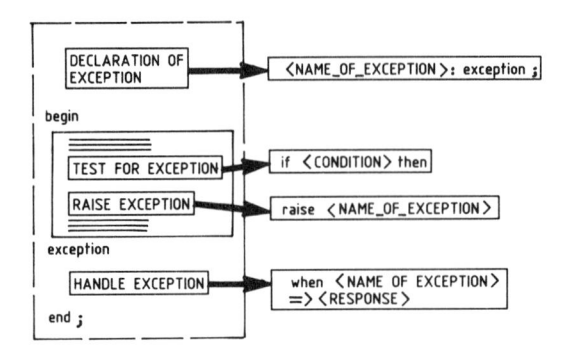

Fig.12.5 Programmed exception mechanism (detailed aspects).

The detailed aspects of this are given in Fig.12.5.

Its form and usage is demonstrated in Listing 12.7, the outline skeleton being

```
declare
    OVERSPEED_ALARM : exception;
begin
    if SPEED >= MAX_SPEED then
        raise OVERSPEED_ALARM;
    end if;
exception
    when OVERSPEED_ALARM =>
        .............................................
end;
```

It should be clear that the test condition used is defined by the programmer.

The declaration format of an exception is much the same as that for a variable. However, these program items are very different beasts. Unlike a variable an exception is not an object – it is a name denoting something. Thus we can't assign values to it, pass it as a parameter or use it in expressions, etc. In fact, the exception name can only be used in a very limited number of places. We will restrict ourselves to using it with **raise** and **when**.

A small, but important, feature of exceptions should be noted. When we declare an exception, its meaning is determined at compile time. Thus it is a static item.

12.2.5 Raising predefined exceptions

Predefined exceptions are normally raised automatically. However, they may also be raised by the programmer, as shown in Listing 12.8.

```ada
with TEXT_IO;                 use TEXT_IO;
procedure USER_DEFINED_EXCEPTION is
  package INT_IO is new INTEGER_IO (INTEGER);
  SPEED             :    INTEGER range 0..130;
  MAX_SPEED         :    constant INTEGER := 70;
begin
  PUT_LINE ("Enter 0 to finish");
  loop
    PUT ("Enter current speed => ");
    INT_IO.GET (SPEED);
 -- if value < 0 or > 130 then constraint exception
 -- raised here!
    SKIP_LINE;
    exit when SPEED = 0;
    declare
      OVERSPEED_ALARM :    exception;
    begin
      if SPEED >= MAX_SPEED then
        raise OVERSPEED_ALARM;
      end if;
      PUT ("Current speed => ");
      INT_IO.PUT (SPEED);
      NEW_LINE;
    exception
      when OVERSPEED_ALARM =>
        PUT_LINE ("Exceeded maximum speed, re-set to 70");
        SPEED := 70;
    end;
  end loop;
  PUT_LINE ("Program finished");
exception
  when CONSTRAINT_ERROR =>
    PUT_LINE ("CONSTRAINT_ERROR raised");
    PUT_LINE ("Number entered did not fall in the range 0..130");
    PUT_LINE ("Program terminated abnormally");
end USER_DEFINED_EXCEPTION;
```

Listing 12.7 The implementation of a user-defined exception mechanism.

We recommend that this should be avoided as it has one major drawback. If such an exception handler is invoked, we don't necessarily know what activated it. It may have been our programmed check, but equally well it may, in some cases, have been a compiler-generated one.

12.3 FRAME CONSTRUCTS – SUBPROGRAMS AND PACKAGES

12.3.1 Introduction

So far we have seen the exception handler used in two forms of program unit: a main program and a block nested within a main program. Now we will

```ada
with TEXT_IO;                    use TEXT_IO;
procedure RAISING_PREDEFINED_EXCEPTIONS is
  package INT_IO is new INTEGER_IO (INTEGER);
  SPEED              :    INTEGER range 0..130;
  MAX_SPEED          :    constant INTEGER := 70;
begin
  PUT ("Enter current speed => ");
  INT_IO.GET (SPEED);
  -- if value < 0 or > 130 then constraint error
  -- raised here!
  SKIP_LINE;
  if SPEED >= MAX_SPEED then
    raise CONSTRAINT_ERROR;
  -- raise our own constraint error. Bad practice!
  end if;
  PUT_LINE ("Program finished");
exception
  when CONSTRAINT_ERROR =>
    PUT_LINE ("CONSTRAINT_ERROR raised");
    PUT_LINE ("In a large program this would be difficult to find");
    PUT_LINE ("Advise against raising predefined exceptions");
end RAISING_PREDEFINED_EXCEPTIONS;
```

Listing 12.8 Raising of a predefined exception by the programmer.

look at the use of exception handlers with procedures, functions and packages. The object is to demonstrate clearly what happens once the exception handler has completed its programmed response. More will be said on this topic when we look at the propagation of exceptions.

12.3.2 Exceptions in procedures

The main program of Listing 12.9 calls a procedure (GET_SPEED) which contains an exception handler.

In fact it calls the procedure twice to bring out clearly the response of the program to exceptions. When the program is run there are four possible outcomes:

- No exceptions.
- Exception raised during the first call of the procedure.
- Exception raised during the second call of the procedure.
- Exceptions raised during both calls of the procedure.

The screen text corresponding to each scenario is given below. Italics are used to indicate keyboard responses.

```
with TEXT_IO;                  use TEXT_IO;
procedure EXCEPTION_IN_A_PROCEDURE is
  package INT_IO is new INTEGER_IO (INTEGER);
  SPEED            :       INTEGER;
  MAX_SPEED        :       constant INTEGER := 70;
  procedure GET_SPEED (CALL_NUMBER  : in     INTEGER) is
    OVERSPEED_ALARM :     exception;
  begin
    PUT ("Enter Speed => ");
    INT_IO.GET (SPEED);
    SKIP_LINE;
    if SPEED >= MAX_SPEED then
      raise OVERSPEED_ALARM;
    end if;
    INT_IO.PUT (CALL_NUMBER,0);
  -- 0 to get rid of blank spaces
    PUT_LINE (":OKAY");
  exception
    when OVERSPEED_ALARM =>
      INT_IO.PUT (CALL_NUMBER,0);
      PUT_LINE (":ERROR");
  end GET_SPEED;
begin
  GET_SPEED (CALL_NUMBER => 1);
  GET_SPEED (CALL_NUMBER => 2);
  PUT_LINE ("Program finished");
end EXCEPTION_IN_A_PROCEDURE;
```

Listing 12.9 Using an exception handler in a procedure.

NO EXCEPTIONS	ON FIRST CALL	ON SECOND CALL	ON BOTH CALLS
Enter Speed =>	Enter Speed =>	Enter Speed =>	Enter Speed =>
key entry reply	key entry reply	key entry reply	key entry reply
20	100	69	110
1:OKAY	1:ERROR	1:OKAY	1:ERROR
Enter Speed =>	Enter Speed =>	Enter Speed =>	Enter Speed =>
key entry reply	key entry reply	key entry reply	key entry reply
30	50	70	120
2:OKAY	2:OKAY	2:ERROR	2:ERROR
Program finished	Program finished	Program finished	Program finished

From this it should be clear that control is passed back to the calling program to the point immediately after the procedure call.

12.3.3 Exceptions in functions

The main program of Listing 12.10 calls a function (GET_NEW_SPEED) which contains an exception handler.

Its reaction to an exception is initially the same as that of the procedure. When the error is detected, the exception is raised and control is transferred

380 Exceptions

```
with TEXT_IO;                use TEXT_IO;
procedure FIRST_FUNCTION_EXCEPTION is
  package INT_IO is new INTEGER_IO (INTEGER);
  SPEED          :       INTEGER             := 0;
  MAX_SPEED      :       constant INTEGER := 70;
  function GET_NEW_SPEED (CALL_NUMBER : in     INTEGER)
    return INTEGER is
    NEW_SPEED        :        INTEGER;
    OVERSPEED_ALARM :        exception;
  begin
    PUT ("Enter new Speed => ");
    INT_IO.GET (NEW_SPEED);
    SKIP_LINE;
    if NEW_SPEED >= MAX_SPEED then
      raise OVERSPEED_ALARM;
    end if;
    return (NEW_SPEED);
  exception
    when OVERSPEED_ALARM =>
      INT_IO.PUT (CALL_NUMBER);
      PUT_LINE (":ERROR");
  -- PROGRAM_ERROR raised here!
  end GET_NEW_SPEED;
begin
  SPEED := GET_NEW_SPEED (CALL_NUMBER => 1);
  INT_IO.PUT (SPEED);
  NEW_LINE;
  SPEED := GET_NEW_SPEED (CALL_NUMBER => 2);
  INT_IO.PUT (SPEED);
  NEW_LINE;
  PUT_LINE ("Program finished");
end FIRST_FUNCTION_EXCEPTION;
```

Listing 12.10 Using an exception handler in a function. The handler does not contain a return statement.

to the error handler. However, the final action of the handler is – surprise – to raise the predefined exception PROGRAM_ERROR. The reason for this? We haven't included a **return** statement in the exception handler. A moment's thought shows that this makes sense. After all, a function has to return some result if the program is to continue running.

Listing 12.11 shows how to remedy this mistake by including a **return** statement in the exception handler.

12.3.4 Exceptions in packages

Here we will look at what happens when exceptions occur in packages. However, we have to be very careful when we discuss and evaluate this problem. Our discussion here is quite specific – it considers the package as

```
with TEXT_IO;                  use TEXT_IO;
procedure SECOND_FUNCTION_EXCEPTION is
  package INT_IO is new INTEGER_IO (INTEGER);
  SPEED          :      INTEGER               := 0;
  MAX_SPEED      :      constant INTEGER := 70;
  function GET_NEW_SPEED (CALL_NUMBER : in       INTEGER)
    return INTEGER is
    NEW_SPEED        :       INTEGER;
    OVERSPEED_ALARM :        exception;
  begin
    PUT ("Enter new Speed => ");
    INT_IO.GET (NEW_SPEED);
    SKIP_LINE;
    if NEW_SPEED >= MAX_SPEED then
      raise OVERSPEED_ALARM;
    end if;
    return (NEW_SPEED);
  exception
    when OVERSPEED_ALARM =>
      INT_IO.PUT (CALL_NUMBER);
      PUT_LINE (":ERROR");
      return (MAX_SPEED);
  end GET_NEW_SPEED;
begin
  SPEED := GET_NEW_SPEED (CALL_NUMBER => 1);
  INT_IO.PUT (SPEED);
  NEW_LINE;
  SPEED := GET_NEW_SPEED (CALL_NUMBER => 2);
  INT_IO.PUT (SPEED);
  NEW_LINE;
  PUT_LINE ("Program finished");
end SECOND_FUNCTION_EXCEPTION;
```

Listing 12.11 Using a 'return' statement in a function's exception handler.

a means of building library facilities. In this role it is a separately compilable program unit, but essentially it is not – in its own right – an executable unit. Primarily it provides resources to users. Thus we need to show what happens when an exported item raises an exception. We also need to investigate the raising of exceptions during package elaboration. This will be dealt with first and then the other cases will be evaluated.

(a) **Raising an exception during package elaboration**

Exceptions can occur in two places during package elaboration: the declarative region and the initialization code. We will deal only with initialization errors for the moment. Declarative errors are discussed separately in section 12.7.

Here we include an exception handler in the initialization code of a package (MESSED_UP), Listing 12.12. For demonstration purposes an error is deliberately induced.

```
package MESSED_UP is
  procedure TEST_1;
end MESSED_UP;

with TEXT_IO;            use TEXT_IO;
package body MESSED_UP is
  procedure TEST_1 is
  begin
    PUT_LINE ("TEST_1 is running");
  end TEST_1;
begin
  raise CONSTRAINT_ERROR;
  PUT_LINE ("Elaborated MESSED_UP");
exception
  when others =>
    PUT_LINE ("We have an initialisation problem");
end MESSED_UP;
```

Listing 12.12 Exception handling in a package initialization section.

```
with TEXT_IO;            use TEXT_IO;
with MESSED_UP;
procedure ELABORATION_EXCEPTION is
begin
  PUT_LINE ("Starting main program");
  PUT_LINE ("Now calling the procedure TEST_1");
  MESSED_UP.TEST_1;
  PUT_LINE ("Finishing the main program");
end ELABORATION_EXCEPTION;
```

Listing 12.13 Using the package of Listing 12.12.

The package contains a single procedure, 'TEST_1', invoked by the program ELABORATION_EXCEPTION of Listing 12.13.

Of course, to do this we have to import package MESSED_UP into program ELABORATION_EXCEPTION (using **with**). When we run ELABORATION_EXCEPTION, package MESSED_UP is elaborated, executing its initialization code. As we have deliberately forced an exception to take place, the resulting screen display is

```
We have an initialisation problem
Starting main program
Now calling the procedure TEST_1
TEST_1 is running
Finishing the main program
```

Frame constructs – subprograms and packages 383

```
package MESSED_UP is
  procedure TEST_1;
end MESSED_UP;

with TEXT_IO;                    use TEXT_IO;
package body MESSED_UP is
  procedure TEST_1 is
    X1                  :        INTEGER;
    X2                  :        INTEGER;
  begin
    X1 := 1;
    X2 := INTEGER'LAST;
    X2 := X1 + X2;
    PUT_LINE ("TEST_1 is running");
  exception
    when others =>
      PUT_LINE ("TEST_1 is faulty");
  end TEST_1;
begin
  -- package elaboration code
  PUT_LINE ("Elaborated MESSED_UP");
end MESSED_UP;
```

Listing 12.14 A modified version of Listing 12.12. Exception handling in a package procedure.

(b) Raising an exception in a package procedure

Let us now modify Listing 12.12 to:

- Remove the exception cause and handler from the initialization code.
- Insert an exception cause and handler into procedure TEST_1.

This is shown in Listing 12.14.

If we now use this with the main program ELABORATION_EXCEPTION, and then run ELABORATION_EXCEPTION, the following print-out is produced:

```
Elaborated MESSED_UP
Starting main program
Now calling the procedure TEST_1
TEST_1 is faulty
Finishing the main program
```

This response from the procedure exception handler is fully consistent with that obtained earlier.

384 Exceptions

```
package MESSED_UP is
  procedure TEST_1;
end MESSED_UP;

with TEXT_IO;              use TEXT_IO;
package body MESSED_UP is
  procedure TEST_1 is
    X1              :      INTEGER;
    X2              :      INTEGER;
  begin
    X1 := 1;
    X2 := INTEGER'LAST;
    X2 := X1 + X2;
    PUT_LINE ("TEST_1 is running");
  exception
    when others =>
      PUT_LINE ("TEST_1 is faulty");
  end TEST_1;
begin
  -- package elaboration code
  raise CONSTRAINT_ERROR;
  PUT_LINE ("Elaborated MESSED_UP");
exception
  when others =>
    PUT_LINE ("We have an initialisation problem");
end MESSED_UP;
```

Listing 12.15 A modified version of Listing 12.14 incorporating two exception handlers.

(c) Two exception handlers – combining cases (a) and (b)

Listing 12.15 is a revised version of Listing 12.14.

Note that we have installed both exception handlers. We have also caused an error in both the elaboration (initialization) code and the procedure TEXT_1 When this is used by ELABORATION_EXCEPTION the result is

```
We have an initialisation problem
Starting main program
Now calling the procedure TEST_1
TEST_1 is faulty
Finishing the main program
```

12.4 SCOPE AND VISIBILITY ASPECTS

The concepts of scope and visibility of declared items were covered earlier in chapter 4. Revise this if necessary. Generally the same rules of scoping and

```
with TEXT_IO;              use TEXT_IO;
procedure EXCEPTION_IN_A_PROCEDURE is
  package INT_IO is new INTEGER_IO (INTEGER);
  SPEED           :   INTEGER;
  MAX_SPEED       :   constant INTEGER := 70;
  -- change from 12.9. Exception we declared local to the procedure GET_VALUE
  OVERSPEED_ALARM :   exception;
  procedure GET_SPEED  (CALL_NUMBER : in      INTEGER) is
  begin
    PUT ("Enter Speed => ");
    INT_IO.GET (SPEED);
    SKIP_LINE;
    if SPEED >= MAX_SPEED then
      raise OVERSPEED_ALARM;
    end if;
    INT_IO.PUT (CALL_NUMBER,0);
  -- 0 to get rid of blank spaces
    PUT_LINE (":OKAY");
  exception
    when OVERSPEED_ALARM =>
      INT_IO.PUT (CALL_NUMBER,0);
      PUT_LINE (":ERROR");
  end GET_SPEED;
begin
  GET_SPEED (CALL_NUMBER => 1);
  GET_SPEED (CALL_NUMBER => 2);
  PUT_LINE ("Program finished");
end EXCEPTION_IN_A_PROCEDURE;
```

Listing 12.16 A modified version of Listing 12.9 declaring an exception at an outer level, having a handler in the inner frame.

visibility apply to exceptions (more strictly we should call them exception identifiers). Review Listing 12.9. Here the exception is declared in the innermost program unit. Everything works fine because we use it only within this unit, but if we tried to raise it in the main program it would fail at compilation time because scoping rules have been broken.

Now, however, amend Listing 12.9 so that the exception is declared at the main program level (Listing 12.16).

You should find that it will compile without problems. Further, at run time, its behaviour will be identical to that of the original version.

If we choose to, we can hide an exception declaration: merely declare one having the same name in an inner program unit. Dot notation can, of course, always be used to make items visible again. Nevertheless, we recommend that all exception handling should be done as simply and as clearly as possible. After all, the whole reason for having exceptions is to handle potentially disastrous situations at run time. The last thing we want to do is to complicate programs at such critical times.

12.5 PROPAGATION OF EXCEPTIONS

12.5.1 Overview

What do we mean by 'propagating an exception'? It describes the situation where an exception is raised within a program unit – but the unit does not handle it. Up to now all our examples have included matched exception raising and handling operations. Suppose we fail to include the handler. What then? The answer is that the exception condition is passed out of the unit in which it was raised – and into its surrounding unit. If there is a handler for the exception at this level then it will, of course, be handled. If not, then the exception is once more passed up a level. This continues until either we reach a handler or the run-time support system is activated. These points are best illustrated by example.

Before doing this a brief comment needs to be made concerning scope and visibility. An exception, when it is propagated, produces some effect. Therefore it is in scope. But that doesn't mean that it is necessarily visible, and it must be visible if it is to be handled. This distinction will become clear in a moment. Note the significant difference between the scoping rules for exceptions and those concerning other program items. The scope of 'normal' items never extends outwards.

12.5.2 Propagation of exceptions from a block

Modify Listing 12.7 so that:

- The exception is declared at the main program level;
- The exception handler is moved from the block to the main program level.

This is shown in Listing 12.17.

Two possible responses at run time are

No exception
Enter current speed => 50 Current speed => 50 Program finished

Exception raised
Enter current speed => 100 Maximum speed exceeded

You can see that when an exception is raised we (Fig.12.6):

- Immediately exit the block and return to the outer unit with the exception raised.

```
with TEXT_IO;                  use TEXT_IO;
procedure EXCEPTION_PROPAGATION is
  package INT_IO is new INTEGER_IO (INTEGER);
  SPEED            :      INTEGER range 0..130 :=  0;
  MAX_SPEED        :      constant INTEGER     := 70;
  OVERSPEED_ALARM  :      exception;
begin
  PUT ("Enter current speed => ");
  INT_IO.GET (SPEED);
  SKIP_LINE;
  begin
  -- block
     if SPEED >= MAX_SPEED then
        raise OVERSPEED_ALARM;
     end if;
     PUT ("Current speed => ");
     INT_IO.PUT (SPEED);
     NEW_LINE;
  end;
  -- block
  PUT_LINE ("Program finished");
exception
  when OVERSPEED_ALARM =>
     PUT_LINE ("Maximum speed exceeded");
end EXCEPTION_PROPAGATION;
```

Listing 12.17 A modified version of Listing 12.7 declaring an exception at an outer level, also having a handler at this level. The exception is raised in the inner block.

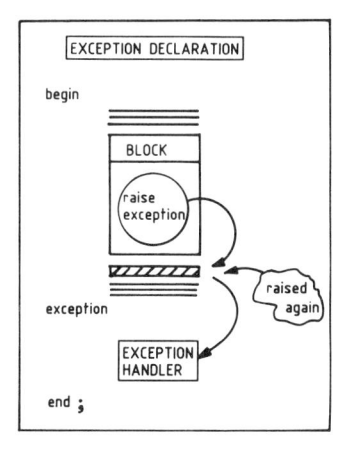

Fig.12.6 Propagation of exceptions from a block.

388 Exceptions

```
RUN-TIME SYSTEM
    procedure MAIN is
        EXCEPTION DECLARATION
    begin
        ═══════
        BLOCK
            raise
            exception
        ▰▰▰▰▰▰▰
        ═══════
        NO EXCEPTION
        HANDLER
    end
    exception
        when CONSTRAINT_ERROR =>
        when NUMERIC_ERROR =>
            •
            •
            •
        when others =>
end RUN-TIME SYSTEM
```

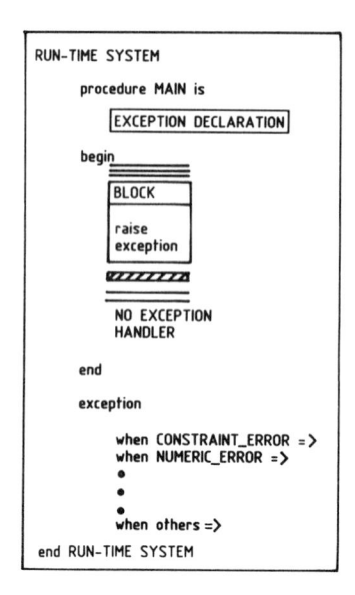

Fig.12.7 Conceptual view of the run-time system.

- Do not execute any statements, but look for the exception handler.
- Enter and execute the handler.

Now modify Listing 12.17 by removing the exception handler. Recompile and run the program. Observe the response when we introduce an error condition. You should find that the complete program aborts once the exception is raised, control being returned to the run-time system. What happened was that when control returned to the outer unit it was unable to handle the exception. It therefore passed control up one level – in this case to the run-time system. You can view this system as being an invisible outermost procedure that calls your main procedure. It always has exception handlers for predefined exceptions (Fig.12.7).

12.5.3 Propagation of exceptions from a subprogram

Listing 12.18 is a modified version of Listing 12.9; the handler has now been located in the procedure calling unit.

When the program is run there are now three (not four) possible outcomes:

- No exceptions;
- Exception raised during the first call of the procedure;
- Exception raised during the second call of the procedure.

```
with TEXT_IO;                    use TEXT_IO;
procedure SUBPROGRAM_EXCEPTION_PROPAGATION is
  package INT_IO is new INTEGER_IO (INTEGER);
  SPEED            :       INTEGER;
  MAX_SPEED        :       constant INTEGER := 70;
  OVERSPEED_ALARM :        exception;
  procedure GET_SPEED (CALL_NUMBER:       INTEGER) is
  begin
    PUT ("Enter Speed => ");
    INT_IO.GET (SPEED);
    SKIP_LINE;
    if SPEED >= MAX_SPEED then
      raise OVERSPEED_ALARM;
    end if;
    INT_IO.PUT (CALL_NUMBER,0);
  -- 0 width reduces unwanted spaces
    PUT_LINE (":OKAY");
  end GET_SPEED;
begin
  GET_SPEED (CALL_NUMBER => 1);
  GET_SPEED (CALL_NUMBER => 2);
  PUT_LINE ("Program Finished");
exception
  when OVERSPEED_ALARM =>
    PUT_LINE (":ERROR");
end SUBPROGRAM_EXCEPTION_PROPAGATION;
```

Listing 12.18 A modified version of Listing 12.9 declaring an exception at an outer level, also having a handler at this level. The exception is raised in a called procedure.

It is impossible to make a second call to the subprogram if it raises an exception on the first call (Fig.12.8).

The example of the screen text corresponding to each scenario is

NO EXCEPTIONS	ON FIRST CALL	ON SECOND CALL
Enter Speed =>	Enter Speed =>	Enter Speed =>
Key entry reply	Key entry reply	Key entry reply
50	150	30
1:OKAY	ERROR	1:OKAY
Enter Speed =>	Program finished	Enter Speed =>
Key entry reply		Key entry reply
45		99
2:OKAY		ERROR
Program finished		Program finished

This brings up an interesting point. Can we tell, by looking at the response of the exception handler, which call produced the exception? No, we can't, unless we build extra code (flags or indicators) into our ('normal') program. This is left as an example for the reader to experiment with.

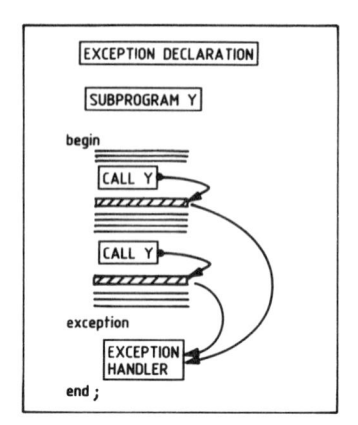

Fig.12.8 Propagation of exceptions from a subprogram.

12.5.4 Exporting an exception from a package

We can, if we wish, export an exception from a package. The purpose is to allow the user (importer) of the package freedom to choose the resulting responses. In the example of Listing 12.19 we have a package (specification and body) named MESSED_UP.

```
package MESSED_UP is
  EXPORTED_EXCEPTION : exception;
  procedure TEST_1;
end MESSED_UP;

package body MESSED_UP is
  procedure TEST_1 is
  begin
    raise EXPORTED_EXCEPTION;
  end TEST_1;
end MESSED_UP;
```

Listing 12.19 Exporting an exception from a package.

Within the specification we declare an exception EXPORTED_EXCEPTION. Procedure TEST_1 raises this exception, but does not have an associated handler.

In Listing 12.20 we have the client (importer) of package MESSED_UP.

This does contain an exception handler, for the exception EXPORTED_EXCEPTION. When this is executed the following screen text appears:

```
with TEXT_IO;                use TEXT_IO;
with MESSED_UP;
procedure IMPORTED_EXCEPTION is
begin
  PUT_LINE ("Starting main program");
  PUT_LINE ("Now calling the procedure TEST_1");
  MESSED_UP.TEST_1;
  PUT_LINE ("Finishing the main program");
exception
  when MESSED_UP.EXPORTED_EXCEPTION =>
    PUT_LINE ("Handled exception raised in MESSED_UP.TEST_1");
end IMPORTED_EXCEPTION;
```

Listing 12.20 Using an imported exception.

```
Starting main program
Now calling the procedure TEST_1
Handled exception raised in MESSED_UP.TEST_1
```

12.5.5 Propagation of exceptions from a package

How are exceptions propagated from a package? Before answering that, we must first define the package type in question. Here we limit ourselves to library packages, these being the most useful ones. The second point to be made is that such packages are used mainly as holders for subprograms. Now, you will recall that unhandled subprogram exceptions always propagate back into their calling programs. Naturally enough this applies to exceptions raised by subprograms contained within packages. From that point of view it is the subprogram, not the package itself, which raises the exception. Consequently, our discussion here applies to exceptions which occur during elaboration (see also section 12.7).

If, during elaboration, a library package raises an exception, the main program is abandoned. Control then returns to the run-time system. Note also that if an exception is raised whilst executing the initialization code – and there isn't an appropriate handler – then the same response occurs. This is demonstrated in Listings 12.25 and 12.26 (see later).

12.5.6 Anonymous exceptions

Examine the situation depicted in Fig.12.9.

Here we have declared and raised an exception in an inner program unit. We haven't, though, included its handler at this level; this is located in the

```
           OUTER PROGRAM UNIT - BETA
          ┌─────────────────────────────────┐
          │ begin                           │
          │     INNER PROGRAM UNIT - DELTA  │
          │   ┌───────────────────────────┐ │
          │   │                           │ │
          │   │     ═══════════════       │ │
          │   │     │DECLARE EXCEPTION│   │ │
          │   │   begin                   │ │
          │   │     ═══════════════       │ │
          │   │     │RAISE EXCEPTION│     │ │
          │   │     ═══════════════       │ │
          │   │                           │ │
          │   │   end ;                   │ │
          │   └───────────────────────────┘ │
          │       ┌───────────────────┐     │
          │       │ EXCEPTION HANDLER │     │
          │       └───────────────────┘     │
          │ end ;                           │
          └─────────────────────────────────┘
```

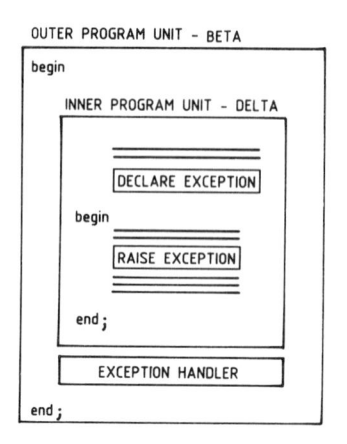

Fig. 12.9 Anonymous ('invisible') exceptions.

outer unit. Because the exception is declared in the inner unit its name cannot be used in the outer unit (although it is in scope it isn't visible). Suppose such an exception is raised. Because there isn't a handler in the inner unit it is immediately propagated to the outer unit. The outer unit realizes that an exception has occurred but it doesn't recognize its name. We say that it is 'anonymous'. The only way to deal with this is to use the **with others** clause, Listing 12.21.

12.5.7 Propagation and nested program units

Let's modify Listing 12.19 to give the structure shown in Fig.12.10 (Listing 12.22).

The exception, as before, is declared and raised in DELTA. This now propagates to BETA. BETA, however, doesn't have an exception handler, and so passes it on to ALPHA. ALPHA has the handler, treating the incoming exception as an anonymous one.

The propagation route in this example is simple. We can predict at compile time precisely what will happen when an exception is raised. Do not, though, be fooled by this simplicity. Consider where an exception occurs in a subprogram. Consider further where this subprogram is called in a number of places, and with different levels of nesting. In this situation the propagation path depends on when the exception is raised. Thus it is a run-time, dynamic event, not a compilation (static) one.

Now let's change the scenario of Fig.12.10 slightly. Declare the exception in the outer unit ALPHA, but raise it, as before, in DELTA. Provide ALPHA

```
with TEXT_IO;              use TEXT_IO;
procedure ANONYMOUS_EXCEPTION is
  package INT_IO is new INTEGER_IO (INTEGER);
  SPEED        :   INTEGER            :=  0;
  MAX_SPEED    :   constant INTEGER := 70;
begin
  PUT ("Enter current speed => ");
  INT_IO.GET (SPEED);
  SKIP_LINE;
  declare
    OVERSPEED_ALARM :   exception;
  begin
    if SPEED >= MAX_SPEED then
      raise OVERSPEED_ALARM;
 -- no exception handler.
    end if;
    PUT ("Current speed => ");
    INT_IO.PUT (SPEED);
    NEW_LINE;
  end;
  PUT_LINE ("Program finished");
exception
 -- cannot see OVERSPEED_ALARM as it's not visible.
 -- when OVERSPEED_ALARM => would cause a compiler error
 -- so we have to do  (as a catch all!) :-
  when others =>
    PUT_LINE ("Exception raised");
end ANONYMOUS_EXCEPTION;
```

Listing 12.21 Dealing with anonymous exceptions.

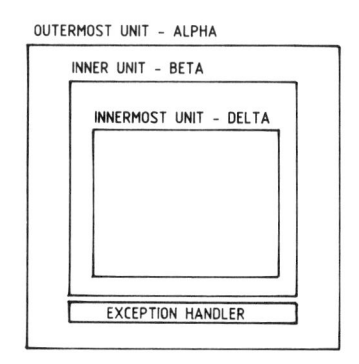

```
OUTERMOST UNIT - ALPHA
  INNER UNIT - BETA
    INNERMOST UNIT - DELTA


    EXCEPTION HANDLER
```

Fig.12.10 Nested program units.

394 Exceptions

```
with TEXT_IO;                use TEXT_IO;
procedure NESTED_EXCEPTIONS is
  package INT_IO is new INTEGER_IO (INTEGER);
  SPEED          :   INTEGER            :=  0;
  MAX_SPEED      :   constant INTEGER := 70;
begin
  ALPHA_BLOCK:
  begin
    PUT ("Enter current speed => ");
    INT_IO.GET (SPEED);
    SKIP_LINE;
    BETA_BLOCK:
    begin
      DELTA_BLOCK:
      declare
        OVERSPEED_ALARM :    exception;
      begin
        if SPEED >= MAX_SPEED then
          raise OVERSPEED_ALARM;
-- no exception handler.
      end if;
    end DELTA_BLOCK;
    PUT ("Current speed => ");
    INT_IO.PUT (SPEED);
    NEW_LINE;
  end BETA_BLOCK;
  exception
-- cannot see OVERSPEED_ALARM as it's not visible.
-- when OVERSPEED_ALARM => would cause a compiler error
-- so we have to do  (as a catch all!) :-
    when others =>
      PUT_LINE ("Exception caught in ALPHA_BLOCK");
  end ALPHA_BLOCK;
  PUT_LINE ("Program finished");
end NESTED_EXCEPTIONS;
```

Listing 12.22 Exceptions in nested units.

with the exception handler, as before. Now the exception name is visible in ALPHA, BETA and DELTA. Moreover, we can use it in the handler of ALPHA. When the exception is raised in DELTA it propagates to BETA. This in turn propagates it to ALPHA, where it is actioned by the handler. The difference now is that the exception handler can be an explicit one (naming the exception), not an anonymous one.

12.6 RAISING EXCEPTIONS IN THE EXCEPTION HANDLER

12.6.1 Re-raising exceptions

We can, if we wish, raise exceptions in the exception handler itself. The syntax for this is exactly the same as in all previous examples. In fact we can re-raise the exception that activated the exception handler in the first instance, for example:

> **when** NUMERIC_ERROR => **raise**;

The result is to re-raise the exception NUMERIC_ERROR.

Let us see how useful this feature can be. Look back to Fig.12.10. Suppose we decide to handle partly within BETA the exception raised by DELTA. We then intend to complete the handling process in ALPHA. Assume also that the exception is declared in DELTA. Therefore an exception handler has to be incorporated, using the **when others** clause in BETA (remember, the exception will be propagated as an anonymous one from DELTA to BETA). The question is: how, after carrying out the handling in BETA, do we propagate the exception to ALPHA? The answer is to use the **raise** clause, as, for example,

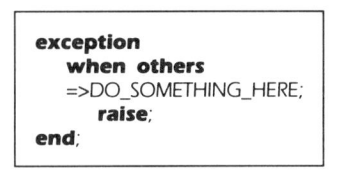

> **exception**
>   **when others**
>   =>DO_SOMETHING_HERE;
>   **raise**;
> **end**;

12.6.2 Raising a new exception in the handler

The section sets out to show that it is the reasons for raising exceptions in the exception handler which are important, not the construct itself. Fundamentally we use this if we can't, or don't wish to, handle the exception completely in the first handler. Let us examine this using a simple example, Fig.12.11.

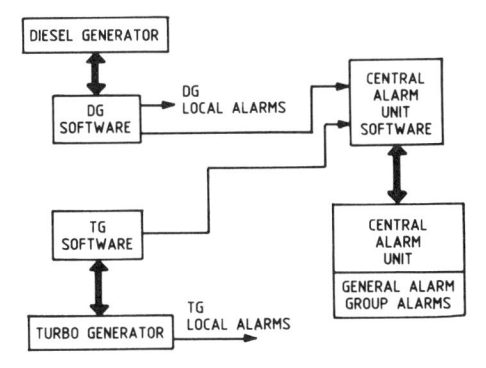

Fig.12.11 Application example.

Here we have a Diesel Generator being controlled and monitored by the DG software routines. Likewise the Turbo Generator has its corresponding TG routines. We decide that should errors occur in either routine various alarms should be raised. These include local, group and master alarms.

Each system has its own local alarm. There are a number of group alarms: one includes the DG system, another the TG system. One master alarm only is fitted. This produces a good partitioning of system functions. Each local operation is defined by the software local to the controlled unit; other units cannot affect its functioning. Likewise, the centralized software is not intermingled with that of the remote units.

A system design decision is made that, when an exception occurs in a control and monitoring routine:

- The routine activates its local alarm;
- It informs the master alarm routine of the event;
- The master alarm routine responds by generating the general alarm together with the appropriate group alarm.

We can implement this in a simple way by raising exceptions in the monitoring routines, Listing 12.23.

You can see that the SYSTEM_ALARM routine operates in a continuous loop. On each run it calls up the routines MONITOR_DG_SYSTEM and MONITOR_TG_SYSTEM as procedures. Both these routines contain exception handlers. In each one there is a **when others** clause to trap fatal errors. Should such an error arise, control is passed to SYSTEM_ALARM using the *raise exception* in the handler. The ensuing response is set by the code of the SYSTEM_ALARM exception handlers.

Raising an exception in an exception handler has allowed us to build well-structured software. For a small example like this the benefits are not all that obvious. Once you develop large programs they will become very clear indeed.

12.7 EXCEPTION RAISING DURING DECLARATION ELABORATION

We met this topic earlier in the context of exception raising and package initialization. Now let's consider the more general case which includes blocks, subprograms and packages.

Suppose we have a declaration in a block of the form

```
declare
    subtype COEFFICIENTS is INTEGER range 0..4095;
    DIGITAL_COEFFICIENTS : COEFFICIENTS := 4096;
```

Exception raising during declaration elaboration 397

```
with TEXT_IO;           use TEXT_IO;
procedure SYSTEM_ALARMS is
  DG_SYSTEM_FAULT :     exception;
  TG_SYSTEM_FAULT :     exception;
  procedure MONITOR_DG_SYSTEM is
    LOCAL_ALARM    :     exception;
  begin
  -- code statements for monitoring the diesel generator
  -- LOCAL_ALARM may be raised here
       null;
  exception
    when LOCAL_ALARM =>
      PUT_LINE ("DG SYSTEM Alarm Set");
  -- raise DG_SYSTEM_FAULT so the master unit can set the other alarms
      raise DG_SYSTEM_FAULT;
  end MONITOR_DG_SYSTEM;
  procedure MONITOR_TG_SYSTEM is
    LOCAL_ALARM    :     exception;
  begin
  -- code statements for monitoring the turbo generator
  -- LOCAL_ALARM may be raised here
       null;
  exception
    when LOCAL_ALARM =>
      PUT_LINE ("TG SYSTEM Alarm Set");
  -- raise TG_SYSTEM_FAULT so the master unit can set the other alarms
      raise TG_SYSTEM_FAULT;
  end MONITOR_TG_SYSTEM;
begin
  MONITOR_DG_SYSTEM;
  MONITOR_TG_SYSTEM;
exception
  when DG_SYSTEM_FAULT =>
    PUT_LINE ("Alarm set DG SYSTEM");
    PUT_LINE ("MASTER alarm set");
  when TG_SYSTEM_FAULT =>
    PUT_LINE ("Alarm set TG SYSTEM");
    PUT_LINE ("MASTER alarm set");
end SYSTEM_ALARMS;
```

Listing 12.23 Raising exceptions in an exception handler.

The preassigned value of DIGITAL_COEFFICIENTS lies outside the defined range. The error will be detected not at compile time but during elaboration (note, though, that some compilers will give you a warning). Therefore, for the above case, we find that a range error is generated when elaboration takes place. At that point the elaboration is abandoned. What happens next depends on the frame type in which the exception was raised. Listing 12.24 demonstrates this for a block construct.

When this program is run the following print-out will result:

```
About to enter block
Exception caught outside of the block
```

```
with TEXT_IO;                 use TEXT_IO;
procedure EXCEPTION_AT_ELABORATION is
begin
  PUT_LINE ("About to enter block");
  declare
  -- block
    subtype COEFFICIENTS is INTEGER range 0..4095;
    DIGITAL_COEFFICIENTS : COEFFICIENTS :=   4096;
  begin
  -- block
    PUT_LINE ("In block");
  exception
    when others =>
  -- catch all condition
      PUT_LINE ("Exception within the block");
  end;
  -- block
  PUT_LINE ("Program finished");
exception
  when others =>
    PUT_LINE ("Exception caught outside of the block");
end EXCEPTION_AT_ELABORATION;
```

Listing 12.24 Raising exceptions at elaboration time.

You can see that when the error is reached elaboration is discontinued and the block is exited – with the exception raised. This then activates the exception handler of the main program. Note that the exception handler local to the block is not activated. We always propagate the exception one level up.

The rules governing this topic are not simple. For detailed information see section 11.4.2 of the LRM. As a rough guide – and sufficiently good enough for us at the moment – the following apply:

- An elaboration exception occurring in a subprogram returns control to the point of call with the exception raised.
- An elaboration exception occurring in a library package causes the main program to be abandoned.

12.8 SUPPRESSING EXCEPTIONS

How do we detect exceptions? By making checks at run time. And how do we know which checks to make? By looking at the program construct in the source code. This means that:

- The check code is produced at compile time;
- Checks are related to constructs, not values.

Therefore any program is going to have a code overhead (which may be substantial) because of exception testing. Further, error checking code is generated even when there is no possibility of an error occurring. For example:

```
package MESSED_UP is
  procedure TEST_1;
end MESSED_UP;

with TEXT_IO;              use TEXT_IO;
package body MESSED_UP is
  GLOBAL_DATA_1   :     INTEGER         := 0;
  GLOBAL_DATA_2   :     INTEGER         := 10;
  -- raise a divide-by-zero error (NUMERIC)
  GLOBAL_DATA_3   :     INTEGER         := GLOBAL_DATA_2 / GLOBAL_DATA_1;
  procedure TEST_1 is
  begin
    PUT_LINE ("TEST_1 is running");
  end TEST_1;
begin
  PUT_LINE ("Elaborated MESSED_UP");
exception
  when others =>
    PUT_LINE ("We have an initialisation problem");
end MESSED_UP;
```

Listing 12.25 Exception during elaboration of a library package.

```
with TEXT_IO;              use TEXT_IO;
with MESSED_UP;
procedure ELABORATION_EXCEPTION is
begin
  PUT_LINE ("Starting main program");
  PUT_LINE ("Now calling the procedure TEST_1");
  MESSED_UP.TEST_1;
  PUT_LINE ("Finishing the main program");
exception
  when others =>
    PUT_LINE ("Exception caught in main program body");
end ELABORATION_EXCEPTION;
```

Listing 12.26 Showing that a library package elaboration exception cannot be handled by ANY exception handler.

```
declare
  type TEMPERATURE_REFERENCE_RANGE is new INTEGER range 0..100;
  DEW_POINT : TEMPERATURE_REFERENCE_RANGE;
begin
  DEW_POINT := 15;
end;
```

When the program is run, the predefined error check relating to CONSTRAINT_ERROR is carried out on this statement. Yet we can clearly see just by looking at the source code that no error exists.

The result of exception testing is a program overhead in two areas: speed of execution and store requirements. For many systems such overheads don't present a problem. But for fast systems, and/or those with limited storage space, these overheads can be unacceptable. Thus Ada allows us to turn off certain run-time checks using a suppression mechanism. We do this using a compiler directive (or *pragma*) called SUPPRESS. In the above case, for instance, we could have used the pragma as follows:

```
declare
    pragma SUPPRESS (RANGE_CHECK);
    type TEMPERATURE_REFERENCE_RANGE is new INTEGER range 0..100;
    DEW_POINT : TEMPERATURE_REFERENCE_RANGE;
begin
    DEW_POINT := 15;
end;
```

As a result of the pragma, all range checks are turned off for the duration of the block.

Variations of the pragma form are allowed, as follows:

```
pragma SUPPRESS (RANGE_CHECK, DEW_POINT);
pragma SUPPRESS (RANGE_CHECK, ON => DEW_POINT);
```

These are selective. They turn off the range check only for the variable DEW_POINT.

We wouldn't expect you to be suppressing exceptions at this stage of your work with Ada. If you need further, detailed, information consult the LRM, section 11.7. However, you should be aware of the effects produced by exception checking. Two other points need to be mentioned:

- Exception suppression is not a mandatory feature of Ada;
- Including the pragma SUPPRESS does not guarantee that an implementation will conform with the directive. It may choose to ignore it.

The best rules to follow concerning the use of error checks are:

- Always leave them on during host development work;
- Always leave them on until the program works correctly (or appears to) in the target system;
- Be selective in their removal;
- Always perform run-time tests after removing any error testing.

12.9 EXCEPTION HANDLING IN EMBEDDED SYSTEMS – A COMMENT

In target embedded systems, exception handling requires much thought, for a number of reasons. First, many of these systems – if not most – do not have operator interfaces like that of a host development system. Embedded applications aren't often run from a computer console. Second, when predefined exceptions occur we rarely have any idea what the root of the problem is. Third, even if we could log the run-time data there isn't usually time to evaluate it. We need to respond to exceptions very quickly because, while the computer is down, the system is out of control. So generally (though not always) we don't differentiate between the different types of automatically detected exceptions. A single, specific, user-defined response is invoked. Various exception handling strategies can be used – it depends on the application. Two particular methods are widely applied:

- Put the system into a fail-safe mode, and suspend the program.
- Reset the program to its initial state, and restart it.

It is also usual to generate external warnings in such cases.

REVIEW

Do you now:

- Understand the concepts and principles of detecting, raising and handling exceptions?
- Appreciate the difference between predefined and user-defined exceptions in Ada, and understand the role of the exception handler?
- Know how to program responses to predefined exceptions, implement user-defined exceptions, and raise predefined exceptions yourself?
- Know how to implement these in blocks, subprograms and packages?
- Understand the basics of scope and visibility rules for exceptions?
- Perceive how exceptions are propagated from inner (enclosed) program units to outer (enclosing) ones and know how to handle them (particularly for nested program units)?
- Recognize the difference between exception raising during statement execution and during declaration elaboration?
- Realize that exceptions can be suppressed, and appreciate why we should want to do so?

Chapter Thirteen
Generics

The major program units of Ada are the subprogram and the package. We've already seen the many benefits to be gained by using these constructs: saving of time and effort, improved software reliability, minimization of redundant code, and the provision of library functions. In this chapter we'll see how we can further improve on these by using the generics feature of Ada.

The basic concept of generics is a simple one. It is the development of generalized program templates from which specific program units can be constructed. On completing this chapter you will:

- Appreciate the fundamental concepts of generics and instantiation;
- Understand the make-up of generic entities in terms of generic units and generic parameters;
- Know how to build generic units (templates) based on the subprogram and the package;
- Be proficient in creating particular instances of the templates (*instantiate* the generic unit);
- Be able to use the instantiations;
- Understand the essential role of generic parameters, and apply these in practice.

13.1   CONCEPTS

At this stage you won't need to be told that the major building blocks of Ada are the subprogram and the package. By now their constructs and uses should be second nature. Further, the benefits of using them to build programs should be absolutely clear (so clear, in fact, that you may wonder why we had to spell it out in such detail). We use them to produce reliable software, minimize redundant code, and provide sets of standard program building blocks. Now we'll see how we can further improve on these by using the generics feature of Ada. But first, a conceptual digression.

In Fig.13.1 we once more repeat the concept of building and using procedures (bear with us – there is a good reason for this).

Here, in Fig.13.1a, we have the English version of a generalized form TICKET (the procedure) for use with the flights of Bled Airways. The ticket only becomes valid for any particular journey when it is filled in (inserting

Concepts   403

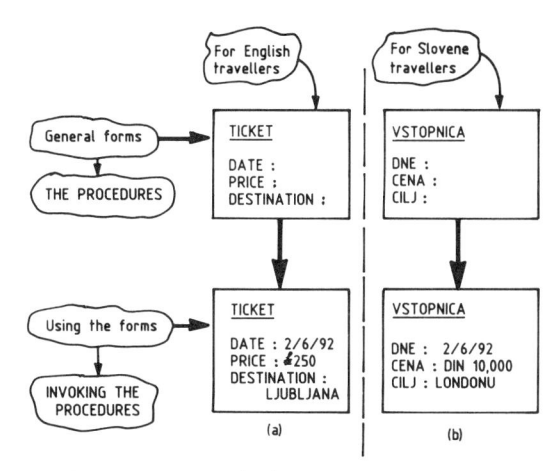

Fig.13.1 The procedure concept revised.

the procedure parameters). Now we can go ahead and use the ticket (call the procedure).

Slovene passengers also use Bled Airways. Thus the company decides to have two sets of tickets, one for each language. But this means that we need a distinct manufacturing blank for the second ticket type (Fig.13.1b). The company then decides to produce tickets in French, Serbo-Croat, Greek, German, Italian, ... The result? Before long the print unit is awash with ticket print blanks. And the consequences of this? We spend considerable time dealing with the problems of storage, issue, modification, etc., of the blanks. How can we simplify this situation?

The key to solving this issue is to recognize that both ticket types do the same job. However, one requires that it is filled in using English, the other in Slovene. Therefore we still need to provide separate ticket types – but we can produce these using only a single print template, Fig.13.2.

First we make the template which will be used to print tickets. This is called a generic unit ('generic: characteristic of a class', *Oxford English Dictionary*). In this we provide a set of placeholders to be filled in before running off the tickets. These placeholders, called fields in the example, are equivalent to formal parameters. To customize the generic unit we insert the customizing data (the actual parameters) into their placeholders (the formal parameters). Then we print off copies – 'instances' – of the template. In Ada terminology, we instantiate the generic unit. Finally we use (invoke) the instantiated item.

This example brings out the essentials of the topic, namely:

- Once we get the template right, it stays right. This minimizes clerical errors in its use.

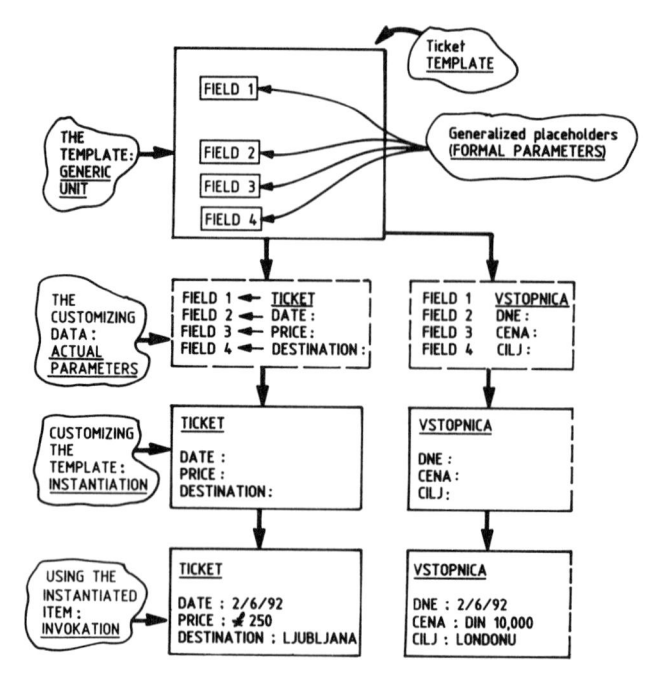

Fig.13.2 Concept – generics and instantiation.

- Mistakes can only be made when it is filled in. Thus the chances of making mistakes are reduced.
- The number of different ticket formats is reduced.
- We cannot use (invoke) the ticket template, only the instantiation.
- This approach does not make any difference to the number of tickets which are used by passengers.

Make sure that you fully appreciate these points before getting into detail concerning Ada and generics.

13.2 GENERICS AND ADA

Suppose we were asked to discuss the reasons for, and qualities of, subprograms. The first three items in the listing of points above would, without doubt, figure strongly. From this you should be able to see that generics is a way of extending the subprogram concept and use. But be careful – it is easy to confuse the two. The following example summarizes, in a simple way, the reason for having generics in Ada.

We are asked to produce a program which will swap two numbers. We produce a procedure for this, where the items to be swapped are identified as A and B. It's executable part is

```
begin
    C := A; -- C is merely a temporary placeholder
    A := B;
    B := C;
end SWAP;
```

A first request is to perform this on integer numbers. Thus we implement the procedure

```
procedure SWAP_1 (A, B : in out INTEGER) is
    C : INTEGER;
begin
    C := A;
    A := B;
    B := C;
end SWAP_1;
```

A second request arrives: do a SWAP procedure for ASCII characters. So diligently we obey, producing:

```
procedure SWAP_2 (A, B : in out CHARACTER) is
    C : CHARACTER;
begin
    C := A;
    A := B;
    B := C;
end SWAP_2;
```

Now, observe that these procedures carry out identical actions. The only difference is in the types used within the calculations. This suggests that perhaps we could base the individual procedures on some common unit. And that is the basis of the Ada generic unit.

There are three distinct operations relating to generics in Ada (Fig.13.3).

First we have to build our generic template or 'model'. Using this we can then instantiate specific program units having the behaviour of the model, but tailored with particular individual qualities. Finally we can apply the instantiated unit by invoking it in the program. In Fig.13.3 these operations are illustrated using the example procedure SWAP. This is the basis of the generic template SWAP. Note that its parameters are defined to be of type SOME_TYPE. Following this are two instantiations, SWAP_1 and SWAP_2.

406 Generics

```
                    ESSENTIAL
                    OPERATIONS

   BUILD THE        INSTANTIATE      INVOKE THE
   TEMPLATE         THE TEMPLATE     INSTANTIATED UNIT

   (The generic    (The particular   (The applied
     model)         implementations)   item)

procedure SWAP                              begin
  ( A , B : in out SOME TYPE ) is             SWAP_1 (X , Y);
  C : SOME TYPE ;                             SWAP_1 (α , β);
begin                                         SWAP_2 (C , D);
  C : = A ;                                 end ;
  A : = B ;
  B : = C ;
end SWAP ;

         procedure SWAP_1              procedure SWAP_2
           ( A , B : in out INTEGER) is  ( A , B : in out CHARACTER) is
           C : INTEGER;                  C : CHARACTER ;
         begin                         begin
           C : = A ;                     C : = A ;
           A : = B ;                     A : = B ;
           B : = C ;                     B : = C ;
         end SWAP_1 ;                  end SWAP_2 ;
```

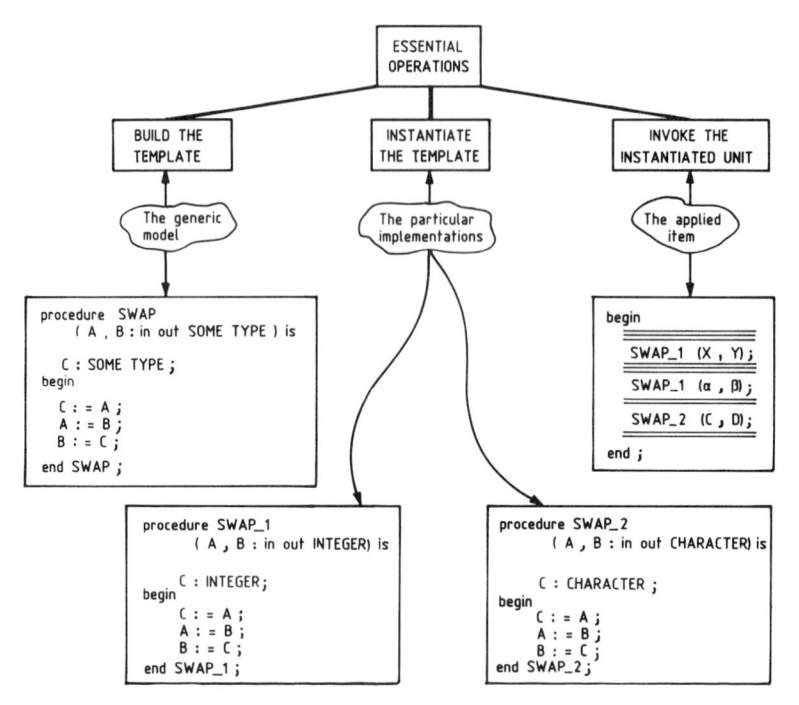

Fig.13.3 Generic program units – the essential operations.

Observe that individual distinct names are used for the separate instantiations. Observe also that for SWAP_1 we use actual parameters of type INTEGER. In SWAP_2 instantiation the actual parameters are of type CHARACTER. We are now in a position to use these procedures by invoking them in the usual way.

In Fig.13.3 the code from the template has been repeated in the instantiations. In practice this is not the case – it was done in the example merely to help the explanation. In a moment you will see how we instantiate a template without replicating its code (otherwise there wouldn't be any point in using generics).

There are two major entities within generics: the program units themselves and the parameters used with these units, Fig.13.4.

The generic program units of Ada are the subprogram (procedures and functions) and the package. Thus we build procedure templates, function templates and package templates. Into these units we insert generic formal parameters: types, objects, subprograms. The formal parameters act as placeholders. We instantiate the template or model by replacing these formal parameters with actual parameters. Replacement is done at compile time – a translation time process. From then on you cannot see any difference between

Introduction using the generic procedure

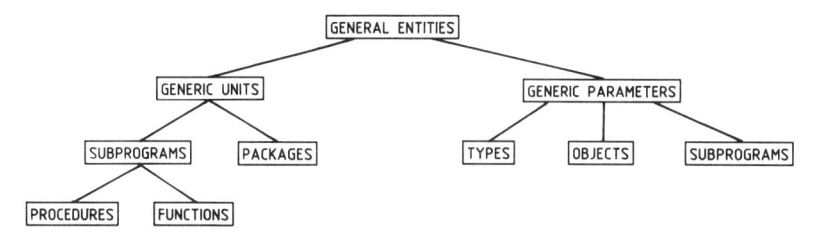

Fig.13.4 Major entities within generics.

the behaviour of a generic program unit and its non-generic counterpart. We invoke both using exactly the same calling mechanisms – a run-time process.

At this point the subject may appear very abstract, so let us flesh it out, using the generic procedure as an example.

13.3 INTRODUCTION USING THE GENERIC PROCEDURE

13.3.1 General

The purpose here is to bring out the essentials of Ada generics as implemented in Ada code:

- Defining (building) the model – the generic declaration;
- Defining an instance of the model – the generic instantiation;
- Using the instance – the invocation.

We will see how this is done using the procedure as the generic unit. Only basic, essential points will be discussed; a fuller description follows later. We also need to have some discussion on types. This, though, will be a limited one, sufficient to make the example understandable.

13.3.2 Building the procedure template – the generic declaration

The template (or generic declaration) of a generic procedure consists of two sections: the generic declaration and the generic body (Fig.13.5).

Let us first look at the generic (procedure) body. The procedure is the 'thingy' that causes something to happen in the program. In formal terms it is 'a template for the bodies of the corresponding procedure obtained by instantiation'. When we write the code for this we don't treat it as anything special. It's just like any ordinary procedure that we've met so far in Ada.

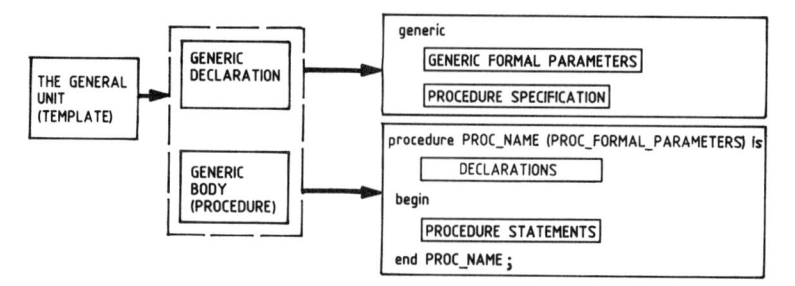

Fig.13.5 Building a generic procedure.

The difference is that we use information from the generic formal part within this procedure.

Now let's turn to the generic declaration. This is identified using the reserved word **generic** and contains two items:

- The generic formal parameters for the procedure;
- The procedure specification.

These formal parameters are used within the procedure body itself. For the example described above the generic declaration is (Fig.13.6)

```
generic
    type SOME_TYPE is (<>); -- this is the generic formal parameter
    procedure SWAP (A, B : in out SOME_TYPE); -- procedure declaration
```

Following this is the procedure body SWAP:

```
procedure SWAP (A, B : in out SOME_TYPE) is
    C : SOME_TYPE;
begin
    C := A;
    A := B;
    B := C;
end SWAP;
```

The symbol (<>) stands for 'any discrete type'. Thus the first line of the declaration can be read as: 'We have a formal parameter named SOME_TYPE. This can be replaced in the instantiation with any discrete type.' In the second line we write out the specification of the procedure SWAP. You can see that the formal parameters of the procedure are declared to be of type SOME_TYPE (try not to confuse generic formal parameters with subprogram formal parameters).

This completes the building of the template.

Introduction using the generic procedure

```
generic
    type SOME_TYPE is (<>);
    procedure SWAP (A , B : in out SOME_TYPE);
```
⟵ The generic declaration

```
procedure SWAP (A , B : in out SOME_TYPE) is
    C : SOME_TYPE;
begin
    C : = A ;
    A : = B ;
    B : = C;
end SWAP;
```
⟵ The procedure body template

`Procedure SWAP_1 is new SWAP (INTEGER);`   `Procedure SWAP_2 is new SWAP (CHARACTER);`

```
Procedure SWAP_1 ( A , B : in out INTEGER ) is
    C : INTEGER ;
begin
    C : = A ;
    A : = B ;
    B : = C ;
end SWAP_1 ;
```

```
Procedure SWAP_2 ( A , B : in out CHARACTER ) is
    C : CHARACTER ;
begin
    C : = A ;
    A : = B ;
    B : = C ;
end SWAP_2;
```

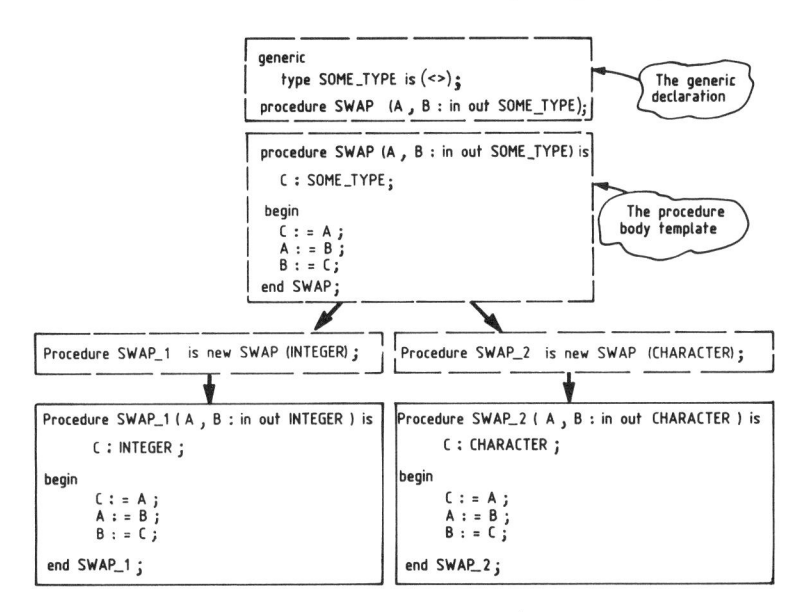

Fig.13.6 Declaring and instantiating a generic procedure.

13.3.3 Implementing the procedure template – the generic instantiation

To create a specific instance of the template SWAP (i.e. to instantiate it) two factors have to be defined:

- The name to be used for the instantiated procedure (replacing SWAP);
- The actual parameter type to be used (replacing SOME_TYPE).

The general format is

```
procedure <NAME_OF_NEW_PROCEDURE> is
    new <NAME_OF_GENERIC_PROCEDURE> <ACTUAL_PARAMETERS>;
```

For the example above we have (Fig.13.6)

```
procedure SWAP_1 is new SWAP (INTEGER);
procedure SWAP_2 is new SWAP (CHARACTER);
```

13.3.4 Using the instantiated procedure – invocation

The procedures SWAP_1 and SWAP_2 are no different to non-generic procedures. Therefore we can go ahead and use them as per normal by invoking

```
with TEXT_IO;              use TEXT_IO;
procedure SINGLE_GENERIC is
  package INT_IO is new INTEGER_IO (INTEGER);
  use INT_IO;
  -- variables must appear here as generic declaration is classed as a
  -- later declaration [LRM 3.9/2]
  FIRST            :       INTEGER        := 1;
  SECOND           :       INTEGER        := 2;
  generic
    type SOME_TYPE is (<>);
  procedure SWAP (A, B     : in out SOME_TYPE);
  procedure SWAP (A, B     : in out SOME_TYPE) is
    C              :       SOME_TYPE;
  begin
    C := A;
    A := B;
    B := C;
  end SWAP;
  procedure SWAP_1 is new SWAP (INTEGER);
begin
  PUT (" FIRST = ");
  PUT (FIRST, 0);
  PUT (" SECOND = ");
  PUT (SECOND, 0);
  NEW_LINE;
  SWAP_1 (FIRST, SECOND);
  PUT (" FIRST = ");
  PUT (FIRST, 0);
  PUT (" SECOND = ");
  PUT (SECOND, 0);
end SINGLE_GENERIC;
```

Listing 13.1 The purpose of this example is to show how to declare, instantiate and invoke a simple generic procedure.

them as executable statements. Listing 13.1 is a simple example which uses only one instantiation of the procedure SWAP. Note that we can call this instantiated procedure as many times as we desire.

This example is extended in Listing 13.2 to show two instantiations of the procedure SWAP.

From these examples you should clearly see that:

- We have one template only;
- We cannot use (invoke) the template, only the instantiation;
- There is no difference between a normal procedure and an instantiated generic one;
- This approach does not make any difference to the number of procedure calls used in the application program;
- We may not save on the amount of program object code. Most current compilers also generate full object code for each and every instantiated procedure;
- We do, however, have less source code;

```
with TEXT_IO;                use TEXT_IO;
procedure DOUBLE_GENERIC is
  package INT_IO is new INTEGER_IO (INTEGER);
  use INT_IO;
  FIRST            :    INTEGER      := 1;
  SECOND           :    INTEGER      := 2;
  ALPHA            :    CHARACTER    := 'A';
  BETA             :    CHARACTER    := 'B';
  generic
    type SOME_TYPE is (<>);
  procedure SWAP (A, B     : in out SOME_TYPE);
  procedure SWAP (A, B     : in out SOME_TYPE) is
    C              :    SOME_TYPE;
  begin
    C := A;
    A := B;
    B := C;
  end SWAP;
  procedure SWAP_1 is new SWAP (INTEGER);
  procedure SWAP_2 is new SWAP (CHARACTER);
begin
  PUT (" FIRST = ");
  PUT (FIRST, 0);
  PUT (" SECOND = ");
  PUT (SECOND, 0);
  PUT (" ALPHA = ");
  PUT (ALPHA);
  PUT (" BETA  = ");
  PUT (BETA);
  NEW_LINE;
  SWAP_1 (FIRST, SECOND);
  SWAP_2 (ALPHA, BETA);
  PUT (" FIRST = ");
  PUT (FIRST, 0);
  PUT (" SECOND = ");
  PUT (SECOND, 0);
  PUT (" ALPHA = ");
  PUT (ALPHA);
  PUT (" BETA  = ");
  PUT (BETA);
end DOUBLE_GENERIC;
```

Listing 13.2 This shows two instantiations of a single generic procedure and their use in a program.

- If the implementation code requires alteration, only one program unit is changed – the generic body.

13.3.5 Overloading

We have already met overloading in a number of applications. Now we come to its use in relationship to instantiated procedures (in fact, to any form of instantiation). For the example above – SWAP – we could have implemented the following:

```
procedure EXCHANGE is new SWAP (INTEGER); -- Instantiation 1
procedure EXCHANGE is new SWAP (CHARACTER); -- Instantiation 2
```

When we call these in a program we leave it to the compiler to sort out which procedure we really want. It does this by looking at the parameter type. Assume that we have

```
ALPHA, BETA : CHARACTER;
begin
    EXCHANGE (ALPHA, BETA);
```

The procedure EXCHANGE must be instantiation 2 as the parameter is of type CHARACTER.

13.4 GENERIC FORMAL PARAMETERS – TYPES

13.4.1 General comment

Generic type parameters are used to define the types passed into a generic unit at instantiation time. These types are collected into two groups, being labelled private type declarations and generic type definitions (Fig.13.7).

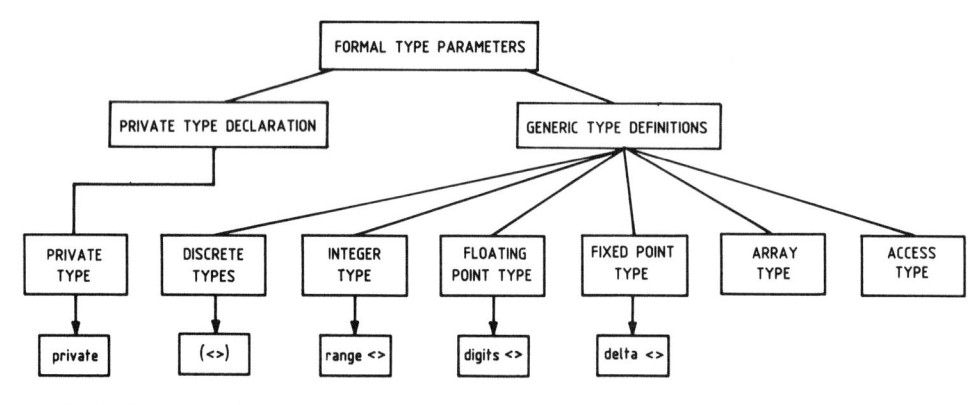

Fig.13.7 Generic formal types.

Very roughly we can say that private type declarations allow us to handle almost any type – but they must obey the rules set down for private types. In contrast the second group spells out precisely which types are involved. Before we look into their use it is well worth while defining the associated operations.

Let us suppose that we produce a procedure which can be used with any

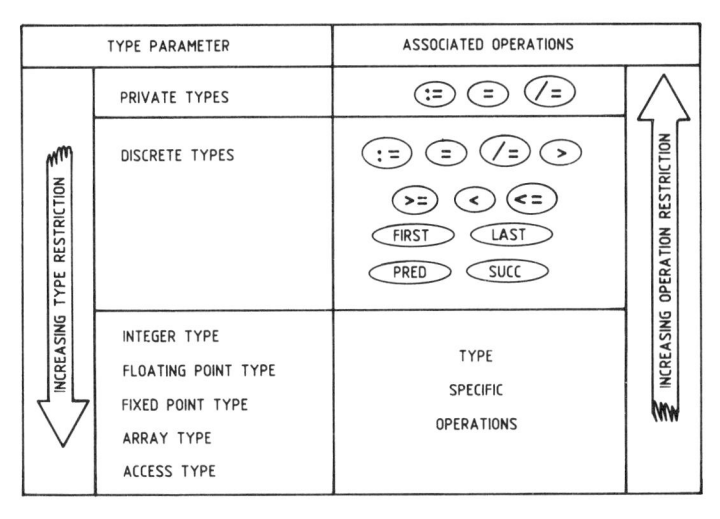

Fig.13.8 Generic units – type parameters and associated operations.

type. Thus, when the body of the procedure is written, the compiler has no knowledge of the types involved. This raises a problem. As Ada is a strongly typed language, the compiler is supposed to check that type rules are followed. Yet, as we've just pointed out, it doesn't know which types are to be used. The simple way out of this is to permit the procedure to use operations applicable to all types. But that limits us to assignment and equality/inequality testing.

Generic type definitions restrict the types which can be used as formal parameters. This restriction has an important consequence – it increases the variety of operations which can be applied within the procedure. For instance, suppose when declaring a generic unit we define its formal parameter type to be INTEGER. We then use objects of this type within the procedure body. As a result, all operations defined for type INTEGER can be used without problem; the compiler knows exactly what to check for.

Fig.13.8 shows the relationship between the formal type parameters and their associated operations.

The parameter declaration format is

```
type PRIVATE_TYPE_NAME is private;
type DISCRETE_TYPE_NAME is (<>);
type INTEGER_TYPE_NAME is range <>;
type FP_TYPE_NAME is digits <>;
type FIXED_TYPE_NAME is delta <>;
type ARRAY_TYPE_NAME is array (INDEX) of A_TYPE;
type UNCONSTRAINED_ARRAY_TYPE_NAME is array (INDEX range <>) of
   A_TYPE;
type ACCESS_TYPE_NAME is access NODE_TYPE;
```

13.4.2 Using generic formal types with the procedure

For the example SWAP given earlier, we could have used a private type declaration, as in

```
generic
    type SOME_TYPE is private; -- this is the generic formal parameter
procedure SWAP (A, B : in out SOME_TYPE);

procedure SWAP (A, B : in out SOME_TYPE) is
    C : SOME_TYPE;
begin
    C := A;
    A := B;
    B := C;
end SWAP;
```

Note, however, that to check if A is greater than B, the formal private type could not be used. The discrete type, at the minimum, would be needed in such a case.

The following examples (Listings 13.3, 13.4) show how a single generic unit can be instantiated with enumeration and record types. Using an enumeration type as a formal parameter is a very straightforward task.

```
with TEXT_IO;                use TEXT_IO;
procedure ENUM_GENERIC is
  type TRAFFIC_LIGHT is (RED, AMBER, GREEN);
  LIGHT_1         :       TRAFFIC_LIGHT   := RED;
  LIGHT_2         :       TRAFFIC_LIGHT   := GREEN;
  generic
    type SOME_TYPE is (<>);
    procedure SWAP (A, B      : in out SOME_TYPE);
    procedure SWAP (A, B      : in out SOME_TYPE) is
      C             :       SOME_TYPE;
  begin
    C := A;
    A := B;
    B := C;
  end SWAP;
    procedure SWAP_LIGHTS is new SWAP (TRAFFIC_LIGHT);
  begin
    SWAP_LIGHTS (LIGHT_1, LIGHT_2);
  end ENUM_GENERIC;
```

Listing 13.3 Instantiating a generic procedure using an enumeration formal parameter.

The record construct looks more complex but again is quite easy to use. The use of array and access types will be demonstrated later.

Generic formal parameters – types 415

```
with TEXT_IO;                    use TEXT_IO;
procedure RECORD_GENERIC is
  type PROPULSION_ENGINE is
    record
       PT_FIRE            :    BOOLEAN;
       GG_OVERSPEED       :    FLOAT;
       GG_VIBRATION       :    INTEGER;
    end record;
  PORT_GAS_TURBINE :    PROPULSION_ENGINE;
  STBD_GAS_TURBINE :    PROPULSION_ENGINE;
  generic
    type SOME_TYPE is private;
  -- note the change of declaration
  procedure SWAP (A, B       : in out SOME_TYPE);
  procedure SWAP (A, B       : in out SOME_TYPE) is
    C              :    SOME_TYPE;
  begin
    C := A;
    A := B;
    B := C;
  end SWAP;
  procedure SWAP_ENGINES is new SWAP (PROPULSION_ENGINE);
begin
  SWAP_ENGINES (PORT_GAS_TURBINE, STBD_GAS_TURBINE);
end RECORD_GENERIC;
```

Listing 13.4 Instantiating a generic procedure using a record formal parameter.

13.4.3 More on the private type parameter

A few more comments are worth making concerning the formal private type parameter. Strictly speaking we have two types, the 'normal' and the limited private one. The declaration formats are

> **type** SOME_TYPE **is private**;
> **type** SOME_LIMITED_TYPE **is limited private**;

There is a major difference, though, in how we can use these. Our original reason for having private types was to hide information contained in some unit. Few, if any, external operations could be carried out on objects of the private type. Within the unit, however, the normal type rules applied. But look at what happens when we use the private type as a formal parameter of a generic unit. These restrictions apply inside the unit.

First consider the use of the limited private type as a formal parameter. Very little can be done with, or to, objects of this type – using predefined operations, that is. Therefore any actual type can be matched up to this formal type. Now take the normal private type. This is less restrictive – formal/actual matches are legal for types which permit assignment and tests for equality/inequality. It should be evident that this construct is very well suited for data shifting and the like.

It might appear that the limited private type parameter is a fairly useless item. But it looked like that when we first met it. Only later did its value become clear. Later still we'll see that it is equally useful in generic units when the subprogram parameter is used.

13.4.4 Matching actual and formal type parameters

All the examples so far have incorporated one formal type parameter only. There is, in fact, no limit to the number of type parameters that can be used. For example, we could have

```
generic
    type TEXT is (<>);
    type LIMITS is range <>;
    type COEFFICIENTS is digits <>;
procedure COMPUTE_CONTROL_LAW (MESSAGE  :  out TEXT;
                               A1       :  in out COEFFICIENTS;
                               PROFILE  :  in     LIMITS;
                               DEADBAND :  in out LIMITS);
```

When this is instantiated we have to pair up the actual parameters with the formal ones. It should be no surprise to find that both positional and named associations can be used. The following constructs are thus legal:

```
procedure LOW_PASS_FILTER is new COMPUTE_CONTROL_LAW
                                 (CHARACTER, INTEGER, FLOAT);
```

```
procedure LOW_PASS_FILTER is new COMPUTE_CONTROL_LAW
                                 (TEXT          => CHARACTER,
                                  LIMITS        => INTEGER,
                                  COEFFICIENTS  => FLOAT);
```

These points are demonstrated in the context of array (Listing 13.5) and access types (Listing 13.6).

Detailed matching rules are beyond the scope of this text. See section 13.3 of the LRM for further information.

13.5 GENERIC FORMAL PARAMETERS – OBJECTS

The simplest type of generic formal parameter is the generic object. This can be a variable or a constant item. Taken in isolation it doesn't appear to have

```
with TEXT_IO;            use TEXT_IO;
procedure ARRAY_GENERIC is
  -- declare an array type
  subtype NUMBER_LIST_LENGTH is INTEGER range 1..10;
  type NUMBER_LIST is array (NUMBER_LIST_LENGTH) of INTEGER;
  NUMBER_LIST_1   :     NUMBER_LIST;
  NUMBER_LIST_2   :     NUMBER_LIST;
  -- declare a generic procedure with an array formal parameter. Note that
  -- formal parameters have been declared for the array index type and the
  -- array element type as well as the array type itself.
  generic
    type SOME_INDEX is (<>);
    type ARRAY_COMPONENT is private;
    type SOME_TYPE is array (SOME_INDEX) of ARRAY_COMPONENT;
  procedure SWAP (A, B     : in out SOME_TYPE);
  procedure SWAP (A, B     : in out SOME_TYPE) is
    C             :     SOME_TYPE;
  begin
    C := A;
    A := B;
    B := C;
  end SWAP;
  -- instantiate the generic. Named association has been used here.
  procedure SWAP_NUMBER_LISTS is new SWAP
                                      (SOME_INDEX      => NUMBER_LIST_LENGTH,
                                       ARRAY_COMPONENT => INTEGER,
                                       SOME_TYPE       => NUMBER_LIST);
begin
  SWAP_NUMBER_LISTS (NUMBER_LIST_1, NUMBER_LIST_2);
end ARRAY_GENERIC;
```

Listing 13.5 Instantiating a generic procedure using an array formal parameter.

```
with TEXT_IO;            use TEXT_IO;
procedure ACCESS_GENERIC is
  type PROPULSION_ENGINE is
    record
      PT_FIRE          :    BOOLEAN;
      GG_OVERSPEED     :    FLOAT;
      GG_VIBRATION     :    INTEGER;
    end record;
  type PE_POINTER is access PROPULSION_ENGINE;
  PORT_GAS_TURBINE :   PE_POINTER;
  STBD_GAS_TURBINE :   PE_POINTER;
  -- The generic procedure. Note that the access type and the type which it
  -- is an access to are both generic formal parameters
  generic
    type NODE_TYPE is private;
    type SOME_TYPE is access NODE_TYPE;
  procedure SWAP (A, B     : in out SOME_TYPE);
  procedure SWAP (A, B     : in out SOME_TYPE) is
    C             :     SOME_TYPE;
  begin
    C := A;
    A := B;
    B := C;
  end SWAP;
  -- match the generic parameters to actual parameters. Positional notation
  -- used here.
  procedure SWAP_ACCESS is new SWAP (PROPULSION_ENGINE, PE_POINTER);
begin
  SWAP_ACCESS (PORT_GAS_TURBINE, STBD_GAS_TURBINE);
end ACCESS_GENERIC;
```

Listing 13.6 Instantiating a generic procedure using an access formal parameter.

418 Generics

much value. To be useful it really needs to be combined with other parameters. This will be demonstrated shortly. For the moment we'll concentrate on the mechanics of declaring and using the object.

The example given below is devised merely to show the key points of the topic. Sensible uses will be covered later in conjunction with generic subprograms. We will only look at the use of the object parameter as a constant value within the generic unit. The use of the object as a variable is an advanced topic, beyond the scope of this book.

For the constant object the declaration format is

```
generic
    HIGH_LIMIT : in INTEGER;
```

Here the formal object is HIGH_LIMIT, its type is INTEGER, and its mode is in. As a result of the mode definition, the object is defined to be a constant. Further, this is the default mode. Therefore it can be omitted from the generic declaration, giving

```
generic
    HIGH_LIMIT : INTEGER;
```

Look back at the basic definition for the generic procedure declaration of a procedure, Fig.13.5. A complete declaration must include a procedure specification, so the above example is extended as follows:

```
generic
    HIGH_LIMIT : INTEGER;
procedure NOT_A_LOT;
```

Next is the generic body:

```
procedure NOT_A_LOT is
begin
    INT_IO.PUT (HIGH_LIMIT);
end NOT_A_LOT;
```

Then instantiate the procedure:

```
procedure DOES_LITTLE is new NOT_A_LOT
                            (HIGH_LIMIT_ => 4096);
```

```
with TEXT_IO;                use TEXT_IO;
procedure GENERIC_IN_OBJECT is
  package INT_IO is new INTEGER_IO (INTEGER);
  generic
    HIGH_LIMIT : INTEGER;
  procedure NOT_A_LOT;
  procedure NOT_A_LOT is
  begin
    INT_IO.PUT (HIGH_LIMIT);
  end NOT_A_LOT;
  procedure DOES_LITTLE is new NOT_A_LOT (HIGH_LIMIT => 4096);
begin
  DOES_LITTLE;
end GENERIC_IN_OBJECT;
```

Listing 13.7 Instantiating and using a generic procedure which incorporates a generic constant object.

We can now use it in the usual way:

```
begin
    DOES_LITTLE;
end;
```

The full code for this is shown in Listing 13.7.

Although this is a fairly pointless exercise it does illustrate the essentials of the subject.

It is permissible to use default values with constants, as in

```
generic
    HIGH_LIMIT : INTEGER := 0;
```

If at instantiation time we provide a value for the parameter the default is overridden. But should we write

```
procedure DOES_LITTLE is new NOT_A_LOT;
```

then the constant HIGH_LIMIT will default to a value of 0.

Two final points concerning formal objects are that:

- Explicit range constraints cannot be applied to formal objects.
- The mode **out** is not allowed.

13.6 GENERIC FORMAL PARAMETERS – SUBPROGRAMS

13.6.1 Main features

The third form of generic formal parameter is the subprogram. The concept is simple:

- First declare a subprogram within the generic unit (this becomes the generic formal subprogram parameter).
- Use (call) this subprogram within the generic subprogram itself.
- Replace the formal subprogram with an actual subprogram at the time of instantiation.

For Ada this is the only situation where we can use a subprogram as a parameter. In this section we'll focus on declaration aspects, and complete it with a simple application. The power and usefulness of this construct will be pointed out in later applications.

Let us return to our first generic example. For this we had the declaration form

```
generic
    type SOME_TYPE is (<>)
procedure SWAP (A, B : in out SOME_TYPE);
```

If we introduce a generic formal subprogram (say a procedure called DEMO), we have a problem. How do we distinguish between this formal procedure and the generic procedure SWAP? The technique adopted is to prefix the name of the formal subprogram using the keyword **with**, as in

```
generic
    type SOME_TYPE is (<>);
    with procedure DEMO; -- declare the formal subprogram parameter
procedure SWAP_NEW (A, B : in out SOME_TYPE);

procedure SWAP_NEW (A, B : in out SOME_TYPE) is
    C : SOME_TYPE;
begin
    DEMO; -- call the formal subprogram
    C := A;
    A := B;
    B := C;
end SWAP_NEW;
```

(It should be appreciated that the keyword **with** has one purpose only – to distinguish formal subprogram parameters from the generic subprogram itself.)

Instantiation follows the usual rules:

Generic formal parameters – subprograms   421

```
with TEXT_IO;              use TEXT_IO;
procedure GENERIC_SUBPROGRAM_PARAMETER is
   X           :      INTEGER      :=  0;
   Y           :      INTEGER      :=  1;
   ALPHA       :      CHARACTER    :=  'A';
   BETA        :      CHARACTER    :=  'B';
   generic
     type SOME_TYPE is (<>);
     with procedure DEMO;
   procedure SWAP_NEW (A, B     : in out SOME_TYPE);
   procedure SWAP_NEW (A, B     : in out SOME_TYPE) is
     C            :     SOME_TYPE;
   begin
     DEMO;
     C := A;
     A := B;
     B := C;
   end SWAP_NEW;
   procedure TEXT_INFO_1 is
   begin
     PUT_LINE ("Text Info 1");
   end TEXT_INFO_1;
   procedure TEXT_INFO_2 is
   begin
     PUT_LINE ("Text Info 2");
   end TEXT_INFO_2;
   procedure SWAP_1 is new SWAP_NEW (SOME_TYPE => INTEGER,
                                     DEMO      => TEXT_INFO_1);
   procedure SWAP_2 is new SWAP_NEW (SOME_TYPE => CHARACTER,
                                     DEMO      => TEXT_INFO_2);
begin
   SWAP_1 (X, Y);
   SWAP_2 (ALPHA, BETA);
end GENERIC_SUBPROGRAM_PARAMETER;
```

Listing 13.8 An introduction to the generic formal subprogram parameter.

```
procedure SWAP_1 is new SWAP_NEW (INTEGER, TEXT_INFO_1);
procedure SWAP_2 is new SWAP_NEW (CHARACTER, TEXT_INFO_2);
```

In the first instantiation the actual subprogram TEXT_INFO_1 is matched up with the formal subprogram DEMO. As a result, when SWAP_1 is invoked, each call of DEMO is replaced by a call of TEXT_INFO_1. Likewise, for each invocation of SWAP_2, DEMO is replaced by a call of TEXT_INFO_2. A full demonstration program for this is given in Listing 13.8.

In the example so far, the generic formal subprogram has not been parameterized. Suppose, though, that we had used the following formal subprogram parameter:

```
with procedure DEMO_1 (A : in INTEGER; B : in out FLOAT);
```

```
with TEXT_IO;                use TEXT_IO;
procedure GENERIC_SUBPROGRAM_WITH_PARAMETERS is
  ALPHA          :      CHARACTER       := 'A';
  BETA           :      CHARACTER       := 'B';
  generic
    type SOME_TYPE is (<>);
    with procedure DEMO (A : in     INTEGER;
                         B : in out FLOAT);
  procedure SWAP_NEW (A, B      : in out SOME_TYPE);
  procedure SWAP_NEW (A, B      : in out SOME_TYPE) is
    C          :      SOME_TYPE;
    D          :      FLOAT           := 0.0;
  begin
    DEMO (5, D);
    C := A;
    A := B;
    B := C;
  end SWAP_NEW;
  procedure CALC (RATE     : in     INTEGER;
                  SKEW     : in out FLOAT) is
  begin
    SKEW := SKEW * FLOAT(RATE / 100);
  end CALC;
  procedure CALC_AND_SWAP is new SWAP_NEW (SOME_TYPE => CHARACTER,
                                           DEMO      => CALC);
begin
  CALC_AND_SWAP (ALPHA, BETA);
end GENERIC_SUBPROGRAM_WITH_PARAMETERS;
```

Listing 13.9 Using parameters with generic subprograms.

What is the instantiation syntax for this case? There is, in fact, no change. But we must make sure that the actual subprogram replacement precisely matches the formal one. That is, it must be a procedure having two parameters, one INTEGER of **in** mode, the other FLOAT of **in out** mode. This is demonstrated in Listing 13.9.

13.6.2 Default parameters

One of the constructs available for use with generic subprogram parameters is that of the default mechanism. More precisely, we can specify a default parameter to be used if the actual subprogram parameter is omitted at instantiation time. This can be done in two ways.

1. First, write out the name of the default subprogram explicitly within the declarations, as:

    with procedure DEMO **is** DEFAULT_PROC;

```
with TEXT_IO;                use TEXT_IO;
procedure GENERIC_SUBPROGRAM_DEFAULT_PARAMETER is
  X          :       INTEGER       := 0;
  Y          :       INTEGER       := 1;
  ALPHA      :       CHARACTER     := 'A';
  BETA       :       CHARACTER     := 'B';
  procedure TEXT_INFO_1 is
  begin
    PUT_LINE ("Text Info 1");
  end TEXT_INFO_1;
  procedure TEXT_INFO_2 is
  begin
    PUT_LINE ("Text Info 2");
  end TEXT_INFO_2;
  generic
    type SOME_TYPE is (<>);
    with procedure DEMO is TEXT_INFO_1;
  procedure SWAP_NEW (A, B     : in out SOME_TYPE);
  procedure SWAP_NEW (A, B     : in out SOME_TYPE) is
    C            :    SOME_TYPE;
  begin
    DEMO;
    C := A;
    A := B;
    B := C;
  end SWAP_NEW;
  procedure SWAP_1 is new SWAP_NEW (SOME_TYPE => INTEGER);
  procedure SWAP_2 is new SWAP_NEW (SOME_TYPE => CHARACTER,
                                    DEMO      => TEXT_INFO_2);
begin
  SWAP_1 (X, Y);
  SWAP_2 (ALPHA, BETA);
end GENERIC_SUBPROGRAM_DEFAULT_PARAMETER;
```

Listing 13.10 The generic formal subprogram and default parameters.

For the example above, we could have

```
generic
    type SOME_TYPE is (<>);
    with procedure DEMO is TEXT_INFO_1;
procedure SWAP_NEW (A, B : in out SOME_TYPE);
```

Next, instantiate the procedure, but leave out the actual subprogram parameter:

```
procedure SWAP_1 is new SWAP_NEW (INTEGER);
```

The actual (instantiated) procedure will thus use procedure TEXT_INFO_1 as its actual subprogram parameter. Listing 13.10 describes this feature.

2. The second method is slightly different. It causes the instantiated unit

to use a default subprogram that is identical (in its specification) to the formal subprogram. Its declaration form is

```
with procedure DEMO is <>;
```

as in

```
generic
    type SOME_TYPE is (<>);
    with procedure DEMO is <>;
procedure SWAP_NEW (A, B : in out SOME_TYPE);
```

Instantiate this without defining the actual subprogram parameter:

```
procedure SWAP_1 is new SWAP_NEW (INTEGER);
```

At translation time the compiler has the task of finding a procedure called DEMO, and inserting it into the actual procedure. As this is a relatively advanced topic, nothing more will be said on the subject.

13.7 GENERIC FUNCTIONS

There is very little new to be said here. The concepts are identical to those of the procedure, with variation of detail to suit the function construct. A single example will clarify the issues involved.

(a) Generic declaration

```
generic
    type SOME_TYPE is (<>);
function IS_IN_ALARM (VALUE, LIMIT : SOME_TYPE) return BOOLEAN;

function IS_IN_ALARM (VALUE, LIMIT : SOME_TYPE) return BOOLEAN is
    ALARM : BOOLEAN;
begin
    ALARM := (VALUE > LIMIT);
    return ALARM;
end IS_IN_ALARM;
```

(b) Generic instantiation

```
function PRESSURE_IS_IN_ALARM is new IS_IN_ALARM
                                    (SOME_TYPE => INTEGER);
```

```
with TEXT_IO;                use TEXT_IO;
procedure GENERIC_FUNCTION is
   X                :        INTEGER;
   Y                :        INTEGER;
   ALARM            :        BOOLEAN;
   generic
      type SOME_TYPE is (<>);
   function IS_IN_ALARM (A, B      : in    SOME_TYPE)
      return BOOLEAN;
   function IS_IN_ALARM (A, B      : in    SOME_TYPE)
      return BOOLEAN is
      C                :        BOOLEAN;
   begin
      C := (A > B);
      return C;
   end IS_IN_ALARM;
   function PRESSURE_IS_IN_ALARM is new IS_IN_ALARM (SOME_TYPE => INTEGER);
begin
   X := 2000;
   Y := 1500;
   ALARM := PRESSURE_IS_IN_ALARM (X, Y);
   if ALARM then
      PUT_LINE ("Alarm conditions !");
   else
      PUT_LINE ("condition safe");
   end if;
end GENERIC_FUNCTION;
```

Listing 13.11 The generic function.

The application of this generic function, together with its full code, is given in Listing 13.11.

13.8 GENERIC PACKAGES

13.8.1 Introduction

The generic declaration for a package is shown in Fig.13.9.

This is virtually the same as that shown in Fig.13.5 for the generic procedure. But, quite deliberately, no reference has been made to the package body. That has been done to reinforce the point that a package does not necessarily have a body (unlike the subprogram). Moreover, a package specification can hold program items which appear nowhere else – objects and types, for instance.

It is highly unlikely that we would use a generic package which consists only of a package specification. However, it does allow us to introduce the topic in a simple way, even if it is slightly artificial. Below we have the generic

Generics

```
             ┌─ generic ──────────────────────────┐
┌──────────┐ │  ┌──────────────────────────────┐  │
│ GENERIC  │ │  │ GENERIC FORMAL PARAMETERS    │  │
│ PACKAGE  │→│  └──────────────────────────────┘  │
│DECLARATION│ │  ┌──────────────────────────────┐  │
└──────────┘ │  │ PACKAGE SPECIFICATION        │  │
             │  └──────────────────────────────┘  │
             └────────────────────────────────────┘
```

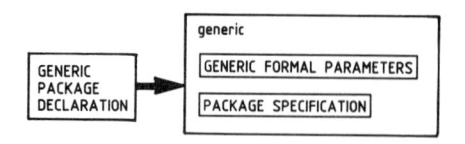

Fig.13.9 Generic package declaration structure (without body).

```
generic
  type PERCENTAGE is private;
package SIGNAL_LIMITS is
  TOP_LIMIT     :      PERCENTAGE;
  BOTTOM_LIMIT  :      PERCENTAGE;
end SIGNAL_LIMITS;
```

Listing 13.12 The generic package – consisting only of a package specification.

package SIGNAL_LIMITS. Within its specification we declare two objects, TOP_LIMIT and BOTTOM_LIMIT:

```
generic
   type PERCENTAGE is private;
package SIGNAL_LIMITS is
   TOP_LIMIT      : PERCENTAGE;
   BOTTOM_LIMIT   : PERCENTAGE;
end SIGNAL_LIMITS;
```

The package is instantiated, using the actual type parameter AP_LIMIT_RANGE:

```
subtype AP_LIMIT_RANGE is INTEGER range 0..100;
package AP_SIGNAL_LIMITS is new SIGNAL_LIMITS
                                  (AP_LIMIT_RANGE);
```

COMMENT: There is no fundamental reason for using a subtype in this example. It's merely for demonstration purposes.

The instantiated package is used in exactly the same way as any non-generic package. We can, for instance, access and manipulate the package objects, as in

```
AP_SIGNAL_LIMITS.TOP_LIMIT    := 80;
AP_SIGNAL_LIMITS.BOTTOM_LIMIT := 10;
```

This is demonstrated in full in Listings 13.12 and 13.13. See also Fig.13.10.

```
with TEXT_IO;              use TEXT_IO;
with SIGNAL_LIMITS;
procedure SIMPLE_GENERIC_PACKAGE is
  package INT_IO is new INTEGER_IO (INTEGER);
  subtype AP_LIMIT_RANGE is INTEGER range 0 .. 100;
  subtype HYD_LIMIT_RANGE is INTEGER range 0..50;
  package AP_SIGNAL_LIMITS is new SIGNAL_LIMITS (AP_LIMIT_RANGE);
  package HYD_SIGNAL_LIMITS is new SIGNAL_LIMITS (HYD_LIMIT_RANGE);
begin
  AP_SIGNAL_LIMITS.TOP_LIMIT := 80;
  AP_SIGNAL_LIMITS.BOTTOM_LIMIT := 10;
  PUT ("The current AP Signal limits are Top: ");
  INT_IO.PUT (AP_SIGNAL_LIMITS.TOP_LIMIT, 0);
  PUT (" Bottom: ");
  INT_IO.PUT (AP_SIGNAL_LIMITS.BOTTOM_LIMIT, 0);
  NEW_LINE;
  HYD_SIGNAL_LIMITS.TOP_LIMIT := 50;
  HYD_SIGNAL_LIMITS.BOTTOM_LIMIT := 5;
  PUT ("The current HYD Signal limits are Top: ");
  INT_IO.PUT (HYD_SIGNAL_LIMITS.TOP_LIMIT, 0);
  PUT (" Bottom: ");
  INT_IO.PUT (HYD_SIGNAL_LIMITS.BOTTOM_LIMIT, 0);
  NEW_LINE;
end SIMPLE_GENERIC_PACKAGE;
```

Listing 13.13 Using the generic package of Listing 13.12.

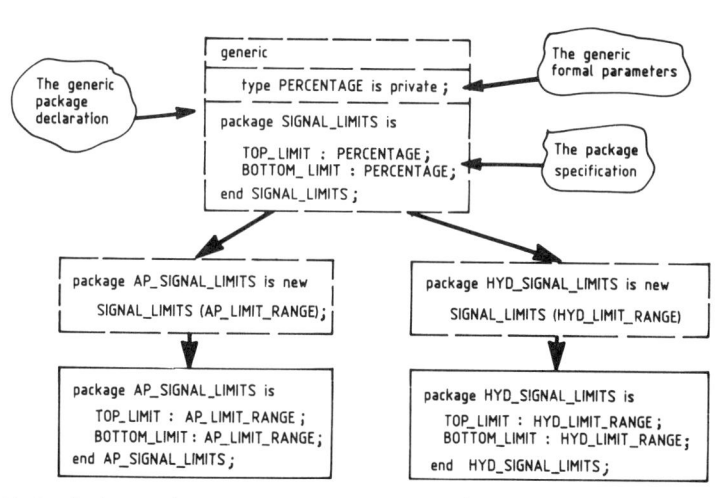

Fig.13.10 Declaring and instantiating a generic package specification.

13.8.2 More on the generic package

The most usual form of generic package includes a body in addition to its specification, Fig.13.11.

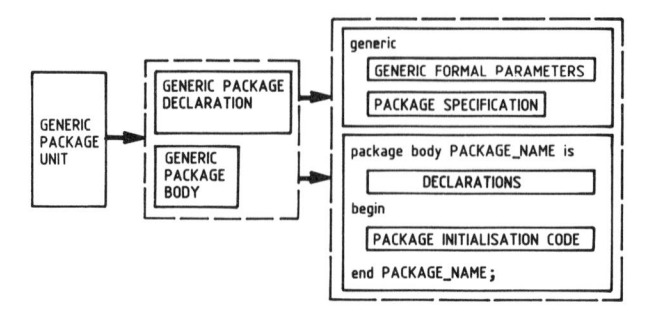

Fig.13.11 Generic package structure – complete.

Before investigating the technical details in depth, let us look at a useful application of this unit.

The scenario is that we have information coming into our system over a serial digital link. The data can be in character or integer form. We first identify the nature of the data. Then it is loaded, object by object, into the appropriate store – character or integer. Loading continues item by item until the information flow ceases. When we want to process this data we extract it, in the same order. Data is thus stored in a first-in first-out manner. The essential ingredients for this operation are:

- The store itself (DATA_STORE);
- Its related size (STORE_SIZE);
- The data units (DATA_ITEM);
- Operations to load data (LOAD_DATA);
- Operations to retrieve data (RETRIEVE_DATA).

For the moment neglect the identification aspect and concentrate only on the storing and retrieving of data. To manipulate characters, for instance, the core software is as given in Listing 13.14.

Now that the package for characters is done, we turn our attention to making one for integers. We could, of course, use our word processor or text editor to copy this package, and then change CHARACTER to INTEGER. But a much better approach is to use a generic package, as demonstrated in Listing 13.15.

This package, COMMS_DATA_STORE, can now be instantiated for the two types, CHARACTER and INTEGER:

```
package CHAR_COMMS_STORE is
  procedure LOAD_DATA (NEXT_ITEM : in     CHARACTER);
  function RETRIEVE_DATA
    return CHARACTER;
end CHAR_COMMS_STORE;

with TEXT_IO;              use TEXT_IO;
package body CHAR_COMMS_STORE is
  type DATA_SIZE is range 1..256;
  DATA_STORE      :     array (DATA_SIZE) of CHARACTER;
  NEXT_IN         :     DATA_SIZE         := DATA_SIZE'FIRST;
  NEXT_OUT        :     DATA_SIZE         := DATA_SIZE'FIRST;
  procedure LOAD_DATA (NEXT_ITEM : in     CHARACTER) is
  begin
    DATA_STORE (NEXT_IN) := NEXT_ITEM;
    if (NEXT_IN = DATA_SIZE'LAST) then
      PUT_LINE ("Data Store full. All new data will be lost");
    else
      NEXT_IN := NEXT_IN + 1;
    end if;
  end LOAD_DATA;
  function RETRIEVE_DATA
    return CHARACTER is
    NEXT_ITEM      :      CHARACTER;
  begin
    if (NEXT_OUT /= NEXT_IN) then
      NEXT_ITEM := DATA_STORE (NEXT_OUT);
      if (NEXT_OUT = DATA_SIZE'LAST) then
        PUT_LINE ("Data Store empty. Next retrieval will cause an error");
      else
        NEXT_OUT := NEXT_OUT + 1;
      end if;
    else
      PUT_LINE ("Error: No data available, return value undefined");
    end if;
    return NEXT_ITEM;
  end RETRIEVE_DATA;
end CHAR_COMMS_STORE;
    DIGIT := INT_COMMS_STORE.RETRIEVE_DATA;
    INT_IO.PUT (DIGIT, 0);
    NEW_LINE;
  end loop;
end COMMS_HANDLER;
```

Listing 13.14 This is a package used to manipulate items of type CHARACTER.

Generics

```ada
generic
  SIZE : INTEGER;
  type DATA_ITEM is private;
package COMMS_DATA_STORE is
  procedure LOAD_DATA (NEXT_ITEM : in     DATA_ITEM);
  function RETRIEVE_DATA
    return DATA_ITEM;
end COMMS_DATA_STORE;

with TEXT_IO;              use TEXT_IO;
package body COMMS_DATA_STORE is
  type DATA_SIZE is new INTEGER range 1..SIZE;
  DATA_STORE       :    array (DATA_SIZE) of DATA_ITEM;
  NEXT_IN          :    DATA_SIZE          := DATA_SIZE'FIRST;
  NEXT_OUT         :    DATA_SIZE          := DATA_SIZE'FIRST;
  procedure LOAD_DATA (NEXT_ITEM : in     DATA_ITEM) is
  begin
    DATA_STORE (NEXT_IN) := NEXT_ITEM;
    if (NEXT_IN = DATA_SIZE'LAST) then
      PUT_LINE ("Data Store full. All new data will be lost");
    else
      NEXT_IN := NEXT_IN + 1;
    end if;
  end LOAD_DATA;
  function RETRIEVE_DATA
    return DATA_ITEM is
    NEXT_ITEM      :       DATA_ITEM;
  begin
    if (NEXT_OUT /= NEXT_IN) then
      NEXT_ITEM := DATA_STORE (NEXT_OUT);
      if (NEXT_OUT = DATA_SIZE'LAST) then
        PUT_LINE ("Data Store empty. Next retrieval will cause an error");
      else
        NEXT_OUT := NEXT_OUT + 1;
      end if;
    else
      PUT_LINE ("Error: No data available, return value undefined");
    end if;
    return NEXT_ITEM;
  end RETRIEVE_DATA;
end COMMS_DATA_STORE;
```

Listing 13.15 This is a generic package used to manipulate items of a generic type.

```ada
package CHAR_COMMS_STORE is new COMMS_DATA_STORE (256, CHARACTER);
package INT_COMMS_STORE is new COMMS_DATA_STORE (4095, INTEGER);
```

In a client program we can use the procedures as shown in Listing 13.16.

Dot notation was used here to define clearly which procedure was being called – it makes the example easier to follow. In this particular case it wasn't necessary. We could just as well have written

```ada
with TEXT_IO;              use TEXT_IO;
with COMMS_DATA_STORE;
procedure COMMS_HANDLER is
 -- instantiate COMMS_DATA_STORE for CHARACTER and INTEGER.
  package CHAR_COMMS_STORE is new COMMS_DATA_STORE (256, CHARACTER);
  package INT_COMMS_STORE is new COMMS_DATA_STORE (4096, INTEGER);
 -- declare type and variables
  type OPTION is (CHAR, INT, QUIT);
  SELECTION        :     OPTION;
  CHAR_COUNT       :     INTEGER        := 0;
  INT_COUNT        :     INTEGER        := 0;
  ASCII            :     CHARACTER;
  DIGIT            :     INTEGER;
 -- IO packages
  package OPTION_IO is new ENUMERATION_IO (OPTION);
  package INT_IO is new INTEGER_IO (INTEGER);
begin
  loop
    PUT ("Char, Int or Quit ? ");
    OPTION_IO.GET (SELECTION);
    SKIP_LINE;
--
    exit when SELECTION = QUIT;
--
    if (SELECTION = CHAR) then
      PUT ("Ascii character => ");
      GET (ASCII);
      SKIP_LINE;
--
      CHAR_COMMS_STORE.LOAD_DATA (ASCII);
--
      CHAR_COUNT := CHAR_COUNT + 1;
    else
      PUT ("Integer value => ");
      INT_IO.GET (DIGIT);
      SKIP_LINE;
--
      INT_COMMS_STORE.LOAD_DATA (DIGIT);
--
      INT_COUNT := INT_COUNT + 1;
    end if;
  end loop;
-- display ASCII stored values
  NEW_LINE;
  PUT_LINE ("ASCII stored values");
  for COUNT in 1..CHAR_COUNT loop
    INT_IO.PUT (COUNT, 0);
    PUT (" : ");
    ASCII := CHAR_COMMS_STORE.RETRIEVE_DATA;
    PUT (ASCII);
    NEW_LINE;
  end loop;
-- display Integer stored values
  PUT_LINE ("Integer stored values");
  for COUNT in 1..INT_COUNT loop
    INT_IO.PUT (COUNT, 0);
    PUT (" : ");
    DIGIT := INT_COMMS_STORE.RETRIEVE_DATA;
    INT_IO.PUT (DIGIT, 0);
    NEW_LINE;
  end loop;
end COMMS_HANDLER;
```

Listing 13.16 This is a complete example which uses a generic package.

432 Generics

```
LOAD_DATA (ASCII);
LOAD_DATA (DIGIT);
etc.
```

and left it at that. This is a classic case of overloading of names, here being applied to procedures. The compiler resolves which LOAD_DATA procedure is being called by assessing the type of its parameter.

13.9 PUTTING VERSATILITY INTO THE GENERIC UNIT

13.9.1 The problem

Generic units, as discussed so far, can be very inflexible. This is clearly shown in Fig.13.8. You can see that as we extend the range of types handled by the instantiated unit, fewer operations are applicable. For example, take the function IS_IN_ALARM, given earlier:

```
generic
   type SOME_TYPE is (<>);
function IS_IN_ALARM (VALUE, LIMIT : SOME_TYPE) return BOOLEAN;

function IS_IN_ALARM (VALUE, LIMIT : SOME_TYPE) return BOOLEAN is
   ALARM : BOOLEAN;
begin
   ALARM := (VALUE > LIMIT);
   return ALARM;
end IS_IN_ALARM;
```

The declaration form of SOME_TYPE defines it to be any discrete type. Thus, for example, we can instantiate this generic function as

```
function SPEED_IS_IN_ALARM is new IS_IN_ALARM
                               (SOME_TYPE => INTEGER);
```

Now suppose that we wish to use this function where SOME_TYPE is of type FLOAT. If we try to instantiate IS_IN_ALARM as

```
function SPEED_IS_IN_ALARM is new IS_IN_ALARM
                               (SOME_TYPE => FLOAT);
```

Putting versatility into the generic unit 433

it will be rejected by the compiler. FLOAT cannot be used with this type definition. We could, of course, build a new generic unit for floating point types, but this seems to negate the whole purpose of generics. Is there an alternative solution? Fortunately there is. First, use a type declaration which will accept any type. Second, ensure that all operations within the generic body are applicable to these types. Third, make sure that the rules of generic type declarations are obeyed.

13.9.2 The versatile generic subprogram parameter

For the example IS_IN_ALARM, the first point to tackle is the relational operator >. Remember, as a predefined operator, it can only be used with specific types. So, let us see how to replace

> ALARM := (VALUE > LIMIT);

with

> ALARM := (VALUE GREATER_THAN LIMIT);

where GREATER_THAN is to be replaced on instantiation by a function which:

- Accepts VALUE and LIMIT as parameters;
- Performs the comparison 'is VALUE greater than LIMIT?'
- Returns a BOOLEAN result – TRUE or FALSE.

Assume that we develop such a function (the details can be ignored just for the moment). Typically its specification would be:

> **function** GREATER_THAN (X, Y : PARAMETER_TYPE) **return** BOOLEAN;

We do this for INTEGERs and real types, using function overloading:

> **function** GREATER_THAN (X, Y : INTEGER) **return** BOOLEAN;
> **function** GREATER_THAN (X, Y : FLOAT) **return** BOOLEAN;

Naturally the formal parameter type has to match the actual parameter type when the function is called. Therefore we form the generic unit:

```
generic
    type SOME_TYPE is limited private; -- declaring a formal type
    with function GREATER_THAN (X, Y : SOME_TYPE) return BOOLEAN;
function IN_ALARM (VALUE, LIMIT : SOME_TYPE) return BOOLEAN;

function IN_ALARM (VALUE, LIMIT : SOME_TYPE) return BOOLEAN is
    ALARM : BOOLEAN;
begin
    ALARM := GREATER_THAN (VALUE, LIMIT);
    return ALARM;
end IN_ALARM;
```

Instantiating this results in

```
function SPEED_IS_IN_ALARM is new IN_ALARM (FLOAT, BIGGER_THAN);
function PRESSURE_IS_IN_ALARM is new IN_ALARM (INTEGER, BIGGER_THAN);
```

The complete program for this is shown in Listing 13.17.

You should see now that we can make our generic units highly flexible by tailoring them using formal subprograms.

13.9.3 Operator symbols and the generic subprogram parameter

At this stage we seem to have accomplished quite a lot. But the approach used here has one significant drawback (or didn't you notice?): that is, we needed to define two different GREATER_THAN procedures to make the instantiation work. Is this progress, we ask? The answer is obvious. In truth what we need is to be able to use a single actual subprogram parameter, one that caters for both INTEGER and FLOAT types.

Examine the details of the package STANDARD in your compiler manual. Here you'll find that the operator '>' is defined for BOOLEAN, INTEGER, FLOAT and STRING (strictly speaking the operations are implemented using the function ">"). This particular example is yet another oft-quoted example of overloading. When we use '>' the compiler selects the appropriate operator by looking at its parameters. So, what would be the effect of using ">" as the actual subprogram parameter (as shown below) in the instantiations of IN_ALARM?

```
function SPEED_IS_IN_ALARM is new IN_ALARM (FLOAT, ">");
function PRESSURE_IS_IN_ALARM is new IN_ALARM (INTEGER, ">");
```

It results in the formal subprogram parameter GREATER_THAN being substituted by the actual parameter ">" at translation time. Moreover, this

```ada
with TEXT_IO;              use TEXT_IO;
procedure FORMAL_SUBPROGRAM is
  -- declare variables
  MAX_VELOCITY      :    FLOAT          :=  70.0;
  CURRENT_VELOCITY  :    FLOAT;
  MAX_PRESSURE      :    INTEGER        :=  1000;
  CURRENT_PRESSURE  :    INTEGER;
  ALARM             :    BOOLEAN;
  function BIGGER_THAN (X, Y         :         INTEGER)
    return BOOLEAN is
  begin
    return (X > Y);
  end BIGGER_THAN;
  function BIGGER_THAN (X, Y         :         FLOAT)
    return BOOLEAN is
  begin
    return (X > Y);
  end BIGGER_THAN;
  -- the generic function
  generic
    type SOME_TYPE is limited private;
    with function GREATER_THAN (X, Y : SOME_TYPE)
    return BOOLEAN;
  function IN_ALARM (VALUE, LIMIT :    SOME_TYPE)
    return BOOLEAN;
  function IN_ALARM (VALUE, LIMIT :    SOME_TYPE)
    return BOOLEAN is
    IN_ALARM         :     BOOLEAN;
  begin
    IN_ALARM := GREATER_THAN (VALUE, LIMIT);
    return IN_ALARM;
  end IN_ALARM;
  function SPEED_IS_IN_ALARM is new IN_ALARM (FLOAT, BIGGER_THAN);
  function PRESSURE_IS_IN_ALARM is new IN_ALARM (INTEGER, BIGGER_THAN);
begin
  CURRENT_VELOCITY := 100.0;
  ALARM := SPEED_IS_IN_ALARM (CURRENT_VELOCITY, MAX_VELOCITY);
  if ALARM then
    PUT_LINE ("Panic !! Velocity too high.");
  else
    PUT_LINE ("Velocity OK");
  end if;
  CURRENT_PRESSURE := 100;
  ALARM := PRESSURE_IS_IN_ALARM (CURRENT_PRESSURE, MAX_PRESSURE);
  if ALARM then
    PUT_LINE ("Panic !! Pressure too high.");
  else
    PUT_LINE ("Pressure OK");
  end if;
end FORMAL_SUBPROGRAM;
```

Listing 13.17 Using a generic subprogram parameter to insert an operator into a generic unit.

436 Generics

```
with TEXT_IO;              use TEXT_IO;
procedure PREDEFINED_OP is
   MAX_VELOCITY       :   FLOAT           :=   70.0;
   CURRENT_VELOCITY   :   FLOAT;
   MAX_PRESSURE       :   INTEGER         :=   1000;
   CURRENT_PRESSURE   :   INTEGER;
   ALARM              :   BOOLEAN;
   generic
     type SOME_TYPE is limited private;
     with function GREATER_THAN (X, Y : SOME_TYPE)
       return BOOLEAN;
   function IN_ALARM (VALUE, LIMIT :     SOME_TYPE)
     return BOOLEAN;
   function IN_ALARM (VALUE, LIMIT :     SOME_TYPE)
     return BOOLEAN is
     IN_ALARM        :   BOOLEAN;
   begin
     IN_ALARM := GREATER_THAN (VALUE, LIMIT);
     return IN_ALARM;
   end IN_ALARM;
   function SPEED_IS_IN_ALARM is new IN_ALARM (FLOAT, ">");
   function PRESSURE_IS_IN_ALARM is new IN_ALARM (INTEGER, ">");
begin
   CURRENT_VELOCITY := 100.0;
   ALARM := SPEED_IS_IN_ALARM (CURRENT_VELOCITY, MAX_VELOCITY);
   if ALARM then
     PUT_LINE ("Panic !! Velocity too high.");
   else
     PUT_LINE ("Velocity OK");
   end if;
   CURRENT_PRESSURE := 100;
   ALARM := PRESSURE_IS_IN_ALARM (CURRENT_PRESSURE, MAX_PRESSURE);
   if ALARM then
     PUT_LINE ("Panic !! Pressure too high.");
   else
     PUT_LINE ("Pressure OK");
   end if;
end PREDEFINED_OP;
```

Listing 13.18 Using a generic subprogram parameter to insert a predefined operator from package STANDARD into a generic unit.

operator can be used with both types INTEGER and FLOAT. Therefore both instantiations are valid. This is shown in full in Listing 13.18.

Naturally enough this technique works with all the predefined overloaded operators.

Let us extend this work relating to predefined operators (take this carefully, it may be slightly confusing at first). Suppose that, in the previous example, we had been able to use the > operator (instead of GREATER_THAN) within the generic function. This would be quite an asset in terms of code readability and comprehension. As it turns out, we can do just that. Look back to the section on overloading of operators. There it was shown how to replace the standard operators with functions of our choice. Why not apply that technique now? Substitute ">" for GREATER_THAN, as in

```
function ">" (X, Y : PARAMETER_TYPE) return BOOLEAN;
```

Rewriting the generic unit, we have

```
generic
    type SOME_TYPE is limited private; -- declaring a formal type
    with function ">" (X, Y : SOME_TYPE) return BOOLEAN;
function IN_ALARM (VALUE, LIMIT : SOME_TYPE) return BOOLEAN;

function IN_ALARM (VALUE, LIMIT : SOME_TYPE) return BOOLEAN is
    ALARM : BOOLEAN;
begin
    ALARM := VALUE > LIMIT; -- using infix notation
    return ALARM;
end IN_ALARM;
```

This can now be instantiated as shown below:

```
function SPEED_IS_IN_ALARM is new IN_ALARM (FLOAT, ">");
function PRESSURE_IS_IN_ALARM is new IN_ALARM (INTEGER, ">");
```

Alternative forms of instantiation which are directly equivalent are:

1.
```
function SPEED_IS_IN_ALARM is new IN_ALARM (SOME_TYPE => FLOAT,
                                             ">" => ">");
```

The parameter named association ">" => ">" looks very strange indeed, but it follows the normal rules for named association. That is, the symbol to the left of the arrow is the formal parameter, the other being the actual parameter.

2.
```
function SPEED_IS_IN_ALARM is new IN_ALARM (SOME_TYPE => FLOAT,
                                             ">" => STANDARD.">");
```

Here the actual parameter is a qualified one. This makes it absolutely clear that we intend to use the predefined operator from package STANDARD. Otherwise it could be that the actual parameter ">" is yet another overloaded one.

3. Using a default parameter. If the declaration was amended to read

438 Generics

```
with function ">" (X, Y : SOME_TYPE) return BOOLEAN is <>;
```

then the following instantiation form may be used:

```
function SPEED_IS_IN_ALARM is new IN_ALARM (FLOAT);
```

Here the second parameter defaults to the formal one.

Listing 13.19 illustrates these approaches.

REVIEW

Do you now:

- Appreciate the fundamental concepts of generics and instantiation?
- Understand the role of generic units and generic parameters?
- Know how to build generic units based on the procedure, the function and the package?
- Realize the purpose and application of types, objects and subprograms as generic parameters?
- See how to instantiate and apply generic units?
- Perceive how subprogram parameters can be used to bring flexibility into generic units?

If you've answered yes to all of these, then you should be able to follow the text below without difficulty.

Go back to the very first chapter. There you'll find that we introduced packages, importing, generics, instantiation and invocation using

```
with TEXT_IO;
procedure EXAMPLE_1 is
package INT_IO is new TEXT_IO.INTEGER_IO (INTEGER);
begin
    ........................;
    INT_IO.GET (X1);
    ........................;
end;
```

This should at last make sense. First, review the text of the example. The opening line imports the package TEXT_IO, part of the predefined language environment. On the third line we instantiate the package INTEGER_IO – which is embedded in the package TEXT_IO – as INT_IO. One actual

```ada
with TEXT_IO;              use TEXT_IO;
procedure OPERATOR_FORMAL_PARAM is
   MAX_VELOCITY         :   FLOAT        := 70.0;
   CURRENT_VELOCITY     :   FLOAT;
   MAX_PRESSURE         :   INTEGER      := 1000;
   CURRENT_PRESSURE     :   INTEGER;
   MAX_TEMPERATURE      :   POSITIVE     := 99;
   CURRENT_TEMPERATURE  :   POSITIVE;
   ALARM                :   BOOLEAN;
   generic
      type SOME_TYPE is limited private;
      with function ">" (X, Y : SOME_TYPE)
         return BOOLEAN is <>;
   function IN_ALARM (VALUE, LIMIT :   SOME_TYPE)
      return BOOLEAN;
   function IN_ALARM (VALUE, LIMIT :   SOME_TYPE)
      return BOOLEAN is
      IN_ALARM      :    BOOLEAN;
   begin
      IN_ALARM := VALUE > LIMIT;
      return IN_ALARM;
   end IN_ALARM;
   function SPEED_IS_IN_ALARM is new IN_ALARM (SOME_TYPE => FLOAT,
                                                ">"       => ">");
   function PRESSURE_IS_IN_ALARM is new IN_ALARM (SOME_TYPE => INTEGER,
                                                   ">"       => STANDARD.">");
   function TEMPERATURE_IS_IN_ALARM is new IN_ALARM (POSITIVE);
begin
   CURRENT_VELOCITY := 100.0;
   ALARM := SPEED_IS_IN_ALARM (CURRENT_VELOCITY, MAX_VELOCITY);
   if ALARM then
      PUT_LINE ("Panic !! Velocity too high.");
   else
      PUT_LINE ("Velocity OK");
   end if;
   CURRENT_PRESSURE := 100;
   ALARM := PRESSURE_IS_IN_ALARM (CURRENT_PRESSURE, MAX_PRESSURE);
   if ALARM then
      PUT_LINE ("Panic !! Pressure too high.");
   else
      PUT_LINE ("Pressure OK");
   end if;
   CURRENT_TEMPERATURE := 100;
   ALARM := TEMPERATURE_IS_IN_ALARM (CURRENT_TEMPERATURE, MAX_TEMPERATURE);
   if ALARM then
      PUT_LINE ("Panic !! Temperature too high.");
   else
      PUT_LINE ("Temperature OK");
   end if;
end OPERATOR_FORMAL_PARAM;
```

Listing 13.19 Using a generic subprogram parameter to insert a predefined operator from package STANDARD into a generic unit.

parameter is defined – INTEGER. Within the program statements the procedure GET is invoked. It has a single parameter.

From this we deduce that procedure GET is located within the package INTEGER_IO, which in turn is located within the package TEXT_IO. INTEGER_IO is a generic unit (but not TEXT_IO).

Now turn to your compiler manual (or the LRM) and review the package TEXT_IO. The important features of its declaration – some aspects have been omitted – are

```
package TEXT_IO is
    subtype FIELD is INTEGER range 0 .. implementation defined;
generic
    type NUM is range <>;
package INTEGER_IO is
    procedure GET (ITEM : out NUM; WIDTH : in FIELD := 0);
end INTEGER_IO;
```

On instantiation of the generic package INTEGER_IO, the actual type parameter used is INTEGER. This replaces the formal type parameter NUM. When the procedure GET is invoked in the application program, a single actual parameter (X1) is passed in. This is substituted for the formal parameter ITEM. For the second procedure parameter, WIDTH, the default value is used.

Chapter Fourteen
Concurrency – the Ada task

Up to this time all our programs have one unifying feature: sequential operation. In other words, they only ever do one thing at a time. And yet, in the real world, most applications consist of a multiplicity of jobs, many of which should be carried out at the same time. For instance, we may wish to use a word processing package and a printer simultaneously under the control of a standard commercial operating system. In an embedded application we may have to run a control loop, a data communications channel and a display system in parallel. Operations such as these are described as being concurrent, the related software being that of concurrent programming. Ada provides a powerful mechanism to help us build and control concurrent programs – the task.

After having studied this chapter you will:

- Understand the difference between sequential and parallel activities;
- Appreciate the use of multiprocessing and multitasking;
- Understand and implement concurrent tasking of independent tasks;
- Understand and implement concurrent tasking of interdependent tasks;
- Understand and implement intertask synchronization using the rendezvous;
- Be able to implement selective acceptor and calling rendezvous;
- Perceive the structure and use of task types and task entry families;
- Know how to implement various task termination techniques;
- Appreciate the way in which exceptions are handled in tasks;
- Understand the use of task priorities and task attributes.

14.1 CONCURRENCY – AN INTRODUCTION

In Fig.14.1 we show two different tasks running under the control of a single computer system.

At this stage nothing has been said about how many separate processors are contained within this system. Further, nothing has been said about task interaction. Assume that both operations are to run simultaneously. This can be shown diagrammatically as in Fig.14.2.

Here we have true parallel task execution; that is, each task actually runs at the same time. To implement this we must have a separate processor dedicated to each function (Fig.14.3).

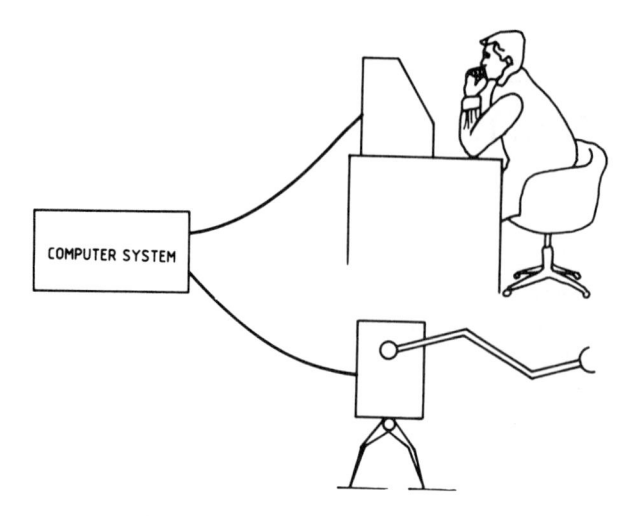

Fig.14.1 Computer-based tasks.

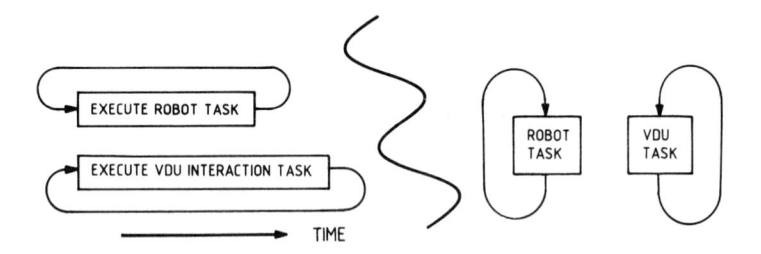

Fig.14.2 Simultaneous task or process operation (parallel execution).

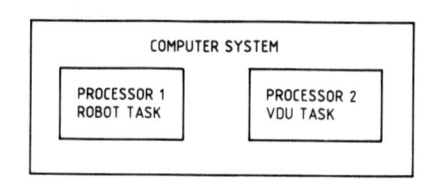

Fig.14.3 Hardware support for parallel processing.

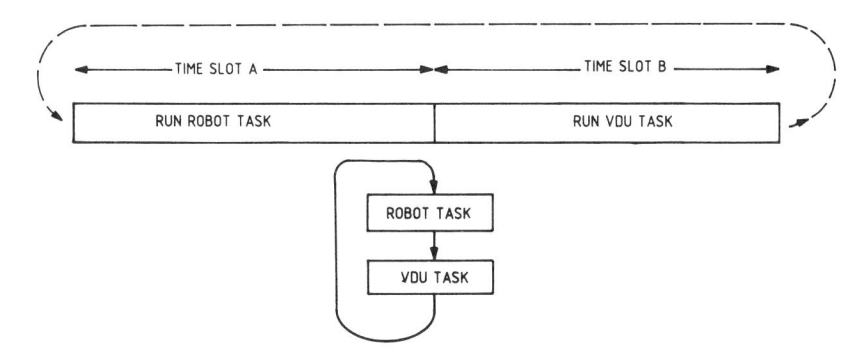

Fig.14.4 Simple sequential task operation.

This is a proper multiprocessor system, being the only way to implement true multiprocessing.

Now take the situation where only one processor is available, yet the two tasks still have to be carried out. One solution might be to use the method shown in Fig.14.4.

Here each task is performed in sequence, the program being a continuous loop. Control merely passes from the robot task to the VDU task to the robot task ... and so on. This is a simple example of *multitasking* on a single processor system (to avoid confusion, the term multitasking will here apply to single processor systems; executing multiple tasks on a number of processors will be referred to as *multiprocessing*).

Using this approach the resulting software is:

- Simple to implement;
- Well controlled;
- Predictable;
- Relatively straightforward to debug.

Such methods have, for instance, been widely used in slow systems such as process control and the like. But there is a significant drawback with the technique. While one task is being serviced by the computer, the other is idle (or out of control). This may make it unacceptable for use in many applications. For example, in fast embedded systems, tasks may be left uncontrolled only for very short periods. At the other extreme, waiting for computer responses in a shared mainframe environment can be totally frustrating. How can we improve system performance in these circumstances?

A number of solutions are available. Underlying many of them is a common factor. For many applications the work does not need to be performed continuously; it can be carried out in short, discontinuous bursts. Even though there is a time gap between activities, the appearance – to the user – is that

444 Concurrency – the Ada task

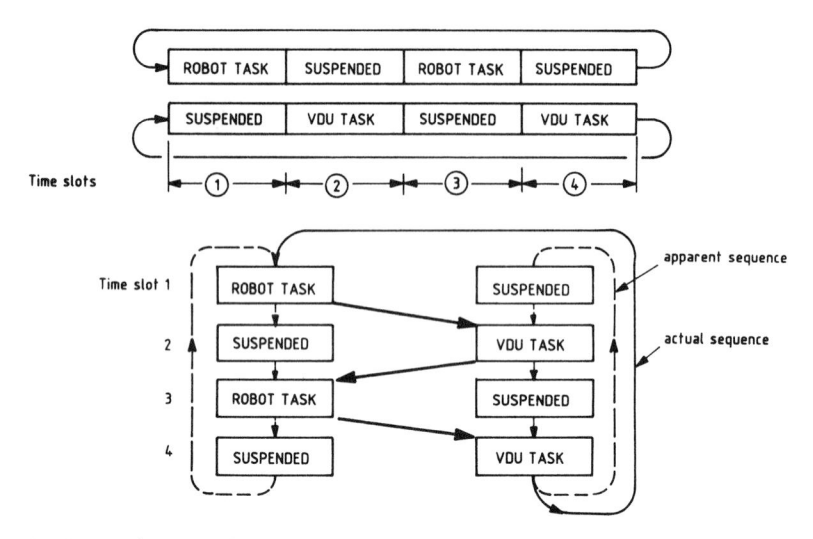

Fig.14.5 Time-sharing of tasks (multitasking).

of one continuous operation. So, to execute more than one task on a single processor, we may be able to time-share its resources as shown in Fig.14.5.

Here each individual task is either running or suspended; the tasks take it in turns to use the computing facilities. This produces the illusion of running two tasks simultaneously in the system. The reality, of course, is quite different.

For either multiprocessing or multitasking, each task may be in one of three possible states, Fig.14.6.

In Ada we use the task construct to build concurrent software. Thus we would have a ROBOT_TASK and a VDU_TASK. But we do not define the execution strategies (scheduling policies) applied to these tasks. That is fixed by our computing environment. We can build tasks, set them running, suspend them and terminate them. We cannot, from our Ada code, control and decree precisely how these tasks are handled by the computer.

14.2 INTERDEPENDENT AND INDEPENDENT TASKS – THEIR CO-ORDINATION

We haven't as yet discussed how the robot and the VDU tasks interact with each other. Clearly, if the VDU operator sends commands to the robot, we have interdependent tasks. If, on the other hand, the VDU is used for word processing only, the tasks are independent ones. But that doesn't mean that

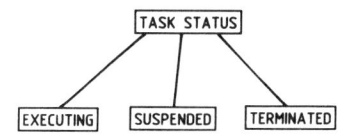

Fig.14.6 Possible task states.

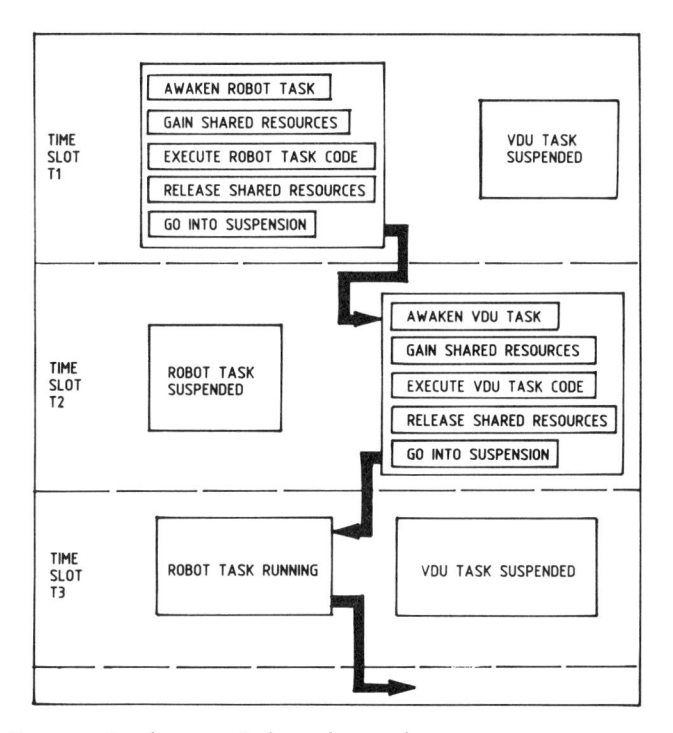

Fig.14.7 Co-operation between independent tasks.

the tasks don't interact with each other. Quite often they have to co-operate when using computer resources.

Let's first assume that the functions performed are independent of each other. Task scheduling and communication could, in this instance, be implemented as shown in Fig.14.7.

Here operations are carried out under the command of a system controller (the scheduler). The suspended task sits waiting for a 'start' command whilst the other is using system resources. The running task carries out part of its total function and is then suspended by the scheduler. It, the scheduler, now activates the other task. At some later stage this process is repeated; a task swap once again takes place. The awoken task resumes execution from where it previously left off.

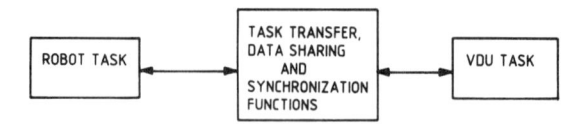

Fig.14.8 Co-operation between interdependent tasks.

This represents a simple form of concurrency, often found in time-shared computer installations. A good example of this is the typical college computer system used by students for programming and similar activities. In such instances each task is essentially an individual, private one. Normally, users do not need, or wish, to interact with each other. As a result the problem – as far as the computer operating system is concerned – is reduced to handling task information and allocating computer time to users.

Let us now assume that the VDU operator can control and monitor the robot from his or her console. Here the tasks must co-operate in a number of ways (Fig.14.8).

Task transfer still has to be implemented: nothing has changed here. However, the tasks now have to communicate with each other. For instance, the operator may set the maximum velocity of movement of the robot via the keyboard input. This data then has to be accessed by the robot servo drive controllers. In the same way, status information acquired by the robot sensors may need to be displayed on the VDU. Such communication functions can be carried out using data-sharing methods.

Finally, the tasks must be co-ordinated or synchronized. The following is a simple example of the need for such co-ordination. The robot is carrying out a delicate operation, based on information supplied by the operator. Assume that changing this information part way through the operation would produce a dangerous situation. Therefore we can time-share both tasks safely, subject to one constraint. It is essential to block updating of the control data during this critical operation. In other words, the update and use of such information must be synchronized.

In a single processor system, only one task runs at any one time. Suspended tasks should normally release all system facilities. Hence there cannot be a direct (i.e. simultaneous) clash for the use of shared resources. This may lull you into thinking that contention for such facilities is a non-problem. Do not fall into this trap. In practice, if such accesses are not carefully controlled, we may end up with a chaotic situation (see later).

A last major issue is that of a deadlock. Deadlocks occur typically when two (or more) tasks come to a complete standstill because of missing information. Consider the case where:

Task A needs the result of a computation from task B before it can proceed; and

Task B is waiting for the result from A before it can complete.

This is a classic deadlock situation.

Deadlocks are much more likely to be met in multiprocessor systems where tasks actually do run simultaneously (and usually asynchronously). Further, there is often extensive sharing of hardware resources in such systems.

14.3 INTRODUCING THE ADA TASK

14.3.1 Implementing independent tasks

Recapping, there are a number of categories of Ada tasks, Fig.14.9.

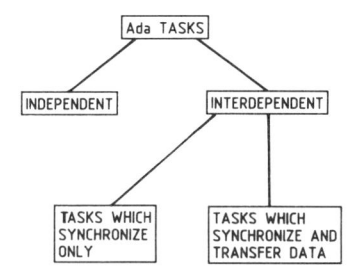

Fig.14.9 Ada task categories.

In this introductory section we will confine ourselves to independent operations. These, as you will discover through experience, are much less common than interdependent ones. However, they allow us to introduce the topic in a relatively simple way. They also highlight several essential points of tasking.

Suppose we are presented with the problem of implementing the VDU and ROBOT operations discussed earlier. It is required that these are performed as two parallel tasks. How should we tackle this problem?

First we have to build the software unit which contains the tasks, the so-called *master*. In this example we will use a procedure (note this point well – a task, by itself, is not a compilable unit). Then we construct the tasks within this. At run time we have to ensure that the tasks are activated as required. Equally important, we need to see that the tasks are deactivated (terminated) correctly. For this example the basic task framework is that of Fig.14.10.

Tasks (more precisely task units) are housed in the declarations section of

448   Concurrency – the Ada task

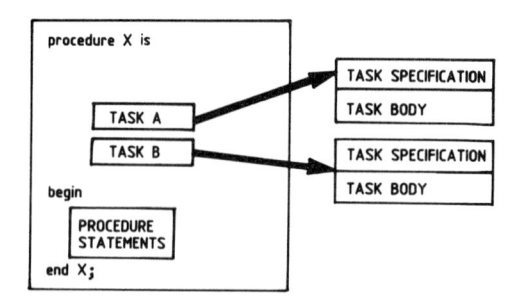

```
procedure X is
                              ┌──────────────────────┐
                              │ TASK SPECIFICATION   │
              ┌────────┐─────▶├──────────────────────┤
              │ TASK A │      │ TASK BODY            │
              └────────┘      └──────────────────────┘
              ┌────────┐      ┌──────────────────────┐
              │ TASK B │─────▶│ TASK SPECIFICATION   │
              └────────┘      ├──────────────────────┤
begin                         │ TASK BODY            │
     ┌────────────┐           └──────────────────────┘
     │ PROCEDURE  │
     │ STATEMENTS │
     └────────────┘
end X;
```

Fig.14.10 Tasks – location and structure.

their master unit. Each task consists of a specification and a body, having the following basic syntax:

```
TASK SPECIFICATION ====> task TASK_NAME;

TASK BODY          ====> task body TASK_NAME is
                             TASK_LOCAL_DECLARATIONS
                         begin
                             TASK_EXECUTABLE_STATEMENTS
                         end TASK_NAME;
```

In this example the task units are

Task A

```
task VDU; -- task declaration (i.e. task_specification;)
task body VDU is
begin
    PUT_LINE ("task VDU is running");
end VDU;
```

Task B

```
task ROBOT;
task body ROBOT is
begin
    PUT_LINE ("task ROBOT is running");
end ROBOT;
```

The task specification acts as its interface. The body contains the statements which are executed when the task is activated.

Now let us include these tasks in a procedure FIRST_TASK_EXAMPLE,

Introducing the Ada task

```
with TEXT_IO;              use TEXT_IO;
procedure MANUFACTURING_SYSTEM is
  procedure FIRST_TASK_EXAMPLE is
    task VDU;
    task ROBOT;
    task body VDU is
    begin
       PUT_LINE ("task VDU is running");
    end VDU;
    task body ROBOT is
    begin
       PUT_LINE ("task ROBOT is running");
    end ROBOT;
  begin
    PUT_LINE ("First task example");
  end FIRST_TASK_EXAMPLE;
begin
  PUT_LINE ("Main progam is running");
  FIRST_TASK_EXAMPLE;
end MANUFACTURING_SYSTEM;
```

Listing 14.1 Demonstrating independent tasks in execution.

Listing 14.1. This procedure is declared within a main program, MANUFACTURING_SYSTEM.

Hence, in Listing 14.1, the procedure FIRST_TASK_EXAMPLE is the master for both the VDU and ROBOT tasks.

Observe that FIRST_TASK_EXAMPLE has just one executable statement. This is needed to comply with the rules of Ada: 'the main program must have at least one executable statement'. We could, of course, use the **null** statement by itself if so desired.

Task activation and execution is automatic. Unlike a subprogram, for instance, it doesn't have to be called explicitly. However, in order to bring the tasks into existence, we first have to run the master. Then, as soon as the master reaches its **begin**, the tasks within it become active. Each task then runs independently to completion (when a task reaches its **end** it is said to be completed). However, the code of the procedure (i.e. between its **begin** and **end**) is also considered to belong to a task. This task therefore executes in parallel with the other tasks. Unfortunately, we can't be sure of the running order.

Only when all tasks are completed can the procedure be left. Control is then returned to the calling program. Note this small but important point. The master may have executed its code, yet it cannot be left until all its dependent tasks are terminated. To demonstrate this put the statements of the VDU task inside an infinite loop and rerun the program.

In this example the tasks were contained in a procedure in order to demonstrate certain specific points. This is not the normal approach.

14.3.2 Task interference – an introduction to the problem

From the previous example we might assume that handling independent tasks is fairly simple. Be warned, it may not be that easy, as shown in Listing 14.2.

```
with TEXT_IO;                  use TEXT_IO;
procedure SECOND_TASK_EXAMPLE is
  task VDU;
  task ROBOT;
  task body VDU is
  begin
    for COUNT in 1..10 loop
      PUT_LINE ("task VDU is running");
    end loop;
  end VDU;
  task body ROBOT is
  begin
    for COUNT in 1..10 loop
      PUT_LINE ("task ROBOT is running");
    end loop;
  end ROBOT;
begin
  PUT_LINE ("Main progam is running");
end SECOND_TASK_EXAMPLE;
```

Listing 14.2 Demonstrating possible interference between independent tasks.

Here we have modified the VDU and ROBOT tasks so that they perform multiple writes to the screen display. Now, although the tasks themselves are independent, they share a common resource, the screen system. How are they going to co-operate in the use of this? Frankly, we really don't know. And to demonstrate this point we urge you to run the example.

The basic problem is that there is no control exercised over access to the screen. So, while the VDU task is executing, it could well be suspended, being replaced by the ROBOT task. Or, the ROBOT task may be replaced (pre-empted) by the VDU task. And so on. clearly, when tasks share resources, access control must be implemented. This is normally called mutual exclusion.

At this point we introduce the delay statement. This enables you to set delays into your program, wherever and whenever you want to. A typical delay statement has the format

delay (10.0);

The result of using this is to suspend program execution for 10 seconds at the statement point.

Strictly speaking, the delay statement is defined as

Introducing the Ada task 451

```
with TEXT_IO;                   use TEXT_IO;
procedure DELAY_TASK_EXAMPLE is
  task VDU;
  task ROBOT;
  task body VDU is
  begin
    for COUNT in 1..10 loop
      PUT_LINE ("task VDU is running");
      delay 1.0;
    end loop;
  end VDU;
  task body ROBOT is
  begin
    for COUNT in 1..10 loop
      PUT_LINE ("task ROBOT is running");
      delay 1.0;
    end loop;
  end ROBOT;
begin
  PUT_LINE ("Main progam is running");
end DELAY_TASK_EXAMPLE;
```

Listing 14.3 This introduces the delay statement, and shows how it affects task execution.

```
delay simple_expression;
```

where simple_expression is a predefined type called DURATION. This is a fixed point one. Thus we could have, for instance,

```
VALVE_OPENING_TIME : DURATION := 2.0;
begin
    .
    delay VALVE_OPENING_TIME;
    .
end;
```

It should be noted that the delay statement is not an integral part of tasking – you can use it anywhere. However, it is widely applied to task operations, a demonstration being given in Listing 14.3.

This will modify the behaviour of the tasks so that they will run in 'lock-step' mode (i.e. A, B, A, B, A, ..., etc.; see Fig.14.11).

Note also that the delay time value is always stated in seconds. Be careful about using **delay** if you want precise timing. You are guaranteed to get at least the value specified in your statement – but not necessarily exactly that value.

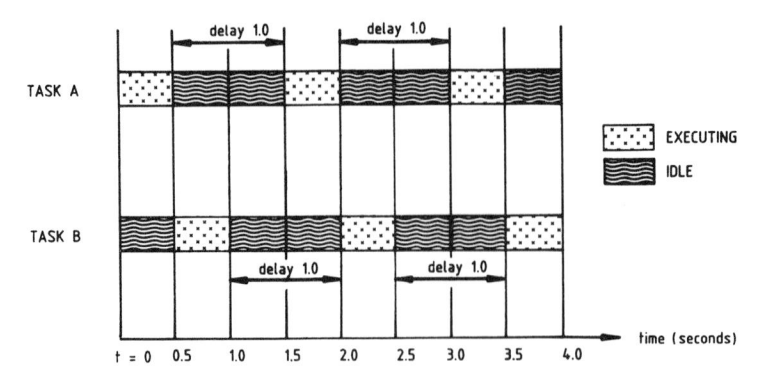

Fig.14.11 The effect of using the delay statement.

14.4 INTERDEPENDENT TASKS, SYNCHRONIZATION AND THE RENDEZVOUS

14.4.1 General concepts

The simplest form of interaction between interdependent tasks occurs when we only want to synchronize their operations. Here there is no requirement to transfer data between them.

Figure 14.12 shows the synchronizing model used in Ada, applicable to a two-task situation.

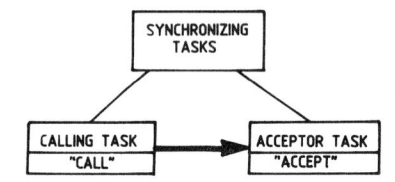

Fig.14.12 The Ada synchronizing model – two tasks.

We treat one as the *calling* task, the other as the *acceptor*. The calling task always defines which acceptor task it wishes to synchronize with. It does this by issuing a signal (*call*) to the acceptor. In contrast, the acceptor task synchronizing signal *accept* indicates that it (the acceptor) will synchronize with any calling task. Both tasks must be active if they are to synchronize. Be clear on one point: the calling task does not activate the acceptor task.

Now let us see, in general terms, how synchronization is attained. Remember, both tasks run quite separately, at their own pace. Therefore we cannot

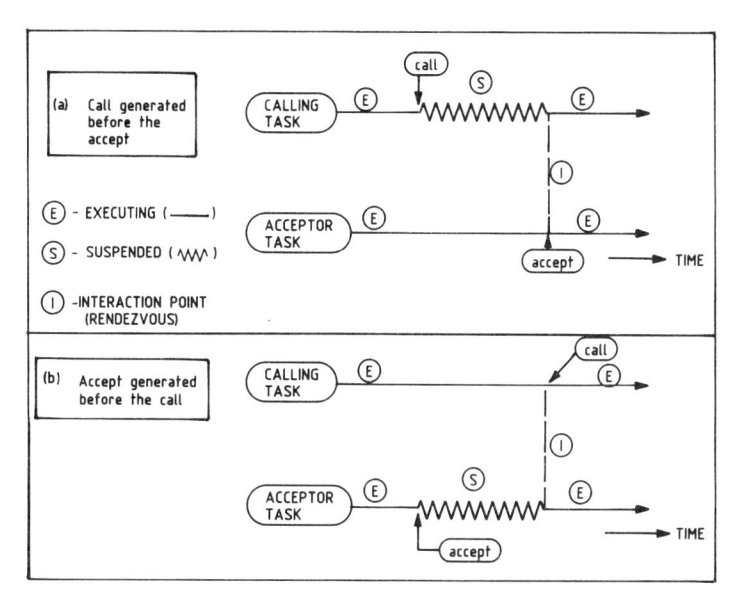

Fig.14.13 Synchronization of two tasks.

predict when synchronizing signals are going to be generated. But when it does happen, the two most likely scenarios are those illustrated in Fig.14.13.

In (a), the calling task issues its call signal before the acceptor has reached its accept point. The caller now waits (suspended) until the acceptor is ready for synchronization. At this point the two tasks interact or *rendezvous*. As a result the acceptor carries on executing, whilst the caller resumes execution of its program.

In (b) the reverse occurs. Here the acceptor task reaches its synchronization point before the caller has generated a call signal. It, the acceptor, now suspends, waiting for the call to reawaken it. Eventually the call arrives. At this point task interaction takes place (again defined as the rendezvous). The caller carries on executing whilst the acceptor resumes execution of its program.

A third scenario is possible – when both call and accept are reached simultaneously. This, although highly unlikely, produces no problems. Both tasks rendezvous, and then continue executing their respective programs.

Of course, tasks are not limited to a single synchronization point. Multiple rendezvous can occur, as shown in Fig.14.14.

In this simple situation there is symmetry of operation. That is, if we interchanged the caller and acceptor, you wouldn't see any difference in system behaviour. It is, though, most unusual to have only two tasks in a system.

It is more precise to say that we build calling and accepting mechanisms

454   Concurrency – the Ada task

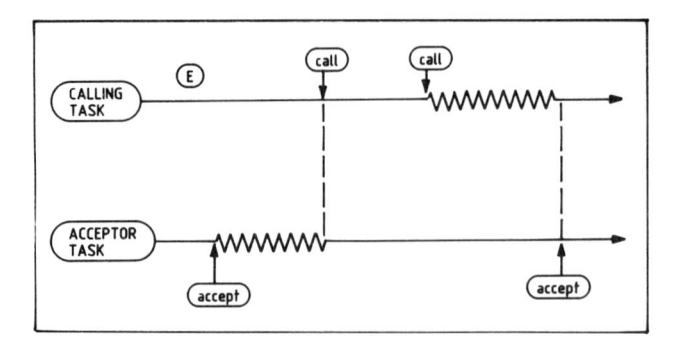

Fig.14.14 Multiple synchronizations of two tasks.

into Ada tasks. Thus any individual task can behave as an acceptor at one point and as a caller at a different point. This is frequently the case in practical systems.

14.4.2   Synchronization mechanisms – basic structure and implementation

The mechanism which provides the link between the calling and called task is the entry clause. Such clauses are written in the specification of the acceptor task. In its simplest form the syntax is

> **entry** ENTRY_NAME;

A specific example is shown in Fig.14.15, where the entry name is RESET_DRILL.

A calling task calls this entry to achieve synchronization. In the call we name both the acceptor task and the entry within that task, as follows:

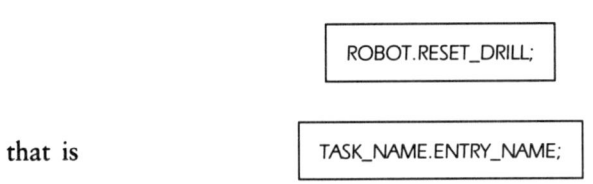

> ROBOT.RESET_DRILL;

that is

> TASK_NAME.ENTRY_NAME;

Note the use of dot notation.

The behaviour of the acceptor task during the rendezvous is determined by an associated accept statement in the task body (Fig.14.15). The example here is, once again, the simplest form:

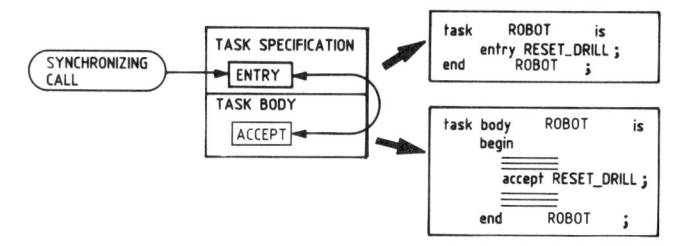

Interdependent tasks, synchronization and the rendezvous 455

Fig.14.15 Entry and accept clauses.

```
with TEXT_IO;              use TEXT_IO;
procedure SIMPLE_ACCEPT is
  -- declare a task with an entry
  task ROBOT is
    entry RESET_DRILL;
  end ROBOT;
  -- declare a second task with no entries - the calling task
  task ROBOT_CONTROLLER;
  -- the task bodies
  task body ROBOT is
  begin
    PUT_LINE ("ROBOT ready");
    accept RESET_DRILL;
    PUT_LINE ("ROBOT received request to reset drill");
  end ROBOT;
  task body ROBOT_CONTROLLER is
  begin
    ROBOT.RESET_DRILL;
  end ROBOT_CONTROLLER;
begin
  null;
end SIMPLE_ACCEPT;
```

Listing 14.4 Demonstrating task synchronization.

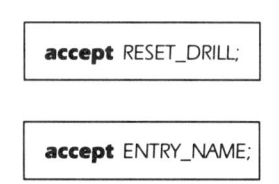

accept RESET_DRILL;

that is

accept ENTRY_NAME;

In this example there is no code attached to the accept statement. Thus the acceptor doesn't do anything during the rendezvous. Our only wish is to 'lock' the tasks together at some particular point in each of the two programs.

This operation is demonstrated in Listing 14.4.

The specification acts as the interface between the task and the outside world. For synchronization, the specific interface point is the entry. Other tasks can only call on the entry (in this way it is like a subprogram call).

What the acceptor then does depends on the corresponding accept statement – which is hidden within the body.

14.4.3 Multiple accept and entry clauses

A task body may have more than one accept statement for its entry, see Listing 14.5.

```
with TEXT_IO;                use TEXT_IO;
procedure MULTIPLE_ACCEPT is
  -- declare a task with an entry
  task ROBOT is
    entry RESET_DRILL;
  end ROBOT;
  -- declare a second task with no entries - the calling task
  task ROBOT_CONTROLLER;
  -- the task bodies
  task body ROBOT is
  begin
    PUT_LINE ("ROBOT ready");
    accept RESET_DRILL;
    PUT_LINE ("ROBOT received first request to reset drill");
    accept RESET_DRILL;
    PUT_LINE ("ROBOT received second request to reset drill");
  end ROBOT;
  task body ROBOT_CONTROLLER is
  begin
    ROBOT.RESET_DRILL;
    ROBOT.RESET_DRILL;
  end ROBOT_CONTROLLER;
begin
  null;
end MULTIPLE_ACCEPT;
```

Listing 14.5 Using multiple accept statements.

In this example there are two accept statements in the acceptor task. The calling task has two identical call statements. Task rendezvous first occurs with the first call and accept, and later with the second pairing. But note that there is only one task entry.

This example is not typical of the way tasking is used in Ada. Yet it clearly shows how the rendezvous mechanism allows us to control task activity carefully. It also shows how tasks behave when they are activated. Each one starts at its first statement, then runs to a rendezvous point. Termination finally occurs when a task reaches its end point – a very simple mode of operation indeed. Unfortunately, for practical applications, this very simplicity has the seeds of disaster in it. The problem? Unless calls and accepts are carefully matched, tasks will get blocked. They will just stop dead at any unfulfilled rendezvous. Needless to say, such a situation is highly undesirable. We will return to this aspect later, covering it within the context of task selection.

A task may have multiple entries, as in

```
with TEXT_IO;                 use TEXT_IO;
procedure MORE_THAN_ONE_ENTRY is
  -- declare a task with several entries
  task ROBOT is
    entry RESET_DRILL;
    entry MOVE_DRILL;
    entry MOVE_ROUTER;
  end ROBOT;
  -- declare a second task with no entries - the calling task
  task ROBOT_CONTROLLER;
  -- the task bodies
  task body ROBOT is
  begin
    PUT_LINE ("ROBOT ready");
    accept RESET_DRILL;
    PUT_LINE ("ROBOT received first request to reset drill");
    accept MOVE_ROUTER;
    PUT_LINE ("ROBOT received request to move router");
    accept RESET_DRILL;
    PUT_LINE ("ROBOT received second request to reset drill");
    accept MOVE_DRILL;
    PUT_LINE ("ROBOT received request to move drill");
  end ROBOT;
  task body ROBOT_CONTROLLER is
  begin
    ROBOT.RESET_DRILL;
    ROBOT.MOVE_ROUTER;
    ROBOT.RESET_DRILL;
    ROBOT.MOVE_DRILL;
  end ROBOT_CONTROLLER;
begin
  null;
end MORE_THAN_ONE_ENTRY;
```

Listing 14.6 Using multiple entry clauses.

```
task ROBOT is
    entry RESET_DRILL;
    entry MOVE_DRILL;
    entry MOVE_ROUTER;
end ROBOT;
```

Each entry has at least one corresponding accept statement in the task body (as shown above, there may well be many accepts for any one entry). A quite artificial example which uses multiple entries is given in Listing 14.6.

This is cumbersome, complex, inflexible and error prone. It shows that we need further tasking constructs to be able to build practical systems.

14.5 EXECUTING CODE DURING THE RENDEZVOUS

In the most recent examples we used the rendezvous for one purpose only – to synchronize tasks. Once the tasks interact they go their own separate ways, doing their own things. But there are cases where we want to:

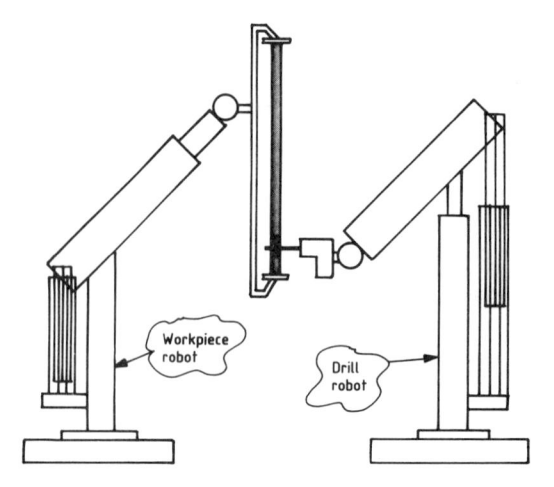

Fig.14.16 Interacting tasks.

- Synchronize tasks (lock them together);
- Perform some action;
- Resume normal operations.

For instance, suppose ROBOT_1 has the task of handling and positioning machine castings. The function of ROBOT_2 is to drill and shape this material, Fig.14.16.

At synchronization time the casting and the drill are aligned. We can now proceed to drill the material – which is splendid, as long as they both stay in position. What we have to do is:

- Position both robots (the synchronization or rendezvous);
- Carry out the drilling operation;
- Resume both robot tasks.

We achieve this by performing the drilling operation during the rendezvous itself, Fig.14.17.

The desired operation (in this case DRILL_CASTING) is implemented in the acceptor task, within the accept statement, as follows:

```
accept BORE_MANIFOLD do
   DRILL_CASTING;
end BORE_MANIFOLD;
```

Code to be executed at rendezvous time is written between the **do** and the **end** of the accept statement. The calling task is forced to wait until this code completes – that is, for the rendezvous period. Listing 14.7 illustrates this feature.

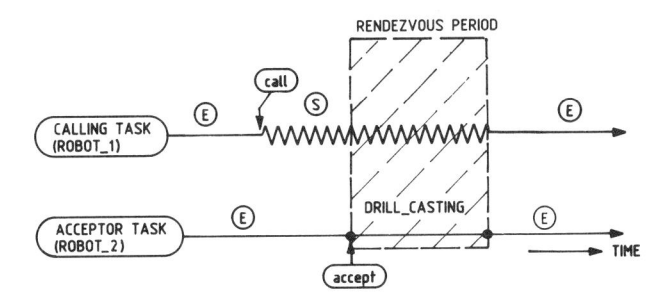

Fig.14.17 Executing operations during the rendezvous.

One last detail: there aren't any particular restrictions placed on statements which can be used in the accept statement.

14.6 SYNCHRONIZATION AND DATA TRANSFER

Suppose that when ROBOT_1 and ROBOT_2 synchronize for drilling operations we want to define the drill size (i.e. we wish to transfer information from one task to the other), and we choose to do it during the rendezvous. How can we tackle this? One possible method is to use global variables – but, as we've stressed many times, avoid these whenever and wherever possible. Earlier (much earlier), to eliminate their use with the subprogram we used parameter passing mechanisms. And, not surprisingly, that is the technique used with tasks.

Parameters are passed during the rendezvous period. Like the subprogram, they can be of type **in**, **out** or **in out**, Fig.14.18.

Those passed from the caller to the acceptor are designated **in**, whilst those passed the other way are **out**. The formal parameters are declared in the acceptor task, as part of the entry and the accept statements:

```
task ROBOT_2 is
    entry BORE_ENGINE_BLOCK (DRILL_SIZE : in INTEGER);
end ROBOT_2;
task body ROBOT_2 is
begin
    STATEMENTS
    accept BORE_ENGINE_BLOCK (DRILL_SIZE : in INTEGER) do
        SELECT_DRILL (DRILL_SIZE);
        DRILL_CASTING;
    end BORE_ENGINE_BLOCK;
    STATEMENTS
end ROBOT_2;
```

```ada
with TEXT_IO;              use TEXT_IO;
procedure CODE_IN_ACCEPT is
  task ROBOT_1;
  task ROBOT_2 is
    entry BORE_MANIFOLD;
  end ROBOT_2;
  -- the task body for ROBOT 1
  task body ROBOT_1 is
  begin
    PUT_LINE ("Moved casting into position");
    ROBOT_2.BORE_MANIFOLD;
    PUT_LINE ("Manifold bore complete");
  end ROBOT_1;
  -- the task body for ROBOT 2
  task body ROBOT_2 is
  -- declare local procedure to drill the casting
    procedure DRILL_CASTING is
    begin
      PUT_LINE ("Drilling Casting");
    end DRILL_CASTING;
  begin
    accept BORE_MANIFOLD do
      DRILL_CASTING;
    end BORE_MANIFOLD;
  end ROBOT_2;
begin
  null;
end CODE_IN_ACCEPT;
        DONE := TRUE;
      else
        DONE := FALSE;
      end if;
    end REBORE_ENGINE_BLOCK;
  --
  -- other ROBOT_2 statements
  -- DRILL_SIZE is not in scope here
  --
  end ROBOT_2;
begin
  null;
end RENDEZVOUS_PARAM;
```

Listing 14.7 Using code statements in the accept statement.

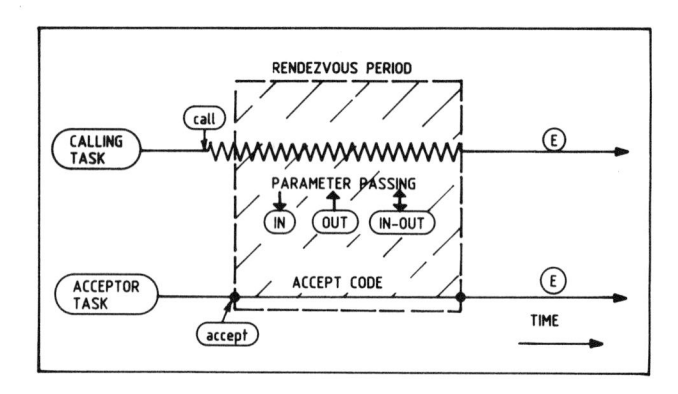

Fig.14.18 Parameter passing during the rendezvous.

Here entry BORE_ENGINE_BLOCK has a single formal parameter DRILL_SIZE, its type being INTEGER, its mode being **in**. Note well that the formal parameter belongs to the entry, not to the task as a whole. It can only be used as part of the corresponding accept statement.

Let us now move to the calling task. To achieve a rendezvous with ROBOT_2 it must call the entry BORE_ENGINE_BLOCK. This is much the same as before, except that now the call includes an actual parameter, as in

```
ROBOT_2.BORE_ENGINE_BLOCK (DRILL_SIZE => 15);
```

An example which uses **in** mode entry parameters is given in Listing 14.8.

Their more general application, using **in**, **out** and **in out** parameters, is shown in Listing 14.9.

If you are unsure about the use of entry parameters, just treat the accept statement as a procedure. Likewise, the entry call is analogous to the procedure call.

14.7 THE SELECTIVE RENDEZVOUS

14.7.1 Why selection is needed

Suppose that we implement the following task:

```
task ROBOT_3 is
    entry MOVE_DRILL;
    entry MOVE_ROUTER;
end ROBOT_3;
task body ROBOT_3 is
begin
   loop
      STATEMENTS
      accept MOVE_DRILL;
      STATEMENTS
      accept MOVE_ROUTER;
      STATEMENTS
   end loop;
end ROBOT_3;
```

As the robot is intended to work continuously we insert its code statements into a continuous loop. This approach will work, but not very well. From a practical point of view we don't mind when drilling or routing is carried out.

```ada
with TEXT_IO;              use TEXT_IO;
procedure DATA_IN_RENDEZVOUS is
  package INT_IO is new INTEGER_IO (INTEGER);
  use INT_IO;
  task ROBOT_1;
  task ROBOT_2 is
    entry BORE_ENGINE_BLOCK (DRILL_SIZE : in    INTEGER);
  end ROBOT_2;
-- the task body for ROBOT 1
  task body ROBOT_1 is
  begin
    PUT_LINE ("Moved casting into position");
    ROBOT_2.BORE_ENGINE_BLOCK (DRILL_SIZE => 15);
    PUT_LINE ("Engine bore complete");
  end ROBOT_1;
-- the task body for ROBOT 2
  task body ROBOT_2 is
-- declare local procedures
    procedure DRILL_CASTING is
    begin
      PUT_LINE ("Drilling Casting");
    end DRILL_CASTING;
    procedure SELECT_DRILL (SIZE     : in     INTEGER) is
    begin
      PUT ("Selected drill size ");
      PUT (SIZE, 0);
      NEW_LINE;
    end SELECT_DRILL;
  begin
--
-- other ROBOT_2 statements
-- DRILL_SIZE is not in scope here
--
    accept BORE_ENGINE_BLOCK (DRILL_SIZE : in    INTEGER) do
      SELECT_DRILL (DRILL_SIZE);
      DRILL_CASTING;
    end BORE_ENGINE_BLOCK;
--
-- other ROBOT_2 statements
-- DRILL_SIZE is not in scope here
--
  end ROBOT_2;
begin
  null;
end DATA_IN_RENDEZVOUS;
```

Listing 14.8 Passing information during the rendezvous – in parameters.

```ada
with TEXT_IO;              use TEXT_IO;
procedure RENDEZVOUS_PARAM is
  package INT_IO is new INTEGER_IO (INTEGER);
  use INT_IO;
  task ROBOT_1;
  task ROBOT_2 is
    entry BORE_ENGINE_BLOCK (DRILL_SIZE : in    INTEGER);
    entry REBORE_ENGINE_BLOCK (DRILL_SIZE : in out INTEGER;
                               DONE       :    out BOOLEAN);
  end ROBOT_2;
  -- the task body for ROBOT 1
  task body ROBOT_1 is
    WHICH_DRILL     :    INTEGER      := 15;
    REBORE_SUCCESS  :    BOOLEAN;
  begin
    PUT_LINE ("Moved casting into position");
    ROBOT_2.BORE_ENGINE_BLOCK (DRILL_SIZE => WHICH_DRILL);
    PUT_LINE ("Engine bore complete");
    PUT_LINE ("Reboring Engine Block");
    ROBOT_2.REBORE_ENGINE_BLOCK (DRILL_SIZE => WHICH_DRILL,
                                 DONE       => REBORE_SUCCESS);
    if REBORE_SUCCESS then
      PUT_LINE ("Rebore successful");
      PUT ("Drill size used : ");
      PUT (WHICH_DRILL, 0);
    end if;
  end ROBOT_1;
  -- the task body for ROBOT 2
  task body ROBOT_2 is
  -- declare local procedures
    procedure DRILL_CASTING is
    begin
      PUT_LINE ("Drilling Casting");
    end DRILL_CASTING;
    procedure SELECT_DRILL (SIZE     : in    INTEGER) is
    begin
      PUT ("Selected drill size ");
      PUT (SIZE, 0);
      NEW_LINE;
    end SELECT_DRILL;
  begin
  --
  -- other ROBOT_2 statements
  -- DRILL_SIZE is not in scope here
  --
    accept BORE_ENGINE_BLOCK (DRILL_SIZE : in    INTEGER) do
      SELECT_DRILL (DRILL_SIZE);
      DRILL_CASTING;
    end BORE_ENGINE_BLOCK;
    accept REBORE_ENGINE_BLOCK (DRILL_SIZE : in out INTEGER;
                                DONE       :    out BOOLEAN) do
      if DRILL_SIZE < 20 then
        DRILL_SIZE := DRILL_SIZE + 1;
        SELECT_DRILL (DRILL_SIZE);
        DRILL_CASTING;
        DONE := TRUE;
      else
        DONE := FALSE;
      end if;
    end REBORE_ENGINE_BLOCK;
  --
  -- other ROBOT_2 statements
  -- DRILL_SIZE is not in scope here
  --
  end ROBOT_2;
begin
  null;
end RENDEZVOUS_PARAM;
```

Listing 14.9 More on passing information during the rendezvous – 'in', 'out', and 'in out' parameters.

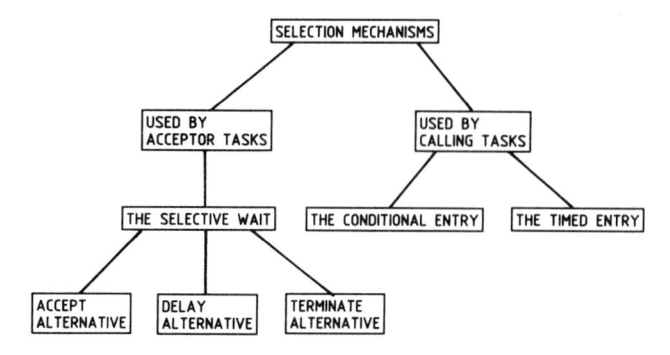

Fig.14.19 Ada task selection mechanisms.

Yet the program structure forces us to work in a specific way. For instance, we cannot go past the accept statement MOVE_DRILL until that entry is called – irrespective of how many requests are made for MOVE_ROUTER. And then, once this entry is called, we must proceed to 'accept MOVE_ROUTER', even if this hasn't been called.

This is a rigid, unnatural, way of working, negating many of the advantages of the task construct. There is, fortunately, a neat way to overcome such limitations: allow the acceptor task some control over its responses to entry calls. That is, it should be able to select its resulting course of action. Moreover, we can further improve matters by making entry calls more flexible.

To satisfy such requirements, Ada has a number of task selection mechanisms, Fig.14.19.

These are split into two major groups: those used by acceptor tasks and those applicable to calling tasks. We will first look at the acceptor task selective wait constructs: accept, delay or terminate. Then selection techniques used by calling tasks will be discussed.

14.7.2 The selective wait accept alternative

In the example above the acceptor task was forced to take entry calls in a predefined order. We can overcome this limitation by using the selective wait construct. This allows the acceptor to decide which entry call it will service – ordering of calls does not apply. Generally the format of the selective wait is

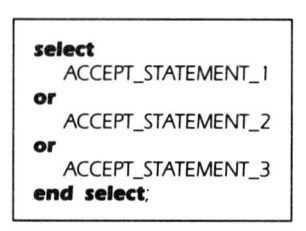

```
select
    ACCEPT_STATEMENT_1
or
    ACCEPT_STATEMENT_2
or
    ACCEPT_STATEMENT_3
end select;
```

Being more precise, this is the accept alternative version of the selective wait (all the alternatives are accepts).

For the earlier example we could have used the selective wait as follows:

```
loop
   select
      accept MOVE_DRILL;
      STATEMENTS
   or
      accept MOVE_ROUTER;
      STATEMENTS
   end select;
end loop;
```

Assume for the moment that no entry calls have been made. The acceptor task simply sits there, doing nothing, waiting for a rendezvous. It will subsequently respond to the first entry call which arrives, accepting that call. Thus it doesn't matter whether MOVE_DRILL or MOVE_ROUTER is called first. Neither is it a problem if a MOVE_DRILL call is followed immediately by another call of MOVE_DRILL. These points are demonstrated in Listing 14.10.

```
with TEXT_IO;              use TEXT_IO;
procedure SELECTIVE_WAIT is
  task ROBOT_3 is
    entry MOVE_DRILL;
    entry MOVE_ROUTER;
  end ROBOT_3;
  task ROBOT_CONTROLLER;
  -- task body ROBOT_3
  task body ROBOT_3 is
  begin
    loop
      select
        accept MOVE_DRILL;
        PUT_LINE ("Received request to move DRILL");
      or
        accept MOVE_ROUTER;
        PUT_LINE ("Received request to move ROUTER");
      end select;
    end loop;
  end ROBOT_3;
  -- task body ROBOT_CONTROLLER
  task body ROBOT_CONTROLLER is
  begin
    ROBOT_3.MOVE_ROUTER;
    ROBOT_3.MOVE_DRILL;
    ROBOT_3.MOVE_DRILL;
    ROBOT_3.MOVE_ROUTER;
  end ROBOT_CONTROLLER;
begin
  null;
end SELECTIVE_WAIT;
```

Listing 14.10 Using the selective wait in an acceptor task.

In essence the select statement offers us a choice of routes into different program branches. Take note that, in the example given, the program contains executable statements after each accept statement. These are executed after each rendezvous. Thus, although not within the rendezvous, they are still part of that particular selection.

One further point needs a mention. If there are calls outstanding to both MOVE_DRILL and MOVE_ROUTER we cannot predict which one will be accepted; selection is arbitrary.

Select statements, as used above, are said to be open. That is, they always provide a rendezvous point. Consequently, the acceptor task always waits for an entry call when it reaches an accept statement, no matter how long this wait may be. Now, instead of waiting, we could put this time to good use. Clean the robot, for instance. But, given the current accept structure, we can't do that. However, just a small addition – the **else** alternative – makes it possible. When **else** is included in the select construction the syntax is

```
loop
   select
      accept MOVE_DRILL;
      STATEMENTS
   or
      accept MOVE_ROUTER;
      STATEMENTS
   else
      CLEAN_ROBOT;
   end select;
end loop;
```

When the acceptor task reaches the select statement it checks out all the accept alternatives (in this case MOVE_DRILL and MOVE_ROUTER). If neither has an outstanding entry call the else part is immediately actioned. This feature is illustrated in Listing 14.11.

14.7.3 Conditional selective waits – the guard

The selective wait statement provides great flexibility in tasking operations. But we still have one problem with it, a significant one for practical applications. In the previous example, once we call an entry (say MOVE_DRILL), a rendezvous is set in motion. Yet we may not want to, or be able to, accept this. For instance, the drill may be out of action. We could, of course, allow for such problems in the task code. But a better way is to refuse to accept the rendezvous unless explicit conditions are met – conditional acceptance. This is loosely referred to as a 'guarded accept' statement. Fig.14.20 shows its syntax.

```
with TEXT_IO;                    use TEXT_IO;
procedure ELSE_ALTERNATIVE is
  task ROBOT_3 is
    entry MOVE_DRILL;
    entry MOVE_ROUTER;
  end ROBOT_3;
  task ROBOT_CONTROLLER;
  -- task body ROBOT_3
  task body ROBOT_3 is
  -- a local procedure
    procedure CLEAN_ROBOT is
    begin
      PUT_LINE ("Cleaning Robot");
    end CLEAN_ROBOT;
  begin
    loop
      select
        accept MOVE_DRILL;
        PUT_LINE ("Received request to move DRILL");
      or
        accept MOVE_ROUTER;
        PUT_LINE ("Recieved request to move ROUTER");
      else
        CLEAN_ROBOT;
      end select;
    end loop;
  end ROBOT_3;
  -- task body ROBOT_CONTROLLER
  task body ROBOT_CONTROLLER is
  begin
    ROBOT_3.MOVE_ROUTER;
    ROBOT_3.MOVE_DRILL;
    ROBOT_3.MOVE_DRILL;
    ROBOT_3.MOVE_ROUTER;
  end ROBOT_CONTROLLER;
begin
  null;
end ELSE_ALTERNATIVE;
```

Listing 14.11 Using the else alternative of a selective wait.

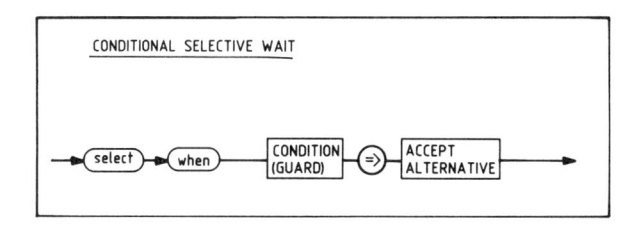

Fig.14.20 Syntax – conditional selective wait statement.

Concurrency – the Ada task

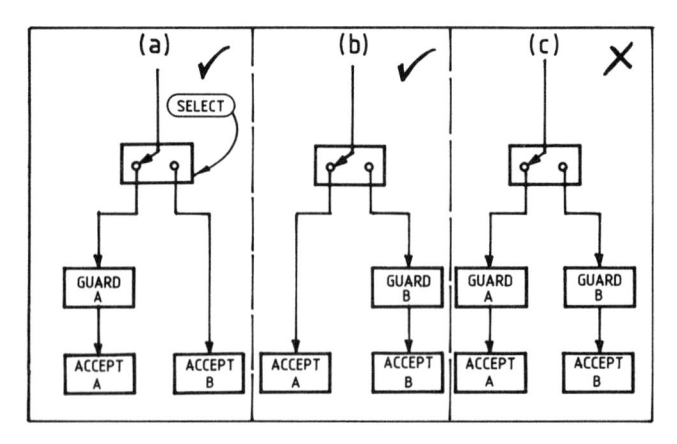

Fig.14.21 Applying guards.

Such a statement is written as

```
select
    when CONDITION =>
        accept SELECT_ALTERNATIVE
```

as in

```
select
    when DRILL_READY =>
        accept MOVE_DRILL;
```

The test conditions (*guarding conditions* or just *guards*) are applied individually to each accept statement. The acceptor program, on reaching the select statement, checks the state of the guard (assume just one guard for the moment). The result is a BOOLEAN value, which must be TRUE or FALSE. If TRUE, the accept statement is actioned, otherwise it is regarded as being closed and cannot be selected. For the example above we first evaluate 'if DRILL_READY'. A TRUE answer means that we accept the rendezvous MOVE_DRILL, otherwise we must reject it.

Consider where we apply this to a task having two accept statements. There are three possible implementations here. Which one we use depends on our particular needs, Fig.14.21.

In (a), accept A is guarded, B being open. The converse is true in (b). In (c), guards are applied to both A and B. Although this may seem a reasonable thing to do it should, in practice, be avoided. We could end up with all guards closed, and the task would stop (if you try this you will get a

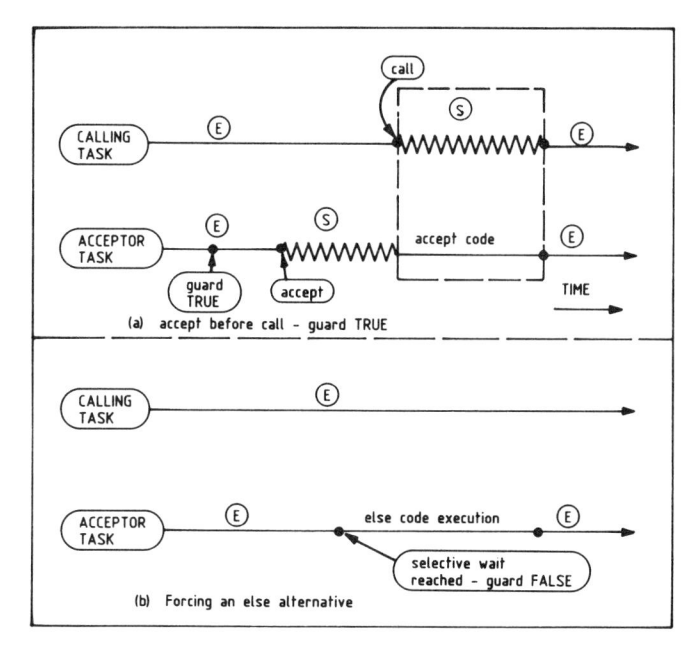

Fig.14.22 Using 'else' in a selective wait.

PROGRAM_ERROR exception message). To prevent this we must include an **else** alternative – which must be unguarded. Program behaviour, when using guards and an **else** statement, takes two forms, Fig.14.22.

Assume, for explanation purposes, that we have one calling and one acceptor task. In (a), an accept is reached before a call (the guard must be true in this case). Normal operation ensues. In (b) the selective wait is reached while all guards are false. Straight away the alternative code (the statements of the else part) is executed. If, after this, the calling task generates a call, it will suspend. Listing 14.12 shows how this construct is applied.

One last point here: when, and how often, do we evaluate the guards? The answer is: on first reaching the selective wait statement, and once only. All guards are evaluated (though the order isn't defined).

14.7.4 The delay alternative of the acceptor task

Suppose we have a rather eccentric drill machine which jams up if it isn't run regularly. We therefore need to make sure that the drill doesn't remain idle for long periods. As shown so far, calling tasks define how often the drill is used. Acceptor tasks have no say in this matter, yet the one task that knows exactly how the drill has been used is the acceptor (remember, in practice there could be many calling tasks for one acceptor task). There is an obvious solution to the drill problem: make the acceptor task exercise the drill if it hasn't been used for some time.

470 Concurrency – the Ada task

```
with TEXT_IO;                      use TEXT_IO;
procedure CONDITIONAL_SELECTIVE_WAIT is
  task ROBOT_3 is
    entry MOVE_DRILL;
    entry MOVE_ROUTER;
  end ROBOT_3;
  task ROBOT_CONTROLLER;
  -- task body ROBOT_3
  task body ROBOT_3 is
    DRILL_READY      :     BOOLEAN        := FALSE;
    ROUTER_READY     :     BOOLEAN        := FALSE;
  -- a local procedure
    procedure CLEAN_ROBOT is
    begin
      PUT_LINE ("Cleaning Robot");
      DRILL_READY := TRUE;
      ROUTER_READY := TRUE;
    end CLEAN_ROBOT;
  begin
    loop
      select
        when DRILL_READY =>
          accept MOVE_DRILL;
          PUT_LINE ("Received request to move DRILL");
      or
        when ROUTER_READY =>
          accept MOVE_ROUTER;
          PUT_LINE ("Received request to move ROUTER");
      else
        CLEAN_ROBOT;
      end select;
    end loop;
  end ROBOT_3;
  -- task body ROBOT_CONTROLLER
  task body ROBOT_CONTROLLER is
  begin
    ROBOT_3.MOVE_ROUTER;
    ROBOT_3.MOVE_DRILL;
  end ROBOT_CONTROLLER;
begin
  null;
end CONDITIONAL_SELECTIVE_WAIT;
```

Listing 14.12 The conditional selective wait construct – guards.

The solution to this problem, as provided by Ada, is the delay alternative. Its outline form is

```
select
    accept MOVE_DRILL;
or
    delay 60.0;
    EXERCISE_DRILL;
end select;
```

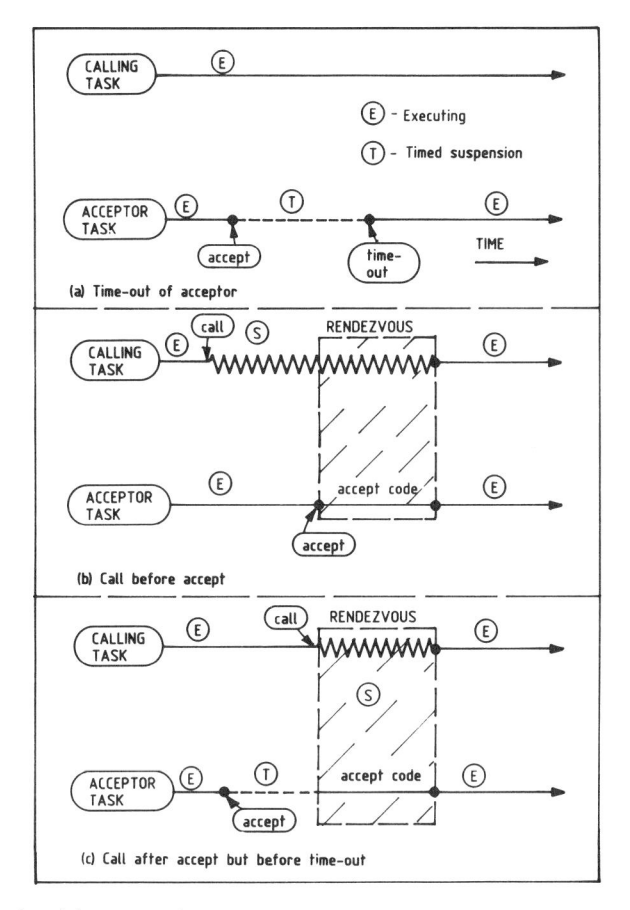

Fig.14.23 The delay operation.

Here the delay action is an alternative to the accept statement. What this select statement means is: accept a rendezvous with an entry call MOVE_DRILL, but if such a call is not made within 60 seconds execute the statement EXERCISE_DRILL. In more general terms, its operation is as described in Fig.14.23.

Part (a) shows a time-out condition, as already described. Part (b) illustrates a call before accept. Clearly the acceptor task will rendezvous as soon as it reaches its accept statement. The first section of part (c) is the same as for part (a). Here the accept is reached before a call is made. A timed suspension is thus entered – but an entry call is made before the time-out ends. Consequently the delay is cancelled and the accept code executed.

Treat the delay statement as a timer which:

```
with TEXT_IO;                    use TEXT_IO;
procedure DELAY_ALTERNATIVE is
  task ROBOT_3 is
    entry MOVE_DRILL;
  end ROBOT_3;
  task body ROBOT_3 is
  -- local procedure
    procedure EXERCISE_DRILL is
    begin
      PUT_LINE ("Drill Exercised");
    end EXERCISE_DRILL;
  begin
    loop
      select
        accept MOVE_DRILL;
        PUT_LINE ("Received request to move DRILL");
      or
        delay 60.0;
        EXERCISE_DRILL;
      end select;
    end loop;
  end ROBOT_3;
begin
  null;
end DELAY_ALTERNATIVE;
```

Listing 14.13 Using the delay alternative in the acceptor task.

- Times out after a defined period (in this case, 60 seconds);
- Is reset after a time-out;
- Is reset if the accept alternative is actioned.

This is demonstrated in Listing 14.13.

14.7.5 The terminate alternative of the acceptor task

As our program examples became more complex we generally formed the task body as a loop. This is by far the most common method used in practice. Unfortunately it has one drawback: it becomes difficult or unwieldy to bring such tasks to completion (i.e. at the task **end** statement). To simplify this operation we can use the **terminate** statement, as part of the selective wait construction. In its simplest form this is

```
select
    accept MOVE_DRILL;
or
    terminate;
end select;
```

Its use is illustrated in Listing 14.14.

```
with TEXT_IO;                    use TEXT_IO;
procedure TASK_TERMINATION is
  task ROBOT_3 is
    entry MOVE_DRILL;
    entry MOVE_ROUTER;
  end ROBOT_3;
  task ROBOT_CONTROLLER;
  -- task body ROBOT_3
  task body ROBOT_3 is
  begin
    loop
      select
        accept MOVE_DRILL;
        PUT_LINE ("Received request to move DRILL");
      or
        accept MOVE_ROUTER;
        PUT_LINE ("Received request to move ROUTER");
      or
        terminate;
      end select;
    end loop;
  end ROBOT_3;
  -- task body ROBOT_CONTROLLER
  task body ROBOT_CONTROLLER is
  begin
    ROBOT_3.MOVE_ROUTER;
    ROBOT_3.MOVE_DRILL;
    ROBOT_3.MOVE_DRILL;
    ROBOT_3.MOVE_ROUTER;
  end ROBOT_CONTROLLER;
begin
  null;
end TASK_TERMINATION;
```

Listing 14.14 Using the terminate alternative in the acceptor task.

14.8 THE CALLING TASK – CONDITIONAL AND TIMED ENTRIES

Let us now return and look into calling task behaviour in a little more depth. Up to now, when a task calls an entry, it is forced into a rendezvous. But a moment's reflection shows that this is a very dogmatic approach. Suppose that in our robot example, Listing 14.7, ROBOT_1 calls for a drilling operation by ROBOT_2. For some reason this service isn't available. As a result ROBOT_1 will cease working, waiting for a rendezvous. Yet it may be that it could perform other jobs. Logically we would proceed with those, otherwise we are wasting useful production time.

This, and similar requirements, can be satisfied by the conditional entry call. If, at rendezvous time, the acceptor task is ready, then the rendezvous is carried out (Fig.14.24(a)). But if this condition isn't met, the caller carries out some alternative course of action, Fig.14.24(b).

In general terms its syntactic form is

474 Concurrency – the Ada task

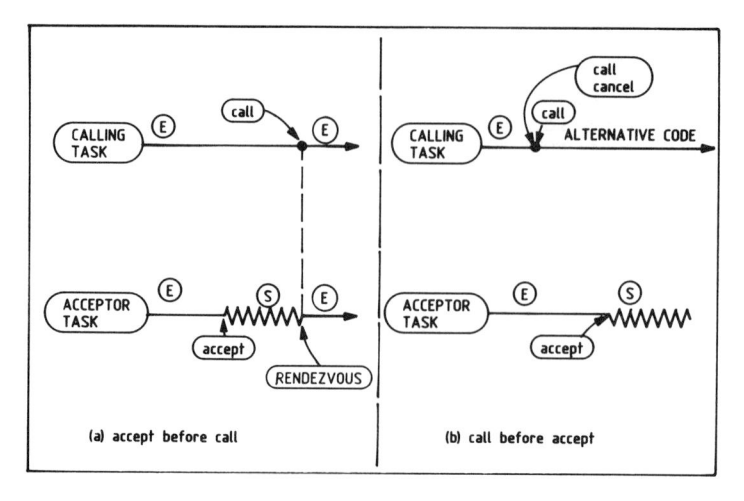

Fig.14.24 The conditional entry call action.

```
select
    ENTRY_CALL
else
    DO_SOMETHING_ELSE
end select;
```

Its structure and use is given in Listing 14.15.

We are allowed to try only one entry call in this select statement. Further, the alternative course of action cannot itself be an entry call.

Sometimes we may be prepared to wait if the acceptor task isn't ready – but not indefinitely; there is a limit to our patience. The way to implement this is to employ the timed entry call:

```
select
    ENTRY_CALL
or
    DELAY_FOR_A_TIME
end select;
```

Using this we can specify the maximum waiting time for a rendezvous. If the entry call is accepted within that time period, fine. But if it isn't, a time-out takes place, and the call is cancelled. Listing 14.16 demonstrates how to use this program feature.

Note that, for all entry calls, if an entry call is made to a task which has completed its execution, the exception TASKING_ERROR is raised, Listing 14.17.

```
with TEXT_IO;              use TEXT_IO;
procedure CONDITIONAL_CALL is
  task ROBOT_2 is
    entry BORE_MANIFOLD;
  end ROBOT_2;
  task ROBOT_1;
  -- the task body for ROBOT 2
  task body ROBOT_2 is
  -- declare local procedure to drill the casting
     procedure DRILL_CASTING is
     begin
        PUT_LINE ("Drilling Casting");
     end DRILL_CASTING;
  begin
  -- delay at the beginning of the task so the rendezvous cannot take place
     delay 5.0;
     accept BORE_MANIFOLD do
        DRILL_CASTING;
     end BORE_MANIFOLD;
  end ROBOT_2;
  -- the task body for ROBOT 1
  task body ROBOT_1 is
  begin
     PUT_LINE ("Moved casting into position");
  -- call ROBOT_2 with a conditional call
     loop
        select
           ROBOT_2.BORE_MANIFOLD;
           exit;
        else
           PUT_LINE ("ROBOT_2.BORE_MANIFOLD not ready, doing something else");
           delay 1.0;
  -- simulate work being done
        end select;
     end loop;
     PUT_LINE ("Manifold bore complete");
  end ROBOT_1;
begin
  null;
end CONDITIONAL_CALL;
```

Listing 14.15 The conditional entry call.

14.9 TASK TYPES

From an earlier example we have the following task declaration:

```
task ROBOT_2 is
    entry BORE_ENGINE_BLOCK (DRILL_SIZE : in INTEGER);
end ROBOT_2;
```

This defined ROBOT_2 to be a task, but did not specify its type. Once again we meet the use of anonymous type declarations (see chapter 8, arrays). There are times, though, when it is useful to be able to declare specific task

```ada
with TEXT_IO;                   use TEXT_IO;
procedure TIMED_CALL is
  task ROBOT_2 is
    entry BORE_MANIFOLD;
  end ROBOT_2;
  task ROBOT_1;
  -- the task body for ROBOT 2
  task body ROBOT_2 is
  -- declare local procedure to drill the casting
    procedure DRILL_CASTING is
    begin
      PUT_LINE ("Drilling Casting");
    end DRILL_CASTING;
  begin
  -- delay at the beginning of the task so the rendezvous cannot take place
    delay 5.0;
    accept BORE_MANIFOLD do
      DRILL_CASTING;
    end BORE_MANIFOLD;
  end ROBOT_2;
  -- the task body for ROBOT 1
  task body ROBOT_1 is
  begin
    PUT_LINE ("Moved casting into position");
  -- call ROBOT_2 with a conditional call
    loop
      select
        ROBOT_2.BORE_MANIFOLD;
        exit;
      or
        delay 1.0;
      end select;
      PUT ("Timed out on call to ROBOT_2.BORE_MANIFOLD ");
      PUT_LINE (" doing something else");
    end loop;
    PUT_LINE ("Manifold bore complete");
  end ROBOT_1;
begin
  null;
end TIMED_CALL;
```

Listing 14.16 The timed entry call.

types. From this task template we can create task objects of the type. Clearly, all objects created from one task type perform the same function. They may, in fact, be identical. The declaration format is

> **task type** NAME_OF_TASK_TYPE **is**
>   **entry** TASK_ENTRY;
> **end** NAME_OF_TASK_TYPE;
>
> <TASK_BODY_DECLARATION>
>
> TASK_OBJECT : NAME_OF_TASK_TYPE;

Details of the task body declaration have been omitted as this is identical to the normal body declaration.

```
with TEXT_IO;              use TEXT_IO;
procedure TASK_ERR is
  -- declare a task with several entries
  task ROBOT is
    entry RESET_DRILL;
    entry MOVE_DRILL;
    entry MOVE_ROUTER;
  end ROBOT;
  -- the task bodies
  task body ROBOT is
  begin
    PUT_LINE ("ROBOT ready");
    accept RESET_DRILL;
    PUT_LINE ("ROBOT received first request to reset drill");
    accept MOVE_ROUTER;
    PUT_LINE ("ROBOT received request to move router");
    accept RESET_DRILL;
    PUT_LINE ("ROBOT received second request to reset drill");
    accept MOVE_DRILL;
    PUT_LINE ("ROBOT received request to move drill");
  end ROBOT;
begin
  ROBOT.RESET_DRILL;
  ROBOT.MOVE_ROUTER;
  ROBOT.RESET_DRILL;
  ROBOT.MOVE_DRILL;
  ROBOT.RESET_DRILL;
end TASK_ERR;
```

Listing 14.17 Calling a completed task.

An important question is: how can we sensibly use task objects in practice? Suppose we have to write the software for a number of robot welders. Suppose also that the control algorithms and routines for each welder are identical. For this we could have a task type, as follows:

```
task type ROBOT_WELDING_TASK is
    entry GO (NO_OF_JOINTS : in POSITIVE);
    entry STOP;
end ROBOT_WELDING_TASK;

<TASK_BODY_DECLARATION>

WELDING_ROBOT_1 : ROBOT_WELDING_TASK;
WELDING_ROBOT_2 : ROBOT_WELDING_TASK;
```

Here, both WELDING_ROBOT_1 and WELDING_ROBOT_2 carry out exactly the same functions. But they are separate from, and independent of, each other. Their use is demonstrated in Listing 14.18.

Observe that they both contain variables. Although these variables are declared in the one task body they are not global variables. They behave as if they are declared local to each task object, being quite separate items. The same remarks apply to task constants.

```ada
with TEXT_IO;                 use TEXT_IO;
procedure TASK_TYPES is
  package POSITIVE_IO is new INTEGER_IO (POSITIVE);
  use POSITIVE_IO;
  task type ROBOT_WELDING_TASK is
    entry GO (NO_OF_JOINTS : in  POSITIVE);
    entry STOP;
  end ROBOT_WELDING_TASK;
 -- declare two objects of this task type
  WELDING_ROBOT_1 :     ROBOT_WELDING_TASK;
  WELDING_ROBOT_2 :     ROBOT_WELDING_TASK;
 -- declare a task which controls the welding robots
  task WELDING_CONTROLLER;
 -- the body of the task type;
  task body ROBOT_WELDING_TASK is
     X_POSITION         :     POSITIVE;
     Y_POSITION         :     POSITIVE;
     MAX_X              :     constant POSITIVE := 50;
     MAX_Y              :     constant POSITIVE := 100;
     JOINTS             :     POSITIVE;
     JOINT_COUNT        :     POSITIVE;
  begin
    loop
      accept GO (NO_OF_JOINTS : in  POSITIVE) do
-- take a copy of the number of joints for use outside
-- the rendezvous
        JOINTS := NO_OF_JOINTS;
      end GO;
      JOINT_COUNT := 1;
      X_POSITION := 1;
      Y_POSITION := 1;
      loop
        select
          accept STOP do
            PUT_LINE ("Received request to stop welding at position ");
            PUT ("X = ");
            PUT (X_POSITION, 0);
            PUT (" Y = ");
            PUT (Y_POSITION, 0);
            NEW_LINE;
          end STOP;
          exit;
        else
          if (JOINT_COUNT <= JOINTS) then
            if X_POSITION = MAX_X then
              X_POSITION := POSITIVE'FIRST;
              if Y_POSITION = MAX_Y then
                Y_POSITION := POSITIVE'FIRST;
              else
                Y_POSITION := Y_POSITION + 1;
              end if;
            else
              X_POSITION := X_POSITION + 1;
            end if;
            JOINT_COUNT := JOINT_COUNT + 1;
            delay 0.1;
          else
             exit;
          end if;
        end select;
      end loop;
 -- STOP loop
    end loop;
 -- GO loop
  end ROBOT_WELDING_TASK;
  task body WELDING_CONTROLLER is
  begin
```

```
         WELDING_ROBOT_1.GO (NO_OF_JOINTS => 150);
         WELDING_ROBOT_2.GO (NO_OF_JOINTS => 200);
         WELDING_ROBOT_1.GO (NO_OF_JOINTS => 150);
         delay 0.5;
         WELDING_ROBOT_1.STOP;
         WELDING_ROBOT_2.STOP;
      end WELDING_CONTROLLER;
   begin
      null;
   end TASK_TYPES;
```

Listing 14.18 The use of task types.

This example shows that the rationale for task types is similar to that for generics. That is, if you have a number of matching tasks, you only need to write the code once – as a task type. Then declare your required number of task objects. It also shows precisely the need for dot notation. Without name qualification we wouldn't be able to identify which task entry was being called.

In conclusion, task objects:

- Are limited private; hence assignment and comparison of such objects are forbidden;
- Behave as constants;
- May be used as subprogram parameters (but not as mode **out**);
- Can be formed as an array.

Many of these points are illustrated in Listing 14.19.

14.10 TASK ENTRY FAMILIES

One way of looking at task objects is to consider them as members of the same task family. We can also apply the concept of family grouping to entries within individual tasks.

In earlier program examples entries had one common factor. Each task entry had a single, unique name which provided a single, specific route into the task. This is defined to be a *single* entry. Any realistic task could have a collection of such single entries, as in

```
task ROBOT_WELDER is
   entry SET_UP;
   entry WELD_BOTTOM_PLATE;
   entry WELD_TOP_PLATE;
   entry WELD_BUTT_JOINTS;
   entry STOP;
end ROBOT_WELDER;
```

```ada
with TEXT_IO;              use TEXT_IO;
procedure ADVANCED_TASK_TYPES is
  package POSITIVE_IO is new INTEGER_IO (POSITIVE);
  use POSITIVE_IO;
  task type ROBOT_WELDING_TASK is
    entry GO (NO_OF_JOINTS : in  POSITIVE);
    entry STOP;
  end ROBOT_WELDING_TASK;
  -- declare a type which is an array of the task type
  type WELDING_ROBOT_GROUP is array (1..10) of ROBOT_WELDING_TASK;
  -- declare object of the array type
  WELDING_ROBOTS   :    WELDING_ROBOT_GROUP;
  -- declare a task which controls the welding robots
  task WELDING_CONTROLLER;
  -- the body of the task type;
  task body ROBOT_WELDING_TASK is
    X_POSITION       :      POSITIVE          := 1;
    Y_POSITION       :      POSITIVE          := 1;
    MAX_X            :      constant POSITIVE := 50;
    MAX_Y            :      constant POSITIVE := 100;
    JOINTS           :      POSITIVE;
  begin
    loop
      select
        accept GO (NO_OF_JOINTS : in  POSITIVE) do
-- take a copy of the number of joints for use outside
-- the rendezvous
          JOINTS := NO_OF_JOINTS;
        end GO;
        for JOINT_COUNT in 1..JOINTS loop
          if X_POSITION = MAX_X then
            X_POSITION := POSITIVE'FIRST;
            if Y_POSITION = MAX_Y then
              Y_POSITION := POSITIVE'FIRST;
            else
              Y_POSITION := Y_POSITION + 1;
            end if;
          else
            X_POSITION := X_POSITION + 1;
          end if;
        end loop;
      or
        accept STOP do
          PUT_LINE ("Received request to stop welding at position ");
          PUT ("X = ");
          PUT (X_POSITION, 0);
          PUT (" Y = ");
          PUT (Y_POSITION, 0);
          NEW_LINE;
        end STOP;
      end select;
    end loop;
  end ROBOT_WELDING_TASK;
  task body WELDING_CONTROLLER is
  -- Local var
    JOINT_COUNT    :    POSITIVE;
  -- local procedure which has a parameter of type ROBOT_WELDING_TASK
    procedure DO_SOME_WELDING (WELDER    : in    ROBOT_WELDING_TASK) is
      JOINT_COUNT     :     POSITIVE;
    begin
      PUT ("Please enter the number of welding joints : ");
      GET (JOINT_COUNT);
      SKIP_LINE;
      WELDER.GO (NO_OF_JOINTS => JOINT_COUNT);
    end DO_SOME_WELDING;
```

```
    begin
      for ROBOT in WELDING_ROBOTS'range loop
    -- do the welding
        DO_SOME_WELDING (WELDER    => WELDING_ROBOTS (ROBOT));
      end loop;
      for ROBOT in WELDING_ROBOTS'range loop
        WELDING_ROBOTS (ROBOT).STOP;
      end loop;
    end WELDING_CONTROLLER;
begin
  null;
end ADVANCED_TASK_TYPES;
      end loop;
   end WELDING_BOSS;
begin
  null;
end ENTRY_FAMILIES;
```

Listing 14.19 Showing a task type formed as an array and used as a parameter of a procedure.

You can see that entries 2, 3 and 4 are all closely related. Clearly it would make sense to highlight this relationship. We can do this by creating a family of entries, all grouped under the same family name. For example, we could have

```
type CHASSIS_PART is (BOTTOM_PLATE, TOP_PLATE, BUTT_JOINT);
task ROBOT_WELDER is
   entry SET_UP;
   entry WELD (CHASSIS_PART);
   entry STOP;
end ROBOT_WELDER;
```

The entry declaration WELD (CHASSIS_PART) represents a family of entries, namely WELD (BOTTOM_PLATE), WELD (TOP_PLATE) and WELD (BUTT_JOINTS). Each entry has a corresponding **accept** statement. The calling task calls on specific entries, as, for instance, ROBOT_WELDER.WELD (BUTT_JOINT) or ROBOT_WELDER.WELD (TOP_PLATE). Listing 14.20 expounds the use of task entry families.

14.11 TERMINATION AND EXCEPTIONS

We will deal with these topics together for one simple reason: when an exception occurs task termination frequently takes place.

We define termination to mean that a task has completed its execution. Normal completion – or just completion – occurs when the task body reaches

```ada
with TEXT_IO;               use TEXT_IO;
procedure ENTRY_FAMILIES is
  type CHASIS_PART is (BOTTOM_PLATE, TOP_PLATE, BUTT_JOINT);
  task ROBOT_WELDER is
    entry SET_UP;
    entry WELD (CHASIS_PART);
    entry STOP;
  end ROBOT_WELDER;
  task WELDING_BOSS;
  task body ROBOT_WELDER is
    type WELDER_IN_ON_STATE is array (CHASIS_PART) of BOOLEAN;
    WELDER_ON        :       WELDER_IN_ON_STATE := (others => FALSE);
  begin
    loop
      select
        accept SET_UP;
        WELDER_ON := (others => TRUE);
        PUT_LINE ("All welders ready to weld");
      or
        when WELDER_ON (BOTTOM_PLATE) =>
          accept WELD (BOTTOM_PLATE);
          PUT_LINE ("Welding BOTTOM PLATE");
      or
        when WELDER_ON (TOP_PLATE) =>
          accept WELD (TOP_PLATE);
          PUT_LINE ("Welding TOP PLATE");
      or
        when WELDER_ON (BUTT_JOINT) =>
          accept WELD (BUTT_JOINT);
          PUT_LINE ("Welding BUTT JOINT");
      or
        accept STOP;
        WELDER_ON := (others => FALSE);
        PUT_LINE ("Stopped all welders");
      end select;
    end loop;
  end ROBOT_WELDER;
 -- task body WELDING BOSS
  task body WELDING_BOSS is
  begin
 -- keep the welders going. If any weld entry is open then
 -- switch that welder on
    loop
      ROBOT_WELDER.SET_UP;
      for PART_ID in CHASIS_PART loop
        select
          ROBOT_WELDER.WELD (PART_ID);
        else
          null;
        end select;
      end loop;
 -- stop all welders after 10 seconds for safety reasons
      delay 10.0;
      ROBOT_WELDER.STOP;
 -- delay for cooling off period
      delay 5.0;
    end loop;
  end WELDING_BOSS;
begin
  null;
end ENTRY_FAMILIES;
```

Listing 14.20 Application of task entry families.

its **end** (for simplicity assume that this task does not itself have dependent tasks). Otherwise we can force completion by using the **terminate** alternative of a select statement, section 14.6.5 (just to confuse the issue, this is often called termination). Both completion and termination are normal ways to end tasks. By contrast we can produce an abnormal completion using the **abort** statement (this is said to cause a task to become *abnormal*). The statement syntax is extremely simple:

> **abort** <TASK_NAME>

as in

> **abort** ROBOT_10;

When this is invoked the task concerned is brought to a halt. Unfortunately, the actual behaviour is quite unpredictable. We can define the program conditions which must occur before the task halts. But what we can't do in a practical application is to define:

- How long a task runs for after the abort is issued;
- The program statements it executes in that time.

Precisely what happens depends on the state of the aborted tasks at the time when abort is invoked. For details on this refer to section 9.10 of the LRM. Because of this, and possible consequential effects, we recommend great caution in its use.

More than one task can be aborted at a time with this statement. We could have, for instance

> **abort** ROBOT_10, ROBOT_5, ROBOT_6;

Remember also that a task will not, in normal circumstances, conclude until all its dependent tasks have also concluded.

Now we come to the topic of exceptions in tasks. We first met exceptions in chapter 11, as applicable to packages, subprograms and blocks. The basic features discussed there also apply to tasks, so, if necessary, revise them before going further.

Task exception handlers are located in the task body. Thus, when using such a handler, the task structure becomes

```
with TEXT_IO;                use TEXT_IO;
procedure TASK_EXCEP_HANDLER is
  subtype NO_OF_MUSIC_TRACKS is INTEGER range 1..15;
  task ROBOT_10 is
    entry PLAY_MUSIC (NO_OF_TRACKS : in  NO_OF_MUSIC_TRACKS := 10);
    entry STOP_MUSIC;
  end ROBOT_10;
  -- a second task - the calling task for ROBOT_10
  task MAKE_SOUND;
  task body ROBOT_10 is
    TRACKS            :     NO_OF_MUSIC_TRACKS;
  begin
    accept PLAY_MUSIC (NO_OF_TRACKS : in  NO_OF_MUSIC_TRACKS := 10) do
      TRACKS := NO_OF_TRACKS;
    end PLAY_MUSIC;
    loop
      select
        accept STOP_MUSIC;
      else
        delay 2.0;
        PUT_LINE ("End of track");
  -- no exit from loop. The next line will eventually cause a
  -- CONSTRAINT_ERROR!
        TRACKS := TRACKS - 1;
      end select;
    end loop;
  exception
    when CONSTRAINT_ERROR =>
      PUT_LINE ("CONSTRAINT_ERROR - ROBOT_10");
  end ROBOT_10;
  task body MAKE_SOUND is
  begin
    ROBOT_10.PLAY_MUSIC;
  end MAKE_SOUND;
begin
  null;
end TASK_EXCEP_HANDLER;
```

Listing 14.21 Tasks and the exception handler.

```
task ROBOT_10;

task body ROBOT_10 is
begin
    <STATEMENTS>
exception
    <EXCEPTION HANDLER>
end ROBOT_10;
```

This is expanded on in Listing 14.21.

Now for an interesting question. How does a task behave when an exception occurs? To answer this we must first define when exceptions can be raised. These are:

```
with TEXT_IO;              use TEXT_IO;
procedure NO_EXCEP_HANDLER is
  subtype NO_OF_MUSIC_TRACKS is INTEGER range 1..15;
  task ROBOT_10 is
    entry PLAY_MUSIC (NO_OF_TRACKS : in  NO_OF_MUSIC_TRACKS := 10);
    entry STOP_MUSIC;
  end ROBOT_10;
  -- a second task - the calling task for ROBOT_10
  task MAKE_SOUND;
  task body ROBOT_10 is
    TRACKS           :    NO_OF_MUSIC_TRACKS;
  begin
    accept PLAY_MUSIC (NO_OF_TRACKS : in  NO_OF_MUSIC_TRACKS := 10) do
      TRACKS := NO_OF_TRACKS;
    end PLAY_MUSIC;
    loop
      select
        accept STOP_MUSIC;
      else
        delay 2.0;
        PUT_LINE ("End of track");
  -- no exit from loop. The next line will eventually cause a
  -- CONSTRAINT_ERROR!
        TRACKS := TRACKS - 1;
      end select;
    end loop;
  -- exception handler has been removed
  end ROBOT_10;
  task body MAKE_SOUND is
  begin
    ROBOT_10.PLAY_MUSIC;
  end MAKE_SOUND;
begin
  null;
end NO_EXCEP_HANDLER;
```

Listing 14.22 Task exception without a handler.

(a) During the execution of a task which has a related exception handler;
(b) During the execution of a task which does not have a related exception handler;
(c) During elaboration of task declarations;
(d) During elaboration of items within a task body;
(e) During task rendezvous.

Let us review each case in turn. Please bear in mind that this does not cover all possible situations. For further information consult the LRM.

(a) If a task has an appropriate handler, then the handler statements are executed. The task then finishes (as for a normal completion). This action occurs for the exception example of Listing 14.21.
(b) If the task has no handler (or no appropriate handler), it completes as soon as the exception is raised. That is, it just grinds to a standstill. No propagation of exceptions takes place (unlike all earlier applications). See Listing 14.22 for an example of this.

```
with TEXT_IO;              use TEXT_IO;
procedure DECL_EXCEPTION is
  subtype NO_OF_MUSIC_TRACKS is INTEGER range 1..15;
  task ROBOT_10 is
    entry PLAY_MUSIC (NO_OF_TRACKS : in  NO_OF_MUSIC_TRACKS := 21);
    entry STOP_MUSIC;
  end ROBOT_10;
  -- a second task - the calling task for ROBOT_10
  task MAKE_SOUND;
  task body ROBOT_10 is
    TRACKS        :     NO_OF_MUSIC_TRACKS;
  begin
    accept PLAY_MUSIC (NO_OF_TRACKS : in  NO_OF_MUSIC_TRACKS := 21) do
      TRACKS := NO_OF_TRACKS;
    end PLAY_MUSIC;
    loop
      select
        accept STOP_MUSIC;
      else
        delay 2.0;
        PUT_LINE ("End of track");
        exit when TRACKS = 1;
   -- EXIT
        TRACKS := TRACKS - 1;
      end select;
    end loop;
  exception
    when CONSTRAINT_ERROR =>
      PUT_LINE ("CONSTRAINT_ERROR - ROBOT_10");
  end ROBOT_10;
  task body MAKE_SOUND is
  begin
    ROBOT_10.PLAY_MUSIC;
  end MAKE_SOUND;
begin
  null;
end DECL_EXCEPTION;
```

Listing 14.23 Task exception during elaboration of declarations.

(c) If exception is raised during elaboration of task declarations, elaboration is abandoned (Listing 14.23).

(d) An exception in the declarative part of a task body isn't raised until the task is executed. More precisely, it is raised during the elaboration of the declarative part of the body – the activation of the task object. In this case the task is immediately completed, Listing 14.24.

(e) During task rendezvous, exceptions can occur in two ways. The first we have already met. That is where a calling task tries to rendezvous with an acceptor task which is unavailable (either the acceptor has already completed, or else it completes before the entry is accepted). In this case the exception TASKING_ERROR is raised in the calling task.

The second way is where the acceptor task raises the exception during the rendezvous. If it is handled within the **accept** statement both tasks

```
with TEXT_IO;              use TEXT_IO;
procedure ACTIVATION_EXCEP is
  subtype NO_OF_MUSIC_TRACKS is INTEGER range 1..15;
  task ROBOT_10 is
    entry PLAY_MUSIC (NO_OF_TRACKS : in  NO_OF_MUSIC_TRACKS := 10);
    entry STOP_MUSIC;
  end ROBOT_10;
  -- a second task - the calling task for ROBOT_10
  task MAKE_SOUND;
  task body ROBOT_10 is
  -- the next line will cause a CONSTRAINT_ERROR
    TRACKS          :       NO_OF_MUSIC_TRACKS := 30;
    begin
      accept PLAY_MUSIC (NO_OF_TRACKS : in  NO_OF_MUSIC_TRACKS := 10) do
        TRACKS := NO_OF_TRACKS;
      end PLAY_MUSIC;
      loop
        select
          accept STOP_MUSIC;
        else
          delay 2.0;
          PUT_LINE ("End of track");
          exit when TRACKS = 1;
  -- EXIT
          TRACKS := TRACKS - 1;
        end select;
      end loop;
    exception
      when CONSTRAINT_ERROR =>
        PUT_LINE ("CONSTRAINT_ERROR - ROBOT_10");
    end ROBOT_10;
    task body MAKE_SOUND is
    begin
      PUT_LINE ("MAKE_SOUND active");
      ROBOT_10.PLAY_MUSIC;
    end MAKE_SOUND;
begin
  null;
end ACTIVATION_EXCEP;
```

Listing 14.24 Task exception during task activation.

continue executing. If it isn't, then execution of the **accept** statement is abandoned. The exception is raised again immediately after the **accept** statement. Moreover, the exception is propagated to the calling task. These points are demonstrated in Listings 14.25 and 14.26.

14.12 TASK PRIORITIES

Task priorities is a small but very important subtopic of tasking in Ada. But to see its importance you need to understand why we have task priorities in the first place.

Suppose in a flight control system we have two tasks. One is a stability

488 Concurrency – the Ada task

```
with TEXT_IO;                  use TEXT_IO;
procedure RENDEZVOUS_EXCEPTION_HANDLER is
  subtype NO_OF_MUSIC_TRACKS is INTEGER range 1..15;
  task ROBOT_10 is
     entry PLAY_MUSIC (NO_OF_TRACKS : in  NO_OF_MUSIC_TRACKS := 10);
     entry STOP_MUSIC;
  end ROBOT_10;
  -- a second task - the calling task for ROBOT_10
  task MAKE_SOUND;
  task body ROBOT_10 is
     TRACKS          :       NO_OF_MUSIC_TRACKS;
  begin
     accept PLAY_MUSIC (NO_OF_TRACKS : in  NO_OF_MUSIC_TRACKS := 10) do
        begin
  -- the next line will cause a constraint error to be raised
           TRACKS := 20;
         exception
           when CONSTRAINT_ERROR =>
              PUT_LINE ("CONSTRAINT_ERROR in PLAY_MUSIC");
         end;
     end PLAY_MUSIC;
     loop
        select
          accept STOP_MUSIC;
        else
          delay 2.0;
          PUT_LINE ("End of track");
          exit when TRACKS = 1;
  -- EXIT
          TRACKS := TRACKS - 1;
        end select;
     end loop;
  exception
     when CONSTRAINT_ERROR =>
        PUT_LINE ("CONSTRAINT_ERROR - ROBOT_10");
  end ROBOT_10;
  task body MAKE_SOUND is
  begin
     ROBOT_10.PLAY_MUSIC;
  exception
     when CONSTRAINT_ERROR =>
        PUT_LINE ("CONSTRAINT_ERROR - MAKE_SOUND");
  end MAKE_SOUND;
begin
  null;
end RENDEZVOUS_EXCEPTION_HANDLER;
```

Listing 14.25 Task exceptions in an acceptor task during a rendezvous – exception handled.

augmentation loop, and the other handles cockpit display data. Visualize the following situation. The aircraft enters a dangerous flight regime, which requires an immediate response. But at the same instant the display unit is due to be updated. The processor decides to update the display. End of aircraft, pilot and story.

Clearly the stability loop task should be actioned. Yet, with the task constructs described so far, we cannot force such a course of action. This is where the priority feature (more correctly, priority pragma) comes into use.

```ada
with TEXT_IO;            use TEXT_IO;
procedure RENDEZVOUS_EXCEPTION is
  subtype NO_OF_MUSIC_TRACKS is INTEGER range 1..15;
  task ROBOT_10 is
    entry PLAY_MUSIC (NO_OF_TRACKS : in  NO_OF_MUSIC_TRACKS := 10);
    entry STOP_MUSIC;
  end ROBOT_10;
  -- a second task - the calling task for ROBOT_10
  task MAKE_SOUND;
  task body ROBOT_10 is
    TRACKS          :      NO_OF_MUSIC_TRACKS;
  begin
    accept PLAY_MUSIC (NO_OF_TRACKS : in  NO_OF_MUSIC_TRACKS := 10) do
  -- the next line will cause a constraint error to be raised
      TRACKS := 20;
    end PLAY_MUSIC;
    loop
      select
        accept STOP_MUSIC;
      else
        delay 2.0;
        PUT_LINE ("End of track");
        exit when TRACKS = 1;
  -- EXIT
        TRACKS := TRACKS - 1;
      end select;
    end loop;
  exception
    when CONSTRAINT_ERROR =>
      PUT_LINE ("CONSTRAINT_ERROR - ROBOT_10");
  end ROBOT_10;
  task body MAKE_SOUND is
  begin
    ROBOT_10.PLAY_MUSIC;
  exception
    when CONSTRAINT_ERROR =>
      PUT_LINE ("CONSTRAINT_ERROR - MAKE_SOUND");
  end MAKE_SOUND;
begin
  null;
end RENDEZVOUS_EXCEPTION;
```

Listing 14.26 Task exceptions in an acceptor task during a rendezvous – exception NOT handled.

Its purpose is to help the processor resolve contention between tasks. We attach a priority rating to a task using the pragma. Then, if contention does occur, the highest priority task is selected for execution.

The general syntax is

```ada
task ROBOT_10;

task body ROBOT_10 is
   pragma PRIORITY (2);
begin
   <STATEMENTS>
end ROBOT_10;
```

Here we have defined the task ROBOT_10 to have a priority of 2. The higher the number, the greater the priority.

Priorities are fixed – except in the case of a rendezvous. This may seem odd, but there is a good reason for it. Assume that a high-priority task makes a rendezvous with one having a very low priority. Assume also that there are a number of other tasks in the system which:

- Have priorities which lie between these two;
- Are ready to run.

If the priorities are left fixed, the low-priority task will be blocked out until these other tasks are serviced. But that means that the high-priority task cannot proceed – it is suspended for the duration of the rendezvous. Here we have the nonsensical situation of low-priority tasks blocking out a high-priority one. To eliminate this we raise the priority setting of the lower one to that of the higher one.

Where a rendezvous takes place between prioritized tasks, we do not distinguish between caller and acceptor. The rendezvous takes place with both tasks set to the same (high) priority. If only one task has a defined priority, the rendezvous takes place at that priority.

When tasks have the same priority we cannot define their run-time order.

14.13 TASK AND ENTRY ATTRIBUTES

We have already met various language attributes. Now we come to those which are applied to tasks. They fall into two groups: those used by callers and that used by acceptors, Fig.14.25.

If a task is called which is 'dead' (completed, terminated or aborted) the exception TASKING_ERROR is raised. Before we can institute appropriate responses we need to identify the cause and source of the exception. This may be lengthy and difficult. In fact we may not always succeed. So, what happens if our system relies on the continued execution of the calling task? We have a major problem, to say the least. Even if we can pin down the source of the exception, the time taken may be unacceptable. In cases like this it is much better for the calling task to find out if the acceptor is 'alive'. We do this using the task attributes CALLABLE and TERMINATED.

To find out if a task is completed, terminated or abnormal, we use the CALLABLE attribute, as in

```
if ROBOT_WELDER'CALLABLE then
    ROBOT_WELDER.WELD (BUTT_JOINT);
end if;
```

Tasks in packages 491

```
                    TASK ATTRIBUTES
                   /               \
            CALLING TASK         ACCEPTOR TASK
           /            \              |
  ACCEPTOR CALLABLE ?  ACCEPTOR TERMINATED ?   HOW MANY CALLS TO AN ENTRY ?
```

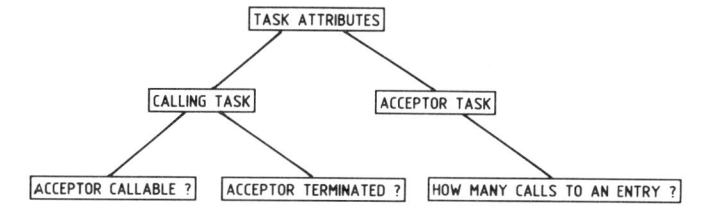

Fig.14.25 Task attributes.

Likewise, to see whether a task has terminated we use the attribute TERMI-NATED:

```
if ROBOT_WELDER'TERMINATED then
    GENERATE_OPERATOR_ALARM;
end if;
```

Now let us turn to the acceptor task. Assume that another task calls on an entry in the acceptor – which the task is not ready to accept. The entry call is queued. A different task now makes a call to the same entry. This too is queued, taking its place behind the first one; that is, queued on a first-come first-served basis. We say that we have a queue of entry calls. An acceptor task can determine the number of entry calls in an entry queue using the attribute COUNT.

14.14 TASKS IN PACKAGES

Tasks, in practice, are most likely to be built within packages. This can be done in two ways. First, the task declaration may be included in the package specification. Alternatively, the task declaration may be located in the package body. Let us consider each in turn.

If you wish to make a task visible to clients it must be declared in the package specification. It can then be directly manipulated by these clients (as long as the rules of tasking are followed). Also, task entries form part of the task declaration. Therefore clients can rendezvous with this (called) task using the entry calls. These points are shown in Listings 14.27 and 14.28.

Note that the task body goes in the package body.

Up to this point no new ideas have been introduced. Now, however, let us declare the task within the package body, as shown in the part program below (Listing 14.29).

As a result, the task – and thus entries – is hidden from clients. If we wish

```ada
with TEXT_IO;                   use TEXT_IO;
package DRILLING_ROBOT is
  -- declare a task with several entries
  task ROBOT is
    entry RESET_DRILL;
    entry MOVE_DRILL;
    entry MOVE_ROUTER;
  end ROBOT;
end DRILLING_ROBOT;

package body DRILLING_ROBOT is
  task body ROBOT is
  begin
    PUT_LINE ("ROBOT ready");
    loop
      select
        accept RESET_DRILL;
        PUT_LINE ("ROBOT received request to reset drill");
      or
        accept MOVE_ROUTER;
        PUT_LINE ("ROBOT received request to move router");
      or
        accept MOVE_DRILL;
        PUT_LINE ("ROBOT received request to move drill");
      end select;
    end loop;
  end ROBOT;
begin
  null;
end DRILLING_ROBOT;
```

Listing 14.27 Task declaration in a package specification.

```ada
with TEXT_IO;                use TEXT_IO;
with DRILLING_ROBOT;
procedure USE_DRILLING_ROBOT is
  -- a calling task
  task ROBOT_CONTROLLER;
  task body ROBOT_CONTROLLER is
  begin
     DRILLING_ROBOT.ROBOT.RESET_DRILL;
     DRILLING_ROBOT.ROBOT.MOVE_ROUTER;
     DRILLING_ROBOT.ROBOT.RESET_DRILL;
     DRILLING_ROBOT.ROBOT.MOVE_DRILL;
  end ROBOT_CONTROLLER;
begin
  null;
end USE_DRILLING_ROBOT;
```

Listing 14.28 Using the task of Listing 14.27.

```ada
with TEXT_IO;                use TEXT_IO;
package body DRILLER_ROBOT is
  -- declare task here
  task ROBOT is
    entry RESET_DRILL;
    entry MOVE_DRILL;
    entry MOVE_ROUTER;
  end ROBOT;
  task body ROBOT is
  begin
    PUT_LINE ("ROBOT ready");
    loop
      select
        accept RESET_DRILL;
        PUT_LINE ("ROBOT received request to reset drill");
      or
        accept MOVE_ROUTER;
        PUT_LINE ("ROBOT received request to move router");
      or
        accept MOVE_DRILL;
        PUT_LINE ("ROBOT received request to move drill");
      end select;
    end loop;
  end ROBOT;
begin
  null;
end DRILLER_ROBOT;
```

Listing 14.29 Part-program – task declaration in a package body.

to use this task we can access it only by using provided subprograms, these being given in Listing 14.30.

Use of the task by clients is illustrated in Listing 14.31.

This demonstrates two features. First, clients cannot directly access the task and so control its behaviour (e.g. aborting it). Second, implementation details are hidden. The client calls on facilities (using subprograms) without being concerned as to how these facilities are provided.

REVIEW

In this chapter we have covered one of the most important advanced topics of Ada. Do you now:

- Understand the difference between sequential and parallel activities?
- Appreciate the use of multiprocessing and multitasking?
- Understand how to implement concurrent tasking of independent tasks?
- Realize that independent tasks may well interact by using shared resources?
- Understand how to implement concurrent tasking of interdependent tasks?
- Understand how to implement intertask synchronization using the rendezvous?

```ada
with TEXT_IO;                   use TEXT_IO;
package DRILLER_ROBOT is
  procedure RESET_ROBOT_DRILL;
  procedure MOVE_ROBOT_DRILL;
  procedure MOVE_ROBOT_ROUTER;
end DRILLER_ROBOT;
package body DRILLER_ROBOT is
  -- declare task here
  task ROBOT is
    entry RESET_DRILL;
    entry MOVE_DRILL;
    entry MOVE_ROUTER;
  end ROBOT;
  task body ROBOT is
  begin
    PUT_LINE ("ROBOT ready");
    loop
      select
        accept RESET_DRILL;
        PUT_LINE ("ROBOT received request to reset drill");
      or
        accept MOVE_ROUTER;
        PUT_LINE ("ROBOT received request to move router");
      or
        accept MOVE_DRILL;
        PUT_LINE ("ROBOT received request to move drill");
      end select;
    end loop;
  end ROBOT;
  -- the procedures
  procedure RESET_ROBOT_DRILL is
  begin
    PUT_LINE ("Resetting Robot Drill");
    ROBOT.RESET_DRILL;
  end RESET_ROBOT_DRILL;
  procedure MOVE_ROBOT_DRILL is
  begin
    PUT_LINE ("Moving Robot Drill");
    ROBOT.MOVE_DRILL;
  end MOVE_ROBOT_DRILL;
  procedure MOVE_ROBOT_ROUTER is
  begin
    PUT_LINE ("Moving Robot Router");
    ROBOT.MOVE_ROUTER;
  end MOVE_ROBOT_ROUTER;
begin
  null;
end DRILLER_ROBOT;
```

Listing 14.30 Task declaration in a package body.

```
with TEXT_IO;                    use TEXT_IO;
with DRILLER_ROBOT;
procedure USE_DRILLER_ROBOT is
  -- a calling task
   task ROBOT_CONTROLLER;
   task body ROBOT_CONTROLLER is
   begin
      DRILLER_ROBOT.RESET_ROBOT_DRILL;
      DRILLER_ROBOT.MOVE_ROBOT_ROUTER;
      DRILLER_ROBOT.RESET_ROBOT_DRILL;
      DRILLER_ROBOT.MOVE_ROBOT_DRILL;
   end ROBOT_CONTROLLER;
begin
   null;
end USE_DRILLER_ROBOT;
```

Listing 14.31 Using the task of Listing 14.30.

- Appreciate what happens before, during and after a rendezvous?
- Know how to transfer data between tasks at rendezvouz time?
- Understand the need for and use of selective waits?
- Recollect the concepts and implementation of conditional and timed entries?
- See the reason for having task types, and know how to apply them?
- Discern the structure and application of task entry families?
- Perceive the methods by which tasks terminate?
- Comprehend the aspects of exception responses and handling in tasks?
- Recognize the need for task priorities?
- See why we have, and how we can use, task attributes?

Chapter Fifteen
Low-level issues

Everything that has been covered so far is standard to Ada. Different compilers may have different library features but, once this is allowed for, any program should run on any computer system. Now, why should this be the case? The answer is that our computer comes with an operating system which provides an interface between the Ada software and machine features. So when we insert a program statement such as PUT ('Hello'), the operating system is responsible for printing out screen information at program run time. To us, the user, the operation is automatic and unseen, that is 'transparent'. But what do we do when we need to use a feature which is non-standard as far as the operating system is concerned? Or what if we are working with a bare board in a target (embedded) system environment? In both cases the only way to achieve our goals is to interact with the system at the chip level. Can this be done in Ada? Generally, yes, although we may not write all the source code in the Ada language itself.

This chapter sets out to show:

- Why we need to access machine facilities;
- What access features are needed;
- How Ada supports operations of this type;
- The unchecked programming aspects of the language;
- Interfacing aspects to other languages.

15.1 INTRODUCTION – THE NEED TO ACCESS MACHINE FACILITIES

Do we need to manipulate hardware at the chip level? Well, if our software is destined to run on a standard operating system, and the system is already installed on our machine, then we don't. In such cases control of the computer devices is done by 'systems software', our own programs being defined as 'applications software' (Fig.15.1).

Unfortunately for the engineer, many computer-based real-time engineering functions don't use standard operating systems. Software tends to be tailor made for the task in hand, with little or no distinction between systems and applications software. In fact, software in smaller embedded systems is considered to be 'applications' only, interacting directly with the computer hardware (Fig.15.2).

Introduction – the need to access machine facilities   497

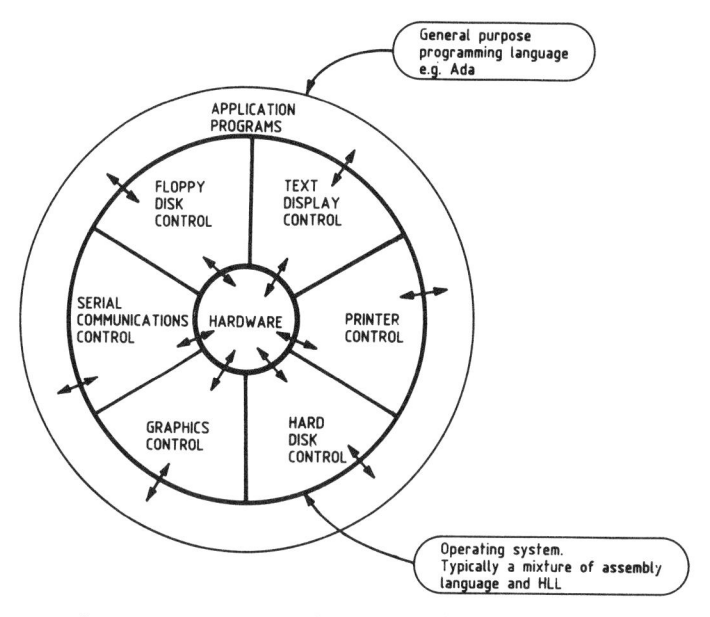

Fig.15.1 General purpose computer – hardware/software structure.

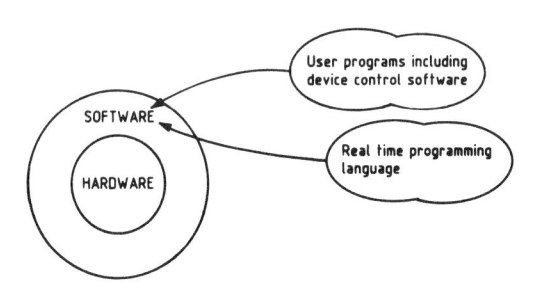

Fig.15.2 Small embedded real-time computer – hardware/software structure.

Systems like these are many and diverse, ranging from aircraft flight controllers to microwave ovens; hence the need for unique, as opposed to general purpose, software.

Adapting hardware behaviour to meet varying requirements is not restricted just to embedded schemes. The systems programmer, for instance, faces similar problems when installing operating systems on new or modified hardware.

A second set of problems arise when dealing with designs which use different processors. A brief comparison is given in Table 15.1 of the Intel 8086 and 386 microprocessors. This shows just how much variation can be found even in devices from the same manufacturer.

498 Low-level issues

Table 15.1 Outline comparison – intel 8086 vs. 386

	8086	*80386DX*
Address range	1 Mbyte	4 Gbytes
Date word size	16 bits	32 bits
Memory management unit	No	Yes
Clock speed (max.)	10 MHz	33 MHz

From this it is clear that operating systems have to be adaptable if they're ever going to work on different processors. Even when the processor is fixed, designs still differ concerning:

- Use of memory space for code, data and stack;
- Amount of code in read-only store;
- Amount of read/write store;
- Special store provisions, such as non-volatile devices;
- Address locations of these devices;
- Location, size and activating methods for interrupt-driven programs.

So, software engineers who wish to venture beyond the comfortable confines of applications programming have to get involved in machine details.

15.2 FACILITIES NEEDED TO ACCESS MACHINE RESOURCES

15.2.1 General comments

Before looking at what Ada offers, let's define what we do need for the access and control of computer resources. Our requirements can be grouped roughly into five areas:

- Memory accesses, for the control of code, data and stack operations;
- Interrupt handling;
- Peripheral device interfacing and control;
- Support of special machine operations, as in I/O mapping methods in Intel processors;
- Software aspects relating to these and other requirements.

These are of particular interest to the embedded (usually microprocessor-based) systems designer (Fig.15.3).

In such applications non-volatile storage is used for the program code. Almost always this is programmed into UV erasable programmable read-only memory (EPROM) integrated circuit devices. Data (i.e. program variables)

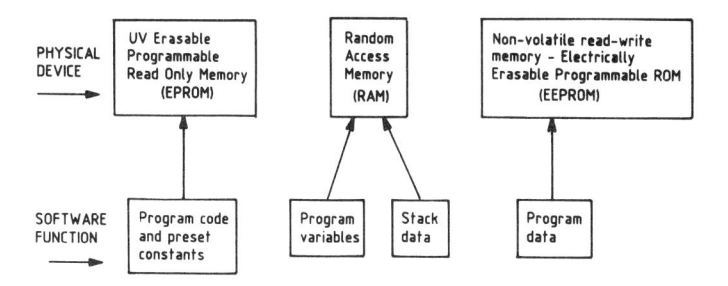

Fig.15.3 Memory devices – their use in processor systems.

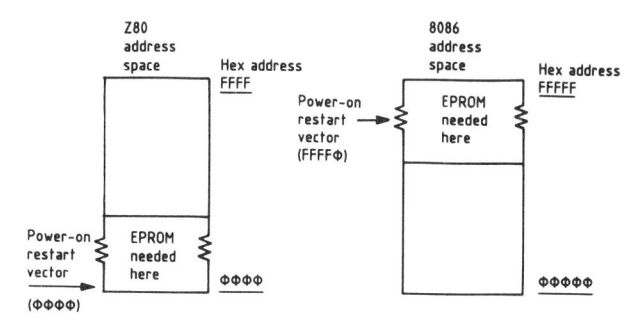

Fig.15.4 Mapping of memory devices.

is held in read/write store, normally random access memory (RAM). Some applications call for the use of non-volatile read/write data stores, this function being performed by battery-backed RAM or electrically erasable programmable ROM (EEPROM). The stack, being a read/write data store, must be located in RAM.

These physical devices are mapped into the processor address space, their locations being determined mainly by processor characteristics. For instance, EPROM must be mapped at the bottom of memory in the Z80 (Fig.15.4).

This comes about because, on power-up, program execution begins at location 0000H. The 8086, however, restarts with its instruction pointer pointing to location FFFF0H. Hence EPROM must be located at the top of memory in this instance. Thus the software engineer must take into account the mapping scheme in use when compiling the program (as it's rather difficult to write information into EPROM).

In other cases it may be that we want to handle information which resides in specific memory locations (absolute addresses). This is, for instance, one way of communicating between devices, the so-called 'shared memory' method (Fig.15.5).

500 Low-level issues

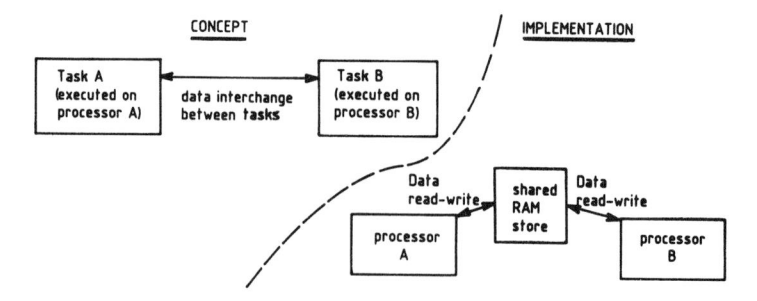

Fig.15.5 Use of shared memory.

Here we need to be able to specify precisely the addresses of the memory locations we're reading from or writing to.

15.2.3 Management of peripheral devices

Virtually everything except processor and memory devices comes into this category. Included are items such as programmable timers, interrupt controllers, serial I/O controllers, maths chips, analogue-to-digital converters, etc.; the list is immense. Generally, though, they have three factors in common:

- They are mapped at specific absolute addresses;
- Both read and write operations are performed on them;
- Individual bits within a data word have specific meanings.

Where peripherals are mapped into memory then, to the processor, they look like RAM. Thus the first two points need no further discussion. However, bit management is a different matter. We need this facility for two main reasons, both associated with programmable devices or processor subsystems. First, we may want to establish the status of the device being accessed. Second, we may wish to change its operational mode. Both status and control information is handled using word (in smaller systems, byte) data transfers. For such applications the information carried by the word is set by individual bits within the word. As an example, Fig.15.6 shows the make-up of two registers from a Signetics serial communications controller.

From this it is obvious that, when interacting with peripherals, we must be able to examine and modify data words bit by bit. And for the sake of clarity and reliability it is better to do this using high-level language statements.

15.2.4 Interrupt handling

Interrupts have three main roles. First, they enable us to guarantee to meet stringent timing requirements of programs. This is a common aspect of closed

STATUS REGISTER							
BIT7	BIT6	BIT5	BIT4	BIT3	BIT2	BIT1	BIT0
RECEIVED BREAK	FRAMING ERROR	PARITY ERROR	OVERRUN ERROR	TxEMT	TxRDY	FFULL	RxRDY
0 = no 1 = yes	0 = no 1 = yes	0 = no 1 = yes	0 = no 1 = yes	0 = no 1 = yes	0 = no 1 = yes	0 = no 1 = yes	0 = no 1 = yes

CONTROL REGISTER						
BIT7	BIT6	BIT5	BIT4 BIT3	BIT2	BIT1 BIT0
RX RTS CONTROL	RX INT SELECT	ERROR MODE	PARITY MODE	PARITY TYPE	BITS PER CHAR
0 = no 1 = yes	0 = RXRDY 1 = FFULL	0 = char 1 = block	00 = with parity 01 = force parity 10 = no parity 11 = multi-drop mode	0 = no 1 = yes	00 = 5 01 = 6 10 = 7 11 = 8

Fig.15.6 Interacting with peripherals – status and control features.

loop control systems. Second, they simplify the implementation of multitasking or handling processor–I/O interaction as asynchronous operations. Finally, they can get us out of dangerous situations, such as loss of program control, dividing by zero, etc. Different processors use different hardware/software interrupt control methods. But no matter how these are actually implemented, we always end up using absolute addressing methods. Typically we locate the interrupt program at a defined absolute address in memory; the processor is then vectored to this address when the interrupt is activated (Fig.15.7).

Alternatively, the compiler fixes the program location. We then 'plant' the necessary reference to this at an absolutely defined address in the interrupt vector area. When an interrupt occurs program control is initially transferred to the appropriate location in the vector area (Fig.15.8).

The program residing here is usually quite short. Normally it performs limited housekeeping functions and then transfers program execution to its interrupt program.

Variations of these exist, of course.

15.2.5 Special machine operations

Occasionally processors provide facilities which are unique to their design. For instance, on Intel processors, data can be transferred quickly and efficiently using their 'IN' and 'OUT' instructions. Peripheral devices which respond to these instructions are mapped into the so-called 'I/O' space. Address decoding is performed in conjunction with a signal generated by the processor on one of its output pins. There is no overlap with the memory space. It would be contradictory to include such instructions as standard in a general

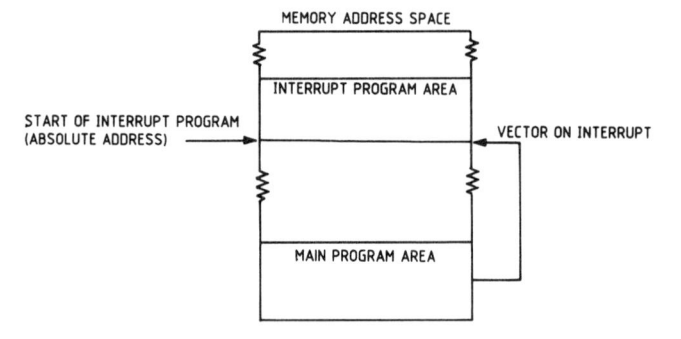

Fig.15.7 Interrupt operation – 1.

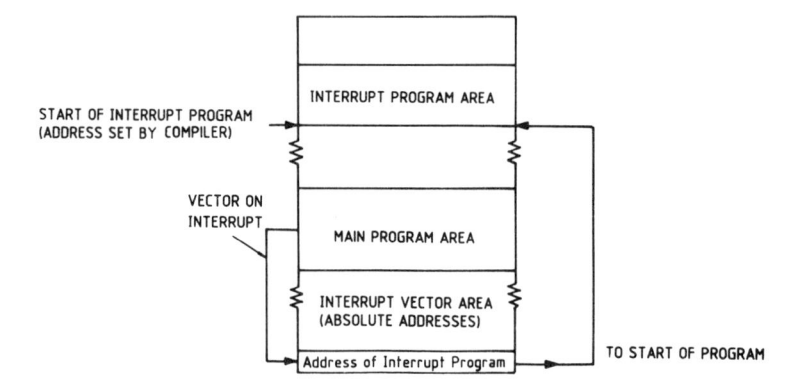

Fig.15.8 Interrupt operation – 2.

purpose high-level language; this would make it much less portable (or else dangerous) in use. Yet we still need to be able to invoke all facilities provided by the processor.

15.2.6 Software issues

The primary requirement is that we should be able to do as much as possible using high-level statements. These are easy to understand, straightforward to maintain, and are much less likely to hold unwitting mistakes. Nevertheless, there will be some occasions when the high-level approach fails. Therefore we must be able to insert low-level statements, either in assembly language or machine (hex) form, into the high-level code.

A second requirement is to have the ability to handle a data object(s) as if it belongs to different types – without changing its bit representation. Hence type transfer facilities must be available.

Mapping Ada on to the machine – representation clauses   503

Finally, it is highly desirable that program modules developed in different languages can be bound (linked) together. At the very least assembler modules must be handled by the linker.

15.3 LOW-LEVEL FACILITIES IN ADA – AN OVERVIEW

Once we've decided to use a particular microprocessor we have to live with its functions. Ideally, all access to such functions would be made using standard high-level code. Unfortunately, this doesn't work in practice.

Software designers can produce compilers for specific processors. But the problem is that the functions and operation of complete computers vary from design to design. Clearly, it is just not feasible for the compiler writer to take such individual designs into account. Hence a fully 'standard' implementation of Ada would fail to meet all our needs – bespoke versions are needed to cope with these design variations. Yet we don't want the language to appear in numerous dialects. Ada is meant to be Ada: no subsets, no supersets. The problem is tackled in two ways: compiler attributes (the package SYSTEM) and language features (representation clauses).

Ada compilers are designed so that machine-dependent (low-level) facilities are supplied within a library package called SYSTEM. Its details are given in section 13.7 of the LRM. Although this is a library package it is closely related to the compiler, being specific to the target processor. As such, it is not provided as a separate item but is part of the Ada compiler suite.

In the following sections we'll look at the use of both representation clauses and SYSTEM facilities. One very important point must be stressed. Great care must be taken when using low-level facilities – these are machine, and sometimes device, dependent. The resulting software is not usually portable; moreover, the compiler error checking power is seriously reduced when handling such facilities. It is recommended that any code so produced is kept in clearly identified packages.

15.4 MAPPING ADA ON TO THE MACHINE – REPRESENTATION CLAUSES

15.4.1 General

The purpose of representation clauses is to map Ada features (abstract) into machine format (concrete), Fig.15.9. They come in two general flavours, address and type representation (Fig.15.10).

504 Low-level issues

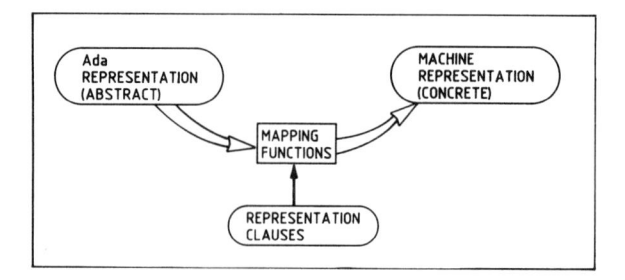

Fig.15.9 Concept – representation clauses.

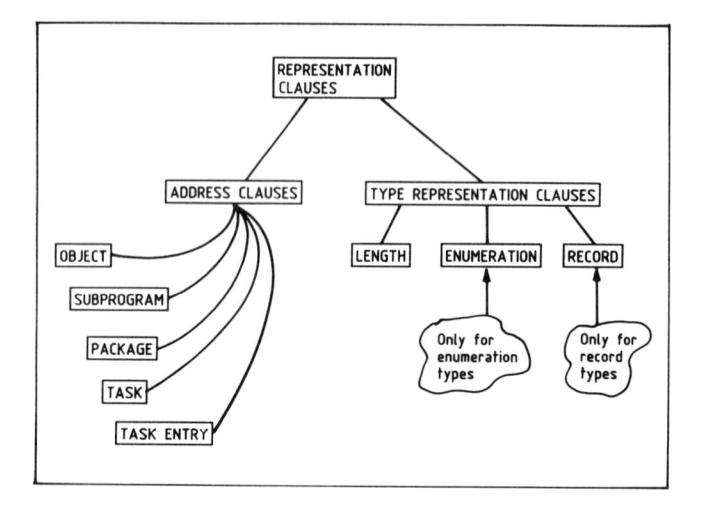

Fig.15.10 Representation clauses.

Address clauses enable us to specify the absolute address of Ada items: objects, subprograms, packages, tasks and task entries. Type representation clauses allow us to define the structure of Ada types within the machine. Observe that enumeration and record types have their own specification rules.

Treat these clauses as system programming features. Using these we can develop application programs without having to take machine details into account. The representation clauses then provide the mapping between the application code and the target machine. Naturally enough, each target system will have its own set of low-level programs.

There is another advantage in using representation clauses: the application code should – if well designed – be highly portable. That is, if it is moved to (ported to) another machine it should work correctly, without modification.

Let us now look at the representation clauses in more detail.

15.4.2 Address clauses

We've already discussed the need to get at specific, absolute, machine addresses. Address clauses allow us to do precisely that. Suppose, for example, we wish to load an INTEGER value into a particular memory location. The address of this location is hexadecimal 1F497. First, use a name for this location, say INT_25, by declaring it. Then give it the desired address. Finally, in the program code, we can write data to it. The outline details for this are as follows:

```
INT_25 : INTEGER;
for INT_25 use at 16#1F497#;
begin
   .
   INT_25 := 895;
   .
end;
```

Here the address clause consists of the reserved word **for**, then the name of the object, followed by **use at**. It is finished off with the address location at which the object is to be located. In this case we have specified the address to be 1F497 hexadecimal (the '16' defines it to be base 16). Addresses of subprograms, packages and tasks are specified in an identical manner. The general syntax is

```
for SIMPLE_NAME use at SIMPLE_EXPRESSION;
```

For example, suppose we have declared a procedure COMPUTE_CONTROL_LAW. We then define its location by writing

```
for COMPUTE_CONTROL_LAW use at 16#20000#;
```

This is a clear, simple construction which is easy to use. Note that SIMPLE_EXPRESSION must be of type ADDRESS, as defined in package SYSTEM (i.e. SYSTEM.ADDRESS). Thus SYSTEM must be imported – using **with** – in order to apply address representation clauses. These points are further illustrated in Listing 15.1.

For task entries the situation is only slightly more complex. We have to define the entry address within the task specification, as, for example,

506   Low-level issues

```
with SYSTEM;                   use SYSTEM;
procedure SPECIFY_ADDRESS is
  REGISTER_1      :     INTEGER        := 0;
  for REGISTER_1 use at 16#10000#;
  REGISTER_2      :     INTEGER        := 0;
  for REGISTER_2 use at 16#10004#;
begin
  -- assign values to the objects. The values will be written to at the
  -- addresses specified
  REGISTER_1 := REGISTER_1 + 1;
  REGISTER_2 := REGISTER_1 + REGISTER_2;
end SPECIFY_ADDRESS;
```

Listing 15.1 Specifying the address of an object using the address representation clause.

```
task ROBOT_2 is
  entry RESET;
  entry MOVE_DRILL;
  for MOVE_DRILL use at 16#10000#;
  entry MOVE_ROUTER;
  for MOVE_ROUTER use at 16#10100#;
end ROBOT_2;
```

Experience has shown that the most widely used address clauses are those for objects and task entries. Further, absolute addressing of task entries is normally related to interrupt handling functions (see later).

A topic closely related to representation clauses is that of representation attributes. These enable us to obtain information about machine-specific items – objects, types and program units. This includes task objects and task types. The attribute of interest here is the one used to find addresses, its syntax being

```
ADA_ITEM'ADDRESS
```

The value returned is of type ADDRESS, as defined in package SYSTEM. Note that we can apply this attribute to objects, subprograms, packages, labels or entries. Its use is demonstrated in Listing 15.2.

15.4.3 Interrupts

In Ada, the standard way to handle an interrupt – either software or hardware generated – is to use an interrupt handler task. The interrupt signal acts

Mapping Ada on to the machine – representation clauses 507

```
with SYSTEM;              use SYSTEM;
procedure ADDRESS_ATTRIB is
   REGISTER_1      :   INTEGER       :=  0;
   for REGISTER_1 use at 16#10000#;
   REGISTER_2      :   INTEGER       :=  0;
   for REGISTER_2 use at REGISTER_1'ADDRESS + 16#00004#;
begin
   -- assign values to the objects. The values will be written to at the
   -- addresses specified
   REGISTER_1 := REGISTER_1 + 1;
   REGISTER_2 := REGISTER_1 + REGISTER_2;
end ADDRESS_ATTRIB;
```

Listing 15.2 Applying the ADDRESS representation attribute.

```
with SYSTEM;                  use SYSTEM;
procedure PROVIDE_INT_HANDLER is
   task TALLY is
      entry INCREMENT;
      for INCREMENT use at 16#00020#;
   end TALLY;
   task body TALLY is
      COUNT           :   INTEGER       :=  0;
      COUNT_MAX       :   constant INTEGER := 999;
   begin
      loop
        accept INCREMENT;
        COUNT := (COUNT + 1) mod COUNT_MAX;
      end loop;
   end TALLY;
begin
   null;
end PROVIDE_INT_HANDLER;
```

Listing 15.3 An interrupt handler task.

as an entry call into the task. What happens subsequently depends on the corresponding accept statement.

The objective here is to show how to associate a task entry with an interrupt. The mechanism is, in fact, that of the address clause. Interrupt signals (vectors) normally have fixed positions in memory. These may, in some cases, be programmable. Even so, we usually decide where these are going to be located, program them, and leave it fixed. We will illustrate this by example.

Suppose we have a timer that can be used to generate an interrupt. Each time it does so, the processor is forced to use the contents of a particular memory location (i.e. it is vectored to that location). Without Ada, our approach would be to plant the address of the interrupt service routine at that location. With Ada, though, we plant the address of the entry to our interrupt handler task. The example of Listing 15.3 is that of an interrupt handler, activated by a hardware timer. Assume that the timer interrupts each millisecond, at store location 20H. The function of the task is to count up to 999, reset, and then recommence counting.

15.4.4 Length clauses

The length clause allows us to control the amount of memory store allocated to program items. More precisely, we define (Fig.15.11) the:

* Store allocation for various program types;
* Working space needed by specific program items.

```
                    STORAGE ALLOCATION
                    /                \
         TYPE SIZE ALLOCATION    WORKING SPACE ALLOCATION
                |                        |
              'SIZE                  'STORAGE_SIZE
           /  |   |   \                /        \
      OBJECT TASK ACCESS FIXED POINT  FOR TASK  FOR ACCESS
      (TYPE) (TYPE)(TYPE)  (TYPE)     OBJECTS   OBJECTS
```

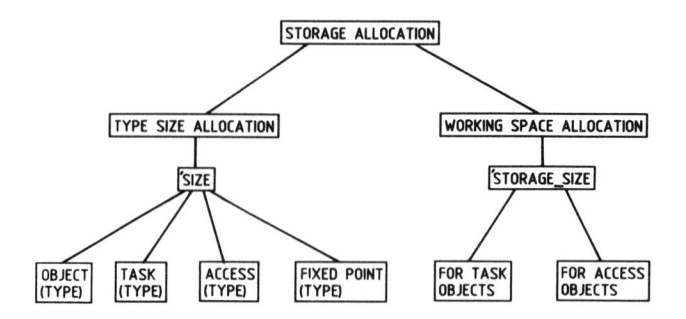

Fig.15.11 Length clauses – storage allocation.

The types we can work with are the object, task, access and fixed point ones. Related to these are the attribute designators SIZE, STORAGE_SIZE and SMALL. Length clauses have the following syntax:

> **for** ATTRIBUTE **use** SIMPLE_EXPRESSION

For simplicity we will use ATTRIBUTE and ATTRIBUTE_DESIGNATOR interchangeably. Strictly speaking, this is wrong, but it does simplify the text. Two attributes are of interest to us, SIZE and STORAGE_SIZE.

(a) **The SIZE attribute**

Using 'SIZE, we can specify the maximum number of bits to be used for a type. Note this well – bits. We should also understand why it is useful (or, in some cases, essential) to define object size. The following example demonstrates the need for such control.

In many microprocessor systems peripheral interfacing is done using byte (8 bit) values. The compiler, left to itself, would not normally generate byte-

```
with TEXT_IO;             use TEXT_IO;
procedure SIZE_ATTRIBUTE is
  type BYTE is range 0..255;
  for BYTE'SIZE use 8;
  UART_DATA       :      BYTE;
  package BYTE_IO is new INTEGER_IO (BYTE);
  use BYTE_IO;
begin
  PUT ("The size in bits of UART_DATA is ");
  PUT (UART_DATA'SIZE, 0);
  NEW_LINE;
  PUT ("The size of an INTEGER in this system is ");
  PUT (INTEGER'SIZE, 0);
  NEW_LINE;
end SIZE_ATTRIBUTE;
```

Listing 15.4 The SIZE attribute.

sized values. Typically it will allocate 16 or 32 bits for simple (i.e. unstructured) objects. This has two effects. First, we waste storage space, though this isn't always a major issue. Second, this allocation may be incompatible with the addressing structure of the peripheral. Therefore, to work with bytes, we first declare the object type and then define its size:

```
type BYTE is range 0..255;
for BYTE'SIZE use 8; -- the size specification
UART_DATA : BYTE;
```

The attribute here is of course BYTE'SIZE.

The SIZE attribute also allows us to obtain the number of bits used by objects, types and subtypes. Consider first an object (say ADA_OBJECT) which is stored as a 16 bit word. The attribute ADA_OBJECT'SIZE returns an answer '16'. For a type (subtype) it yields the minimum number of bits needed to hold objects of that type (subtype). Listing 15.4 illustrates the use of the SIZE attribute.

(b) The STORAGE_SIZE attribute

A preamble. In Ada, a storage unit is defined as the smallest addressable memory unit. When handling memory storage – as with access types, for instance – it is more logical to use storage units rather than bits. This is compiler dependent, and detailed in package SYSTEM as the object STORAGE_UNIT (i.e. SYSTEM.STORAGE_UNIT). Typical sizes are byte (8 bits), word (16 bits), double word (32 bits) and quad word (64 bits). However, in the authors' experience a storage unit is normally a byte – regardless of the target machine data structure. Warning: the meaning of word can vary.

Let us now return to the main topic of this section. To make sure that sufficient storage is available for

- the running of tasks, and;
- holding access type objects

we invoke the attribute STORAGE_SIZE. This is used in conjunction with access types, task types and task objects. It allows us to specify and identify the number of storage units required for these items.

Assume that LIST_POINTER is an access type. Then LIST_POINTER 'STORAGE_SIZE imparts the number of storage units reserved for variables pointed to by LIST_POINTER. To specify the storage space needed for objects we write

> **for** LIST_POINTER'STORAGE_SIZE **use** <NUMBER_OF_STORAGE_UNITS>;

as for example, in

> **for** LIST_POINTER'STORAGE_SIZE **use** 256;

This defines that a total storage space of 256 units is allocated to objects of type LIST_POINTER (whether such units are bytes, words, etc., depends on your compiler). As a result a data 'pool' is set aside to hold all the objects pointed to by LIST_POINTER. Clearly, this sets a limit on the number of items which can be stored. That is, it defines the maximum size of the list.

In this example we used a literal value to specify the storage space. Alternatively it could have been specified using an expression. This may be a more flexible approach – the expression need not be static (see Listing 15.5).

Now take the case of tasks. Assume we have a task type ADA_TASK. Then the operation

> **for** ADA_TASK'STORAGE_SIZE **use** 4096;

defines the number of storage units set aside for each activation of tasks of that type. Naturally we can use the attribute to obtain task storage information.

(c) **The SMALL attribute**

SMALL is used to define the representation of fixed point types. It has been mentioned here for completeness only. For further details see section 13.2 of the LRM.

Mapping Ada on to the machine – representation clauses 511

```
with TEXT_IO;              use TEXT_IO;
procedure ACCESS_STORAGE_ALLOC is
   type LIST is array (1..8) of CHARACTER;
   type LIST_POINTER is access LIST;
   for LIST_POINTER'STORAGE_SIZE use 256;
   NEXT_LIST_POINTER : LIST_POINTER;
   package INT_IO is new INTEGER_IO (INTEGER);
begin
   for I in 1..100 loop
      NEXT_LIST_POINTER := new LIST;
      INT_IO.PUT (I, 4);
   end loop;
exception
   when STORAGE_ERROR =>
      NEW_LINE;
      PUT_LINE ("Run out of storage space for LIST_POINTER");
end ACCESS_STORAGE_ALLOC;
```

Listing 15.5 Defining the storage allocation for an access type using the STORAGE_SIZE attribute.

15.4.5 Enumeration representation clauses

Consider the following scenario. We have a data communications device which produces four status messages:

> Transmitter ready (TX_RDY)
> Receiver ready (RX_RDY)
> Parity error (PE)
> Overrun error (OE)

Logically we would form an enumerated type DATA_COMMS_STATUS, as

> **type** DATA_COMMS_STATUS **is** (TX_RDY, RX_RDY, PE, OE);

Remember, we use enumeration for reasons of program readability, comprehension and reliability. Question: How are the individual elements (literals) represented in the machine? Answer: This will depend on the compiler, but, most likely, TX_RDY will be assigned a value of 0, RX_RDY a value of 1, and so on. Does the actual representation matter? No – until we start to interact at the machine level, that is. Then it does become important.

We find, on investigation, that the communication device produces the following status codes:

512 Low-level issues

STATUS	BINARY CODE	DECIMAL VALUE
TX_RDY	00000001	1
RX_RDY	00000010	2
PE	00000100	4
OE	00001000	8

Unluckily, this gives a mismatch between the concrete and the abstract representations of the same items. We can, though, overcome this in Ada by using the enumeration representation clause. Applying this to the above example we have

```
for DATA_COMMS_STATUS use (TX_RDY => 2#00000001#,
                           RX_RDY => 2#00000010#,
                           PE     => 2#00000100#,
                           OE     => 2#00001000#);
```

What we have done is to specify the machine codes for the literals of the enumeration type. An aggregate must be used for this. Three other important points should be noted. First, we cannot use the same code value for two (or more) literals – they must be distinct. Second, code values do not have to be contiguous. Third, the values in the aggregate must be listed in ascending order. This last item is important in practical terms. It means that we first need to define enumeration at the device level. Then we can specify high-level abstract enumerated types.

Positional notation can, of course, be used with the aggregate, giving

```
for DATA_COMMS_STATUS use (2#00000001#,
                           2#00000010#,
                           2#00000100#,
                           2#00001000#);
```

Also, the code values can be written in base 10 (decimal) form:

```
for DATA_COMMS_STATUS use (1, 2, 4, 8);
```

This is more compact and readable. However, for machine-level work, it is not so helpful – bit patterns are much more meaningful.

We can also apply the attributes SUCC, PRED, POS and VAL to these, even though values are not contiguous. These, and the aspects discussed earlier, are illustrated in Listing 15.6.

Mapping Ada on to the machine – representation clauses 513

```
with TEXT_IO;              use TEXT_IO;
procedure ENUM_REP is
  type DATA_COMMS_STATUS is (TX_RDY, RX_RDY, PE, OE);
  for DATA_COMMS_STATUS use (TX_RDY => 2#00000001#,
                             RX_RDY => 2#00000010#,
                             PE     => 2#00000100#,
                             OE     => 2#00001000#);
  DATA_COMMS_INPUT :    DATA_COMMS_STATUS;
  package INT_IO is new INTEGER_IO (INTEGER);
  use INT_IO;
  package DATA_COMMS_IO is new ENUMERATION_IO (DATA_COMMS_STATUS);
  use DATA_COMMS_IO;
begin
  -- we can use objects of the enumeration type as per normal
  DATA_COMMS_INPUT := RX_RDY;
  -- and the associated attributes give the same results
  PUT ("DATA_COMMS_STATUS'VAL (0)                  => ");
  PUT (DATA_COMMS_STATUS'VAL (0), 0);
  NEW_LINE;
  PUT ("DATA_COMMS_STATUS'POS (DATA_COMMS_INPUT)   => ");
  PUT (DATA_COMMS_STATUS'POS (DATA_COMMS_INPUT), 0);
  NEW_LINE;
  PUT ("DATA_COMMS_STATUS'SUCC (DATA_COMMS_INPUT)  => ");
  PUT (DATA_COMMS_STATUS'SUCC (DATA_COMMS_INPUT), 0);
  NEW_LINE;
  PUT ("DATA_COMMS_STATUS'PRED (DATA_COMMS_INPUT)  => ");
  PUT (DATA_COMMS_STATUS'PRED (DATA_COMMS_INPUT), 0);
  NEW_LINE;
end ENUM_REP;
```

Listing 15.6 Applying the enumeration representation clause.

15.4.6 Record representation clauses

Once more we will start off by using a practical example to illustrate our points. Suppose that we have to manage digital data communications between a master device and a remote telemetry station. One function carried out by the master is the collection of messages from the remote station. Such messages consist of 4 bytes, carrying the following information:

> Station identification (STATION_NUMBER)
> Message type (MESSAGE)
> Measured parameter (PARAMETER)
> Parameter value (VALUE)

We decide to hold this information as a record, a fairly logical move. First, though, examine the actual bit/byte pattern corresponding to the data, Fig.15.12. This structure doesn't map simply on to standard Ada types. Fortunately, the record representation clause allows us to overcome this problem. Using this we can specify the order, position and size of record

514 Low-level issues

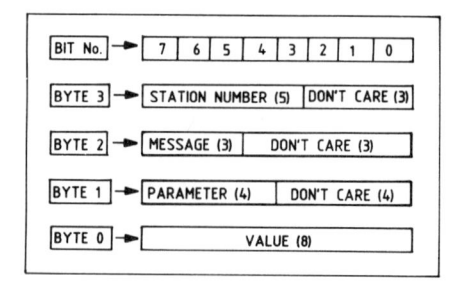

```
BIT No. →  7 | 6 | 5 | 4 | 3 | 2 | 1 | 0
BYTE 3 → STATION NUMBER (5) | DON'T CARE (3)
BYTE 2 → MESSAGE (3)        | DON'T CARE (3)
BYTE 1 → PARAMETER (4)      | DON'T CARE (4)
BYTE 0 →          VALUE (8)
```

Fig.15.12 Example – digital data protocol format.

components. Let us see how this works by applying it to the problem outlined above. First, though, some more system information:

Station numbers:	0 to 31 inclusive
Message types:	Analogue, identified by binary code 001
	Digital, identified by binary code 010
Parameters:	Pressure, code 0001
	Temperature, code 0010
	Speed, code 0011
Parameter values:	In the range 0 to 255 units

(a) **Operations at the abstract level**

First define all types and subtypes needed in the record structure:

```
type STATION is range 0..31;
type MESSAGE_TYPE is (ANALOGUE_IN, DIGITAL_IN);
type PARAMETER_TYPE is (PRESSURE, TEMPERATURE, SPEED);
type MEASUREMENT is range 0..255;
```

Now define the record structure itself:

```
type TELEMETRY_INPUT_DATA is
   record
      STATION_NUMBER : STATION;
      MESSAGE        : MESSAGE_TYPE;
      PARAMETER      : PARAMETER_TYPE;
      VALUE          : MEASUREMENT;
   end record;
```

(b) **Operations at the concrete level**

What was given above is the abstract representation of the record. Now tackle the machine-dependent parts. The record, remember, is a collection of

Mapping Ada on to the machine – representation clauses 515

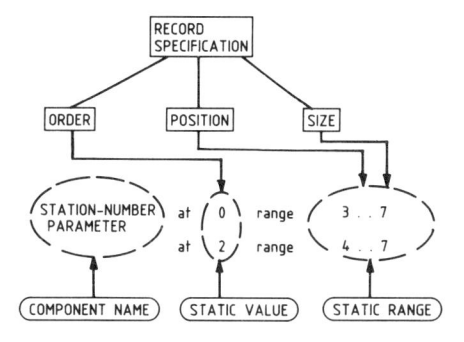

Fig.15.13 Record representation clause – overview.

heterogeneous objects. Therefore the first action is to specify the basic type representations for these components:

-- Length clause

```
for STATION'SIZE use 5;
```

-- Enumeration clauses

```
for MESSAGE_TYPE use (ANALOGUE_IN => 2#001#
                      DIGITAL_IN   => 2#010#);
```

```
for PARAMETER_TYPE use (PRESSURE    => 2#0001#,
                        TEMPERATURE => 2#0010#,
                        SPEED       => 2#0011#);
```

-- Length clause

```
for MEASUREMENT'SIZE use 8;
```

Now define the record representation, that is the ordering, position and size of record components (we will assume that the SYSTEM.STORAGE_UNIT is a byte in this example). To do this we use the format shown in Fig.15.13.

Here we have shown part of the representation clause – the component clauses. These are used to link the (abstract) components with their hardware details. Here, for instance, component STATION_NUMBER is designated – using the static value – to occupy storage unit zero. It begins at bit number 3 of this storage unit, having a range of 5 bits. Likewise, component PARAMETER uses bits 4 to 7 of storage unit 2.

Thus, assuming that the basic storage unit is a byte, the total record representation clause becomes

516 Low-level issues

```
procedure RECORD_REP is
  -- define types for the record components
  type STATION is range 0..31;
  for STATION'SIZE use 5;
  type MESSAGE_TYPE is (ANALOGUE_IN, DIGITAL_IN);
  for MESSAGE_TYPE use (ANALOGUE_IN => 2#001#,
                        DIGITAL_IN  => 2#010#);
  type PARAMETER_TYPE is (PRESSURE, TEMPERATURE, SPEED);
  for PARAMETER_TYPE use (PRESSURE    => 2#0001#,
                          TEMPERATURE => 2#0010#,
                          SPEED       => 2#0011#);
  type MEASUREMENT is range 0..255;
  for MEASUREMENT'SIZE use 8;
  -- define the record structure
  type TELEMETRY_INPUT_DATA is
    record
      STATION_NUMBER  :   STATION;
      MESSAGE         :   MESSAGE_TYPE;
      PARAMETER       :   PARAMETER_TYPE;
      VALUE           :   MEASUREMENT;
    end record;
  -- now define the internal representation of the record structure
  for TELEMETRY_INPUT_DATA use
    record at mod 4;
      STATION_NUMBER at 0 range 3..7;
      MESSAGE        at 1 range 5..7;
      PARAMETER      at 2 range 4..7;
      VALUE          at 3 range 0..7;
    end record;
  -- declare an object of this type
  COMMS_PACKET    :     TELEMETRY_INPUT_DATA;
begin
  -- now work with the record just as any other record structure
  COMMS_PACKET := (STATION_NUMBER => 1,
                   MESSAGE        => DIGITAL_IN,
                   PARAMETER      => SPEED,
                   VALUE          => 100);
end RECORD_REP;
```

Listing 15.7 Applying the record representation clause.

```
for TELEMETRY_INPUT_DATA use
  record
    STATION_NUMBER at 0 range 3..7;
    MESSAGE        at 1 range 5..7;
    PARAMETER      at 2 range 4..7;
    VALUE          at 3 range 0..7;
  end record;
```

To use this, declare objects of type TELEMETRY_INPUT_DATA in the normal way. Then, at the high (abstract) level, the low-level details can be completely ignored, see Listing 15.7.

Observe that in this example we have used the construct **at mod 4**. This is called an alignment clause. It directs the compiler to locate the start of the record in a particular manner. You can read it as 'set the beginning of the record to an address which is a multiple of four storage units'. In this example, valid addresses would be at byte 0, 4, 8, etc. Thus, if our computer used 32 bit (4 byte) word operation, each record would be aligned on a word boundary. We do this to improve the efficiency of machine addressing operations.

The first storage unit of a record is always numbered zero. All other component positions are specified in relationship to this first component. This, however, does not mean that we have to write out the record components in this same order (in the example above this was done for clarity). We could just as well have used the following specification:

```
for TELEMETRY_INPUT_DATA use
    record
        VALUE           at 3 range 0..7;
        MESSAGE         at 1 range 5..7;
        PARAMETER       at 2 range 4..7;
        STATION_NUMBER  at 0 range 3..7;
    end record;
```

However, we strongly recommend that clear, logical ordering methods should always be used.

15.4.7 Record attributes – POSITION, FIRST_BIT and LAST_BIT

These are taken together as they apply to records only. We use them to identify how components of a record are located in memory store. Let us apply these representation attributes to objects of record type TELEMETRY_INPUT_DATA of Listing 15.7. Being more correct, we use the attributes with each of the object components. For example, declaring

```
COMMS_PACKET : TELEMETRY_INPUT_DATA;
```

then

```
COMMS_PACKET.STATION_NUMBER'POSITION  yields  0.
```

The POSITION attribute tells us the offset of STATION_NUMBER from the start of the record. This value is given in storage units (here, bytes). In this case STATION_NUMBER is the first component, and thus it has no offset. However,

518 Low-level issues

> COMMS_PACKET.MESSAGE'POSITION yields 1.

The record component MESSAGE is at byte 1. Hence its offset is 1. Moving on to the FIRST_BIT attribute, we find that

> COMMS_PACKET.STATION_NUMBER'FIRST_BIT yields 3.

This defines the offset of the first bit of STATION_NUMBER from its 0 bit position. Likewise:

> COMMS_PACKET.MESSAGE'FIRST_BIT yields 5.

Finally we have the attribute LAST_BIT. Applying this we find that

> COMMS_PACKET.STATION_NUMBER'LAST_BIT yields 7.

This defines the offset of the last bit of STATION_NUMBER from its 0 bit position. Hence:

> COMMS_PACKET.MESSAGE'LAST_BIT also yields 7.

Listing 15.8 demonstrates the use of representation attributes.

15.4.8 Pragma PACK

Assume that we have made the following declaration:

```
type STATUS is
   record
        EXTRA_LOW   : BOOLEAN;
        LOW         : BOOLEAN;
        NORMAL      : BOOLEAN;
        HIGH        : BOOLEAN;
        EXTRA_HIGH  : BOOLEAN;
   end record


   PRESSURE_ALARM : STATUS;
```

```
with TEXT_IO;                    use TEXT_IO;
procedure RECORD_ATTRIB is
  -- define types for the record components
  type STATION is range 0..31;
  for STATION'SIZE use 5;
  type MESSAGE_TYPE is (ANALOGUE_IN, DIGITAL_IN);
  for MESSAGE_TYPE use (ANALOGUE_IN => 2#001#,
                        DIGITAL_IN  => 2#010#);
  type PARAMETER_TYPE is (PRESSURE, TEMPERATURE, SPEED);
  for PARAMETER_TYPE use (PRESSURE    => 2#0001#,
                          TEMPERATURE => 2#0010#,
                          SPEED       => 2#0011#);
  type MEASUREMENT is range 0..255;
  for MEASUREMENT'SIZE use 8;
  -- define the record structure
  type TELEMETRY_INPUT_DATA is
    record
      STATION_NUMBER  :    STATION;
      MESSAGE         :    MESSAGE_TYPE;
      PARAMETER       :    PARAMETER_TYPE;
      VALUE           :    MEASUREMENT;
    end record;
  -- now define the internal representation of the record structure
  for TELEMETRY_INPUT_DATA use
    record at mod 4;
      STATION_NUMBER at 0 range 3..7;
      MESSAGE        at 1 range 5..7;
      PARAMETER      at 2 range 4..7;
      VALUE          at 3 range 0..7;
    end record;
  -- declare an object of this type
  COMMS_PACKET    :       TELEMETRY_INPUT_DATA;
  package INT_IO is new INTEGER_IO (INTEGER);
  use INT_IO;
begin
  PUT ("COMMS_PACKET.PARAMETER'POSITION => ");
  PUT (COMMS_PACKET.PARAMETER'POSITION);
  NEW_LINE;
  PUT ("COMMS_PACKET.PARAMETER'FIRST_BIT => ");
  PUT (COMMS_PACKET.PARAMETER'FIRST_BIT);
  NEW_LINE;
  PUT ("COMMS_PACKET.PARAMETER'LAST_BIT => ");
  PUT (COMMS_PACKET.PARAMETER'LAST_BIT);
  NEW_LINE;
end RECORD_ATTRIB;
```

Listing 15.8 Applying the representation attributes – records.

You may well find that the compiler allocates 1 byte for each component of PRESSURE_ALARM. Thus we consume 40 bits of storage when only 5 bits are needed. Fortunately, with Ada, we can tell the compiler to use the minimum amount of storage necessary. Here the pragma PACK is invoked, as, for instance

```
pragma PACK (STATUS);
```

520 Low-level issues

Unfortunately, we cannot force the compiler to comply with this request. It may just ignore it. And be wary – it may not tell you of its refusal.

15.5 UNCHECKED PROGRAMMING

15.5.1 Unchecked type conversion

One of the major features of Ada is its strong typing. This, at times, has proved to be somewhat of a nuisance. In the examples thus far, we've overcome such problems by using type conversion (see chapter 5). When using this we convert object representation from one type to another – which is grand, provided that is what we really want to do. But suppose we wish to intermingle objects of different types without changing the representation (type transfer). What then?

First, consider where such a situation could occur. Once again we can use serial data communications to illustrate this point. Assume that messages are formatted as packages of bytes for communication purposes. The total message packet is 5 bytes in size, Fig.15.14.

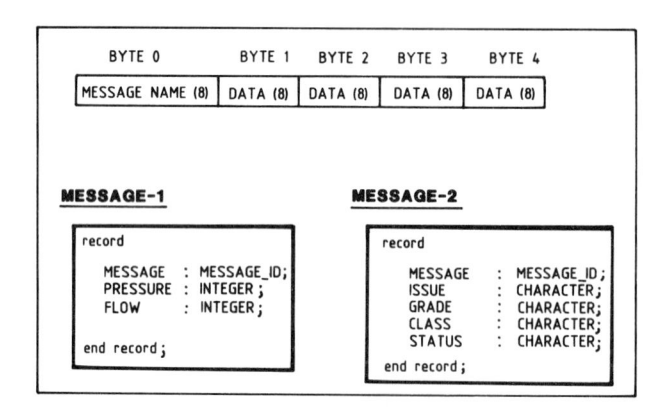

```
 BYTE 0          BYTE 1    BYTE 2    BYTE 3    BYTE 4
 MESSAGE NAME (8) DATA (8)  DATA (8)  DATA (8)  DATA (8)
```

MESSAGE-1
```
record
    MESSAGE  : MESSAGE_ID;
    PRESSURE : INTEGER;
    FLOW     : INTEGER;
end record;
```

MESSAGE-2
```
record
    MESSAGE : MESSAGE_ID;
    ISSUE   : CHARACTER;
    GRADE   : CHARACTER;
    CLASS   : CHARACTER;
    STATUS  : CHARACTER;
end record;
```

Fig.15.14 Mapping byte information to record information.

Also, the first byte in the message packet defines the name of the message. This packet may be used to handle the data of two different messages, MESSAGE_1 or MESSAGE_2. Both messages are, within the computer, structured as records. MESSAGE_1 consists of two components, of type INTEGER. By contrast MESSAGE_2 is a four-component record, each one being a character.

When we receive an incoming message it first has to be identified. Then each byte has to be inserted into its related record, at the correct point, without change of representation. It is in processes like this that UNCHECKED_CONVERSION – a predefined generic library function – is used. Its specification is

> **generic**
>   **type** SOURCE **is limited private**;
>   **type** TARGET **is limited private**;
> **function** UNCHECKED_CONVERSION (S: SOURCE) **return** TARGET;

In the instantiated function we input an object ('S') of one type to the function. This returns a value having the same bit pattern, but now defined to be of the target type.

The application of unchecked conversion to the problem given above is demonstrated in Listing 15.9.

When using UNCHECKED_CONVERSION it is safest if both types are the same size (number of bits). If they aren't then the results are compiler dependent – and sometimes unpredictable. One compiler manual states: 'Conversions between objects whose sizes do not conform may result in storage areas with undefined values.' Check your manual, appendix F.

You must be extremely careful when using unchecked conversion. Take the type DATA_COMMS_STATUS. This has been defined to have the following structure:

> **for** DATA_COMMS_STATUS **use** (TX_RDY => 2#00000001#,
>   RX_RDY => 2#00000010#,
>   PE   => 2#00000100#,
>   OE   => 2#00001000#);

We now produce a new function BYTE_TO_DATA_COMMS_STATUS to perform conversion from machine format to that of the enumeration literals:

> **function** BYTE_TO_DATA_COMMS_STATUS **is new**
>   UNCHECKED_CONVERSION (BYTE, DATA_COMMS_STATUS);

This is applied to status data obtained from the communication device. As long as the data bytes have the values decimal 1, 2, 4 or 8, all is well. But what would happen if, due to a fault, the value 5 arrives? We really don't know – experiments have shown that different compilers produce different results. The only safe way of operating is to confine your working to safe values, as shown in Listing 15.10.

```ada
with UNCHECKED_CONVERSION;
procedure CONVERT is
  type MESSAGE_TYPE is (MESS_1, MESS_2);
  type BYTE is range 0..255;
  for BYTE'SIZE use 8;
  type INPUT_STREAM is array (0..4) of BYTE;
  type MESSAGE_1 is
    record
      MESSAGE_ID    :    MESSAGE_TYPE;
      PRESSURE      :    INTEGER;
      FLOW          :    INTEGER;
    end record;
  for MESSAGE_1 use
    record
      MESSAGE_ID at 0 range 0..7;
      PRESSURE   at 1 range 0..15;
      FLOW       at 3 range 0..15;
    end record;
  for MESSAGE_1'SIZE use 40;
  type MESSAGE_2 is
    record
      MESSAGE_ID    :    MESSAGE_TYPE;
      ISSUE         :    CHARACTER;
      GRADE         :    CHARACTER;
      CLASS         :    CHARACTER;
      STATUS        :    CHARACTER;
    end record;
  for MESSAGE_2 use
    record
      MESSAGE_ID at 0 range 0..7;
      ISSUE      at 1 range 0..7;
      GRADE      at 2 range 0..7;
      CLASS      at 3 range 0..7;
      STATUS     at 4 range 0..7;
    end record;
  for MESSAGE_2'SIZE use 40;
  INPUT_DATA     :     INPUT_STREAM    :=  (0 => 16#00#,
                                            1 => 16#0A#,
                                            2 => 16#10#,
                                            3 => 16#32#,
                                            4 => 16#50#);
  FIRST_MESSAGE   :    MESSAGE_1;
  SECOND_MESSAGE  :    MESSAGE_2;
  MESSAGE_ID      :    MESSAGE_TYPE;
  function BYTES_TO_MESSAGE_1 is new UNCHECKED_CONVERSION (INPUT_STREAM,
                                                           MESSAGE_1);
  function BYTES_TO_MESSAGE_2 is new UNCHECKED_CONVERSION (INPUT_STREAM,
                                                           MESSAGE_2);
  function BYTE_TO_MESSAGE_TYPE is new UNCHECKED_CONVERSION (BYTE,
                                                             MESSAGE_TYPE);
begin
  MESSAGE_ID := BYTE_TO_MESSAGE_TYPE (INPUT_DATA (0));
  case MESSAGE_ID is
    when MESS_1 =>
      FIRST_MESSAGE := BYTES_TO_MESSAGE_1 (INPUT_DATA);
    when MESS_2 =>
      SECOND_MESSAGE := BYTES_TO_MESSAGE_2 (INPUT_DATA);
  end case;
end CONVERT;
```

Listing 15.9 Performing unchecked type conversion.

```ada
with TEXT_IO;                use TEXT_IO;
with UNCHECKED_CONVERSION;
procedure ENUM_CONVERT is
  type DATA_COMMS_STATUS is (TX_RDY, RX_RDY, PE, OE);
  for DATA_COMMS_STATUS use (TX_RDY => 2#00000001#,
                             RX_RDY => 2#00000010#,
                             PE     => 2#00000100#,
                             OE     => 2#00001000#);
  for DATA_COMMS_STATUS'SIZE use 8;
  type BYTE is range 0..255;
  for BYTE'SIZE use 8;
  DATA_COMMS_OUTPUT : DATA_COMMS_STATUS;
  INPUT_BYTE        : BYTE;
  function BYTE_TO_DATA_COMMS_STATUS is new UNCHECKED_CONVERSION
                                            (BYTE, DATA_COMMS_STATUS);
  package BYTE_IO is new INTEGER_IO (BYTE);
  use BYTE_IO;
  package DATA_COMMS_IO is new ENUMERATION_IO (DATA_COMMS_STATUS);
  use DATA_COMMS_IO;
begin
  PUT ("Please enter the input byte (0..255) : ");
  GET (INPUT_BYTE);
  SKIP_LINE;
  case INPUT_BYTE is
    when 1 | 2 | 4 | 8 =>
      DATA_COMMS_OUTPUT := BYTE_TO_DATA_COMMS_STATUS (INPUT_BYTE);
      PUT ("This represents the comms status ");
      PUT (DATA_COMMS_OUTPUT);
      NEW_LINE;
    when others =>
      PUT_LINE ("The byte does not contain a valid comms status value");
  end case;
end ENUM_CONVERT;
```

Listing 15.10 Performing safe conversion of an enumeration type with non-contiguous representation.

15.5.2 Unchecked storage deallocation

The subject of dynamic data objects was dealt with in chapter 9. There we met the problem of allocated but inaccessible storage, and the need for garbage collection. It was pointed out that garbage collection would normally be made using a library subprogram UNCHECKED_DEALLOCATION. Here a more detailed look is taken at this subprogram.

UNCHECKED_DEALLOCATION is, in reality, a generic procedure. Its purpose is simple: to retrieve space which had been allocated to dynamic objects and is now unused. Thus the procedure need only know two factors: the objects in question and the pointers to such objects.

Its generic declaration is (in part)

```ada
generic
   type DYNAMIC_OBJECT_TYPE is limited private;
   type POINTER_TYPE is access DYNAMIC_OBJECT_TYPE;
procedure UNCHECKED_DEALLOCATION (POINTER : in out POINTER_TYPE);
```

Instantiating it:

```
type INTEGER_POINTER is access INTEGER;
procedure DISPOSE is new UNCHECKED_DEALLOCATION
                              (INTEGER, INTEGER_POINTER);
```

Using it:

```
LIST_VALUE : INTEGER_POINTER;
.
begin
    .
    LIST_VALUE : = new INTEGER;
    .
    DISPOSE (LIST_VALUE);
    .
end;
```

After executing this the value of LIST_VALUE is **null**. This tells the run-time system that the object pointed to by LIST_VALUE is no longer needed. Thus its storage space may be reclaimed.

Be careful with the use of UNCHECKED_DEALLOCATION. If, by mistake, we deallocate a pointer which should be left in use, it will be deallocated. No checks are made by the compiler; all are left to the programmer.

15.6 MACHINE CODE INSERTIONS

First, let us be clear what is meant by machine code. Each machine instruction is made up of a sequence of binary values (in the Intel 386 processor, for example, the binary pattern 00011110 means 'save the contents of the DS register'). These occupy one or more basic storage units, typically bytes, words or double words. For simplicity we usually write these machine instructions in hexadecimal format. This gives us 1E(H) for the above instruction (sometimes octal format is used instead of hexadecimal).

We are allowed to use machine code in Ada programs, subject to certain rules:

- The machine code inserts must be housed within a procedure body;
- All statements in the procedure must be in machine code;
- All expressions must be static;
- The procedure has to import (**with**) the predefined library package MACHINE_CODE;
- The only declarative items allowed are **use** clauses;
- Exception handlers are forbidden.

Machine code operations are very machine specific. For detailed information refer to section 13.8 of the LRM and appendix F of your compiler manual. However, just to give a flavour of such operations, we include the following example. This pushes the contents of the DS register on to the stack in an Intel 86 series machine:

```
with SYSTEM;
with MACHINE_CODE

procedure PUSH_DS is
    use MACHINE_CODE;

begin
    inst'(b1 => 16#1E#);
end PUSH_DS;
```

15.7 INTERFACING TO OTHER LANGUAGES

There are two reasons for using 'foreign' languages with Ada programs. First, we may be unable to access machine or peripheral device features from Ada code. In that case the usual alternative is assembly language programming. Second, we may wish to use existing software (such as Fortran numerical libraries or Borland C graphics facilities). To do this we treat the foreign code as a subprogram, specifying it using the pragma INTERFACE. The pragma form, in general, is

```
pragma INTERFACE (language_name, subprogram_name);
```

All communication with the subprogram of interest is made using parameters and function results.

Once again this is an area of work which is very machine and compiler dependent. For that reason no more will be said here on this topic. In practice your major source of information and guidance will be the compiler manual.

REVIEW

Do you now appreciate:

- Why we need to access machine facilities?
- What access features are needed?
- What representation clauses are and how they are used?
- The reasons for using representation clauses?
- The concepts involved in interrupt handling?

- How to minimize machine storage requirements?
- How to carry out type transfer operations?
- How to reclaim dynamic storage?
- The general usage of machine code inserts?
- How to use assembly language programming in Ada programs?
- How to interface to other languages from inside an Ada program?
- How to obtain low-level machine-specific information?

Chapter Sixteen
Data input–output

A program which does not (or cannot) communicate with its external world is useless. Now, this may seem so obvious that it need not be stated. The trouble is we get so involved in programming *per se* that we often overlook this simple fact. Inputting and outputting of information is an essential feature of all software-based systems. Thus it may seem surprising that input–output processing facilities are not built into the Ada language itself. In fact they are supplied as library packages: TEXT_IO, SEQUENTIAL_IO and DIRECT_IO. These are standard items, being supplied with each and every Ada compiler.

In this chapter you will:

- Be introduced to the ideas of Ada file handling and data storage;
- Learn how to create, manipulate and delete files;
- See how to apply package TEXT_IO (and packages within this) to the handling of human-readable data;
- Understand how machine-readable data is handled using packages SEQUENTIAL_IO and DIRECT_IO;
- Be introduced to the basics of handling low-level input–output activities.

16.1 INPUTTING–OUTPUTTING OF DATA – AN OVERVIEW

We have already met this topic in a number of places. For instance, in chapter 15, peripheral devices provided the communication path with the outside world. Further, in most of the specimen programs, we have used console facilities extensively. Thus the basics of the subject should be familiar. Here, though, the objectives are to study in much more detail the mechanisms for handling data input–output (I/O). It is important to stress that it is the handling of the data itself which is important. We are not concerned with its subsequent use, or its consequential effects. The issue, conceptually, is one of transferring data between an Ada program and a data file store, Fig.16.1.

This 'store' may, in practice, be many things – console, keyboard, floppy disk, hard disk, network interface, etc. It really doesn't matter as long as the correct I/O operations are invoked.

Data I/O operations can be grouped into two classes, Fig.16.2. In the first there is data that can be read by people. Essentially it is a collection of (encoded) language characters. In the second the data is meant to be 'under-

528 Data input–output

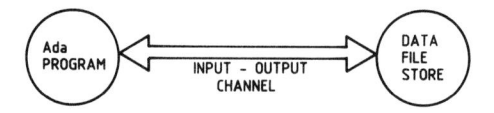

Fig.16.1 Data I/O – conceptual view.

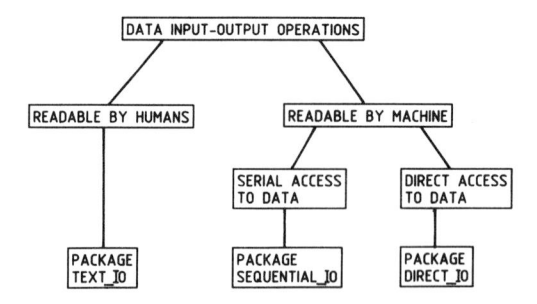

Fig.16.2 Support for data I/O.

stood' only by the computer. Moreover, such data can be accessed in two ways, serially or at random. In the first instance sequential accessing of data is used; in the second, direct access methods are employed. These aspects are covered in detail in later sections.

As stated above, the facilities needed for I/O processing are not built into the Ada language itself. They are supplied in three library packages: TEXT_IO, SEQUENTIAL_IO and DIRECT_IO.

16.2 FILE MANAGEMENT

16.2.1 Introduction

At this stage we take a small detour to cover points essential to later sections – file handling. Think of it as learning how to construct building blocks, not the application of such features. Within this section we will use a set of file handling procedures from package TEXT_IO (this is discussed in detail later). Note that these procedures are also supplied in packages SEQUENTIAL_IO and DIRECT_IO.

Fig.16.3 shows the basic concept involved in file handling.

This figure is merely a more detailed view of Fig.16.1. However, it is important to understand that there are two views of the file: internal and external. The internal view is that seen by, and within, the program; the

File management 529

Fig.16.3 File handling concept.

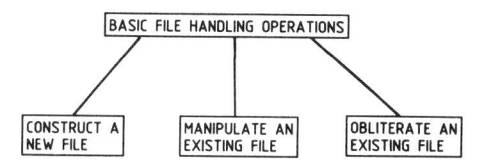

Fig.16.4 Basic file handling operations.

external view is that seen by users of the system (more on this later). Basic file handling operations consist of (Fig.16.4):

1. Constructing a file in the first place, and defining its attributes;
2. Operating on (manipulating) data in an existing file;
3. Removing (obliterating) a file when it is no longer needed.

16.2.2 Constructing a new file

Before using a file to store data, we first need to construct it (Fig.16.5).

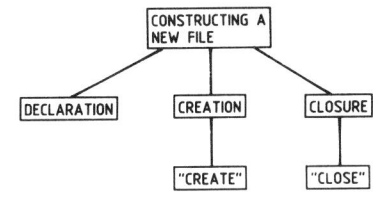

Fig.16.5 File construction features.

The central (core) action is that of creating the physical (external) file, using a standard procedure 'CREATE'. But, before this can be invoked, we need to declare the existence of the internal file object. Finally, after making the file, it is closed up, ready for future use. For this we use the standard procedure CLOSE.

Note that when a file is created it is also opened for use. That is, it is perfectly legal to transfer data to/from the file immediately after creating it. At this point we will, for simplicity, close it up as part of the construction operation.

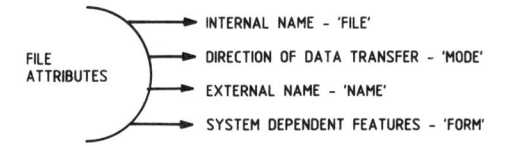

```
                                  ┌─► INTERNAL NAME - 'FILE'
                    FILE          ├─► DIRECTION OF DATA TRANSFER - 'MODE'
                    ATTRIBUTES    ├─► EXTERNAL NAME - 'NAME'
                                  └─► SYSTEM DEPENDENT FEATURES - 'FORM'
```

Fig.16.6 Attributes defined at creation time.

At creation time we have to define specific file attributes, Fig.16.6. Procedure CREATE is used for this purpose, its specification being

```
procedure CREATE (FILE : in out FILE_TYPE;
                  MODE : in FILE_MODE := OUT_FILE;
                  NAME : in STRING := " ";
                  FORM : in STRING := " ");
```

First, we specify the name of the file object used by the program. For the procedure CREATE this is done using the formal parameter FILE, its type being FILE_TYPE.

Next we define the direction of data transfer between the Ada program and the physical file, the MODE. Type FILE_MODE is an enumerated type, its elements in TEXT_IO being:

IN_FILE – reading only from the physical file
OUT_FILE – writing only to the physical file

The third attribute – NAME – is the name by which the file is known in the external world. It is defined using a character string.

Finally we specify system-dependent characteristics associated with the file using the FORM parameter. This is also defined using a character string. Its default value is an empty string. Use this value for working with the standard type of file for your system. However, if you intend to use anything else it will need changing (the details are application dependent).

Procedure CLOSE is specified as

```
procedure CLOSE (FILE : in out FILE_TYPE);
```

The actual parameter corresponding to FILE obviously has to be the same as that in CREATE. CLOSE tells the operating system to close up the physical file. However – and most importantly – it also breaks the link between the internal and external files. As a result we can form new internal/external links of our choice.

A complete, small and simple program based on this is shown in Listing 16.1.

```
with TEXT_IO;
procedure FIRST_FILE is
  -- declare an internal file
  ENGINE_FILE      :     TEXT_IO.FILE_TYPE;
begin
  -- create the file and associate it with an external file (i.e. create
  -- the file in your file system)
  TEXT_IO.CREATE (ENGINE_FILE, TEXT_IO.OUT_FILE, "PORT_GT.TXT");
  -- close the file
  TEXT_IO.CLOSE (ENGINE_FILE);
end FIRST_FILE;
```

Listing 16.1 Constructing a file.

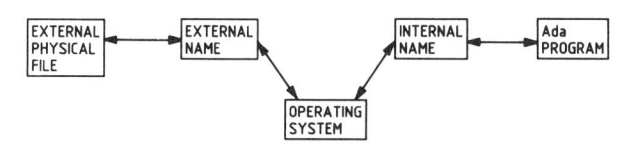

Fig.16.7 Concept − external/internal name association.

Compile and run this program. Now check that the file PORT_GT.TXT exists in your file system.

You may, at this stage, wonder why two names are needed to identify a file. It does seem rather pointless. To understand this we need to consider how file input−output is controlled within our computer system. It's all very well for us to write a program to create a file, but what ensures that our instructions are acted on? The answer is: the file handling software of our operating system (OS). Each and every external physical file is known to the OS as a named item, Fig.16.7.

This has to conform with the naming rules of the OS which interfaces to the Ada program using the internal name of the file. You, the programmer, are free to choose the most suitable name for this − without regard to the naming conventions of the OS. It is also possible to associate many internal names with one external one, Fig.16.8.

We will return to this in a moment. More (much more) important than the flexibility of file naming is the aspect of program portability. A primary design aim of Ada is to allow us to build portable code. Suppose that we write a file handling program, destined to run under an OS called MY_DOS. We later decide to use it on a computer which uses YOUR_DOS. Clearly, if the two operating systems use differing naming rules, we have portability problems. But by separating the internal (program) view from the external (physical) view we can minimize these problems. In fact we can limit changes to the internal/external name relationship only. Contrast this with the use of a single file name. Here, on porting the program from MY_DOS to

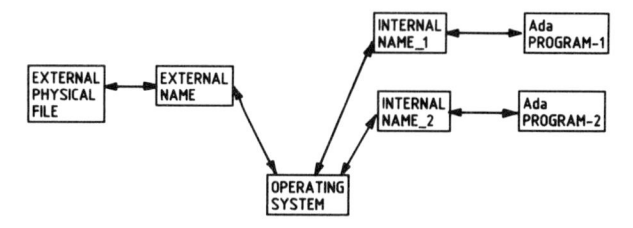

Fig.16.8 Single external/multiple internal names.

YOUR_DOS, every named reference would have to be altered. Enough said, we think.

16.2.3 File manipulation

Now that we have constructed a file we can proceed to use it for the storage of data. This involves three elementary actions: OPEN, RESET and CLOSE, Fig.16.9.

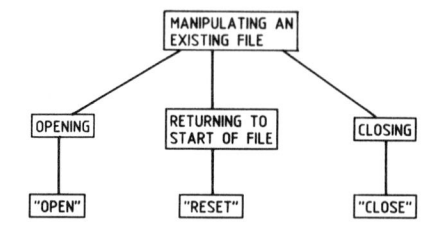

Fig.16.9 File manipulation – elementary operations.

We are only allowed to transfer data to and from an open file. Hence the first operation is to open an existing file, using the procedure OPEN. Its specification is

```
procedure OPEN (FILE : in out FILE_TYPE;
                MODE : in FILE_MODE;
                NAME : in STRING;
                FORM : in STRING := " ");
```

It can be seen that the parameters are the same as those of CREATE. A minor difference is that MODE and NAME do not have default values.

Once a file has been opened we can begin data transfer operations. The operating system ensures that this initial access is always made to a predefined storage location (clearly, if this is the very first access to that file, the operation

```
with TEXT_IO;             use TEXT_IO;
procedure ELEM_FILE_OP is
  ENGINE_FILE       :      FILE_TYPE;
begin
  -- Note: We have created a new file with exactly the same name as the
  --       one of Listing 16.1. This will overwrite the existing one to
  --       create a new file.
  CREATE (ENGINE_FILE, OUT_FILE, "PORT_GT.TXT");
  CLOSE (ENGINE_FILE);
  OPEN (ENGINE_FILE, OUT_FILE, "PORT_GT.TXT");
  RESET (ENGINE_FILE);
  CLOSE (ENGINE_FILE);
end ELEM_FILE_OP;
```

Listing 16.2 Constructing and manipulating a file – elementary operations.

must be a write one). As data is loaded into the file the access locations are automatically changed (by the file handling software). If for any reason we wish to change the mode of the file without closing it, we invoke RESET. Its specification is

> **procedure** RESET (FILE : **in out** FILE_TYPE; MODE : **in** FILE_MODE);
> **procedure** RESET (FILE : **in out** FILE_TYPE);

Invoking RESET also takes us back to the start of the file. Its use will be demonstrated shortly.

Finally, we can close up the file after use by invoking CLOSE. As described earlier, this also severs the link between the internal file and the external one.

Listing 16.2 is a simple example of file manipulation, starting off with the creation of a file.

This ensures that before OPEN is used, an external file actually exists. We have omitted data transfer operations at this stage – they will be covered in the following sections. Observe that we have created a new file which has exactly the same name as the one of Listing 16.1. The effect of this is to replace the old file with this most recent one, so be careful in file naming and creation.

Listing 16.3 is a modified version of Listing 16.2. Here as in the previous example, the files are closed. Now, though, we reopen the external file, but connect it with a different internal file.

16.2.4 Deleting a file

When we say 'delete the file', we really mean the deletion of the external file. The internal file (or file object) is a static object. As such it exists for the

534 Data input–output

```
with TEXT_IO;               use TEXT_IO;
procedure FILE_RELATIONSHIP is
  ENGINE_FILE    :    FILE_TYPE;
  DATA_FILE      :    FILE_TYPE;
begin
  CREATE (ENGINE_FILE, OUT_FILE, "PORT_GT.TXT");
  CLOSE (ENGINE_FILE);
  OPEN (DATA_FILE, OUT_FILE, "PORT_GT.TXT");
  RESET (DATA_FILE);
  CLOSE (DATA_FILE);
end FILE_RELATIONSHIP;
```

Listing 16.3 Changing the internal/external file relationship.

```
with TEXT_IO;          use TEXT_IO;
procedure MANAGE_FILE is
  ENGINE_FILE    :    FILE_TYPE;
begin
 -- Create the file.
  CREATE (ENGINE_FILE, OUT_FILE, "STBD_GT.TXT");
  CLOSE (ENGINE_FILE);
  OPEN (ENGINE_FILE, OUT_FILE, "STBD_GT.TXT");
  RESET (ENGINE_FILE);
  -- Delete the file. This will delete the external file from your system.
  -- Note that the file must be open before we can delete it
  DELETE (ENGINE_FILE);
end MANAGE_FILE;
```

Listing 16.4 Simple demonstration of file management.

duration of the program. As long as the program is live it also exists, but when the program terminates it ceases to exist. The external file, in contrast, does not come into existence until we CREATE it. It continues to exist, irrespective of the state of the Ada program. To delete the external file we have to use the DELETE procedure, its specification being

```
procedure DELETE (FILE : in out FILE_TYPE);
```

Listing 16.4 takes us through the complete (though basic) file management process: creation, opening, closing and eventual deletion of an external file. Note that a file must be open before it can be deleted. You cannot delete a closed file.

Prior to executing this program the external file 'STBD_GT.TXT' does not exist. It is brought into existence at creation time. Finally, it disappears when DELETE is invoked.

What would happen if we created a file without defining an external name? In this case a temporary external file is created. This exists until the program terminates, at which point it disappears from our system.

Various subprograms are supplied in SEQUENTIAL_IO, DIRECT_IO and TEXT_IO to support file activities. These (or, at least, the most relevant ones) will be introduced as and when appropriate.

16.3 READABLE TEXT

16.3.1 General aspects

The topic dealt with here is the handling of I/O data which can be understood by humans. That is, all information exchange to and from the outside world is shown as letters and numbers: alpha-numerics. Such data may come from, or terminate in, another machine – it doesn't have to involve people. Bear in mind, though, that, ultimately, it is intended to be read and understood.

In Ada, readable text may be sorted into three groups: 'text', numbers and enumerated values, Fig.16.10.

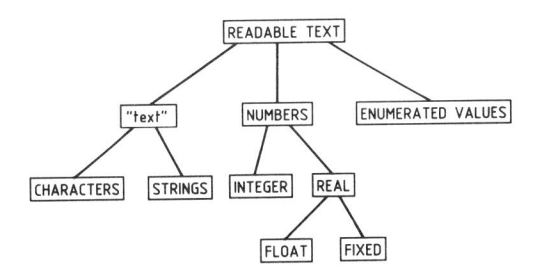

Fig.16.10 The component parts of readable text.

We have used these features extensively in our specimen programs, so there should be no surprises here.

'Text' is made up of individual characters or strings of characters, these being defined by us, the programmer. Such items are represented internally in ASCII format. When we output information of this type to terminals or printers, readable text is automatically produced. However, for numbers (integer, float and fixed) and enumerated values, this is not the case. Inside the computer each type is represented by an appropriate – non-ASCII – format. Further, these formats may well be implementation dependent. Suppose we wish to print out the values of number or enumerated items. Before doing so we first have to convert their normal format into ASCII. Likewise, when we input such values to the computer, the representation will be in ASCII

536   Data input-output

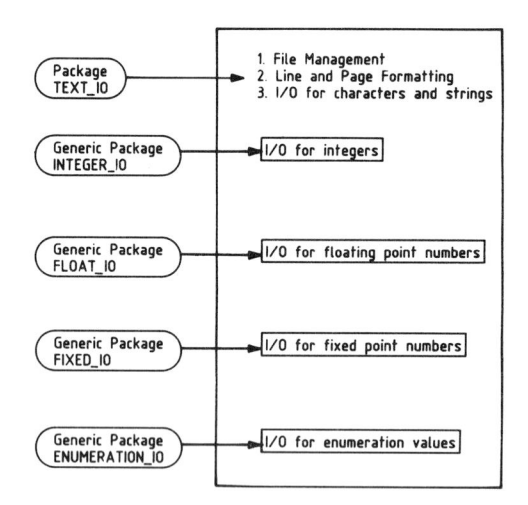

```
    ┌─────────────┐    ┌──────────────────────────────┐
    │   Package   │───▶│ 1. File Management           │
    │   TEXT_IO   │    │ 2. Line and Page Formatting  │
    └─────────────┘    │ 3. I/O for characters and strings │
                       │                              │
  ┌───────────────┐    │  ┌──────────────────┐        │
  │Generic Package│───▶│  │ I/O for integers │        │
  │  INTEGER_IO   │    │  └──────────────────┘        │
  └───────────────┘    │                              │
                       │                              │
  ┌───────────────┐    │  ┌─────────────────────────────┐│
  │Generic Package│───▶│  │ I/O for floating point numbers││
  │   FLOAT_IO    │    │  └─────────────────────────────┘│
  └───────────────┘    │                              │
                       │                              │
  ┌───────────────┐    │  ┌──────────────────────────┐ │
  │Generic Package│───▶│  │ I/O for fixed point numbers│ │
  │   FIXED_IO    │    │  └──────────────────────────┘ │
  └───────────────┘    │                              │
                       │                              │
  ┌────────────────┐   │  ┌────────────────────────┐  │
  │Generic Package │──▶│  │ I/O for enumeration values│  │
  │ ENUMERATION_IO │   │  └────────────────────────┘  │
  └────────────────┘   └──────────────────────────────┘
```

Fig.16.11 The package text_IO.

code. This will then need changing into the correct internal code format for that machine.

Input-output operations involving readable text are implemented using the facilities of package TEXT_IO, Fig.16.11. We discussed this earlier – in part – in chapter 13.

Character and string handling is supported directly in this package. The other operations are provided by generic packages INTEGER_IO, FLOAT_IO, FIXED_IO and ENUMERATION_IO housed within TEXT_IO. At first sight it may seem surprising that generic units are used in these applications. Remember, though, that we somehow have to manage the I/O of derived types, subtypes and user-defined enumeration types. Generics are the solution to this problem. They allow us to instantiate different flavours of the same basic operation.

This has set the outlines of the topic. Now let us look into it in more detail.

16.3.2 Character and string I/O – general

Very roughly we can say that two file types are used with character and string I/O operations: 'default' files and 'other' data files, Fig.16.12.

For simplicity, default files are here referred to as 'I/O devices', the others being denoted as 'data' files. A typical I/O device is a console or a printer, whilst a data file is just what it says – a data file. Usually such files are stored on tape, floppy disk or hard disk.

Four procedures are used to handle these I/O activities: PUT, PUT_LINE,

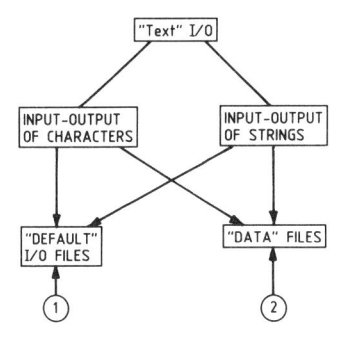

Fig.16.12 I/O of characters and strings.

GET and GET_LINE. These are overloaded to provide the following operations:

1(a) Input a character from an I/O device.
1(b) Output a character to an I/O device.
1(c) Input a string from an I/O device.
1(d) Output a string to an I/O device.

2(a) Input a character from a data file.
2(b) Output a character to a data file.
2(c) Input a string from a data file.
2(d) Output a string to a data file.

16.3.3 Data exchange with I/O devices

There should be few surprises here. After all, these are the operations we've been using all the way through this book. Therefore the review is brief.

When interacting with I/O devices, we do not specify any files. As a result default files are used. These are 'invisible' to the programmer, which should be clear from your earlier use of PUT and GET. Observe that, as usual, positional or named association can be used with procedure parameters.

1(a) Input a character from an I/O device

> **procedure** GET (ITEM : **out** CHARACTER);
> Example : GET (DIGIT_1); where DIGIT_1 is a CHARACTER
> or   GET (ITEM => DIGIT_1); using named notation

You may find that, for GET to work correctly, it must be followed immediately by a SKIP_LINE (described in section 16.3.9). This is compiler dependent. Including it, however, guarantees that GET will produce the correct action. The specimen programs follow this rule.

1(b) Output a character to an I/O device

> **procedure** PUT (ITEM : **in** CHARACTER);
> Example : PUT ('a'); or PUT (ITEM => 'a');
> or   PUT (DIGIT_1) or PUT (ITEM => DIGIT_1);

1(c) Input a string from an I/O device

> **procedure** GET (ITEM : **out** STRING);
> Example: GET (INPUT_TEXT);

Here INPUT_TEXT is of type STRING. This (actual) procedure will input the number of characters corresponding to the length of INPUT_TEXT. We can also use the procedure GET_LINE with strings to input lines of text:

> **procedure** GET_LINE (ITEM : **out** STRING; LAST : **out** NATURAL);

The first parameter is a string, the second gives the length of the line of text. When GET_LINE is used, input characters are read in until an end-of-line character is found. Reading also stops if the end of the string is met. The difference between the two is that, in the first case, we just stop reading. In the second we stop reading and then skip to the next line. The important difference between these is illustrated in Listing 16.5.

1(d) Output a string to an I/O device

> **procedure** PUT (ITEM : **in** STRING);
> Example : PUT ("Hello"); or PUT (MESSAGE);

Here MESSAGE is of type STRING:

> **procedure** PUT_LINE (ITEM : **in** STRING);
> Example: PUT_LINE ("Hello");

```
with TEXT_IO;                use TEXT_IO;
procedure SIMPLE_TEXT_IO is
  SURNAME         :    STRING (1..10);
  CHRISTIAN_NAME  :    STRING (1..10);
  INITIAL         :    CHARACTER;
  LAST_CHAR       :    NATURAL;
begin
  PUT ("Please enter your christian name (10 chars) : ");
  GET (CHRISTIAN_NAME);
  SKIP_LINE;
  PUT ("your surname : ");
  GET_LINE (SURNAME, LAST_CHAR);
  PUT ("your middle initial : ");
  GET (INITIAL);
  PUT ("Your name is ");
  PUT (CHRISTIAN_NAME);
  PUT (' ');
  PUT (INITIAL);
  PUT (' ');
  PUT_LINE (SURNAME (1..LAST_CHAR));
end SIMPLE_TEXT_IO;
```

Listing 16.5 Simple demonstration of 'text' handling with I/O devices.

The only difference between these two is that PUT_LINE terminates the line output and then increments the current line number by one (equivalent to carriage return/line feed).

Compile and run the program in Listing 16.5. Test its response by using the following inputs:

- Surname less than 10 characters;
- Surname equal to 10 characters;
- Surname greater than 10 characters.

IMPORTANT: When program execution begins, the default files are the 'standard' ones. These are provided as part of the system environment, being associated with two implementation-defined external files.

16.3.4 Data exchange with files

2(a) Input a character from a data file

```
procedure GET (FILE : in FILE_TYPE; ITEM : out CHARACTER);
  Example: GET (TREND_RECORDING_FILE, INPUT_DIGIT);
  or       GET (FILE => TREND_RECORDING_FILE,
                ITEM => INPUT_DIGIT);
```

2(b) Output a character to a data file

> **procedure** PUT (FILE : **in** FILE_TYPE; ITEM : **in** CHARACTER);
> Example: PUT (TREND_RECORDING_FILE, OUTPUT_DIGIT);
> or   PUT (FILE => TREND_RECORDING_FILE,
>   ITEM => INPUT_DIGIT);

2(c) Input a string from a data file

> **procedure** GET (FILE : **in** FILE_TYPE; ITEM : **out** STRING);
> Example: GET (FILE => ENGINE_DATA,
>   ITEM => NAME_OF_ENGINE);

> **procedure** GET_LINE (FILE : **in** FILE_TYPE;
>   ITEM : **out** STRING;
>   LAST : **out** NATURAL);
> Example: GET_LINE (FILE => ENGINE_DATA,
>   ITEM => NAME_OF_ENGINE,
>   LAST => NUM_OF_CHARS);

2(d) Output a string to a data file

> **procedure** PUT (FILE : **in** FILE_TYPE; ITEM : **in** STRING);
> Example: PUT (FILE => ENGINE_DATA,
>   ITEM => NAME_OF_ENGINE);

> **procedure** PUT_LINE (FILE : **in** FILE_TYPE; ITEM : **in** STRING);

Basic data file operations are demonstrated in Listing 16.6 which includes a RESET with a mode change.

This example has one limitation: we cannot view progress or results of the program. To do this we need to incorporate device I/O operation – Listing 16.7.

16.3.5 TEXT_IO – Some useful management and control subprograms

The subprograms discussed here fall into two categories. The first are used to obtain information pertaining to files – a query function. The second are employed for the control of default files in text I/O operations.

```
with TEXT_IO;              use TEXT_IO;
procedure TEXT_TO_FILE_IO is
  NAME_FILE       :    FILE_TYPE;
  SURNAME         :    STRING (1..10) := "Cooling   ";
  CHRISTIAN_NAME  :    STRING (1..10) := "Pauline   ";
  INITIAL         :    CHARACTER      := 'M';
  LAST_CHAR       :    NATURAL;
begin
 -- create a file to output data to
  CREATE (NAME_FILE, OUT_FILE, "NAME.TXT");
 -- output name to file
  PUT (NAME_FILE, CHRISTIAN_NAME);
  PUT (NAME_FILE, INITIAL);
  PUT_LINE (NAME_FILE, SURNAME);
 -- reset the file to be an IN_FILE
  RESET (NAME_FILE, IN_FILE);
 -- read the name back in from the file
  GET (NAME_FILE, CHRISTIAN_NAME);
  GET (NAME_FILE, INITIAL);
  GET_LINE (NAME_FILE, SURNAME, LAST_CHAR);
 -- close the file
  CLOSE (NAME_FILE);
end TEXT_TO_FILE_IO;
```

Listing 16.6 Basic text I/O handling with data files – strings and characters.

```
with TEXT_IO;              use TEXT_IO;
procedure COMBINATION_TEXT_IO is
  NAME_FILE       :    FILE_TYPE;
  SURNAME         :    STRING (1..10) := "Cooling   ";
  CHRISTIAN_NAME  :    STRING (1..10) := "Pauline   ";
  INITIAL         :    CHARACTER      := 'M';
  LAST_CHAR       :    NATURAL;
begin
 -- create a file to output data to
  CREATE (NAME_FILE, OUT_FILE, "NAME.TXT");
 -- output name to file
  PUT (NAME_FILE, CHRISTIAN_NAME);
  PUT (NAME_FILE, INITIAL);
  PUT_LINE (NAME_FILE, SURNAME);
 -- reset the file to an IN_FILE in read mode
  RESET (NAME_FILE, IN_FILE);
 -- read the name back in from the file
  GET (NAME_FILE, CHRISTIAN_NAME);
  GET (NAME_FILE, INITIAL);
  GET_LINE (NAME_FILE, SURNAME, LAST_CHAR);
 -- close the file
  CLOSE (NAME_FILE);
 -- print the data read from the file to the screen
  PUT ("The data read from the file was ");
  PUT (CHRISTIAN_NAME);
  PUT (' ');
  PUT (INITIAL);
  PUT (' ');
  PUT_LINE (SURNAME (1..LAST_CHAR));
end COMBINATION_TEXT_IO;
```

Listing 16.7 'text' I/O handling – combining data file and I/O device operations.

542 Data input–output

(a) Query functions: MODE, NAME, FORM and IS_OPEN

(i) MODE This is used to find the current mode of a defined file. Its specification is

> **function** MODE (FILE : **in** FILE_TYPE) **return** FILE_MODE;

Note that this operation can only be applied to a file which is open.

(ii) NAME This is used to find the name (i.e. the string identifier) of the external physical file. Its specification is

> **function** NAME (FILE : **in** FILE_TYPE) **return** STRING;

This operation, too, applies only to an open file.

(iii) FORM This is used to determine system-specific attributes defined by the FORM parameter. Its specification is

> **function** FORM (FILE : **in** FILE_TYPE) **return** STRING;

As with (i) and (ii), the file must be open to use this feature.

(iv) IS_OPEN This is used to determine whether a file is open or closed. Its specification is

> **function** IS_OPEN (FILE : **in** FILE_TYPE) **return** BOOLEAN;

Listing 16.8 demonstrates their use.

(b) Control of default file values

We have used PUT and GET extensively in earlier chapters for console and keyboard interaction. From what has been said above you will now realize that these items are our standard I/O (default) devices. This raises a number of interesting questions. First, can we find out what the standard default files are? Second, can we change the default files? Third, can we determine precisely what default files we are using at any particular time? The answer is yes, by using the following six subprograms:

```
with TEXT_IO;              use TEXT_IO;
procedure FILE_QUERY_FUNC is
  ENGINE_FILE      :     FILE_TYPE;
begin
  CREATE (ENGINE_FILE, OUT_FILE, "PORT_GT.TXT");
  -- determining the mode of a file
  if MODE (ENGINE_FILE) = OUT_FILE then
    PUT_LINE ("ENGINE FILE is set to mode OUT_FILE");
  else
    PUT_LINE ("ENGINE FILE is set to mode IN_FILE");
  end if;
  -- determining the external name of a file
  PUT ("The file ENGINE_FILE is named ");
  PUT_LINE (NAME (ENGINE_FILE));
  -- determining the form of a file
  PUT ("The file ENGINE_FILE has the following form ");
  PUT_LINE (FORM (ENGINE_FILE));
  -- determining if a file is open
  if IS_OPEN (ENGINE_FILE) then
    PUT_LINE ("ENGINE_FILE is open");
  else
    PUT_LINE ("ENGINE_FILE is closed");
  end if;
  CLOSE (ENGINE_FILE);
end FILE_QUERY_FUNC;
```

Listing 16.8 This demonstrates the use of the functions MODE, NAME, FORM and IS_OPEN.

- STANDARD_INPUT
- STANDARD_OUTPUT
- SET_INPUT
- SET_OUTPUT
- CURRENT_INPUT
- CURRENT_OUTPUT

(i) STANDARD_INPUT This is used to find the internal name of the standard input file. Its specification is

> **function** STANDARD_INPUT **return** FILE_TYPE;

(ii) STANDARD_OUTPUT This is used to find the internal name of the standard output file. Its specification is

> **function** STANDARD_OUTPUT **return** FILE_TYPE;

(iii) SET_INPUT This is used to define the file to be used as the default input file. Its specification is

544   Data input–output

> **procedure** SET_INPUT (FILE : **in** FILE_TYPE);

(iv) SET_OUTPUT This is used to define the file to be used as the output default file. Its specification is

> **procedure** SET_OUTPUT (FILE : **in** FILE_TYPE);

(v) CURRENT_INPUT This is used to find the name of the current input default file. Its specification is

> **function** CURRENT_INPUT **return** FILE_TYPE;

(vi) CURRENT_OUTPUT This is used to find the name of the current output default file. Its specification is

> **function** CURRENT_OUTPUT **return** FILE_TYPE;

The use of these subprograms is illustrated in Listing 16.9.

16.3.6   Inputting and outputting integer types

We have already stated that I/O operations involving integer types (i.e. type INTEGER and its subtype/derived type offspring) use the facilities of package INTEGER_IO. This is a generic package, and hence it must be instantiated before it can be used. Central to this is a set of overloaded PUT and GET procedures. However, before looking into the package in detail, certain basic ideas need to be dealt with.

First, a recapitulation: our I/O files must have an agreed coding standard for all readable text, otherwise screen or printer outputs would bear little relationship to the information contained within our programs. Let us assume that we use ASCII for this purpose. Therefore, internally in the computer, all characters and strings are encoded in this format. As a result, we can pass such information directly to I/O devices – no coding changes are needed. However, numerical values are not normally coded in ASCII; different coding formats are used (see chapter 6 for further detail). Therefore translation between the internal and external (ASCII) representations must be carried out, Fig.16.13.

Consider, for instance, how we would represent the decimal value '24' inside the machine. The binary pattern would very likely be 00011000. Its

```
with TEXT_IO;              use TEXT_IO;
procedure DEFAULT_IO_FILE is
  NAME_FILE       :   FILE_TYPE;
  SURNAME         :   STRING (1..10) := "Cooling   ";
  CHRISTIAN_NAME  :   STRING (1..10) := "Pauline   ";
  INITIAL         :   CHARACTER      := 'M';
  LAST_CHAR       :   NATURAL;
begin
  -- create a file to output data to
  CREATE (NAME_FILE, OUT_FILE, "NAME.TXT");
  -- make this the standard output file
  SET_OUTPUT (NAME_FILE);
  -- output name to NAME_FILE
  PUT (CHRISTIAN_NAME);
  PUT (INITIAL);
  PUT_LINE (SURNAME);
  -- reset file to be an IN_FILE
  RESET (NAME_FILE, IN_FILE);
  -- set the standard input file to NAME_FILE
  SET_INPUT (NAME_FILE);
  -- read the name back in from NAME_FILE
  GET (CHRISTIAN_NAME);
  GET (INITIAL);
  GET_LINE (SURNAME, LAST_CHAR);
  -- close the file
  CLOSE (NAME_FILE);
  -- reassign STANDARD_OUT_FILE as the standard output file
  SET_OUTPUT (TEXT_IO.STANDARD_OUTPUT);
  -- reassign STANDARD_IN_FILE as the standard input file
  SET_INPUT (TEXT_IO.STANDARD_INPUT);
  -- print out name to the screen
  PUT ("The name read from NAME_FILE is ");
  PUT (CHRISTIAN_NAME);
  PUT (' ');
  PUT (INITIAL);
  PUT (' ');
  PUT_LINE (SURNAME (1..LAST_CHAR));
end DEFAULT_IO_FILE;
```

Listing 16.9 This demonstrates the use of the subprograms provided for the control of default files.

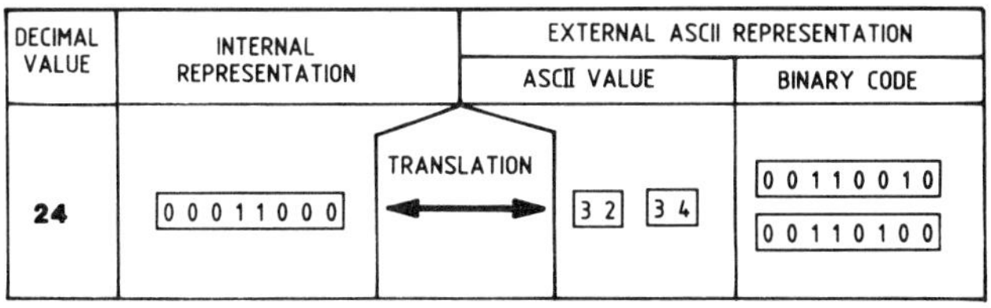

DECIMAL VALUE	INTERNAL REPRESENTATION	EXTERNAL ASCII REPRESENTATION	
		ASCII VALUE	BINARY CODE
24	0 0 0 1 1 0 0 0	TRANSLATION 3 2 3 4	0 0 1 1 0 0 1 0 0 0 1 1 0 1 0 0

Fig.16.13 The internal/external representation problem.

546 Data input-output

DECIMAL VALUE	INTERNAL REPRESENTATION	HEXADECIMAL VALUE	ASCII VALUE
24	0 0 0 1 1 0 0 0	18 (H)	[3 1] [3 8]

Fig.16.14 Change of number base.

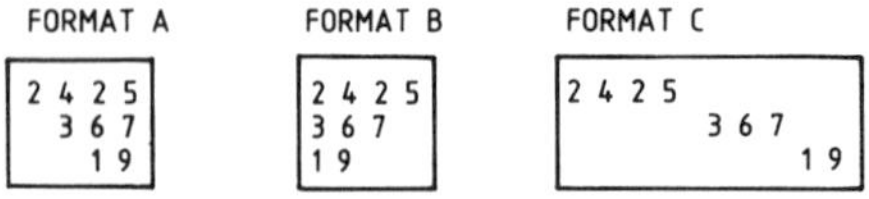

```
   FORMAT A      FORMAT B      FORMAT C
   2 4 2 5       2 4 2 5       2 4 2 5
   3 6 7         3 6 7               3 6 7
     1 9           1 9                   1 9
```

Fig.16.15 Some layout formats.

corresponding ASCII code is a two-digit one, having values 32 and 34 (the equivalent binary codes are shown in Fig.16.13). Therefore, at the machine level we have to translate binary 00011000 to binary 00110010, 00110100 (and vice versa).

Now suppose that we wish to show the internal number on the screen in hexadecimal (base 16) format, Fig.16.14.

This will be written up as '18', having the corresponding ASCII values '31', '38'. Thus you can see that the translation used at any one time depends on number base. This explains why we need to involve number bases – using a parameter BASE – in the handling of integer I/O.

Now let us look at a quite different aspect of this topic – layout formats. Suppose we wish to print out three numbers – 2425, 367 and 19 – as shown in Fig.16.15.

How can we define the required format styles? This is done by including a further parameter in the output command – WIDTH (it is also used in inputting data, see later). WIDTH defines the minimum number of spaces allocated for the print-out of numbers. The rules relating to it are (see also Fig.16.16):

(a) When the number of characters to be output is equal to or greater than the WIDTH setting, the value is output as an integer literal.
(b) When the number of characters is less than the WIDTH setting, leading spaces are inserted to make up the total to the value of WIDTH.
(c) Leading zeros are not output.
(d) Underscores are also ignored.
(e) For negative numbers, a leading minus sign is output.

Now let us return to the package INTEGER_IO. Part of its declaration, which illustrates its most important points, is

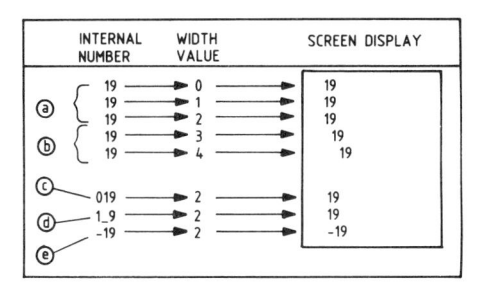

```
              INTERNAL    WIDTH         SCREEN DISPLAY
              NUMBER      VALUE
               19    ────▶  0   ────▶       19
        ⓐ  {   19    ────▶  1   ────▶       19
               19    ────▶  2   ────▶       19
               19    ────▶  3   ────▶      19
        ⓑ  {   19    ────▶  4   ────▶       19
        ⓒ
               019   ────▶  2   ────▶       19
        ⓓ      1_9   ────▶  2   ────▶       19
               -19   ────▶  2   ────▶      -19
        ⓔ
```

Fig.16.16 Use of width parameter.

```
subtype FIELD            is INTEGER range 0 .. implementation_defined
subtype NUMBER_BASE is INTEGER range 2 ..16

generic
   type NUM is range <>;
package INTEGER_IO is

   DEFAULT_WIDTH : FIELD       := NUM'WIDTH;
   DEFAULT_BASE  : NUMBER_BASE := 10;

   procedure PUT (ITEM  : in NUM;
                  WIDTH : in FIELD       := DEFAULT_WIDTH;
                  BASE  : in NUMBER_BASE := DEFAULT_BASE);
```

Here:

- NUM, from its declaration format, is an integer type;
- ITEM is the number to be output;
- WIDTH defines the number of spaces allocated on the screen/paper;
- BASE is the number base used in the output value.

Instantiation of this was demonstrated as an example in the chapter on generics. And, of course, we have used an instantiated version – INT_IO – right from chapter 1. From the above you can see that the default width setting is implementation dependent – check your compiler for details. The default base is 10, giving us standard decimal notation. Listing 16.10 shows different aspects of outputting data to a standard I/O device. This includes changes to format and base, using both positional and named association.

The other procedures for use with integer I/O are:

- PUT, for use with data files;
- GET, for use with default I/O;
- GET, for use with data files.

Their use is shown in Listing 16.11.

One last feature: the default values can be reset under program control, as in

```
with TEXT_IO;              use TEXT_IO;
procedure STANDARD_INT_OUTPUT is
  package INT_IO is new INTEGER_IO (INTEGER);
begin
  INT_IO.PUT (19);
  PUT_LINE (" (used default WIDTH)");
  INT_IO.PUT (19, 0);
  PUT_LINE (" (WIDTH is less than number of characters to be output)");
  INT_IO.PUT (19, 4);
  PUT_LINE (" (WIDTH is greater than number of characters to be output)");
  INT_IO.PUT (ITEM     => 19,
              WIDTH    => 2,
              BASE     => 16);
  PUT_LINE (" (HEXADECIMAL)");
  INT_IO.PUT (ITEM     => 19,
              WIDTH    => 5,
              BASE     => 2);
  PUT_LINE (" (BINARY)");
end STANDARD_INT_OUTPUT;
```

Listing 16.10 This demonstrates the outputting of integer values to a standard I/O device.

```
with TEXT_IO;              use TEXT_IO;
procedure MORE_INTEGER_IO is
  OUTPUT_VALUE   :     INTEGER        :=  255;
  INPUT_VALUE    :     INTEGER        :=  0;
  VALUE_FILE     :     FILE_TYPE;
  package INT_IO is new INTEGER_IO (INTEGER);
  use INT_IO;
begin
  -- create a file and write OUTPUT_VALUE to it
  CREATE (VALUE_FILE, OUT_FILE, "VALUE.INT");
  PUT (VALUE_FILE, OUTPUT_VALUE);
  -- reset the file to an IN_FILE and read the value in it into INPUT_VALUE
  RESET (VALUE_FILE, IN_FILE);
  GET (VALUE_FILE, INPUT_VALUE);
  -- close the file
  CLOSE (VALUE_FILE);
  -- output the number read from the file to the screen
  PUT ("The value ");
  PUT (INPUT_VALUE, 3);
  PUT_LINE (" was read from VALUE_FILE");
end MORE_INTEGER_IO;
```

Listing 16.11 This is a further demonstration of integer I/O using PUT and GET.

```
DEFAULT_WIDTH := 4;
DEFAULT_BASE  := 16;
```

It may, in some instances, be necessary to use dot notation to avoid ambiguity:

```
INT_IO.DEFAULT_WIDTH := 4;
```

16.3.7 Inputting and outputting real types

First, a brief recap of notation for real types, followed by further definitions.

Real numbers are those which contain a radix point, even if this is implicit (however, in Ada syntax, the point must appear). Their values can be expressed in two ways: fixed point and floating point notation (for detailed information, see chapter 6). Thus the following two numbers are equivalent:

Fixed point: 234.5678   Floating point: $2.345\,678 \times 10^2$

In Ada we define various parts of these numbers as FORE, AFT, E and EXP, Fig.16.17.

Digits before the radix point form the FORE field. Those after the point lie in the AFT field. The radix (here, 10) is defined as E, and the exponent forms the EXP field. Thus all values output are decimal ones.

Floating point numbers are handled using the facilities of package FLOAT_IO. Fixed point types are manipulated using FIXED_IO. All operations are performed using a set of overloaded PUT and GET procedures.

(a) **Floating point types**

The essential features of package FLOAT_IO are highlighted by the following part declaration:

```
subtype FIELD is INTEGER range 0 .. implementation_defined
generic
   type NUM is digits <>;
package FLOAT_IO is

   DEFAULT_FORE : FIELD := 2;
   DEFAULT_AFT  : FIELD := NUM'DIGITS – 1;
   DEFAULT_EXP  : FIELD := 3;

procedure PUT (ITEM : in NUM;
               FORE : in FIELD := DEFAULT_FORE;
               AFT  : in FIELD := DEFAULT_AFT;
               EXP  : in FIELD := (DEFAULT_EXP);
```

550   Data input–output

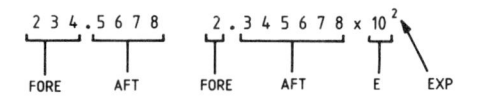

$$\underbrace{234}_{\text{FORE}}.\underbrace{5678}_{\text{AFT}} \qquad \underbrace{2}_{\text{FORE}}.\underbrace{345678}_{\text{AFT}} \underbrace{\times 10}_{E} \underbrace{^{2}}_{\text{EXP}}$$

Fig.16.17 Real number format definitions.

Here:

- NUM, from its declaration format, is a floating point type.
- ITEM is the number to be output.
- FORE defines the number of spaces allocated in the print-out for digits preceding the decimal point (its default value is 2). Where appropriate this includes leading spaces (blanks) and the minus sign.
- AFT serves the same function as FORE, but applies to digits following the decimal point (the default value is system dependent). This contains only decimal digits and, where applicable, trailing zeros.
- EXP defines the number of spaces allocated for print-out of the exponent (default value is 3). This includes the exponent value itself, its sign (+ or −) and, where applicable, leading zeros.

To clarify these points, let us first print out numbers using the default values only, Listing 16.12.

Following this we have an example (Listing 16.13) showing the use of the PUT procedure parameters FORE, AFT and EXP.

Note the following features (the radix E is always 10):

1. If the number of digits output is less than that specified by FORE, padding blanks are used.
2. If the number of digits output is less than that specified by AFT, padding zeros are used.
3. If AFT is set to zero, one digit is always placed to the right of the decimal point (required by Ada syntax).
4. A plus or minus sign always precedes the exponent value.
5. If EXP is set to zero, there is no exponent part.
6. If EXP is set to zero, then the system outputs sufficient characters to represent fully the fore value – if necessary, overriding the set value of FORE.
7. If EXP is zero and the number has no fore value (i.e. it only has a decimal fractional part) then a zero digit is placed before the decimal point.
8. If EXP is not zero, then a single digit is put out as the fore field value. This digit must not be a zero except where the number value is actually zero. In that case the number '0.0' is output.

```
with TEXT_IO;              use TEXT_IO;
procedure FLOAT_DEFAULT_FORMAT is
   OUTPUT_NUM_1   :   FLOAT         := 20.239;
   OUTPUT_NUM_2   :   FLOAT         := 0.00000000005;
   OUTPUT_NUM_3   :   FLOAT         := 1000.3;
   OUTPUT_NUM_4   :   FLOAT         := 5.0;
   package OUTPUT_NUM_IO is new FLOAT_IO (FLOAT);
begin
   OUTPUT_NUM_IO.PUT (OUTPUT_NUM_1);
   PUT_LINE (" (OUTPUT_NUM_1)");
   OUTPUT_NUM_IO.PUT (OUTPUT_NUM_2);
   PUT_LINE (" (OUTPUT_NUM_2)");
   OUTPUT_NUM_IO.PUT (OUTPUT_NUM_3);
   PUT_LINE (" (OUTPUT_NUM_3)");
   OUTPUT_NUM_IO.PUT (OUTPUT_NUM_4);
   PUT_LINE (" (OUTPUT_NUM_4)");
end FLOAT_DEFAULT_FORMAT;
```

Listing 16.12 This is a simple demonstration which outputs floating point numbers using default settings of the PUT procedure.

```
with TEXT_IO;              use TEXT_IO;
procedure FLOAT_OUTPUT_FORMAT is
   OUTPUT_NUM_1   :   FLOAT         := 20.239;
   OUTPUT_NUM_2   :   FLOAT         := 0.00000000005;
   OUTPUT_NUM_3   :   FLOAT         := 1000.3;
   OUTPUT_NUM_4   :   FLOAT         := 5.0;
   package OUTPUT_NUM_IO is new FLOAT_IO (FLOAT);
   use OUTPUT_NUM_IO;
begin
   PUT (OUTPUT_NUM_1,
        FORE      =>   1,
        AFT       =>   4,
        EXP       =>   1);
   PUT_LINE ("          (FORE = 1, AFT = 4,  EXP = 1)");
   PUT (OUTPUT_NUM_2,
        FORE      =>   0,
        AFT       =>   11,
        EXP       =>   2);
   PUT_LINE ("     (FORE = 0, AFT = 11, EXP = 2)");
   PUT (OUTPUT_NUM_3,
        FORE      =>   4,
        AFT       =>   1,
        EXP       =>   1);
   PUT_LINE ("       (FORE = 4, AFT = 1,  EXP = 1)");
   PUT (OUTPUT_NUM_4,
        FORE      =>   1,
        AFT       =>   1,
        EXP       =>   0);
   PUT_LINE ("            (FORE = 1, AFT = 1,  EXP = 0)");
end FLOAT_OUTPUT_FORMAT;
```

Listing 16.13 This demonstrates the use of FORE, AFT and EXP with a PUT procedure for floating point values.

```
with TEXT_IO;                   use TEXT_IO;
procedure FLOAT_GET_PUT is
  FLOAT_OUT       :   FLOAT          := 0.067;
  FLOAT_IN        :   FLOAT          := 0.0;
  FLOAT_FILE      :   FILE_TYPE;
  package FP_NUM_IO is new FLOAT_IO (FLOAT);
begin
  -- create a file and write FLOAT_OUT to it
  CREATE (FLOAT_FILE, OUT_FILE, "VALUE.FP");
  FP_NUM_IO.PUT (FLOAT_FILE, FLOAT_OUT);
  -- reset the file to an IN_FILE and read the value in it into FLOAT_IN
  RESET (FLOAT_FILE, IN_FILE);
  FP_NUM_IO.GET (FLOAT_FILE, FLOAT_IN);
  -- close the file
  CLOSE (FLOAT_FILE);
  -- output the number read from the file to the screen
  PUT ("The value ");
  FP_NUM_IO.PUT (FLOAT_IN,
                 FORE    => 1,
                 AFT     => 1,
                 EXP     => 1);
  PUT_LINE (" was read from FLOAT_FILE");
end FLOAT_GET_PUT;
```

Listing 16.14 This demonstrates the use of GET and PUT procedures for floating point values.

9. If the number of digits defined by EXP is too small for the actual exponent, the setting is overridden. All the exponent digits are output.
10. If the internal (program) fractional part has more digits than AFT, the output value is rounded. A value of one-half in the last place may be rounded up or down.

Listing 16.14 shows further aspects of I/O operations for floating point numbers.

(b) **Fixed point types**

Part of the declaration of package FIXED_IO reads:

```
generic
   type NUM is delta <>;
package FIXED_IO is

   DEFAULT_FORE : FIELD := NUM'FORE;
   DEFAULT_AFT  : FIELD := NUM'AFT;
   DEFAULT_EXP  : FIELD := 0;

   procedure PUT (ITEM : in NUM;
                  FORE : in FIELD := DEFAULT_FORE;
                  AFT  : in FIELD := DEFAULT_AFT;
                  EXP  : in FIELD := DEFAULT_EXP);
```

```
with TEXT_IO;               use TEXT_IO;
procedure FIXED_GET_PUT is
  type DISTANCE is delta 0.1 range 0.0 .. 200.0;
  DISTANCE_OUT   :   DISTANCE       := 100.0;
  DISTANCE_IN    :   DISTANCE       := 0.0;
  DISTANCE_FILE  :   FILE_TYPE;
  package DISTANCE_IO is new FIXED_IO (DISTANCE);
begin
  -- create a file and write DISTANCE_OUT to it
  CREATE (DISTANCE_FILE, OUT_FILE, "VALUE.FX");
  DISTANCE_IO.PUT (DISTANCE_FILE, DISTANCE_OUT);
  -- reset the file to an IN_FILE and read the value in it into DISTANCE_IN
  RESET (DISTANCE_FILE, IN_FILE);
  DISTANCE_IO.GET (DISTANCE_FILE, DISTANCE_IN);
  -- close the file
  CLOSE (DISTANCE_FILE);
  -- output the number read from the file to the screen
  PUT ("The value ");
  DISTANCE_IO.PUT (DISTANCE_IN,
                   FORE      => 3,
                   AFT       => 0);
  PUT_LINE (" was read from DISTANCE_FILE");
end FIXED_GET_PUT;
```

Listing 16.15 Using GET and PUT procedures for fixed point values.

This should be self-explanatory from what has been said previously. The use of parameter EXP in PUT is mysterious (but what else would you expect by now?). Listing 16.15 illustrates various aspects of fixed point I/O operations.

16.3.8 Inputting and outputting enumeration types

For I/O operations involving enumeration types we use the package ENUMERATION_IO. Once again we can show its essential points with the following part declaration:

```
             type TYPE_SET is (LOWER_CASE, UPPER_CASE);


generic
   type ENUM is (< >);
package ENUMERATION_IO is

   DEFAULT_WIDTH    : FIELD := 0;
   DEFAULT_SETTING  : TYPE_SET := UPPER_CASE;

   procedure PUT (ITEM  : in ENUM;
                  WIDTH : in FIELD    := DEFAULT_WIDTH;
                  SET   : in TYPE_SET := DEFAULT_SETTING);
```

554 Data input–output

```
with TEXT_IO;                   use TEXT_IO;
procedure ENUM_GET_PUT is
  type HOUSE is (BUNGALOW, SEMI_DETACHED, DETACHED, COTTAGE);
  OUTPUT_HOUSE     :      HOUSE         := COTTAGE;
  INPUT_HOUSE      :      HOUSE         := BUNGALOW;
  HOUSE_FILE       :      FILE_TYPE;
  package HOUSE_IO is new ENUMERATION_IO (HOUSE);
begin
  -- create a file and write OUTPUT_HOUSE to it
  CREATE (HOUSE_FILE, OUT_FILE, "HOUSE.INT");
  HOUSE_IO.PUT (HOUSE_FILE, OUTPUT_HOUSE);
  -- reset the file to an IN_FILE and read the value in it into INPUT_HOUSE
  RESET (HOUSE_FILE, IN_FILE);
  HOUSE_IO.GET (HOUSE_FILE, INPUT_HOUSE);
  -- close the file
  CLOSE (HOUSE_FILE);
  -- output the enumeral read from the file to the screen
  PUT ("The value ");
  HOUSE_IO.PUT (INPUT_HOUSE,
                WIDTH     => 7,
                SET       => LOWER_CASE);
  PUT_LINE (" was read from HOUSE_FILE");
end ENUM_GET_PUT;
```

Listing 16.16 Using GET and PUT procedures for enumeration types.

Here:

- The declaration format for ENUM denotes it to be an enumeration type.
- ITEM represents an enumeration literal value.
- WIDTH defines the minimum number of spaces to be allocated for output values.
- SET defines the case of the text (upper or lower, as selected).

We must, of course, instantiate this package as it is a generic one. Listing 16.16 demonstrates the important features of enumeration I/O.

16.3.9 Structuring text files – 'Formatting'

Suppose that you had to write – using pen and paper – a lengthy report. You could, if you so wished, use a single continuous roll of paper as the medium. This may appeal to the artist in you. Moreover, it minimizes the amount of paper needed, thus saving trees (an important eco-factor). Unfortunately it is highly unlikely to impress your superiors. Such documents are 'write-easy read-with-great-difficulty' types (you may well have met something like this with computer print-outs). A structure must be imposed on the document to make it usable.

We can apply exactly the same arguments to file structuring. The analogy to our single sheet of paper is an unformatted file, Fig.16.18.

Readable text 555

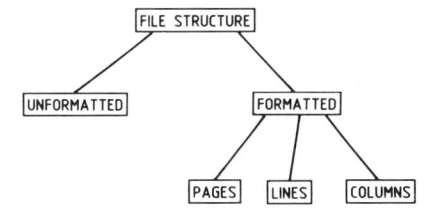

Fig.16.18 Text file structure.

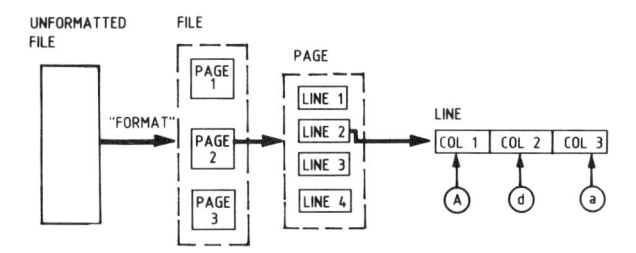

Fig.16.19 File format.

By contrast, a formatted file is the equivalent of a structured document. We take the analogy further by talking of pages, lines and columns. The formatting organizes the file information so that (Fig.16.19):

- The complete file is a sequence of pages;
- Each page is a sequence of lines (the first line number is 1);
- Each line is a sequence of columns (the first column number is 1).

Observe that each column holds a single character (though this is not necessarily a printable one). Compare this organization with that of the unformatted file, which is merely an unstructured sequence of characters.

Our reason for structuring files is simple: to make them usable for the human reader. We have already seen how to create files. Now comes the issues of specifying their structures and then operating on such structures, Fig.16.20.

(a) **Specifying file structures**

There are two aspects in specifying or building file structures. First, we need to define them in terms of line and page lengths. Second, we must be able to find out what the existing structure (if any) is.

The procedures SET_LINE_LENGTH and SET_PAGE_LENGTH are used to set the maximum line and page lengths. The specifications are

556   Data input–output

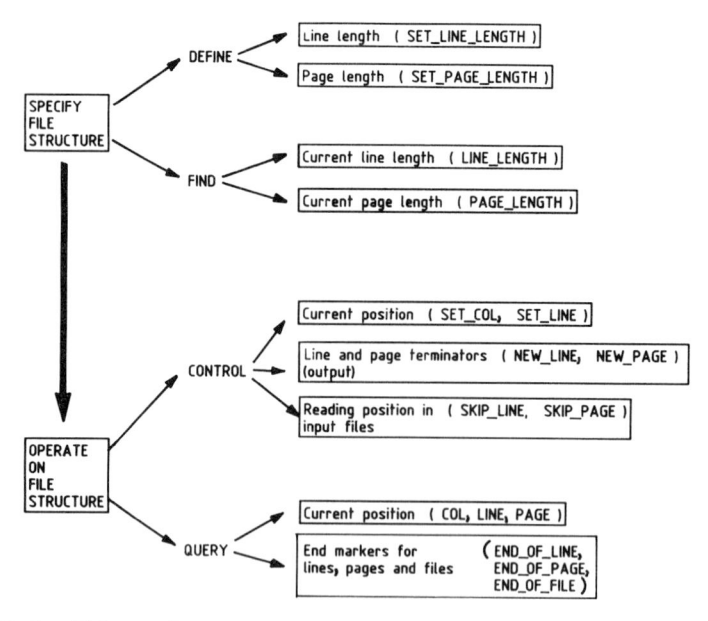

Fig.16.20 Specifying and operating on file structures.

```
procedure SET_LINE_LENGTH (FILE : in FILE_TYPE; TO : in COUNT);
procedure SET_LINE_LENGTH (TO : in COUNT); -- uses the default file
```

SET_PAGE_LENGTH has the same parameters (see your compiler manual).

For line length settings, the value of TO defines the maximum number of characters in a line. For instance,

```
SET_LINE_LENGTH (65);
```

sets a maximum line length of 65 characters. With this setting, the Ada system automatically produces a line terminator after 65 characters are output. As written above it applies to the default file only, of course.

For page settings, TO specifies the maximum number of lines per page. Thus

```
SET_PAGE_LENGTH (55);
```

sets a maximum of 55 lines per page. With this, the system automatically produces a page terminator and a line terminator.

```
with TEXT_IO;                        use TEXT_IO;
procedure SET_PAGE_AND_LINE is
begin
  SET_LINE_LENGTH (15);
  SET_PAGE_LENGTH (10);
  for I in 1..PAGE_LENGTH loop
    for J in 1..LINE_LENGTH loop
      PUT ("*");
    end loop;
  end loop;
end SET_PAGE_AND_LINE;
```

Listing 16.17 Specifying file structures.

If a value for TO is zero, the lengths are unbounded. This is the default condition for newly opened files.

Information concerning current settings is obtained using the functions LINE_LENGTH and PAGE_LENGTH. Their specifications are

```
LINE_LENGTH (FILE : in FILE_TYPE) return COUNT;
LINE_LENGTH return COUNT; -- used with the default file
```

PAGE_LENGTH has the same parameters and return type.

The value returned is the current setting for maximum line (page) length. Listing 16.17 illustrates the major features of file specification.

(b) Operating on file structures

Once we have defined a file structure, we can then proceed to operate on and within it. Very broadly we can say there are two aspects here: controlling what happens and obtaining system information.

(i) Control operations These fall into three categories:

- Changes to the current position in the file;
- Manually inserting line and page terminators into an output file;
- Moving forward (by lines and/or pages) through an input file.

Procedures SET_COL and SET_LINE are used to change our current position in the file (note that there is no corresponding page procedure). Their specifications are

```
procedure SET_COL (FILE : in FILE_TYPE; TO : in POSITIVE_COUNT);
procedure SET_COL (TO : in POSITIVE_COUNT); -- default file
```

SET_LINE has the same parameters.

Assume that we are currently at page 1, line 1, column 1 of the default file. Then the statement

> SET_LINE (23);

will move us to line 23, column 1 of page 1. If this is followed by

> SET_COL (15);

the current position now becomes page 1, line 23, column 15. Now use the statement

> SET_LINE (25);

This moves us to line 25, at (and note this well) column 1 of that line.

Be aware that these numbers only move us in a forward direction through the file. So if we were now to invoke the statement

> SET_LINE (10);

we do not go back to line 10 of the current page. Instead we would find ourselves at line 10, column 1 of the next page; that is, page 2. Likewise, following this with

> SET_COL (14);

takes us to column 15 of line 1, page 2. Applying

> SET_COL (10);

would move us to column 10, line 1 of page 3.

Procedures NEW_LINE and NEW_PAGE are used manually to insert terminators into output files. Their specifications are

```
procedure NEW_LINE (FILE : in FILE_TYPE; SPACING : in POSITIVE_COUNT :=1);
procedure NEW_LINE (SPACING : in POSITIVE_COUNT :=1);

procedure NEW_PAGE (FILE : in FILE_TYPE);
procedure NEW_PAGE;
```

Note an important difference between these two procedures: we can output as many line terminators per statement as we like, but only one page terminator. To output three line terminators to the default file we write

```
NEW_LINE (3);
```

but to output three page terminators we have to use

```
NEW_PAGE;
NEW_PAGE;
NEW_PAGE;
```

(or its equivalent).

When reading information from an input file we can move ('skip') forward lines or pages using SKIP_LINE and SKIP_PAGE. Their declarations are similar to NEW_LINE and NEW_PAGE. Thus

```
SKIP_LINE (5);
```

moves us forward by five lines, to column 1 of that line. Similarly, SKIP_PAGE moves us forward to line 1, column 1 of the next page. This, and the other points discussed above, are illustrated in Listing 16.18.

(ii) Query operations These allow us to obtain file information concerning:

- The current position;
- Terminators in input files.

To find our current position in a file we use the functions COL, LINE and PAGE. Their specifications are virtually identical; only that for COL is given here:

```
function COL (FILE : in FILE_TYPE) return POSITIVE_COUNT;
```

560 Data input-output

```
with TEXT_IO;            use TEXT_IO;
procedure MOVE_THROUGH_FILE is
  EXAMPLE_FILE    :    FILE_TYPE;
  OUTPUT_CHAR     :    CHARACTER      := 'Q';
  INPUT_CHAR      :    CHARACTER      := ' ';
  package COUNT_IO is new INTEGER_IO (TEXT_IO.COUNT);
  use COUNT_IO;
begin
  -- create the ouput file
  CREATE (EXAMPLE_FILE, OUT_FILE, "EXAMPLE.TXT");
  -- set the column and line in the file
  SET_LINE (EXAMPLE_FILE, 15);
  SET_COL (EXAMPLE_FILE, 23);
  -- write a character to this position
  PUT (EXAMPLE_FILE, OUTPUT_CHAR);
  -- reset EXAMPLE_FILE to an IN_FILE
  RESET (EXAMPLE_FILE, IN_FILE);
  -- read the character written to it
  SET_LINE (EXAMPLE_FILE, 15);
  SET_COL (EXAMPLE_FILE, 23);
  GET (EXAMPLE_FILE, INPUT_CHAR);
  -- print out the character found, to the screen
  PUT ("The character read from EXAMPLE_FILE was ");
  PUT (INPUT_CHAR);
  -- move to a new line on the screen
  NEW_LINE;
  -- text output to the screen will now appear on the next line
  PUT ("This is the next line");
  -- move on 3 lines in the output file
  NEW_LINE (3);
  PUT_LINE ("This is three lines from the text above");
  -- move to the next page and output some text
  NEW_PAGE;
  PUT_LINE ("This is the first line of the next page");
  -- we can only move on one page at a time. To move two pages
  -- call NEW_PAGE twice
  NEW_PAGE;
  NEW_PAGE;
  PUT_LINE ("This is the first line of the 4th page of output to the screen");
end MOVE_THROUGH_FILE;
```

Listing 16.18 Moving through a file structure.

This function returns the current column number. LINE and PAGE perform the same function for the current line and page numbers.

To identify the terminators we use the functions END_OF_LINE, END_OF_PAGE and END_OF_FILE. The specification for END_OF_LINE is

```
function END_OF_LINE (FILE : in FILE_TYPE) return BOOLEAN;
function END_OF_LINE return BOOLEAN; -- default file
```

The other two functions have similar specifications. A typical application is for the control of reading operations, as in

```
while not END_OF_LINE loop
  GET (COUNT);
  NEW_COUNT := NEW_COUNT + COUNT;
end loop;
```

Listing 16.19 demonstrates these and related topics.

```
with TEXT_IO;            use TEXT_IO;
procedure OPERATE_ON_FILE is
  EXAMPLE_FILE   :   FILE_TYPE;
  INPUT_CHAR     :   CHARACTER;
  CHAR_COUNT     :   NATURAL      :=  0;
  package COUNT_IO is new INTEGER_IO (TEXT_IO.COUNT);
  use COUNT_IO;
  package NATURAL_IO is new INTEGER_IO (NATURAL);
  use NATURAL_IO;
begin
-- create the ouput file. Do not give it an external name (i.e. the
-- file is only temporary).
  CREATE (EXAMPLE_FILE, OUT_FILE, "");
-- set the column and line
  SET_LINE (EXAMPLE_FILE, 15);
  SET_COL (EXAMPLE_FILE, 23);
-- output the page, column and line numbers, to the screen
  PUT ("The current position is line ");
  PUT (LINE (EXAMPLE_FILE), 0);
  PUT (", page ");
  PUT (PAGE (EXAMPLE_FILE), 0);
  PUT (", column ");
  PUT (COL (EXAMPLE_FILE), 0);
  PUT_LINE (" of EXAMPLE_FILE");
-- move on in the file, remember we can only move forward
  SET_LINE (EXAMPLE_FILE, 10);
  SET_COL (EXAMPLE_FILE, 14);
-- output the page position to the screen
  PUT ("The current page position is ");
  PUT (PAGE (EXAMPLE_FILE), 0);
  PUT_LINE (" in EXAMPLE_FILE");
-- close EXAMPLE_FILE
  CLOSE (EXAMPLE_FILE);
-- read in characters from the keyboard until the end of the line.
-- Output the number of characters read.
  PUT_LINE ("Please enter some characters followed by return");
  PUT ("=> ");
  while not END_OF_LINE loop
    GET (INPUT_CHAR);
    CHAR_COUNT := CHAR_COUNT + 1;
  end loop;
  PUT ("You entered ");
  PUT (CHAR_COUNT, 0);
  PUT_LINE (" characters");
end OPERATE_ON_FILE;
```

Listing 16.19 Operating on a file structure.

16.4 SEQUENTIAL INPUT–OUTPUT OF MACHINE-READABLE DATA

There are many instances where internal machine data needs to be transferred to or obtained from other devices. Such applications include network communications, distributed databases and remote data stores. Here there is no need to present information in human-readable form – machine representation is perfectly acceptable. The advantage with this method is that we eliminate encoding/decoding operations. Further, this minimizes the number of bits needed, so improving system efficiency.

File information is held as a collection of data objects within some external data store. We are not concerned, in these next sections, about the data storage itself. Our interest lies in the means of writing to and reading from such stores. These operations, it turns out, fall into two groupings: sequential (serial) access and direct access. Here these are treated only at the conceptual level; physical aspects are ignored. How data is moved around the computer is not important. Neither is it relevant whether tape or floppy disk or RAM store is used.

Sequential access, the topic of this section, is nothing new. All PUT and GET operations described earlier use serial write and read techniques. What we will do here is extend this knowledge, in the context of machine-readable data. The basic ideas are illustrated – conceptually – in Fig.16.21.

In all file operations, the first operation is to create the file itself, (a). For sequential I/O this is somewhat like making a book storage box, where each book is a data item. One end of the 'box' is identified as the beginning of the file, (b). All new operations start at this point. Putting an item into the store is defined as a write operation. The first write loads a data item into the first storage space, the second into the next space, the third into ... and so on, (c). Note that there is no idea of the 'box' having numbered store locations. Each data item is loaded in a contiguous manner, that is [A] followed by [B] followed by [C] etc. This, at first, may seem trivial. It is, in fact, a very important point. It means that all information relating to data locations is relative, not absolute. The only fixed reference point in our file system is the beginning of the file. One further note: files must be designated OUT_MODE during writing.

Now close the file, (d), and then reopen it, (e). The next read or write operation will commence at the beginning of the file. A single read, (f), 'copies' the data at the front of the store, in this case data item [A]. Now [B] is designated as the next item to be read out, and so on for successive reads.

Let us go back to the file state shown in (e). Suppose now that instead of reading the file, we carried out further writing operations, (g). In this case the new data item – [D] – replaces all existing file items.

When a sequential file is RESET, operations recommence at the beginning of the file.

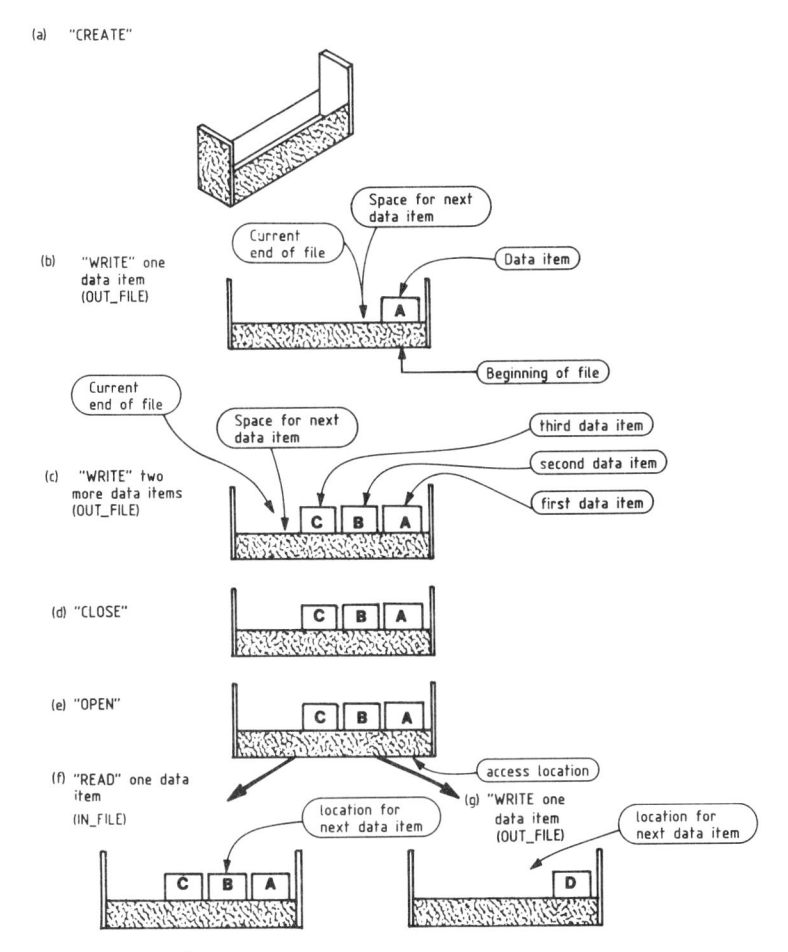

Fig.16.21 Sequential file I/O – basic concepts.

Serial I/O transactions are implemented using the features of package SEQUENTIAL_IO. This is a generic one, its listing, in part, being

```
generic
   type ELEMENT_TYPE is private;
package SEQUENTIAL_IO is
   type FILE_TYPE is limited private;
   type FILE_MODE is (IN_FILE, OUT_FILE);

   procedure READ (FILE : in FILE_TYPE; ITEM : out ELEMENT_TYPE);
   procedure WRITE (FILE : in FILE_TYPE; ITEM : out ELEMENT_TYPE);
```

564   Data input–output

Its instantiation and use is given in Listing 16.20. Note that the data objects to be stored are a simple scalar type.

The major points demonstrated in this section are that:

- All data items must be the same type;
- Data is stored on a first-in first-out basis;
- Reading is non-destructive;
- Writing is destructive (overwrites old data);
- For writing, the file mode must be OUT_FILE;
- For reading, the file mode must be IN_FILE;

16.5   DIRECT INPUT–OUTPUT OF MACHINE-READABLE DATA

In many applications the best way to handle file data is to use the serial input–output approach. When compressing text, for instance, we store information away as a sequence of digital words. Here the sequence is important, rarely individual words. However, there are many times when we need to be able to insert or extract data at specific store locations. For example, suppose that we have a data file which is a list of books on loan. Each data item is a record which contains the book name, borrower name and due-date. Now consider how we normally use this information. 'Is this book out on loan?', 'who has it?', 'when is it due back' are the sort of questions to be answered. So, when we access the data file, our interest concerns specific items of data.

We could handle this using SEQUENTIAL_IO. Unfortunately it has serious limitations in such applications. Remember, locations can only be identified relative to the beginning of the file. Thus, in general, we have to start accesses at the start position. Then we have to work our way through the file until we find the required data. Visualize the time taken to traverse a large database – and the resulting queues of frustrated library customers. The solution to this problem is one which enables us to access file stores directly in a random manner – direct input–output of data. In Ada this is provided by the facilities of package DIRECT_IO.

The basic concept of a direct file store is given in Fig.16.22.

As before, the store can be thought of as a 'box'. Now, though, the box is formed as a set of compartments or slots. Each slot is intended to hold one data item (again, all data items must be the same type). The first slot is designated number 1. This is also called its index value. The current index denotes the slot to be used for the next file access.

When a file is created using DIRECT_IO, the current index is set to 1, (a) in Fig.16.23. Also, the file is opened for use. If we write one data item into the file, it is stored in location 1, (b). The current index is then incremented by 1, setting it to 2. The effects of two more writes are shown in (c). Now

```ada
with TEXT_IO;              use TEXT_IO;
with SEQUENTIAL_IO;
procedure FIRST_SEQ is
  -- Instantiate SEQUENTIAL_IO with type INTEGER;
  package INTEGER_SEQ_IO is new SEQUENTIAL_IO (INTEGER);
  use INTEGER_SEQ_IO;
  -- declare a sequential_file
  TEST_FILE       :      INTEGER_SEQ_IO.FILE_TYPE;
  NEXT_NUM        :      INTEGER;
  package INT_IO is new INTEGER_IO (INTEGER);
begin
  -- create the sequential file
  INTEGER_SEQ_IO.CREATE (TEST_FILE, OUT_FILE, "TRY_SEQ.TXT");
  -- write integers 1 to 10 to the file
  for I in 1..10 loop
    INTEGER_SEQ_IO.WRITE (TEST_FILE, I);
  end loop;
  -- close the file and reopen it as an OUT_FILE again
  INTEGER_SEQ_IO.CLOSE (TEST_FILE);
  INTEGER_SEQ_IO.OPEN (TEST_FILE, OUT_FILE, "TRY_SEQ.TXT");
  -- now write numbers 20 to 30 to the file
  for I in 20..30 loop
    INTEGER_SEQ_IO.WRITE (TEST_FILE, I);
  end loop;
  -- close the file and reopen it as an IN_FILE
  INTEGER_SEQ_IO.CLOSE (TEST_FILE);
  INTEGER_SEQ_IO.OPEN (TEST_FILE, IN_FILE, "TRY_SEQ.TXT");
  -- read its contents and print them to the screen
  PUT_LINE ("The file contains these numbers : ");
  for COUNT in 1..11 loop
    INTEGER_SEQ_IO.READ (TEST_FILE, NEXT_NUM);
    INT_IO.PUT (NEXT_NUM, 3);
  end loop;
  NEW_LINE;
  -- close the file
  INTEGER_SEQ_IO.CLOSE (TEST_FILE);
end FIRST_SEQ;
   -- read the record at this position
      WEATHER_IO.READ (WEATHER_FILE, DAYS_WEATHER);
   -- print its contents to the screen
      PUT ("The maximum temperature on that day was ");
      PUT (DAYS_WEATHER.MAX_TEMPERATURE, 0);
      PUT_LINE (" Centigrade");
      PUT ("The rainfall on that day was ");
      PUT (DAYS_WEATHER.RAINFALL, 0);
      PUT_LINE (" mm");
      PUT ("exit (y/n) ? ");
      GET (EXIT_CHAR);
      SKIP_LINE;
      exit when (EXIT_CHAR = 'y') or (EXIT_CHAR = 'Y');
   end loop;
end LOG_WEATHER;
```

Listing 16.20 File operations using package SEQUENTIAL_IO.

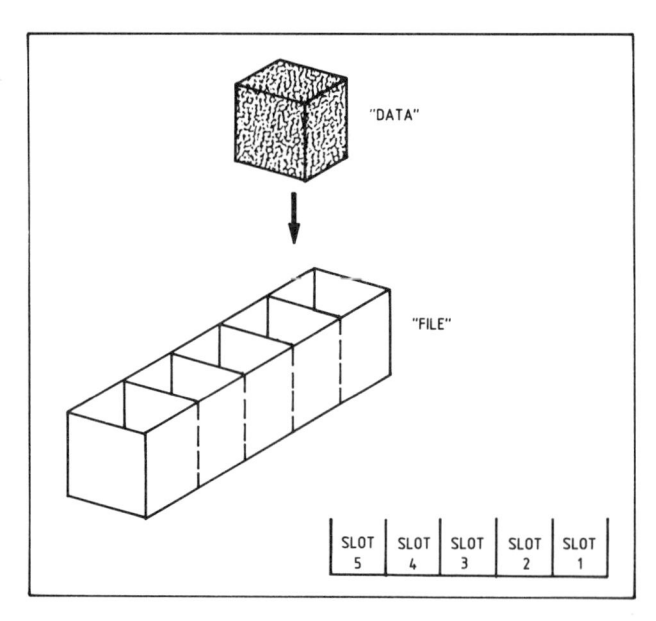

Fig.16.22 Direct file – concept.

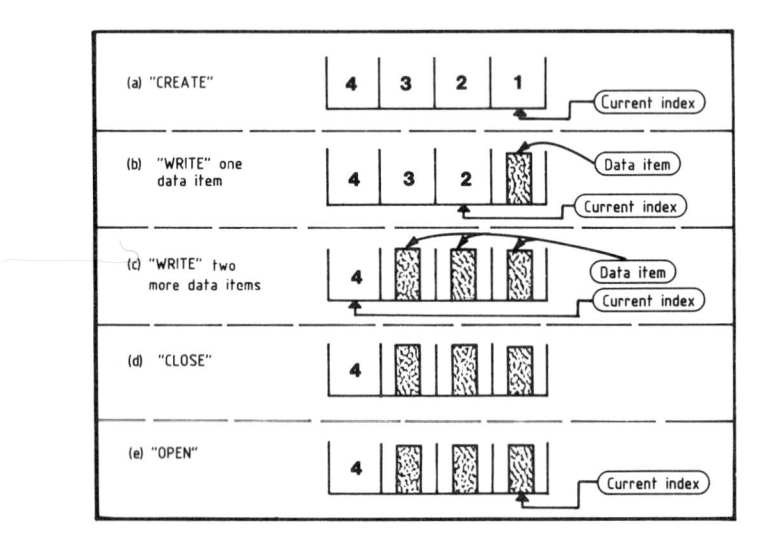

Fig.16.23 Basic direct file operations.

Direct input–output of machine-readable data   567

```
with TEXT_IO;              use TEXT_IO;
with DIRECT_IO;
procedure FIRST_DIRECT is
  -- Instantiate DIRECT_IO with type INTEGER;
  package INTEGER_DIRECT_IO is new DIRECT_IO (INTEGER);
  use INTEGER_DIRECT_IO;
  -- declare a direct file
  TEST_FILE       :   INTEGER_DIRECT_IO.FILE_TYPE;
  NEXT_NUM        :   INTEGER;
  package INT_IO is new INTEGER_IO (INTEGER);
begin
  -- create the direct file
  INTEGER_DIRECT_IO.CREATE (TEST_FILE, OUT_FILE, "TRY_DIRECT.TXT");
  -- write integers 1 to 10 to the file
  for I in 1..10 loop
     INTEGER_DIRECT_IO.WRITE (TEST_FILE, I);
  end loop;
  -- close the file and reopen it as an OUT_FILE again
  INTEGER_DIRECT_IO.CLOSE (TEST_FILE);
  INTEGER_DIRECT_IO.OPEN (TEST_FILE, OUT_FILE, "TRY_DIRECT.TXT");
  -- now write numbers 20 to 30 to the file
  for I in 20..30 loop
     INTEGER_DIRECT_IO.WRITE (TEST_FILE, I);
  end loop;
  -- close the file and reopen it as an IN_FILE
  INTEGER_DIRECT_IO.CLOSE (TEST_FILE);
  INTEGER_DIRECT_IO.OPEN (TEST_FILE, IN_FILE, "TRY_DIRECT.TXT");
  -- read its contents and print them to the screen
  PUT_LINE ("The file contains these numbers : ");
  for COUNT in 1..11 loop
     INTEGER_DIRECT_IO.READ (TEST_FILE, NEXT_NUM);
     INT_IO.PUT (NEXT_NUM, 3);
  end loop;
  NEW_LINE;
  -- close the file
  INTEGER_DIRECT_IO.CLOSE (TEST_FILE);
end FIRST_DIRECT;
```

Listing 16.21 File operations of Listing 16.20, but now using the facilities of package DIRECT_IO.

close the file, (d), and reopen it, (e). Note that the current index is reset to 1.

As shown so far, there is little difference between sequential and direct input–output. To demonstrate this, Listing 16.21 is an abridged form of Listing 16.20, but using the facilities of package DIRECT_IO.

The file is set to IN_FILE and OUT_FILE modes as appropriate. RESET is used for mode changing. This also has the effect of setting the current index value to 1.

The real flexibility of DIRECT_IO is due to two particular features. First, we can set the index value under program control. Second, files can be defined to be of mode IN_OUT. Therefore, we can access store locations at random, performing read and writes as desired. Before demonstrating this, it is worth looking at part of the package specification for DIRECT_IO:

568   Data input–output

```
generic
   type ELEMENT_TYPE is private;
package DIRECT_IO is
   type FILE_TYPE   is limited private;
   type FILE_MODE is (IN_FILE, INOUT_FILE, OUT_FILE);
   type COUNT       is range 0 .. implementation_defined;
   subtype POSITIVE_COUNT is COUNT range 1 .. COUNT'LAST;

   procedure READ (FILE  : in   FILE_TYPE;
                   ITEM  : out  ELEMENT_TYPE;
                   FROM  : in   POSITIVE_COUNT);

   procedure WRITE (FILE : in FILE_TYPE;
                    ITEM : in ELEMENT_TYPE;
                    TO   : in POSITIVE_COUNT);

   procedure SET_INDEX (FILE : in FILE_TYPE; To : in POSITIVE_COUNT);

   function INDEX (FILE : in FILE_TYPE) return POSITIVE_COUNT;
```

POSITIVE_COUNT is used to define the current index value.

From this specification you can see how READ and WRITE designate the data item to be accessed. Moreover, both these procedures are valid for a file of mode INOUT_FILE. The procedure SET_INDEX enables us to set the current index value. Conversely, to find the current index value, we use the function INDEX. These points are illustrated in Listing 16.22, a simple library record for borrowed books.

16.6   LOW-LEVEL INPUT–OUTPUT

Here we consider input–output facilities denoted as 'low level'. Now, in chapter 15 we covered many low-level issues, including access to, and use of, peripheral devices. How then does low-level I/O relate to low-level programming? Remember, what we are striving to achieve is separation of concept from implementation. This is especially true for the applications programmer, who deals essentially with conceptual devices. For this we provide the high-level abstract devices using low-level facilities. But, for low-level I/O, we do recognize that real devices are involved. And, when using such devices, we want to avoid using low-level programming whenever possible. Low-level I/O is a means to that end.

Within the package LOW_LEVEL_IO, two procedures are defined, SEND_CONTROL and RECEIVE_CONTROL. SEND_CONTROL is used to send data out to a device; RECEIVE_CONTROL performs the reverse operation – getting data from a device. Thus, at a high level, programming can be done without needing to know details of the devices.

LOW_LEVEL_IO is hardware specific. As such it is not particularly portable. In fact you may find that your compiler does not implement it.

```ada
with TEXT_IO;            use TEXT_IO;
with DIRECT_IO;
procedure LOG_WEATHER is
  -- define types to hold the maximum temperature (centigrade) and
  -- rainfall (mm) for each day of the week
  subtype DAY_NUM is INTEGER range 1..7;
  subtype TEMPERATURE is INTEGER range -20..120;
  subtype RAINFALL_DEPTH is INTEGER range 0..500;
  type WEATHER_RECORD is
    record
      DAY              :  DAY_NUM;
      MAX_TEMPERATURE  :  TEMPERATURE;
      RAINFALL         :  RAINFALL_DEPTH;
    end record;
  -- Instantiate DIRECT_IO to hold WEATHER_RECORD
  package WEATHER_IO is new DIRECT_IO (WEATHER_RECORD);
  use WEATHER_IO;
  -- declare a DIRECT file and a variable to hold the index into it
  WEATHER_FILE   :  WEATHER_IO.FILE_TYPE;
  CURRENT_INDEX  :  WEATHER_IO.POSITIVE_COUNT;
  -- other variables
  DAYS_WEATHER   :  WEATHER_RECORD;
  DAY            :  DAY_NUM;
  EXIT_CHAR      :  CHARACTER;
  package INT_IO is new INTEGER_IO (INTEGER);
  use INT_IO;
begin
  -- open WEATHER_FILE
  WEATHER_IO.CREATE (WEATHER_FILE, INOUT_FILE, "WEATHER.LOG");
  -- get the readings for the 7 days
  for DAY_COUNT in DAY_NUM loop
    DAYS_WEATHER.DAY := DAY_COUNT;
    PUT ("Enter the Maximum temperature for day ");
    PUT (DAY_COUNT, 0);
    PUT (" : ");
    GET (DAYS_WEATHER.MAX_TEMPERATURE);
    SKIP_LINE;
    PUT ("Enter the Rainfall for day ");
    PUT (DAY_COUNT, 0);
    PUT (" : ");
    GET (DAYS_WEATHER.RAINFALL);
    SKIP_LINE;
  -- write DAYS_WEATHER to WEATHER_FILE, first establishing the index
  -- into the file
    CURRENT_INDEX := WEATHER_IO.POSITIVE_COUNT (DAY_COUNT);
    WEATHER_IO.WRITE (WEATHER_FILE, DAYS_WEATHER, CURRENT_INDEX);
  end loop;
  -- retrieve weather records
  loop
    PUT ("Please enter a day of the week : ");
    GET (DAY);
    SKIP_LINE;
  -- set the index into the file
    CURRENT_INDEX := WEATHER_IO.POSITIVE_COUNT (DAY);
    WEATHER_IO.SET_INDEX (WEATHER_FILE, CURRENT_INDEX);
  -- read the record at this position
    WEATHER_IO.READ (WEATHER_FILE, DAYS_WEATHER);
  -- print its contents to the screen
    PUT ("The maximum temperature on that day was ");
    PUT (DAYS_WEATHER.MAX_TEMPERATURE, 0);
    PUT_LINE (" Centigrade");
    PUT ("The rainfall on that day was ");
    PUT (DAYS_WEATHER.RAINFALL, 0);
    PUT_LINE (" mm");
    PUT ("exit (y/n) ? ");
    GET (EXIT_CHAR);
    SKIP_LINE;
    exit when (EXIT_CHAR = 'y') or (EXIT_CHAR = 'Y');
  end loop;
end LOG_WEATHER;
```

Listing 16.22 A more extensive demonstration of the facilities of package DIRECT_IO.

16.7 EXCEPTIONS IN INPUT–OUTPUT

Exceptions applicable to input-output operations are defined in package IO_EXCEPTIONS. These are:

>STATUS_ERROR
>MODE_ERROR
>NAME_ERROR
>USE_ERROR
>DEVICE_ERROR
>END_ERROR
>DATA_ERROR
>LAYOUT_ERROR

Check your compiler for details of these.

REVIEW

Do you now understand:

- The concepts and methods of creating, opening, closing, resetting and deleting files?
- The essential attributes of files?
- How internal and external files are related, and how to control this relationship?
- The role of package TEXT_IO?
- How to use the features of the generic packages (INTEGER_IO, FLOAT_IO, FIXED_IO and ENUMERATION_IO) contained within TEXT_IO?
- How to exchange human-readable data, using characters and strings, with external devices?
- How to format readable text?
- How to format text files as pages, lines and columns?
- How to input/output machine-readable data using the facilities of packages SEQUENTIAL_IO and DIRECT_IO?

Chapter Seventeen
Program structure and compilation issues

Much of this chapter is concerned with recapitulation and consolidation of knowledge. In particular, it deals with the structure of Ada programs and associated compilation issues. It brings together in one place many aspects covered throughout the text. If you intend to progress to advanced Ada programming you must fully grasp its content.

A real Ada program will be constructed using many different types of program units. The purpose of this chapter is to:

- Review the details of the software components of Ada;
- Define those which are compilable units;
- Review the context clause;
- Define and describe the library and secondary compilation units of the language;
- Show how these relate to, and depend on, each other;
- Illustrate the use of subunits – separate compilation;
- Demonstrate compilation dependencies between program units;
- Outline the essential aspects of elaboration;
- Illustrate the use and benefits of the renaming of program entities.

17.1 INTRODUCTION – COMPILATION UNITS

A compiler is a program that converts (translates) high-level source code into machine code. The process of translation is called compilation. In our case the high-level code will be written in Ada. By contrast, the machine (or object) code output cannot be defined so clearly. It depends both on your software development system and the machine for which the software is destined (the target). If your programs are compiled and executed on the same machine (a host development system) then machine code details are likely to be unimportant. In this chapter we are concerned with the structuring of Ada program units so that they can be compiled – that is, compilation units.

An Ada program can be built as a single compilation unit. This approach is very unlikely to be used in real (as opposed to teaching) applications. We

572 Program structure and compilation issues

```
            ┌─────────────────┐
            │ COMPILATION UNITS│
            └────────┬────────┘
              ┌─────┴─────┐
    ┌─────────────────┐  ┌─────────────────┐
    │ CONTEXT CLAUSE  │  │ CONTEXT CLAUSE  │
    │ LIBRARY UNIT    │  │ SECONDARY UNIT  │
    └─────────────────┘  └─────────────────┘
```

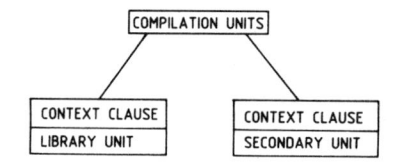

Fig.17.1 Ada compilation units.

spelt out the reasons for this in chapter 7; re-read this if in doubt. Practical programs will, without a doubt, be constructed using a collection of program units. Further, from the way that Ada works, each unit must – at some stage of program development – be compiled. Thus, the complete program is made up of a number of compilation units. But what are the compilation units of Ada?

In Ada we have two types of compilation unit, library and secondary (Fig.17.1).

Strictly speaking, a compilation unit is either a library unit preceded by a context clause or a secondary unit also preceded by a context clause. From now on take the inclusion of the context clauses for granted. The important point to realize is that only certain types of Ada program units are compilable. Let us now identify them and their characteristics.

First take the library unit. This comes in five forms, Fig.17.2a. Fundamentally, we use library units to define the resources provided in our software system. When we compile such a unit it is automatically inserted into a resource facility called the 'Ada program library'. It then becomes available for general use within our Ada system (in the same way that a book can be borrowed by library users). Potential users of the program library see only library – and not secondary – units. Further, the library unit provides the interfacing between client programs and the resource implementation, Fig.17.2b. This has, of course, been explicitly demonstrated throughout the text with the use of package specifications. It should also be obvious that all library units must have unique names.

A secondary unit houses implementation code. It consists of subprogram bodies, package bodies and *subunits*. More will be said about the subunit later. You can see that, for the subprogram body, there is some overlap between library and secondary units (we will return to this point in a moment).

Now the context clause. As noted above, each compilation unit must contain one such clause. Its purpose is simple – to specify any units of the program library used by a compilation unit. It is possible, of course, that no use is made of the library. In this case the context clause, Fig.17.3, is a null one.

If we do wish to access something in the library, we use the **with** clause.

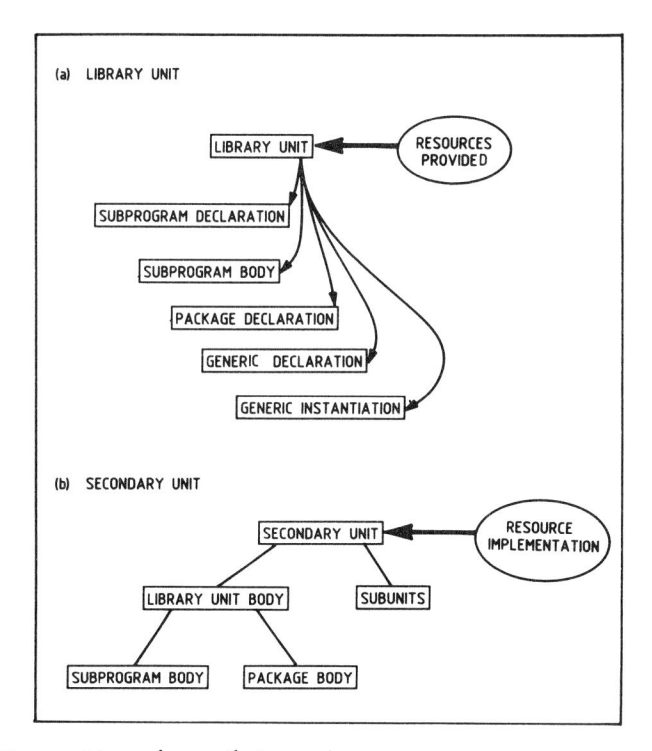

Fig.17.2 Composition of compilation units.

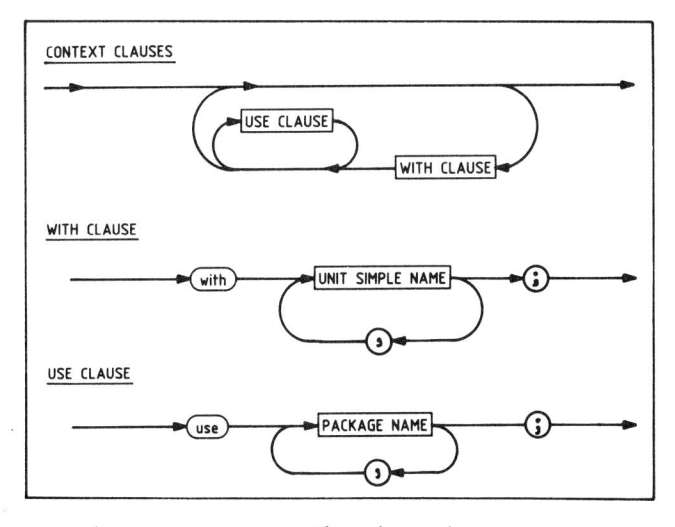

Fig.17.3 Syntax diagram – context, **with** and **use** clauses.

You can view this as a connecting link between a compilation unit and those units named inside it using **with**. At compilation time, the compiler uses the information of the **with** clause to:

- Search for each named item, and confirm its presence in the system;
- Discern its interfacing structure and requirements;
- Make it visible for use within the unit being compiled.

The **use** clause is quite different in function. Its purpose is to make directly visible identifiers within packages named in the **with** clause. Note this well. The only names allowed in **use** clauses are those mentioned in the **with** clause – and they must be packages.

Note, by the way, that blocks are not compilation units. Therefore anything nested within a block – such as a package – cannot be a compilation unit.

17.2 LIBRARY UNITS

A library unit, as stated earlier, may be one of the following:

- Subprogram declaration;
- Subprogram body;
- Package declaration;
- Generic declaration;
- Generic instantiation.

Let us review these in turn, starting with the subprogram.

(a) The subprogram as a library unit

We'll assess the subprogram declaration and body together because of the subprogram definition Fig.17.4.

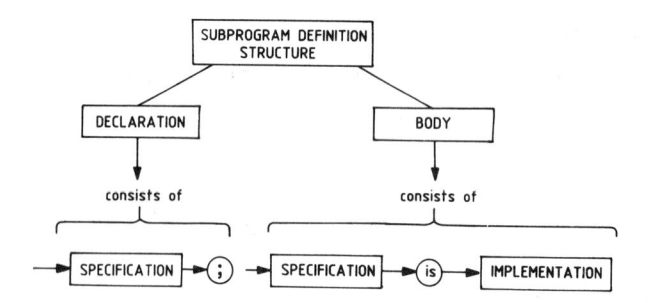

Fig.17.4 Subprogram definition.

Library units 575

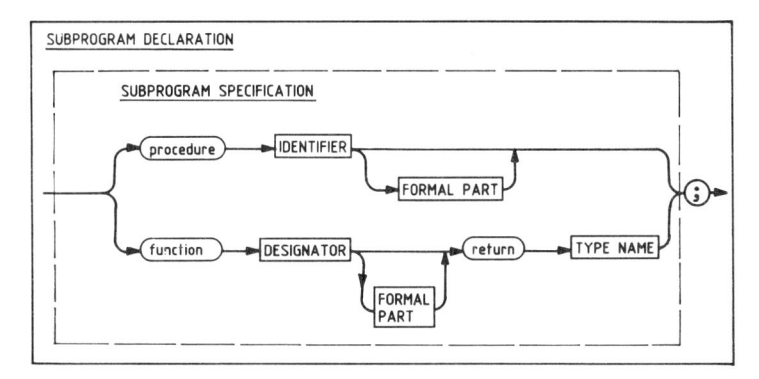

[Figure: Syntax diagram showing SUBPROGRAM DECLARATION containing SUBPROGRAM SPECIFICATION with two branches: procedure → IDENTIFIER → FORMAL PART, and function → DESIGNATOR → FORMAL PART → return → TYPE NAME, ending with ;]

Fig.17.5 Syntax diagram – subprogram declaration.

```
procedure INC (VALUE    : in out INTEGER);
```

Listing 17.1 Example of a library compilation unit – subprogram declaration.

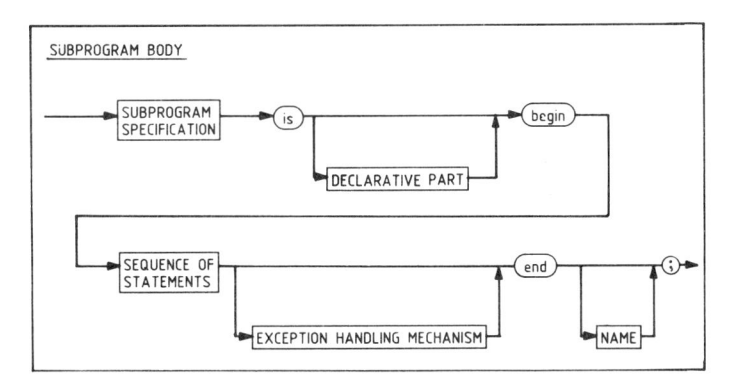

[Figure: Syntax diagram showing SUBPROGRAM BODY containing SUBPROGRAM SPECIFICATION → is → DECLARATIVE PART → begin → SEQUENCE OF STATEMENTS → EXCEPTION HANDLING MECHANISM → end → NAME → ;]

Fig.17.6 Syntax diagram – subprogram body.

The declaration consists of the subprogram specification terminated by the semi-colon delimiter. The body, which contains the implementation code, repeats this specification. Thus we always have to have a subprogram body. The declaration is optional. In such a case the body acts as its declaration.

First, the declaration. The syntax diagram for this is given in Fig.17.5.

An example subprogram declaration compilation unit is given in Listing 17.1.

A subprogram body has the structure specified by the syntax diagram of Fig.17.6.

```
procedure DEC (VALUE    : in out INTEGER) is
begin
  VALUE := VALUE - 1;
end DEC;
```

Listing 17.2 Example of a library compilation unit – subprogram body.

An example of a subprogram body is given in Listing 17.2. Remember, this also acts as its declaration if a separate declaration has not previously been made.

If we write and compile a subprogram declaration, this becomes the subprogram library unit. If we later compile the corresponding body, that body becomes a secondary unit. However, if we do not compile a declaration but go straight to the body, that body becomes the library unit (it is also taken to be a secondary unit).

Be careful if you first compile a subprogram declaration and then the corresponding body. In this case the specification in the body must completely conform to that of the declaration (the text in each case must be identical).

(b) The package declaration as a library unit

A package declaration consists of its specification followed by the semi-colon delimiter, Fig.17.7.

This is the same definition as that of the subprogram (Ada is consistent in its definitions declarations, but not with those for bodies). Listing 17.3 illustrates the package declaration as a compilation unit.

(c) The generic declaration as a library unit

A generic declaration is defined to be a generic specification terminated by a semi-colon. Its syntax is given in Fig.17.8, whilst an example compilation unit is shown in Listing 17.4.

Observe that the declaration does not include implementation code. This is contained within the body of the subprogram (or package) specification listed in the generic specification.

(d) The generic instantiation as a library unit

You may, at first, wonder why a generic instantiation is treated as a library unit. In fact the reason for this is quite logical. Once a generic subprogram (package) is instantiated it becomes exactly the same as a normal subprogram (package) specification. And these normal subprograms or packages are defined

[Syntax diagram]

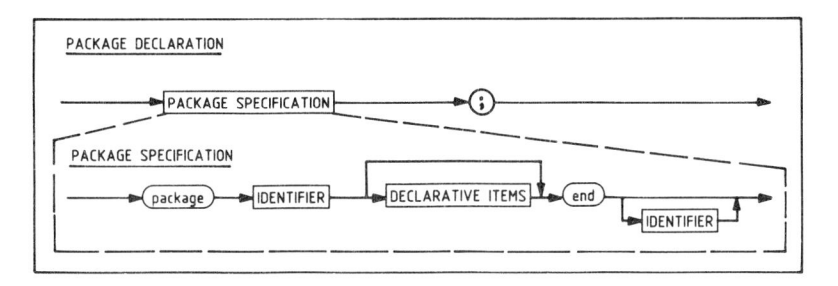

Fig.17.7 Syntax diagram – package declaration.

```
package TEMPERATURE is
  -- Declare constant values for safe working values
  SAFE_MAXIMUM   :   constant   :=  150;
  SAFE_MINIMUM   :   constant   :=   -5;
end TEMPERATURE;
```

Listing 17.3 Example of a compilation library unit – package declaration.

[Syntax diagram]

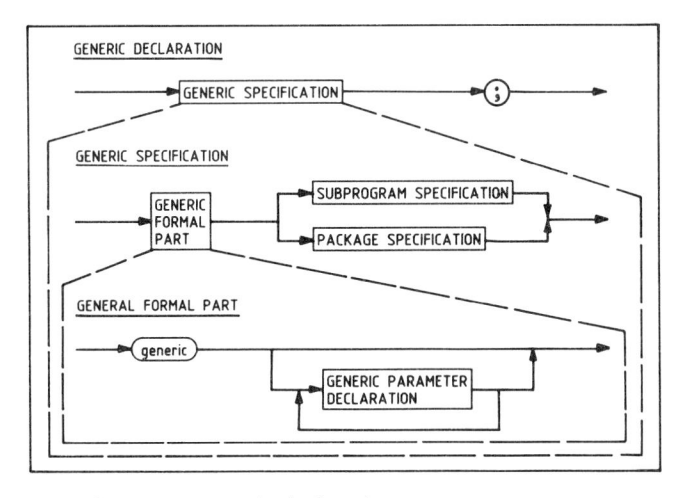

Fig.17.8 Syntax diagram – generic declaration.

```
generic
  type SOME_TYPE is (<>);
procedure SWAP (A, B     : in out SOME_TYPE);
```

Listing 17.4 Example of a library compilation unit – generic declaration.

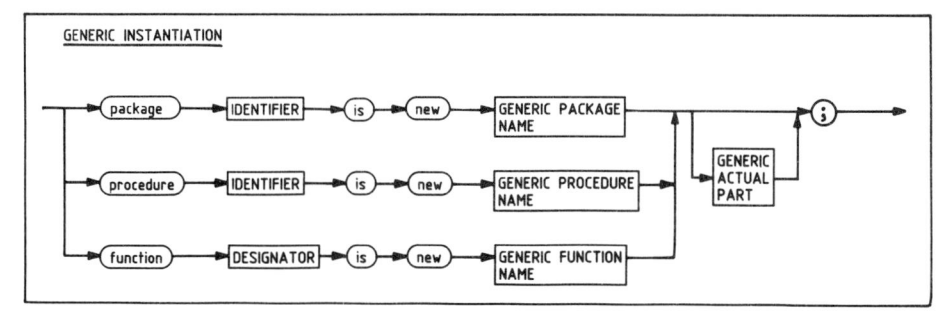

Fig.17.9 Syntax diagram – generic instantiation.

```
with TEXT_IO;
with SWAP;
procedure SWAP_INT is new SWAP (INTEGER);
```

Listing 17.5 Example of a library compilation unit – generic instantiation.

to be library units. The syntax of the generic instantiation is given in Fig.17.9, an example compilation unit being that of Listing 17.5.

17.3 SECONDARY UNITS

Secondary compilation units consist of subprogram bodies, package bodies and subunits. Remember, a secondary unit supplies the actual implementation details. Such a unit must have some related program unit – more on this under compilation dependencies. Before reviewing these units, a few points need discussing.

First, suppose you are presented with the code for the body of a generic subprogram or package. Would you be able to distinguish it from a normal subprogram or package? The answer is no. Thus the body of a generic unit is logically a secondary unit.

Second – to reinforce a point – a subprogram body does not need a separate declaration. But if it is declared separately, then the body becomes a secondary unit.

(a) The subprogram body as a secondary unit

The subprogram body corresponding to the declaration of Listing 17.1 is shown in Listing 17.6.

```
procedure INC (VALUE     : in out INTEGER) is
begin
   VALUE := VALUE + 1;
end INC;
```

Listing 17.6 Example of a secondary compilation unit – subprogram body (the related library unit is Listing 17.1).

```
procedure SWAP (A, B     : in out SOME_TYPE) is
   C              :        SOME_TYPE;
begin
   C := A;
   A := B;
   B := C;
end SWAP;
```

Listing 17.7 Example of a secondary compilation unit – procedure body for a subprogram specified in a generic declaration (the related library unit is Listing 17.4).

Listing 17.7 presents the code for the body of the generic subprogram specified in the generic declaration of Listing 17.4.

(b) The package body as a secondary unit

A package body cannot exist in isolation – there must be a separate, related package declaration. However, the converse is not true. We can have package declarations without the need for a corresponding body. Once more, note that this can never be the case for a subprogram. The syntax of the package body is defined in Fig.17.10. Listing 17.8 carries the code for the package body which matches the package declaration of Listing 17.3.

(c) Subunits

Subunits are, in themselves, nothing new, Fig.17.11 (though note that one of the subunits is a task body).

What is different is the way in which these are used (this will be discussed later). They enable us to compile separately bodies of program units which are declared within other compilation units. Let us illustrate this by comparing program compilation using two approaches: a simple 'normal' one and one using the subunit (Fig.17.12).

Fig.17.12(a) outlines the structure of a compilation unit which should be

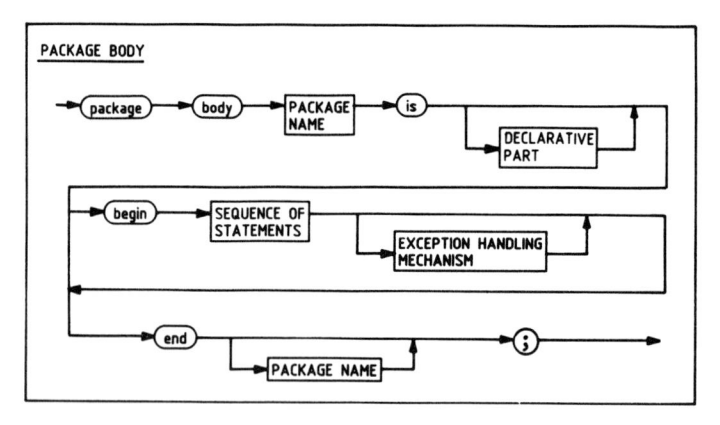

Fig.17.10 Syntax diagram – package body.

```
with TEXT_IO;
package body TEMPERATURE is
begin
   TEXT_IO.PUT_LINE ("Package Temperature elaborated");
end TEMPERATURE;
```

Listing 17.8 Example of a secondary unit – the package body (the related library unit is Listing 17.3).

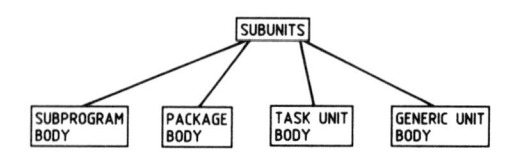

Fig.17.11 Types of subunit.

Secondary units 581

```
┌─────────────────────────────┬─────────────────────────────┐
│  COMPILATION UNIT A         │  COMPILATION UNIT B         │
│  ┌───────────────────────┐  │  ┌───────────────────────┐  │
│  │ Procedure ALPHA is    │  │  │ Procedure ALPHA is    │  │
│  │   ┌─────────────┐     │  │  │   ┌─────┐             │  │
│  │   │ PROCEDURE   │     │  │  │   │BODY │             │  │
│  │   │ BETA        │     │  │  │   │STUB │             │  │
│  │   └─────────────┘     │  │  │   │ OF  │             │  │
│  │                       │  │  │   │BETA │             │  │
│  │ begin                 │  │  │   └─────┘             │  │
│  │   .                   │  │  │                       │  │
│  │   .                   │  │  │ begin                 │  │
│  │   CALL_BETA;          │  │  │   .                   │  │
│  │   .                   │  │  │   .                   │  │
│  │ end ALPHA;            │  │  │   CALL_BETA;          │  │
│  └───────────────────────┘  │  │   .                   │  │
│                             │  │ end ALPHA;            │  │
│                             │  └───────────────────────┘  │
│                             │                             │
│                             │  COMPILATION UNIT C         │
│                             │  ┌───────────────────────┐  │
│                             │  │   ┌─────────┐         │  │
│                             │  │   │ SUBUNIT │         │  │
│                             │  │   │ BETA    │         │  │
│                             │  │   └─────────┘         │  │
│                             │  └───────────────────────┘  │
│                             │                             │
│ (a) Normal program structure│ (b) Program structure using │
│                             │     a subunit               │
└─────────────────────────────┴─────────────────────────────┘
```

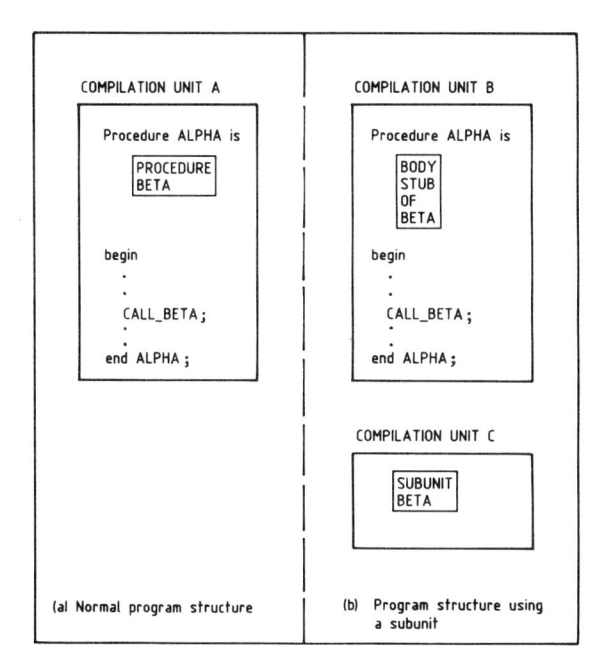

Fig.17.12 Compilation units – the role of the subunit.

well and truly familiar to you. Inside this compilation unit – procedure ALPHA – we declare and use a procedure BETA. Now redo this using the subunit approach, Fig.17.12(b). Here the compilation unit B carries out exactly the same function as A. That is, their executable statements – those between **begin** and **end** – are identical. However, in compilation unit B we have replaced the procedure BETA by a *body stub* of BETA. This, essentially, is the declaration of the procedure. However, it does not hold the implementation code – that is contained within a new compilation unit, C, defined to be a subunit. Procedure ALPHA is called the parent unit of BETA. The syntax for a body stub is given in Fig.17.13 and that for a subunit in Fig.17.14.

For example, we have, in outline form,

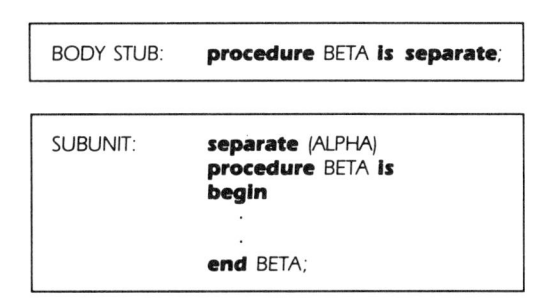

```
┌──────────────────────────────────────────────┐
│  BODY STUB:    procedure BETA is separate;   │
└──────────────────────────────────────────────┘

┌──────────────────────────────────────────────┐
│  SUBUNIT:      separate (ALPHA)              │
│                procedure BETA is             │
│                begin                         │
│                   .                          │
│                end BETA;                     │
└──────────────────────────────────────────────┘
```

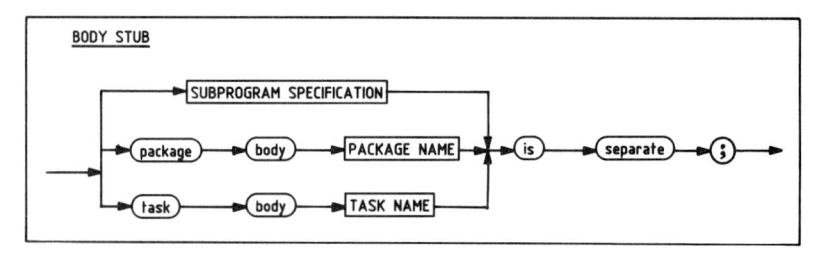

Fig.17.13 Syntax diagram – body stub.

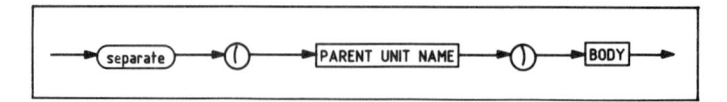

Fig.17.14 Syntax diagram – subunit.

```
with TEXT_IO;
procedure ALPHA is
  procedure BETA is separate;
begin
  TEXT_IO.PUT_LINE ("Calling body stub BETA");
  BETA;
end ALPHA;
```

Listing 17.9 Example of the use of a body stub.

```
separate (ALPHA)
procedure BETA is
begin
  TEXT_IO.PUT_LINE ("This is the body stub BETA");
end BETA;
```

Listing 17.10 Subunit example – the related parent unit is given in Listing 17.9.

These aspects are illustrated in Listings 17.9 and 17.10.

This subject will be discussed further under the topic of Ada program development. For now just remember one – most important – point. Subunits allow us to compile separately bodies which have been declared within other compilation units. Note this phrase well – declared within other compilation units.

You can see that the other secondary unit types have corresponding library units. This is not the case for the subunit – this has a parent unit. The parent unit could be a library unit, for instance a subprogram body. Alternatively it could be a secondary unit, as with a subprogram body compiled after its declaration.

17.4 COMPILATION DEPENDENCIES AND ORDER

17.4.1 General aspects

How do we define the order in which the different units should be compiled? To answer that, we need to consider another factor. How does the compilation of any one unit depend on the compilation of the others?

Four forms of dependency can be defined, Fig.17.15. At the highest level we have the **with** clause. This can be used in both library and secondary units (e.g. a package declaration and a package body). A unit which includes this clause thus depends on those units named in the clause (which, remember, must be library units). Clearly these library units have to be compiled before the importing unit is compiled.

```
LIBRARY UNIT ──────▶ with
LIBRARY UNIT ──────▶ SECONDARY UNIT
PARENT UNIT ───────▶ SUBUNIT
SECONDARY UNIT ────▶ SECONDARY UNIT
```

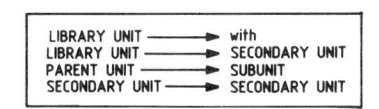

Fig.17.15 Compilation dependencies.

Next consider where a program unit consists of a library unit and a secondary unit. In this case the secondary unit depends on its related library unit. Therefore the library unit must be compiled first.

Third, take the use of subunits. It has been shown how the subunit depends on its parent unit. Therefore the parent must be compiled first.

The final case is where a secondary unit depends on a secondary unit. For instance, a package body A could house a package declaration B which has a separate body. Package body B is thus another secondary unit. It is clear that this secondary unit depends on package A, which is also a secondary unit.

Compilation dependencies can become very complex. Let us justify this using two simple examples.

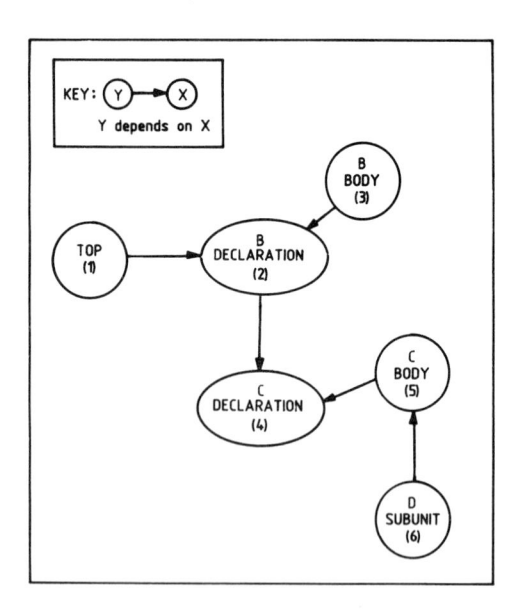

Fig.17.16 Compilation dependency – Example 1.

EXAMPLE 1:

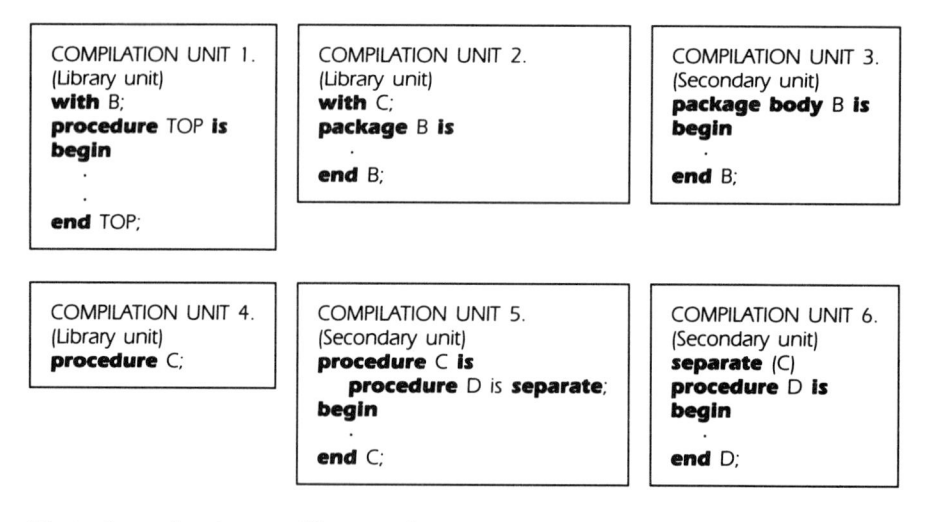

```
COMPILATION UNIT 1.
(Library unit)
with B;
procedure TOP is
begin
   .
   .
end TOP;
```

```
COMPILATION UNIT 2.
(Library unit)
with C;
package B is
   .
   .
end B;
```

```
COMPILATION UNIT 3.
(Secondary unit)
package body B is
begin
   .
   .
end B;
```

```
COMPILATION UNIT 4.
(Library unit)
procedure C;
```

```
COMPILATION UNIT 5.
(Secondary unit)
procedure C is
   procedure D is separate;
begin
   .
   .
end C;
```

```
COMPILATION UNIT 6.
(Secondary unit)
separate (C)
procedure D is
begin
   .
   .
end D;
```

Their dependencies are illustrated in Fig.17.16.

Here procedure TOP is the main program. It can be seen that the key compilation unit is the declaration of procedure C – this must be compiled first. After this we have several options for the order of compilation, for example:

Compilation dependencies and order

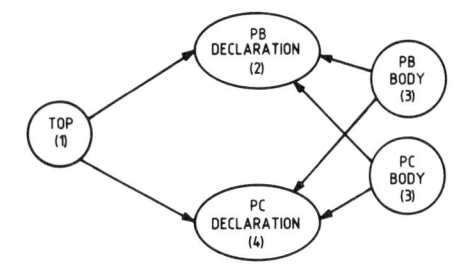

Fig.17.17 Compilation dependencies – Example 2.

$$4 \to 2 \to 5 \to 6 \to 3 \to 1$$
$$4 \to 2 \to 1 \to 3 \to 5 \to 6$$
$$4 \to 5 \to 2 \to 1 \to 3 \to 6$$
$$4 \to 5 \to 6 \to 2 \to 1 \to 3$$

and so on.

EXAMPLE 2:

```
COMPILATION UNIT 1.
(Library unit)
with PB, PC;
procedure TOP is
begin
    .
    .
    .
end TOP;
```

```
COMPILATION UNIT 2.
(Library unit)
package PB is
    .
    .
end PB;
```

```
COMPILATION UNIT 3.
(Secondary unit)
with PC;
package body PB is
being
    .
    .
end PB;
```

```
COMPILATION UNIT 4.
(Library unit)
package PC is
    .
    .
end PC;
```

```
COMPILATION UNIT 5.
(Secondary unit)
with PB;
package body PC is
begin
    .
    .
end PC;
```

Their dependencies are shown in Fig.17.17.

Here the main program TOP **withs** packages PB and PC. Package PB uses resources from the body of PC. Likewise, PC uses resources provided by PB. Now, the two packages' declarations cannot simultaneously call on each other's resources. That is, PB specification cannot **with** PC while specification PC **withs** PB. But the bodies can. From this you can see that either PB or PC declaration can be compiled first – it doesn't matter. They must, though, be

586 Program structure and compilation issues

the first two units to be compiled, leading to the following valid declaration orders:

$$2 \rightarrow 4 \rightarrow 1 \rightarrow 3 \rightarrow 5$$
$$2 \rightarrow 4 \rightarrow 3 \rightarrow 5 \rightarrow 1$$
$$4 \rightarrow 2 \rightarrow 1 \rightarrow 5 \rightarrow 3$$
$$4 \rightarrow 2 \rightarrow 3 \rightarrow 5 \rightarrow 1$$

etc. We strongly recommend that mutual dependencies are avoided wherever possible.

17.4.2 Dependencies involving generic units

Recompiling generic units may produce unpleasant surprises if you aren't fully familiar with your compiler. Consider the following situation. We declare a generic procedure SWAP:

```
generic
    type SOME_TYPE is (<>);
procedure SWAP (A, B : in out SOME_TYPE);
```

We then form the subprogram body and compile it as a secondary unit:

```
procedure SWAP (A, B: in out SOME_TYPE) is
    C : SOME_TYPE;
begin
    C := A;
    A := B;
    B := C;
end SWAP;
```

At some stage this is instantiated in another program unit:

```
with SWAP;
procedure INTEGER_SWAP is new SWAP (DIGIT_1, DIGIT_2);
procedure CHARACTER_SWAP is new SWAP (CHAR_A, CHAR_B);
```

Now it is decided to amend the code of the body:

```
begin
   C := A;
   A := B;
   B := C;
   PUT_LINE ("Swap done");
end SWAP;
```

The question is: what units have to be recompiled? The body of SWAP must, of course, be submitted to the compiler. And, if this was a normal body, we would only have to relink the code. But for the body of a generic unit, this may not be the case. It depends on whether the compiler generates actual object code for each instantiation. If this is the case, the unit containing the instantiation must be recompiled. And suppose that this happens to be, say, a package declaration which has dependencies, and these in turn have further dependencies. What then? The message here is: be cautious in the use of generic units.

17.4.3 Pragma INLINE

Two overheads are incurred when using subprograms: time and data storage (memory) space. The time penalty occurs because, when a subprogram is invoked (called):

- The current state of the computer system is saved;
- Parameter information is set up for the subprogram;
- Its code is then activated.

On its completion, the system has to be restored to its original state (i.e. the state prior to invocation). The storage penalty is caused by the need to provide a temporary store to:

- Save system information;
- Hold parameter data.

Lack of storage is not normally a problem except in small – typically microcontroller – systems. It is especially troublesome when deep nesting of subprograms is done; we may well run out of RAM space. However, time is a different matter. Whenever our programs must produce responses within short timescales (hard, fast real-time applications), the time overhead may be excessive. The way we get round the problem is quite simple. At the object code level we don't use the call mechanism – there is no branching to the subprogram code. Instead, this code follows on in sequence from that which precedes it. If we use the subprogram a second time, then the subprogram object code is once more inserted at that point. You can see that we are trading off program object code size against execution speed. The operation described here is called inline expansion.

At the source code level, that is the Ada code, we use the name of the subprogram in the usual way. However, to tell the compiler that we wish to use inline expansion, the pragma INLINE in used. Its format is

> **pragma** INLINE (NAME_OF_SUBPROGRAM);

INLINE can also be used with generic subprograms.

IMPORTANT: You cannot tell if inline expansion occurs just by inspecting the Ada code where the subprogram is called.

What are the compilation issues associated with the use of pragma INLINE? Suppose we change the body of the subprogram defined by the pragma. We have to recompile the body of course. And, without the pragma, that would be that. Now, however, we must recompile each and every program unit that uses this subprogram – otherwise the inline code will not be updated.

17.4.4 A comment

From these examples it should be obvious that keeping track of compilation units is not a simple task. Doing it manually in a small project is feasible but difficult. For a large project it becomes a major task in its own right. And it is an error-prone one. Now add in the problems caused when changes are made to a program. We have to recompile the affected unit – and all those that depend on it. Take even the simple case of Fig.17.16. A change to compilation unit 4 means that it and all the other units have to be recompiled. In many applications this could result in a massive program recompilation effort. So, for professional Ada programming, the very minimum requirement is a good program 'make' facility. This will automatically invoke compilations and linkages in the event of source file changes.

17.5 DECLARATION AND ELABORATION

17.5.1 Background

The LRM defines elaboration to be 'the process by which a declaration achieves its effect'. In simple terms, elaboration can be viewed as the execution of declarations. Unfortunately, this simple definition hides the extreme complexity of the elaboration issue. Our purpose here is to give an insight into elaboration to lay the foundations for advanced work. While reading this section always keep one point in mind: elaboration takes place when the program is executed, not during compilation. Program malfunctions due to elaboration errors are some of the hardest to track down. You have been warned.

To gain a better understanding of elaboration, a review of declarations is required. More precisely, we need to define the following:

- Declaration;
- Declarative item;
- Declarative part;
- Declarative region.

17.5.2 Declaration aspects

(a) Declaration

The Oxford Dictionary of Computing states: 'A declaration introduces an entity for part of the program, giving it a name and establishing its static properties.' For 'entity', read 'item' in Ada.

(b) Declarative item

A declarative item is one which is named by a declaration. Within Ada there are many different items, including:

(i) Objects   (ii) Numbers   (iii) Types   (iv) Subtypes
(v) Subprograms   (vi) Packages   (vii) Tasks   (viii) Generics
(ix) Exceptions   (x) Generic instantiations

Each item has a specific form of declaration.

(c) Declarative part

A declarative part is a section of the program which contains declarative items (such as those listed above). Note that:

- It contains only declarative items;
- The location of such declarative parts are clearly defined by the language syntax rules.

These items are declared explicitly. Remember, though, that implicit declarations occur in Ada – label names, loop names and block names, for instance.

(d) Declarative region

A declarative region is defined to be a portion of the program text. At first this may appear to clash with the definition of a declarative part – but it doesn't. This is best illustrated by example. Assume that a subprogram consists of a declaration and a corresponding body. Further assume that the body has a body stub, and thus a separate subunit. Then the declarative region for this subprogram consists of the declaration, the body and the subunit.

We say that a declarative region is associated with its corresponding declarations and statements. In the subprogram example, the declarations within its declarative region are said to be local to the subprogram.

Examples of declarative regions include:

(i) Package declarations (ii) Task declarations
(iii) Generic declarations (iv) Entry declarations
(v) Block statements (vi) Loop statements

(e) Order of declarative items

The rules of Ada concerning the order of declarative items are quite simple – with one exception. The simple aspect? You have a free choice in how you order the items in your declaration lists. And the complication? Ada defines the declarative part to consist of two sets of items. First there are the *basic* declarative items, then after this come the *later* declarative ones. The moment you declare a later item you cannot introduce another basic one in that same list. One of the most common mistakes made by beginners is similar to the following:

> TYPE declaration
> OBJECT declaration
> SUBPROGRAM_1 declaration
> SUBPROGRAM_1 BODY declaration
> SUBTYPE declaration
> etc.

Unfortunately, this will generate a compiler error. Why? Because SUBPROGRAM_1 BODY is defined to be a later declarative item whilst a subtype declaration is a basic one.

This is one of the more advanced topics of Ada. However, we have included it here in case you suffer from (apparently) mysterious compilation failures.

17.5.3 Elaboration aspects

There are two distinct issues relating to elaboration. The first concerns declarations, declarative parts and declarative items (loosely, and for brevity, declarations). The second applies to compilation units.

(a) Elaboration of declarations

The elaboration of a declarative part consists of the elaboration of its declarative items. These are elaborated in the order in which they are written. Precisely what happens during item elaboration depends on the item itself. Suppose, for instance, we have

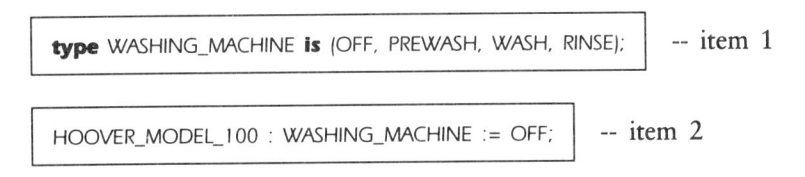

```
type WASHING_MACHINE is (OFF, PREWASH, WASH, RINSE);
```
-- item 1

```
HOOVER_MODEL_100 : WASHING_MACHINE := OFF;
```
-- item 2

The first item to be elaborated is 1, the type declaration. The system creates an enumeration type consisting of OFF, PREWASH, WASH and RINSE – the enumeration literals.

Now item 2, the object declaration, is elaborated. First, the initial value (OFF) is obtained. Then the object (HOOVER_MODEL_100) is created. Finally the object is assigned the initial value.

The rules governing elaboration of declarations are complex. For further information refer to your LRM, section 3.

(b) Elaboration of compilation (library) units

Let us once again reinforce a point. Elaboration takes place at run time. It has nothing to do with compilation order and dependencies.

To execute a program – which must be a main program – we activate a set of compilation units. Therefore, to have reached this point, the main program must have compiled correctly. Now, though, how does elaboration proceed? Before execution begins, all library units needed by the main program are elaborated. These, remember, are named by the **with** clauses of the main program. All corresponding bodies are also elaborated. Elaboration order is defined by the order in which the **with** clauses are written.

Of course, a library unit (say LIB_UNIT) used by the main program may itself have **with** clauses. In this case, the units mentioned in that clause are themselves elaborated before LIB_UNIT is elaborated. So, for example, if we have

```
    Main program                            Library unit
 with COMPUTE;                           with CONTROL_ALGORITHMS;
 with FILTER;                            with NUMERICAL_LIB;
 procedure PROCESS_SIGNAL is             procedure COMPUTE is
    <DECLARATIVE PART>                      <DECLARATIVE PART>
 begin                                   begin
     .                                       .
 end PROCESS_SIGNAL;                     end COMPUTE;
```

the elaboration order is

```
 CONTROL ALGORITHMS
 NUMERICAL_LIB
 COMPUTE
 FILTER
 Declarations of PROCESS_SIGNAL
```

or

```
 FILTER
 CONTROL ALGORITHMS
 NUMERICAL_LIB
 COMPUTE
 Declarations of PROCESS_SIGNAL
```

Unfortunately, we cannot predict which order will be produced by the compiler.

So far, so good. Unfortunately, this does not guarantee that library unit bodies are elaborated by the time they are needed. This can be overcome by using the pragma ELABORATE. For the above main program example we could have

```
 with COMPUTE;
 with FILTER;
 pragma ELABORATE (FILTER);
 procedure PROCESS_SIGNAL is
```

This will cause the body of FILTER to be elaborated before PROCESS_SIGNAL is elaborated.

We said at the beginning of this section that elaboration is a complex issue. What you have seen here is a broad-brush view. But it has, we hope, made you aware of its importance for advanced Ada programming.

17.6 RENAMING ADA ENTITIES

We can rename

- object names;
- subprogram names;
- package names;
- exception names.

using the renaming declaration. Why rename? The reasons are to simplify program text and to resolve name conflicts. Let us illustrate this by example, applying it only to the more common situations.

(a) **Renaming an imported variable**

```
package OIL_SYSTEM is
    ALARM : INTEGER;
end OIL_SYSTEM;
```

```
package AIR_SYSTEM is
    ALARM : INTEGER;
end AIR_SYSTEM;
```

```
with OIL_SYSTEM; use OIL_SYSTEM;
with AIR_SYSTEM; use AIR_SYSTEM;
procedure TOP is
begin
    OIL_SYSTEM.ALARM := 0;
    AIR_SYSTEM.ALARM := 1;
end TOP;
```

Because the **use** clause has been applied to package OIL_SYSTEM, its variable ALARM is directly visible in the procedure TOP. Unfortunately, the same is true of ALARM of package AIR_SYSTEM. Thus we have to use dot notation to eliminate possible name clashes with ALARM. As a result the text has become somewhat cumbersome. In this tiny example it isn't really something to worry about. But, in practical programs, it does cause problems in the reading and comprehension of the source text. Let us now rename these two variables:

```
with OIL_SYSTEM; use OIL_SYSTEM;
with AIR_SYSTEM; use AIR_SYSTEM;
procedure TOP is
    OIL_ALARM : INTEGER renames OIL_SYSTEM.ALARM; -- renaming
    AIR_ALARM : INTEGER renames AIR_SYSTEM.ALARM; -- and again
begin
    OIL_ALARM := 0;
    AIR_ALARM := 1;
end TOP;
```

The formal syntax for renaming objects is

> identifier : type **renames** object_name;

(b) **Renaming a nested record component**

```
type ENGINE_DATA is
   record
      FUEL     : STRING (1..10);
      HOURS    : INTEGER;
   end record;
type PROPULSION_UNIT is
   record
      SHIP     : STRING (1..10);
      ENGINES  : ENGINE_DATA;
   end record;
OLYMPUS_55     : PROPULSION_UNIT;
ENGINE_HOURS : INTEGER renames OLYMPUS_55.ENGINES.HOURS; -- renaming
```

Therefore, instead of writing

> OLYMPUS_55.ENGINES.HOURS := 25000;

we could use

> ENGINE_HOURS := 25000;

One important point to be aware of is that renaming does not hide the original declaration. So, for the example above, both statements could be used within the same code section. Be careful with this, the so-called alias problem.

(c) **Renaming a procedure**

Suppose for some reason we wanted Ada code to look like Modula-2 code. We can turn standard predefined procedures into a Modula-2 lookalike in the following way:

> **procedure** WRITE (ITEM: **in** CHARACTER) **renames** TEXT_IO.PUT;

You will see that we have had to supply the formal parameter information when renaming the procedure. More precisely, the renamed procedure must have the same parameter profile. We don't have to use the same parameter names, but the mode must be identical. Thus, for the above example, we could have written

> **procedure** WRITE (ch : **in** CHARACTER) **renames** TEXT_IO.PUT;

Formally this is:

> subprogram_specification **renames** subprogram_name;

(d) **Renaming functions and operators**

A function can be renamed as a function or as an operator. Take the following part declaration:

> **type** VECTOR **is array** (INTEGER **range** <>) **of** FLOAT;
> **function** CROSS_PRODUCT (VEC_1, VEC_2 : VECTOR) **return** FLOAT;

Then renaming can be applied as follows:

> (i) **function** FORCE (CURRENT, FIELD : VECTOR) **return** FLOAT **renames** CROSS_PRODUCT;

> (ii) **function** " * " (CURRENT, FIELD : VECTOR) **return** FLOAT **renames** CROSS_PRODUCT;

In the same way an operator can be renamed as an operator or as a function.

(e) **Renaming a package**

Package renaming is a simple process. It becomes especially useful when packages are embedded within packages, as in

> **package** MATHS_LIB **is**
>   **package** REAL_MATH **is**
>   **function** ARC_SIN (X : FLOAT) **return** FLOAT;
>   **end** REAL_MATH;
>   **package** INTEGER_MATH **is**
>   **function** ARC_SIN (X : INTEGER) **return** INTEGER;
>   **end** INTEGER_MATH;
> **end** MATHS_LIB;

Without a **use** clause we end up with statements like

```
Y := MATHS_LIB.INTEGER_MATH.ARC_SIN (X);
```

Now rename:

```
package INT_MATHS renames MATHS_LIB.INTEGER_MATH;
```

As a result we could replace the above statement with

```
Y := INT_MATHS.ARC_SIN (X);
```

REVIEW

Do you now:

- Fully understand the details of the software components of Ada?
- See which of these are compilable units?
- Appreciate properly the use of **with** and **use** clauses?
- Know what the library and secondary compilation units of the language are, and what their role is in program development?
- Show how these relate to, and depend on, each other?
- Know how and why to use subunits?
- Recognize the compilation dependencies that can occur between program units?
- Understand the basics of elaboration?
- Appreciate the use and benefits of the renaming of program entities?
- Realize how 'programming in the large' can be implemented?
- Perceive the basics of top-down and bottom-up programming, and see how Ada supports both approaches?

We would like to leave you on a note of sound advice. At the beginning of this book we said that Ada is a complex language. By now you will have truly appreciated that comment. So, when designing Ada programs, keep things simple. Use clear structures. Maintain a consistent, logical style. Make your programs clear and straightforward. Avoid 'clever' programming tricks. And, if this means adopting an *ad hoc* subset of the language, so be it. You will find yourself in some very illustrious company. Good luck.

Appendix: Reserved words

The identifiers listed below are called *reserved words* and are reserved for special significance in the language.

abort	declare	generic	of	select
abs	delay	goto	or	separate
accept	delta		others	subtype
assess	digits	if	out	
all	do	in		task
and		is	package	terminate
array			pragma	then
at	else		private	type
	elsif	limited	procedure	
	end	loop		
begin	entry		raise	use
body	exception		range	
	exit	mod	record	when
			rem	while
		new	renames	with
case	for	not	return	
constant	function	null	reverse	xor

A reserved word must not be used as a declared identifier.

Index

abort 483
ABS 33
Absolute values 33–4
Absolute addressing 499–501
accept 455, 458, 459
access 320
Access object
  assignment 321–2
  creating 321
  deallocation 322
  default initial value 325
  initialization 327
Access type
  arrays of 330
  compatibility 330
  constant 328
  creation 320
  as generic parameter 416
  in real-time system 336–43
  range constraints 330
  see also Access object
Accuracy, in numerical operations
  161–2, 180
Addition 28, 36, 164, 170–2, 182
ADDRESS
  the attribute 506
  the type 505
Address clause 505–6
Aggregate
  arrays 239–41, 258–66
  discriminant record 300–1
  nested record 290–93
  qualification 260
  record 279–83
  variant record 313
all 322
and 41, 131
and then 135
array 228

Array
  of access types 330
  aggregates 239–41, 258–66
  anonymous 234
  array-of- 251–6, 266
  attributes 266–8
  bounds 228, 232, 234, 237, 244
  of characters 242–3
  constant 241
  constrained 234–5
  dynamic 246
  elements 228–9
  as generic parameter 416
  index 229, 237, 244, 262–3
  multidimensional 249–51, 263–5
  of records 289–90
  one-dimensional 244
  operations on 269
  as a parameter 256–8
  slices 241
  subtypes 237–8
  unconstrained 235–9, 242
ASCII 125, 130, 535, 544–6
Assembly language 502, 525
Assignment symbol 8
Attributes
  of arrays 266–8
  CHARACTER 127–30
  FLOAT 177
  INTEGER 123–4
  of records 517–18
  representation 506, 508–10
  of tasks 490–1
  subtype 145

BASE 546
Base type 143
begin 8, 107
Binary representation 173–6

Bit 508
Block structure 10, 106–11
Body stub 581
BOOLEAN 22, 40, 131–6
Boolean logic 41–3, 131–6
Bottom-up design, see Service decomposition
Brackets, see Parentheses
Byte 508

CALLABLE 490
Cardinality 120, 138
case 53–7
CHARACTER 22–3, 124–30, 536–40
Client 195, 198, 199–203, 215–16, 351
CLOSE 529–30
COL 559–60
Comments 13
Compilation 192, 198–9, 206, 207, 215–19, 501
Compilation dependencies 583–7
Compilation order 583–6
Compilation unit 571–4
Compiler 571
Compiler directive, see pragma
Concurrency 441–7
  see also Task
constant 19
Constants 18–19, 241, 284, 328, 352–54
CONSTRAINED 306
CONSTRAINT_ERROR 306, 368
Context clause 14, 572
COUNT 491
CREATE 529–30
CURRENT_INPUT 544
CURRENT_OUTPUT 544

Date types
  access, see Access type
  array, see Array
  Boolean 22
  character 22–3, 536–40
  enumeration 138–41, 553–4
  fixed point 180–5, 552–3
  floating point 176–80, 549–52
  heterogeneous 224, 275

homogeneous 224, 226
integer 20–21
pointer, see Access type
private, see Private type
real 21–2, 176, 549
scalar 20–3, 120–57
string 22, 536–40
Deadlock, see Task
Declaration order 219, 590
Declarations 7, 199, 204, 396–8, 589–90
declare 108
Deferred constant 354
delay 450
DELETE 534
Delimiters 8
delta 180–1
Derived types 152–7
DIGITS 177
DIRECT_IO 528, 535, 564–8
Discriminant record 293–306
Divsion 29–32, 36, 164–5, 172–3, 182–3
Dot notation, see Qualified notation
DURATION 451

Elaboration
  aspects 591–2
  definition 212–13, 588–89
  exceptions 381–2, 391, 396–8, 486
  order 219
elsif 50–2
EMAX 177
Embedded packages 213–315
Encapsulation 202
end 9, 107
END_OF_FILE 560
END_OF_LINE 560
END_OF_PAGE 560
entry 454
Entry family 479–81
Entry queue 491
Enumeration 120
ENUMERATION_IO 536, 553–4
Enumeration types
  defining 138–41
  in generic instantiation 414

overloading 141–3
representation clause 511–12
subtypes 145–50
EPSILON 177
Errors
  in numerical operations 159–61, 165–76, 185
  compile time 12, 86, 91, 106, 206–7
  constraint 156
  I/O 570
  overflow 21, 36, 172
  run-time 17, 300, 336–43, 347–8
  type incompatibility 141, 269
  underflow 172–3
  see also Exceptions
exception
Exceptions
  anonymous 391
  in elaboration 381–2, 391, 396–8, 486
  in embedded systems 401
  exporting from a package 390
  in functions 379–80
  handler 370–5, 378, 379, 384, 394–6, 483–5
  introduction 365–8
  I/O 570
  nested propagation 392–8
  in packages 380–4
  predefined 368–72
  in procedures 378–9, 383
  propagation 386–94
  re-raising 394–5
  suppression 398–400
  in tasks 483–7
  user defined 375–6
  within a block 372
exit 59–61, 67–8
Exponent 164–5, 174, 177
Exponentiation 32–3, 36
Expression 25, 40, 122

FALSE 22, 131
Fieldwidth 15
FIFO, *see* Linked list
File
  deletion 533–5

  external 531–5
  formatting 554–61
  machine readable 561–8
  management 528–35
  manipulation 532–3
  query functions 542, 544
  sequential 561–4
  text 528–35
FILE_MODE 530
FILE_TYPE 530
FIRST 123, 266–8
FIRST_BIT 518
FIXED 175
FIXED_IO 536, 552–3
Fixed point form 21, 166–7, 169, 174–6, 180–5
FLOAT 21, 177–8
FLOAT_IO 22, 536, 549, 52
Floating point form 21, 167–9, 174
  see also Data types
for 61–5
FORM 542
function 94
Function
  body 104–6
  declaration 104–6
  as a generic 424–5
  introduction 94–9
  vs. procedure 97–9
  specification 104–6
  see also Subprograms

generic 408
Generic
  body 407–8, 428
  compilation dependencies 586–7
  declaration 407–8, 576
  default parameters 419, 422–4
  functions 424–5
  instantiation 405–6, 409, 420–2, 426, 576–8
  introduction 402–7
  invocation 409–11
  object 416–19
  operator symbol as parameters 434–8
  overloading 411–12, 432, 434–6

package 425-32
parameters 408, 412-24
procedure 407-11, 414
program unit 406-7
with subprogram parameters 420-24
GET 17, 537, 538, 539, 540
GET_LINE 538, 540
goto 68-70
Guards 466-9

Hexadecimal 505
Hidden entries 491-4
Hierarchical decomposition 195

I/O, see Input/output
Identifiers 11
if-then 45
if-then-else 45-7
in 136
IN_FILE 530, 564
Independent design 189, 191-2
INDEX 568
Infix notation 114-15
Information hiding 196, 207-210
INOUT_FILE 567
Input 17-18
Input/output 13-18, 527-8
Instantiation, see Generic
INTEGER 20-1, 27, 121-4, 154-7
INTEGER_IO 10, 16, 438-40, 536, 544, 546-9
Interrupts 500-1, 506-8
IO_EXCEPTIONS 570
IS_OPEN 542

Label 70, 108-9
Language Reference Manual 4, 10, 213
LARGE 177
LAST 123, 266-8
LAST_BIT 518
LENGTH 266-8
Library features 14, 39, 195, 198-9
Library package, see Package
Library unit 574-8
Limited private type, see Private type
LINE_LENGTH 557

Linkage of a software program 192, 207, 503
Linked list 318, 330-43
Literal
 character 23
 constant 18
 enumeration 138, 142
 integer 123
 string 22
LONG_INTEGER 21, 154-7
loop 59-61
LOW_LEVEL_IO 568
LRM, see Language Reference Manual

MACHINE_CODE 524
Main program 4-10, 107, 187, 391
Mantissa 164-5, 167-74, 177
MANTISSA 177
mod 30, 36, 516
MODE 542
Model numbers 166, 173, 178
Modular design 189, 191
Modulo arithmetic 30-2
Modulus, see Absolute values
Monolithic design 188, 190
Multiplication 29, 36, 164-5, 172-3, 182-3
Multiprocessing 443, 447
Multitasking 443
 see also Task
Mutual exclusion 450

NAME 542
Named association 100-3, 260-2, 281, 296-7, 300-1
Named loop 67
Nested
 block 107
 exception propagation 392-4
 if statements 48
 loops 65-8
 packages, see Embedded packages
 records 287-93, 304
 subprograms 81-4, 99
new 16, 321
NEW_LINE 14-15, 558-9
NEW_PAGE 558-9

Normalization 172, 174
not 41, 131, 134, 136
null 55, 313, 325
Number representation 162–76
NUMERIC_ERROR 369

OPEN 532
Operands 25
Operations
  on arrays 269
  on generic parameters 413
  on record 284–7
Operator 25, 40, 41
  arithmetic 26
  binary 36
  as generic parameters 434–8
  introduction 25, 40, 41
  relational 41, 132
  short-circuit 135
  unary 36
or 41, 131
or else 135
Ordinality 120, 138
others
  in aggregates 259–60, 261, 263, 282–3
  case statement 53
  exception handlers 373–4, 392
  variant record 313
OUT_FILE 530, 564
Output 13–16
Overflow, *see* Errors
Overloading
  enumeration types 141–3
  operators 112–15, 434–6
  subprograms 111–12, 411–12, 432

package 199
Package
  body 195–6, 203–7, 210–13, 215–16, 579
  compilation order 215–19
  declaration 576
  elaboration 212–13, 381–2, 391
  embedded, *see* Embedded package
  generic 425–32
  library 198–9, 215, 391

role and structure 195–6
specification 195–6, 199–207, 215–16, 348–9
PAGE_LENGTH 557
Parameters
  actual 85, 88, 100–1, 112
  formal 85, 88, 100–1
  generic, *see* Generic
  in 87–90, 94, 103
  in-out 92–4
  introduction 85–6
  limited private 363
  list 86
  named 100–3
  out 90–2
  positional 100–4
  rendezvous 459–61
Parent type 152
Parent unit 583
Parentheses 37–39, 132
Pointer, *see* Access type
Portability 207, 504, 531–32, 568
POS 127, 130
POSITION 517–18
Positional notation 100–4, 258–60, 281, 296–7, 300–1
POSITIVE 242
pragma
  ELABORATE 592
  INLINE 587–8
  INTERFACE 525
  PACK 518–20
  PRIORITY 489
  SUPPRESS 400
Precedence 34–7, 38, 131
Precision
  fixed point form 166–7, 175, 180–1
  floating point form 167–8, 177–8
  in numerical operations 161–2
PRED 123, 130
Prefix notation 114–15
private 349
Private type
  as generic parameter 415–16
  constants 352–4, 363
  initialization 363
  introduction 349–51

limited 349–50, 363–4
normal 349–50, 351–7
standard operations 350, 363
procedure 8
Procedure
  body 104–6
  declaration 104–6
  vs. function 97–9
  generic 407–11, 414
  introduction 76–7
  nested 81–4
  parameters 85–94
  specification 104–6
  see also Subprograms
PROGRAM_ERROR 369, 380
Program modularity 10
Program name 8
Program statements 7
Program unit 4, 193–5, 406–7
Propagation of exceptions, see Exceptions
PUT 14–15, 538, 540
PUT_LINE 16, 538–9, 540

Qualified notation 15, 16, 84, 201–2, 323, 454, 479

Radix 163–5, 170
raise 376, 395
range 144, 178, 181, 419
RANGE 266–8
READ 563, 568
Real types, see Data types
record 275
Record
  aggregate 279–83, 290–3, 300–1
  alignment clause 516–17
  array of 289–90
  attributes 517–18
  changing discriminants 301–2
  component identifer 278
  component list 278
  component range constraints 284
  component type 278
  as a composite unit 284–7
  constants 284
  declaration 275–9

default discriminant 298–300
default values 283–4
discriminant 293–306
  in generic instantiation 414
initialization 281–2, 303
nested 287–93, 304
operations on 284–7
representation clause 513–20
variable designator 278
variant 306–14
Recursion 99–100
rem 30, 36
Rename
  functions and operator 595
  package 595–6
  procedure 594–5
  record component 594
  variable 593–4
renames 593
Rendezvous
  delay alternative 469–72
  exceptions 486–7
  executing code 457–9
  the guard 466–9
  introduction 453–6, 461–4
  open alternative 465, 468
  parameters 459–61
  selective call 473–4
  selective wait 464–6
  time-out 471–2
Representation attributes 506, 508–10
Representation clauses
  address 505–6
  enumeration 511–12
  introduction 503–4
  length 508–10
  records 513–20
Reserved words 5, 12
RESET 533, 567
Resolution, see Precision
return 94–6, 380
reverse 64
Rounding 166–7

Scheduling, see Task
Scope 78–84, 107, 384–5, 477
Secondary units 578–83

select
   in acceptor task 464
   in caller task 474
   with guards 468
   with terminate 472
   with time-out 470
Selected component 12
Semantics 25
separate 581
Sequential I/O 561–4
SEQUENTIAL_IO 528, 535, 563–4
Service decomposition 195
SET_COL 557–8
SET_INDEX 568
SET_INPUT 543–4
SET_LINE 557–8
SET_LINE_LENGTH 555–6
SET_OUTPUT 544
SET_PAGE_LENGTH 555–6
SHORT_INTEGER 21, 154–6
Significant bit 175
Significant digit 163, 167–70, 175
'SIZE 508–509
SKIP_LINE 17, 559
SMALL 177, 510
Software construction 192–193
STANDARD 242, 434
Standard I/O 542–4
STANDARD_INPUT 543
STANDARD_OUTPUT 543
Statement 25, 40
STORAGE_ERROR 369
STORAGE_SIZE 509–10
STORAGE_UNIT 515
STRING 22, 242–3, 536–40
Subprograms 4, 187–8, 204, 420–4, 574–6, 578–9
Subtraction 29, 36, 164, 170–2, 182
Subtypes 143–51, 179–80, 237–8
Subunits 579–83
SUCC 123, 130
SUPPRESS 400
Syntax diagrams
   body stub 582
   case 56
   conditional selective wait 467
   context clause 573
   definition of 10
   derived type 154
   enumeration type declaration 140
   for 63
   generic declaration 577
   generic instantiation 578
   identifer 12
   if 52
   if-then 46
   if-then-else 47
   integer literal 123
   loop 58
   main program 11
   package body 580
   package declaration 577
   procedure specification 106
   record type 279
   scalar subtype 145
   subprogram body 575
   subprogram declaration 105, 575
   subunit 582
   use clause 573
   while-loop 65
   with clause 573
Syntax rules 25
SYSTEM 503, 505

task 448
Task
   abnormal 483
   accept 454
   acceptor 452–4, 464–72
   activation 449
   attributes 490–1
   body 448
   caller 452–4, 473–4
   completion 449, 472, 481–3
   deadlock 446–7
   dependent 449, 483
   entry 454
   entry families 479–81
   execution 449
   independent 444–6, 447–51
   interdependent 446–7, 452–7
   interrupt handler 506–8
   multiple accept and entry 456–7
   mutual exclusion 450

object 476–9
in packages 491–4
priorities 487–90
rendezvous, see Rendezvous
scheduling 444–7
specification 448
synchronization 446–7, 452–7
termination 481–7
types 475–9
TASKING_ERROR 369, 490
terminate 472
TERMINATED 490
TEXT_IO 9–10, 14–16, 438–40, 528, 536, 540–4
Top-down design, see Hierarchical decomposition
TRUE 22, 131
Truncation 166–7
Type
conversion 27–8, 119, 157, 520–1
mixing 26–7
see also Date type

UNCHECKED_CONVERSION 521
UNCHECKED_DEALLOCATION 322, 523–4

Universal static expression 19
use 14, 199–202, 214, 574

VAL 128–30
Variable list 8
Variables
declaration 8
global 81–4, 98, 219–22
local 81–4
scope 78–84
Variant record 306–14
Visibility
block structure 107–8
definition 81
exceptions 384–5, 392
package 199, 204, 215–22
tasks 491

when 53–7, 61
while-loop 65
WIDTH 546, 554
with 14, 199–202, 420, 572–4
Word 509–10
WRITE 563, 568

xor 41, 131